ECONOMICS OF ACCOUNTING

Volume I - Information in Markets

Kluwer Series in Accounting Scholarship

Series Editor:

Joel S. Demski
Fisher School of Accounting
University of Florida

Books in the series:

Christensen, Peter O., Feltham, Gerald A.
Economics of Accounting - Volume I
Information in Markets

ECONOMICS OF ACCOUNTING
Volume I - Information in Markets

Peter O. Christensen
University of Southern Denmark-Odense

Gerald A. Feltham
The University of British Columbia, Canada

KLUWER ACADEMIC PUBLISHERS
Boston / Dordrecht / London

Distributors for North, Central and South America:
Kluwer Academic Publishers
101 Philip Drive
Assinippi Park
Norwell, Massachusetts 02061 USA
Telephone (781) 871-6600
Fax (781) 681-9045
E-Mail < kluwer@wkap.com>
Distributors for all other countries:
Kluwer Academic Publishers Group
Distribution Centre
Post Office Box 17
3300 AH Dordrecht, THE NETHERLANDS
Tel.: + 31 (0) 78 657 60 00
Fax: + 31 (0) 78 657 62 54

E-Mail < services@wkap.nl>

Electronic Services < http://www.wkap.nl>

Economics of Accounting -Volume I, Information in Markets
Peter O. Christensen and Gerald A. Feltham
ISBN 1-4020-7229-5

Printed on acid-free paper.
Printed in the United States of America

To Else and June

CONTENTS

Foreword by Joel S. Demski .... *xv*
Preface .... *xvii*

1. Introduction to Information in Markets 1
1.1 Basic Decision-facilitating Role of Information 2
1.2 Public Information in Equity Markets 6
1.2.1 Impact of Public Information in Pure-exchange Setting 6
1.2.2 Impact of Public Information in a Production Choice Setting 7
1.2.3 Market Values and Accounting Information 9
1.3 Private Investor Information in Equity Markets 14
1.4 Disclosure of Private Owner Information in Equity and Product Markets 18
1.4.1 Disclosure by a Risk-averse Owner 19
1.4.2 Disclosure on Behalf of Risk-neutral Owners 21
1.4.3 Disclosure in a Duopoly 23
1.5 Concluding Remarks 24

PART A
BASIC DECISION-FACILITATING ROLE OF INFORMATION

2. Single Person Decision Making under Uncertainty 29
2.1 Representation of Uncertainty 30
2.2 Random Variables 33
2.3 Representation of Preferences 38
2.4 Risk Aversion 43
2.5 HARA Utility Functions 49
2.6 Mean-variance Preferences 51
2.7 Basic Hurdle Models 56
2.8 Stochastic Dominance 60
Appendix 2A: Proofs of Stochastic Dominance Propositions 66
Appendix 2B: One-parameter Exponential Family of Distributions 69
References 70

3. Decision-Facilitating Information 71
3.1 Representation of Information 72
3.1.1 Conditional Probability 72
3.1.2 Posterior Beliefs with Random Variables 74
3.1.3 Multi-variate Normal Distributions 77
3.1.4 Sufficient Statistics 78
3.2 Value of Decision-facilitating Information Systems 81
3.2.1 Partitions and Measurable Functions 81
3.2.2 Basic Information Economic Model 84
3.2.3 Value of Information 90
3.3 Comparison of Information Systems 93
3.3.1 Generally at Least as Valuable Information Systems 93
3.3.2 Informativeness 94
3.4 Impact of Risk and Risk Aversion on the Value of Information 101
3.4.1 Financial Investment Example 101
3.4.2 The Hurdle Model 104
Appendix 3A: Expected Values of Exponential Functions with Normal Distributions 106
References 108

4. Risk Sharing, Congruent Preferences, and Information in Partnerships 111
4.1 Efficient Risk Sharing 112
4.1.1 Efficient Risk Sharing with Homogeneous Beliefs 112
4.1.2 HARA Utility Functions and Linear Risk Sharing 122
4.1.3 Side-betting with Heterogeneous Beliefs 125
4.2 Congruent Preferences 126
4.2.1 Action Choice 127
4.2.2 Information System Choice 132
4.3 Distributed Information in Teams 135
Appendix 4A: Congruent Preferences with Exponential Utility and Heterogeneous Beliefs 136
References 139

PART B
PUBLIC INFORMATION IN EQUITY MARKETS

5. Arbitrage and Risk Sharing in Single-period Markets 143
5.1 Market Value Implications of No Arbitrage 144
5.1.1 Basic Elements of the Single-period Models 144
5.1.2 No Arbitrage in Single-period Markets 145
5.1.3 Alternative Representations of No-arbitrage Prices 149

5.2 Optimal Portfolio Choice 152
5.3 Market Equilibrium and Efficient Risk Sharing 154
5.4 Effectively Complete Markets 161
5.4.1 Linear Risk Sharing 161
5.4.2 Diversifiable Risks 165
5.5 Impact of Public Information 175
5.5.1 *Ex Post* Information 176
5.5.2 *Ex Ante* Information 180
5.6 Concluding Remarks 181
References 182

6. Arbitrage and Risk Sharing in Multi-period Markets 185
6.1 Market Value Implications of No Arbitrage in Multi-period Settings 186
6.1.1 Basic Elements of the Multi-period Model 186
6.1.2 No Arbitrage in Multi-period Markets 188
6.1.3 Alternative Representations of No-arbitrage Prices 192
6.2 Optimal Portfolio Plans 196
6.3 Equilibrium and Efficient Risk Sharing 201
6.4 Effectively Dynamically Complete Markets 206
6.4.1 Linear Risk Sharing 206
6.4.2 Diversifiable Risks 209
6.5 Concluding Remarks 218
Appendix 6A: Risk-neutral Probabilities Based on the Return on a Bank Account 219
References 221

7. Public Information in Multi-period Markets 223
7.1 Efficiency of Information Systems 224
7.2 Impact of Public Information in Securities Markets 228
7.3 Information and Prices 233
7.4 Information and Trades 236
7.5 Exponential Utility and Normally Distributed Dividends 238
7.5.1 Investor Portfolio Choice 238
7.5.2 Equilibrium Prices and Investment Portfolios 240
7.5.3 Impact of Public Information 243
7.6 Concluding Remarks 245
Appendix 7A: Value of Additional Information 246
References 251

8. Production Choice in Efficient Markets 253
8.1 Production Alternatives and Efficiency 254
8.2 Efficient Production Choice with Private Ownership 259
8.2.1 Complete Multi-period Securities Markets 259
8.2.2 Dynamically Complete Securities Markets 260
8.3 Impact of Public Information 262
8.4 Efficient Production Choice in Two-period Economies 265
8.4.1 Basic Two-period Model 265
8.4.2 Impact of Additional Information 266
8.4.3 Production Choice in a Dynamically Quasi-complete Market 268
8.4.4 Information and Firm Value in a Dynamically Quasi-complete Market 269
8.4.5 The Value of Windfall and Productivity Information ... 269
8.4.6 Optimal Behavior when Managers have Private Firm-specific Information 271
8.5 Concluding Remarks 272
References 274

9. Relation Between Market Values and Future Accounting Numbers 277
9.1 No-arbitrage Accounting-value Relations 279
9.1.1 Clean Surplus Relation 279
9.1.2 Accounting-value Relation 281
9.1.3 Alternative Accounting-value Relations 283
9.2 Separation of Financial and Operating Activities 286
9.2.1 Accounting Relations 287
9.2.2 Operating Income-value Relation 289
9.2.3 Operating Cash Flow-value Relation 290
9.3 Truncated Forecasts 291
9.4 Anticipated Equity Transactions 293
9.4.1 Pure- Versus Mixed-equity Concepts 294
9.4.2 Accounting Valuation Model 295
9.4.3 Accounting for the Issuance of New Equity 296
9.4.4 Treating Contingent Claims as Debt 302
9.4.5 Per-share Calculations 304
9.5 Concluding Remarks 305
Appendix 9A: Tax Effects 306
9A.1 Distribution of Earnings and Contributed Capital 307
9A.2 Differential Taxes on Dividends and Interest 309
References 311

10. Relation Between Market Values and Contemporaneous Accounting Numbers 315
10.1 Some Basics of Dynamic Models 319
10.1.1 Stationary Dividend-value Relation 319
10.1.2 A General Linear Dividend Valuation Model 321
10.1.3 A Simple Auto-regressive Dividend Model 323
10.1.4 Stationary Accounting-value Relations 326
10.2 A Capital Investment Model 330
10.2.1 Capital Investment and Depreciation 330
10.2.2 Information and Accounting Accruals 339
10.2.3 Inferring Information from Analysts' Forecasts 343
10.3 Other Factors Influencing Accounting-value Relations 349
10.3.1 Transitory Earnings and Investments 349
10.3.2 Receivables and Bad Debt Expense 352
10.3.3 Research and Development 356
10.4 Concluding Remarks 358
Appendix 10A: Proofs 360
References 361

PART C
PRIVATE INVESTOR INFORMATION IN EQUITY MARKETS

11. Impact of Private Investor Information in Equity Markets ... 367
11.1 Revelation of Private Investor Information Through Prices .. 369
11.1.1 Unsophisticated Versus Fully Informed Equilibria ... 369
11.1.2 Rational Expectations Equilibria 374
11.1.3 Expected Utility from Competitive Acquisition of Risk 375
11.2 Acquisition of Private Information by Price-taking Investors 377
11.2.1 Exogenous Set of Informed Investors 378
11.2.2 Endogenous Information Acquisition 381
11.3 Public Reports and the Concurrent Demand for Private Information 388
11.4 Public Reports and the Prior Demand for Private Information 397
11.5 Concluding Remarks 409
Appendix 11A: Private Information in a Complete Market 410
Appendix 11B: Proofs 414
References 416

12. Strategic Use of Private Investor Information in Equity Markets 419
12.1 The Basic Strategic Investor Model 420
12.1.1 Exogenous Informativeness of the Private Signal 421
12.1.2 Endogenous Informativeness of the Private Signal ... 423

12.2 Public Reports and the Concurrent Demand for Private Information ... 424
12.2.1 Multiple Informed Investors ... 424
12.2.2 Private Investor Information in an Infinite Horizon, Residual Income Model ... 431
12.2.3 Endogenous Informativeness of the Public Report ... 434
12.3 Public Reports and the Prior Demand for Private Information 437
12.4 Concluding Remarks ... 443
References ... 443

PART D
DISCLOSURE OF PRIVATE OWNER INFORMATION IN EQUITY AND PRODUCT MARKETS

13. Disclosure of Private Information by an Undiversified Owner . 447
13.1 Basic Disclosure Issues ... 448
13.2 Equilibria in Disclosure Games ... 452
13.2.1 Sequential Equilibria ... 453
13.2.2 A Simple Risk-sharing Example ... 454
13.2.3 Stable Equilibria ... 459
13.3 Signaling with Outcome-contingent Contracts ... 466
13.3.1 Outcome-contingent Contracts with Finite Sets of Outcomes and Signals ... 467
13.3.2 Equity Retention with Normally Distributed Outcomes 471
13.3.3 Correlated Outcomes among Firms ... 475
13.4 Verified *Ex Ante* Reports ... 480
13.4.1 Perfect *Ex Ante* Reports ... 480
13.4.2 Imperfect *Ex Ante* Reports ... 483
13.5 Verified *Ex Post* Reports ... 492
13.6 Equity Retention and Report Choice as Bivariate Signals ... 494
13.7 Concluding Remarks ... 496
Appendix 13A: Optimal Contracts in the LP-Model ... 497
References ... 499

14. Disclosure of Private Information by Diversified Owners ... 501
14.1 Some Basic Disclosure Model Elements and Issues ... 501
14.2 Verifiable Disclosure to One Recipient ... 506
14.2.1 Full Disclosure with Costless Verification ... 507
14.2.2 Partial Disclosure with Costly Verification ... 511
14.3 Verifiable Disclosure to Two Recipients ... 516
14.3.1 New Equity/Potential Entrant Model ... 517
14.3.2 Other Two-recipient Models ... 520

14.4 Positive Probability the Manager is Uninformed 522
14.4.1 Single Recipient Models 523
14.4.2 Litigation 527
14.4.3 Endogenous Information Acquisition 531
14.4.4 Endogenous Investment Choice 532
14.5 Unverified Disclosure to Two Recipients 535
14.6 Concluding Remarks 539
References 539

15. Disclosure of Private Information in Product Markets 543
15.1 *Ex Ante* Disclosure Policies 545
15.1.1 Cournot Competition 547
15.1.2 Bertrand Competition 555
15.1.3 Discussion and Extension of Results 560
15.2 *Ex Post* Disclosure Choices 567
15.2.1 The Basic *Ex Post* Disclosure Model 568
15.2.2 Positive Probability Manager *i* is Uninformed 571
15.2.3 New Equity Model 572
15.3 Concluding Remarks 576
References 578

Author Index 581
Subject Index 585

Foreword
Joel S. Demski

It has long been recognized that accounting is a source of information. At the same time, accounting thought has developed with a casual if not vicarious view of this fundamental fact, simply because the economics of uncertainty was not well developed until the past four decades. Naturally, these developments in our understanding of uncertainty call for a renewed look at accounting thought, one that formally as opposed to casually carries along the information perspective.

Once this path is entered, one is struck by several facts: Information is central to functioning of organizations and markets, the use to which information is put becomes thoroughly endogenous in a well crafted economic analysis, and uncertainty and risk sharing are fundamental to our understanding of accounting issues.

This is the path offered by the remarkable Christensen and Feltham volumes. Their path takes us through equity and product markets (Volume I) and labor markets (Volume II), and offers the reader a wide-ranging, thorough view of what it means to take seriously the idea that accounting is a source of information. That said, this is not academic technology for technology's sake. Rather it cuts at the very core of the way we teach and research accounting. Once we admit to multiple sources and multiple uses of information, we are forced to test whether our understanding of accounting is affected seriously by ignoring those other sources and uses of information, both in terms of combining information from various sources for some particular use and in terms of reactive response to other sources when one, the accounting source, is altered. It is here that the importance of thinking broadly in terms of the various sources and uses comes into play, and the message is unmistakable: accounting simply cannot be understood, taught, or well researched without placing it in its natural environment of multiple users and multiple sources of information.

The challenge Peter and Jerry provide is not simply to master this material. It is to digest it and act upon it, to offer accounting thought that is matched, so to speak, to the importance of accounting institutions.

We are deeply indebted to Peter and Jerry. That debt will go unattended until we significantly broaden and deepen our collective understanding of accounting.

Preface

In 1977, Tom Dyckman, then Director of Research for the American Accounting Association (AAA) encouraged Joel Demski and Jerry Feltham to submit a proposal for a monograph in the AAA Research Monograph series, "on the state of the art in information economics as it impacts on accounting." Joel and Jerry prepared a proposal entitled:

"Economic Returns to Accounting Information in a Multiperson Setting"

The proposal was accepted by the AAA in 1978, and Joel and Jerry worked on the monograph for the next few years, producing several of the proposed chapters. However, the task went more slowly and proved more daunting than expected. They were at separate universities and both found that, as they wrote and taught, they kept finding "holes" in the literature that they felt "needed to be filled" before completing the monograph. This, plus the rapid expansion of the field, meant they were continually chasing an elusive goal.

In the early nineties, Joel and Jerry faced up to the fact that they would never complete the monograph. However, rather than agree to total abandonment, Jerry "reserved the right" to return to the project. While, at that time, he did not expect to do so, he did have 500 pages of lecture notes that had been developed in teaching two analytical Ph.D. seminars in accounting: "Economic Analysis of Accounting Information in Markets," and "Economic Analysis of Accounting Information in Organizations."

Over the years, Jerry had received several requests for his teaching notes. These notes had the advantage of pulling together the major work in the field and of being done in one notation. However, they were very terse and mathematical, having been designed for use in class where Jerry could personally present the intuition behind the various models and their results. To produce a book based on the notes would require integration of the "words" and "graphs" used in the lectures into the notes (and there were still holes to fill).

Peter Christensen had been a student in one of Jerry's classes in 1986. In 1997, Peter asked Jerry if he was going to write a book based on his lecture notes. When Jerry stated it was too big a task to tackle alone, Peter indicated his willingness to become a coauthor. This was an important factor in Jerry's decision to return to the book, since he had worked effectively with Peter in publishing several papers over the preceding 10 years. Also of significance was our assessment that young researchers and Ph.D. students would benefit from a book that provides efficient access to the basic work in the field. The book need not try to provide all the latest results and it need not "fill the holes". The objective is to lay an integrated foundation that provides young researchers with the tools necessary to insightfully read the latest work in the field, and to develop their own theoretical analyses.

Parallel to Jerry's two Ph.D. courses, the book is divided into two volumes.

Economics of Accounting: Volume I - Information in Markets
Economics of Accounting: Volume II - Performance Evaluation

Chapter 1 gives an overview of the content of Volume I, while Chapter 16 gives an overview of the content of Volume II. Each volume is divided into several parts.

Volume I - Information in Markets
- Part A. Basic Decision-Facilitating Role of Information
- Part B. Public Information in Equity Markets
- Part C. Private Investor Information in Equity Markets
- Part D. Disclosure of Private Owner Information in Equity and Product Markets

Volume II - Performance Evaluation
- Part E. Performance Evaluation in Single-Period/Single-Agent Settings
- Part F. Disclosure of Private Management Information in Single-Period/Single-Agent Settings
- Part G. Contracting in Multi-Period/Single-Agent Settings
- Part H. Contracting with Multiple Agents

The three chapters in Part A are foundational to both volumes. However, with occasional exceptions, one can read the material in Volume II without having read Parts B, C, and D of Volume I. Jerry begins both of his Ph.D. courses by ensuring all students understand the fundamental concepts covered in Part A, since these courses are offered in alternate years and the students differ with respect to which course they take first.

Students often seem to find it easier to grasp the material in Volume II, so there is some advantage to doing it first. However, conceptually, we prefer to cover the information in markets material first, and then consider management incentives. The advantage of this sequence is that management incentive models assume the manager contracts with a principal acting on behalf of the owners. The owners are investors, and Volume I explicitly considers investor preferences with respect to the firm's operations. Furthermore, while most principal-agent models implicitly assume incentive risks are firm-specific, there are models that recognize that incentive risks are influenced by both market-wide and firm-specific factors. To fully understand the impact of the market-wide factors on management incentives, one needs to understand how the manager can personally invest in the market so as to efficiently share market-wide risks with other investors. The first volume provides the necessary background for this type of analysis.

Acknowledgments
Our greatest debt is to Joel Demski. Joel and Jerry were colleagues at Stanford from 1967 to 1971, and collaborated on some of the early information economics research in accounting. Their initial work focused on the role of accounting information in facilitating management decisions, and culminated in the book, *Cost Determination: A Conceptual Approach.* In that book they recognized that accounting had both a decision-facilitating and a decision-influencing role, but the book focused on the former. While completing that book, Joel and Jerry were exposed to work in economics which explicitly considered information asymmetries with respect to management's information and actions. They recognized that this type of economic analysis had much to contribute to our knowledge about the decision-influencing role of accounting. In 1978 they published a paper in *The Accounting Review*, "Economic Incentives in Budgetary Control Systems," which would later receive the AAA 1994 Seminal Contribution to Accounting Literature Award. One of Joel's many Ph.D. students, John Christensen, was instrumental to Peter's interest in accounting research. In recent years, Peter, as with Jerry, has had the opportunity to learn much from working with Joel on joint research.

We also want to acknowledge our debt to other coauthors who have significantly contributed to our knowledge through the joint research process. These include Joy Begley, Hans Frimor, Jack Hughes, Jim Ohlson, Jinhan Pae, Martin Wu, and Jim Xie. Their names are mentioned frequently throughout the two volumes, as we describe some of the models and results from the associated papers.

As noted above, Jerry's Ph.D. lecture notes provide the foundation for much of the material in our two volumes. Jerry acknowledges that he has learned much from preparing the notes for his students and interacting with them as they sought to learn how to apply economic analysis to accounting. The accounting Ph.D. students who have been in Jerry's classes as he developed the notes include Amin Amershi, Derek Chan, Peter Clarkson, Lucie Courteau, Hans Frimor, Pat Hughes, Jennifer Kao, Claude Laurin, Xiaohong Liu, Ella Mae Matsumura, Jinhan Pae, Suil Pae, Florin Sabac, Jane Saly, Mandira Sankar, Mike Stein, Pat Tan, Martin Wu, and Jim Xie. Some have been Jerry's research assistants, some have been his coauthors (see above), and Jerry has supervised the dissertations of many of these students. In addition to the accounting Ph.D.

students, Jerry's Ph.D. seminars have been attended by graduate students in economics, finance, and management science, as well as a number of visiting scholars. All have contributed to the development of the material used in this book.

We are particularly appreciative of colleagues who have read some draft chapters and given us feedback that directly helped us to improve the book. These include Hans Frimor, Jim Ohlson, Alex Thevaranjan, and Martin Wu. Recently, Anne Adithipyangkul, Yanmin Gao, and Yinghua Li (three current Ph.D. students) have served as Jerry's research assistants and have carefully read through the recent drafts of all of the chapters. We are thankful for their diligence and enthusiasm. We are grateful to Peter's secretary, Lene Holbæk, for her substantial editorial assistance.

Jerry's research has been supported by funds from the American Accounting Association, his Arthur Andersen Professorship, and the Social Sciences and Humanities Research Council of Canada. Peter's research has been supported by funds from the Danish Association of Certified Public Accountants, and the Social Sciences Research Council of Denmark.

The writing of a book is a time consuming process. Moreover, every stage takes more time than planned. One must be optimistic to take on the challenge, and then one must constantly refocus as various self imposed deadlines are past. We are particularly thankful for the loving patience and good humor of our wives, Else and June, who had to put up with our constant compulsion to work on the book. Also, Peter has three sons at home, Kasper, Esben, and Anders. They had to share Peter's time with the book, but they also enjoyed a sabbatical year in Vancouver.

Peter O. Christensen

Gerald A. Feltham

CHAPTER 1

INTRODUCTION TO INFORMATION IN MARKETS

In their book on cost determination, Demski and Feltham (1977) characterize accounting as playing both *decision-facilitating* and *decision-influencing* roles within organizations. In its decision-facilitating role, accounting reports provide information that affects a decision maker's beliefs about the consequences of his actions, and accounting forecasts may be used to represent the predicted consequences. On the other hand, in its decision-influencing role, anticipated accounting reports pertaining to the consequences of a decision maker's actions may influence his action choices (particularly if his future compensation will be influenced by those reports).

We adopt these two themes, but broaden the perspective to consider the impact of accounting on investors, as well as managers. We view accounting as an economic activity – it requires the expenditure of resources, and affects the well-being of those who participate in the economy. Obviously, to understand the economic impact of accounting requires economic analysis.

The relevant economic analysis is often referred to as *information economics*. It is a relatively broad field that began to develop in the nineteen-fifties, with significant expansion in the nineteen-eighties. Much of information economic analysis makes no explicit reference to accounting reports. In fact, even the information economic analyses conducted by accounting researchers often do not model the specific form of an accounting report. Nonetheless, many generic results apply to accounting reports. Furthermore, the impact of accounting reports depends on the other information received by the economy's participants. Hence, it is essential that accounting researchers have a broad understanding of the impact of publicly reported information within settings in which there are multiple sources of public and private information.

In our two volumes, we consider the fundamentals of a variety of economic analyses of the decision-influencing and decision-facilitating roles of information. While many of these analyses do not model the details of accounting reports, our choices reflect our convictions as to the analyses that are relevant for understanding the economic impact of accounting.

While the two volumes contain many references to recent research, we do not seek to comprehensively cover recent research. Information economic research has grown significantly, and our focus is on fundamentals. New researchers, particularly Ph.D. students, find it difficult to find time to read the fundamental work in the field, and this makes it difficult for them to fully grasp the recent work. Our two volumes stem from two Ph.D. seminars at The University of British Columbia. The first considers economic analyses that are pertinent to the examination of the role of accounting information in capital markets. The second considers economic analyses that are pertinent to the examination of the role of accounting information in motivating managers. Hopefully, by developing an understanding of the fundamentals in these two areas, new researchers will be able to gain a broad understanding of the field, and then will be able to efficiently read and understand the recent work that is of interest to them.

The focus in this first volume is on the decision-facilitating role of information, with emphasis on the impact of public and private information on the equilibria and investor welfare in capital and product markets. A key distinction between the analyses in the two volumes is that in the first volume, managers of firms are not explicitly modeled as economic agents – they do what they are told by shareholders, and do not require any incentives to do so. In the second volume, managers are economic agents with personal preferences, and the theme is the role of information for performance evaluation.

This first volume is divided into four parts. In Part A, we set the stage in terms of representation of uncertainty, preferences, decisions, and information. The important concept of risk sharing is also introduced in a partnership setting. Risk sharing is a key concept both in the market setting and in the analyses of performance evaluation in the second volume. Part B extends the analysis to a competitive market setting with public information, whereas Part C considers settings in which investors may acquire private information. Finally, Part D considers settings in which managers (or owners) of firms have private information that they can publicly disclose to the capital and product markets. This first chapter provides a brief overview of each of the four parts.

1.1 BASIC DECISION-FACILITATING ROLE OF INFORMATION

If accounting reports are to be informative about the future, a decision maker must believe there are multiple events that can occur, he must be uncertain about which events have occurred or will occur, and he must believe there is a relation between past and future events. A report is informative if it changes the decision maker's beliefs about the possible events. In Chapter 2 we summarize the key elements of the representation of uncertainty and decision maker preferences under uncertainty. The representation of information and its decision-facilitating role are introduced in Chapter 3.

To represent uncertainty we introduce the concept of a *state*. The state is a complete description of all possible past and future events that are beyond the decision maker's control. There are many possible states, but "in the end" only one is realized. The outcome of any action (or sequence of actions) can be represented as a function of the decision maker's actions and the state.

An *event* is a collection of states to which we can assign *probabilities*, which represent the decision maker's beliefs about the likelihood of the events occurring. The specification of the set of states, the set of events, and the decision maker's probabilities is the *probability space* on which economic decision problems under uncertainty can be defined.

Decision-making under uncertainty is a choice among gambles (i.e., outcome probability distributions). Based on assumptions of rational choice under uncertainty, a decision maker's preferences can be represented by a utility function which assigns a real number to each possible outcome, such that the decision maker's optimal action (i.e., preferred gamble) maximizes his expected utility.

Throughout this volume, an outcome is often described in terms of some physical or monetary measure of wealth or consumption (possibly at multiple dates). A decision maker is always assumed to *prefer more outcome to less*, and is generally assumed to be either risk neutral or strictly risk averse. That is, the decision maker's utility function is increasing and either linear or strictly concave. Preferences among gambles (actions) are often decision maker specific, but the *first*- and *second-order dominance relations* provide partial orderings of gambles such that one gamble dominates another if it is preferred by all decision makers who have increasing or have increasing, concave utility functions, respectively.

In Chapter 3 we consider *decision-facilitating information systems* in the context of *single-person decision making under uncertainty.* An information system is represented as a set of signals (e.g., accounting reports) that might be generated and the likelihood of the possible signals given the possible events that affect the outcomes generated by the decision maker's actions. A signal (e.g., an accounting report) potentially changes a decision maker's beliefs about the outcomes from his action alternatives and, hence, potentially changes his action preferences. To have economic value to a decision maker, he must believe that his outcome beliefs will be changed by some of the possible signals and, for at least some of the signals, those changes in beliefs will be sufficient to change his preferred action.

The key characteristic of a signal is the *posterior* event beliefs it generates. The representation of that information is, to some extent, arbitrary. For example, we can report income in Canadian dollars or Euros, but the information content is exactly the same (if we know the exchange rate). Furthermore, in some settings, the decision maker's posterior beliefs are not influenced by details – a summary measure such as net income might result in the same beliefs as a report with all the components of net income. This leads to the concept of a *sufficient statistic* – knowing a sufficient statistic is as good as knowing any other representation of the information, and there are always many possible sufficient statistics. A key characteristic of a sufficient statistic is that it is not sensitive to the decision maker's utility function or prior event beliefs, it only depends on his beliefs about the likelihood of the possible signals given the possible events of interest.

For a given decision maker and information system, there is an *optimal decision rule* specifying the optimal action for each signal the information system might generate. The choice among information systems is based on the decision maker's expected utilities that result from using the optimal decision rules for each information system. In general, the preference ordering among information systems depends on the characteristics of the decision problem, i.e., the decision maker's preferences and beliefs, and the relation between outcomes and actions. However, if the signals from one information system tell at least as much about the likelihood of the outcome-relevant events as the signals from another information system, the former is weakly preferred to the latter independently of the characteristics of the decision problem.[1] This result is commonly referred to as the *Blackwell Theorem*.

Accounting information has many different roles. The analyses in Chapters 2 and 3 focus on decision making under uncertainty by a single decision maker – the only role for information in that setting is to facilitate the decision maker's decisions. In the remainder of the book, we consider settings in which there are multiple decision makers. While the use of accounting information for facilitating decisions continues to be important, the role of accounting information in the contractual arrangements within the organization and between the firm and the markets in which it operates becomes an additional key issue.

We begin our examination of the economics of accounting information in multi-person decision making in Chapter 4 by considering a simple setting that we call a *partnership* (also referred to in the literature as a syndicate). The key concepts introduced are *efficient risk sharing* and *congruent preferences* for action and information system choices.

In Chapter 4, a partnership is assumed to have the following key characteristics. There are two or more partners who contract to share an aggregate outcome that depends on random outcome-relevant events and, possibly, also on actions taken by one or more partners. Each partner has personal preferences depending on his personal share of the aggregate outcome, i.e., his piece of the

---

[1] Of course, this ignores differences in the costs of implementing the various information systems.

total pie. The partners have no direct preferences with respect to the actions that are taken. The size of the total pie available to the partnership is contractible information, so that the partners can agree to a *sharing rule* that specifies how each partner's share of the total will be determined.

For a given action, uncertainty with respect to the outcome-relevant events creates uncertainty about the size of the total pie. How should that risk be shared between the partners? Obviously, the partners would like the sharing rule (i.e., the allocation of the event-contingent aggregate outcome between partners) to be *Pareto efficient*. That is, it is not possible to find another allocation that makes at least one partner better off and no partner worse off. If beliefs are homogeneous, each partner's event-contingent consumption only depends on the size of the total, i.e., each partner's consumption can be written as a function of aggregate consumption. Furthermore, the slope of this function is given by the ratio of the partner's risk tolerance (the inverse of the risk aversion) relative to the aggregate risk tolerance of all partners. That is, the more risk tolerant partners bear bigger shares of the risk in the aggregate outcome.

The information system is assumed to report the outcome that is to be shared, i.e., the outcome is contractible information. With homogeneous beliefs, the reporting of other post-decision information, such as the events that affect the outcome, is irrelevant. However, if beliefs are heterogeneous, the partners can benefit from making "side-bets" on events that will be reported in addition to the aggregate outcome.

HARA utility functions constitute an important class of utility functions that we consider in many different contexts throughout the book. This class consists of utility functions for which the risk tolerance is a linear function of the decision maker's consumption, and includes the exponential, the logarithmic, and the power utility functions. The slope coefficient in this linear function is termed the *risk cautiousness*. If all partners have homogeneous beliefs and the same risk cautiousness, then each partner's efficient consumption is a linear function of the aggregate outcome, i.e., there is *linear risk sharing*.

Interestingly, the conditions that result in linear risk sharing also result in congruent (i.e., identical) preferences over actions and pre-decision information systems if the sharing rule is efficient. Furthermore, those preferences can be represented by a "partnership utility function." Hence, the analyses of information systems in Chapter 3 apply in a straightforward manner to partnerships for which there are congruent preferences.

It should be noted that although we only present the sufficiency of linear sharing for congruent preferences, the conditions for linear risk sharing are (in most cases) also necessary conditions for congruent preferences. Furthermore, we also reiterate that we have assumed the partners have no direct preferences with respect to their actions. Models in which there are direct action preferences are typically called agency models. These are examined in Volume II.

1.2 PUBLIC INFORMATION IN EQUITY MARKETS

In Part A we consider the basic economic model of single-person decision making, and we extend the analysis to partnerships with multiple decision makers. In both settings, pre-decision information reduces the uncertainty about the future consequences of current actions and, thus, helps make better decisions. In Part B we move to a competitive market setting in which firms are owned by equityholders (investors) and the information is public, i.e., known to all investors.

1.2.1 Impact of Public Information in Pure-exchange Setting

There are three key differences between our partnership and market settings. First, in our partnership setting, there is a single firm and the partners have no other random sources of consumption. On the other hand, in our market setting, there are multiple firms and a partner may have other random sources of consumption (e.g., compensation for labor). Second, the form of the partnership contract is unrestricted, whereas, in the market setting, there is no direct contracting and the risk sharing possibilities are constrained by the available set of marketed securities (e.g., equity in the firms). Third, the "weights" used in determining the size of each partner's share of the partnership outcome are exogenous, whereas, in the market settings, the investors' "weights" are endogenously determined and depend on their exogenously endowed ownership of marketed securities and non-tradeable claims to consumption.

In the market setting, the investors need not trade. Hence, each investor's share of the risky aggregate outcome after trading must give him at least as high an expected utility as the expected utility of his endowed position (i.e., *individual rationality*). The market is assumed to be competitive, so that investors take the market prices of securities as given, and choose their portfolio of securities to maximize their expected utility subject to their budget constraints (i.e., *individual optimality*). The security prices are determined such that demand equals supply for each security (i.e., *market clearing*). If there are production choices, efficient production choices maximize the market value of the firm's current and future dividends (to all its claimants).

In our market setting, information can affect the market prices of the marketed securities and the trades made by investors, as well as the production choices by the firms' managers. We initially (Chapters 5, 6, and 7) focus on pure exchange settings in which the managers' production choices are treated as exogenous and unaffected by changes in the information system. Furthermore, we assume that all investors receive the same information at the same time (e.g., publicly reported dividends and financial statements).

All information systems (even the null system) report the dividends received by investors. A key issue in the pure exchange setting is the identification of conditions under which additional public information does or does not have economic value. Interestingly, in any risk sharing setting, public information can have a negative effect if it comes before the investors have had an opportunity to share their risks. For example, you cannot insure a risk if you and the insurer already know the outcome.

This negative effect is avoided if investors can trade claims before public information is released. Interestingly, while the subsequent release of public information will cause equilibrium prices to change (if investor beliefs change), this does not imply that the information has economic value to investors. That is, price changes (or even trading) do not imply changes in consumption plans. In particular, in a pure exchange setting, changes in public information will not facilitate a Pareto improvement if endowments are measurable with respect to the less informative system, and the investors have homogeneous beliefs and time-additive preferences. Hence, additional public information can only be valuable to investors if it facilitates better insurance of personally endowed consumption risks, more side-betting due to heterogeneous beliefs, or improved coordination of consumption across periods due to diverse non-time-additive preferences. None of the above seem to be key sources of value for publicly reported accounting information. Hence, we extend our pure-exchange, public information model to consider endogenous production choice.

1.2.2 Impact of Public Information in a Production Choice Setting

While information induced price changes imply investor beliefs have changed, the key issue is whether those changes in beliefs result in changes in production plans by the firms (and, hence, affect the investors' consumption plans). That is, does the information facilitate a more efficient use of the economy's resources? We explore this role for information in Chapter 8.

In the pure exchange setting we introduce a distinction between economy-wide and firm-specific events. The former are events that affect the aggregate supply of consumption in the economy, and thereby create risks which investors must share. The latter, on the other hand, are events that affect the outcomes of specific firms, and create risks which investors can avoid by holding well-diversified portfolios. In the production setting, we consider information about both economy-wide and firm-specific events, and allow for the possibility that managers might have firm-specific information that is not known by investors.

A manager is exogenously assumed to select the production plan that maximizes the intrinsic value of the firm. The intrinsic value equals the market value that would hold if the managers and investors had the same information. The analysis establishes that, in the production setting, it is valuable for managers and investors to have information about economy-wide events, even though this information was not valuable in the pure-exchange setting. On the other hand, while it is valuable for managers to have firm-specific information about the firm's productivity, it is irrelevant whether this information is reported or not reported to investors (assuming that investors trade well-diversified portfolios at prices that reflect the fact that managers have firm-specific productivity information).

In sum, information that facilitates managers' production decisions is valuable. Nonetheless, there is no benefit to mandating managers to report their private firm-specific information to investors if the investors trade well-diversified portfolios in a competitive market in which they all will receive the same information (and they have homogeneous beliefs, as well as time-additive preferences). That is, while reporting firm-specific information may appear to facilitate the investors' investment decisions because it influences market prices, the investors gain no benefit from that information.

Given these results, one may question whether it is worthwhile for accounting researchers to study general equilibrium models of competitive markets. We obviously feel that it is. First, it is important for accounting researchers to understand the nature of these results so that we do not use arguments for the value of accounting information that are incorrect. For example, establishing that accounting reports or earnings forecasts affect prices establishes that the report or forecast influences investors' beliefs, but it does not establish that reporting this information to investors makes them better off.

Second, general equilibrium models are essential for understanding the implications of the investors' opportunity to trade claims, particularly in contexts in which there are both diversifiable and non-diversifiable risks. In Parts C and D of this volume, and in the second volume, we consider partial equilibrium models of settings in which markets are not perfectly competitive, due, for example, to private investor information, imperfect competition in product markets, and incentive issues for managers. In those settings there is greater scope for financial reporting to investors to have value. Partial equilibrium models are used for tractability reasons. However, their appropriateness depends on how well they reflect the prices that would result from a general equilibrium model. We believe the big picture is important and understanding general equilibrium prices and investor welfare in a perfectly competitive market is useful for understanding prices and investor welfare in imperfectly competitive markets.

For example, the agency literature commonly assumes a risk-neutral principal without any further justification. That assumption can be justified in a general equilibrium setting if the contractible information is viewed as pertaining to firm-specific events, and the principal is viewed as a partnership of investors who hold a diversified portfolio of firms. On the other hand, if there are both firm-specific and economy-wide risks, the latter type of risk must be recognized when we specify the principal's utility function.

Part B is structured as follows. Chapters 5, 6, and 7 consider pure-exchange settings in which production and dividend decisions are fixed, so that the event-contingent dividends from marketed securities are exogenous. Chapter 5 provides some basic insights by focusing on a single-period setting while Chapters 6 and 7 extend the analysis to settings with multiple consumption and trading dates. In Chapter 6 the public information structure is fixed and it provides the basis for the examination in Chapter 7 of the impact of changes in public information systems (e.g., the rules governing published accounting reports) in a pure-exchange setting. Chapter 8 extends the analysis to settings in which production/dividend decisions are endogenous. In Chapters 9 and 10 we consider the relation between accounting information and market values of firms. We review that analysis in the following section.

1.2.3 Market Values and Accounting Information

We draw heavily from the basic theory of finance for our understanding of the relation between public information and the market prices of marketed securities. Investors consume dividends, and are assumed to prefer more consumption to less. Dividends are publicly reported and future dividends are assumed to depend on uncertain future events, so that a marketed security is described as a sequence of event contingent dividends. At any given date, the history of information provided by the public reporting system is represented by a signal that equals the set of events that have a positive probability of occurring in the future. Each marketed security has a signal/date contingent market price.

An *arbitrage* opportunity exists if an investor can get "something for nothing," e.g., he can find a trading strategy of marketed securities that requires no investment and is guaranteed to provide a non-negative return with a positive probability of a positive return. A basic assumption for a competitive market is that security prices and, in particular, the relative security prices, are such that there are *no arbitrage opportunities*. Otherwise, the security prices cannot be sustained as part of an equilibrium in which demand equals supply. If there are no market frictions, the assumption of no arbitrage has important implications for how security prices are determined, and these implications do not require specification of the investors' endowments, beliefs, or preferences (beyond non-satiation). The key implication of no arbitrage is that for each date and signal at that date, the price of a security can be expressed as the weighted sum of all possible future date-event contingent dividends. The weights, which are referred to as *event prices*, apply to all marketed securities at a given date, but change with time and the publicly reported signals.

Two alternative representations of no-arbitrage market values are instructive. First, the event prices for each date can be normalized so that they sum to one, and can be interpreted as *risk-neutral probabilities.* The current market price of a market security can then be expressed as the net present value of the *risk-adjusted expected dividends*, with the riskless discount rate for each date set equal to the current price of a *zero-coupon bond* for that date. This valuation relation is *as if* investors are risk neutral and hold homogeneous beliefs given by the *risk-neutral probabilities.* However, the existence of the risk-neutral probabilities follows solely from the no-arbitrage condition – investors may be risk averse or risk lovers, and they may hold heterogeneous beliefs.

Second, if the investors have homogeneous beliefs, then an event-contingent *valuation index* can be computed for each event by dividing the risk-neutral probability by the investors' probability. The risk-adjusted expected dividend for a marketed security can then be computed by applying the investors' beliefs and adding the covariance between the security's dividend and the valuation index. The valuation index is based on the no-arbitrage event prices, and cannot be given any additional economic interpretation based solely on the no-arbitrage assumptions. However, in an equilibrium context with homogeneous beliefs and time-additive preferences, the valuation index is a measure of the scarcity of consumption, i.e., if aggregate consumption is relatively scarce in a future event, the valuation index for that event is relatively high. In other words, the price of a security increases as the covariance of the dividend with the scarcity of consumption increases, *ceteris paribus.* Furthermore, the event prices are determined by three factors: the discount factor, the conditional probability of the event, and the relative scarcity of consumption in that event.

Clean Surplus Accounting

The analyses in Chapters 5 through 8 are based on a *dividend-value relation* in which security prices are expressed in terms of future date-event contingent dividends. Chapter 9 introduces an *accounting-value relation* in which security prices are expressed in terms of the current book value of equity and future date-event contingent residual income, where residual income equals net accounting income minus the spot interest rate times the opening book value of equity. The accounting-value relation is based on the no-arbitrage dividend-value relation plus an assumption that the predicted accounting numbers satisfy a *clean surplus relation.* This latter relation states that, except for the dividends, all changes in the book value of equity are recorded in the income statement.

Interestingly, changing the accounting policy affects the current book value of equity and future date-event contingent residual income but, nonetheless, the market value of equity stays the same. This holds as long as the clean surplus relation is satisfied by the accounting policy used in deriving forecasts, and the accounting policy has no economic consequences (e.g., tax effects). Changing the accounting policy such that more value is recognized in one period will always result in the recognition of less value in some other periods, and the effects are precisely offsetting. In other words, the accounting-value relation does not depend on the use of "proper" accounting, e.g., accounting that reflects changes in economic value.

The accounting-value relation is simply a restatement of the dividend-value relation using the clean surplus relation. However, the accounting-value relation provides interesting insights as more assumptions are imposed. For example, if we assume mark-to-market accounting for financial assets, and there is dividend policy irrelevance, then the market value relation can be restated as an *operating income value relation* in which the market value of equity is equal to the book value of equity plus the net present value of the future risk-adjusted expected *residual operating income*. The key insight is that we only need forecasts of the operating activities. The distribution of value to equityholders through the choice of dividend policy (and, thus, retained earnings) is irrelevant – it only affects the financial assets, and they are marked-to-market. Another insight from this analysis is that the discounted operating cash flow model, which is often used in corporate finance, can be viewed as a special case of the residual operating income model. Under "cash accounting," the book value of operating assets is zero, so that the capital charge used in computing residual operating income equals zero.

Conceptually, the current market value of equity depends on the forecasts of dividends, residual income, residual operating income, or operating cash flows for the entire anticipated life of the firm. However, it is always possible to express that value as a function of forecasts for some shorter period, and then make an appropriate truncation adjustment. The nature of that adjustment is identified in Section 9.3 for the dividend model and the various forms of accounting models.

Most of the value relations developed in Chapters 5 through 10 assume the number of shares will remain constant, and all exchanges of cash between the firm and its equityholders are encompassed by the dividends (which may be positive or negative). This is readily extended to the issuance or repurchase of shares for cash, if the exchange takes place at the current market price of the shares. However, the issuance of contingent claims to shares (e.g., warrants, convertible debt, and employee stock options) presents non-trivial valuation issues. The analysis in Section 9.4 considers these types of transactions and identifies a class of "super clean" surplus accounting policies such that discounting the risk-adjusted expected residual income based on these policies yields the market value of the current equity outstanding. In addition, a class of "mixed" surplus accounting policies are identified which yield the aggregate market value of the equity outstanding plus the current contingent claims to equity.

Dividend policy irrelevance is not assumed in our basic no-arbitrage valuation models, but it is assumed in all of the analyses in which we separate the book value of equity into financial and operating assets, and assume financial assets are marked-to-market. Taxes can create frictions such that the dividend policy is not irrelevant. In Appendix 9A, we illustrate the care that must be taken in specifying the accounting numbers used in specifying accounting-value relation in the presence of taxes.

Information Dynamics

Chapter 9 establishes relations between the current market value of equity and forecasts of future residual income numbers (and current book value). Obviously, those forecasts depend on the investors' current information. Chapter 10 develops several examples of the relation between market values and representations of investor information that use current and past accounting numbers. The representations in each example are not unique. They depend on the accounting policies used to determine the accounting numbers employed in representing that information.

In each example we assume a stationary economy in which some sufficient statistic for the investors' information is given by a linear process – *a linear information dynamic*. The linear information dynamic and no arbitrage imply that the market value of equity is a linear function of the information variables. A key feature of our analysis is that the statistic representing investor information need not involve accounting numbers. In fact, the initial statistic we consider is expressed in terms of operating cash flows (such as net cash receipts from operations and cash investments in operating assets), as well as other non-accounting information. We then develop alternative statistics that involve accounting numbers derived by applying explicit accounting policies to the initially specified dynamics. This approach facilitates exploration of the impact of accounting policies on the relation between equity value and contemporaneous accounting numbers.

In our basic model (Section 10.2), there is a one-period lag between capital investment and a randomly decaying sequence of net cash receipts. The investors' information can be represented by either the current cash flow information or accrual accounting numbers. The accounting is defined to be unbiased if the difference between the market and book value of the firm's operating assets is expected to equal zero in the long-run (i.e., after any current idiosyncratic differences have been eliminated). On the other hand, if that difference is expected to be positive, then the accounting is defined to be conservative. In our basic model, there are two potential sources of accounting conservatism: the depreciation rate and the anticipated existence of current and future positive net present value (NPV) investment opportunities. The former can be avoided by depreciating capital investments at the same rate as the expected rate of decay in the cash receipts from prior investments. However, the latter is endemic if we record investments only when they are made, and then only at their cost.

The initial discussion of linear models identifies a set of assumptions under which market risk can be recognized and still maintain linearity. While we assume risk neutrality in virtually all the examples in Chapter 10, we do illustrate the recognition of market risk in our basic model. As in Chapter 9, the discount factor and the capital charged used in computing residual operating income are based on the riskless interest rate (which is assumed to be constant in our examples). The adjustment for risk is encapsulated entirely in the linear coefficients applied to residual income, start-of-period book value (if the depreciation rate is conservative), and current investments (if there are positive NPV investments).

The basic model is extended in Section 10.2.2 to include the possibility of "other" investment information about the random persistence of cash receipts from prior investments and the random growth in investment opportunities. This gives greater scope for the use of accrual accounting to reflect the investors' "other" information, and thereby reduce the dimensionality of the statistic used to represent the investors' information. Accounting policies are defined to be "efficient" if the current market value of a firm's equity can be expressed as its current book value plus a multiple of its current residual operating income. While efficiency is possible, it is not achieved if there are positive NPV investments and they are recorded at the cost when incurred.

"Other" information is ubiquitous and is unlikely to be "efficiently" impounded in accounting numbers. This creates difficulties for empirical researchers, since it forces them to find proxies for the "other" information. Many empirical studies have merely ignored the "other" information and "hoped" this did not create an omitted variables problem. As discussed in Section 10.2.3, an alternative approach is to use analysts' forecasts as a means of inferring the investors' "other" information. This effectively integrates approaches that relate current market value to accounting income forecasts, with approaches that relate current market value to current accounting income. The existence of "other" information about both the random persistence of net cash receipts from prior investments and the random growth in investment opportunities play a central role in these results.

Section 10.3 considers examples based on models that are similar to our basic capital investment model, but introduce some key differences. The basic model assumes that net cash receipts randomly persist and cash investments randomly grow. However, in many settings the random cash receipts and cash investments contain both persistent and transitory elements. The example in Section 10.3.1 illustrates that in relating market values to current residual income it is useful to separate out (and ignore) transitory cash receipts. This may appear to be a violation of the clean surplus relation, but it is not. We emphasize that the clean surplus relation must hold for forecasted accounting numbers, but that it is appropriate to omit transitory components of current residual income if they are uninformative about future residual income. Information about current cash investments has no impact if the firm invests in zero NPV projects. On the other hand, if the firm invests in positive NPV projects, it is important to consider both transitory and persistent investments.

The coefficients will be positive for both types, but the former will be smaller than the latter.

The example in Section 10.3.2 introduces a two-period lag between net cash receipts and cash investments. This additional lag is depicted as arising from a one period delay in receiving cash from customer sales. This allows us to illustrate a working capital accrual represented by accounts receivable adjusted for an allowance for bad debts (based on "other" investor information). This model further illustrates the impact of transitory cash receipts, since it is sales that persist in this model, rather than the cash receipts *per se*.

The final example (Section 10.3.3) introduces research and development (R&D) expenditures. They constitute a significant source of conservative accounting, since GAAP requires expensing, rather than capitalizing, significant portions of R&D. Merely expensing the cash investments in our basic model does not adequately illustrate the R&D effect, since that merely results in "cash accounting." In our R&D example we recognize that R&D expenditures often result in capital investments in production facilities, which are capitalized and subsequently result in cash receipts. In our linear value relation, the R&D expenditures must effectively be removed from residual operating income and handled separately – we refer to this as a line-item approach (which is illustrated in earlier examples, e.g., those involving conservative depreciation and transitory cash receipts). We do not consider capitalization of R&D, although that could be done. Instead, we merely illustrate a linear value relation in which R&D is excluded from residual income and used separately to the extent it reflects information about current and future positive NPV investments in R&D. Interestingly, if R&D is a non-negative NPV investment, then implementation investments must be positive NPV investments, thereby providing another source of conservative accounting in this example.

1.3 PRIVATE INVESTOR INFORMATION IN EQUITY MARKETS

Part B considers the impact of public information in competitive capital markets in which all investors receive the same information and are price takers. In Part C we consider the impact of private investor information and non-price taking behavior. The interactive effect of public reports and private investor information is of particular interest to accounting researchers. We are interested in private investor information for two reasons. First, it is widely recognized that investors often know much of the information content in an accounting report before it is released. One reason for this is private information acquisition by investors. The gain from private information comes from going long or short in a firm's shares immediately before the release of public information that causes the price to increase or decrease (and then reversing the position after the information is impounded in the price). Thus, intuitively, one expects investor demand for private information to increase immediately prior to an anticipated public report. Second, the timely release of earnings forecasts and other management information may reduce the incremental informativeness of a private signal and, thus, reduce the incentive to acquire the private signal. Recognizing that investors may acquire private information allows us to examine the relation between public reports, private information acquisition, price changes, price informativeness, and trading volume. The identified relations provide insights that are potentially useful in explaining the relations observed in empirical studies.

In perfectly competitive capital markets with no private information, market prices depend only on the publicly reported information and, thus, equilibrium prices carry no additional information about the occurrence of the uncertain events. However, if some investors know more about future events than is publicly reported, they will utilize that information in determining their demands for individual securities. Hence, the aggregate demand for individual securities and, thus, the market clearing prices, depend on the investors' private information. Obviously, rational investors realize that there is a dependence between private investor information and equilibrium prices. This means that rational investors use the equilibrium prices as signals about the other investors' private information. Hence, the equilibrium concept must recognize that the equilibrium prices of securities themselves are a source of information that affects the investors' demand for individual securities. Equilibria that reflect attempts by investors to infer other investors' information from the equilibrium prices are termed *rational expectations equilibria.*

If the set of available securities is sufficiently rich and private information is the only random factor affecting prices, then the equilibrium prices fully reveal a sufficient statistic for the investors' information, i.e., the resulting equilibrium is *a fully revealing rational expectations equilibrium.* This implies that any anticipated attempt to use the private information will result in the impounding of the private information in the market price, so that there will be no private gain from acquiring the information. This eliminates any incentive to acquire costly private information. However, there would be a private gain if everyone believed that no one is acquiring private information. This implies a lack of an equilibrium due to what is called the *private information paradox.*

In the real world, investors do expend resources on acquiring private information, implying they believe that they will be able to trade on this information without fully revealing it in the trading process. The common approach in the accounting literature (and much of the economics and finance literature as well) is to assume that there is some unobservable, exogenous random factor that influences prices and precludes investors from perfectly inferring the information acquired by other investors. The resulting equilibria are referred to as *noisy rational expectations equilibria.*

A key question is how much of the private information can be inferred from equilibrium prices. In turn, the informativeness of equilibrium prices affects the investors' incentives to acquire private information themselves. Hence, we must examine both the formation of equilibrium security prices and the equilibrium amount of private information acquisition. The informativeness of equilibrium prices depends on how aggressively investors react to their private information, i.e., price informativeness and trading volume are closely related. This analysis ties into the empirical accounting literature examining the relation between, for example, earnings announcements and trading volume.

In most cases, a partial equilibrium analysis is employed in which there is a riskless security and a single risky security, and the unobservable random factor is the supply of the risky security by *liquidity or noise traders*, who trade for reasons independent of public and private information. The fact that the random supply is not observable implies that rational investors cannot determine whether a high price of the risky security is due to other rational investors having favorable information or a low supply from the liquidity traders. Unfortunately, using this approach to introduce noise implies that the analysis does not allow social welfare statements because the preferences of the liquidity traders are not explicitly modeled.[2] Nevertheless, this type of model serves to provide a simple means of introducing noise into the price process, and thereby permits examination of the interactive effect of public and private information acquisition, as well as the response of prices and trading volume to the two types of information. Of course, we can examine how the public reporting system affects the expected utilities of the rational investors, but any gain to the rational investors may be offset by a loss for the liquidity traders.

There are two broad types of analyses in this literature. The models we consider in Chapter 11 assume the rational investors are risk-averse price takers. There are two basic models of this type. The first (referred to as the GS type model) assumes investors have the same constant risk aversion, and they can acquire a common private signal. The uninformed investors imperfectly infer the common private signal from the price. The second (referred to as the HV type model) assumes investors have different risk aversion, and they can acquire differentially precise private signals and make imperfect inferences about the other investors' information from the price. The GS and HV type models obtain similar results since both assume investors are risk-averse price takers. Several

---

[2] Another common approach is to assume the rational investors are randomly endowed with shares of the risky security. Their preferences are modeled, but social welfare statements are equally problematic because the model precludes trading before the investors acquire their private information. Hence, the investors face information risk created by their acquisition of information, and the fact that it is partially impounded in the price.

papers in the accounting literature use HV type models, but we focus on the GS type models because they tend to be less complex.

Risk aversion plays a key role in the GS (and HV) models examined in Chapter 11 since it determines how aggressively the informed investors react to their private information and, thus, how much of the information is impounded in the price. The informed investors are assumed to act as price takers when they trade on their private information. This implies that even though the informed investors rationally anticipate the relation between the equilibrium prices and the private information, they ignore the effect their trades will have on the information conveyed to uninformed investors through the resulting price. This may be a reasonable assumption in settings in which many competing investors become informed and their individual actions have a relatively small impact on the price. However, in some settings there are only a few investors who become informed (e.g., insiders). If their trades have a significant impact on the total trades in the market, they will restrain their trades so as to partially "hide" their private information while still making a profit from its use in their trades.

This latter type of analysis is examined in Chapter 12. The informed investors and the liquidity traders place orders for shares with a "market-maker," who sets the price so that he is expected to breakeven given his inferences about the informed investors' private information based on the total orders received. The informed investors and the market-maker are risk neutral, and the informed investors act strategically in that they anticipate the market-maker's rational inferences from the total orders received. The risk neutrality assumption makes the model relatively simple to use, and provides somewhat different results because of its focus on trading volume and strategic trading by the informed investors.

In both chapters we examine the impact of the informativeness of a public report on price informativeness, price variability, and trading volume in the presence of private information acquisition. The impact of the informativeness of the public report depends on whether the public report is released prior or subsequent to investors acquiring private information. Increasing the informativeness of the public report about the final dividend is likely to reduce the incremental informativeness of the private signal. Hence, if the public report is released prior to private information acquisition, fewer investors acquire the private signal, and they trade less aggressively on their private information. This implies that the increased informativeness of the public report may be partially offset by a reduced informativeness of the price. On the other hand, if the public report is released subsequent to private information acquisition, the advantage of privately acquiring information about the forthcoming public information increases, resulting in a more informative equilibrium price prior to the release of the public report. The price reaction to the public report when it is released will be reduced. That is, in this setting, there can be a negative relation between the informativeness of the public report and the price reaction to the release of the report.

This analysis highlights the fact that the impact of the informativeness of a public report depends on the timing of the release of public reports relative to the acquisition of private information. Obviously, private information can be acquired both prior and subsequent to the release of public reports. Hence, we only point to partial effects that may occur in a more general setting.

The interactive effect of public reports and private information have been used in exploring the use of public reports and market prices in incentive contracts within settings in which the market price is influenced by both accounting reports and private investor information. In that analysis, both the accounting report and the investors' private information are assumed to be useful for incentive contracting, but the latter is not contractible information. The stock price is contractible and reflects both the accounting report and the investors' private information. However, the price may not efficiently aggregate these two sources of information from an incentive contracting perspective. Hence, both the market price and the accounting report are used in optimal contracts. We explore these issues in Chapter 21 in Volume II.

1.4 DISCLOSURE OF PRIVATE OWNER INFORMATION IN EQUITY AND PRODUCT MARKETS

In Part D (Chapters 13, 14, and 15), we assume a firm's current owners (or their representative – the firm's manager) have private information relative to potential new investors or the owners (managers) of other firms. We consider a number of models that examine the informed owners' incentives to reveal their information to others, particularly to investors in new equity that is issued and/or competitors in the firm's product market. This revelation may take place through verified reports (e.g., audited accounting statements), unverified reports (e.g., earnings forecasts), or costly "signals" (e.g., the retention of risk by risk-averse owners). Furthermore, even if a report is not verified, we often assume (as is common in the literature) that the reporting manager is motivated to report truthfully if he reports (e.g., due to unmodeled threats of litigation that may reveal lies).

In Chapter 13 we assume there is a single risk-averse owner, who has decided to take his firm public for the purpose of sharing his risks with well-diversified investors, and to possibly obtain capital from those investors. In Chapters 14 and 15, on the other hand, the current owners are assumed to be risk neutral (e.g., they are well-diversified and the risks are firm-specific) and they are issuing new equity to obtain capital for investments and/or they are concerned about the actions of competitors. In Chapter 14, if there is a competitor, he takes the form of a potential entrant into the product market, whereas in Chapter 15 the firm competes in a duopoly in which the two firms simultaneously choose either production quantities (Cournot competition) or selling prices (Bertrand competition).

1.4.1 Disclosure by a Risk-averse Owner

In the risk-averse owner model in Chapter 13, we do not consider why the owner has not been well-diversified, but merely consider his actions given that he has decided to become as well-diversified as possible. If he had no private information, he would merely sell virtually all the shares in his firm, retaining only the fraction that constitutes his efficient share of market risk. However, as in many initial public offerings (IPOs), the existing owner has private information, and the new investors know he has private information. If the investors will underprice the shares relative to their intrinsic value (i.e., the market price that would hold if the investors knew the owner's private information), then the owner will be motivated to find a mechanism for communicating his private information to the investors.

The owner can always retain some or all of his shares but, obviously, this is costly to the owner since he retains firm-specific risk that he cannot insure through the market. The fraction he retains at a given price is an increasing function of the intrinsic value of the shares. Rational investors will anticipate the relation between price and the fraction sold, thereby making the price a function of that fraction. On the other hand, a rational owner will anticipate the investors' response to his choices. Consequently, in a rational expectations equilibrium (generally referred to as a signaling equilibrium in this type of setting), the fraction of shares retained is a mechanism that can be used to communicate the owner's private information.

In Section 13.2 we discuss some general concepts of equilibria in disclosure (signaling) games. There are typically many Nash equilibria in these games, but many are sustained by non-credible threats as to how investors will react to the owner's off-equilibrium signals (e.g., a retained fraction he is not expected to choose given any information). Hence, refinements of the Nash equilibrium concept are introduced so as to identify credible equilibria (and exclude non-credible equilibria). We refer to the equilibria that satisfy the refinements as "stable." Within our models, these refinements generally serve to support separating equilibria (e.g., equilibria in which there is a separate level of ownership retention for each possible intrinsic value) and to exclude pooling equilibria (e.g., equilibria in which the owner selects the same ownership retention level given all possible intrinsic values, and the price reflects the investors' prior beliefs).

With the requisite game theoretic concepts in hand, Section 13.3 examines two settings in which it is assumed risk retention is the owner's only available mechanism for communicating his private information. In the first setting (Section 13.3.1), the owner's private information is represented by a finite number of possible intrinsic values and there are a finite number of possible outcomes. Instead of merely choosing the number of shares to retain, the owner is able to offer contracts to investors that specify how his compensation will vary with each possible outcome. The contracts in the optimal menu are non-linear functions of the outcome. The owner bears no risk with his worst signal (or for any signal for which he chooses not to operate the firm), and the riskiness of the contract to the owner increases as the intrinsic values increase. That is, the stable equilibrium is a separating equilibrium.

In the second setting (Section 13.3.2), we assume the owner is restricted to choosing his level of ownership retention (i.e., the contract is a linear function of the outcome). This provides the basis for interesting comparative statics when applied in a setting in which the owner's set of possible information is represented by a continua of intrinsic values, the outcome is normally distributed (with a known variance), and the owner's preferences are represented by an exponential utility function. For example, the level of ownership retained is an increasing function of the intrinsic value (a separating equilibrium), and the equilibrium levels are decreasing functions of the variance, i.e., it takes less ownership retention to signal a given intrinsic value if ownership retention is more costly.

In virtually all the models in Part D, we assume that all risk is firm-specific. However, Section 13.3.3 considers the impact of market risk. This analysis establishes that the level of ownership used to signal the owner's information depends only on the firm-specific risk – the market risk is offset, to the extent that it is efficient to do so, through adjustment to the owner's personal investment in the market portfolio.

Risk retention is costly to a risk-averse owner. Hence, he has an incentive to find mechanisms for reducing his risk retention, and still obtain a market price for his shares that is at least as high as their intrinsic value. Section 13.4 considers the possibility of issuing verified reports (e.g., audited financial statements) at the time the shares are issued. If the report can perfectly and costlessly reveal the owner's information (or lack thereof), then the owner will always issue the report and retain no risk. However, a combination of verified reports and risk retention are used if there are frictions, e.g., a report cannot verify the lack of information, the issuance of a verified report is costly, or a verified report imperfectly reveals the owner's information. We characterize the optimal combination in each setting.

Section 13.5 briefly examines the value of verified reports that will be issued at the time the outcome is realized (rather than when the contract is issued). If the report will be incrementally informative about the owner's prior information, it will be optimal for the owner to issue risk sharing contracts in which his compensation is contingent on both the outcome and the *ex post* report.

Finally, Section 13.6 concludes our analysis of reporting by a risk-averse owner with an examination of a setting in which the owner is privately informed about both the intrinsic value of his firm and the risk he will bear if he retains shares. The report is unverified, but is subject to possible litigation and the expected cost of the litigation is a function of the riskiness of the outcome.

1.4.2 Disclosure on Behalf of Risk-neutral Owners

In Chapter 8 we assume investors all have the same information and can efficiently share their risks by trading in well-diversified portfolios of equities in a set of perfectly competitive firms. The manager of each firm is assumed to select the production plan that maximizes his firm's intrinsic value given his information. Since investors trade in well-diversified portfolios, they obtain no benefit from disclosure of the managers' firm-specific information, even though it is beneficial to the investors if the managers have firm-specific information about the productivity of capital invested in their firms.

Chapter 14 considers a similar setting, but focuses on a single firm in which the manager is assumed to act, given his information, so as to maximize the intrinsic value of the shares held by the firm's current owners. Of particular interest to accounting researchers is the manager's decision to disclose his private information. We consider both the *ex post* disclosure choice made after the manager has received his information and the *ex ante* disclosure policy that would be preferred by the current owners.

Risk aversion plays no role in this analysis and, hence, risk retention is not a signaling device. We assume there are no other costly signals available to the manager. His only disclosure device is his report to investors. Throughout most of the chapter, any report made by a manager is assumed to be truthful. This may be because it is audited, or because of threats of future litigation if the manager lies. In any event, recipients believe what the manager says if he discloses information, and a key issue is their response if he does not disclose information.

The current owners are assumed to retain their shares. However, the firm may issue new shares to new investors in order to finance some capital investment in the firm. In that case the value of the current equity depends on the price paid by the new investors (since that will affect the fraction of the firm's ownership retained by the current owners). The higher the price, the larger the retained ownership.

We also consider settings in which the product market is not perfectly competitive. The firm is currently a monopolist but faces a potential competitor. The better the market, the greater is the firm's intrinsic value if it remains a monopolist, but if that is known to the potential competitor, the more likely he is to enter (and thereby reduce the value of the current owners' equity).

The disclosure equilibria depend on whether the recipients of interest are investors in new equity, a potential competitor, or both. The equilibria also depend on whether the available reports are costless and complete, costless and incomplete, or costly. Section 14.2 considers settings in which there is a single type of recipient – either new investors or a potential competitor. If the reports are costless and complete, then the manager will fully disclose all his information even though he would like to "hide" bad news from new investors or "hide" good news from a potential competitor. On the other hand, if the reports are costly, the manager will choose to disclose only good news to new investors, or only bad news to the potential competitor.

Section 14.3 demonstrates that the results can change significantly if the reports are costless and there are two types of recipients. For example, there can exist a disclosure equilibrium in which the manager does not disclose either very bad news (so as not to significantly lower the price of new equity) or very good news (so as not to significantly increase the probability of entry of the competitor), but does disclose information between the two extremes.

Section 14.4 considers settings in which the reports are costless and incomplete, in the sense that the manager cannot issue a report verifying he has no information, and there is a positive probability that it is the case. If there is a single type of recipient, Section 14.4.1 establishes that the manager again discloses only good news if the recipients are new investors, or discloses only bad news if the recipient is a potential competitor. Section 14.4.2 extends the new equity setting to consider the impact of a lawyer who will undertake a lawsuit if there is no report, a bad outcome, and the lawyer believes there is a sufficiently high probability the manager has withheld bad news (as opposed to merely having no information). In that setting, there is an equilibrium in which the manager discloses good news (to obtain a high price for the new equity) and very bad news (to avoid a future law suit), but "hides" the remaining information.

In the basic new equity model, the manager's information system is exogenous and he is assumed to undertake the investment irrespective of the information received (i.e., his information is not decision-facilitating). Further extensions to the new equity setting include the endogenous acquisition of information by the manager (Section 14.4.3) and endogenous investment choice (Section 14.4.4). Interestingly, if the production choice is exogenous, the current owners would prefer, *ex ante*, to preclude the manager from acquiring costly information, but the manager will acquire private information if he is acting in the current owners' best interests *ex post*. On the other hand, the current owners strictly benefit from the manager's private information if it facilitates better investment decisions. Disclosure or lack of disclosure has no *ex ante* benefit to the current owners if the manager makes the production decision. However, if all shares are sold to the new investors and they make the investment decision, the expected market price will be greater the more information the manager discloses to the new investors.

Chapter 14 concludes (in Section 14.5) with a brief discussion of what are called "cheap talk" equilibria. This is a setting where the manager's report is not verified and there are no exogenous incentives for him to tell the truth. Instead, the reporting incentives are all endogenous. If there is only one type of recipient, then there will be effectively no disclosure. However, with two types of recipients, there can exist reporting tensions such that the manager imperfectly reveals his information.

1.4.3 Disclosure in a Duopoly

Chapter 15 continues the analysis in Chapter 14 in that we again assume the current owners are well-diversified and all risk is diversifiable. There are now two firms, with different sets of owners, competing in an industry with downward sloping demand curves for the firms' products. The managers receive private information, which they may disclose, and then simultaneously choose either production quantities (Cournot competition) or prices (Bertrand competition). The managers' information may pertain to either the intercepts of the demand curves or the variable costs of production, and either type of information may be firm-specific or industry-wide.

Under Cournot competition, the owners of the first firm prefer that the second produces less rather than more. This implies that, *ex post*, the first manager prefers to reveal to the second that he has observed good news about either the first firm's demand or costs, or he has observed bad news about either the industry-wide demand or costs. On the other hand, under Bertrand competition, the owners of the first firm prefer that the second sets a higher price rather than a lower price. This implies that, *ex post*, the first manager prefers to reveal to the second that he has observed good news about demand or bad news about costs, irrespective of whether the information is industry-wide or firm specific. Of course, if the managers' information is costlessly and completely verifiable, the *ex post* disclosure equilibrium will be full disclosure.

Interestingly, while there is full disclosure *ex post*, that is not always the *ex ante* preference of the firms' owners. In fact, we begin Chapter 15 (Section 15.1) with an examination of the owners' *ex ante* choice among disclosure policies, assuming the manager can be committed to follow these policies. In each case, there are gains to disclosure of either good news or bad news, with losses to disclosure of the converse (all relative to the results with no disclosure). If the gain from disclosure is a concave (convex) function of the manager's signal, then the optimal *ex ante* disclosure choice is no (full) disclosure. This yields the result that no disclosure is preferred *ex ante* if the information is industry-wide with Cournot competition or firm-specific with Bertrand competition. On the other hand, full disclosure is preferred *ex ante* if the information is firm-specific with Cournot competition or industry-wide with Bertrand competition.

Section 15.2 considers *ex post* disclosure under Cournot competition. Section 15.2.1 provides the full disclosure results described above, assuming production choice is positive for all information. However, there can be a partial disclosure equilibrium if some information results in zero or negative production (if that is feasible). Section 15.2.2 then integrates the analysis of disclosure in a duopoly with the analysis in Section 14.4 that assumes there is a positive probability a manager is uninformed and he cannot verify that fact to his competitor. The results are comparable to those for the single recipient models in Section 14.4.1.

Similarly, Section 15.2.3 integrates the analysis of disclosure in a duopoly with the two-recipient model in Section 14.3.1 in which the firm must obtain capital by issuing equity to new investors. The manager's disclosure preferences are the same for both recipients if the private information pertains to either firm-specific demand or cost information under Cournot competition, or to firm-specific or industry-wide demand information under Bertrand competition. Hence, in these settings there is full disclosure. However, in the other settings (i.e., industry-wide demand or cost information with Cournot competition or firm-specific or industry-wide cost information under Bertrand competition), there is a tension similar to the tension in Section 14.3.1 (where the competitor is a potential entrant). However, while the equilibrium in Section 14.3.1 involves no disclosure of very bad and very good news, in the duopoly setting the equilibrium may be such that, for example, the manager only discloses good industry-wide information.

1.5 CONCLUDING REMARKS

Our focus in this volume is on the economic analysis of information in capital and product markets, with particular emphasis on the impact of public reports. In laying the foundation, we considered settings in which there is no private information. However, to fully understand the impact of public reports we must consider them in the context of settings in which investors and managers acquire private information. Except for the liquidity traders in Chapters 11 and 12, and the managers in Chapters 8, 14, and 15, the "players" in our analysis are rational, expected utility maximizers. If some players have private information, then it is common knowledge that they may have such information, and everyone "plays" accordingly. The uninformed players make inferences about the private information of the informed players based on the observable consequences of the informed players' choices. The informed players, on the other hand, are aware that the uninformed will be making such inferences, and act accordingly.

While there is a developing body of research referred to as behavioral economics and finance, we have restricted our attention to classical information economic analysis. Even so, we have not attempted to provide an exhaustive survey of all the relevant literature, particularly with respect to recent research. Our objective has been to provide an integrated exploration of the basic information economic research that we perceive is relevant for understanding the economic impact of accounting information. The material is quite technical, rather than being an intuitive survey. The content is designed to help develop the technical background and skills of new accounting researchers who wish to be able to efficiently read the current information economic literature in accounting, and to carry out their own information economic research. If a reader develops a strong interest in a particular area, then they should read the original research in that area. It should be much easier to do so if you have carefully gone through this book.

There are gaps in the material covered in this book. In some cases, we have omitted models that we view as interesting, but which we view as relatively idiosyncratic. That is, while many papers provide interesting insights relative to our area of interest, some stand alone in the literature. We have focused on work in which there are a number of related papers.

In other cases, there are relevant areas of research which constitute a sufficiently large body of research that they require separate volumes, e.g., papers that explore the economics of auditing. An obvious area of research that fits into this latter category is the use of public reports as performance measures in motivating managers. We assume in this volume that the manager is either irrelevant or is exogenously motivated to act (rationally) in the best interests of the owners. However, managers are more appropriately viewed as rational players who act in their own best interests. Their authority in operating a firm is delegated to them by the owners. This is a contractual arrangement, and the terms of that contract often provide incentives by making a manager's compensation conditional on his reported performance. Hence, public reports potentially play an important role in a firm's operations by serving as performance measures in contracting with managers. We view this as a very significant role for accounting reports and, hence, explore this area in Volume II of this book.

Finally, some of the gaps in this book reflect gaps in the available literature. The reader is encouraged to undertake research to fill those gaps. Of particular note is the use of accounting reports in contracting with debtholders. Throughout this book we focus on equityholders, and often assume that the firm is exclusively financed by equity or that the existence of debt does not affect the manager's actions. For example, in Chapters 9 and 10 we explicitly consider the possibility of debt, but put it into the background by assuming dividend policy irrelevance and mark-to-market accounting for debt (which is viewed as a negative financial asset). Tax and bankruptcy issues raise questions about the dividend policy irrelevance assumption. Furthermore, the existence of debt is likely to affect the choices made by managers, whether they are acting in the best interests of the equityholders or of themselves. There is very little theoretical work in accounting with respect to the role of accounting information in the pricing of debt or in the determination of debt covenants. This is an area of potentially useful information economics research in accounting.

PART A

BASIC DECISION-FACILITATING ROLE OF INFORMATION

CHAPTER 2

SINGLE PERSON DECISION MAKING UNDER UNCERTAINTY

If there is no uncertainty, there is no role for information. Hence, any examination of the role of accounting information in markets and organizations must recognize that decision makers face uncertainty about the consequences of their actions. In this chapter we summarize some key elements of the representation of uncertainty and decision maker preferences under uncertainty. The representation of information and its decision-facilitating role is introduced in Chapter 3. Chapters 2 and 3 consider settings with a single decision maker, while Chapter 4 considers a setting with multiple decision makers, and it introduces the key concepts of efficient risk sharing, and congruent preferences over actions.

The chapters in Part A (Chapters 2, 3, and 4) are foundational chapters for the subsequent analyses in both volumes. They introduce key economic concepts that are the basis for both the examination of information in markets in this volume and the examination of performance evaluation in Volume II.

The structure of the remainder of this chapter is as follows. In Section 2.1 we introduce uncertainty based on the theory of probability. In order to represent uncertainty we introduce the concept of a *state*. The state is a complete description of all possible past and future events that are beyond the decision maker's control. There are many possible states, but "in the end" only one is realized. The outcome of any action (or sequence of actions) can be represented as a function of the decision maker's actions and the state. An *event* is a collection of states to which we can assign *probabilities*, which represent the decision maker's beliefs about the likelihood of the events occurring. The specification of the set of states, the set of events, and the decision maker's probabilities is the *probability space* on which economic decision problems under uncertainty can be defined.

In many settings we focus on the outcomes instead of the states directly. This is facilitated by the introduction of *random variables* in Section 2.2. A random variable is a function from the set of states to the set of possible values it may take. Each action specifies its own random variable, and the *probability distribution over outcomes* is parameterized by the action.

In Section 2.3 we introduce decision making under uncertainty. Decision making under uncertainty is a choice among gambles (i.e., outcome probability distributions). Based on assumptions of rational choice under uncertainty, a decision maker's preferences can be represented by a utility function which assigns a real number to each possible outcome, such that the decision maker's optimal action (i.e., preferred gamble) maximizes his expected utility.

Throughout this volume, an outcome is often described in terms of some physical or monetary measure of wealth or consumption (possibly at multiple dates). A decision maker is always assumed to *prefer more outcome to less*, but his attitudes towards risk is less obvious. This is discussed in Section 2.4. We generally assume decision makers to be either risk neutral or strictly risk averse. That is, the decision maker's utility function is increasing and either linear or strictly concave. Sections 2.5 and 2.6 introduce specific classes of preferences used throughout both volumes, i.e., HARA utilities and mean-variance preferences, respectively. Section 2.7 introduces a specific parametric model, known as the hurdle model, that we use (primarily in Volume II) to illustrate some of the general theory. The models we consider in this volume assume that the decision makers' preferences only depend on the monetary outcome. However, the need for performance evaluation derives from the fact that the decision makers' preferences may also depend on the action itself. This is a key assumption for most of the settings examined in Volume II.

Preferences among gambles (actions) are often decision maker specific. In Section 2.8 we derive *first-* and *second-order dominance relations* that provide partial orderings of gambles. One gamble first- or second-order dominates another if it is preferred by all decision makers who have increasing or have increasing, concave utility functions, respectively.

2.1 REPRESENTATION OF UNCERTAINTY

Uncertainty can pertain to both the past and the future. In particular, a decision maker is uncertain about some past or future event if he believes there is more than one possible substantive description or characterization of what has occurred or will occur. For example, a decision maker in Vancouver may be "interested in" the weather at the Toronto airport. He is uncertain about yesterday's, today's, and tomorrow's weather if he believes it may have been, is, or will be clear, cloudy with zero rain, or cloudy with a strictly positive amount of rain.

In representing uncertainty it is useful to introduce the rather abstract concept of a *state*. We can think of a state as a complete description of all possible past and future events that are beyond the decision maker's control, but may influence his information or the consequences of his actions. There are many possible states (e.g., an infinite number) that may occur, but "in the end" only one is realized. In the following discussion we let s represent a specific state and let S represent the set of possible states. The "completeness" assumption implies that s depicts all relevant aspects of the uncontrollable events that occur over the time frame of the analysis. Hence, the outcome of any action (or sequence of actions) can be represented as a function of the decision maker's actions and the state. The "non-controllability" assumption implies that the decision maker's beliefs about the state are independent of his actions. Of course, the decision maker's belief about an event that is a function of the state and his actions depends on his past or planned future actions.

Probabilities are numbers in the interval from zero to one that represent the decision maker's belief about the likelihood of an event occurring. If the decision maker is absolutely certain that an event is impossible, then the decision maker's probability for the event is zero. Conversely, if the decision maker is absolutely certain that an event has occurred or will occur, then the decision maker's probability for the event is one. More generally, the decision maker is uncertain about the event and assigns a probability between zero and one.

The probabilities we consider are often referred to as being *subjective* and, as noted above, are described as being specific to a decision maker. That is, probabilities can vary across individuals. This can occur because of differences in their experiences (i.e., past information) or in their fundamental characteristics (e.g., DNA). As we see later in the book, the existence and source of differences can significantly affect our analysis.

A decision maker may never fully know the state s, i.e., even at the "end" the decision maker may be uncertain as to what has in fact occurred. However, a decision maker observes events (e.g., the weather on a given day in a given location) and receives reports of the observations of others (e.g., a published weather report). Inherently, there are many possible states that will result in the same observed or reported event, i.e., an event is a collection of states (for example, there are many possible states that have the same weather on a given day at the Toronto airport).

Probability theory describes uncertainty in terms of a *probability space* (S, Ξ, P), which consists of a *state space*, a *sigma-field*, and a *probability distribution*. The state space $S = \{ s \}$ describes the basic events that serve as the foundation for the specification of probabilities. If the set of possible states has a finite number of elements, then positive probabilities can be assigned directly to each possible state. However, if the number of possible states is infinite (e.g., all the real numbers from $-\infty$ to $+\infty$) then it may well be that no one state has a positive probability of occurring, and clearly it is not possible to assign a positive probability to all states (since their sum must equal one).[1] Nonetheless, while specific states may not have a positive probability of occurring (such states are often referred to as being of *measure zero*), sets of states can have a positive probability of occurring.

A *sigma-field*, denoted $\Xi = \{ \xi \}$, consists of the empty set and all *probabilizable* events, i.e., the events to which the decision maker can assign zero or positive probability. Every probabilizable event is a subset of the state space, i.e., $\xi \subseteq S, \forall \xi \in \Xi$,[2] and logical consistency requires that the following sets belong to the sigma-field:

- the entire state space, i.e., $S \in \Xi$;

- any complimentary event, i.e., if $\xi \in \Xi$, then $\xi^c \in \Xi$ (where $\xi^c = S \backslash \xi$, represents the elements in S that remain after "subtracting" the elements in ξ);

- for any sequence of events $\{ \xi_1, \xi_2, ... \}$ in Ξ, the union $\bigcup_{i=1}^{\infty} \xi_i$ is in Ξ.

The probabilities assigned by a decision maker to the probabilizable events $\xi \in \Xi$ constitute the decision maker's *probability distribution.* The function P is a probability distribution on (S,Ξ), where Ξ is a sigma-field on S, if:

- P: $\Xi \rightarrow [0,1]$, $P(\xi) \geq 0, \forall \xi \in \Xi$, i.e., a non-negative real number is assigned to every event ξ;

- $P(S) = 1$ and $P(\emptyset) = 0$, where $\emptyset$ is the empty set, i.e., the probability that the state is in the designated state space is one;

- if $\{ \xi_1, \xi_2, ... \}$ is a sequence of disjoint events, then

$$P\left(\bigcup_{i=1}^{\infty} \xi_i\right) = \sum_{i=1}^{\infty} P(\xi_i).$$

The specification of a probability function is relatively straightforward if S has a finite number of elements and Ξ consists of all possible sets that can be constructed from those basic elements. For example, if $S = \{$ red, green, blue $\}$,

[1] Of course, if the number of states is countably infinite, then it is possible to assign a positive probability to each state, although the probabilities of some states will have to go to zero in the limit, e.g., if $S = \{ s_1, s_2, ... \}$ and $P(s_i) = 2^{-i}$, then the probability of each state is positive and the sum of the probabilities for the infinite number of states equals one, with $\lim_{i \rightarrow \infty} P(s_i) = 0$.

[2] The symbol $\forall$ represents "for every."

then $\Xi = \{ \xi_r, \xi_g, \xi_b, \xi_{rg}, \xi_{rb}, \xi_{bg}, \xi_{rgb}, \emptyset \}$ where the subscripts indicate the colors that are in the set. In this case, $P(\xi_{rgb}) = P(\xi_r) + P(\xi_g) + P(\xi_b) = 1$ since $S = \xi_{rgb}$.

On the other hand, specifying the probability distribution is conceptually more complex if S has an infinite number of elements. For example, suppose the state space is the set of real numbers, i.e., $S = (-\infty,+\infty)$, and no number has a positive probability of occurring.[3] However, the decision maker could assign positive probabilities to all open or closed intervals, e.g., $B = (\underline{b},\bar{b})$, and all sequences of disjoint open or closed intervals. The smallest sigma-field that contains all open (or closed) intervals in $\mathbb{R}$ is referred to as the sigma-field of *Borel sets*.[4] The probability assigned to Borel set $B \subseteq S$ is denoted $P(B)$.

2.2 RANDOM VARIABLES

A random variable is a variable whose "value" depends on the state s. It is defined by a function from S to the set of possible "values" the variable may take on. (The term random variable is often restricted to a variable whose value is described by a real number or vector of real numbers, and if a non-numerical description such as color is used, it is termed a random object.)

Consider a random variable x, with $\boldsymbol{x}: S \to X \subseteq \mathbb{R}$ (the concepts are readily extended to a random vector). Given the probability space (S,Ξ,P), the probability of event $B \subseteq X$ is

$$\Pr(x \in B) = P\{s \in S \mid \boldsymbol{x}(s) \in B\},$$

i.e., the probability of all states that result in the event $x \in B$. The probabilities for a random variable can be fully characterized by a distribution function, denoted $\Phi(t)$, that describes the probability that the value of the random variable is less than or equal to some value t, for all $t \in \mathbb{R}$. For example, if x is the total rainfall at the Toronto airport in a given month, then $\Phi(t)$ is the probability the total rainfall does not exceed t. Any distribution function has the following characteristics.

Distribution Function (d.f.): If $\Phi(t) = \Pr(x \in (-\infty,t])$, it is a distribution function for the random variable x with the following characteristics:

- $\Phi(t') \le \Phi(t'')$ if $t' \le t''$, i.e., a d.f. is non-decreasing (more events have larger probability);

---

[3] The concepts described here can be readily extended to include vectors of real numbers.

[4] Note that any arbitrary number b in $\mathbb{R}$ is also a Borel set, since $\{ b \} = ((-\infty,b)\cup(b,\infty))^c$. However, these sets may have zero probability.

- $\Phi(\cdot)$ is right continuous, i.e., $\Phi(t^+) = \Phi(t)$, where $\Phi(t^+)$ denotes the limit of values of $\Phi(x)$ as x converges to t through values greater than t;

- $\lim_{t \to -\infty} \Phi(t) = 0 \quad$ and $\quad \lim_{t \to \infty} \Phi(t) = 1.$

An important characteristic of a distribution function is how it changes as t increases. It can increase in "jumps" or in a continuous fashion. If it increases only in jumps at a countable number of points, we refer to the distribution as *discrete* and can characterize it with a probability frequency function.

Probability (Frequency) Function (p.f.): If $X = \{ x_1, x_2, ... \}$ is a countable (perhaps finite) number of distinct values, then we have a discrete distribution

$$\varphi(x_i) = \Pr(x \in \{x_i\}),$$

which is termed a probability (frequency) function (p.f.) and is such that

$$\Phi(t) = \sum_{\{i: x_i \le t\}} \varphi(x_i),$$

$$\Pr(x \in B) = \sum_{\{i: x_i \in B\}} \varphi(x_i).$$

If the distribution function is absolutely continuous over the entire range of x, it can be characterized by a probability density function (see, for example, Billingsley, 1986, Theorem 31.8).[5]

Probability Density Function (p.d.f.): The random variable x has an absolutely continuous distribution if there exists a non-negative probability density function (p.d.f.) φ such that for any Borel set $B \subseteq \mathbb{R}$,

$$\Pr(x \in B) = \int_B \varphi(x)\, dx,$$

[5] If no number has a positive probability, the distribution function is continuous. However, to facilitate a density representation (by the Radon-Nikodym Theorem) the distribution function must be absolutely continuous (see Billingsley, 1986, Example 31.1, for an example in which the distribution function is continuous and differentiable almost everywhere, but integrating $\Phi'(x)$ does not lead back to $\Phi(x)$).

i.e., the probability of $x \in B$ is obtained by integrating $\varphi(x)$ over the Borel set B. Furthermore, the distribution function for x can be differentiated almost everywhere, and at any continuity point x of the p.d.f. φ, $\Phi'(x) = \varphi(x)$.

In most examples in this book the distributions are either discrete or absolutely continuous. However, in some cases they are a mixture of the two and most of our theoretical results apply to settings with a mixture, i.e., there are a countable number of "jumps" and there are intervals between the jumps at which the distribution is absolutely continuous. Hence, we assume $\varphi(x)$ is a generalized probability density function.

Generalized Probability Density Function (g.p.d.f.)*:** We refer to $\varphi(x)$ as a ***g.p.d.f. if, at any given value of x, it can be either a p.f. or a p.d.f. In that case, for an arbitrary function $g(x)$ and Borel set B, we let

$$\int_B g(x)\, d\Phi(x)$$

denote the general Lebesgue-Stieltjes integral, which applies to discrete, absolutely continuous, and mixed distributions. (It is essentially a generalized summation operator.)

To illustrate the above, we consider three examples and compute the expectation of $g(x) = x^2$, denoted $E[g(x)]$.

(a) *Discrete Distribution*: $X = \{ x_1=2, x_2=4, x_3=6 \}$, with $\varphi(x_1) = .2$, $\varphi(x_2) = .5$, and $\varphi(x_3) = .3$. Figure 2.1a depicts the distribution function, which is a series of discrete steps.

$$E[g(x)] = \int_{-\infty}^{+\infty} x^2\, d\Phi(x) = .2 \times 2^2 + .5 \times 4^2 + .3 \times 6^2 = 19.6;$$

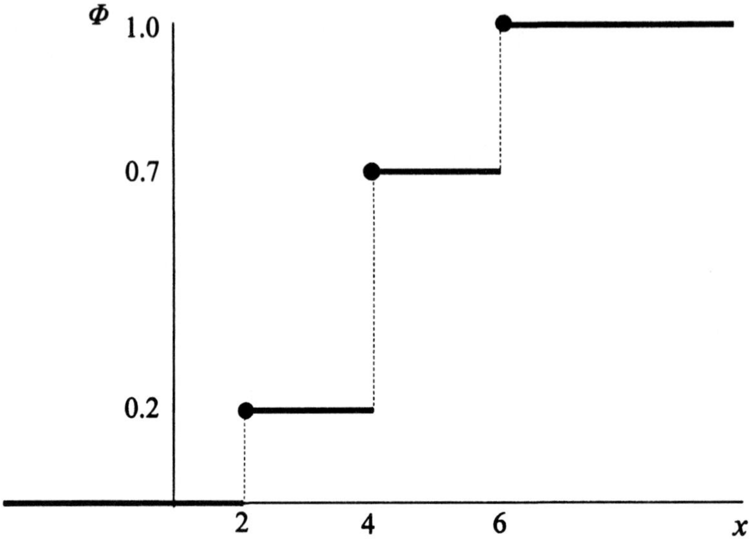

Figure 2.1a: Discrete probability distribution function.

(b) *Absolutely Continuous Distribution*: $X = [0, 10]$, with $\varphi(x) = .1$, for $x \in [0, 10]$, and zero otherwise.

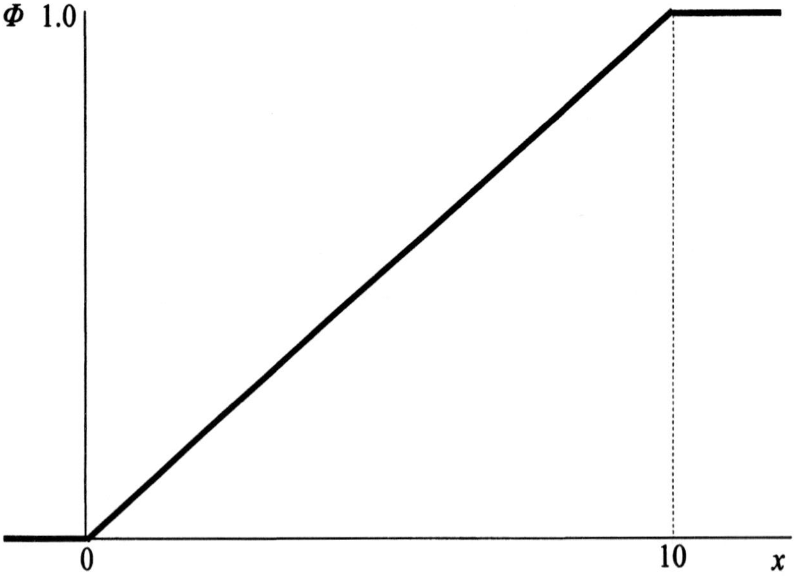

Figure 2.1b: Absolutely continuous probability distribution function.

Figure 2.1b depicts the distribution function, which is a continuous function that is differentiable at all points except $x = 0$ and $x = 10$.

$$E[g(x)] = \int_{-\infty}^{+\infty} x^2 \, d\Phi(x) = \int_{0}^{10} x^2 \times .1 \, dx = 33.33333;$$

(c) *Mixed Distribution*: $X = [0, 10]$, with $\varphi(x) = .1$ for all $x \in (2,4) \cup (4,6)$, $\varphi(x_1{=}2) = .1$, $\varphi(x_2{=}4) = .3$, $\varphi(x_3{=}6) = .2$, and zero otherwise. Figure 2.1c depicts the distribution function, which is continuous except at the three "jump" points.

$$E[g(x)] = \int_{-\infty}^{+\infty} x^2 \, d\Phi(x)$$

$$= .1 \times 2^2 + .3 \times 4^2 + .2 \times 6^2 + \int_{2}^{4} x^2 \times .1 \, dx + \int_{4}^{6} x^2 \times .1 \, dx$$

$$= 19.33333.$$

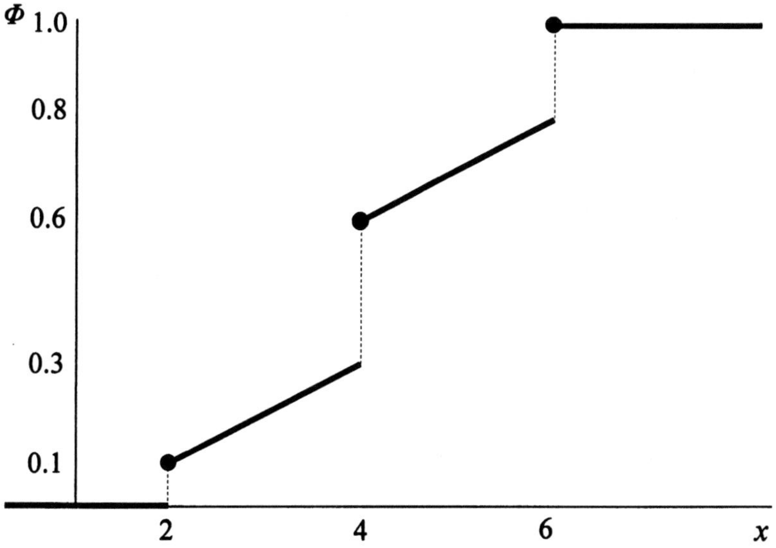

Figure 2.1c: Mixed probability distribution function.

In each case we use the expression $d\Phi(x)$. In case (a) that is equivalent to summing over the values of x for which $\Phi(x)$ has a discrete increase (i.e., $d\Phi(x)$

= $\varphi(x)$ for x at which $\Phi(x)$ has a discrete increase, and zero otherwise). In case (b), $d\Phi(x) = \varphi(x)dx$ applies to the values of x over which $\Phi(x)$ increases continuously. And in case (c), we apply the first approach to the values of x for which $\Phi(x)$ has a discrete increase and apply the second approach over the values of x for which $\Phi(x)$ increases continuously.

2.3 REPRESENTATION OF PREFERENCES

A decision is a choice from among a set of actions. We assume the decision maker's preferences are based upon the consequences of those actions, including any preference relevant descriptions of the actions (e.g., the amount of time required to undertake a given task). The set of possible actions is denoted $A = \{ a \}$, and can include either specific acts or strategies that specify event contingent acts. The preference relevant description of the set of possible consequences of those acts is denoted X. This description can have many dimensions, e.g., the decision maker's consumption and effort at a sequence of future dates.

We assume that the decision maker can express a preference ordering over the set of possible outcomes (consequences) and across the set of possible actions. Our objective is to develop a numerical representation of the decision maker's preferences across outcomes and a numerical representation of the relation between actions and outcomes such that we can compute a number for each action that is consistent with the decision maker's preferences across those actions.

In a "certainty" setting, the decision maker identifies a unique outcome for each action. Therefore, any system that assigns a higher number to a more preferred outcome will also assign a higher number to a more preferred action. Only the ordering of the outcomes is significant.

In an "uncertainty" setting, we assume that the decision maker identifies a set of possible outcomes and views each action as a gamble across the set of possible outcomes. The connection between the decision maker's preferences across outcomes and his preferences across actions is now less clear. In this setting, our objective is to develop two real valued functions:

$u: X \rightarrow \mathbb{R}$	a utility function that assigns a utility number to each possible outcome;
$\Phi: X \times A \rightarrow [0,1]$	a family of probability distribution functions, where $\Phi(x \mid a)$ is the distribution function over $x \in X$ given action $a \in A$ and $\varphi(x \mid a)$ is the corresponding generalized probability density function.

We then want those two functions to be such that the following relations hold:

- $u(x') \geq u(x'')$ if, and only if, x' is at least as preferred as x'';

- $U(a') \equiv \int_X u(x)\, d\Phi(x|a') \geq U(a'') \equiv \int_X u(x)\, d\Phi(x|a'')$ if, and only if, a' is at least as preferred as a''.

The big advantage of this type of preference representation is that we can assign a real number to each gamble (i.e., its expected utility) such that the preference relation among gambles can be represented as a comparison between real numbers for which there is a natural ordering. Another advantage is that we can later introduce information that influences the probabilities of the gambles but not the utility numbers for the outcomes, allowing us to readily recompute the decision maker's preferences across actions given a particular signal (revision of probabilities).

The literature contains a variety of axiomatic systems (sets of assumptions) that are used as a basis for supporting the above representation of preferences. The following is essentially the same as that found in DeGroot (1970). These follow from the path breaking work of von Neumann and Morgenstern (1944) and assume that the probability functions φ are known (i.e., in a sense they are objective) and do not have to be elicited from the decision maker.[6]

To simplify the discussion we assume the set of preference relevant outcomes, $X = \{ x_1, ..., x_n \}$, is finite and we let $\varphi(\cdot)$ represent a lottery (i.e., a probability function) defined over X. The set of all possible lotteries over the elements of X is denoted

$$\Delta(X) \equiv \{ \varphi: X \to \mathbb{R} \mid \textstyle\sum_{x \in X} \varphi(x) = 1 \text{ and } \varphi(x) \geq 0, \forall\, x \in X \}.$$

If outcome $x_i \in X$ occurs with certainty, then it is a lottery in which $\varphi(x) = 1$ for $x = x_i$ and zero otherwise. In the following discussion, this lottery is succinctly represented by $[x_i]$, which is in the set $\Delta(X)$. Preferences are expressed in terms of lotteries, where $\varphi^1 \succ (\succeq, \sim)\ \varphi^2$ is used to represent the fact that the decision maker strictly prefers (weakly prefers, is indifferent between) lottery φ^1 to (to, and) lottery φ^2.

---

[6] An alternative approach is to use axioms (often referred to as the Savage axioms) which consider the elicitation of both the decision maker's preferences over outcomes and beliefs about the likelihoods of the outcomes for the alternative action choices. Hence, the system develops both a utility function and subjective probability functions (see Savage, 1972).

Preference Assumptions

The decision maker's preferences over lotteries are assumed to be such that the following conditions hold.

1. **Interest:** There exists a worst and best possible outcome x_1, $x_n \in X$ such that the decision maker strictly prefers the latter to the former, i.e., $[x_1] \preceq [x] \preceq [x_n]$, $\forall\, x \in X$, and $[x_1] \prec [x_n]$.

2. **Completeness:** The decision maker can provide a complete ordering of all lotteries, i.e., for every pair of lotteries φ^1, $\varphi^2 \in \Delta(X)$, either $\varphi^1 \succeq \varphi^2$ or $\varphi^1 \preceq \varphi^2$ or both (i.e., $\varphi^1 \sim \varphi^2$).

3. **Transitivity:** There are no incongruities in the ordering in (2), i.e., if $\varphi^1 \preceq \varphi^2$ and $\varphi^2 \preceq \varphi^3$, then $\varphi^1 \preceq \varphi^3$.

4. **Monotonicity:** In a two-stage gamble, the decision maker prefers a higher probability of obtaining a preferred lottery relative to a lower probability, i.e., if $\varphi^1 \prec \varphi^2$ and $0 \le \gamma' < \gamma'' \le 1$, then $\gamma'\varphi^2 + (1-\gamma')\varphi^1 \prec \gamma''\varphi^2 + (1-\gamma'')\varphi^1$, where γ is the first-stage probability of obtaining the second-stage lottery φ^2.

5. **Continuity:** For any three lotteries there exists a two-stage gamble between the most and least preferred lottery for which the decision maker is indifferent to the intermediate lottery, i.e., if $\varphi^1 \preceq \varphi^2$ and $\varphi^2 \preceq \varphi^3$, then there exists a first-stage probability $\gamma \in [0,1]$ such that $\varphi^2 \sim \gamma\varphi^1 + (1-\gamma)\varphi^3$.

6. **Substitution:** The decision maker is indifferent between lottery $\varphi \in \Delta(X)$ and lottery $\beta[x_n] + (1-\beta)[x_1]$, where

$$\beta = \sum_{x \in X} \gamma(x)\, \varphi(x),$$

   and $\gamma(x) \in [0,1]$ is such that $[x] \sim \gamma(x)[x_n] + (1-\gamma(x))[x_1]$.

Observe that the existence of $\gamma(x)$ in (6) follows from (1) and (5).

Proposition 2.1 (DeGroot 1970, p. 108)
The above preference assumptions are jointly satisfied if, and only if, there exists a utility function u: $X \rightarrow \mathbb{R}$ such that $\varphi^1 \preceq \varphi^2$ if, and only if, the expected utility of outcomes is lower for φ^1 than for φ^2, i.e., $U(\varphi^1) \leq U(\varphi^2)$,

where $$U(\varphi) \equiv \sum_{x \in X} u(x)\, \varphi(x).$$

Proof: The first step is to develop a utility function using the following procedure:

(a) Find x_1 and x_n such that $[x_n] \succeq [x] \succeq [x_1], \quad \forall\, x \in X$ (by (1));

(b) Let $u(x_1) = 0$ and $u(x_n) = 1$ ($x_n \succ x_1$ by (1));

(c) For each $x \in X$ find the number $\gamma(x) \in [0,1]$ (by (5)) such that $[x] \sim (1\text{-}\gamma(x))[x_1] + \gamma(x)[x_n]$;

(d) Let $u(x) = \gamma(x), \quad \forall\, x \in X$.

The second step is to prove that the above utility function satisfies the proposition. This follows directly from (4) and (6).

To complete the proof it remains to be shown that the existence of u satisfying the condition in the proposition is sufficient to imply all the assumptions. It is straightforward to verify this using the basic mathematical properties of the expected utility formula. **Q.E.D.**

A utility function u describes the preferences for a given decision maker and can be used to assess the decision maker's preferences among action alternatives. However, it is not appropriate to make comparisons of one decision maker's utility relative to that of another. This can be seen by the fact that the utility function used to represent the preferences of a given decision maker is not unique. While we used $u(x_1) = 0$ and $u(x_n) = 1$ in proving the preceding proposition, the use of 0 and 1 was arbitrary – we could have used any pair of numbers. Interestingly, if we had used a different pair of minimum and maximum utility numbers, then the new utility function would be a positive linear transformation of the old (i.e., it is a positive multiple of the old, plus a constant which could be positive or negative). The following proposition establishes that all utility functions that represent the preference orderings of a given decision maker are positive linear transformations of each other.

Proposition 2.2 (DeGroot 1970, p. 108)

Suppose that u^1 and u^2 are real-valued functions on X each of which satisfies the property stated in Proposition 2.1. Then there exist constants $f \in \mathbb{R}$ and $v > 0$ such that

$$u^1(x) = f + v\, u^2(x), \quad \forall\, x \in X.$$

Proof: Since $[x_1] \prec [x_n]$, it follows that: $u^1(x_1) < u^1(x_n)$ and $u^2(x_1) < u^2(x_n)$. Therefore, we can always find f and $v > 0$ such that

$$u^1(x_1) = f + v\, u^2(x_1),$$

$$u^1(x_n) = f + v\, u^2(x_n).$$

Let $\gamma(x)$ be such that $[x] \sim \gamma(x)[x_n] + (1\text{-}\gamma(x))[x_1]$, which implies

$$u^1(x) = \gamma(x)u^1(x_n) + (1\text{-}\gamma(x))u^1(x_1),$$

and

$$u^2(x) = \gamma(x)u^2(x_n) + (1\text{-}\gamma(x))u^2(x_1).$$

It then follows that

$$\begin{aligned} u^1(x) &= \gamma(x)[f + v\, u^2(x_n)] + (1\text{-}\gamma(x))[f + v\, u^2(x_1)] \\ &= f + v[\gamma(x)u^2(x_n) + (1\text{-}\gamma(x))u^2(x_1)] \\ &= f + v\, u^2(x). \end{aligned}$$

Q.E.D.

The above set of preference assumptions is one of the most basic in the literature. The assumptions can be modified so as to consider infinite sets of possible outcomes with bounded or unbounded preferences, as well subjective probabilities and the role of information. Technical considerations arise in these settings that result in slightly more complex structures and some additional assumptions. However, the basic thrust of these assumptions is essentially the same as the above. If the decision maker has consistent preferences that are fundamentally based on the potential outcomes and the likelihood of those outcomes, then we can represent his preferences by a utility function and his beliefs by a probability function, such that his preferences across actions (strategies) are represented by the expected utility of each action.

2.4 RISK AVERSION

In the preceding analysis the outcome descriptions in X reflect any aspect of the outcome that influences the decision maker's preferences, including qualitative characteristics. In this section we focus on settings in which the outcome is a real valued, single dimensional number, i.e., $X = \{ x \} \subseteq \mathbb{R}$, and the set of outcomes over which the decision maker's preferences are defined is an interval on the real line (e.g., $(-\infty,+\infty)$ or $[0,+\infty)$). Furthermore, the outcome represents some attribute for which the decision maker prefers more to less, i.e., $x^1 \preceq x^2$ if, and only if, $x^1 \leq x^2$. For example, the outcome could be the decision maker's terminal wealth or the firm's profit, and the decision maker prefers more wealth or profit to less. To simplify the discussion, we refer to x as the decision maker's outcome, but keep in mind that the concept applies to a broad class of single-dimensional measures.

The decision maker's preferences over his outcome are represented by the utility function $u(x)$, which is increasing in x, i.e., $u(x^1) \leq u(x^2)$ if, and only if, $x^1 \leq x^2$. The "shape" of $u(x)$ is an important characteristic of the decision maker's preferences in many analyses. Let $I = [\underline{x}, \bar{x}\,]$ represent a closed interval of outcomes.

Definition *Concavity and Convexity of Preferences*

The decision maker's preferences are defined to be *concave* (*convex*) on the interval I if, for every pair of outcomes x^1, $x^2 \in I$ and every $\lambda \in (0,1)$,

$$u(x) \geq (\leq)\ \lambda\, u(x^1) + (1\text{-}\lambda)\, u(x^2),$$

where $$x = \lambda\, x^1 + (1\text{-}\lambda)\, x^2 \in I.$$

The decision maker's preferences are *strictly* concave (convex) on I if strict inequality holds for every x^1, $x^2 \in I$.

We are primarily interested in concave utility functions, for the reasons explained below.

Figure 2.2 depicts three concave utility functions: (a) is linear over the entire interval, (b) is piece-wise linear, and (c) increases at a decreasing rate over the entire interval. Over the linear segments the utility function is both weakly concave and weakly convex, so that in (a) we have $u(x) = \lambda\, u(x^1) + (1\text{-}\lambda)\, u(x^2)$. The utility function in (c) is strictly concave over the entire interval $[\underline{x}, \bar{x}\,]$, so that $u(x) > \lambda\, u(x^1) + (1\text{-}\lambda)\, u(x^2)$ for all $x \in (x^1, x^2)$ holds for any interval. In (b) the utility function is not strictly concave, since $u(x) = \lambda\, u(x^1) + (1\text{-}\lambda) u(x^2)$ whenever x^1 and x^2 are chosen such that they belong to the same linear segment for the utility function.

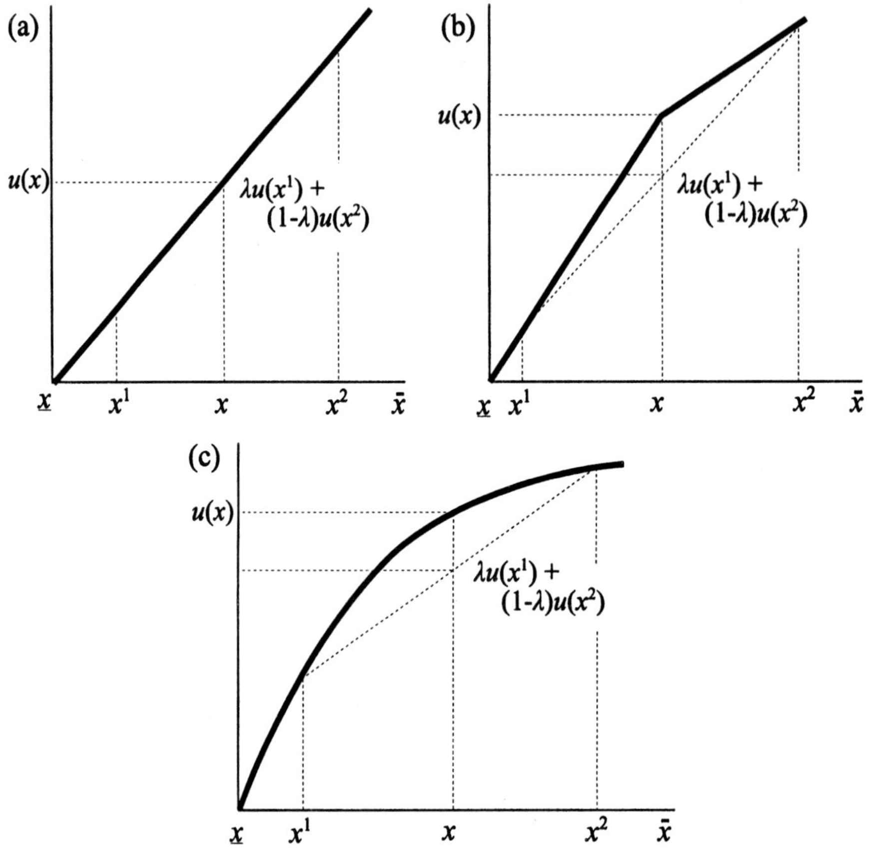

Figure 2.2: Concave utility functions.

If $u(x)$ is continuous and twice differentiable on I, then $u(x)$ is concave (convex) on I if, and only if, $u''(x) \leq (\geq)\ 0$ for $x \in (x^1,x^2)$. Strict concavity (convexity) holds if, and only if, the strict inequality holds. The latter is depicted in Figure 2.2(c) where we observe that $u(x)$ is increasing at an ever decreasing rate, i.e., its slope is strictly decreasing.

Jensen's inequality is used extensively throughout this book. It establishes that a concave (convex) utility function represents a weakly risk-averse (seeking) individual in the sense that if the decision maker's utility function is concave (convex), then he weakly prefers (does not prefer) to receive with certainty the expected value of a lottery instead of the lottery. Furthermore, those preferences are strict if the utility function is strictly concave (convex).

Proposition 2.3 (Jensen's Inequality)

Let $u(x)$ be a concave (convex) function on I and let x be a random variable such that $\Pr\{ x \in I \} = 1$, and suppose the expectations $U(a)$ and $E[x|a]$ associated with a given action (lottery) a exist. Then

$$U(a) = \int_X u(x)\, d\Phi(x|a) \leq (\geq)\, u(E[x|a]),$$

where
$$E[x|a] = \int_X x\, d\Phi(x|a).$$

Furthermore, if $u(x)$ is strictly concave (convex) and $\Pr\{ x = E[x|a] \} < 1$, the inequality is strict.

Proof: Assume $u(x)$ is concave. If $\Pr\{ x = E[x|a] \} = 1$, then $U(a) = u(E[x|a])$. If $\Pr\{ x = E[x|a] \} < 1$, then there exists an interval $I = [x^1, x^2]$ such that $\Pr\{ x \in I \} = 1$ and $x^1 < E[x|a] < x^2$. The concavity of $u(x)$ ensures that there exist parameters f and v such that $u(x) \leq f + v\,x$ and $u(E[x|a]) = f + v\,E[x|a]$.[7] It then follows that

$$U(a) \leq f + v\,E[x|a] = u(E[x|a]).$$

Strict concavity implies the inequalities are strict. Furthermore, the same arguments can be applied when $u(x)$ is convex, since in that case $-u(x)$ is concave.

Q.E.D.

Assuming $u(x)$ is a continuous function, there exists, for any action (lottery) a, a *certainty equivalent*, denoted $CE(a) \in \mathbb{R}$, such that the decision maker is indifferent between receiving the *certainty equivalent* with certainty and taking the lottery, i.e., the certainty equivalent is defined by

$$u(CE(a)) = U(a).$$

Figure 2.3 depicts the certainty equivalent for a lottery in which there is a ⅔ probability of receiving x^1 and a ⅓ probability of receiving x^2.

---

[7] That is, given the concavity of $u(x)$, there is a linear function of x that is "tangent" to $u(x)$ at $x = E[x|a]$, and lies on or above $u(x)$ for all $x \in I$.

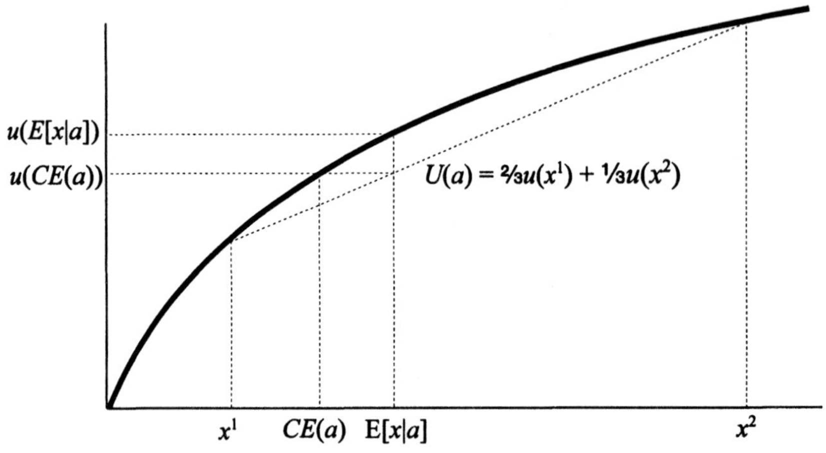

Figure 2.3: Certainty equivalent.

The difference between the expected outcome and the certainty equivalent is referred to as the *risk premium*, and is represented by

$$\pi(a) = \mathrm{E}[x|a] - CE(a),$$

so that

$$u(\mathrm{E}[x|a] - \pi(a)) = U(a).$$

The risk premium can be viewed as the maximum amount the decision maker would be willing to pay (i.e., reduce his expected payoff) in order to transfer the risk of the outcome to another party.

Now consider a setting in which $x = w + \varepsilon$, where w is the decision maker's known wealth which is independent of a and ε is a random variable with probability function $\varphi(\varepsilon|a)$. We refer to π_a as the (minimum) *asking price* (or cash equivalent value) of lottery a, where

$$u(w+\pi_a) = \mathrm{E}[u(w+\varepsilon)|a].$$

π_a is the smallest amount at which the individual would sell lottery a. It should be distinguished from the (maximum) *bid price* π_b, which is the largest amount an individual would pay for the lottery a:

$$u(w) = \mathrm{E}[u(w+\varepsilon-\pi_b)|a].$$

If wealth affects an individual's risk preferences, then $\pi_a \neq \pi_b$. However, $\pi_a = \pi_b$ if there is no wealth effect. This occurs if the decision maker is risk neutral or if $u(x)$ is an exponential utility function, as defined later. In the risk-neutral case, $\pi_a = \pi_b = \mathrm{E}[\varepsilon|a]$.

If the lottery is actuarially neutral, i.e., $\mathrm{E}[\varepsilon|a] = 0$, and the decision maker is risk averse, then both π_a and π_b are negative, i.e., the decision maker will pay to avoid the risk and must be paid to undertake the risk. In this setting, the previously defined risk premium π is equal to $-\pi_a$. The magnitude of the risk premium is a measure of the decision maker's risk aversion, and we use that connection to develop the following measure of risk aversion.

Local Risk Aversion

Consider the risk premium associated with a small gamble given a wealth level w. The payoff from the gamble is ε, where $\Phi(\varepsilon|a)$ is the probability distribution over ε and $\mathrm{E}[\varepsilon|a] = 0$ and $\mathrm{Var}[\varepsilon|a] = \sigma_\varepsilon^2 > 0$. Let π represent the risk premium associated with this gamble, i.e., $u(w-\pi) = \mathrm{E}[u(w+\varepsilon)|a]$.

To develop a succinct measure of the decision maker's aversion to "local" risk at a given wealth level, we first obtain the following Taylor approximation to his utility function at w:

$$\begin{aligned} u(w-\pi) &= u(w) - u'(w)\pi + u''(w)\pi^2/2! - u'''(w)\pi^3/3! + \ldots \\ &= u(w) - u'(w)\pi + O(\pi^2) \qquad (2.1) \end{aligned}$$

where $O(\cdot)$ = "terms of order at most".[8] Now we use a similar approximation to $u(w+\varepsilon)$ in the decision maker's expected utility for $w + \varepsilon$:

$$\begin{aligned} \mathrm{E}[u(w+\varepsilon)|a] &= \mathrm{E}[u(w) + u'(w)\varepsilon + \tfrac{1}{2}u''(w)\varepsilon^2 + O(\varepsilon^3)|a] \\ &= u(w) + \tfrac{1}{2}u''(w)\sigma_\varepsilon^2 + o(\sigma_\varepsilon^2). \qquad (2.2) \end{aligned}$$

where $o(\cdot)$ = "terms of smaller order than". Substituting the above expressions into $u(w-\pi) = \mathrm{E}[u(w+\varepsilon)|a]$ and solving for π yields:

$$\pi = -\frac{1}{2}\sigma_\varepsilon^2 \frac{u''(w)}{u'(w)} + O(\pi^2) - o(\sigma_\varepsilon^2) \approx \frac{1}{2}\sigma_\varepsilon^2 r(w),$$

[8] If g is a real-valued function of a real variable, the notation $g(x) = O(x)$ means that $g(x)$ goes to zero at least as fast as x does. More precisely, it means that there is a constant $K \geq 0$ such that

$$\left|\frac{g(x)}{x}\right| \leq K \quad \text{as} \quad x \to 0.$$

The notation $g(x) = o(x)$ means that $g(x)$ goes to zero faster than x does; or equivalently, that the constant K above is zero.

where $$r(w) \equiv - u''(w)/u'(w)$$

is the *measure of local risk aversion.*

Hence, the decision maker's risk premium for a *small*, actuarially neutral gamble ε is approximately equal to $r(w)$ times ½ the variance of ε. That is, $r(w)$ is twice the risk premium per unit of variance for infinitesimal risk.

The above measure of local risk aversion is often termed the Pratt/Arrow measure of risk aversion, in recognition of its development by Pratt (1964) and Arrow (1970). The following two propositions come from Pratt (1964). We present them without proofs.

Proposition 2.4 (Pratt 1964, Theorem 2)

Let $r(w)$ be the local risk aversion and $\pi(w,a)$ be the risk premium for any gamble a (small or large, actuarially neutral or not) at initial wealth w. The following conditions are equivalent:

(a) $r(w)$ is a (strictly) decreasing function of w;

(b) $\pi(w,a)$ is a (strictly) decreasing function of w for all a.

Proposition 2.5 (Pratt 1964, Theorem 1)

Consider a gamble $\Phi(\varepsilon|a)$ and two utility functions u_1 and u_2. Let $r_i(w)$ and $\pi_i(w,a)$ be the local risk aversion and risk premia corresponding to i=1,2. The following conditions are equivalent:

(a) $r_1(w) \geq r_2(w), \quad \forall\, w$;

(b) $\pi_1(w,a) \geq \pi_2(w,a), \quad \forall\, w$ and a;

(c) There exists a concave function G, $G' \geq 0$ and $G'' \leq 0$ such that $u_1(x) = G(u_2(x))$, i.e., u_1 is "more concave" than u_2.

Proposition 2.4 considers the effect of an individual's wealth – if his risk aversion decreases with wealth, then his risk premium also decreases. Proposition 2.5, on the other hand, compares one individual with another. If one is more risk averse than the other, then the former has a higher risk premium, and has a more concave utility function.

Earlier we stated that it was inappropriate to make comparisons of utility functions across individuals, yet we appear to be doing so in the above proposition. However, comparisons of risk aversion are not the same as comparing utility levels. The former are statements about choices among gambles, whereas the latter compares levels or differences in utility levels that are subject to an arbitrary scaling of the utility functions (see Proposition 2.2). Of particular note is the fact that if two decision makers would make the same choices among all gambles (i.e., they have the same preference relations), then they have the same risk aversion, irrespective of the scale of their utility functions.

Proposition 2.6

If there exist parameters f and v such that $u_1(x) = f + v\, u_2(x)$ for all x, then $r_1(w) = r_2(w)$ for all w.

Proof: The key here is that $u_1' = v\, u_2'$ and $u_1'' = v\, u_2''$, so that $r_1 = -v\, u_2''/v\, u_2' = r_2$. **Q.E.D.**

The above result implies that a decision maker's risk aversion function $r(x)$ is sufficient to determine a positive linear transformation of his utility function $u(x)$, i.e., if you know the decision maker's risk aversion at each $x \in X$, you know his preferences over lotteries. This can be seen by observing that

$$r(x) = -\frac{d}{dx} \ln u'(x),$$

which implies

$$-\int r(x)\, dx = \ln u'(x) + C, \tag{2.3}$$

where C is the constant of integration. Then, using the fact that $e^{\ln u'(x) + C} = e^C u'(x)$, and integrating, provides

$$\int e^{-\int r(x) dx} dx = f + v\, u(x), \tag{2.4}$$

where f is a constant of integration and $v = e^C$.

2.5 HARA UTILITY FUNCTIONS

We now consider an important special class of utility functions for risk-averse decision makers. In specifying these functions it is useful to introduce two other risk measures.

***Risk Tolerance*:** Risk tolerance is the inverse of the decision maker's risk aversion, i.e.,

$$\rho(x) \equiv \frac{1}{r(x)} = -\frac{u'(x)}{u''(x)}.$$

Hence, the larger is $\rho(x)$, the smaller is the decision maker's risk premium and the more willing he is to take on risk.

***Risk cautiousness*:** Risk cautiousness describes the rate of change in the decision maker's risk tolerance, i.e.,

$$\rho'(x) = -\frac{r'(x)}{r(x)^2} = \frac{u'(x)u'''(x)}{[u''(x)]^2} - 1.$$

Definition *HARA Utility Functions*
The class of utility functions that have *linear risk tolerances*, i.e., there exist two parameters α and β such that

$$\rho(x) = \alpha x + \beta > 0,$$

are termed the class of HARA utility functions.

Observe that all utility functions in this class have *constant risk cautiousness*, i.e.,

$$\rho'(x) = \alpha.$$

In addition, graphically, the measure of local risk aversion is an hyperbola, i.e.,

$$r(x) = \frac{1}{\alpha x + \beta}.$$

Due to the hyperbolic shape of $r(x)$, which is often termed *absolute risk aversion*, the utility functions with linear risk tolerances are generally referred to as the HARA class, where HARA stands for "hyperbolic absolute risk aversion."

We now use $r(x) = (\alpha x + \beta)^{-1}$ to characterize $u(x)$. From (2.3) we obtain:

$$\ln u'(x) + C = -\int r(x)\,dx = \begin{cases} -\dfrac{x}{\beta} & \text{if } \alpha = 0,\ \beta > 0, \\[2ex] -\dfrac{1}{\alpha}\ln(\alpha x + \beta) & \text{if } \alpha \neq 0,\ \alpha x + \beta > 0. \end{cases}$$

Deleting the constant of integration and taking both sides up as powers of e yields:

$$u'(x) = \begin{cases} e^{-\frac{x}{\beta}} & \text{if } \alpha = 0,\ \beta > 0, \\ [\alpha x + \beta]^{-\frac{1}{\alpha}} & \text{if } \alpha \neq 0,\ \alpha x + \beta > 0. \end{cases}$$

Next, following (2.4), we integrate both sides to obtain $f + u(x)$.[9]

$$u(x) \sim \begin{cases} -\beta e^{-x/\beta} + f & \text{if } \alpha = 0,\ \beta > 0, \\ \ln(x + \beta) + f & \text{if } \alpha = 1,\ x + \beta > 0, \\ \dfrac{1}{\alpha - 1}[\alpha x + \beta]^{1-1/\alpha} + f & \text{if } \alpha \neq 0,1,\ \alpha x + \beta > 0. \end{cases}$$

Removing "irrelevant" constants results in the characteristics of HARA utility functions shown in Table 2.1.

Risk tolerance is increasing in β for all types. In the exponential utility function, $\alpha = 0$ and risk tolerance is fully characterized by β, i.e., it is independent of x and there is *no wealth effect*. With the logarithmic and power utility functions with $\alpha > 0$, the decision maker's risk tolerance is increasing in x, while it is decreasing in x for power utility functions with $\alpha < 0$.

2.6 MEAN-VARIANCE PREFERENCES

If the decision maker has a quadratic utility function, i.e., a HARA utility function with $\alpha = -1$, then

$$u(x) = -\tfrac{1}{2}[\beta - x]^2 \sim \beta x - \tfrac{1}{2}x^2, \quad \text{for } \beta - x \geq 0.$$

Hence,

$$U(a) = \beta\, E[x|a] - \tfrac{1}{2}E[x^2|a] = \beta\, E[x|a] - \tfrac{1}{2}\{E[x|a]^2 + \text{Var}[x|a]\},$$

---

[9] For the power utility functions with $\alpha \notin [0,1]$ we typically also include the case in which $\alpha x + \beta$ is equal to zero even though the risk aversion is infinity at that point.

Type	Parameter Restrictions	Utility Function $u(x)$	Risk Aversion $r(x)$	Risk Tolerance $\rho(x)$	Risk Cautiousness $\rho'(x)$
Exponential	$\alpha = 0, \beta > 0$	$- e^{-x/\beta}$	$\frac{1}{\beta}$	β	0
Logarithmic	$\alpha = 1, x+\beta > 0$	$\ln (x+\beta)$	$\frac{1}{x+\beta}$	$x + \beta$	1
Power	$\alpha \neq 0,1, \alpha x+\beta > 0$	$\frac{1}{\alpha - 1} [\alpha x + \beta]^{1 - 1/\alpha}$	$\frac{1}{\alpha x + \beta}$	$\alpha x + \beta$	α

Table 2.1: Characteristics of HARA utility functions.

i.e., the decision maker's expected utility for a given lottery is a function of the lottery's mean and variance. A mean-variance representation does not apply in general to other utility functions. However, if the outcomes from the alternative lotteries are normally distributed, then the decision maker's preferences can be expressed as a function of the mean and variance, $E[x|a]$ and $Var[x|a]$. This holds for any utility function since normal distributions are fully characterized by their means and variances. Of course, the functional relation may be more complex than in the quadratic utility case.

Mean-Variance Approximations

In some settings, there is a simple linear mean-variance representation of a decision maker's preferences, or this type of representation provides a "close" approximation to those preferences. To develop this perspective we note that the ordering of preferences over lotteries in terms of the certainty equivalent $CE(a)$ is identical to the ordering in terms of the expected utility. From (2.1) and (2.2) we obtain Taylor approximations to the decision maker's utility for his certainty equivalent $CE(a) = E[x|a] - \pi(a)$ and his expected utility for any lottery a:

$$u(CE(a)) = u(E[x|a]) - u'(E[x|a])(E[x|a] - CE(a)) + O((E[x|a] - CE(a))^2).$$

$$U(a) = u(E[x|a]) + \tfrac{1}{2}u''(E[x|a])Var[x|a] + o(Var[x|a]).$$

In order to obtain an approximate closed form expression for the certainty equivalent we note that the utility for the certainty equivalent equals the expected utility of the gamble. Hence, by dropping the $O(\cdot)$ and $o(\cdot)$ terms in the two approximations we get

$$u(E[x|a]) - u'(E[x|a])(E[x|a] - CE(a)) \approx u(E[x|a]) + \tfrac{1}{2}u''(E[x|a])Var[x|a],$$

from which we obtain the following approximation of the certainty equivalent:

$$CE(a) \approx E[x|a] + \frac{1}{2}\frac{u''(E[x|a])}{u'(E[x|a])} Var[x|a]$$

$$= E[x|a] - \tfrac{1}{2}r(E[x|a])Var[x|a]. \tag{2.5}$$

Since the ordering of preferences over lotteries in terms of the certainty equivalent $CE(a)$ is identical to the ordering in terms of the expected utility $U(a)$, we observe that, in approximation, the decision maker trades off the expected outcome of a lottery with its uncertainty as measured by its variance. The relative weight in that trade-off is the decision maker's risk aversion at the expected outcome of the lottery.

Exponential Utility with Normally Distributed Outcomes

The exponential utility function $u(x) = - e^{-rx}$ is particularly interesting because the decision maker's risk aversion is a constant r, i.e., it is independent of the outcome, so that for the approximation in (2.5) we obtain

$$CE(a) \approx \mathrm{E}[x|a] - \tfrac{1}{2}r\mathrm{Var}[x|a]. \tag{2.6}$$

Hence, the decision maker's indifference curves in (Var[$x|a$],E[$x|a$])-space are increasing straight lines (and the increasing part of a parabola when risk is measured by standard deviations). Furthermore, and more importantly, this approximation is exact if x is a normally distributed random variable.

Proposition 2.7

If $u(x) = -\exp[-rx]$ and $x \sim \mathrm{N}(m(a),\sigma^2(a))$, then

$$U(a) = u(CE(a)),$$

where
$$CE(a) = m(a) - \tfrac{1}{2}r\sigma^2(a).$$

Proof: Using the specific form of the exponential utility function and the normal distribution, we obtain

$$U(a) = \int_{-\infty}^{+\infty} -\exp[-rx]\left(\frac{1}{[2\pi]^{1/2}\sigma(a)}\exp\left[-\frac{1}{2}\left(\frac{x-m(a)}{\sigma(a)}\right)^2\right]\right)dx$$

$$= -\exp[-r(m(a) - \tfrac{1}{2}r\sigma^2(a))]$$

$$\int_{-\infty}^{+\infty} \frac{1}{[2\pi]^{1/2}\sigma(a)}\exp\left[-\frac{1}{2}\left(\frac{x-[m(a)-r\sigma^2(a)]}{\sigma(a)}\right)^2\right]dx$$

$$= -\exp[-r(m(a) - \tfrac{1}{2}r\sigma^2(a))].$$

The first equality holds because

$$-rx - \frac{1}{2}\left(\frac{x-m(a)}{\sigma(a)}\right)^2 = -r[m(a) - \tfrac{1}{2}r\sigma^2(a)] - \frac{1}{2}\left(\frac{x-[m(a)-r\sigma^2(a)]}{\sigma(a)}\right)^2,$$

and the second equality holds because the term following the integral is a normal density function with mean $m(a) - r\sigma^2(a)$ and variance $\sigma^2(a)$, which integrates to 1. **Q.E.D.**

This exponential utility/normal distribution model is used extensively in subsequent chapters. Here we use it to demonstrate the impact of the decision maker's risk aversion on his action choices.

A Simple Investment Choice Example

Consider a simple financial investment setting in which the decision maker has wealth w that he can allocate between a riskless asset (e.g., a zero-coupon bond) that will return one dollar for each dollar invested (i.e., the risk-free interest rate is zero) and a risky asset that will provide, for each dollar invested, a return of $1 + \varepsilon$, where $\varepsilon \sim N(\mu,\sigma^2)$, with $\mu > 0$. Let a equal the number of dollars invested in the risky asset so that $x = w + a\varepsilon$, with $E[x|a] = w + a\mu$ and $Var[x|a] = a^2\sigma^2$. If the decision maker's utility function is $u(x) = -\exp[-rx]$, it follows from Proposition 2.7 that

$$U(a) = -\exp[-rCE(a)]$$

where $$CE(a) = w + a\mu - \tfrac{1}{2}ra^2\sigma^2.$$

Assuming that the decision maker can go long or short in the riskless asset, his optimal action can be obtained from the first-order condition for maximizing the certainty equivalent,[10]

$$CE'(a) = \mu - ra\sigma^2 = 0,$$

which implies that the optimal action is

$$a^* = \mu/[r\sigma^2]. \tag{2.7}$$

Note that the number of dollars invested in the risky asset is independent of the decision maker's initial wealth w. This is a direct consequence of the fact that a decision maker with an exponential utility function has constant (absolute) risk aversion, which implies that his preferences for gambles (large or small) are independent of his wealth level.[11] While constant risk aversion may not be

---

[10] The second-order condition $CE''(a) = -r\sigma^2$ establishes CE is strictly concave, so that the first-order condition identifies a global maximum.

[11] It is frequently argued that the risk aversion for most decision makers is decreasing in wealth. This condition is satisfied for HARA utility functions with $\alpha > 0$. If we also have $\beta = 0$, then

(continued...)

descriptive of most decision makers, the literature and the analysis in this book frequently use the exponential utility function precisely because there is no wealth effect. This is justified if the wealth effect for a given individual is a minor aspect of the phenomena being examined. Differences in risk aversion across individuals can be represented in these analyses by differences in r.

Substituting (2.7) into $U(a)$ establishes that the decision maker's maximum expected utility is

$$U(a^*) = -\exp[-r(w + \tfrac{1}{2}\mu^2/[r\sigma^2])]. \tag{2.8}$$

Differentiating (2.7) and (2.8) with respect to μ and σ^2 establishes that the investment in the risky asset and the decision maker's expected utility increase with μ and decrease with σ^2. This reflects the natural impact of shifts in the mean return and riskiness from a risky asset. Differentiating (2.7) with respect to r establishes that a more risk-averse decision maker will invest less in the risky asset. It is inappropriate to make inferences from the derivative of (2.8) with respect to r, since that involves making statements about the impact of r on the level of a decision maker's utility, and we earlier established that utility levels are not unique. However, in Chapter 3 we return to this example and consider how a decision maker's risk aversion affects his demand for information about the risky return.

2.7 BASIC HURDLE MODELS

In general, the mean-variance approximation of the certainty equivalent is not exact, even if the decision maker has exponential utility. To illustrate this and to provide further exploration of the impact of risk, we introduce a basic version of a simple model that will be used extensively in future chapters (particularly in Volume II).

In this model, the decision maker chooses an action $a \in A = [0,1]$, which we refer to as his *effort* level. There is a random variable h (called the *hurdle)* that is uniformly distributed on the unit interval, i.e., Φ is absolutely continuous with density function $\varphi(h) = 1$ for $h \in [0,1]$. The decision maker's preference relevant outcome consists of a gross payoff $x \in X = \{ x_g, x_b \}$, which can be

[11] (...continued)
HARA utility functions with $\alpha > 0$ have *constant relative risk aversion*, where relative risk aversion is defined as $r(x)x$. These utility functions have the property that *the fraction of wealth* invested in the risky asset is independent of the decision maker's initial wealth.

either good or bad, as well as the decision maker's effort level a.[12] In the basic model, the good payoff is achieved if $a \geq h$ (i.e., the decision maker "clears" the hurdle). Otherwise, the bad outcome obtains. Hence, $\varphi(x=x_g) = a$, $E[x|a] = x_b + a\Delta_x$, and $Var[x|a] = a(1-a)\Delta_x^2$, where $\Delta_x = x_g - x_b$.

The decision maker's utility function has two arguments, i.e., $u(x,a)$ is defined over the decision maker's monetary payoff x and his action a. We initially assume the decision maker's utility function is exponential and defined over the net monetary payoff $x - \kappa(a)$, i.e.,

$$u(x,a) = -\exp[-r(x - \kappa(a))],$$

where $\kappa(a) = \frac{1}{2}\gamma a^2$ is an increasing, strictly convex personal monetary cost of effort. This utility function is *multiplicatively separable* since

$$u(x,a) = -\exp[-rx]\exp[r\kappa(a)].$$

In the analysis that follows we let $x_b = w$ and $x_g = w + \Delta_x$. With multiplicatively separable exponential preferences, the decision maker's expected utility is

$$U(a) = -\exp[-r(w + \Delta_x - \kappa(a))]a - \exp[-r(w - \kappa(a))](1-a),$$

$$= -\exp[-r(w - \kappa(a))]\{\exp[-r\Delta_x]a + (1-a)\}.$$

The first-order condition for the decision maker's optimal choice of a, if $a \in (0,1)$, is

$$U'(a) = -\exp[-r(w - \kappa(a))]\Big(r\kappa'(a)\{\exp[-r\Delta_x]a + (1-a)\} + \exp[-r\Delta_x] - 1\Big)$$

$$= 0.$$

Since $\kappa'(a) = \gamma a$, the decision maker's optimal effort level (if less than one) is[13]

$$a^* = \frac{r\gamma - \sqrt{(r\gamma)^2 - 4r\gamma(1-\exp[-r\Delta_x])^2}}{2r\gamma(1-\exp[-r\Delta_x])}.$$

---

[12] It would be more consistent with our earlier notation to let $x = (x_1,x_2)$, where $x_1 \in \{x_{1g}, x_{1b}\}$ represents the payoff and $x_2 = a$ represents the effort level. However, letting x and a represent the two dimensions is simpler and should not be confusing in this specific example.

[13] Since $U'(0) > 0$ and the "negative root" is greater than zero, any "positive root" less than one is a local minimum. If the risk aversion is sufficiently high the decision maker's optimal effort level is $a^* = 1$.

Now compare the above result to the action based on the mean-variance approximation. The approximate certainty equivalent is

$$CE(a) \approx w + a\Delta_x - \tfrac{1}{2}ra(1-a)\Delta_x^2 - \kappa(a),$$

for which the first-order condition is

$$\Delta_x - \tfrac{1}{2}r\Delta_x^2 + ra\Delta_x^2 - \kappa'(a) = 0.$$

Hence, the mean-variance approximation results in the action choice

$$a^{mv} = [\tfrac{1}{2}r\Delta_x^2 - \Delta_x]/[r\Delta_x^2 - \gamma].$$

Observe that w has no impact on the effort choice. This is because there is no wealth effect on the choice of gambles when the utility for the net return from effort is exponential. However, the optimal effort does depend on the decision maker's risk aversion r, the potential gain from effort Δ_x, and the cost of effort γ.

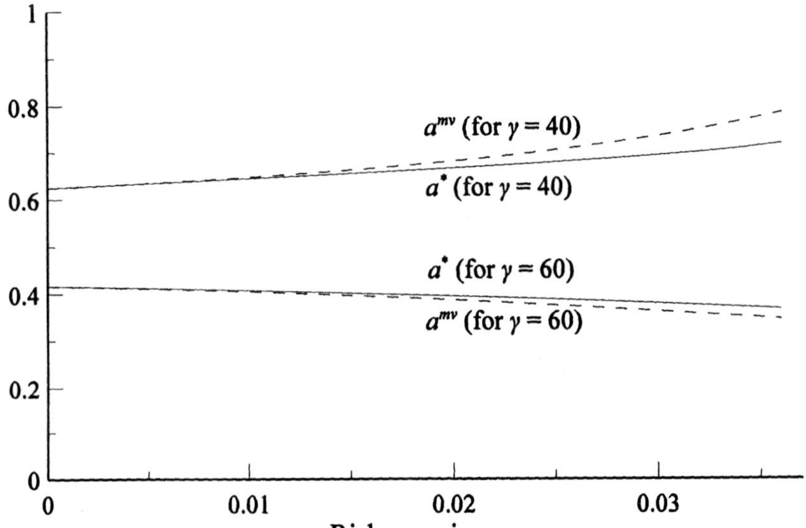

Figure 2.4: Multiplicative hurdle model effort ($\Delta_x = 25$).

Figure 2.4 depicts the relation between a^* and a^{mv} for two levels of γ and a range of values for r. Observe that for $\Delta_x/\gamma > 0.5$, both the optimal action a^* and a^{mv} are increasing in r, but decreasing for $\Delta_x/\gamma < 0.5$. The reason for this is that the outcome risk (e.g., outcome variance) is highest for $a = \tfrac{1}{2}$. If $a^* > \tfrac{1}{2}$, then increasing the risk aversion creates a stronger incentive to reduce risk, which in this case is achieved by increasing a. The converse holds if $a^* < ½$. In either case, the mean-variance approximation generates an action choice a^{mv} close to a^* for small risk aversions, but the difference increases as r increases.

The utility function $u(x,a)$ used above is referred to as *multiplicatively separable*. The utility function is referred to as *additively separable* if there exist functions u_x and v such that

$$u(x,a) = u_x(x) - v(a),$$

where $u_x(x)$ is the decision maker's utility for monetary outcome x and $v(a)$ is the decision maker's disutility for effort. In the hurdle model, the expected additively separable utility is

$$U(a) = u_x(x_g)a + u_x(x_b)\,(1- a) - v(a) = u_x(w) + \Delta_u a - v(a),$$

where $w \equiv x_b$ and $\Delta_u \equiv u_x(x_g) - u_x(x_b)$. Assuming an interior solution with $v(a)$ increasing and strictly convex, i.e., $v'(a) > 0$ and $v''(a) > 0$, the decision maker's optimal effort is characterized by the first-order condition

$$v'(a^*) = \Delta_u.$$

To illustrate, assume that $u_x(x) = -\exp[-rx]$ and $v(a) = \gamma a/(1- a)$, so that $\Delta_u = e^{-rw}[1 - e^{-r\Delta_x}]$ and $v'(a) = \gamma/(1- a)^2$. Hence, assuming γ is sufficiently small to induce positive effort, the optimal effort level is

$$a^* = 1 - \gamma^{½}e^{½rw}[1 - e^{-r\Delta_x}]^{-½}.$$

Observe that a^* is increasing in Δ_x, decreasing in both w and γ, and increasing (decreasing) in r if

$$r < (>)\ \frac{1}{\Delta_x}[\ln(w+\Delta_x) - \ln w].$$

The impact of Δ_x and γ is not surprising, since increasing the former increases the benefit of more effort, while increasing the latter increases the cost. Perhaps somewhat surprisingly, increasing w reduces the optimal effort! Wealth does not affect the decision maker's risk aversion and, hence, has no effect on the effort choice with multiplicatively separable exponential utility. However, that is not the case here. The reason that increasing w reduces a^* with additively separable utility is that the outcome utility is concave, so that increasing w decreases Δ_u, i.e., the *incremental* utility for the outcome increase Δ_x is reduced.

The impact of the risk aversion parameter r is also rather subtle. Recall that $\Delta_u = e^{-rw}[1 - e^{-r\Delta_x}]$. Increasing r reduces e^{-rw} reflecting the reduction in the outcome utility u_x relative to the disutility for effort v. Conversely, increasing r increases $[1 - e^{-r\Delta_x}]$, which has the reverse effect on Δ_u. If r is small, the latter impact dominates, while the former dominates if r is large.

We extensively use various versions of the hurdle model in subsequent chapters (particularly in Volume II). Here we have used it to illustrate the impact of wealth and risk aversion for both multiplicatively and additively separable utility functions. The examples highlight the fact that one must be careful in making generalizations about the impact of utility function characteristics on the decision maker's choices.

2.8 STOCHASTIC DOMINANCE

We now consider two partial orderings over alternative gambles (outcome probability distributions) that depend only on limited assumptions regarding the shape of the decision maker's utility function. The analysis is restricted to the case in which the uncertain outcome is *single-dimensional.*[14] We initially consider *first-order stochastic dominance*, which provides a partial ordering of gambles that only requires the decision maker to prefer more outcome to less. We then consider *second-order stochastic dominance*, which provides a more complete partial ordering that also requires the decision maker to be weakly risk averse.

We consider a set of gambles that are characterized by parameters $\omega \in \Omega$ (e.g., the set of parameters could be a set of actions $a \in A$). The initial question addressed is: if all we know is that the decision maker prefers more outcome to less (i.e., $x' \succeq x''$ if, and only if, $x' \geq x''$), when can we say that he will prefer gamble ω_2 to ω_1 irrespective of the other characteristics of his preferences? To examine this we first observe that the decision maker's preferences can be represented by a utility function $u: X \rightarrow \mathbb{R}$ that is a *non-decreasing function* of x.

Now consider a probability space (S,Ξ,P) and a random variable $\boldsymbol{x}: S\times\Omega \rightarrow X$, parameterized by $\omega \in \Omega$, with a corresponding family of generalized probability density functions $\{ \varphi(\cdot|\omega), \omega \in \Omega \}$. The probability distribution corresponding to $\varphi(\cdot|\omega)$ is denoted $\Phi(\cdot|\omega)$. Now consider the following potential comparison of the distribution functions of two gambles.

---

[14] Although we do not formally allow for multi-dimensional preference relevant outcomes in this analysis, we could allow for an additional component such as effort. However, in that case the additional component must be non-stochastic (see below).

Definition *First-order Stochastic (FS) Dominance*

The probability function given ω_2 *FS*-dominates ω_1 if, and only if, $\Phi(x|\omega_1) \geq \Phi(x|\omega_2), \forall x \in X$.

That is, we say ω_2 *FS*-dominates ω_1 if the former is less likely to generate outcomes in the "lower tail" than is the latter, for all possible "lower tails". Of course, this comparison is often not possible, since the inequality may hold for some x but not for others. Hence, the *FS* dominance criterion only provides a partial ordering of the set of possible gambles. To illustrate, consider the following probability functions:

(ω_1): $\varphi(x|\omega_1) = .20$ for $x \in [0,5]$, and zero otherwise;

(ω_2): $\varphi(x|\omega_2) = .10$ for $x \in [0,10]$, and zero otherwise;

(ω_3): $\varphi(x|\omega_3) = .20$ for $x \in [2.5, 7.5]$, and zero otherwise.

The distribution functions are depicted in Figure 2.5. Obviously, ω_2 and ω_3 both *FS*-dominate ω_1, but neither ω_2 nor ω_3 *FS*-dominates the other.

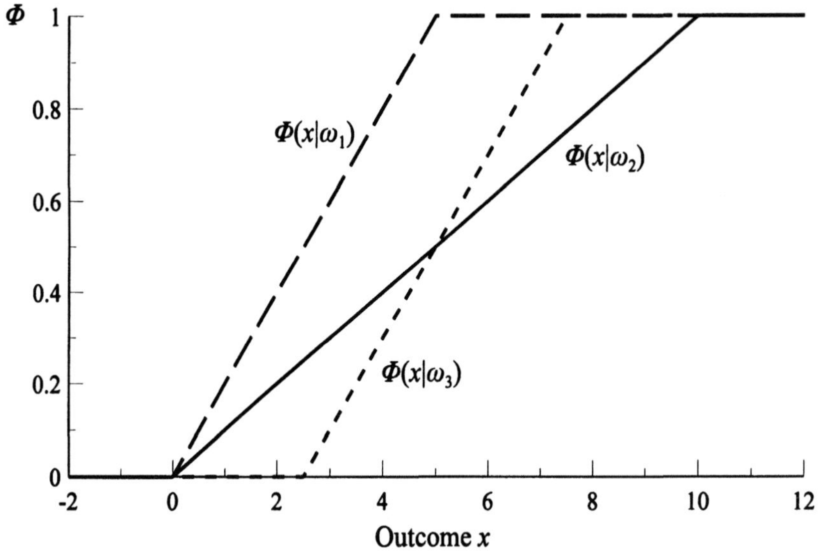

Figure 2.5: *FS*-dominance.

The key result here is that if one gamble *FS*-dominates the other, then the former is preferred by any decision maker who prefers more to less. Early analyses containing this and other widely known results can be found in Hadar and Russell (1969) and Hanoch and Levy (1969), and proofs of this and the other stochastic dominance results that follow are provided in Appendix 2A.

Proposition 2.8 (Hadar and Russell 1969, Theorems 1, 1′, 2, & 2′; Hanoch and Levy 1969, Theorem 1)

Given any two gambles ω_1 and ω_2, $\omega_2 \succeq \omega_1$ for *all* non-decreasing utility functions if, and only if, ω_2 *FS*-dominates ω_1.

As noted above, one gamble *FS*-dominates another if the distribution for the former has uniformly smaller lower tails than the latter. Instead of comparing distribution functions it is often useful to compare the ratio of the generalized probability density functions, i.e., the likelihood ratio $\varphi(x|\omega_1)/\varphi(x|\omega_2)$. This ratio will be less than one for some x and greater than one for others. For some distributions, such as those in the one-parameter exponential family (see below), the ratio is a uniformly decreasing function of x if the mean of ω_1 is less than for ω_2. To illustrate, consider the family of normal distributions for which $\omega \in \Omega \subseteq \mathbb{R}$ is the mean and σ^2 is the variance; in this case,

$$\varphi(x|\omega) = [2\pi\sigma^2]^{-½} \exp[-½(x-\omega)^2/\sigma^2] ,$$

and
$$\frac{\varphi(x|\omega_1)}{\varphi(x|\omega_2)} = \exp[½(\omega_2 - \omega_1)(\omega_2 + \omega_1 - 2x)/\sigma^2],$$

which is decreasing in x if $\omega_2 \geq \omega_1$. Distributions that have this property are said to satisfy the monotone likelihood ratio property.

Definition *Monotone Likelihood Ratio Property (MLRP)*

The family of probability functions $\{ \varphi(\cdot|\omega), \omega \in \Omega \}$ satisfies (strict) MLRP if for every $x_1 < x_2$ and $\omega_1 < \omega_2$ the following condition holds:

$$\frac{\varphi(x_1|\omega_1)}{\varphi(x_1|\omega_2)} \geq (>) \frac{\varphi(x_2|\omega_1)}{\varphi(x_2|\omega_2)}.$$

If the probability function $\varphi(\cdot|\omega)$ is continuous and differentiable with respect to ω, then from Milgrom (1981) we learn that we can determine whether MLRP is satisfied by computing the rate of change in $\varphi(x|\omega)$ relative to $\varphi(x|\omega)$.

Proposition 2.9 (Milgrom 1981, Prop. 5)

If $\Omega = [\underline{\omega},\bar{\omega}]$ and $\varphi(\cdot|\omega)$ is continuous and differentiable with respect to ω, then $\{ \varphi(\cdot|\omega), \omega \in \Omega \}$ satisfies MLRP if, and only if, for all $\omega \in \Omega$:

$$\frac{\varphi_\omega(x|\omega)}{\varphi(x|\omega)} \text{ is non-decreasing in } x, \text{ where } \varphi_\omega(x|\omega) = \frac{\partial\varphi(x|\omega)}{\partial\omega}.$$

Returning to the normal distribution case, we observe that

$$\frac{\varphi_\omega(x|\omega)}{\varphi(x|\omega)} = \frac{x - \omega}{\sigma^2},$$

which is strictly increasing in x, thereby supporting our earlier demonstration that the normal distribution satisfies MLRP if ω represents the mean of the distribution (or the mean is an increasing function of ω).

The normal distribution in which ω represents the mean and the variance is fixed is a specific example of what is called the *one-parameter exponential family of distributions*. Members of this family are frequently used in this book, and some results apply to the entire family.

Definition *One-Parameter Exponential Family of Distributions*

A probability distribution is a member of the one-parameter exponential family if there exist functions $\theta(x)$, $\psi(x)$, $\alpha(\omega)$, and $\beta(\omega)$ such that

$$\varphi(x|\omega) = \theta(x)\,\beta(\omega)\exp[\alpha(\omega)\,\psi(x)].$$

Proposition 2.10

The one-parameter exponential family of distributions satisfies MLRP if $\alpha(\omega)$ is non-decreasing in ω and $\psi(x)$ is non-decreasing in x.

Proof: Assume $\Omega = [\underline{\omega},\overline{\omega}]$ and both $\alpha(\omega)$ and $\beta(\omega)$ are continuous and differentiable with respect to ω. It then follows that

$$\frac{\varphi_\omega(x|\omega)}{\varphi(x|\omega)} = \alpha'(\omega)\,\psi(x) + \frac{\beta'(\omega)}{\beta(\omega)},$$

which is increasing in x. **Q.E.D.**

Appendix 2B states the specific forms of several members of this family (exponential, normal, gamma, Poisson, and binomial). In these examples, $\psi(x) = x$ and there exists a function $B(\alpha)$ such that $\beta(\omega) = \exp[-B(\alpha(\omega))]$, which implies

$$\frac{\varphi_\omega(x|\omega)}{\varphi(x|\omega)} = [x - B'(\alpha(\omega))]\alpha'(\omega)$$

is an increasing linear function of x (given that $\alpha'(\omega) \geq 0$).

MLRP suggests that increasing ω is desirable since it implies that larger values of x are relatively more likely to occur if ω is larger. This intuition is correct.

Proposition 2.11

If $\{ \varphi(\cdot|\omega), \omega \in \Omega \}$ satisfies (strict) MLRP, then ω_2 (strictly) *FS*-dominates ω_1, for all $\omega_1 < \omega_2$.

Observe that MLRP is sufficient, but not necessary, for first-order stochastic dominance. The following example illustrates that the latter can hold without the former. The likelihood ratio is not monotonic, even though a comparison of $\Phi(x|\omega_1)$ and $\Phi(x|\omega_2)$ establishes that ω_2 first-order stochastic dominates ω_1.

	x_1	x_2	x_3
$\varphi(x\|\omega_1)$	0.5	0.3	0.2
$\varphi(x\|\omega_2)$	0.2	0.5	0.3
$\varphi(x\|\omega_1)/\varphi(x\|\omega_2)$	2.5	0.6	0.667
$\Phi(x\|\omega_1)$	0.5	0.8	1
$\Phi(x\|\omega_2)$	0.2	0.7	1

First-order stochastic dominance provides a preference ordering among gambles that holds for all non-decreasing utility functions, and ignores whether the decision maker is risk averse or not. As noted, *FS*-dominance is a partial ordering, e.g., we cannot compare gambles ω_2 and ω_3 in Figure 2.5 on the basis of *FS*-dominance. However, we observe that these two gambles both have means of 5.0 and, intuitively, ω_3 is less risky than ω_2, which suggests that a risk-averse decision maker may prefer ω_3 to ω_2. This type of observation leads to the concept of second-order stochastic dominance, which provides a more extensive ordering of gambles than does first-order stochastic dominance, if we restrict our analysis to settings in which the decision maker is risk averse.

Definition *Second-order Stochastic (SS) Dominance*

The probability function given ω_2 *SS*-dominates ω_1 if, and only if, $G(x|\omega_1) \geq G(x|\omega_2)$, $\forall\, x \in X$, where

$$G(x|\omega) = \int_{-\infty}^{x} \Phi(y|\omega)\, dy.$$

To illustrate *SS*-dominance, again consider the three gambles depicted in Figure 2.5.

$$(\omega_1):\ G(x|\omega_1) = \int_0^x .2y\,dy = .1x^2,\ \text{for } x \in [0,5],$$

$$0 \text{ for } x \le 0, \text{ and } x - 2.5 \text{ for } x \ge 5;$$

$$(\omega_2):\ G(x|\omega_2) = \int_0^x .1y\,dy = .05x^2,\ \text{for } x \in [0,10],$$

$$0 \text{ for } x \le 0, \text{ and } x - 5 \text{ for } x \ge 10;$$

$$(\omega_3):\ G(x|\omega_3) = \int_{2.5}^x .2(y - 2.5)\,dy = .1x^2 - .5x + .625 \text{ for } x \in [2.5, 7.5],$$

$$0 \text{ for } x \le 2.5, \text{ and } x - 5 \text{ for } x \ge 7.5.$$

Figure 2.6 depicts these three functions, clearly illustrating that ω_3 *SS*-dominates both ω_2 and ω_1, and ω_2 *SS*-dominates ω_1.

The key result for *SS*-dominance is that if a gamble *SS*-dominates another gamble, any risk-averse decision maker (that prefers more outcome to less) prefers the former to the latter.

Proposition 2.12 (Hadar and Russell 1969, Theorems 3, 3′, 4, & 4′; Hanoch and Levy 1969, Theorem 2)

Given any two gambles ω_1 and ω_2, $\omega_2 \succeq \omega_1$ for *all* non-decreasing, concave utility functions if, and only if, ω_2 *SS*-dominates ω_1.

It should be noted that if one gamble *FS*-dominates another, then the former also *SS*-dominates the latter. However, *SS*-dominance does not imply *FS*-dominance, as our example illustrates.

In general, while *SS*-dominance provides a more complete ordering of gambles than does *FS*-dominance, both are partial orderings. Moreover, the two stochastic dominance criteria only apply to the distributions for the decision maker's "total" outcome from risky gambles. For example, if the decision maker considers investing in a number of different risky assets, then an asset which is *FS*-dominated by another asset may very well be part of the decision maker's optimal portfolio. This can occur, for example, in a mean-variance portfolio problem if the dominated asset's return has a sufficiently low correlation with the returns of the other assets, so that including the asset in the

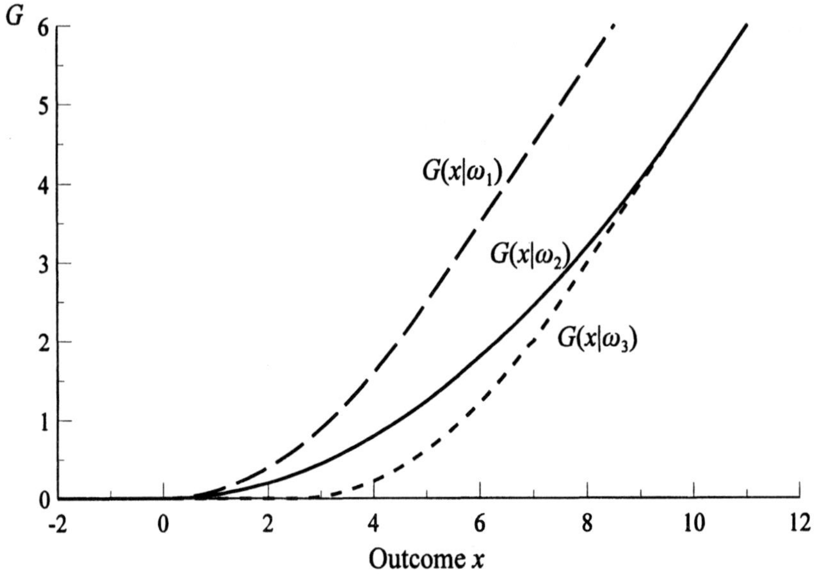

Figure 2.6: *SS*-dominance.

portfolio reduces the total risk of the portfolio sufficiently to make up for its low expected return relatively to its variance.[15]

APPENDIX 2A: Proofs of Stochastic Dominance Propositions

To simplify the proofs, we assume throughout this appendix that the generalized probability density functions are absolutely continuous on $X = [\underline{x}, \bar{x}]$. It is straightforward to generalize the proofs to discrete and mixed distributions.

Proof of Proposition 2.8:

if: $U(\omega_2) - U(\omega_1)$

$$= \int_X u(x)\, [\varphi(x|\omega_2) - \varphi(x|\omega_1)]\, dx$$

$$= u(x)\,[\Phi(x|\omega_2) - \Phi(x|\omega_1)]\Big|_{\underline{x}}^{\bar{x}} - \int_X u'(x)\, [\Phi(x|\omega_2) - \Phi(x|\omega_1)]\, dx$$

[15] In the context of the CAPM, stocks with negative beta are *FS*-dominated by the riskless asset, in equilibrium.

$$= - \int_X u'(x)\,[\Phi(x|\omega_2) - \Phi(x|\omega_1)]\,dx \geq 0,$$

where the first equality follows from integration by parts, and the inequality follows from the fact that $u'(x) \geq 0$ and $\Phi(x|\omega_2) \leq \Phi(x|\omega_1)$.
only if: Proof is by contradiction. Assume there is some interval $[x_1,x_2]$ such that $\Phi(x|\omega_2) > \Phi(x|\omega_1)$ for $x \in (x_1,x_2)$. Construct a utility function as follows: $u(x) = 0$ for $x \leq x_1$, $(x - x_1)/(x_2 - x_1)$ for $x \in (x_1,x_2)$, and 1 for $x \geq x_2$. The argument used to prove "if" then implies that $U(\omega_2) < U(\omega_1)$. **Q.E.D.**

Proof of Proposition 2.9:
if: Observe that

$$\int \varphi_\omega(x|\omega)/\varphi(x|\omega)\,d\omega = \ln \varphi(x|\omega)$$

$$\Rightarrow \quad \varphi(x|\omega_1)/\varphi(x|\omega_2) = \exp[\ln \varphi(x|\omega_1) - \ln \varphi(x|\omega_2)]$$

$$= \exp\left[- \int_{\omega_1}^{\omega_2} \varphi_\omega(x|\omega)/\varphi(x|\omega)\,d\omega\right].$$

Therefore, if $\varphi_\omega(x|\omega)/\varphi(x|\omega)$ is non-decreasing in x, then $\varphi(x|\omega_1)/\varphi(x|\omega_2)$ is non- increasing in x, for $\omega_2 > \omega_1$.
only if: The above equality also establishes that if $\varphi(x|\omega_1)/\varphi(x|\omega_2)$ is non-increasing in x, then

$$\int_{\omega_1}^{\omega_2} \varphi_\omega(x|\omega)/\varphi(x|\omega)\,d\omega$$

is non-decreasing in x. For this to be true for all $\omega_2 > \omega_1$, it must be that $\varphi_\omega(x|\omega)/\varphi(x|\omega)$ is non-decreasing in x for all ω. **Q.E.D.**

Proof of Proposition 2.11:
From Proposition 2.9 it follows that if Ω is an interval and φ is differentiable with respect to ω, then MLRP implies $\varphi_\omega(x|\omega)/\varphi(x|\omega)$ is increasing in x for any ω. Let x_ω be such that $\varphi_\omega(x|\omega) < 0$ for all $x < x_\omega$ and ≥ 0 otherwise. We want to prove that $\Phi_\omega(x|\omega) \leq 0$ for all x and ω, where

$$\Phi_\omega(x|\omega) \equiv \int_{\underline{x}}^{x} \varphi_\omega(y|\omega)\, dy.$$

$\Phi_\omega(x|\omega) < 0$ follows immediately if $x < x_\omega$. Therefore, consider $x > x_\omega$. Since φ is a probability function which always sums (integrates) to one, it follows that

$$\int_{\underline{x}}^{\bar{x}} \varphi_\omega(y|\omega)\, dy = 0.$$

Therefore,

$$\Phi_\omega(x|\omega) = \int_{\underline{x}}^{x} \varphi_\omega(y|\omega)\, dy = 0 - \int_{x}^{\bar{x}} \varphi_\omega(y|\omega)\, dy \le 0. \qquad \textbf{Q.E.D.}$$

Proof of Proposition 2.12:
if: From the proof of proposition 2.8 we get that

$$U(\omega_2) - U(\omega_1) = - \int_X u'(x)\, [\Phi(x|\omega_2) - \Phi(x|\omega_1)]\, dx.$$

Integration by parts gives

$$U(\omega_2) - U(\omega_1)$$

$$= - u'(x)[G(x|\omega_2) - G(x|\omega_1)]\Big|_{\underline{x}}^{\bar{x}} + \int_X u''(x)\, [G(x|\omega_2) - G(x|\omega_1)]\, dx$$

$$= - u'(\bar{x})[G(\bar{x}|\omega_2) - G(\bar{x}|\omega_1)] + \int_X u''(x)\, [G(x|\omega_2) - G(x|\omega_1)]\, dx \ge 0,$$

where the inequality follows from $u'(x) \ge 0$, $u''(x) \le 0$, and $G(x|\omega_1) \ge G(x|\omega_2)$ for all $x \in X$.
only if: Proof is by contradiction. Assume by continuity of G that there is some interval $[x_1,x_2]$ such that $G(x|\omega_1) < G(x|\omega_2)$ for $x \in (x_1,x_2)$. Construct a utility function as follows: $u'(x) = x_2 - x_1$ for $x \le x_1$, $u'(x) = (x_2 - x)$ for $x \in (x_1,x_2)$, and $u'(x) = 0$ for $x \ge x_2$. The argument used to prove "if" then implies that $U(\omega_2) < U(\omega_1)$. **Q.E.D.**

APPENDIX 2B
One-parameter Exponential Family of Distributions

$$\varphi(x|\omega) = \theta(x)\beta(\omega)\exp[\alpha(\omega)\psi(x)],$$

Examples with $\beta(\omega) = \exp[-B(\alpha(\omega))]$ and $\psi(x) = x$

	Exponential	Normal	Gamma	Poisson	Binomial
$\varphi(x\|\omega)$	$\frac{1}{\bar{x}(\omega)}\exp\left[\frac{-x}{\bar{x}(\omega)}\right]$	$\left[\frac{1}{2\pi\sigma^2}\right]^{1/2}\exp\left[-\frac{(x-\bar{x}(\omega))^2}{2\sigma^2}\right]$	$\frac{1}{(n-1)!}\lambda^n x^{n-1} e^{-\lambda x}$	$\exp[-\bar{x}(\omega)]\,\frac{1}{x!}\,\bar{x}(\omega)^x$	$\binom{n}{x}\left(\frac{\bar{x}(\omega)}{n}\right)^x\left(1-\frac{\bar{x}(\omega)}{n}\right)^{n-x}$
$\theta(x)$	1	$\left[\frac{1}{2\pi\sigma^2}\right]^{1/2}\exp\left[-\frac{x^2}{2\sigma^2}\right]$	$\frac{n^n}{(n-1)!}x^{n-1}$	$\frac{1}{x!}$	$\binom{n}{x} n^{-n}$
$\alpha(\omega)$	$-1/\bar{x}(\omega)$	$\bar{x}(\omega)/\sigma^2$	$-n/\bar{x}(\omega)$	$\ln \bar{x}(\omega)$	$\ln \bar{x}(\omega) - \ln(n - \bar{x}(\omega))$
$B(\alpha)$	$-\ln[-\alpha]$	$\frac{1}{2}\sigma^2\alpha^2$	$n \ln\left[-\frac{n}{\alpha}\right]$	$\exp[\alpha]$	$n\alpha - n\ln\left[\frac{ne^\alpha}{1+e^\alpha}\right]$
$\frac{\varphi_\omega(x\|\omega)}{\varphi(x\|\omega)}$	$\frac{\bar{x}'(\omega)}{\bar{x}(\omega)^2}(x-\bar{x}(\omega))$	$\frac{\bar{x}'(\omega)}{\sigma^2}(x-\bar{x}(\omega))$	$n\frac{\bar{x}'(\omega)}{\bar{x}(\omega)^2}(x-\bar{x}(\omega))$	$\frac{E_\omega[x\|\omega]}{E[x\|\omega]}(x - E[x\|\omega])$	$\left[\frac{\bar{x}'(\omega)}{\bar{x}(\omega)}+\frac{\bar{x}'(\omega)}{n-\bar{x}(\omega)}\right](x-\bar{x}(\omega))$

Note: $\bar{x}(\omega) \equiv E[x|\omega]$. In the gamma distribution, $\lambda = n/\bar{x}(\omega)$, and the exponential distribution is a special case in which $n = 1$.

REFERENCES

Arrow, K. (1970) *Essays in the Theory of Risk-Bearing.* Amsterdam: North-Holland.

Billingsley, P. (1986) *Probability and Measure.* New York: John Wiley & Sons.

DeGroot, M. H. (1970) *Optimal Statistical Decisions.* New York: McGraw-Hill.

Diamond, P. A., and J. E. Stiglitz. (1974) "Increases in Risk and in Risk Aversion," *Journal of Economic Theory* 8, 605-620.

Hadar, J., and W. R. Russell. (1969) "Rules for Ordering Uncertain Prospects," *American Economic Review* 59, 25-34.

Hanock, G., and H. Levy. (1969) "Efficiency Analysis of Choices Involving Risks," *Review of Economic Studies* 36, 335-346.

Milgrom, P. (1981) "Good News and Bad News: Representation Theorems and Application," *Bell Journal of Economics* 12, 380-391.

Pratt, J. (1964) "Risk Aversion in the Small and the Large," *Econometrica* 32, 122-136.

Rothschild, M., and J. E. Stiglitz. (1970) "Increasing Risk I: A Definition," *Journal of Economic Theory* 2, 225-243.

Rothschild, M., and J. E. Stiglitz. (1971) "Increasing Risk II: Its Economic Consequences," *Journal of Economic Theory* 3, 66-84.

Savage, L. (1972) *Foundations of Statistics.* Dover. New York.

von Neumann, J., and O. Morgenstern. (1944) *Theory of Games and Economic Behavior.* Princeton, New Jersey: Princeton University Press.

CHAPTER 3

DECISION-FACILITATING INFORMATION

An accounting system potentially reports information to decision makers. Consequently, to understand the economic role of accounting systems it is useful to understand the economic role of information systems. In our basic economic model of decision making, the decision maker faces uncertainty about the outcomes from his actions. We generally view information as a mechanism for reducing uncertainty, and in single-person decision making the reduction of outcome uncertainty has economic value (which may or may not exceed its costs) if it influences the decision maker's action choices. Hence, the key characteristic of an information system is how the signals (information) it generates affect the decision maker's beliefs about outcome relevant events.

We characterize an information system in terms of the signals it might generate, and the relation between the possible signals and the possible events of interest. A system can only be informative about uncertain events if it can generate more than one signal and the signal generated is correlated with those events. An information system that provides signals to a decision maker *prior* to making a decision, and *affects his decision*, is referred to as a *decision-facilitating information system.* The decision maker can always ignore the signals when he makes his decision. Hence, if his decision is affected by the signal received, it must be that he believes it helps him to make a better decision.

The structure of the remainder of this chapter is as follows. Section 3.1 describes the representation of information systems and signals. The key characteristic of a signal is the *posterior* event beliefs it generates. The representation of that information is, to some extent, arbitrary. For example, we can report income in millions of dollars or thousands of dollars, but the information content is exactly the same, i.e., scaling of signals does not affect the posterior event beliefs. Furthermore, in some settings, the decision maker's posterior beliefs are not influenced by details – a summary measure such as net income might result in the same beliefs as a report with all the components of net income. This leads to the concept of a *sufficient statistic* – knowing a sufficient statistic is as good as knowing any other representation of the information, and there are always many possible sufficient statistics. A key characteristic of a sufficient statistic is that it is not sensitive to the decision maker's utility function or prior event beliefs, it only depends on his beliefs about the likelihood of the possible signals given the possible events of interest.

Section 3.2 introduces information into economic decision problems under uncertainty. For a given decision maker and information system, there is an optimal decision rule specifying the optimal action for each signal the information system might generate. The choice among information systems is based on the decision maker's expected utilities that result from using the optimal decision rules for each information system. In general, the preference ordering among information systems depends on the characteristics of the decision problem, i.e., the decision maker's preferences and beliefs, and the relation between outcomes and actions. In Section 3.3 we consider statements about the relative preferences among information systems given only the statistical characteristics of these systems. If the signals from one information system tell at least as much about the likelihood of the outcome-relevant events as the signals from another information system, the former is weakly preferred to the latter independently of the characteristics of the decision problem (assuming the implementation of information systems is costless). This result is commonly referred to as the *Blackwell Theorem.*

Section 3.4 concludes the chapter with an examination of the impact of risk and risk aversion on the value of information in two specific parametric models, i.e., in a financial investment model, and in the hurdle model.

3.1 REPRESENTATION OF INFORMATION

This section discusses the formal representation of information systems and the relations between the system's signals and the uncertain events of interest. This includes specification of the decision maker's beliefs after receiving a signal – which are generally referred to as his *posterior* beliefs – and specification of alternative representations of signals that do not change the information content – which are generally referred to as *sufficient statistics.*

3.1.1 Conditional Probability

Before introducing formal representation of an information system, we briefly consider the concept of a *conditional probability*, which is one of the basic elements of probability theory that is important in representing the effect of information.

The underlying probability space is again represented by (S,Ξ,P). Recall that each probabilizable event $\xi \in \Xi$ is a subset of the state space, i.e., $\xi \subseteq S$. Let $y \in \Xi$ represent an *observed* event and consider how the observation of y affects the decision maker's beliefs about all other events $\xi \in \Xi$. If y and ξ have no states in common, i.e., $y \cap \xi = \emptyset$, then observing y reveals that ξ could not have occurred. At the other extreme, if all the states in y are also in ξ, i.e., $y \subseteq \xi$, then observing y reveals that ξ has definitely occurred. In between these two extremes we have settings in which some states in y are also in ξ, but there are some states in y that are not in ξ, i.e., $y \cap \xi \neq \emptyset$ and $y \not\subset \xi$. In this case, observing y potentially changes the decision maker's beliefs about ξ, but not to the extremes of zero or one.

The belief about ξ given y is referred to as the conditional probability of ξ given y, and is written $P(\xi|y)$. If y has a positive probability of occurring, i.e., $P(y) > 0$, then the conditional probability is

$$P(\xi|y) = \frac{P(y \cap \xi)}{P(y)}. \tag{3.1}$$

Observe that this statement is sufficiently general to include the two extreme cases, since $P(y \cap \xi) = 0$ if $y \cap \xi = \emptyset$ and $P(y \cap \xi) = P(y)$ if $y \subseteq \xi$.

Bayes' theorem is a widely used application of relation (3.1). It begins with "prior" beliefs about a set of events that partition the state space and with the "likelihood" of observing a "signal" y given each of the possible events of interest. It then uses these elements to compute the "posterior" beliefs about the events of interest given the signal y.

Definition *Partition*

A set of events $\Omega = \{ \omega_1, \omega_2, \omega_3 \ldots \}$, which could have a finite or countably infinite number of elements, defines a probabilizable partition on the state space S if $\omega_i \in \Xi$, $\omega_i \cap \omega_j = \emptyset$, for all i, j, $i \neq j$, and $\omega_1 \cup \omega_2 \cup \omega_3 \cup \ldots = S$.

That is, Ω divides S into an exhaustive set of disjoint events. We can think of these events as the decision relevant events. The prior beliefs about the elements in Ω are represented by $P(\omega_i)$ and the likelihood of the event y given ω_i is the conditional probability $P(y|\omega_i)$. The widely used Bayes' theorem states how to compute the posterior probability $P(\omega_i|y)$.

Proposition 3.1 *Bayes' Theorem*

Let Ω partition S such that $P(\omega_i) > 0$ for all $i = 1, 2, 3, \ldots$. Also, let $y \in \Xi$ be such that $P(y) > 0$. Then

$$P(\omega_i|y) = \frac{P(y|\omega_i)\, P(\omega_i)}{\sum_{j=1}^{\infty} P(y|\omega_j)\, P(\omega_j)}, \quad i = 1, 2, 3, \ldots \tag{3.2}$$

Proof: From (3.1) we obtain both $P(\omega_i|y) = P(\omega_i \cap y)/P(y)$ and $P(\omega_i \cap y) = P(y|\omega_i)P(\omega_i)$. Given that Ω partitions S, it follows that

$$P(y) = \sum_{j=1}^{\infty} P(\omega_j \cap y) = \sum_{j=1}^{\infty} P(y|\omega_j)\, P(\omega_j). \qquad \textbf{Q.E.D.}$$

The signal y is defined to be *independent* of the events in Ω if the likelihood $P(y|\omega_i) = P(y)$, $\forall\, y \in Y$, $\omega_i \in \Omega$. In that case it immediately follows from (3.2) that $P(\omega_i|y) = P(\omega_i)$, $\forall\, y \in Y$, $\omega_i \in \Omega$, i.e., the decision maker's posterior belief about the events of interest is the same as his prior belief – the signal has no impact.

3.1.2 Posterior Beliefs with Random Variables

Throughout this book we let η represent an information system and let $Y = \{y\}$ represent the set of possible signals that might be generated by η. Generally, the information system is a function from the set of states S to the set of signals Y, i.e., η: $S \rightarrow Y$. (In some cases it is important to recognize that the set of possible signals can vary with the information system, in which case we let Y^η represent the set of possible signals for system η.) In the discussion that follows we let $\Omega = \{\omega\}$ represent the set of events about which the decision maker wishes to make inferences based on the signal y from system η. These events are often referred to as the *parameters* of interest.

Throughout our subsequent analysis $y \in Y$ is a random variable and we initially assume that $\omega \in \Omega$ is also a random variable, i.e., they are real numbers (or vectors of real numbers) and are functions of the state $s \in S$. The set Y and its relation to S are the characteristics of the information system. The relation between the random variable y and S is given by the subset of states defined by $\eta^{-1}(y) \equiv \{\, s \in S \mid \eta(s) = y \,\}$.[1] Conditional on observing y, the decision maker knows that the true state is in the subset $\eta^{-1}(y) \subseteq S$. It is important to recognize that from a decision making perspective the key characteristic of an information system is *not* the values the signals may take, but rather what the signals tell the decision maker about the state.

Treating η as implicit, we represent the joint distribution function for these two random variables by $\Phi(y,\omega)$ and the marginal distribution functions by $\Phi(y)$ and $\Phi(\omega)$, where

$$\Phi(y) = \int_\Omega d\Phi(y,\omega),$$

and

$$\Phi(\omega) = \int_Y d\Phi(y,\omega).$$

[1] Note that if $\eta(\cdot)$ is not an invertible function, then $\eta^{-1}(\cdot)$ is a correspondence, i.e., it maps into sets.

The corresponding generalized probability density functions are $\varphi(y,\omega)$, $\varphi(y)$, and $\varphi(\omega)$.

Now consider the decision maker's belief about the unknown parameter ω given the receipt of signal y. That *posterior* belief is represented by $\Phi(\omega|y)$, which has a generalized probability density function $\varphi(\omega|y)$. In deriving posterior beliefs we typically use the density functions. In particular, assuming $\varphi(y) > 0$, we have the following counterpart to (3.1):

$$\varphi(\omega|y) = \frac{\varphi(y,\omega)}{\varphi(y)}. \tag{3.3}$$

Of course, as in the preceding section, if the decision maker's beliefs are initially expressed in terms of his prior marginal density function $\varphi(\omega)$ and a likelihood function $\varphi(y|\omega)$, then Bayes' theorem implies

$$\varphi(\omega|y) = \frac{\varphi(y|\omega)\,\varphi(\omega)}{\int_{\Omega} \varphi(y|\omega)\, d\Phi(\omega)}. \tag{3.4}$$

The following simple example illustrates the two approaches for updating the decision maker's beliefs about the events of interest based on observation of y. In this example, Y and Ω are assumed to be finite, with 2 and 3 elements each, respectively. In the first approach, the decision maker's beliefs are represented by the joint probability function $\varphi(y,\omega)$, which is specified in Table 3.1.

	ω_1	ω_2	ω_3
y_1	0.3	0.2	0.1
y_2	0.1	0.1	0.2

Table 3.1: Joint probabilities $\varphi(y,\omega)$.

From this table we can derive the marginal probabilities for the two signals y_1 and y_2 by adding across the rows to obtain $\varphi(y_1) = .6$ and $\varphi(y_2) = .4$. The conditional probabilities obtained using (3.3) are summarized in Table 3.2. Observe that the rows sum to one, as they should given that the probabilities are conditional on y. The joint probabilities are simply normalized with the probability of y, which changes from row to row.

	ω_1	ω_2	ω_3
y_1	.3/.6 = 1/2	.2/.6 = 1/3	.1/.6 = 1/6
y_2	.1/.4 = 1/4	.1/.4 = 1/4	.2/.4 = 1/2

Table 3.2: Conditional probabilities $\varphi(\omega|y)$.

Under the second approach, the decision maker's prior belief is represented by the prior probability function $\varphi(\omega_1) = .4$, $\varphi(\omega_2) = .3$, and $\varphi(\omega_3) = .3$, and the likelihood function $\varphi(y|\omega)$, which is summarized in Table 3.3:

	ω_1	ω_2	ω_3
y_1	36222	36193	36162
y_2	36163	36162	36193

Table 3.3: Likelihood function $\varphi(y|\omega)$.

Observe that the columns sum to one, since the probabilities are conditional on ω, which changes from column to column. In this case we obtain the marginal probabilities for the signals as follows:

$$\varphi(y_1) = \int_\Omega \varphi(y_1|\omega)\, d\Phi(\omega) = 3/4 \times .4 + 2/3 \times .3 + 1/3 \times .3 = .6,$$

$$\varphi(y_2) = \int_\Omega \varphi(y_2|\omega)\, d\Phi(\omega) = 1/4 \times .4 + 1/3 \times .3 + 2/3 \times .3 = .4.$$

Now we apply (3.4) and summarize the results for $\varphi(\omega|y)$ in the Table 3.4.

	ω_1	ω_2	ω_3
y_1	$3/4 \times .4 \div .6 = 1/2$	$2/3 \times .3 \div .6 = 1/3$	$1/3 \times .3 \div .6 = 1/6$
y_2	$1/4 \times .4 \div .4 = 1/4$	$1/3 \times .3 \div .4 = 1/4$	$2/3 \times .3 \div .4 = 1/2$

Table 3.4: Posterior probability $\varphi(\omega|y)$.

Observe that the computed probabilities are consistent with the first approach. This illustrates that the two approaches are equivalent provided that the joint probability function $\varphi(y,\omega)$ specified in the first approach is consistent with the marginal probability $\varphi(\omega)$ and likelihood $\varphi(y|\omega)$ specified in the second approach.

3.1.3 Multi-variate Normal Distributions

In many analyses throughout this book we assume the random variables are normally distributed vectors. In those analyses we use $\mathbf{x} \sim N(\boldsymbol{\mu},\boldsymbol{\Sigma})$ to indicate that the $k\times 1$ random vector $\mathbf{x}$ is normally distributed with $k\times 1$ mean vector $\boldsymbol{\mu}$ and $k\times k$ covariance matrix $\boldsymbol{\Sigma}$, i.e.,

$$\varphi(\mathbf{x}) = (2\pi)^{-\frac{1}{2}k}\, |\mathbf{H}|^{\frac{1}{2}} \exp[-\tfrac{1}{2}(\mathbf{x} - \boldsymbol{\mu})^t\, \mathbf{H}\, (\mathbf{x} - \boldsymbol{\mu})],$$

where $\mathbf{H} = \boldsymbol{\Sigma}^{-1}$ is the $k\times k$ *precision* matrix for $\mathbf{x}$.[2]

To illustrate the posterior beliefs when variables are normally distributed we assume $\mathbf{y}$ and $\boldsymbol{\omega}$ represent $n\times 1$ and $m\times 1$ vectors of jointly normally distributed random variables. Two approaches are considered and proofs of the various relations can be found in Raiffa and Schlaifer (1961). In the first approach, the decision maker's prior belief is represented by the joint density function $\varphi(\mathbf{y},\boldsymbol{\omega}) \sim N(\boldsymbol{\mu},\boldsymbol{\Sigma})$.[3] In this setting, $\boldsymbol{\mu}$ is an $(n+m) \times 1$ mean vector and $\boldsymbol{\Sigma}$ is an $(n+m) \times (n+m)$ covariance matrix, with

$$\boldsymbol{\mu} = \begin{bmatrix} \boldsymbol{\mu}_y \\ \boldsymbol{\mu}_\omega \end{bmatrix} \qquad \boldsymbol{\Sigma} = \begin{bmatrix} \boldsymbol{\Sigma}_{yy} & \boldsymbol{\Sigma}_{y\omega} \\ \boldsymbol{\Sigma}_{\omega y} & \boldsymbol{\Sigma}_{\omega\omega} \end{bmatrix} \qquad \mathbf{H} = \boldsymbol{\Sigma}^{-1} = \begin{bmatrix} \mathbf{H}_{yy} & \mathbf{H}_{y\omega} \\ \mathbf{H}_{\omega y} & \mathbf{H}_{\omega\omega} \end{bmatrix}.$$

The marginal distributions are:

$$\varphi(\mathbf{y}) = \int_{R_m} \varphi(\mathbf{y},\boldsymbol{\omega})\, d\boldsymbol{\omega} \sim N(\boldsymbol{\mu}_y,\boldsymbol{\Sigma}_{yy}),$$

$$\varphi(\boldsymbol{\omega}) = \int_{R_n} \varphi(\mathbf{y},\boldsymbol{\omega})\, d\mathbf{y} \sim N(\boldsymbol{\mu}_\omega,\boldsymbol{\Sigma}_{\omega\omega}).$$

In this approach, the conditional probability density function for $\boldsymbol{\omega}$ given $\mathbf{y}$ is $\varphi(\boldsymbol{\omega}|\mathbf{y}) \sim N(\boldsymbol{\mu}_{\omega|y}, \boldsymbol{\Sigma}_{\omega|y})$, where

---

[2] For more extensive derivation of various relations using normal distributions see, for example, Raiffa and Schlaifer (1961) and DeGroot (1970).

[3] It would be more precise to write $\varphi(\mathbf{y},\boldsymbol{\omega})$ as $\varphi\begin{pmatrix}\mathbf{y}\\ \boldsymbol{\omega}\end{pmatrix}$, but the former should not cause any confusion and is less cumbersome.

$$\boldsymbol{\mu}_{\omega|y} = \boldsymbol{\mu}_{\omega} + \boldsymbol{\Sigma}_{\omega y}\, \boldsymbol{\Sigma}_{yy}^{-1}(\mathbf{y} - \boldsymbol{\mu}_{y}), \tag{3.5a}$$

$$\boldsymbol{\Sigma}_{\omega|y} = \boldsymbol{\Sigma}_{\omega\omega} - \boldsymbol{\Sigma}_{\omega y}\, \boldsymbol{\Sigma}_{yy}^{-1}\, \boldsymbol{\Sigma}_{y\omega} = \mathbf{H}_{\omega\omega}^{-1}. \tag{3.5b}$$

That is, the signal **y** shifts the prior mean for $\boldsymbol{\omega}$ based on the difference between **y** and its prior mean, times its covariance with $\boldsymbol{\omega}$ adjusted for the variance of **y**. Furthermore, the reduction in the prior variance for $\boldsymbol{\omega}$ depends on the covariance between **y** and $\boldsymbol{\omega}$, adjusted for the variance of **y**. Observe that with normal distributions, the specific signal **y** received by the decision maker affects his conditional mean for $\boldsymbol{\omega}$ but *it does not affect his conditional variance*. The latter is only affected by the covariance and variance characteristics of the signal, not the specific signal. This feature simplifies analyses that are based on normal distributions.

The second approach is frequently used in settings in which $\boldsymbol{\omega}$ represents the unknown mean of a process generating independent, identically distributed random variables (vectors) for which N vectors have been observed (i.e., a sample size of N). That is, $\mathbf{y} = (\mathbf{y}_1,...,\mathbf{y}_N)$, $\varphi(\mathbf{y}|\boldsymbol{\omega}) = \varphi(\mathbf{y}_1|\boldsymbol{\omega})\times...\times\varphi(\mathbf{y}_N|\boldsymbol{\omega})$, and $\varphi(\mathbf{y}_i|\boldsymbol{\omega}) \sim \mathrm{N}(\boldsymbol{\omega},\boldsymbol{\Sigma}_{y|\omega})$, where $\boldsymbol{\omega}$ and $\mathbf{y}_i$ are $m\times 1$ vectors and $\boldsymbol{\Sigma}_{y|\omega}$ is an $m\times m$ covariance matrix. In this setting, if the prior is $\varphi(\boldsymbol{\omega}) \sim \mathrm{N}(\boldsymbol{\mu}_{\omega},\boldsymbol{\Sigma}_{\omega\omega})$, then the posterior is $\varphi(\boldsymbol{\omega}|\mathbf{y}) \sim \mathrm{N}(\boldsymbol{\mu}_{\omega|y}, \boldsymbol{\Sigma}_{\omega|y})$, where

$$\boldsymbol{\mu}_{\omega|y} = \left[\boldsymbol{\Sigma}_{\omega\omega}^{-1} + N\boldsymbol{\Sigma}_{y|\omega}^{-1}\right]^{-1}\left[\boldsymbol{\Sigma}_{\omega\omega}^{-1}\boldsymbol{\mu}_{\omega} + \boldsymbol{\Sigma}_{y|\omega}^{-1}\sum_{i=1}^{N} \mathbf{y}_j\right]$$

$$\boldsymbol{\Sigma}_{\omega|y} = \left[\boldsymbol{\Sigma}_{\omega\omega}^{-1} + N\boldsymbol{\Sigma}_{y|\omega}^{-1}\right]^{-1}.$$

Observe that the precision (i.e., the inverse of the variance) increases as the sample size N increases, and the posterior mean is a weighted average of the prior mean and the total observations, with weights equal to the precision of the prior and the precision of each signal.

3.1.4 Sufficient Statistics

The information generated by an information system can be represented in a variety of ways. In this section we consider a *statistic* $\psi \in \Psi$ that is a function of the signal y, i.e., it is defined by a function ψ: $Y \to \Psi$. We define ψ to be an *equivalent statistic* to y if ψ is invertible. In that case, one can infer y from ψ.

For example, assume $y = \mathbf{y}$ and $\psi = \boldsymbol{\psi}$ are $n\times 1$ and $n'\times 1$ random vectors, respectively, with $\boldsymbol{\psi} = \mathbf{f} + \mathbf{v}\mathbf{y}$, where **f** is an $n'\times 1$ parameter vector and **v** is an $n'\times n$ parameter matrix. In that setting, **y** and $\boldsymbol{\psi}$ are equivalent representations of the decision maker's information if $n \le n'$ and **v** has rank n, since the decision maker knows

$$\mathbf{y} = (\mathbf{v}^t\mathbf{v})^{-1}\,\mathbf{v}^t\,(\boldsymbol{\psi} - \mathbf{f})$$

if $\boldsymbol{\psi}$ is reported (since the fact that $\mathbf{v}$ has rank n implies that the inverse of $\mathbf{v}^t\mathbf{v}$ exists). To illustrate, assume $\mathbf{y}$ is a 2×1 vector and $\boldsymbol{\psi}$ is a 3×1 vector with

$$\mathbf{f} = \begin{bmatrix} 10 \\ 0 \\ -5 \end{bmatrix} \qquad \mathbf{v} = \begin{bmatrix} 1 & 0 \\ 1 & 1 \\ 0 & 1 \end{bmatrix},$$

which implies

$$(\mathbf{v}^t\mathbf{v})^{-1}\mathbf{v}^t = \begin{bmatrix} 2 & 1 \\ 1 & 2 \end{bmatrix}^{-1} \begin{bmatrix} 1 & 1 & 0 \\ 0 & 1 & 1 \end{bmatrix} = \begin{bmatrix} 2/3 & -1/3 \\ -1/3 & 2/3 \end{bmatrix} \begin{bmatrix} 1 & 1 & 0 \\ 0 & 1 & 1 \end{bmatrix} = \begin{bmatrix} 2/3 & 1/3 & -1/3 \\ -1/3 & 1/3 & 2/3 \end{bmatrix}.$$

If $\mathbf{y} = [2, 4]^t$, then $\boldsymbol{\psi} = \mathbf{f} + \mathbf{v}\mathbf{y} = [12, 6, -1]^t$ and

$$\mathbf{y} = (\mathbf{v}^t\mathbf{v})^{-1}\,\mathbf{v}^t\,(\boldsymbol{\psi} - \mathbf{f}) = \begin{bmatrix} 2/3 & 1/3 & -1/3 \\ -1/3 & 1/3 & 2/3 \end{bmatrix} \begin{bmatrix} 12 - 10 \\ 6 - 0 \\ -1 + 5 \end{bmatrix} = \begin{bmatrix} 2 \\ 4 \end{bmatrix}.$$

Now consider a setting in which ψ is not invertible, so that y cannot be inferred from ψ. A key point here is that a decision maker is not directly concerned with determining y. Instead, he is concerned about making inferences about some decision relevant event ω given y. We refer to ψ as a *sufficient statistic* if it yields the same inferences about ω as does y.

In defining a sufficient statistic we consider a "family" of likelihood functions $\{\, \varphi(y|\omega), y \in Y, \omega \in \Omega \,\}$. In this analysis $y \in Y$ is a random variable, but $\omega \in \Omega$ can be either a random variable or a set of possible parameter values. The latter interpretation is important when, in Volume II, we consider agency theory models in which one decision maker (the principal) pays incentive compensation to motivate the action chosen by another decision maker (the agent). In that setting Ω is the set of possible actions that might be chosen by the agent. The principal assigns probability one to the action induced by the incentive contract, but the incentive contract depends crucially on the likelihood function for the set of alternative actions the agent could select.

While ω need not be a random variable, it is useful to define a sufficient statistic in terms of the posterior beliefs that would be generated by prior beliefs about ω. To be a sufficient statistic, using ψ instead of y must not affect the decision maker's posterior beliefs no matter what prior beliefs he holds. That is, identification of a sufficient statistic depends only on the characteristics of the likelihood function and not on the characteristics of the prior beliefs.

Definition *Sufficient Statistic*

The statistic ψ: $Y \rightarrow \Psi$ is *sufficient for y with respect to* ω, where the relation between y and ω is characterized by the family of likelihood functions $\{ \varphi(y|\omega), y \in Y, \omega \in \Omega \}$, if the posterior beliefs are such that

$$\varphi(\omega|y') = \varphi(\omega|y''), \quad \forall\, \omega \in \Omega,$$

for any prior belief $\varphi(\omega)$, $\omega \in \Omega$, and any two signals y', $y'' \in Y$ such that

$$\psi(y') = \psi(y'').$$

The following well known result identifies the key characteristic of a sufficient statistic for a given family of likelihood functions (see DeGroot ,1970, p. 156).

Proposition 3.2 *Sufficient Statistic Factorization Theorem*

A statistic ψ: $Y \rightarrow \Psi$ is sufficient for y with respect to ω, given the family of likelihood functions $\{ \varphi(y|\omega), y \in Y, \omega \in \Omega \}$, if, and only if, there exist real valued functions $g(y)$ and $h(\psi,\omega)$ such that

$$\varphi(y|\omega) = g(y)\, h(\psi(y),\omega), \quad \forall\, y \in Y, \omega \in \Omega.$$

In general, there are an infinite number of possible sufficient statistics, and any statistic that is equivalent to y is a sufficient statistic. The more interesting statistics are those that simplify the representation of the information by eliminating unnecessary details. A sufficient statistic ψ^*: $Y \rightarrow \Psi^*$ is called a *minimal sufficient statistic* if for *every* sufficient statistic ψ there exists a function G_ψ: $\Psi \rightarrow \Psi^*$ such that $\psi^*(y) = G_\psi(\psi(y))$ for all $y \in Y$.[4]

To illustrate the above, consider the setting in which $y = (y_1, ..., y_n)$ and $y_i \sim N(\omega,\sigma^2)$, i.e., ω is an unknown parameter and y is a sequence of n independent draws from a normal distribution with mean ω and known variance σ^2. In that setting,

$$\begin{aligned}\varphi(y|\omega) &= (2\pi\sigma^2)^{-n/2} \exp\left[-\frac{1}{2\sigma^2}\sum_{i=1}^{n} (y_i - \omega)^2\right] \\ &= (2\pi\sigma^2)^{-n/2} \exp\left[-\frac{1}{2\sigma^2}\left(\sum_{i=1}^{n} (y_i - \bar{y})^2 + n(\bar{y} - \omega)^2\right)\right] \\ &= g(y)\; h(\bar{y},\omega),\end{aligned}$$

[4] In Appendix 18A we return to some key characteristics of sufficient statistics within the exponential family of distributions.

where

$$\bar{y} = \frac{1}{n}\sum_{i=1}^{n} y_i,$$

$$g(y) = (2\pi\sigma^2)^{-n/2}\exp\left[-\frac{1}{2\sigma^2}\sum_{i=1}^{n}(y_i - \bar{y})^2\right],$$

$$h(\bar{y},\omega) = \exp\left[-\frac{n}{2\sigma^2}(\bar{y} - \omega)^2\right].$$

Hence, the mean of the sample is a sufficient statistic for the detailed sample results (i.e., $\psi = \bar{y}$) if the sample is normally distributed and the unknown parameter ω is the mean.

Now consider how the above result changes if the decision maker is uncertain about both the mean and the variance of the normal distribution, i.e., $\varphi(y_i|\omega) \sim N(\mu,\sigma^2)$, with $\omega = (\mu,\sigma)$. We leave the proof to the reader, and merely state that the sufficient statistic ψ cannot be reduced to a single element, as in the preceding case, but it can be reduced to two elements. The first element is the mean (i.e., $\psi_1 = \bar{y}$) and the second is the following measure of the dispersion of the observations:

$$\psi_2 = \sum_{i=1}^{n}(y_i - \bar{y})^2.$$

3.2 VALUE OF DECISION-FACILITATING INFORMATION SYSTEMS

We now examine how information can improve decisions. However, before relating information to decisions we introduce the concepts of partitions and measurable functions, which is useful in characterizing the decision-facilitating role of information.

3.2.1 Partitions and Measurable Functions

In the following analysis we use the concept of a partition for representing both information and events that affect outcomes. Recall from the definition in Section 3.1.1 that a set of events defines a probabilizable partition of the state space S if the elements divide S into an exhaustive set of disjoint probabilizable events. A probabilizable partition is not a sigma-field, but a partition can be used to generate a unique minimal sigma-field. In particular, a sigma-field Ξ is the minimal sigma-field generated by the partition if it is the sigma-field with the fewest elements such that the elements of the partition are (subsets of the) elements in Ξ.

An information system η defines a partition of the state space as the set of subsets of states that result in particular signal for each subset, i.e., the set $\{ \eta^{-1}(y) \subseteq S, y \in Y \}$. This partition is an equivalent representation of the information system. If the number of elements in this partition is finite, it is often more convenient to represent the information system as the partition of the state space it generates instead of its random variable representation. Hence, (with a slight abuse of notation) we let Y denote the set of signals as well as the partition generated by the information system, and $y \in Y$ represent the information signal as well as the set of states that result in this signal, i.e., $y = \{ s \in S \mid \eta(s) = y \}$.[5]

In some cases two information systems can be compared on the basis of the relative fineness (or coarseness) of their partitions of S.

Definition *Fineness and Coarseness of Partitions*

Partition Y' is *at least as fine* a partition of S as partition Y'' if, for every $y' \in Y'$ there exists a $y'' \in Y''$ such that $y' \subseteq y''$. (Equivalently, Y'' is at least as coarse a partition as Y'.)

Partition Y' is a *finer* partition than Y'' if Y' is at least as fine as Y'' and the converse is not true.

The fineness/coarseness relation provides an *incomplete ordering* of partitions. To illustrate, assume S is an interval on the real line and the information systems Y', Y'', and Y''' divide S into sequences of intervals as represented in Figure 3.1.

Consider a function $f\colon S \to X$, i.e., $f(s) = x$ specifies the element of X associated with each state $s \in S$. Now consider whether a partition Y tells us enough about S to determine the value of the function f. If that is the case, then the function is defined to be measurable with respect to the partition.[6]

---

[5] Alternatively, we can directly define the set of information signals as $Y = \{ y \mid y = \eta^{-1}(\eta(s)), s \in S \}$.

[6] More generally, a random variable $f(\cdot)$ is measurable with respect to the sigma-field generated by the information system $\eta(\cdot)$ if $\{ s \mid f(s) = x \}$ is an element in that sigma-field for all x. Hence, every element in sigma-field generated by $f(\cdot)$ is also an element in the sigma-field generated by the information system $\eta(\cdot)$. However, if the number of elements in the partition generated by the information system is finite, our definition of Y-measurability and the more general definition of measurability are equivalent statements.

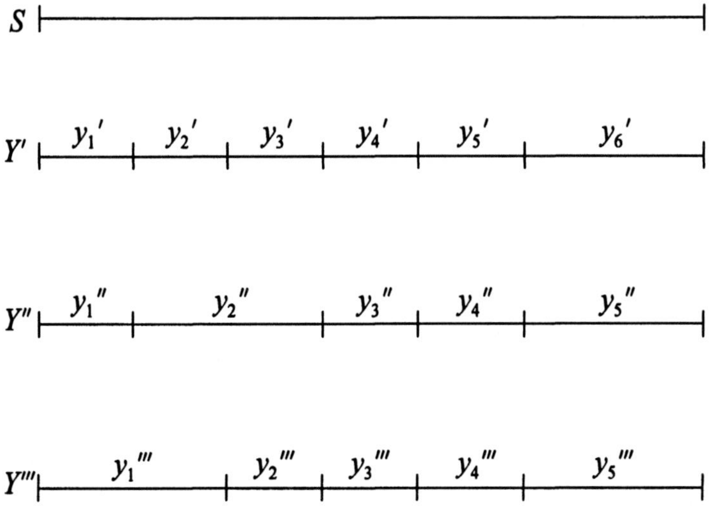

Figure 3.1: Comparison of partitions.

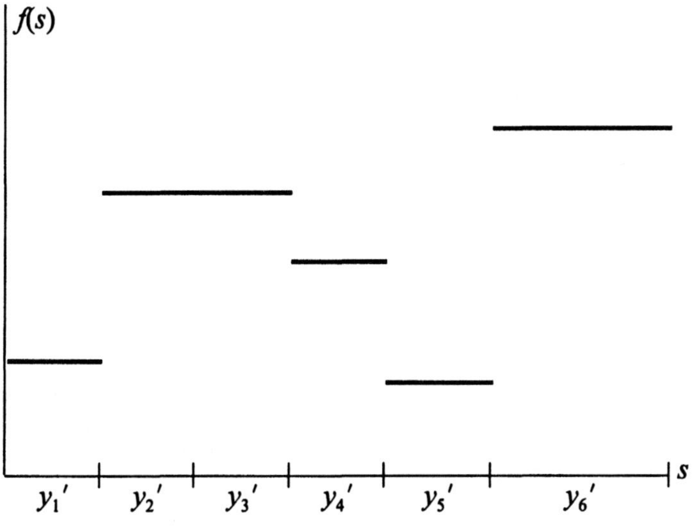

Figure 3.2: Y'-measurable function.

Definition *Y-measurable Functions*

A function f: $S \rightarrow X$ is *Y-measurable* with respect to a partition Y of S if $f(s') = f(s'')$ for every pair of states $s', s'' \in y$, in every partition element $y \in Y$. We can then express f as a function from Y to X, i.e., $f(y) = f(s)$, for $s \in y$.

To illustrate, consider the function depicted in Figure 3.2, and relate it to the partitions in Figure 3.1. This function is such that it is measurable with respect to Y', which is specified in the figure. This follows from the fact that the function has the same value for all states in each element of Y'. The fact that $f(y_2') = f(y_3')$ implies that f is also measurable with respect to Y''. However, the fact that $f(y_1') \neq f(y_2')$ implies that f is *not measurable* with respect to Y'''.

The preceding characterizes the measurability of a function with respect to a specified partition Y. We can go in the opposite direction and specify which partitions are sufficient to sustain a given function, or class of functions. Furthermore, we can identify the coarsest partition that sustains a given class.[7]

Definition *f-sufficient and f-relevant Partitions*

Given an arbitrary family of functions f: $S \times \Omega \rightarrow X$ (where $\omega \in \Omega$ is a "parameter" of the function from S to X), a partition Y is *f-sufficient* with respect to Ω if $f(s,\omega)$ is Y-measurable for all $\omega \in \Omega$. Furthermore, Y is *f-relevant* with respect to Ω if Y is the coarsest partition that is f-sufficient.

For example, for the function f in Figure 3.2, both Y' and Y'' are f-sufficient, while Y'' is f-relevant since Y'' is coarser than Y' and there is no partition coarser than Y'' that is f-sufficient.

3.2.2 Basic Information Economic Model

In this model there are potentially two individuals of interest. The first is an *information system evaluator* who selects an information system η from a set of alternative systems H. Our analysis is conducted from the perspective of that individual. The second is a *decision maker* who selects and implements an action a from among a set of actions A after observing a signal $y \in Y$ from the system η chosen by the evaluator. While we frequently assume the evaluator

[7] With general state spaces and sigma-fields, a sigma-field is f-sufficient if the random variables $f(\cdot,\omega)$ parameterized by ω are all measurable with respect to that sigma-field (see previous footnote). A sigma-field is f-relevant if it is the minimal sigma-field generated by the random variables $f(\cdot,\omega)$, for all ω.

is also the decision maker, we allow for the possibility that they may be two different individuals.[8]

The model is based on a probability space (S, Ξ, P), where S encompasses all sources of uncertainty. In particular, S represents all uncertainty with respect to the outcomes that will result from the alternative information systems and actions, and all uncertainty with respect to the information signals that may be received.

Outcomes and Utilities: The evaluator chooses an information system $\eta \in H$ and the decision maker chooses an action (or strategy) $a \in A$ given the signal $y \in Y$ from the information system. The preferences of direct interest are those of the evaluator. His preferences are assumed to depend on an outcome that can be divided into two components. The first component is the "gross" outcome $x \in X$ which is assumed to depend on the state $s \in S$ and the action $a \in A$ as specified by the outcome function

$$\boldsymbol{x}: S \times A \rightarrow X.$$

The second is the cost of the information system $\eta \in H$, which we assume for simplicity is independent of the state and the action. The cost function is represented by $\boldsymbol{\kappa}(\eta)$ and has the same dimension as x so that the evaluator's von Neumann/Morgenstern utility function with respect to the net outcome is expressed as $u(x\text{-}\kappa)$.

Some aspects of the state do not affect the outcome x, and it is at times useful to focus on outcome-adequate or outcome-relevant partitions of the state space.

Definition *Outcome-adequate and Outcome-relevant Partitions*

A partition $\Theta = \{\ \theta\ \}$ of the state space S is *outcome-adequate* if it is $\boldsymbol{x}$-sufficient, i.e.,

$$\boldsymbol{x}(s^1,a) = \boldsymbol{x}(s^2,a), \quad \forall\, s^1,s^2 \in \theta, \quad \forall\, \theta \in \Theta, \quad \forall\, a \in A.$$

A partition Θ is *outcome-relevant* if it is the coarsest outcome-adequate partition.

Observe that we can express the outcome functions as $\boldsymbol{x}$: $\Theta \times A \rightarrow X$ if Θ is outcome-adequate, where $\boldsymbol{x}(\theta,a) = \boldsymbol{x}(s,a)$, for $s \in \theta$.

---

[8] For an early discussion of this type of model in the accounting literature, see Feltham (1968, 1972) and Feltham and Demski (1970).

Information: The information received by the decision maker before he chooses his action is represented by a signal $y \in Y$, where Y is the set of possible signals. The fact that S is assumed to represent all sources of uncertainty, including any factors that affect the information received, implies that the set of signals defines a partition of S. The set Y and the partition it defines on S both depend on the information system $\eta \in H$ that is chosen.

Beliefs: To simplify the following discussion we assume that S and A are finite, with all $s \in \Xi$, i.e., each state is a probabilizable event. The evaluator's prior belief about the states is represented by the probability function $P(s)$, and his prior belief with respect to the outcome-relevant events is

$$P(\theta) = \sum_{s \in \theta} P(s).$$

Similarly, the marginal probability of the signal y is

$$P(y) = \sum_{s \in y} P(s),$$

and the likelihood function relating the outcome-relevant events to signals is

$$\varphi(y|\theta) = \begin{cases} \dfrac{P(y \cap \theta)}{P(\theta)} & y \cap \theta \neq \emptyset \\ 0 & y \cap \theta = \emptyset. \end{cases}$$

The evaluator's posterior beliefs given signal y are

$$\varphi(s|y) = \begin{cases} \dfrac{P(s)}{P(y)} & s \in y \\ 0 & s \notin y \end{cases}$$

$$\varphi(\theta|y) = \begin{cases} \dfrac{P(y \cap \theta)}{P(y)} & y \cap \theta \neq \emptyset \\ 0 & y \cap \theta = \emptyset. \end{cases}$$

Figure 3.3 illustrates the two partitions defined by Y and Θ on S. In this illustration there are five possible states and the information system reports one of two signals, y_1 or y_2, where y_1 is reported if the state is "odd numbered" and y_2 is reported if the state is "even numbered."

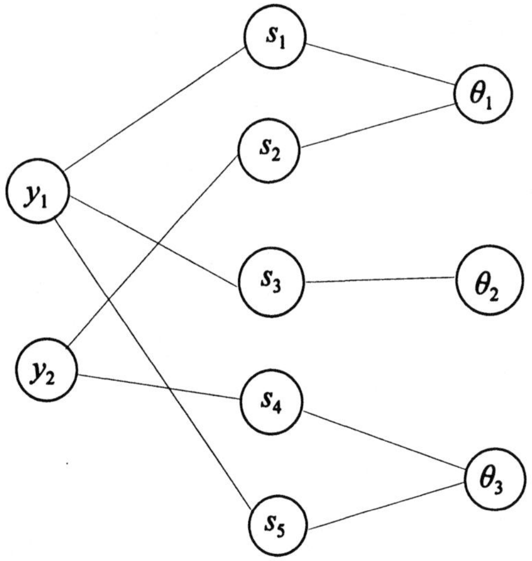

Figure 3.3: Information and outcome-relevant partitions.

There are two possible actions, a_1 and a_2, and the outcome function is

$$\boldsymbol{x}(s_1,a_1) = \boldsymbol{x}(s_2,a_1) = \boldsymbol{x}(s_3,a_1) = 10; \quad \boldsymbol{x}(s_4,a_1) = \boldsymbol{x}(s_5,a_1) = 30;$$

$$\boldsymbol{x}(s_1,a_2) = \boldsymbol{x}(s_2,a_2) = 25; \quad \boldsymbol{x}(s_3,a_2) = \boldsymbol{x}(s_4,a_2) = \boldsymbol{x}(s_5,a_2) = 15.$$

Hence, the outcome-relevant partition of S is $\Theta = \{ \theta_1, \theta_2, \theta_3 \}$, with $\theta_1 = \{ s_1, s_2 \}$, $\theta_2 = \{ s_3 \}$, and $\theta_3 = \{ s_4, s_5 \}$. If the states are equally likely, then the prior probabilities for the outcome-relevant events, the likelihood function conditional on those events, and the resulting posterior probabilities are as summarized in Table 3.5. The marginal probabilities for the two signals are $\varphi(y_1) = .2 + .2 + .2 = .6$ and $\varphi(y_2) = .2 + .2 = .4$. Observe that signal y_1 increases the probability that event θ_2 has occurred and reduces the probabilities of the other two events, whereas signal y_2 has the reverse effect.

		θ_1	θ_2	θ_3
Prior:	$P(\theta)$	$.2 + .2 = .4$	0.2	$.2 + .2 = .4$
Likelihood:	$\varphi(y_1\|\theta)$	$.2 \div .4 = .5$	$.2 \div .2 = 1$	$.2 \div .4 = .5$
	$\varphi(y_2\|\theta)$	$.2 \div .4 = .5$	$0 \div .2 = 0$	$.2 \div .4 = .5$
Posterior:	$\varphi(\theta\|y_1)$	$.2 \div .6 = 1/3$	$.2 \div .6 = 1/3$	$.2 \div .6 = 1/3$
	$\varphi(\theta\|y_2)$	$.2 \div .4 = .5$	$0 \div .4 = 0$	$.2 \div .4 = .5$

Table 3.5: Prior and posterior beliefs, and the likelihood function for the outcome-relevant events.

Decision Strategies: The analysis is stated from the *ex ante* perspective of the information system evaluator. To evaluate system η he must predict the action the decision maker will select given each possible signal $y \in Y$. This prediction may be either deterministic or stochastic. If it is deterministic, the prediction is represented by a function $\boldsymbol{a}$: $Y \rightarrow A$, where $a = \boldsymbol{a}(y)$ represents the action the decision maker is predicted to select if he receives signal y. On the other hand, if the prediction is stochastic, it is represented by a probability function $\boldsymbol{\alpha}$: $A \times Y \rightarrow [0,1]$, where $\boldsymbol{\alpha}(a|y)$ is the probability action a will be selected if the decision maker receives signal y, with

$$\sum_{a \in A} \boldsymbol{\alpha}(a|y) = 1.$$

The latter is more general in that it permits consideration of random action choice. If the decision choice is not random, then

$$\boldsymbol{\alpha}(a|y) = \begin{cases} 1 & \boldsymbol{a}(y) = a, \\ 0 & \boldsymbol{a}(y) \neq a. \end{cases}$$

Expected Utility for given Decision Rules and Information Structures: The evaluator's expected utility for a given decision rule and a given information structure can be stated using either the likelihood function $\varphi(y|\theta)$ or the posterior belief $\varphi(\theta|y)$. The expressions are slightly different if the decision rule is deterministic versus stochastic.

Deterministic decision rule:

$$U(\boldsymbol{a},\eta) = \sum_{\theta\in\Theta}\sum_{y\in Y} u(\boldsymbol{x}(\theta,\boldsymbol{a}(y)) - \boldsymbol{\kappa}(\eta))\,\varphi(y|\theta)\,P(\theta)$$

$$= \sum_{y\in Y}\sum_{\theta\in\Theta} u(\boldsymbol{x}(\theta,\boldsymbol{a}(y)) - \boldsymbol{\kappa}(\eta))\,\varphi(\theta|y)\,P(y).$$

Stochastic decision rule:

$$U(\boldsymbol{\alpha},\eta) = \sum_{\theta\in\Theta}\sum_{y\in Y}\sum_{a\in A} u(\boldsymbol{x}(\theta,a) - \boldsymbol{\kappa}(\eta))\,\boldsymbol{\alpha}(a|y)\,\varphi(y|\theta)\,P(\theta)$$

$$= \sum_{y\in Y}\sum_{\theta\in\Theta}\sum_{a\in A} u(\boldsymbol{x}(\theta,a) - \boldsymbol{\kappa}(\eta))\,\boldsymbol{\alpha}(a|y)\,\varphi(\theta|y)\,P(y).$$

Optimal Decision Rules: From the perspective of the information system evaluator, $\boldsymbol{a}_\eta^*$ is an optimal deterministic decision rule for information system η if

$$U(\boldsymbol{a}_\eta^*,\eta) \geq U(\boldsymbol{a},\eta), \quad \forall\, \boldsymbol{a} \in \{\, \boldsymbol{a}: Y \rightarrow A \,\}.$$

Similarly, $\boldsymbol{\alpha}_\eta^*$ is an optimal stochastic decision rule for information system η if

$$U(\boldsymbol{\alpha}_\eta^*,\eta) \geq U(\boldsymbol{\alpha},\eta), \quad \forall\, \boldsymbol{\alpha} \in \{\, \boldsymbol{\alpha}: A\times Y \rightarrow [0,1] \mid \textstyle\sum_{a\in A} \boldsymbol{\alpha}(a,y) = 1,\, y \in Y \,\}.$$

Proposition 3.3

If an optimal stochastic decision rule $\boldsymbol{\alpha}_\eta^*$ exists, there is an optimal deterministic decision rule $\boldsymbol{a}_\eta^*$ such that

$$U^*(\eta) \equiv U(\boldsymbol{a}_\eta^*,\eta) = \sum_{y\in Y}\left[\max_{a\in A}\left(\sum_{\theta\in\Theta} u(\boldsymbol{x}(\theta,a) - \boldsymbol{\kappa}(\eta))\,\varphi(\theta|y)\right)\right]P(y).$$

That is, *randomization over A given y is never necessary*, and $\boldsymbol{a}_\eta^*(y)$ is an action that provides the evaluator with the maximum expected utility conditional on having observed signal y. The key here is that an optimal stochastic decision rule only assigns non-zero probabilities to actions that have maximum expected utility conditional on having observed signal y.

We now consider two extreme information systems: the null and perfect systems. These serve as useful benchmarks in some of the subsequent analyses.

Null information system: The *null information system* η^o sends a constant (null) signal represented by $Y^o = \{y^o\}$. The optimal decision for this system is $\boldsymbol{a}^o(y^o) = a^o$, where a^o is such that

$$U^*(\eta^o) \equiv U(a^o,\eta^o) = \max_{a\in A} \left(\sum_{\theta\in\Theta} u(\boldsymbol{x}(\theta,a) - \kappa(\eta^o))\, P(\theta) \right).$$

Perfect information system: The *perfect information system* η^p reveals the outcome-relevant events (which is essentially equivalent to revealing the state), so that $Y^p = \Theta$. The optimal decision rule $\boldsymbol{a}^p$: $\Theta \rightarrow A$ is such that

$$U^*(\eta^p) \equiv U(\boldsymbol{a}^p,\eta^p) = \sum_{\theta\in\Theta} \left(\max_{a\in A} u(\boldsymbol{x}(\theta,a) - \kappa(\eta^p)) \right) P(\theta).$$

Observe that the maximization operator and the summation over outcome-relevant events are reversed between the null and perfect information systems. The optimal null action maximizes the expected utility, whereas the optimal perfect information action potentially differs for each outcome-relevant event.

Optimal Information System: If the optimal decision rule is implemented for each information system, the system most preferred by the information system evaluator, denoted η^*, is characterized by

$$U^*(\eta^*) \geq U^*(\eta) \quad \forall\, \eta \in H.$$

Alternatively, if decision rule $\boldsymbol{\alpha}(\eta)$: $A \times Y^\eta \rightarrow [0,1]$ is predicted to be implemented with information system $\eta \in H$, the system most preferred by the evaluator is characterized by

$$U(\boldsymbol{\alpha}(\eta^*),\eta^*) \geq U(\boldsymbol{\alpha}(\eta),\eta) \quad \forall\, \eta \in H.$$

3.2.3 Value of Information

In the discussion that follows we drop the cost of the information system and examine the value of a system η relative to the null system η^o. This should not be construed as ignoring costs, but merely as determining whether a system might be sufficiently valuable to offset additional costs. If it has no incremental value, then it is not preferred if there are incremental costs. Throughout this analysis we assume that the information evaluator is the decision maker, so that the optimal deterministic decision rule is implemented for each information system.

Let $\pi(\eta)$ represent the value of η relative to η^o, *expressed in the same units as the outcome x.* In particular, $\pi(\eta)$ is the maximum amount the information system evaluator would pay (i.e., the *buying price*) to implement η instead of η^o (which is assumed to have zero cost). That is, $\pi(\eta)$ is such that

$$U^*(\eta^o) = \sum_{y\in Y}\left[\max_{a\in A}\left(\sum_{\theta\in\Theta} u(\boldsymbol{x}(\theta,a)-\pi(\eta))\,\varphi(\theta|y)\right)\right]P(y).$$

If the evaluator is risk neutral, then the value is equal to the optimal expected gross outcome for information system η minus the optimal outcome with the null system, i.e.,

$$\pi(\eta) = \sum_{y\in Y}\left[\max_{a\in A}\left(\sum_{\theta\in\Theta} \boldsymbol{x}(\theta,a)\,\varphi(\theta|y)\right)\right]P(y) - \max_{a\in A}\left(\sum_{\theta\in\Theta} \boldsymbol{x}(\theta,a)\,P(\theta)\right).$$

A somewhat similar calculation is also possible if the evaluator has an exponential utility function, i.e., $u(x\text{-}\kappa) = -\exp[-r(x\text{-}\kappa)] = -\exp[-rx]\exp[r\kappa]$, in which case[9]

$$\pi(\eta) = \frac{1}{r}\left\{\ln\left[\max_{a\in A}\left(\sum_{\theta\in\Theta} -\exp[-r\boldsymbol{x}(\theta,a)]\,P(\theta)\right)\right]\right.$$
$$\left. - \ln\left(\sum_{y\in Y}\left[\max_{a\in A}\left(\sum_{\theta\in\Theta} -\exp[-r\boldsymbol{x}(\theta,a)]\,\varphi(\theta|y)\right)\right]P(y)\right)\right\}.$$

A key factor permitting a closed form expression for $\pi(\eta)$ in the risk-neutral and exponential-utility settings is that in those settings the size of the cost of the information system has no impact on the decisions that are made, i.e., there are no wealth effects on the choices among gambles. As we saw in Chapter 2, that is not the case for other risk-averse utility functions, so that the value of a information system must be expressed as an implicit function.

Given that the evaluator selects the optimal action for each signal, the value of η relative to η^o is always *non-negative.* This follows from the fact that it is always possible for the decision maker to ignore the signal received and select a^o for each signal $y \in Y$. Furthermore, the value of information system η can never exceed the value of the perfect information system η^P, since $\boldsymbol{a}^P(\theta)$ identifies the best action in each state $\theta \in \Theta$. These statements are summarized in the following proposition, along with conditions that are necessary for η to have strictly positive value.

---

[9] Note that in this case the value of the information system is equal to the difference between the certainty equivalents for η and η^o with no information costs for both.

Proposition 3.4

The value of η is non-negative and less than the value of the perfect information system, i.e., $\pi(\eta^p) \geq \pi(\eta) \geq 0$, and the following are *necessary conditions* for η to have *strictly positive value:*

(a) A cannot be a singleton, i.e., there must be alternative actions.

(b) $\boldsymbol{a}^p(\theta) \neq a^o$ for at least some $\theta \in \Theta$, i.e., one action cannot be optimal for all outcome-relevant events – there must be some desire to choose better actions.

(c) $\boldsymbol{a}_\eta^*(y) \neq a^o$ for at least some $y \in Y$, i.e., the change in beliefs must be sufficient for at least one signal (more generally, a measurable set of signals) to induce the decision maker to choose a different action.

A *sufficient condition* for η to have *strictly positive value* is that a^o is not an optimal action for at least some $y \in Y$.[10]

Finally, to identify information systems that have a value equal to the value of the perfect information system, let $\hat{\Theta}$ represent an $\boldsymbol{a}^p$-relevant partition of Θ (and, hence, of S), i.e., $\hat{\Theta}$ is the coarsest partition of Θ such that

$$\boldsymbol{a}^p(\theta') = \boldsymbol{a}^p(\theta'') \quad \text{if } \theta', \theta'' \subseteq \hat{\theta} \in \hat{\Theta}.$$

Observe that different events θ' and θ'' must result in different outcomes for at least some actions (since Θ is an outcome-relevant partition of S), but they can result in the same optimal action choice. Therefore, from a decision-facilitating perspective there is no need to distinguish between those two events.

Proposition 3.5

The value of information system η is equal to the value of perfect information, i.e., $\pi(\eta) = \pi(\eta^p)$, if Y is at least as fine a partition of S as is the $\boldsymbol{a}^p$-relevant partition $\hat{\Theta}$.

[10] As stated in the proposition, the value of perfect information is an upper bound on the value of any imperfect information system η and zero is a lower bound. There are a number of papers in the early seventies that identify other bounds that are "sharper" than these two. They are all developed for the case in which the information evaluator/decision maker is risk neutral. See, for example, Demski (1972), Ziemba and Butterworth (1975) and Huang, Vertinsky, and Ziemba (1977).

3.3 COMPARISON OF INFORMATION SYSTEMS

We now consider statements about relative preferences among information systems given only the statistical characteristics of these systems, knowing very little about the evaluator and the decision context in which he will use the system. In these statements we examine the evaluator's preference under the assumption that both systems are *costless* and that the information will be used to make *optimal decisions* from the evaluator's perspective.

3.3.1 Generally at Least as Valuable Information Systems

In the following discussion we use the term *payoff function* to refer to the function $\boldsymbol{w}$: $\Theta \times A \to \mathbb{R}$, where $\boldsymbol{w} = u \circ \boldsymbol{x}$, i.e., the payoff function is obtained by combining the evaluator's utility function u with the outcome function $\boldsymbol{x}$ as follows:

$$\boldsymbol{w}(\theta,a) = u(\boldsymbol{x}(\theta,a)).$$

To explicitly recognize the role of the payoff function $\boldsymbol{w}$: $\Theta \times A \to \mathbb{R}$ and prior probability function P: $\Theta \to [0,1]$ in the expected utility calculation, we let

$$U(\boldsymbol{w},P,\boldsymbol{a},\eta) \equiv \sum_{\theta\in\Theta}\sum_{y\in Y} \boldsymbol{w}(\theta,\boldsymbol{a}(y))\, \varphi(y|\theta)\, P(\theta),$$

and

$$U^*(\boldsymbol{w},P,\eta) \equiv \sum_{\theta\in\Theta}\sum_{y\in Y} \boldsymbol{w}(\theta,\boldsymbol{a}^*(y))\, \varphi(y|\theta)\, P(\theta),$$

where $\boldsymbol{a}^*$ is the optimal decision rule given $\boldsymbol{w}$, P, and η.

The following analysis makes statements about the relative value of information systems that are independent of the payoff and prior probability functions. Hence, we require some notation to represent the set of possible functions that are being considered. In all cases, the state partition Θ is taken as given – the functions are those that apply to that partition. The set of all possible prior beliefs over the events in Θ is denoted

$$\Delta(\Theta) = \{\, P: \Theta \to \mathbb{R} \mid \textstyle\sum_{\theta\in\Theta} P(\theta) = 1,\ P(\theta) \geq 0, \quad \forall\, \theta \in \Theta \,\},$$

and the set of bounded, *relative* payoff functions given Θ and the set of actions A is denoted

$$W(\Theta,A) = \{\, \boldsymbol{w}: \Theta \times A \to [0,1] \,\}.$$

Observe that if the evaluator's utility function is bounded, there is no loss of generality in assuming that it has been scaled such that it has a minimum of zero and a maximum of one (see Proposition 2.2).

Now we focus on a comparison of pairs of information systems. We define one information system to be "generally at least as valuable" as the other if the former would not be of less value in any decision context for which Θ is outcome-adequate.[11] The actions do not play a central role here, but the set A must be sufficiently diverse. We assume the set of actions A has a cardinality at least as great as Θ, so that there could conceivably be a different optimal action for each event θ.

While the basis for much of the analysis reported below can be found in Blackwell (1951, 1953) and Blackwell and Girshick (1954), the specific form of the analysis relates more closely to Marschak and Miyasawa (MM) (1968), and frequent reference is made to that paper.

Definition *Generally at Least as Valuable - MM Condition (A)*

Given Θ and A, η^2 is generally at least as valuable as η^1 if, and only if,

$$U^*(w,P,\eta^2) \geq U^*(w,P,\eta^1), \quad \forall\, w \in W(\Theta,A),\ P \in \Delta(\Theta).$$

3.3.2 Informativeness

At Least As Informative: The following is a very important condition for comparing information systems on the basis of their likelihood functions. In this discussion we refer to information system η^i in terms of the $|\Theta|\times|Y^i|$ Markov matrix $\boldsymbol{\eta}^i$, whose element in row θ and column y^i is the likelihood $\varphi^i(y^i|\theta)$. Observe that, as with any Markov matrix, the elements of $\boldsymbol{\eta}^i$ are non-negative and its rows sum to one.

Definition *At Least as Θ-informative - MM Condition (B)*

Information system $\boldsymbol{\eta}^2$ is *at least as Θ-informative* as $\boldsymbol{\eta}^1$ if, and only if, there exists a $|Y^2|\times|Y^1|$ *Markov matrix* **B** with elements $b(y^1|y^2) \geq 0$ such that

$$\boldsymbol{\eta}^1 = \boldsymbol{\eta}^2\, \mathbf{B}.$$

The relation between y^1 and y^2 is statistical, not necessarily physical. However, the process generating y^1 acts "as if" y^2 were generated and then either

[11] Blackwell (1951, 1953) uses the term "more informative" for what we have defined to be "generally at least as valuable." Our terminology seems to fit more closely to its intuitive meaning.

some noise is added to that signal to obtain y^1 or information is deleted through aggregation (which MM refer to as collapsing).

Definition *Collapsing Information - MM Condition (C)*
Information system $\boldsymbol{\eta}^1$ is a collapsing of $\boldsymbol{\eta}^2$ if Y^2 is a partition of Y^1 (i.e., Y^2 is a finer partition of S than Y^1).

Proposition 3.6
If information system $\boldsymbol{\eta}^1$ is a collapsing of $\boldsymbol{\eta}^2$, then $\boldsymbol{\eta}^2$ is at least as Θ-informative as $\boldsymbol{\eta}^1$.

Illustrations: To illustrate the above, consider the following three systems (Θ has three elements):

$$\boldsymbol{\eta}^1 = \begin{bmatrix} 1 & 0 \\ .1 & .9 \\ .1 & .9 \end{bmatrix}; \quad \boldsymbol{\eta}^2 = \begin{bmatrix} 1 & 0 & 0 \\ .1 & .6 & .3 \\ .1 & .3 & .6 \end{bmatrix}; \quad \boldsymbol{\eta}^3 = \begin{bmatrix} .60 & .40 & 0 \\ .06 & .50 & .44 \\ .06 & .44 & .50 \end{bmatrix}.$$

Observe that $\boldsymbol{\eta}^1$ is a collapsing of $\boldsymbol{\eta}^2$ since the second signal of $\boldsymbol{\eta}^1$ aggregates (collapses) the second and third signals of $\boldsymbol{\eta}^2$. The latter is at least as informative as the former because $\boldsymbol{\eta}^1 = \boldsymbol{\eta}^2\mathbf{B}$ with

$$\mathbf{B} = \begin{bmatrix} 1 & 0 \\ 0 & 1 \\ 0 & 1 \end{bmatrix}.$$

This illustrates the fact that in a collapsing, **B** is all zeros and ones, and the number of signals are reduced. On the other hand, $\boldsymbol{\eta}^3$ has the same number of signals as $\boldsymbol{\eta}^2$ but is less informative, as demonstrated by the fact that $\boldsymbol{\eta}^3 = \boldsymbol{\eta}^2\mathbf{B}$ with

$$\mathbf{B} = \begin{bmatrix} .6 & .2 & .2 \\ 0 & .6 & .4 \\ 0 & .4 & .6 \end{bmatrix},$$

and there does not exist a Markov matrix **B** such that $\boldsymbol{\eta}^2 = \boldsymbol{\eta}^3\mathbf{B}$.

Is $\boldsymbol{\eta}^1$ at least as informative as $\boldsymbol{\eta}^3$, or vice-versa? The answer is no! To illustrate, first consider whether there exists a 2×3 Markov matrix **B** such that $\boldsymbol{\eta}^3 = \boldsymbol{\eta}^1\mathbf{B}$. The non-existence of **B** follows from the fact that it would require that both $\varphi(y_2^3|\theta_2) = .50$ and $\varphi(y_2^3|\theta_3) = .44$ equal $.1 \times b_{12} + .9 \times b_{22}$, which is obviously impossible. Now consider whether there exists a 3×2 Markov matrix such that $\boldsymbol{\eta}^1 = \boldsymbol{\eta}^3\mathbf{B}$. Observe that $\boldsymbol{\eta}^3$ is invertible and, hence, we can solve for $\mathbf{B}$:

$$\mathbf{B} = [\boldsymbol{\eta}^3]^{-1}\,\boldsymbol{\eta}^1 = \frac{1}{3}\begin{bmatrix} 5 & -2 \\ 0 & 3 \\ 0 & 3 \end{bmatrix}.$$

The problem is that $\mathbf{B}$ is not a Markov matrix – while the rows sum to one, one of the elements is negative.

This example illustrates that "informativeness" provides only a partial ordering of information systems – not all systems can be compared on the basis of informativeness.

Infinite Sets: If the set of signals is not finite, then we can use the likelihood distribution functions and the informativeness relation holds if there exists a *Markov kernel* $b(y^1|y^2)$ such that

$$\varphi^1(y^1|\theta) = \int_{Y^2} b(y^1|y^2)\, d\Phi^2(y^2|\theta).$$

A Markov kernel a is non-negative function that integrates over Y^1 to one, i.e.,

$$\int_{Y^1} b(y^1|y^2)\, dy^1 = 1.$$

To illustrate this type of relation consider a decision setting in which θ represents an unknown mean μ of a normally distributed process that generates an independent sample of size η with known variance σ^2. In that setting, $\mathbf{y}^\eta$ is an η×1 vector of observations and the likelihood function is

$$\varphi(\mathbf{y}^\eta|\mu) = (2\pi\sigma^2)^{-\eta/2} \exp\left[\frac{1}{2\sigma^2}\sum_{i=1}^{\eta} (y_i^\eta - \mu)^2\right].$$

Now consider two information systems with sample sizes $\eta^1 < \eta^2$. In this setting, $b(\mathbf{y}^1|\mathbf{y}^2)$ equals zero if $\mathbf{y}^1$has some observations that are not the same as in $\mathbf{y}^2$, whereas $b(\mathbf{y}^1|\mathbf{y}^2) = 1$ if $\mathbf{y}^2$ has η^1 elements in common with $\mathbf{y}^1$. Assume, for example, that $\eta^2 = n + 1$ and $\eta^1 = n$, then (letting the first n elements of $\mathbf{y}^2$ correspond with the n elements in $\mathbf{y}^1$) we have $b(\mathbf{y}^1|\mathbf{y}^1, y_{n+1}^2) = 1$ for all $y_{n+1}^2 \in (-\infty,\infty)$ and

$$\varphi(\mathbf{y}^1|\mu) = \int_{-\infty}^{\infty} b(\mathbf{y}^1|\mathbf{y}^1, y_{n+1}^2)\, \varphi(\mathbf{y}^1, y_{n+1}^2|\mu)\, dy_{n+1}^2$$

$$= (2\pi\sigma^2)^{-n/2} \exp\left[\frac{1}{2\sigma^2} \sum_{i=1}^{n} (y_i^1 - \mu)^2\right].$$

Relation Between Informativeness and Value: Now we relate informativeness to value, which is Blackwell's key result. An information system that is at least as Θ-informative as another is at least as valuable, for all decision settings in which Θ is an outcome-relevant partition of S.

Proposition 3.7 (MM Theorem 6.3)*: (B) ⇒ (A)*
If η^2 is at least as Θ-informative as η^1, then η^2 is generally at least as valuable as η^1.

Proof: Let $w^*(\theta,y) \equiv w(\theta,a^*(y))$, so that

$$\sum_{\theta\in\Theta} w^*(\theta,y)\, \varphi(\theta|y) \geq \sum_{\theta\in\Theta} w(\theta,a)\, \varphi(\theta|y), \quad \forall\, a \in A.$$

Multiply both sides by $P(y)$ and use $\varphi(\theta|y)\, P(y) = \varphi(y|\theta)\, P(\theta)$:

$$\sum_{\theta\in\Theta} w^*(\theta,y)\, \varphi(y|\theta)\, P(\theta) \geq \sum_{\theta\in\Theta} w(\theta,a)\, \varphi(y|\theta)\, P(\theta), \quad \forall\, a \in A. \tag{3.6}$$

Assume η^2 is at least as Θ-informative as η^1. We then obtain

$$U^*(w, P, \eta^1) = \sum_{\theta\in\Theta} \sum_{y^1\in Y^1} w^*(\theta,y^1)\left[\sum_{y^2\in Y^2} b(y^1|y^2)\, \varphi(y^2|\theta)\right] P(\theta)$$

$$= \sum_{y^2\in Y^2} \sum_{y^1\in Y^1} b(y^1|y^2)\left[\sum_{\theta\in\Theta} w^*(\theta,y^1)\, \varphi(y^2|\theta)\, P(\theta)\right]$$

$$\leq \sum_{y^2\in Y^2} \sum_{y^1\in Y^1} b(y^1|y^2)\left[\sum_{\theta\in\Theta} w^*(\theta,y^2)\, \varphi(y^2|\theta)\, P(\theta)\right]$$

$$= \sum_{y^2\in Y^2} \sum_{\theta\in\Theta} w^*(\theta,y^2)\, \varphi(y^2|\theta)\, P(\theta) = U^*(w,P,\eta^2).$$

The first equality follows from the fact that η^2 is at least as informative as η^1. The second equality is merely a rearranging of terms. The inequality is obtained by switching to a potentially better decision rule, given that the expression in the square brackets is the same as in (3.6). The final equality holds because y^1 only appears in $b(y^1|y^2)$ and the sum for all y^1 equals one. **Q.E.D.**

Observe that the informativeness relation we have been using is a weak relation. The fact that system η^2 is at least as informative as η^1 does not preclude the converse. Hence, it is not surprising that the resulting value relation is also weak. However, a stronger informativeness relation will not, in general, result in a stronger value relation. To illustrate, consider the following definition of *more informative*.

Definition *More Θ-informative*
Information system $\boldsymbol{\eta}^2$ is *more Θ-informative* than $\boldsymbol{\eta}^1$ if, and only if, the former is at least as informative as the latter and the converse does not hold.

Now consider the two illustrative matrices $\boldsymbol{\eta}^1$ and $\boldsymbol{\eta}^2$ introduced earlier. We have already demonstrated that the latter is at least as informative as the former and it is straightforward to prove the converse does not hold. Hence, $\boldsymbol{\eta}^2$ is *more Θ-informative* than $\boldsymbol{\eta}^1$. Now consider two decision problems which differ with respect to the payoffs associated with three actions and the three payoff-relevant events, but which have the same prior beliefs and hence the same posterior beliefs. The prior and posterior beliefs are summarized in Table 3.6.

		θ_1	θ_2	θ_3
Prior:	$P(\theta)$	0.3	0.4	0.3
Posterior:	$\boldsymbol{\eta}^1$: y_1^1	30/37	4/37	3/37
	y_2^1	0	4/7	3/7
	$\boldsymbol{\eta}^2$: y_1^2	30/37	4/37	3/37
	y_2^2	0	8/11	3/11
	y_3^2	0	2/5	3/5

Table 3.6: Prior $P(\theta)$ and posterior $\varphi(\theta|y)$ beliefs.

Table 3.7 specifies the payoff functions for the two decision problems.

	Problem (a)			Problem (b)		
	θ_1	θ_2	θ_3	θ_1	θ_2	θ_3
Action a_1	1	0	0	1	0	0
a_2	0	1	0	0	1	0.4
a_3	0	0	1	0	0	1

Table 3.7: Payoff functions $w(\theta,a)$.

Observe that in both problems, a_i is the optimal action given event θ_i, so that each event has a different optimal action. In problem (a), information system η^2 generates a different action choice for each signal, with $\mathbf{a}^*(y_i^2) = a_i$, while the optimal action choices for information system η^1 are $a^*(y_1^1) = a_1$ and $a^*(y_2^1) = a_2$. The expected payoffs for η^1 and η^2 are .66 and .72, respectively. Hence, in this problem, the additional signal in η^2 results in a higher expected payoff, due to the fact the optimal decisions differ between y_2^2 and y_3^2.

In problem (b) the optimal action choices for the signals from η^1 are the same as in problem (a). However, the optimal action choices for the signals from η^2 are $a^*(y_1^2) = a_1$ and $a^*(y_2^2) = a^*(y_3^2) = a_2$, i.e., the second and third signals induce the same action choice as the second signal in η^1. Consequently, the expected payoff is .768 for both information systems, which implies the more informative system is no more valuable than the less informative system.

Noiseless Information Systems: In some settings the signals define a partition on the event space Θ. These systems are defined to be noiseless and the informativeness relation takes a particularly simple form. However, one must be careful here. Information systems always define partitions on the underlying state space S, but two factors hinder a comparison on the basis of partitions. First, the partition defined by one system may be neither coarser nor finer than the partition defined by another system. Second, information systems may not define partitions on the events that influence the payoff from alternative actions.

Definition *Noiseless Information Systems - MM Condition (N)*

Information system η is noiseless relative to Θ if, and only if, Y defines a partition on Θ.

Observe that a noiseless system is such that the likelihood function $\varphi(y|\theta)$ is equal to either zero or one. Earlier we introduced MM's collapsing condition (C). It plays a particularly important role if the information systems are noiseless.

Proposition 3.8 (MM Theorem 11.4): *(N) ⇒ [(A) ⇔ (C)]*

If η^1 and η^2 are noiseless information structures with respect to Θ, then η^2 is at least as Θ-informative as η^1 if, and only if, η^1 is a collapsing of η^2.

Redundant Information: In the preceding analysis we implicitly assume that the evaluator can only choose between two information systems. Now consider the possibility of selecting η^1, η^2, or η^{12}, where η^{12} reports both y^1 and y^2. Marschak and Miyasawa refer to η^1 as a garbling of η^2 if the following relations hold.

Definition *Garbling: MM Condition (G)*

Information system η^1 is a *garbling* of η^2 if each of the following three equivalent conditions are true (where each of the conditional probability functions are derived from a joint probability function $\varphi(y^1,y^2,\theta)$):

(a) $\varphi(y^1|y^2,\theta) = \varphi(y^1|y^2)$;

(b) $\varphi(\theta|y^1,y^2) = \varphi(\theta|y^2)$;

(c) $\varphi(y^1,y^2|\theta) = \varphi(y^1|y^2)\,\varphi(y^2|\theta)$.

The first condition can be interpreted as stating that the evaluator's belief about y^1 is independent of θ given y^2. The second condition states that the evaluator's belief about θ is independent of y^1 given y^2. The third is perhaps the most interesting because, based on Proposition 3.2, it implies that y^2 is a *sufficient statistic* for (y^1,y^2) with respect to θ.[12]

Now consider the relation between garbling and informativeness.

Proposition 3.9 (MM Theorem 6.2)

If η^1 is a garbling of η^2, then η^2 is at least as informative as both η^1 and η^{12}.

Effectively, garbling implies that y^1 adds nothing to y^2.

[12] See Amershi (1988) for an extensive discussion of the relation between informativeness and sufficient statistics, including consideration of generalized probability spaces.

3.4 IMPACT OF RISK AND RISK AVERSION ON THE VALUE OF INFORMATION

To illustrate the potential impact of risk aversion on the value of information we return to the simple financial investment and hurdle model examples introduced in Chapter 2.

3.4.1 Financial Investment Example[13]

Recall that in the financial investment example the decision maker is an investor with w units of capital and chooses between investing in a riskless and a risky asset (investment). The wealth level w does not play any role, due to the lack of a wealth effect with exponential utility. Hence, in the following discussion we assume, for simplicity, that the investor has zero wealth (i.e., $w = 0$).

The Basic Model: The investor can invest a units of capital in a risky asset by borrowing a units of capital ($a < 0$ represents going short in the risky asset and investing $|a|$ in the riskless asset). The net return per unit invested in the risky asset is represented by the random variable ε and the cost of riskless borrowing is normalized to be one per unit. Hence, the net outcome is $x = a\varepsilon$.

The investor's prior belief with respect to the net return ε is normally distributed with mean μ_0 and variance σ_0^2. He has an exponential utility function with risk aversion r. Hence, with normally distributed returns, he selects his investment level so as to maximize his certainty equivalent:

$$CE(a) = \mathrm{E}[x|a] - \tfrac{1}{2}r\mathrm{Var}[x|a].$$

If the investor chooses his action based on his prior beliefs, then his optimal decision (see equation (2.7)) is

$$a^o = \mu_0/[r\sigma_0^2] \tag{3.7}$$

and his expected utility is

$$U(a^o) = -\exp[-rCE(a^o)]$$

where

$$CE(a^o) = \tfrac{1}{2}\mu_0^2/[r\sigma_0^2]. \tag{3.8}$$

Impact of Information: Now assume that information system η provides the investor with a signal y prior to making his investment decision. We assume

[13] Gould (1974) provides an analysis of a similar example.

that y and ε are jointly normally distributed, and the signal is scaled so that both y and ε have mean μ_0. Furthermore, the variance of y is σ_y^2 and this is also the covariance between y and ε, i.e., we assume that y is measured such that it equals the investor's posterior mean and ε is essentially y plus unanticipated randomness in returns.[14] Hence, the investor's posterior belief about ε given y is $\varepsilon|y \sim N(y,\sigma_1^2)$, where $\sigma_1^2 = \sigma_0^2 - \sigma_y^2$ is the posterior variance, i.e., the unanticipated randomness in returns.

From (3.7) and (3.8) it follows that

$$\boldsymbol{a}^*(y) = y/[r\sigma_1^2]$$

$$CE(\boldsymbol{a}^*(y)|y) = \tfrac{1}{2}y^2/[r\sigma_1^2].$$

From this (and the analysis in Appendix 3A) we obtain the following expected utility for system η:

$$U^*(\eta) = -\int_{-\infty}^{+\infty} \exp\left[-\frac{1}{2\sigma_1^2}y^2\right](2\pi\sigma_y^2)^{-\frac{1}{2}} \exp\left[-\frac{1}{2\sigma_y^2}(y - \mu_0)^2\right]dy$$

$$= -\frac{\sigma_1}{\sigma_0}\exp\left[-\frac{1}{2\sigma_0^2}\mu_0^2\right].$$

Value of Information: In the exponential utility function case the optimal action is independent of the cost of the information system since there is no wealth effect. The value of the information is equal to the amount π such that

$$U(a^o) = U^*(\eta)\exp[r\pi].$$

Taking the log of both sides, using $\sigma_1^2 = \sigma_0^2 - \sigma_y^2$, and solving for π yields:

$$\pi = \frac{1}{2r}\left[\ln\sigma_0^2 - \ln(\sigma_0^2 - \sigma_y^2)\right].$$

From the above, we obtain the following comparative statics. The value of the information is:

---

[14] The representation of information is somewhat arbitrary. Assume that (δ, ε) are jointly normally distributed random variables with means (μ_δ,μ_0), variances $(\sigma_\delta^2,\sigma_0^2)$ and covariance $\sigma_{\delta\varepsilon}$. Now let $y = \mu_0 + (\delta - \mu_\delta)\,\sigma_0/\sigma_\delta^2$, which implies that y has mean μ_0 and variance $\sigma_y^2 = \sigma_0^2/\sigma_\delta^2$. Hence, if the underlying signal and ε are jointly normally distributed, one can always redefine the signal so that y and ε have the assumed relation.

(a) independent of the prior mean μ_0;

(b) decreasing in the prior uncertainty σ_0^2, given that the uncertainty resolved by the information (σ_y^2) is held constant;

(c) increasing in the uncertainty resolved by the information (σ_y^2), given that the prior uncertainty (σ_0^2) is held constant;

(d) decreasing in the decision maker's risk aversion r.

Results (a), (b), and (c) are not surprising. The investor is undertaking a gamble both in his investment decision and in acquiring information; with exponential utility there is no wealth effect on the preferences among gambles, so μ_0 has no impact. More prior uncertainty, holding σ_y^2 constant, implies that there is greater unresolved uncertainty after the signal is received and, hence, it is less valuable. Conversely, increasing σ_y^2 while holding σ_0^2 constant implies that there is less unresolved uncertainty after the signal is received and, hence, the signal is more valuable. One can view increasing σ_y^2 as increasing the informativeness of the information system. In this example, even a small increase in informativeness has value. A key aspect of that result is that the investor's set of possible actions is a convex set and the optimal action is a continuous variable of the investor's posterior mean, i.e., any change in expectation leads to a change in action. That type of "fine tuning" was not possible in our earlier example with a finite action space (recall that there were only three possible actions).

Students often find result (d) to be surprising. The usual intuition is that risk-averse investors dislike risk so they will be willing to pay more for the information so as to reduce their risk. However, this fails to recognize that an investor can reduce his risk by investing less in the risky asset. If he is less willing to invest in the risky asset, independent of the information, then the information is less valuable. Furthermore, "buying" information is itself a gamble, with an outcome that is greatest if y is either very large or very small. A more risk-averse investor is less willing to undertake that gamble.

In concluding this example it is important to note that this has been a partial equilibrium analysis. In particular, the information received by the investor is assumed to have no impact on the market price of the risky asset. In Chapters 5 and 7 we re-examine the impact of acquiring information in a pure exchange market setting – considering the case in which all investors receive a report of y. In that setting, a public signal has zero value if the investors have equilibrium holdings prior to receiving the information – the prices adjust (whereas here the price is fixed at one) so that the investors choose to retain their prior equilibrium holdings. This result changes in Chapter 8 when we introduce production choice, and changes again in Chapters 11 and 12 when we consider an equilibrium in which only some investors receive y and the others seek to infer y from the equilibrium price.

3.4.2 The Hurdle Model

Recall that in the hurdle model the decision maker chooses an action $a \in [0,1]$ and obtains a good outcome x_g if a is greater than the hurdle $h \in [0,1]$, and receives a bad outcome x_b otherwise. The decision maker's prior belief about the hurdle h is assumed to be uniformly distributed over the unit interval [0,1], and his utility function depends both on the outcome net of the information cost $x - \kappa$ and the effort (action) a, i.e., the utility function is $u(x\text{-}\kappa,a)$. In the following analysis we assume the agent has an additively separable utility function such that

$$u(x\text{-}\kappa,a) = u_x(x\text{-}\kappa) - v(a),$$

where $u_x' > 0$, $u_x'' < 0$, $v' > 0$ and $v(0) = 0$. We consider a simple version of the model in which the decision maker can acquire perfect information about the hurdle.

With perfect information about the hurdle before choosing the action, the decision maker can choose his optimal action with a perfect knowledge of how high he must jump to clear the hurdle. Since it is costly for the agent to jump, his optimal action strategy is either to precisely clear the hurdle, i.e., $\mathbf{a}^p(h) = h$, if $u_x(x_g\text{-}\kappa) - v(h) \geq u_x(x_b\text{-}\kappa)$, or not to jump at all, i.e., $\mathbf{a}^p(h) = 0$. Hence, we can characterize the optimal action strategy by a cutoff $\hat{h}^p(\kappa) \in [0,1]$ such that

$$\mathbf{a}^p(h) = \begin{cases} h & \text{if } h \leq \hat{h}^p(\kappa), \\ 0 & \text{if } h \geq \hat{h}^p(\kappa). \end{cases}$$

The optimal cutoff $\hat{h}^p(\kappa) \in (0,1)$ is the hurdle for which the agent is indifferent between clearing the hurdle (and obtaining the good outcome), and not jumping (and obtaining the bad outcome), i.e.,

$$\Delta_u(\kappa) = v(\hat{h}^p(\kappa)), \tag{3.9}$$

where $\Delta_u(\kappa) \equiv u_x(x_g\text{-}\kappa) - u_x(x_b\text{-}\kappa)$. Note that $\Delta_u'(\kappa) > 0$ if the decision maker is risk averse. Hence, he clears higher hurdles, the higher is the information cost. That is, even though the information cost is sunk when the decision maker makes his action choice, that cost affects his optimal action. On the other hand, if the decision maker is risk neutral or has a multiplicatively separable exponential utility function, the optimal cutoff is independent of the information cost.

Since the hurdle h is assumed to be uniformly distributed over the unit interval [0,1], we can write the decision maker's expected utility as follows:

$$U^*(\eta^p) = \hat{h}^p(\kappa)\Delta_u(\kappa) + u_x(x_b - \kappa) - \int_0^{\hat{h}^p(\kappa)} v(h)\,dh.$$

Without information the agent does not spend κ and must choose an optimal action a^o independent of h; his expected utility is given by

$$U^*(\eta^o) = a^o\Delta_u(0) + u_x(x_b) - v(a^o),$$

where a^o is given by

$$v'(a^o) = \Delta_u(0). \tag{3.10}$$

To illustrate, assume $u_x(x\text{-}\kappa) = -\exp[-r(x\text{-}\kappa)]$ and $v(a) = \gamma a/(1-a)$. Hence, $\Delta_u(\kappa) = \Delta_u(0)\exp[r\kappa]$ and (3.9) and (3.10) then imply that

$$\hat{h}^p(\kappa) = \frac{\Delta_u(0)\exp[r\kappa]}{\Delta_u(0)\exp[r\kappa] + \gamma},$$

and
$$a^o = 1 - \gamma^{1/2}\Delta_u(0)^{-1/2}.$$

Figure 3.4 shows the decision maker's expected utility with perfect and no information along with the optimal cutoff for varying information costs for the perfect information system ($x_g = 20$; $x_b = 10$; $r = .1$; $\gamma = .1$). The optimal action with no information is $a^o = .34$. With perfect information the agent clears substantially higher hurdles, and the maximum hurdle he clears increases with the information cost. The value of perfect information is the information cost for which the expected utility with perfect information is equal to the expected utility with no information, which in this example is $\pi = 3.6$. Hence, while we plot the cutoffs for costs of κ greater than 3.6, the decision maker would not choose to acquire the information for those cost levels.

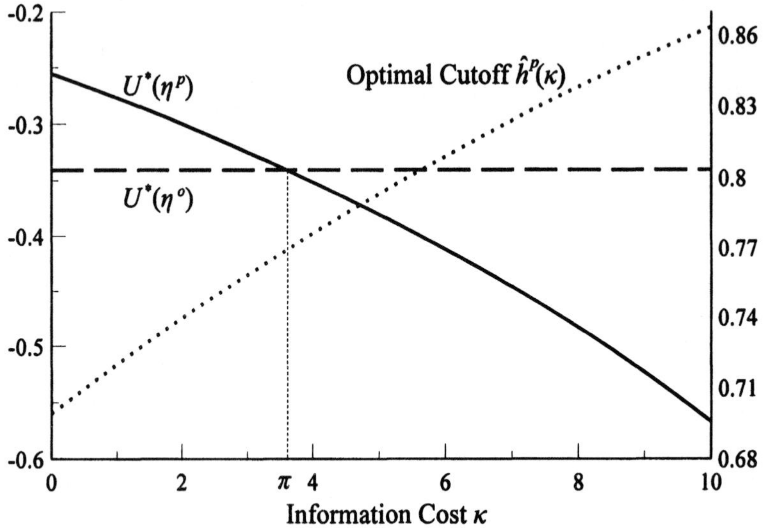

Figure 3.4: Optimal action strategy with perfect information and expected utilities for perfect and no information for varying information costs κ. ($a^o = .34$; $\pi = 3.6$).

APPENDIX 3A: Expected Values of Exponential Functions with Normal Distributions

In a number of settings in this book, exponential utility is combined with normal distributions to obtain relatively simple decision rules and expected utility levels (see, for example, Proposition 2.7). In the simplest of these settings, the decision maker's outcome is a linear function of the normally distributed random variables. In others, the outcome function is quadratic.

Let $\mathbf{x} \sim \mathrm{N}(\boldsymbol{\mu},\boldsymbol{\Sigma})$ be an $n\times1$ random vector, where $\mathrm{N}(\boldsymbol{\mu},\boldsymbol{\Sigma})$ represents the normal distribution function with mean $\boldsymbol{\mu}$ and covariance matrix $\boldsymbol{\Sigma}$. The precision matrix is represented by $\mathbf{H} = \boldsymbol{\Sigma}^{-1}$. In the following analysis, the function parameters are represented by constants β, r, and f, $n\times1$ vector $\mathbf{v}$, and $n\times n$ positive definite symmetric matrix $\mathbf{Q}$.

Expectation of a exponential-linear function of a normally distributed vector:

$$\mathrm{E}[\beta \exp[-r(f+\mathbf{v}^t\mathbf{x})]]$$

$$= \int \beta \exp[-r(f+\mathbf{v}^t\mathbf{x})]\, d\,\mathrm{N}(\boldsymbol{\mu},\boldsymbol{\Sigma})$$

$$= \beta\,[2\pi]^{-\frac{1}{2}n}|\mathbf{H}|^{\frac{1}{2}} \int \exp[-\,r(f + \mathbf{v}^t\mathbf{x}) - \tfrac{1}{2}(\mathbf{x} - \boldsymbol{\mu})^t\mathbf{H}(\mathbf{x} - \boldsymbol{\mu})]\,d\mathbf{x}$$

$$= \beta\,[2\pi]^{-\frac{1}{2}n}|\mathbf{H}|^{\frac{1}{2}} \int \exp[-\,r(f + \mathbf{v}^t\boldsymbol{\mu} - \tfrac{1}{2}r\mathbf{v}^t\boldsymbol{\Sigma}\mathbf{v})$$

$$- \tfrac{1}{2}(\mathbf{x} - \boldsymbol{\mu} + r\boldsymbol{\Sigma}\mathbf{v})^t\mathbf{H}(\mathbf{x} - \boldsymbol{\mu} + r\boldsymbol{\Sigma}\mathbf{v})]\,d\mathbf{x}$$

$$= \beta\exp[-\,r(f + \mathbf{v}^t\boldsymbol{\mu} - \tfrac{1}{2}r\mathbf{v}^t\boldsymbol{\Sigma}\mathbf{v})] \int d\mathrm{N}(\boldsymbol{\mu} - r\boldsymbol{\Sigma}\mathbf{v}, \boldsymbol{\Sigma})$$

$$= \beta\exp[-\,r(f + \mathbf{v}^t\boldsymbol{\mu} - \tfrac{1}{2}r\mathbf{v}^t\boldsymbol{\Sigma}\mathbf{v})].$$

Expectation of an exponential-quadratic function of a normally distributed vector:

In this analysis it is useful to let $\hat{\mathbf{x}} \equiv \mathbf{x} + (r\mathbf{Q} + \mathbf{H})^{-1}(r\mathbf{v} - \mathbf{H}\boldsymbol{\mu})$, which is a normally distributed vector with the same covariance $\boldsymbol{\Sigma}$ as $\mathbf{x}$, but with mean $\boldsymbol{\mu} + (r\mathbf{Q} + \mathbf{H})^{-1}(r\mathbf{v} - \mathbf{H}\boldsymbol{\mu})$.

$$\mathrm{E}[\beta\exp[-\,r(f + \mathbf{v}^t\mathbf{x} + \tfrac{1}{2}\mathbf{x}^t\mathbf{Q}\mathbf{x})]]$$

$$= \int \beta\exp[-\,r(f + \mathbf{v}^t\mathbf{x} + \tfrac{1}{2}\mathbf{x}^t\mathbf{Q}\mathbf{x})]\,d\,\mathrm{N}(\boldsymbol{\mu},\boldsymbol{\Sigma})$$

$$= \beta\,[2\pi]^{-\frac{1}{2}n}|\mathbf{H}|^{\frac{1}{2}} \int \exp[-\,r(f + \mathbf{v}^t\mathbf{x} + \tfrac{1}{2}\mathbf{x}^t\mathbf{Q}\mathbf{x}) - \tfrac{1}{2}(\mathbf{x} - \boldsymbol{\mu})^t\mathbf{H}(\mathbf{x} - \boldsymbol{\mu})]\,d\mathbf{x}$$

$$= \beta\,[2\pi]^{-\frac{1}{2}n}|\mathbf{H}|^{\frac{1}{2}} \int \exp[-\,(rf + (r\mathbf{v} - \mathbf{H}\boldsymbol{\mu})^t\mathbf{x} + \tfrac{1}{2}\mathbf{x}^t(r\mathbf{Q} + \mathbf{H})\mathbf{x} + \tfrac{1}{2}\boldsymbol{\mu}^t\mathbf{H}\boldsymbol{\mu})]\,d\mathbf{x}$$

$$= \beta\,[2\pi]^{-\frac{1}{2}n}|\mathbf{H}|^{\frac{1}{2}}\exp[-\,(rf + \tfrac{1}{2}\boldsymbol{\mu}^t\mathbf{H}\boldsymbol{\mu} - \tfrac{1}{2}(r\mathbf{v} - \mathbf{H}\boldsymbol{\mu})^t(r\mathbf{Q} + \mathbf{H})^{-1}(r\mathbf{v} - \mathbf{H}\boldsymbol{\mu}))]$$

$$\times \int \exp[-\,\tfrac{1}{2}\hat{\mathbf{x}}^t(r\mathbf{Q} + \mathbf{H})\,\hat{\mathbf{x}}]\,d\hat{\mathbf{x}}$$

$$= \beta\exp[-\,(rf + \tfrac{1}{2}\boldsymbol{\mu}^t\mathbf{H}\boldsymbol{\mu} - \tfrac{1}{2}(r\mathbf{v} - \mathbf{H}\boldsymbol{\mu})^t(r\mathbf{Q} + \mathbf{H})^{-1}(r\mathbf{v} - \mathbf{H}\boldsymbol{\mu}))]$$

$$\times\,|\mathbf{H}|^{\frac{1}{2}}\,|r\mathbf{Q} + \mathbf{H}|^{-\frac{1}{2}} \int [2\pi]^{-\frac{1}{2}n}\,|r\mathbf{Q} + \mathbf{H}|^{\frac{1}{2}}\exp[-\,\tfrac{1}{2}\hat{\mathbf{x}}^t(r\mathbf{Q} + \mathbf{H})\,\hat{\mathbf{x}}]\,d\hat{\mathbf{x}}$$

$$= \beta\,|\mathbf{H}|^{\frac{1}{2}}|r\mathbf{Q} + \mathbf{H}|^{-\frac{1}{2}}\exp[-\,(rf + \tfrac{1}{2}\boldsymbol{\mu}^t\mathbf{H}\boldsymbol{\mu} - \tfrac{1}{2}(r\mathbf{v} - \mathbf{H}\boldsymbol{\mu})^t(r\mathbf{Q} + \mathbf{H})^{-1}(r\mathbf{v} - \mathbf{H}\boldsymbol{\mu}))].$$

To illustrate the use of the above expression, consider the financial investment model in Section 3.4.1. In that model, $U^*(\eta)$ has a very simple quadratic form in which $\mathbf{x} = y$, with $\mathbf{x} \sim N(\mu_0,\sigma_y^2)$, and $f + \mathbf{v}^t\mathbf{x} + \frac{1}{2}\mathbf{x}^t\mathbf{Q}\mathbf{x} = \frac{1}{2}y^2[r\sigma_1^2]^{-1}$. Hence, $\boldsymbol{\mu} = \mu_0$, $\mathbf{H} = \sigma_y^{-2}$, $f = 0$, $\mathbf{v} = 0$, and $\mathbf{Q} = [r\sigma_1^2]^{-1}$, and the preceding result implies

$$U^*(\eta) = -\sigma_y^{-1} \times (\sigma_1^{-2} + \sigma_y^{-2})^{-\frac{1}{2}} \times \exp[-\tfrac{1}{2}\mu_0^2\sigma_y^{-2} + \tfrac{1}{2}\mu_0^2\sigma_y^{-4}(\sigma_1^{-2} + \sigma_y^{-2})^{-1}]$$

$$= -(\sigma_1/\sigma_0)\exp[-\tfrac{1}{2}\mu_0^2\sigma_0^{-2}]$$

given that $\sigma_y^2 + \sigma_1^2 = \sigma_0^2$.

REFERENCES

Amershi, A. H. (1988) "Blackwell Informativeness and Sufficient Statistics with Application to Financial Markets and Multiperson Agencies," *Economic Analysis of Information and Contracts*, edited by G. A. Feltham, A. H. Amershi, and W. T. Ziemba. Boston: Kluwer Publishers, 25-93.

Blackwell, D. (1951) "Comparison of Experiments," *Proceedings of the Second Berkeley Symposium on Mathematical Statistics and Probability*. Berkeley: University of California Press, 93-102.

Blackwell, D. (1953) "Equivalent Comparison of Experiments," *Annals of Mathematical Statistics* 24, 267-272.

Blackwell, D., and M. A. Girshick. (1954) *Theory of Games and Statistical Decisions*. New York: John Wiley.

DeGroot, M. H. (1970) *Optimal Statistical Decisions*. New York: McGraw-Hill.

Demski, J. S. (1972) "Information Improvement Bounds," *Journal of Accounting Research* 10, 58-76.

Demski, J. S., and G. A. Feltham. (1976) *Cost Determination: A Conceptual Approach*. Ames, Iowa: Iowa State University Press.

Feltham, G. A. (1968) "The Value of Information," *The Accounting Review* 43, 684-696.

Feltham, G. A. (1972) *Information Evaluation*, Studies in Accounting Research #5. Sarasota, Florida: American Accounting Association.

Feltham, G. A., and J. S. Demski. (1970) "The Use of Models in Information Evaluation," *The Accounting Review* 45, 623-640.

Gould, J. P. (1974) "Risk, Stochastic Preference, and the Value of Information," *Journal of Economic Theory* 8, 64-84.

Huang, C. C., I. Vertinsky, and W. T. Ziemba. (1977) "Sharp Bounds on the Value of Perfect Information," *Operations Research* 25, 128-139.

Marschak, J., and K. Miyasawa. (1968) "Economic Comparability of Information Systems," *International Economic Review* 9, 137-174.

Raiffa, H., and R. Schlaifer. (1961) *Applied Statistical Decision Theory.* Boston: Graduate School of Business Administration, Harvard University.

Ziemba, W. T., and J. E. Butterworth. (1975) "Bounds on the Value of Information in Uncertain Decision Problems," *Stochastics* 1, 361-378.

CHAPTER 4

RISK SHARING, CONGRUENT PREFERENCES, AND INFORMATION IN PARTNERSHIPS

Chapters 2 and 3 focus on decision making under uncertainty by a single decision maker. In the remainder of the book all analyses consider settings in which there are multiple decision makers. This chapter considers a simple setting that we call a *partnership*, although in the literature it is often called a *syndicate* (e.g., Wilson, 1968). The key concepts introduced are *efficient risk sharing* and *congruent preferences* for action and information system choices.

In this chapter, a partnership has the following key characteristics. First, there are two or more partners who contract to share an aggregate outcome, which we can represent as end-of-period consumption or wealth. Second, the aggregate outcome depends on random outcome-relevant events and may also depend on actions taken by one or more partners. Uncertainty with respect to the outcome-relevant events creates uncertainty about total consumption. Third, each partner has personal preferences and a partner's preferences depend on his personal share of the aggregate outcome, i.e., his piece of the total pie. Fourth, the partners have no direct preferences with respect to the actions that are taken, only for their share of the end-of-period consumption. Fifth, the aggregate outcome available to the partnership is contractible information, so that the partners can agree to a contract that specifies how each partner's share of the total will be determined. This implies, for example, that any personal sources of consumption are considered in determining the aggregate outcome (consumption) to be shared.

In Section 4.1 we identify the characteristics of a contract that specifies a Pareto efficient sharing of the aggregate outcome resulting from a given action. A general characterization of the setting in which the partners have the same (i.e., *homogeneous*) beliefs is provided in Section 4.1.1. Section 4.1.2 identifies special cases in which Pareto efficient contracts are linear functions of the aggregate outcome. Section 4.1.3 considers settings in which partners can have different (i.e., *heterogeneous*) beliefs.

Section 4.2.1 considers the partners' preferences among alternative actions. A key issue here is whether the partners have the same preferences over alternative actions given their contract with respect to how the outcome is to be shared. Interestingly, the conditions that result in linear risk sharing also result in congruent preferences over actions. Although we only present the sufficiency of linear sharing for congruent preferences, the conditions for linear risk sharing are (in most cases) also necessary conditions for congruent preferences.

In Section 4.2.1, the partner's beliefs at the time of the action choice are taken as exogenous (as well as homogeneous). In Section 4.2.2, we extend the analysis to consider the impact of pre-decision information and the partners' preferences with respect to alternative information systems.

Finally, in Section 4.3 we briefly consider what has been termed a *team* in the literature. Essentially, a team is a partnership in which the partners have congruent preferences and homogeneous prior beliefs, and the team members can, at a cost, personally acquire information and communicate it to other partners before they take their personal actions.

Before proceeding, we reiterate that the partners have no direct preferences with respect to their actions. Models in which there are direct preferences for actions are typically called agency models. These are examined in Volume II.

4.1 EFFICIENT RISK SHARING

The partnership consists of n partners who share an aggregate outcome $x \in X \subseteq \mathbb{R}$. This outcome is a single dimensional real number, which we can think of as money or a single type of consumption good. It may come from several sources, but the specific sources are not of direct concern for most of our analysis. The key feature of the aggregate outcome is that it is uncertain (and later we consider the possibility that it may be influenced by the partners' actions). As in preceding chapters, uncertainty is represented by a probability space. A key issue is whether partners have *homogeneous beliefs*, so that the probability space $\{ S, \Xi, P \}$ is common to all partners, or they have *heterogeneous beliefs*, represented by $\{ S, \Xi, P_i \}$, $i = 1,...,n$. Observe that we assume that the state space S and the set of probabilizable events Ξ are the same for all partners – if they have heterogeneous beliefs it is only with respect to the probability functions P_i defined on Ξ. In Sections 4.1.1 and 4.1.2 we assume the partners have homogeneous beliefs, and in Section 4.1.3 we extend the analysis to consider heterogeneous beliefs.

4.1.1 Efficient Risk Sharing with Homogeneous Beliefs

Throughout Section 4.1 we ignore action choices and focus on the efficient sharing of an uncertain aggregate outcome denoted $x \in X$. All uncertainty is reflected in a state space S, so that the aggregate outcome (wealth) is a function of the state $s \in S$. The state is not directly observed, but the aggregate outcome is *contractible information* along with an outcome-adequate partition of S

denoted by $\Theta = \{ \theta \}$. (That is, x and θ are observed at the end of the period and can be verified before the "court" enforcing the partnership contract.) Hence, the aggregate outcome can be represented by the following function:

$$\boldsymbol{x}: \Theta \rightarrow X.$$

Since x is a function of θ and θ is contractible information, we express the partnership contract as a function of θ. In particular, we let $\boldsymbol{c} = (\boldsymbol{c}_1,...,\boldsymbol{c}_n)$ represent the partnership contract (i.e., the contract for sharing the aggregate outcome), where

$$\boldsymbol{c}_i: \Theta \rightarrow C_i$$

specifies partner i's share of the aggregate outcome, with C_i representing the set of possible consumption levels for partner i (e.g., if consumption must be non-negative, then $C_i = [0,\infty)$). Similarly, we can represent the full specification of the partnership contract as a sharing rule (specifying each individual partner's share) of the form

$$\boldsymbol{c}: \Theta \rightarrow C,$$

where $$C = C_1 \times ... \times C_n.$$

To be feasible, a sharing rule $\boldsymbol{c}$ must specify shares that are individually feasible (i.e., are in the set C_i for each partner $i = 1,...,n$) and feasible in aggregate (i.e., does not distribute more than the total pie x).

Definition *Sharing Rule Feasibility*

A partnership sharing rule $\boldsymbol{c}$ is *feasible* if, and only if,

$$\boldsymbol{c} \in \boldsymbol{C} \equiv \left\{ \boldsymbol{c} \;\middle|\; \sum_{i=1}^{n} \boldsymbol{c}_i(\theta) \leq \boldsymbol{x}(\theta),\ \boldsymbol{c}_i(\theta) \in C_i,\ \forall\, i = 1,...,n,\ \forall\, \theta \in \Theta \right\}.$$

In our basic model we assume that the partners have homogeneous beliefs P. From this we can determine a homogeneous probability distribution $\Phi(\theta)$ with respect to the outcome-adequate partition Θ, and a homogeneous outcome distribution function $\Phi(x)$. The corresponding generalized probability density functions are $\varphi(\theta)$ and $\varphi(x)$, respectively.

We assume partner i's preferences depend on his share of the aggregate outcome in each state and his beliefs. Furthermore, we assume that those preferences can be expressed as an increasing, concave von Neumann/Morgenstern utility function u_i: $C_i \rightarrow \mathbb{R}$, with $u_i'(c_i) > 0$ and $u_i''(c_i) \leq 0$, so that his expected utility given his personal sharing rule $\boldsymbol{c}_i$ is

$$U_i(\boldsymbol{c}_i) \equiv \int_{\Theta} u_i(\boldsymbol{c}_i(\theta))\, d\Phi(\theta).$$

Our focus in this chapter is on characterizing Pareto efficient contracts among the n partners. That is, we are concerned with identifying contracts that are not dominated by any other contract when considered from the perspective of all the partners as individuals. There is no concept of fairness and, for much of our analysis, we ignore factors that affect the partners' bargaining positions when they join the partnership.

Definition *Pareto Preference and Efficiency*

Partnership contract $\boldsymbol{c}^2$ is *Pareto preferred* to $\boldsymbol{c}^1$ if, and only if,

$$U_i(\boldsymbol{c}_i^2) \geq U_i(\boldsymbol{c}_i^1), \quad \forall\, i = 1,...,n.$$

The Pareto preference is *strict* if there is a strict inequality for *at least* one partner.

Partnership contract $\boldsymbol{c}^*$ is *Pareto efficient* if, and only if, there does not exist any other feasible plan $\boldsymbol{c}$ that is strictly Pareto preferred to $\boldsymbol{c}^*$.

In characterizing Pareto efficient risk sharing it is useful to consider the set of possible feasible sharing rules and the set of possible vectors of expected utility levels for the n partners:

$$\boldsymbol{C} \equiv \left\{ \boldsymbol{c} \;\middle|\; \sum_{i=1}^{n} \boldsymbol{c}_i(\theta) \leq \boldsymbol{x}(\theta),\ \boldsymbol{c}_i(\theta) \in C_i,\ \forall\, i = 1,...,n,\ \forall\, \theta \in \Theta \right\},$$

$$\boldsymbol{U} \equiv \left\{ \mathbf{U} = (U_1,...,U_n) \;\middle|\; U_i = U_i(\boldsymbol{c}_i),\ \forall\, i = 1,...,n,\ \forall \boldsymbol{c} \in \boldsymbol{C} \right\}.$$

A key feature of $\boldsymbol{C}$ is that it permits the partnership to throw away some of the outcome, so that the total of the individual shares can be less than x. This condition implies that $\boldsymbol{C}$ is a convex set and this, combined with the concavity of the partners' utility functions, implies that $\boldsymbol{U}$ is a convex set.[1]

---

[1] A set G is defined to be convex if for any two members g^1 and g^2, any convex combination $g = \lambda g^1 + (1-\lambda)g^2$, for $\lambda \in (0,1)$, is a member of the set G.

Lemma 4.1

The sets $\boldsymbol{C}$ and $\boldsymbol{U}$ are both convex.

We leave the proof as an exercise for the reader. However, we depict these two sets in Figures 4.1 and 4.2. Assume that individual consumption cannot be negative (i.e., $C_i = [0,\infty)$), there is no uncertainty (i.e., $\boldsymbol{x}(\theta) = 16$ for all θ), and there are only two partners (i.e., $n = 2$). In Figure 4.1, $\boldsymbol{C}$ consists of all pairs of numbers $\boldsymbol{c} = (c_1,c_2)$ such that $c_1 \geq 0$, $c_2 \geq 0$, and $c_1 + c_2 \leq x$.

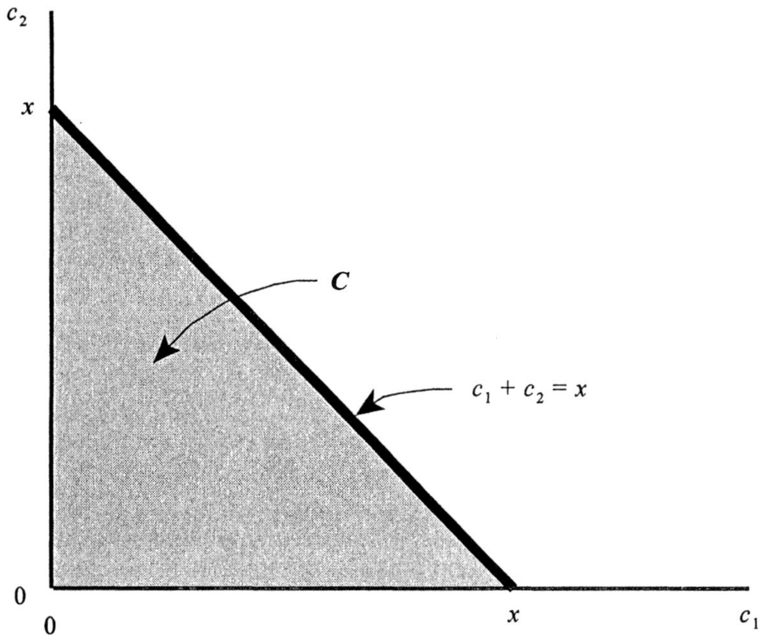

Figure 4.1: Set of possible sharing rules for a single outcome.

Now assume that the partners have square-root utility functions $u_1(c_1) = c_1^{1/2}$ and $u_2(c_2) = [9 + c_2]^{1/2}$. Hence, as depicted in Figure 4.2, $\boldsymbol{U}$ consists of all pairs of numbers $\mathbf{U} = (U_1,U_2)$ such that $U_1 = c_1^{1/2}$, $U_2 = [9 + c_2]^{1/2}$, and $(c_1,c_2) \in \boldsymbol{C}$.

Let $\boldsymbol{U}^*$ represent the set of Pareto efficient utility levels, i.e.,

$$\boldsymbol{U}^* \equiv \{\ \mathbf{U} \in \boldsymbol{U} \mid \nexists\ \mathbf{U}' \in \boldsymbol{U} \text{ such that } U_i' \geq U_i,\quad \forall\ i=1,\ldots n, \text{ and } > \text{ for some } i\ \}.$$

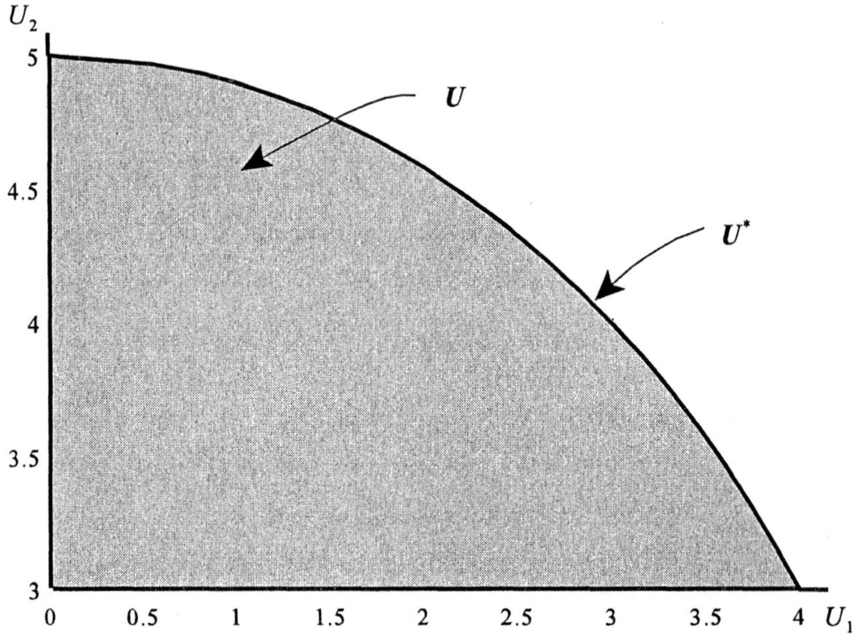

Figure 4.2: Feasible and Pareto efficient expected utility levels for the single outcome case.

In Figure 4.2, the set of Pareto efficient utility levels $\boldsymbol{U}^*$ consists of the points on the curved, "northwest" frontier of $\boldsymbol{U}$. The convexity of the set implies that any point on the frontier (i.e., in $\boldsymbol{U}^*$) is such that if a line is drawn tangent to the frontier at that point it will not intersect the frontier at any other point. As a result, for any Pareto efficient partnership contract $\boldsymbol{c}^*$ there exist non-negative partner utility weights $\lambda_1,...,\lambda_n$ such that the $\boldsymbol{c}^*$ is a solution to the following problem.

***Efficient Risk Sharing Problem*:**

$$\underset{c \in C}{\text{maximize}} \quad \sum_{i=1}^{n} \lambda_i \, U_i(\boldsymbol{c}_i) \tag{4.1a}$$

$$\text{subject to} \quad \sum_{i=1}^{n} \boldsymbol{c}_i(\theta) \le \boldsymbol{x}(\theta), \quad \forall\, \theta \in \Theta, \tag{4.1b}$$

$$\boldsymbol{c}_i(\theta) \in C_i, \quad \forall\, \theta \in \Theta,\, i = 1,...,n. \tag{4.1c}$$

If we assume the feasible individual consumption set has the form $C_i = [\underline{c}_i, \infty)$ and Θ is a finite set, the efficient risk sharing problem can be represented by the following Lagrangian:

$$\mathcal{L} = \sum_{i=1}^{n} \lambda_i U_i(\mathbf{c}_i) - \sum_{\theta \in \Theta} \mu(\theta) \left[\sum_{i=1}^{n} \mathbf{c}_i(\theta) - \mathbf{x}(\theta) \right] + \sum_{\theta \in \Theta} \sum_{i=1}^{n} \zeta_i(\theta) \, [\mathbf{c}_i(\theta) - \underline{c}_i],$$

where $\mu(\theta)$ and $\zeta_i(\theta)$ are Lagrange multipliers for the event-contingent aggregate outcome and event/partner contingent individual consumption constraints, respectively. Differentiating the Lagrangian by $c_i = \mathbf{c}_i(\theta)$ for a given event and partner yields the following first-order conditions:[2]

$$\lambda_i \, u_i'(\mathbf{c}_i(\theta)) \, \varphi(\theta) - \mu(\theta) + \zeta_i(\theta) = 0, \quad \forall \, \theta \in \Theta, i = 1,...,n. \tag{4.2}$$

The problem has a concave objective function and linear constraints. Hence, the Kuhn-Tucker conditions identify a global maximum, and the following proposition due to Wilson (1968) characterizes a Pareto efficient contract.

Proposition 4.1 (Wilson 1968, Theorems 1 and 5)

A necessary and sufficient condition for $\mathbf{c}^*$ to be a *Pareto efficient partnership contract* is that there exist non-negative weights $\lambda = (\lambda_1,...,\lambda_n)$ such that $\mathbf{c}^*$ is a solution to efficient risk sharing problem (4.1). If all partners are strictly risk averse, then the solution has the following characteristics.

(a) All of the aggregate outcome is distributed to the partners, i.e.,

$$\sum_{i=1}^{n} \mathbf{c}_i^*(\theta) = \mathbf{x}(\theta), \quad \forall \, \theta \in \Theta.$$

(b) Individual consumption only varies with the outcome, i.e., $\mathbf{c}_i^*(\theta^1) = \mathbf{c}_i^*(\theta^2)$ if $\mathbf{x}(\theta^1) = \mathbf{x}(\theta^2)$, and, hence, the contract can be expressed as a function of the aggregate outcomes x instead of the events θ, i.e., $\mathbf{c}_i^*(x) \equiv \mathbf{c}_i^*(\theta)$ for θ such that $\mathbf{x}(\theta) = x$.

---

[2] These conditions are sometimes referred to as the Borch first-order conditions since Borch (1962) was the first to derive the necessary and sufficient conditions for Pareto efficient risk sharing.

(c) There exist positive weights $\lambda_1,...,\lambda_n$ and a positive multiplier $\mu(x)$ for each aggregate outcome $x \in X$ such that

$$u_i'(c_i^*(x)) = \frac{\mu(x)}{\lambda_i\,\varphi(x)} \quad \text{if } c_i^*(x) > \underline{c}_i, \quad \forall\, i = 1,...,n. \tag{4.3}$$

(d) If $c_i^*(x) > \underline{c}_i$, then the partner's consumption is a strictly increasing function of the aggregate outcome, i.e., $c_i^*(x^1) < c_i^*(x^2)$, for all $i = 1,...,n$, if $x^1 < x^2$. Furthermore, if X is a convex set and $c_i^*(x)$ is differentiable, then

$$c_i^{*\prime}(x) = \frac{\rho_i(c_i^*(x))}{\rho_o(c^*(x))}, \quad \forall\, x \in X,\ i = 1,...,n,$$

where
$$\rho_i(c_i) = -\frac{u_i'(c_i)}{u_i''(c_i)}$$

$$\rho_o(c) = \sum_{i=1}^{n} \rho_i(c_i),$$

i.e., the slope of a partner's consumption function is equal to the ratio of the partner's risk tolerance relative to the aggregate risk tolerance of all partners.

Proof:
(a): The proof is straightforward since all partners prefer more to less (i.e., $u_i'(c_i) > 0$) and, hence, it can never be efficient to throw away some of the pie.

(b): The fact that all partners have strictly concave utility functions and homogeneous beliefs is important for this result. If c_i differs between θ^1 and θ^2 even though they produce the same x, then that implies that at least two partners are bearing unnecessary risk. Proof is by contradiction. Assume there are two events such that $x(\theta^1) = x(\theta^2)$ with at least two partners with $c_i^*(\theta^1) \neq c_i^*(\theta^2)$. Replace these consumption shares with $c_i(\theta^1) = [\varphi(\theta^1)c_i^*(\theta^1) + \varphi(\theta^2)c_i^*(\theta^2)] \div [\varphi(\theta^1)+\varphi(\theta^2)]$. The revised contract is feasible and, by Jensen's inequality, it provides every partner with at least as high an expected utility, with some strictly higher.

(c): Expression (4.3) follows from (4.2) given condition (b).

(d): Let $g(x) = \mu(x)/\varphi(x)$ so that (4.3) can be written as

$$\lambda_i\, u_i'(c_i^*(x)) = g(x). \tag{4.4}$$

Differentiate both sides: $\lambda_i\, u_i''(c_i^*(x))\, c_i^{*\prime}(x) = g'(x).$ (4.5)

Divide (4.5) by (4.4):

$$u_i''(c_i^*(x))\, c_i^{*\prime}(x) \div u_i'(c_i^*(x)) = g'(x) \div g(x). \tag{4.6}$$

Rearrange terms: $$c_i^{*\prime}(x) = \rho_i(c_i^*(x))\left[-\frac{g'(x)}{g(x)} \right]. \tag{4.7}$$

Summing both sides of (4.7) and recognizing that the left-hand side must equal one, since the total consumption sums to x, implies:

$$-\frac{g'(x)}{g(x)} = \left[\sum_{i=1}^{n} \rho_i(c_i^*(x)) \right]^{-1}.$$ **Q.E.D.**

The expression $g(x) = \mu(x)/\varphi(x)$ is introduced in the proof of (d) and will appear several times in subsequent analysis. It can be interpreted as the marginal utility (scaled by λ_i) to each member of the syndicate of an increase in the aggregate outcome at the level x. The multiplier $\mu(x)$ is influenced by the probability of x, and dividing through by $\varphi(x)$ removes that effect. Hence, $g(x)$ reflects the scarcity of consumption, but not its likelihood.

Observe that the following ratios follow directly from (4.3) in condition (c).

Corollary 4.1

If $c_i^*(x) > \underline{c}_i$, then

$$\frac{u_i'(c_i^*(x^1))}{u_i'(c_i^*(x^2))} = \frac{g(x^1)}{g(x^2)}, \quad \forall\, i = 1,\ldots,n, \tag{4.8}$$

$$\frac{u_1'(c_1^*(x))}{u_2'(c_2^*(x))} = \frac{\lambda_1^{-1}}{\lambda_2^{-1}}, \quad \forall\, x \in X. \tag{4.9}$$

The first ratio establishes that every partner has precisely the same marginal rate of substitution (in terms of utility of consumption) across any pair of outcomes. This is depicted in the Edgeworth box in Figure 4.3, which has two partners and two outcomes, with $x^1 = 20 > x^2 = 10$. The points in the box indicate each partner's share of the aggregate outcome, with partner 1's share being measured from the bottom left corner and partner 2's share being measured from the top right corner. The indifference curve for partner *i* represents the set of consumption levels $c_i^1 = c_i(x^1)$ and $c_i^2 = c_i(x^2)$ that provide partner *i* with the same expected utility. Condition (4.8) establishes that an efficient contract always occurs at points at which the indifference curves for the two partners are tangent to each other (unless there is a corner solution). The set of all such points is depicted by the bold line and is referred to as the "contract curve." In this figure we assume $\underline{c}_i = 0$ and the partners both have square-root utility functions, but partner 1 is more risk averse than partner 2, with $u_1(c_1) = c_1^{½}$ and $u_2(c_2) = [9 + c_2]^{½}$. This is reflected in two ways. First, partner 1's indifference curve is more curved than for partner 2 (it is linear if a partner is risk neutral).[3] Second, if partner 1 receives a much larger share, we have a corner solution in which partner 2 receives zero in the second (low) outcome (as reflected by the contract curve in the upper right-hand corner of the box).

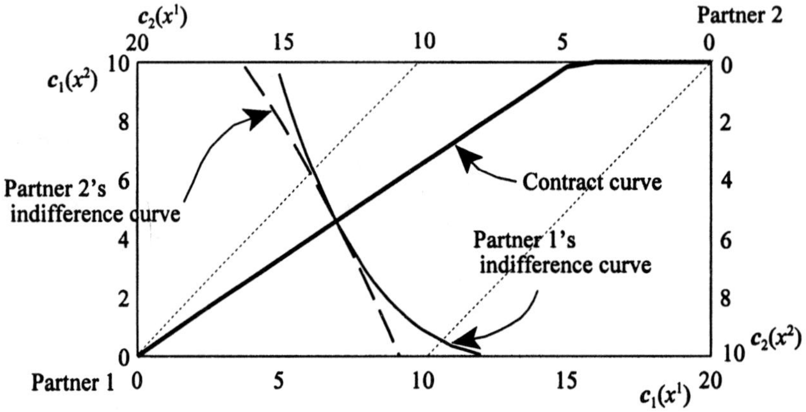

Figure 4.3: Edgeworth box – efficient sharing of uncertain binary outcome.

The second ratio (i.e., expression 4.9) reveals that for any given outcome, the marginal rate of substitution of utility across partners is equal to the ratio of their weights in the efficient risk sharing problem. The fact that u_i' is decreasing in c_i implies that for any given outcome *x* the partner with the largest weight receives the largest share of the pie. In Figure 4.3 that characteristic is repres-

[3] The "slant" of an indifference curve depends on the probability function. In this example we assume $\varphi(x^1) = .7$.

ented by the fact that the contract curve is non-decreasing, with the points close to the lower left corner representing settings in which the ratio λ_1/λ_2 is small, and the points close to the upper right corner representing settings in which that ratio is large.

Observe that since all partners are risk averse, every partner bears some risk reflected by the contract curve falling between the two 45-degree lines in Figure 4.3, c.f., Proposition 4.1(d). This implies, for example, that it is always beneficial to expand the partnership to include more partners (assuming, as we have, that there are no administrative costs or incentive problems). Even a highly risk-averse partner can efficiently absorb some risk.

Our analysis has assumed that all partners are strictly risk averse. What happens if there are risk-neutral partners? In the Edgeworth box, a risk-neutral partner has a linear indifference curve with a slope equal to $-\varphi(x^1)/\varphi(x^2)$. If both partners are risk neutral then their indifference curves coincide, so that all the points in the box are on the contract curve, i.e., all are efficient. On the other hand, if one partner is strictly risk averse and the other is risk neutral, the contract curve is such that the risk-averse partner receives the same consumption for both values of x if that is feasible. The latter is depicted in Figure 4.4, in which partner 1 is the same as in Figure 4.3, while partner 2 is risk neutral.

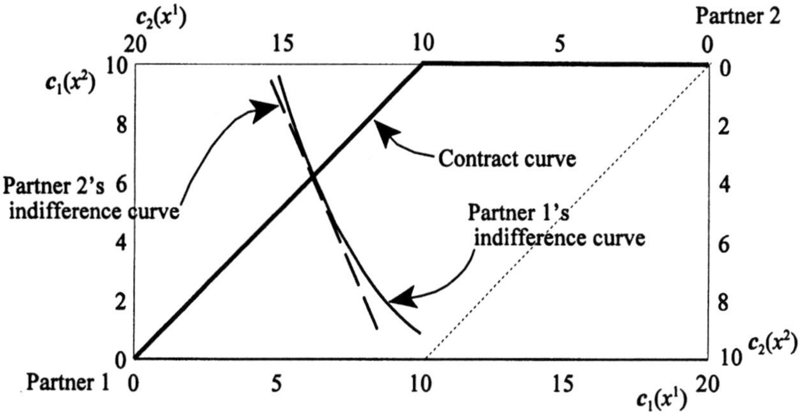

Figure 4.4: Edgeworth box – efficient sharing of uncertain binary outcome with partner 2 risk neutral.

Proposition 4.2

If a subset of the partners are risk neutral and they have sufficient capacity to absorb all risk, then the strictly risk-averse partners bear no risk (i.e., $c_i(x)$ is constant for all x).

In Volume II we consider a variety of settings in which one or more partners (referred to as the principal) are risk neutral (e.g., wealthy) owners of the firm, and they contract with a risk-averse partner (referred to as the agent) to operate the firm. If the agent has no direct preferences with respect to his actions, Proposition 4.2 applies and he bears no risk. However, in most principal-agent models we assume the agent has direct preferences with respect to his actions (e.g., a disutility or personal cost of effort) and the optimal contract is such that risk is imposed on the agent for incentive purposes.

4.1.2 HARA Utility Functions and Linear Risk Sharing

Efficient risk sharing when the partners have HARA utility functions (see Chapter 2) is particularly interesting, if we assume that they have the same "type" of HARA utility function with *identical risk cautiousness.* Recall that the HARA utility functions have linear risk tolerances, which are expressed in Table 2.1 as $\alpha x + \beta$,and hence have constant risk cautiousness of α. There are three basic types: exponential ($\alpha = 0$), logarithmic ($\alpha = 1$), and power ($\alpha \neq 0,1$ and the power equals $1 - 1/\alpha$).

The risk tolerance for the exponential utility function is a constant (i.e., ρ is equal to β in Table 2.1). Hence, if all partners have exponential utility functions, ρ_i is partner i's risk tolerance, $\rho_o = \rho_1 + \ldots + \rho_n$ is the partners' aggregate risk tolerance, and $\underline{c}_i = -\infty$, then Proposition 4.1(d) implies

$$\mathbf{c}_i^{*\prime}(x) = \frac{\rho_i}{\rho_o}, \qquad \forall\, i = 1,\ldots,n.$$

Consequently, with exponential utility a Pareto efficient partnership contract gives each partner a linear share of the aggregate outcome and the partners share risk in proportion to their risk tolerances. The lack of a wealth effect on the partners' risk preferences implies that the partners' utility weights $\lambda_1,\ldots,\lambda_n$ do not affect their share of the risk – the weights only affect the fixed portions of their linear consumption functions.

Definition *Linear partnership contract*

A partnership contract is defined to be *linear* if it is characterized by parameters v_i and f_i such that $\mathbf{c}_i(x) = f_i + v_i x$, for all $i = 1,\ldots,n$, and $\Sigma_{i=1}^n v_i = 1$ and $\Sigma_{i=1}^n f_i = 0$.

While not as obvious as in the exponential utility function case, the Pareto efficient contracts are linear if all partners have logarithmic utility functions or all have power utility functions with the same risk cautiousness, subject to appropriate boundary conditions. To avoid the problems created by the lower bounds on partner consumption we assume $C_i = (-\infty,\infty)$ in the exponential utility case, $C_i = (-\beta_i/\alpha_i,\infty)$ in the logarithmic utility case, and $C_i = [-\beta_i/\alpha_i,\infty)$ in the power utility case with $\alpha_i > 0$. Observe that these conditions are such that

$$\lim_{c_i \to \underline{c}_i} u_i'(c_i) = \infty, \quad \forall\, i = 1,\ldots,n,$$

which induces interior solutions in all cases.

Proposition 4.3

If the partners have homogeneous beliefs and their preferences are represented by HARA utility functions with *identical risk cautiousness*, then any Pareto efficient partnership contract is linear.

Proof: The exponential case ($\alpha = 0$) follows from the above discussion. We provide a proof for the logarithmic case ($\alpha = 1$) and leave the proof for the power case ($\alpha \neq 0,1$) to the reader since it is similar to the logarithmic case.

Proposition 4.1(c) specifies that (4.3) is a characteristic of an efficient contract $\boldsymbol{c}$. Letting $g(x) = \mu(x)/\varphi(x)$ and using the derivative of a logarithmic utility function yields

$$\lambda_i \frac{1}{c_i(x) + \beta_i} = g(x), \quad \forall\, x \in X,\, i = 1,\ldots,n. \tag{4.10}$$

Solve (4.10) for c_i:

$$c_i(x) = \frac{\lambda_i}{g(x)} - \beta_i, \quad \forall\, x \in X,\, i = 1,\ldots,n. \tag{4.11}$$

Sum both sides of (4.11) over all i and use Proposition 4.1(a) to set the sum of the left-hand-side equal to x:

$$\sum_{i=1}^{n} c_i(x) = x = \frac{\lambda_o}{g(x)} - \beta_o, \quad \forall\, x \in X, \tag{4.12}$$

where $\lambda_o \equiv \sum_{i=1}^{n} \lambda_i$ and $\beta_o \equiv \sum_{i=1}^{n} \beta_i$. Solve (4.12) for $g(x)$:

$$g(x) = \frac{\lambda_o}{x + \beta_o}, \quad \forall\, x \in X. \tag{4.13}$$

Substitute (4.13) into (4.11):

$$c_i(x) = \frac{\lambda_i}{\lambda_o}(x + \beta_o) - \beta_i, \quad \forall\, x \in X,\ i = 1,...,n\,.$$

Hence, a Pareto efficient contract $\boldsymbol{c}$ is linear, with the parameters specified in Table 4.1. **Q.E.D.**

	Utility Function	Share of Risk (v_i)	Intercept (f_i)
Exponential:	$-\exp[-c_i/\rho_i]$	$\frac{\rho_i}{\rho_o}$	$\rho_i\left[\sum_{j=1}^{n} v_j \ln\left(\frac{\rho_j}{\lambda_j}\right) - \ln\left(\frac{\rho_i}{\lambda_i}\right)\right]$
Logarithmic:	$\ln(c_i + \beta_i)$	$\frac{\lambda_i}{\lambda_o},\ \lambda_o \equiv \sum_{i=1}^{n} \lambda_i$	$v_i\beta_o - \beta_i$
Power:	$\frac{1}{\alpha - 1}[\alpha c_i + \beta_i]^{\frac{\alpha-1}{\alpha}}$	$\frac{\lambda_i^\alpha}{\lambda_o^\alpha},\ \lambda_o^\alpha \equiv \sum_{i=1}^{n} \lambda_i^\alpha$	$(v_i\beta_o - \beta_i)/\alpha$

Table 4.1: Linear sharing rules for HARA utility functions with identical risk cautiousness.

Observe that the variable rates $v_i \in (0,1)$ represents the share of the risk born by partner i. Each partner's share is independent of the weights $\lambda_1,...,\lambda_n$ in the exponential case, but is an increasing function of the relative weight in the logarithmic and power utility cases with positive risk cautiousness and is a decreasing function of the relative weight in the power utility case with negative risk cautiousness. The key is that, if the risk cautiousness is positive, the partners' risk tolerances are increasing in "wealth" and the partners with the largest weights effectively receive the largest "wealth". On the other hand, if the risk cautiousness is negative, then the partners' risk tolerances are decreasing in "wealth" and the reverse holds.

In the logarithmic and power utility function cases, the β_i parameter also affects partner i's risk aversion. The effect is relatively simple in the logarithmic utility case. Here we observe that β_i impacts the analysis in essentially the same way as a personal source of consumption. In particular, it is "as if" the total consumption is $x + \beta_o$ and partner i receives λ_i/λ_o of that total.

4.1.3 Side-betting with Heterogeneous Beliefs

Partners often have differences in beliefs, so that the homogeneous beliefs assumption may appear unrealistic. Later in this book we consider a number of settings in which individuals have differences in beliefs due to differences in information. Those differences have a profound effect on the analysis and are generally characterized by one individual attempting to infer the other individuals' "private" information based on their observed actions or observed variables, such as market price, that are influenced by their actions. We leave all consideration of the impact of differences in information until subsequent chapters. However, here we briefly consider the impact of what are commonly referred to as *heterogeneous beliefs*. These differences in partner beliefs are assumed to be due to fundamental differences in the partners' personal characteristics – differences that are irrelevant to the preferences and beliefs of the other partners (e.g., it is part of their DNA).

In our setting, heterogeneous beliefs are represented by differences in the probability function $P_i(\xi)$ that characterizes partner i's probability space. In this analysis it is important to assume that the state space S and the set of probabilizable events Ξ are common to all partners. Furthermore, the probability functions must have the same "null sets", i.e., if $P_i(\xi) = 0$ for some partner i and event $\xi \in \Xi$, then $P_j(\xi) = 0$ for all partners j. If this was not the case, then one partner could believe an event has a positive probability of occurring while another believes it has zero probability, i.e., it is impossible. This would lead the latter to be willing to undertake an "infinite" bet that the event will not occur.

The probability function $P_i(\xi)$ is used to derive partner i's probability distribution function $\Phi_i(\theta)$ and generalized probability density function $\varphi_i(\theta)$ with respect to the outcome-relevant events, as well as the outcome probability functions $\Phi_i(x)$ and $\varphi_i(x)$. Partner i's expected utility for sharing rule $\boldsymbol{c}_i$ is

$$U_i(\boldsymbol{c}_i) \equiv \int_{\Theta} u_i(\boldsymbol{c}_i(\theta))\, d\Phi_i(\theta).$$

Using this in efficient risk sharing problem (4.1) leads to a slight change in first-order condition (4.2):

$$\lambda_i\, u_i'(\boldsymbol{c}_i(\theta))\, \varphi_i(\theta) - \mu(\theta) + \zeta_i(\theta) = 0, \quad \forall\, \theta \in \Theta,\ i = 1,...,n. \qquad (4.14)$$

While the change is slight, the impact is potentially significant.

To see the impact of heterogeneous beliefs consider Proposition 4.1. There is no change in result (a) – it is still efficient to fully distribute the aggregate outcome since all partners still prefer more to less. However, result (b) does not hold – the partners' consumption may differ between two events even though they produce the same outcome. The key issue is whether the partners' beliefs lead them to efficiently "bet" on the event as well as efficiently share the outcome. We obtain some insight into this by considering (4.14) for events in which $\mathbf{c}_i(\theta) > \underline{c}_i$ and hence $\zeta_i(\theta) = 0$. The ratio of partner i's marginal utilities for two events θ^1 and θ^2 such that $\mathbf{x}(\theta^1) = \mathbf{x}(\theta^2)$ is

$$\frac{u_i'(\mathbf{c}_i(\theta^1))}{u_i'(\mathbf{c}_i(\theta^2))} = \frac{\mu(\theta^1)/\varphi_i(\theta^1)}{\mu(\theta^2)/\varphi_i(\theta^2)}, \quad \forall\, i = 1,...,n. \tag{4.15}$$

In the homogeneous beliefs case, the right-hand-side of (4.15) is the same for all partners and all partners have the same marginal rate of substitution between the two events. If the two events result in the same aggregate outcome, the latter is only possible if the ratio is equal to one, i.e., each partner has identical consumption in the two events. However, in the heterogeneous beliefs case, the right-hand-side differs across partners unless $\varphi_i(\theta^1)/\varphi_i(\theta^2)$ is constant. If the latter ratio is constant across partners, each partner again has identical consumption for the two events. This occurs because the partners have homogeneous beliefs about θ^1 and θ^2 *given* that they know that either θ^1 or θ^2 has occurred! On the other hand, if $\varphi_i(\theta^1)/\varphi_i(\theta^2)$ varies across partners, then (4.15) implies that efficient consumption must vary across events. In particular, assume partners i and j are such that $\varphi_i(\theta^1)/\varphi_i(\theta^2) > \varphi_j(\theta^1)/\varphi_j(\theta^2)$, i.e., i believes θ^1 is relatively more likely than does j. This implies, from (4.15), that the marginal rate of substitution for i must be less than for j. If i and j were the only two partners (or they represented two subsets of partners with two types of beliefs), partner i would consume more in state θ^1 than in state θ^2, whereas partner j would do the reverse. We refer to this as *side-betting*. Figure 4.5 depicts a setting in which there is no risk, but the partners bear risk because partner i attaches a higher probability to θ^1 than does partner j.

4.2 CONGRUENT PREFERENCES

In section 4.1 the relation between the state s and the aggregate outcome x is exogenous – the partners have no action choices. We now assume the partners must choose an action a from a set A and then consider the choice of a decision-facilitating information system η from a set H.

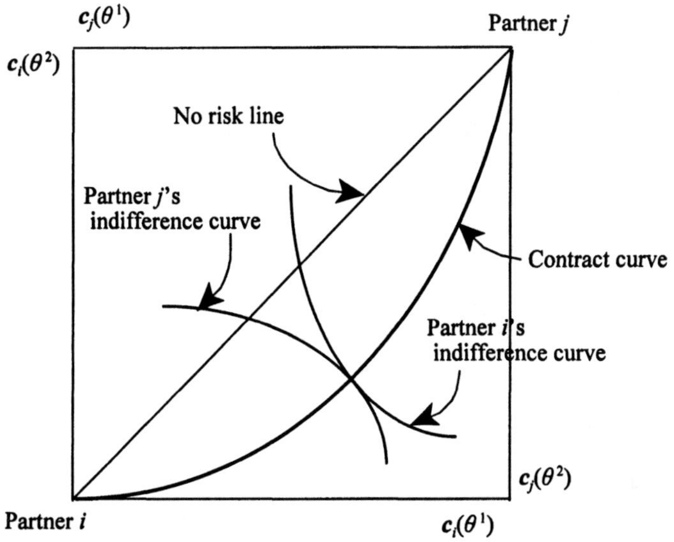

Figure 4.5: Edgeworth box – side-betting with heterogeneous beliefs and $x(\theta^1) = x(\theta^2)$.

4.2.1 Action Choice

The aggregate outcome is now a function of the random event $\theta \in \Theta$ and the partners' action $a \in A$, and is represented by

$$\boldsymbol{x}: \Theta \times A \rightarrow X.$$

We assume the partners beliefs are homogeneous so that probability distribution over the outcome-adequate events in Θ are again represented by $\Phi(\theta)$. Of course, since the outcome function depends on the partners' action a, the probability distribution over the outcomes in X is conditional on that action, and is represented by $\Phi(x|a)$.

The event θ, action a, and outcome x are all contractible information. However, since the partners' beliefs are homogeneous, Proposition 4.1 characterizes efficient risk sharing contracts for a given action a and the contract can be expressed as a function of x and a, i.e., partner i's sharing rule is $\boldsymbol{c}_i(x,a)$. In this case, partner i's expected utility from contract $\boldsymbol{c}_i$ and action a is

$$U_i(\boldsymbol{c}_i,a) = \int_X u_i(\boldsymbol{c}_i(x,a))\, d\Phi(x|a).$$

For purposes of this analysis we adopt a slightly different approach to the specification of the efficient partnership contract. Partner 1 is depicted as having control. He selects the action a to be implemented and the risk sharing contract $\boldsymbol{c}$. Of course, he can only obtain the participation of the other partners if he makes it "worth their while." In this regard, each partner i, $i = 2,...,n$ is assumed to have an expected utility level $\bar{U}_i$ that he must receive from the partnership in order to induce him to participate. This minimum expected utility level is often referred to as partner i's *reservation utility* level. The optimal action and contract are obtained by solving the following problem.

***Optimal Partnership Contract Problem*:**

$$\underset{\boldsymbol{c} \in C,\, a \in A}{\text{maximize}} \quad U_1(\boldsymbol{c}_1,a) \tag{4.16a}$$

$$\text{subject to} \quad U_i(\boldsymbol{c}_i,a) \geq \bar{U}_i, \quad \forall\, i = 2,...,n, \tag{4.16b}$$

$$\sum_{i=1}^{n} \boldsymbol{c}_i(x,a) \leq x, \quad \forall\, x \in X, \tag{4.16c}$$

$$\boldsymbol{c}_i(x,a) \in C_i, \quad \forall\, x \in X,\ i = 1,...,n. \tag{4.16d}$$

The Lagrangian for this problem is

$$\mathcal{L} = U_1(\boldsymbol{c}_1,a) + \sum_{i=2}^{n} \lambda_i\, [U_i(\boldsymbol{c}_i,a) - \bar{U}_i] - \sum_{x \in X} \mu(x) \left[\sum_{i=1}^{n} \boldsymbol{c}_i(x,a) - x \right]$$

$$+ \sum_{x \in X} \sum_{i=1}^{n} \zeta_i(x)\, [\boldsymbol{c}_i(x,a) - \underline{c}_i], \tag{4.17}$$

where λ_i is now a Lagrange multiplier for partner i's participation constraint (4.16b), $\mu(x)$ is the multiplier for constraint (4.16c), and $\zeta_i(x)$ is the multiplier for constraint (4.16d).

Solving problem (4.16) for the optimal risk sharing contract given the optimal action a^* is effectively the same as solving problem (4.1) using $\boldsymbol{x}(\theta) = \boldsymbol{x}(\theta,a^*)$. The main difference is that in (4.16) the "weight" assigned to the first partner is implicitly $\lambda_1 = 1$ and "weights" for the other partners equal the endogenously determined Lagrange multipliers for each partner's participation constraint.[4] Hence, the characterization of the efficient risk sharing contract is effectively the same (with $\boldsymbol{c}_i^*(x) = \boldsymbol{c}_i^*(x,a^*)$ and $\Phi(x) = \Phi(x|a^*)$).

Optimal partnership contract problem (4.16) assumes that the first partner selects both the action and the risk sharing contract for that action. Assume that the action potentially consists of n tasks, where task a_i is implemented by partner i, i.e., $a = (a_1,...,a_n) \in A = A_1 \times ... \times A_n$ (if partner i is not assigned a task, i.e., he is merely a risk sharer, then $A_i = \emptyset$). If all elements of a are contractible information, we can view $\boldsymbol{c}_i^*(x,a_i)$ as specifying the optimal risk sharing contract if $a_i = a_i^*$, and imposing the minimum consumption $\underline{c}_i$ if $a_i \neq a_i^*$ (which we assume will be sufficient to deter him from selecting $a_i \neq a_i^*$). That is, each partner receives their efficient share of the outcome if, and only if, they implement the optimal task assigned to them. Of course, this type of penalty contract is not feasible if a is not contractible information since in that setting the contract can only depend on the outcome x, i.e., $\boldsymbol{c}_i$: $X \to C_i$.

Let $a_{-i} = (a_1,...,a_{i-1},a_{i+1},...,a_n)$ represent all actions other than that of partner i, so that $a = (a_{-i},a_i)$. If each partner i selects action $a_i \in A_i$ based on his personal preferences given his sharing rule $\boldsymbol{c}_i$ and his conjecture as to the actions a_{-i} taken by the other partners, we must add the following *incentive constraints* to the optimal partnership contract problem:[5]

$$a_i \in \underset{\hat{a}_i \in A_i}{\operatorname{argmax}} \; U_i(\boldsymbol{c}_i, a_{-i}, \hat{a}_i), \quad \forall\, i = 1,...,n. \tag{4.16e}$$

That is, to be feasible, the contract and action selected by the first partner must be such that each partner i has *no incentive not to implement the action a_i specified by the first partner* given that partner i conjectures that all other partners will be induced to implement action a_{-i}. We include a_1 in the incentive constraints since the action the first partner chooses for his task must be consistent with his personal preferences once the sharing rules are fixed – otherwise, the other partners will not conjecture that partner 1 will implement a_1 and that may affect their action choices.

---

[4] Earlier we stated that for any Pareto efficient risk sharing contract there exist exogenous weights $\lambda_1,...,\lambda_n$ such that the contract is a solution to problem (4.1). It can also be shown that for any Pareto efficient risk sharing contract there exist exogenous reservation utility levels $\bar{U}_2,...,\bar{U}_n$ such that the contract is a solution to problem (4.16). The Lagrange multipliers in the latter problem will be equivalent to the weights used in problem (4.1), subject only to possible differences in scaling, and the expected utilities obtained in solving (4.1) will be the reservation utility levels used in (4.16).

[5] "argmax" is the subset of the set of choice variables that maximize the function that follows, i.e., in this case, the set of actions $a_i \in A_i$ that maximize $U_i(a_{-i},a_i)$. A maximum is assumed to exist, but it need not be unique.

While we could provide a general characterization of the optimal solution to problem (4.16) with the incentive constraints (4.16e), we will not do so. Incentive problems become much more significant when we assume that the partners have direct preferences with respect to the tasks assigned to them. These types of incentive problems are examined in the analysis of principal/agent problems in Volume II. Here we focus on identifying conditions that are sufficient for the incentive constraints (4.16e) to be non-binding. That is, conditions such that the solution to (4.16a-d) is the same as the solution to (4.16a-e).

In the following analysis we consider a slightly stronger condition, which we call *congruent preferences*. A partnership contract induces congruent preferences if, after specifying the sharing rule $\boldsymbol{c}$ all partners would make the same action choice (assuming they could control all elements of a).

Definition *Congruent Preferences*

A partnership contract $\boldsymbol{c}: X \rightarrow C$ induces *congruent preferences* for action a if

$$a \in \underset{\hat{a} \in A}{\operatorname{argmax}} \; U_i(\boldsymbol{c}_i, \hat{a}), \quad \forall\, i = 1,\dots,n.$$

From Wilson (1968) we know that the efficient risk sharing contract for optimal action a^* induces congruent preferences for a^* if the partners have HARA utility functions with identical risk cautiousness.

Proposition 4.4 (Wilson 1968, Theorem 11)

Assume that for each HARA utility function, C_i is such that the optimal risk sharing contract induces $\boldsymbol{c}_i(x) > \underline{c}_i$ for all $x \in X$ and $i = 1,\dots,n$.[6] If the partners have homogeneous beliefs and their preferences are represented by HARA utility functions with *identical risk cautiousness*, the Pareto efficient partnership contract for action a^* induces congruent preferences with respect to a^*.

Proof: We limit our proof to the case of logarithmic utility functions since the proofs for exponential and power utility functions are essentially the same. Let $w_i(x) = u_i \circ \boldsymbol{c}_i^*$ represent partner i's payoff as a function of x, where $\boldsymbol{c}_i^*(x) = v_i x + f_i$, where v_i and f_i are as specified in Table 4.1. For logarithmic utility this composite function is given by

[6] This is a crucial assumption for the result. If some partners receive the lower bound compensation for some outcomes while other partners do not, their risk preferences are not aligned (through their sharing rules).

$$w_i(x) = \ln\left[\left(\frac{\lambda_i}{\lambda_o}x + \frac{\lambda_i}{\lambda_o}\beta_o - \beta_i\right) + \beta_i\right]$$

$$= \ln\left[\frac{\lambda_i}{\lambda_o}\right] + \ln\left[x + \beta_o\right] \sim \ln\left[x + \beta_o\right]. \tag{4.18}$$

This implies that all partners' induced preferences over the outcome x are the same, i.e., the induced utilities by the optimal risk sharing contract, $w_i(x)$, are equivalent (up to a positive linear transformation) and, hence, the partners will all be induced to select the same action. **Q.E.D.**

Observe that the weighted sum of the payoff functions in (4.18) takes the following form:

$$w_o(x) = \sum_{i=1}^{n} \lambda_i w_i(x)$$

$$= \lambda_o\left(\sum_{i=1}^{n} \frac{\lambda_i}{\lambda_o} \ln(\lambda_i) - \ln(\lambda_o) + \ln\left[x + \beta_o\right]\right) \sim \ln\left[x + \beta_o\right]$$

This can be viewed as a *partnership utility function* with respect to the aggregate outcome x, and the partners' choice of the optimal action maximizes the following partnership expected utility:

$$U_o(x,a) = \int_X w_o(x)\, d\Phi(x|a).$$

Observe that the weights $\lambda_1,\ldots,\lambda_n$ have no effect on the partnership's utility function – they only introduce irrelevant constants. The key factors affecting the partnership's action choice are the aggregate "risk tolerance" parameter β_o and the outcome distribution functions $\Phi(x|a)$ for each action. The weights will affect the distribution of the outcome among the partners, but not their efficient action choice.

The same results hold for the exponential and power utility functions, and Table 4.2 summarizes the partnership utility functions for each HARA type (omitting the irrelevant constants associated with the weights).[7]

exponential:	$w_o(x) \sim w_i(x) \sim -\exp\left[-\dfrac{x}{\rho_o}\right]$,	
logarithmic:	$w_o(x) \sim w_i(x) \sim \ln[x + \beta_o]$,	$x + \beta_o > 0$,
power:	$w_o(x) \sim w_i(x) \sim \dfrac{1}{\alpha - 1}[\alpha x + \beta_o]^{\frac{\alpha-1}{\alpha}}$,	$\alpha x + \beta_o \geq 0$.

Table 4.2: Partnership utility functions.

In the exponential utility function case, the partnership preferences depend only on the partners' aggregate risk tolerance, ρ_o. As in the logarithmic utility function case, the partnership preferences for the power utility function case depend on the "aggregate risk" tolerance parameter β_o, but also the partners' risk cautiousness α.

4.2.2 Information System Choice

We briefly consider information choice in a partnership.[8] In this analysis we assume that the action and information system choice are centrally determined. Information system η provides a signal $y \in Y$ to the partnership before the action is selected. Beliefs are homogeneous and the partners' prior beliefs about the signal are represented by $\Phi(y|\eta)$ and their posterior beliefs about x given y and a are denoted $\Phi(x|y,a,\eta)$. The information system affects the outcome, since some systems are more costly than others and, hence, η is an argument in $\Phi(x|y,a,\eta)$ both because of its associated costs and because the posterior belief about x given y depends on the system that generates the signal y. We could include the event θ, but for the reasons discussed above it is irrelevant.

The contractible information consists of x, y, a, and η. So that partner i's sharing rule is expressed as $\mathbf{c}_i$: $X \times Y \times A \times H \rightarrow C_i$. Partner i's expected utility given $\mathbf{c}_i$, y, a, and η is

[7] See Amershi and Stoeckenius (1983) and Amershi (1988) for further discussion of partnership (syndicate) preferences and utility functions.

[8] See Demski (1973) and Verrecchia (1978) for more detailed analysis based on the work of Wilson (1968).

$$U_i(\boldsymbol{c}_i,y,a,\eta) = \int_X u_i(\boldsymbol{c}_i(x,y,a,\eta))\, d\Phi(x|y,a,\eta),$$

and his *ex ante* expected utility given $\boldsymbol{c}_i$ and η, as well as decision rule $\boldsymbol{a}$: $Y \to A$, is

$$U_i(\boldsymbol{c}_i,\boldsymbol{a},\eta) = \int_Y U_i(\boldsymbol{c}_i,y,\boldsymbol{a}(y),\eta)\, d\Phi(y|\eta).$$

Using these expressions, we restate the optimal partnership contract problem as follows, where $\boldsymbol{A}$ is the set of all possible decision rules.

Optimal Partnership Contract Problem with Information System Choice:

$$\underset{\boldsymbol{c}\in\boldsymbol{C},\,\boldsymbol{a}\in\boldsymbol{A},\,\eta\in H}{\text{maximize}} \quad U_1(\boldsymbol{c}_1,\boldsymbol{a},\eta) \tag{4.19a}$$

$$\text{subject to} \quad U_i(\boldsymbol{c}_i,\boldsymbol{a},\eta) \geq \bar{U}_i, \quad \forall\, i = 2,\dots,n, \tag{4.19b}$$

$$\sum_{i=1}^{n} \boldsymbol{c}_i(x,y,a,\eta) \leq x, \quad \forall\, x \in X,\, y \in Y \tag{4.19c}$$

$$\boldsymbol{c}_i(x,y,a,\eta) \in C_i, \quad \forall\, x \in X,\, y \in Y,\, i = 1,\dots,n. \tag{4.19d}$$

Given that $\boldsymbol{a}$ and η are under the direct control of the first partner, we can treat the optimal choices $\boldsymbol{a}^*$ and η as implicit in $\boldsymbol{c}_i^*$. Hence, for our purposes we only need to consider how $\boldsymbol{c}_i^*$ varies with x and y. The Lagrangian for this problem is

$$\begin{aligned}\mathcal{L} = {} & U_1(\boldsymbol{c}_1,\boldsymbol{a},\eta) + \sum_{i=2}^{n} \lambda_i \left[U_i(\boldsymbol{c}_i,\boldsymbol{a},\eta) - \bar{U}_i\right] \\ & - \sum_{x\in X}\sum_{y\in Y} \mu(x,y)\left[\sum_{i=1}^{n} \boldsymbol{c}_i(x,y) - x\right] \\ & + \sum_{x\in X}\sum_{y\in Y}\sum_{i=1}^{n} \zeta_i(x,y)\left[\boldsymbol{c}_i(x,y) - \underline{c}_i\right].\end{aligned} \tag{4.20}$$

Differentiating the Lagrangian with respect to $c_i = \boldsymbol{c}_i(x,y)$ for a given outcome, signal and partner yields the following first-order condition:

$$\lambda_i\, u_i'(\boldsymbol{c}_i(x,y))\, \varphi(x|y,\boldsymbol{a}(y),\eta)\, \varphi(y|\eta) - \mu(x,y) + \zeta_i(x,y) = 0. \tag{4.21}$$

It is again obvious that the optimal contract will fully distribute all of the outcome, i.e.,

$$\sum_{i=1}^{n} \boldsymbol{c}_i(x,y) = x, \quad \forall\, x \in X, y \in Y, i = 1,...,n.$$

What is perhaps less obvious is that the partners' shares depend only on the outcome x, and are independent of the signal y.

Proposition 4.5

If beliefs are homogeneous and the partners are strictly risk averse, the optimal risk sharing contract for the problem with information system choice is independent of y, and there exist positive multipliers λ_i and $g(x)$ such that $\boldsymbol{c}_i^*(x)$ is characterized by

$$u_i'(\boldsymbol{c}_i^*(x)) = \frac{g(x)}{\lambda_i}, \quad \text{if } \boldsymbol{c}_i^*(x) > \underline{c}_i, \quad \forall\, i = 1, ..., n. \tag{4.22}$$

Proof: The argument that $\boldsymbol{c}_i^*$ is independent of y is essentially the same as the argument that it is independent of θ in Proposition 4.1. Any variations in $\boldsymbol{c}_i^*$ due to y for a given x represent unnecessary side-betting on y. Given homogeneous beliefs, eliminating those variations makes the strictly risk-averse partners better off (due to Jensen's inequality). Condition (4.22) then follows from (4.21), since the preceding argument and the assumption $\boldsymbol{c}_i^*(x) > \underline{c}_i$ imply

$$\mu(x,y) \div [\varphi(x|y,\boldsymbol{a}(y),\eta)\, \varphi(y|\eta)]$$

is a constant, which is the multiplier $g(x)$ in (4.22). **Q.E.D.**

In concluding this section we make the observation that if the partners have homogeneous beliefs and HARA utility functions with identical risk cautiousness (and efficient contracts are interior), there exists a partnership utility function $w_o(x)$ (see Table 4.2) such that $\boldsymbol{c}^*$ induces all partners to choose decision rule $\boldsymbol{a}^*$ and information system η^* so as to maximize:

$$U_o(\boldsymbol{a},\eta) = \int_Y \int_X w_o(x)\, d\Phi(x|y,\boldsymbol{a}(y),\eta)\, d\Phi(y|\eta).$$

Consequently, if the information systems are costless, the informativeness conditions discussed in Chapter 3 apply in a straightforward manner to partnerships for which there are congruent preferences.

4.3 DISTRIBUTED INFORMATION IN TEAMS

The work by Marschak and Radner (MR72), which is reported in their book *Theory of Teams* (1972), was very important in initiating and developing the general area of information economics. Most of their work was done in the early sixties, even though the book was not published until 1972. It was this work that led to the early work on information economics in accounting.

The initial chapters of MR72 review single person decision making under uncertainty. The later chapters examine the use of information in a multi-person setting called a team. A team consists of two or more members who have the *homogeneous prior beliefs* and *identical preferences* over a *common outcome.* The members of the team differ with respect to the set of actions they can take, the information they can observe, and the communication channels through which they can communicate information to (or receive from) other members of the team. The analysis identifies the optimal communication and decision rules for a given information/decision making structure, and examines the impact of changes in that structure.

MR72 exogenously assume that the team members have identical preferences over a common outcome. The analysis in this chapter identifies settings in which a partnership will act like a team even though their personal preferences depend only on their share of the aggregate outcome. Hence, we can interpret the MR72 analysis as one in which the team members have homogeneous beliefs, HARA utility functions with identical risk cautiousness with respect to their share of the aggregate outcome, and no direct preferences with respect to their actions.

The work on team theory has been largely dormant over the past twenty years. In the early seventies it was recognized that the personal preferences of decision makers in a multi-person setting is an extremely important ingredient in that decision context. Hence, most subsequent work has assumed that a decision maker's preferences are defined over his share of an organization's outcome and the actions they personally must take. And up until the mid eighties there was little consideration of organizations with multiple decision makers. Hence, issues of decentralized information acquisition, communication, and decision making have received only limited attention. In the later chapters in Volume II, we examine some principal/agent models with multiple decision makers. There may be scope for some interesting future research that returns to some of the central concerns of team theory, but which addresses these issues within a principal/agent framework.

APPENDIX 4A: Congruent Preferences with Exponential Utility and Heterogeneous Beliefs

Efficient partnership contracts with heterogeneous beliefs involve what is commonly termed side-betting. The characteristics of efficient side-betting are provided in section 4.1.3. We did not consider heterogeneous beliefs in the discussion of congruent preferences over actions and information in Section 4.2. In this appendix we briefly consider the congruency of preferences with heterogeneous beliefs in settings in which the partners have exponential utility functions.

Sufficient Conditions for Congruent Preferences

With homogeneous beliefs, HARA utility functions with identical risk cautiousness are sufficient to result in efficient contracts that yield congruent preferences (see Section 4.2). In general, that result does not hold when the partners' beliefs are heterogeneous. Here we need the stronger condition that all partners have zero risk cautiousness. We present the "sufficiency" component of Wilson's (1968) result. The precise nature of the necessity condition is somewhat complex and is not of sufficient general interest for us to explore it here. (See Amershi and Stoeckenius, 1983, for further discussion.)

Proposition 4A.1 (Wilson 1968, Theorem 11)

If the partners' beliefs are heterogeneous and their preferences are represented by HARA utility functions with *zero risk cautiousness*, then the Pareto efficient contract for action a^* induces congruent preferences with respect to a^*.

Proof: Partner i's beliefs and preferences are represented by $\varphi_i(\theta)$ and $u_i(c_i) = -\exp[-c_i/\rho_i]$. Assuming $\underline{c}_i = -\infty$, first-order condition (4.14) implies

$$u_i'(\mathbf{c}_i(x,\theta)) = \frac{1}{\rho_i}\exp\left[-\frac{\mathbf{c}_i(x,\theta)}{\rho_i}\right] = \frac{\mu(\theta)}{\lambda_i\,\varphi_i(\theta)}. \tag{4A.1}$$

Solving for $\mathbf{c}_i(x,\theta)$ yields

$$\mathbf{c}_i(x,\theta) = -\rho_i \ln(\mu(\theta)) - \rho_i \ln\left[\frac{\rho_i}{\lambda_i\,\varphi_i(\theta)}\right]. \tag{4A.2}$$

Summing over all partners, setting the sum of the left-hand-side equal to x, and solving for $\ln(\mu(\theta))$ yields

$$\ln(\mu(\theta)) = -\frac{1}{\rho_o}\left(x + \sum_{i=1}^{n} \rho_i \ln\left[\frac{\rho_i}{\lambda_i \varphi_i(\theta)}\right]\right). \qquad (4A.3)$$

Substituting (4A.3) into (4A.2) yields

$$\mathbf{c}_i^*(x,\theta) = v_i x + f_i(\theta),$$

where $$v_i = \frac{\rho_i}{\rho_o}, \quad f_i(\theta) = \rho_i\left(f_o(\theta) - \ln\left[\frac{\rho_i}{\lambda_i \varphi_i(\theta)}\right]\right),$$

and $$f_o(\theta) = \sum_{j=1}^{n} \frac{\rho_j}{\rho_o} \ln\left[\frac{\rho_j}{\lambda_j \varphi_j(\theta)}\right].$$

Hence, $$U_i(\mathbf{c}_i^*,a) = -\frac{\rho_i}{\lambda_i} \sum_{\theta\in\Theta} \exp\left[-\frac{x(\theta,a)}{\rho_o}\right] \exp[-f_o(\theta)]. \qquad (4A.4)$$

Observe that partner i's expected utility given the optimal contract and action a is the same as partner j's expected utility except for the initial constants, ρ_i/λ_i versus ρ_j/λ_j, which will not affect their action choices. **Q.E.D.**

Observe that with exponential utility, the optimal contract is again, in some sense, linear with respect to x. The important feature for congruency of action preferences is that the variable rate $v_i = \rho_i/\rho_o$ is independent of the state. The fixed component, $f_i(\theta)$, depends on the state, but this does not affect action preferences because with exponential utility there is no wealth effect. Of course, it is important that Θ is an outcome-adequate partition of S and the *ex post* observation of θ is contractible information. As a result all side-betting can be expressed in terms of θ, independent of x (which depends on both θ and a).

Homogeneous Information Beliefs

Now consider the acquisition of information when the partners have heterogeneous beliefs about θ. With homogeneous beliefs we found that the optimal contract is a function of only x even though θ and y are also contractible information. From the analysis in Section 4.1.3, with heterogeneous beliefs we expect the optimal contract to be a function of at least x and θ. The question is whether heterogeneous beliefs can also make it optimal to contract on the signal y. The answer is *yes*!

Interestingly, with heterogeneous beliefs, an information system η can have positive value (in the sense that there is a Pareto preferred contract with the system versus without) even if the signals from η are completely uninformative about the outcome from alternative actions. The key here is that, with heterogeneous beliefs about events which are not fully revealed by θ, a signal y can provide the basis for "beneficial" side-betting. For example, assume Y = {heads, tails}, which is the result of the flip of a biased coin. If there is no information (i.e., no flipping of the coin), the two "partners" will equally share a certain outcome of $x = 40$. They have square-root utility functions, $u_i(c_i) = c_i^{1/2}$ and have no action alternatives. If they had homogeneous beliefs about the coin, e.g., both believe φ(heads) = .7, they would attach no value to flipping the coin since at least one partner would be made worse-off by any feasible change in the contract in which $\boldsymbol{c}_1$ and $\boldsymbol{c}_2$ vary with y. However, if φ_1(heads) = .7 and φ_2(heads) = .6, the following contract will be preferred by both partners: $\boldsymbol{c}_1$(heads) = 40 - $\boldsymbol{c}_2$(heads) = 23.059 and $\boldsymbol{c}_1$(tails) = 40 - $\boldsymbol{c}_2$(tails) = 14.4. This is the efficient contract in which $\lambda_1 = \lambda_2$, and it is characterized by

$$[\boldsymbol{c}_1(\text{heads})/\boldsymbol{c}_2(\text{heads})]^{1/2} = .7/.6$$

and

$$[\boldsymbol{c}_1(\text{tails})/\boldsymbol{c}_2(\text{tails})]^{1/2} = .3/.4.$$

While horse-races (and the like) may provide the efficient side-betting based on heterogeneous beliefs, that does not seem to us to be an attractive role for accounting reports. Hence, even if we choose to admit heterogeneous beliefs about events affecting outcomes, we prefer to limit our analysis to settings in which there are homogeneous information beliefs.[9]

Definition *Homogeneous Information Beliefs*

Partners have *homogeneous information beliefs* (HIB) if the likelihood function $\varphi(y|\theta,\eta)$ is the same for all partners. In that case, if Θ and Y are finite, the information structure is represented by the $|\Theta|\times|Y|$ Markov matrix:

$$\boldsymbol{\eta} = [\ \varphi(y|\theta,\eta)\ ].$$

Observe that HIB does not imply that the marginal probability $\varphi_i(y|\eta)$ is homogeneous, unless we also assume the beliefs about θ are homogeneous.

With HIB there is no gambling on the signal, even though the partners may have heterogeneous beliefs about the signal. The key is that all efficient side-betting can be conditioned on θ. We state the following result without proof since it is a relatively straightforward combination of the arguments used above.

---

[9] Hakansson, Kunkel, and Ohlson (1982) introduce this concept in their exploration of efficient risk sharing in a market setting. We comment on their results in Chapter 7.

Proposition 4A.2

If partners have heterogeneous event beliefs but homogeneous information beliefs, then any Pareto efficient contract is independent of y and there exist positive multipliers λ_i and $\mu(x,\theta)$ such that

$$u_i'(\mathbf{c}_i(x,\theta)) = \frac{\mu(x,\theta)}{\lambda_i\,\varphi_i(\theta)}.$$

Recall that the informativeness conditions considered in Chapter 3 were independent of the prior beliefs. Hence, if all partners have exponential utility functions and homogeneous information beliefs, it follows that an efficient contract will induce congruent information system choices and system η^2 is weakly preferred to η^1 if η^2 is at least as informative as and no more costly than η^1, even if the partners have heterogeneous event beliefs.

REFERENCES

Amershi, A. H. (1988) "Blackwell Informativeness and Sufficient Statistics with Applications to Financial Markets and Multiperson Agencies," *Economic Analysis of Information and Contracts*, edited by G. A. Feltham, A. H. Amershi, and W. T. Ziemba. Boston: Kluwer Publishers.

Amershi, A. H., and J. H. W. Stoeckenius. (1983) "The Theory of Syndicates and Linear Sharing Rules," *Econometrica* 51, 1407-1416.

Borch, K. (1962) "Equilibrium in a Reinsurance Market," *Econometrica* 30, 424-444.

Demski, J. S. (1973) "Rational Choice of Accounting Method for a Class of Partnerships," *Journal of Accounting Research* 11, 176-190.

Hakansson, N. H., J. G. Kunkel, and J. A. Ohlson. (1982) "Sufficient and Necessary Conditions for Information to Have Social Value in Pure Exchange," *Journal of Finance* 37, 1169-1181.

Kobayashi, T. (1980) "Equilibrium Contracts for Syndicates with Differential Information," *Econometrica* 48, 1635-1665.

Marschak, J., and R. Radner. (1972) *Theory of Teams*. New Haven: Yale University Press.

Raiffa, H. (1970) "Risk Sharing and Group Decisions," *Decision Analysis*, Chapter 8. Addison-Wesley.

Rosing, J. (1970) "The Formation of Groups for Cooperative Decision Making Under Uncertainty," *Econometrica* 38, 430-448.

Verrecchia, R. (1978) "On the Choice of Accounting Method for Partnerships," *Journal of Accounting Research* 16, 150-168.

Wilson, R. (1968) "The Theory of Syndicates," *Econometrica* 36, 119-132.

PART B

PUBLIC INFORMATION IN EQUITY MARKETS

CHAPTER 5

ARBITRAGE AND RISK SHARING IN SINGLE-PERIOD MARKETS

In Chapter 4 we consider the use of a sharing rule (i.e., a contract) to efficiently share a partnership's aggregate uncertain outcome among its members. We now consider risk sharing and market prices in a competitive financial market in which investors share the economy's risky aggregate outcome by means of trading in securities, with investors taking the market prices as given.

There are three key differences between the partnership and market settings. First, in the partnership setting, there is a single firm and the partners have no other random sources of consumption. In the market setting, there are multiple firms and a partner may have other random sources of consumption (e.g., compensation for labor). Second, the form of the partnership contract is unrestricted, whereas, in the market setting, there is no direct contracting and the risk sharing possibilities are constrained by the available set of marketed securities (e.g., equity in the firms). Third, the "weights" used in determining the size of each partner's share of the partnership outcome are exogenous, whereas, in the market settings, the investors' "weights" are endogenously determined and depend on their exogenously endowed ownership of marketed securities and non-tradeable claims to consumption.

The market is assumed to be competitive, so that investors take the market prices of securities as given, and choose their portfolio of securities to maximize their expected utility subject to their budget constraints (i.e., *individual optimality*). A necessary condition for optimal portfolios to exist is that there are no arbitrage opportunities, i.e., it is not possible to "get something for nothing." The security prices are determined such that demand equals supply for each security (i.e., *market clearing*). In the market setting, the investors need not trade. Hence, each investor's share of the risky aggregate outcome after trading must give him at least as high an expected utility as the expected utility of his endowed position (i.e., *individual rationality*). If there are production choices, efficient production choices maximize the market value of the firm's current and future dividends (to all its claimants).

This chapter begins Part B (Chapters 5 through 10) by providing some basic insights obtained from examining a single-period, pure-exchange setting. In particular, there is a single trading date (at the start of the period) and a single consumption date (at the end of the period), and the event-contingent dividends of the marketed securities are exogenous. The single-period setting is extended to a setting with multiple consumption and trading dates in Chapter 6. This setting provides the basis for the examination in Chapter 7 of the impact of public information (e.g., published accounting reports) in a pure-exchange setting.

In the pure-exchange settings, production and dividend decisions are fixed, so that the event-contingent dividends from marketed securities are exogenous. Chapter 8 extends the analysis to settings in which production/dividend decisions are endogenous.

Chapters 9 and 10 consider the relation between accounting information and market values of firms in the setting of Chapters 6 and 7. This analysis draws heavily on the no-arbitrage value relations established in Chapter 6, and it adds assumptions on the accounting and the representations of the investors' information dynamics.

5.1 MARKET VALUE IMPLICATIONS OF NO ARBITRAGE

An arbitrage opportunity exists if an investor can get a "free lunch," e.g., he can make a trade that requires no investment and is guaranteed to provide a non-negative return with a positive probability of a positive return. The assumption that there are no arbitrage opportunities is a minimal requirement for a rational market. Section 5.1.1 specifies some basic elements of the single-period models considered in this chapter, and then Section 5.1.2 examines the price implications of the no-arbitrage requirement. These implications do not require specification of the investors' beliefs or preferences (beyond non-satiation).

5.1.1 Basic Elements of the Single-period Models

There are I investors, and uncertainty is represented by their probability spaces $\{ S, \Xi, P_i \}$, $i = 1, ..., I$. To simplify the discussion, we generally assume that the set of states S is finite so that the probabilizable events can be represented as finite partitions of S. The set of states and the probabilizable events are common to all investors, but the investors can have personal subjective probability measures P_i, $i = 1, ..., I$. However, we assume that all probability measures attach zero probabilities to the same events.[1] In this chapter we assume that all information is public, i.e., all investors have the same information system.

[1] We make this assumption to avoid "infinite side-betting" by investors.

Initially, we consider a single-period (two date) setting in which investors receive no information prior to trading at the start of the period ($t = 0$). However, they receive information at the end of the period ($t = 1$), represented by the information system $\eta: S \to Y$. The set of signals Y partitions the set of states into M possible events $y \in \{ y_1, ..., y_M \}$, and the investors' subjective beliefs about these events are represented by strictly positive probability functions $\varphi_i(y_m) > 0$, $i = 1, ..., I$, $m = 1, ..., M$.

There is a finite set of securities $j = 1,..., J$. The securities' dividends (or payoffs) are, of course, observable at $t = 1$, and, thus, measurable with respect to the partition Y, i.e., we can write security j's dividend as a function of the event y, $d_j(y) \in \mathbb{R}$. We represent security j as the vector of dividends in the M possible events, i.e., $\mathbf{d}_j = \{ d_j(y_m) \}_{m=1,...,M}$, and the event-contingent dividends of all securities are represented by the $J \times M$ matrix $\mathbf{D}$. The price of security j at $t = 0$ is denoted v_j and the prices of all securities are represented by the $J \times 1$ vector $\mathbf{v}$.

At the initial date $t = 0$, investors choose a portfolio $\mathbf{z} \in \mathbb{R}^J$ where z_j is the number of units of security j acquired, i.e., the portfolio has market value $\mathbf{v}^t\mathbf{z}$ at $t = 0$ and yields the $M \times 1$ event-contingent dividend vector $\mathbf{D}^t\mathbf{z}$ at $t = 1$.

In the first three sections of this chapter we review the theory of asset pricing under three increasingly restrictive assumptions: *no arbitrage*, *single-agent optimality*, and *market equilibrium*.[2]

5.1.2 No Arbitrage in Single-period Markets

The no-arbitrage assumption is a basic requirement for security prices. It states that the security prices must be such that it is not possible to "get something for nothing."

Definition *Arbitrage*

An arbitrage is a portfolio $\mathbf{z} \in \mathbb{R}^J$ with $\mathbf{v}^t\mathbf{z} \le 0$ and $\mathbf{D}^t\mathbf{z} > \mathbf{0}$, i.e., a portfolio with non-positive market value, non-negative dividends in all events, and a strictly positive dividend in at least one event, or $\mathbf{v}^t\mathbf{z} < 0$ and $\mathbf{D}^t\mathbf{z} \ge \mathbf{0}$, i.e., a portfolio with strictly negative market value and non-negative dividends in all events.[3]

---

[2] The approach is similar to that found in Duffie (1996).

[3] We use the following conventions. If $\mathbf{x}$ is a vector in $\mathbb{R}^N$, then $\mathbf{x} \ge \mathbf{0}$ means that each coordinate is non-negative or, equivalently, $\mathbf{x} \in \mathbb{R}^N_+$. On the other hand, $\mathbf{x} > \mathbf{0}$ means that each coordinate is non-negative but the vector is not the "null" vector. If all coordinates are strictly positive, we write $\mathbf{x} \gg \mathbf{0}$ or, equivalently, $\mathbf{x} \in \mathbb{R}^N_{++}$.

An arbitrage is a portfolio giving the investor something positive at $t = 1$ or $t = 0$ for nothing. A basic requirement for an equilibrium in a competitive market is that no such portfolio exists if investors prefer more dividend to less. Otherwise, investors would find it optimal to change their portfolios. The absence of arbitrage opportunities implies that security prices can be characterized as a linear function of their event-contingent dividends by applying a strictly positive $M\times 1$ vector of *event-prices* **p**.

Proposition 5.1[4]

There is no arbitrage if, and only if, there is an event-price vector $\mathbf{p} \in \mathbb{R}^M_{++}$, i.e., $p(y_m) > 0, \forall\, m = 1, ..., M$, i.e.,

$$\mathbf{v} = \mathbf{D}\mathbf{p}. \tag{5.1}$$

Note that no arbitrage implies that the price of security j can be written as a sum of its event-contingent dividends times the event-prices, i.e.,

$$v_j = \sum_{m=1}^{M} d_j(y_m)\, p(y_m), \quad j = 1, 2, ..., J. \tag{5.2}$$

The event-price for event y_m can therefore be interpreted as the implicit price at $t = 0$ of acquiring a claim to an additional unit of account (i.e., return or dividend) at $t = 1$ if event y_m occurs.

Complete Securities Market

The no-arbitrage condition *does not* imply that the event-prices are unique. This will only be the case if the securities market is *complete*, that is, there are as many linearly independent dividend vectors as there are events.

---

[4] The proof is a straightforward application of the following lemma (let $\mathbf{A} = \{\ \mathbf{D}, -\mathbf{v}\ \}$).

> **Stiemke's Lemma:** Suppose **A** is an $n\times m$ matrix. Then one and only one of the following is true:
>
> (a) There exists $\mathbf{x} \in \mathbb{R}^m_{++}$ with $\mathbf{A}\mathbf{x} = \mathbf{0}$.
>
> (b) There exists $\mathbf{y} \in \mathbb{R}^n$ with $\mathbf{y}'\mathbf{A} > \mathbf{0}$.

Definition *Complete Securities Market*

The securities market is said to be complete if the dividend matrix **D** has rank M, i.e., span $(\mathbf{D}^t) = \mathbb{R}^M$.[5]

If the securities market is complete, the $M \times M$ matrix $\mathbf{D}^t\mathbf{D}$ is invertible. It then follows from (5.1) that the event-prices are uniquely determined.

Corollary

If the securities market is complete, the event-prices are uniquely determined by

$$\mathbf{p} = (\mathbf{D}^t\mathbf{D})^{-1}\mathbf{D}^t\mathbf{v}. \tag{5.3}$$

To illustrate the previous analysis, consider a simple setting with three events. Initially, suppose the marketed securities consist of a stock and a call option on the stock with exercise price 80. The stock is trading at the price $v_1^s = 95$, and its dividend in the three events are $\mathbf{d}_1^s = (80, 100, 125)$. The option has dividends $d_2^{80} = \max\{0, d_1^s - 80\}$, i.e., $\mathbf{d}_2^{80} = (0, 20, 45)$, and suppose it is trading at the price 23. Consequently, the market price vector and the dividend matrix are

$$\mathbf{v} = \begin{bmatrix} 95 \\ 23 \end{bmatrix}, \quad \mathbf{D} = \begin{bmatrix} 80 & 100 & 125 \\ 0 & 20 & 45 \end{bmatrix}.$$

Of course, this securities market is not complete (since the rank of **D** equals two, which is less than the three possible events), but there exist event-price vectors **p** that solves the two-equation, three-unknown problem (5.1), i.e., $\mathbf{v} = \mathbf{D}\mathbf{p}$. For example, $\mathbf{p} = (.25, .25, .40)^t$ is a solution, and so is $\mathbf{p} = (.125, .475, .300)^t$.[6] Even though we cannot determine the event-prices uniquely, we can, for example, determine the riskless interest rate uniquely. Note that the riskless asset with dividend vector $\mathbf{d}_f = (1, 1, 1)$ can be implicitly created as a portfolio of the two marketed securities, i.e.,

$$\mathbf{d}_f = (1/80)\,(\mathbf{d}_1^s - \mathbf{d}_2^{80}), \qquad \mathbf{z}_f = (1/80, -1/80)^t.$$

No arbitrage implies that the price of the riskless asset must be $v_f = (95 - 23)/80 = 9/10$. Hence, the riskless interest rate is $\imath = 10/9 - 1 = 1/9$. This illustrates the

---

[5] Span $(\mathbf{D}^t)$ denotes the set of all vectors in $\mathbb{R}^M$ that can be obtained as linear combinations of the J columns of $\mathbf{D}^t$.

[6] These event-prices are members of a one-dimensional linear subspace in $\mathbb{R}^3$ that solves $\mathbf{v} = \mathbf{D}\mathbf{p}$.

general point that even though the securities market may not be complete, the no-arbitrage assumption implies that we can uniquely "price" securities with dividend vectors in the span of the dividend matrix $\mathbf{D}^t$ for the marketed securities.

Suppose that we expand the set of marketed securities with an additional option on the stock with exercise price 100, and that it is trading at 10. Hence, the market price vector and the dividend matrix now become

$$\mathbf{v} = \begin{bmatrix} 95 \\ 23 \\ 10 \end{bmatrix}, \quad \mathbf{D} = \begin{bmatrix} 80 & 100 & 125 \\ 0 & 20 & 45 \\ 0 & 0 & 25 \end{bmatrix}.$$

The expanded securities market is complete, and it is a particularly simple task to solve for the unique event-prices in this example (given the upper-triangular structure of the dividend matrix), i.e.,[7]

$$\mathbf{v} = \mathbf{Dp} \quad \Leftrightarrow \quad \mathbf{p} = (.25, .25, .40)^t.$$

Note that (5.3) can be used to determine the event-prices if there are more securities than states, e.g., the securities include the riskless asset as well as the stock and the two options. However, it is not necessary to use all four securities and, as demonstrated above, we can follow the (simpler) approach of determining the event-prices from the stock and the two options (a subset of securities that constitute a complete market). No arbitrage implies that the price of the riskless asset must be consistent with those event-prices.

Since there are as many linearly independent dividend vectors as there are events in a complete securities market, any $1 \times M$ dividend vector $\mathbf{d}$ can be obtained as a portfolio $\mathbf{z}$ of marketed securities (even though the portfolio may not be unique if $J > M$), i.e., there exists a portfolio $\mathbf{z}$ such that $\mathbf{d}^t = \mathbf{D}^t\mathbf{z}$. It follows from (5.1) that the *unique* price of any such portfolio is

$$\mathbf{v}^t\mathbf{z} = (\mathbf{Dp})^t\mathbf{z} = \mathbf{p}^t\mathbf{D}^t\mathbf{z} = \mathbf{p}^t\mathbf{d}^t, \tag{5.4}$$

i.e., although the portfolio may not be unique, its price is.

In particular, consider an implicit *event-security* that pays one unit of account if, and only if, event y occurs, i.e., the dividend vector $\mathbf{d}_y$ is given by,

---

[7] Find the event-price for y_3 from the option with exercise price 100 (i.e., $p(y_3) = 10/25 = .4$), and substitute that event-price into the price relation for the option with exercise price 80 to find the event-price for y_2 and so on.

$$d_y(y') = \begin{cases} 1 & \text{if } y' = y, \\ 0 & \text{otherwise.} \end{cases}$$

This security is also commonly referred to as the *Arrow/Debreu security* for event y. The unique price of the event-security for event y is, by (5.4), precisely the unique event-price for event y.

Note also that any marketed security j can be viewed as a portfolio of M event-securities with portfolio weights $z_m = d_j(y_m)$, and the price of that portfolio is given by (5.2).

5.1.3 Alternative Representations of No-arbitrage Prices

The preceding analysis establishes that event-contingent prices can be used to characterize prices that satisfy the no-arbitrage condition. We now consider two other equivalent representations. The first uses what are called risk-neutral probabilities, whereas the second uses the covariance of dividends with a valuation index.

Risk-neutral Probabilities

The event-prices are strictly positive and, hence, if we normalize the event-prices by the sum of the event-prices, i.e.,

$$\hat{\varphi}(y_m) \equiv \frac{p(y_m)}{\beta}, \quad \beta \equiv \sum_{m=1}^{M} p(y_m), \tag{5.5}$$

then the normalized event-prices $\hat{\varphi}(y_m)$ satisfy the properties of a probability function over the set of events. That is, since the event-prices are all strictly positive, the normalized event-prices are strictly positive ($\hat{\varphi}(y_m) > 0$) for all events, and dividing by β implies that they sum to one. Note that β is the price of a security paying one unit of account in each event, i.e., a riskless security which we will generally assume to be one of the marketed securities. Hence, the riskless return (i.e., one plus the riskless interest rate) is $R = \beta^{-1}$ or, equivalently, β is the riskless discount factor, i.e., $\beta = R^{-1}$. Therefore, if there is no arbitrage, we can write the price of any security j as the discounted value of its expected dividend using the normalized event-prices as probabilities, i.e.,

$$v_j = \beta\, \hat{\mathrm{E}}[d_j] = \beta \sum_{m=1}^{M} d_j(y_m)\hat{\varphi}(y_m). \tag{5.6}$$

The normalized event-prices are often referred to as "*the risk-neutral probabilities,*" since the pricing of securities is *as if* investors are risk neutral with beliefs given by these probabilities. Note that no investor may actually hold these beliefs – their existence is a direct consequence of no arbitrage. Another important property of the risk-neutral probabilities is that they are *not* subjective probabilities even though investors may have heterogeneous subjective beliefs – they are determined by the market prices of securities and their event-contingent dividends. The investors' beliefs and risk preferences are embedded in the market prices of securities and, thus, in the event-prices. The normalized event-prices are therefore also commonly referred to as "*risk-adjusted probabilities.*"

Valuation Index

The preceding analysis establishes that, if there is no arbitrage, the price of any marketed security is a linear function of its event-contingent dividends. Based on this result, the following mathematical result is useful to obtain yet another representation of security prices when there is no arbitrage.

This representation can be based on any strictly positive probability vector $\boldsymbol{\varphi} \in \mathbb{R}^M_{++}$ of interest (e.g., the beliefs of a "representative" investor), and the following lemma.

Lemma *Riesz Representation Theorem*

Suppose the function F: $\mathbb{R}^M \rightarrow \mathbb{R}$ is linear, e.g., $F(\mathbf{x}) = \mathbf{p}^t\mathbf{x}$ for some vector $\mathbf{p} \in \mathbb{R}^M$, and let $\boldsymbol{\varphi} \in \mathbb{R}^M_{++}$ be a strictly positive probability vector. Then there is a unique vector $\boldsymbol{\pi} \in \mathbb{R}^M$ such that for all $\mathbf{x} \in \mathbb{R}^M$ we have[8]

$$F(\mathbf{x}) = \sum_{m=1}^{M} \pi_m x_m \varphi_m = \mathrm{E}[\, \pi\, x \,].$$

Moreover, F is strictly increasing if, and only if, $\boldsymbol{\pi}$ is strictly positive, i.e., $\boldsymbol{\pi} \in \mathbb{R}^M_{++}$.

Using Proposition 5.1, the following is an immediate corollary to this lemma.

Corollary

There is no arbitrage with prices $\mathbf{v}$ and dividends $\mathbf{D}$ if, and only if, there exists some $\boldsymbol{\pi} \gg \mathbf{0}$ such that

$$v_j = \mathrm{E}[\, \pi\, d_j \,], \quad j = 1, ..., J,$$

for any fixed strictly positive probability vector $\boldsymbol{\varphi} \gg \mathbf{0}$.

---

[8] Here linear means that there are constants a_m such that $F(\mathbf{x}) = a_1x_1 + ... + a_Mx_M$, i.e., there is no "intercept" term. Hence, $\pi_m = a_m/\varphi_m$, $m = 1, ..., M$.

The vector $\boldsymbol{\pi}$ is commonly referred to as an *event-price deflator* for (**v**,**D**) and is given by

$$\pi(y_m) = p(y_m)/\varphi(y_m), \quad m = 1, ..., M.$$

That is, an event-price deflator is the vector of event-prices adjusted for the probabilities of the events for some given strictly positive probability distribution. If we normalize the event-price deflator by the riskless discount factor,

$$\begin{aligned} q(y_m) &\equiv \pi(y_m)/\beta \\ &= p(y_m)/\beta\varphi(y_m) \\ &= \frac{\hat{\varphi}(y_m)}{\varphi(y_m)}, \quad m = 1, ..., M, \end{aligned}$$

then both the "probability" and "time-value" effects are removed from the event-prices. Hence, as we see later, in an equilibrium setting with homogeneous beliefs, the normalized event-price deflator measures the "scarcity" of consumption in the different events as measured by the investors' marginal utility of consumption. We refer to the normalized event-price deflator q as the *valuation index*.[9]

Note that the expected value of the valuation index is equal to one, i.e.,

$$\mathrm{E}[\, q \,] = \sum_{m=1}^{M} \frac{\hat{\varphi}(y_m)}{\varphi(y_m)} \varphi(y_m) = 1.$$

Hence, using the valuation index, we can write the price of any security as

$$\begin{aligned} v_j &= \beta\, \mathrm{E}[\, q\, d_j \,] \\ &= \beta \left\{ \mathrm{E}[\, q \,]\, \mathrm{E}[\, d_j \,] + \mathrm{Cov}[\, q, d_j \,] \right\} \\ &= \beta \left\{ \mathrm{E}[\, d_j \,] + \mathrm{Cov}[\, q, d_j \,] \right\}, \quad j = 1, ..., J. \end{aligned} \tag{5.7}$$

---

[9] In the more technical (finance) literature, the valuation index is also referred to as the *Radon-Nikodym* derivative of the "risk-neutralized" probability distribution $\hat{\Phi}$ with respect to the "original" probability distribution Φ since it describes the transformation between the two distributions.

That is, we can view the securities as being priced as their discounted risk-adjusted dividends, where the risk adjustment is the covariance between the dividends of the security and the valuation index. As we see later, the valuation index is typically decreasing in the economy's aggregate dividend, so that if a firm's dividend is positively correlated with the economy's aggregate dividend, then the covariance term is negative. That is, the market value is less than the discounted expected dividend, reflecting the firm's market risk premium.

Note that, as with the event-prices, and the risk-neutral probabilities, the valuation index is not unique, in general. Even with complete markets, the valuation index is only unique up to the choice of any strictly positive probability vector $\boldsymbol{\varphi}$. Of course, if investors have homogeneous beliefs, the natural choice of $\boldsymbol{\varphi}$ is to take it to be the investors' probability function.

5.2 OPTIMAL PORTFOLIO CHOICE

Investors are characterized by their event-contingent, strictly positive endowments $\mathbf{e}_i \in \mathbb{R}^M_{++}$ of units of consumption at $t = 1$, their event beliefs $\varphi_i(y_m)$, and a strictly increasing and strictly concave utility function defined on their non-negative consumption at $t = 1$, i.e., u_i: $\mathbb{R}_+ \to \mathbb{R}$, $u_i' > 0$, and $u_i'' < 0$. Endowments may consist of the dividend on an endowed portfolio, $\bar{\mathbf{z}}_i$, and consumption endowments from other sources, $\bar{\mathbf{c}}_i$, such as compensation contracts and non-marketed assets, i.e.,

$$\mathbf{e}_i = \mathbf{D}^t\bar{\mathbf{z}}_i + \bar{\mathbf{c}}_i.$$

An investor can make transfers of consumption $\boldsymbol{\delta}_i$ between the different events by acquiring a portfolio $\mathbf{z}_i$, i.e., $\boldsymbol{\delta}_i = \mathbf{D}^t\mathbf{z}_i$, such that he gets event-contingent consumption $\mathbf{c}_i = \boldsymbol{\delta}_i + \mathbf{e}_i$. Since he has no wealth at $t = 0$, he must effectively sell securities to buy securities and the price of any such portfolio must be non-positive, i.e., $\mathbf{v}^t\mathbf{z}_i \le 0$. Hence, the investor i's feasible consumption set given his endowment and his budget constraint at $t = 0$ is

$$C_i(\mathbf{e}_i,\mathbf{v},\mathbf{D}) \equiv \left\{\mathbf{c}_i \mid \mathbf{c}_i = \mathbf{D}^t\mathbf{z}_i + \mathbf{e}_i \in \mathbb{R}^M_+ \text{ where } \mathbf{v}^t\mathbf{z}_i \le 0\right\},$$

and investor i's decision problem can be formulated as follows.

***Investor i's optimal portfolio choice problem*:**

$$\underset{\mathbf{c}_i \in C_i(\mathbf{e}_i,\mathbf{v},\mathbf{D})}{\text{maximize}}\; U_i(\mathbf{c}_i) = \underset{\mathbf{z}_i \in \{\mathbf{z} \in \mathbb{R}^J \mid \mathbf{D}^t\mathbf{z} + \mathbf{e}_i \in \mathbb{R}^M_+,\, \mathbf{v}^t\mathbf{z} \le 0\}}{\text{maximize}}\; U_i(\mathbf{D}^t\mathbf{z}_i + \mathbf{e}_i),$$

where $U_i(\mathbf{c}_i)$ is the investor's expected utility, i.e.,

$$U_i(\mathbf{c}_i) = \sum_{m=1}^{M} u_i(c_i(y_m))\varphi_i(y_m).$$

Clearly, this decision problem only has a solution if there is no arbitrage. Otherwise, the investor would engage in infinite arbitrage (since he has a strictly increasing utility function). Moreover, if there exists a portfolio with non-negative dividends in all events and strictly positive dividends in at least one event, the $t = 0$ budget constraint will be binding, i.e., $\mathbf{v}^t\mathbf{z}_i = 0$.

The Lagrangian for investor i's optimal portfolio choice problem is

$$\mathcal{L}_i = \sum_{m=1}^{M}\Big[u_i\Big(e_i(y_m) + \sum_{j=1}^{J} z_{ij}d_j(y_m)\Big)\varphi_i(y_m)$$
$$+ \zeta_i(y_m)\Big(e_i(y_m) + \sum_{j=1}^{J} z_{ij}d_j(y_m)\Big)\Big] - \lambda_i \sum_{j=1}^{J} z_{ij}v_j,$$

where $\zeta_i(y_m)$ is the multiplier on the non-negativity constraint on consumption in event y_m and λ_i is the multiplier on the $t = 0$ budget constraint. The first-order condition for an optimal investment in security j is

$$v_j = \sum_{m=1}^{M} \frac{u_i'(c_i(y_m))\,\varphi_i(y_m) + \zeta_i(y_m)}{\lambda_i} d_j(y_m), \quad j = 1, 2, ..., J. \tag{5.8}$$

Note that $\zeta_i(y_m) = 0$, if $c_i(y_m) > 0$. Hence, if the investor's optimal portfolio is such that his consumption is strictly positive, i.e., $\mathbf{c}_i \in \mathbb{R}^M_{++}$, then the normalized expected utility gradient is an event-price vector. i.e.,

$$\mathbf{v} = \mathbf{D}(\nabla \mathbf{U}_i/\lambda_i)$$

where

$$\nabla \mathbf{U}_i/\lambda_i \equiv \left\{\frac{u_i'(c_i(y_m))\,\varphi_i(y_m)}{\lambda_i}\right\}_{m = 1,...,M.}$$

If, furthermore, there is a riskless security paying one unit of account in each event, then (5.8) implies

$$\beta = \mathrm{E}_i[\, u_i'(c_i)/\lambda_i \,],$$

and we may write the price of any marketed security as

$$v_j = \beta \sum_{m=1}^{M} \frac{u_i'(c_i(y_m))\,\varphi_i(y_m)}{\mathrm{E}_i[\,u_i'(c_i)\,]} d_j(y_m), \quad j = 1, 2, ..., J.$$

Therefore, we can define risk-neutral probabilities for investor i such that

$$v_j = \beta\, \hat{\mathrm{E}}_i[d_j], \quad j = 1, 2, ..., J,$$

where the expectation is taken with respect to the probabilities

$$\hat{\varphi}_i(y_m) \equiv \frac{u_i'(c_i(y_m))\,\varphi_i(y_m)}{\mathrm{E}_i[\,u_i'(c_i)\,]}, \quad m = 1, 2, ..., M.$$

In general, these risk-neutral probabilities may vary across investors. However, for any investor they constitute a set of normalized event-prices. Furthermore, note that it follows from the Corollary to Proposition 5.1, that if the securities market is complete, then the risk-neutral probabilities must be the same for all investors even though they may have heterogeneous subjective beliefs.

5.3 MARKET EQUILIBRIUM AND EFFICIENT RISK SHARING

In the analysis above, each investor takes the security prices as given. However, in equilibrium, those prices must induce investors to have a zero net demand for marketed securities. Hence, the equilibrium prices (and the resulting investor portfolio choices) depend on the fundamentals of the economy, i.e., endowments, preferences, and beliefs. More specifically, an equilibrium in the securities market is a collection of investor portfolio choices and security prices, $\mathscr{E} \equiv \{\, \mathbf{z}_1, ..., \mathbf{z}_I; v_1, ..., v_J \,\}$, such that, given the security prices, the investors' portfolio choices are individually optimal, and such that the securities market "clear." That is, an equilibrium can be characterized as satisfying the following two sets of conditions:

Individual Optimality: $\mathbf{z}_i \in \underset{\{\mathbf{z} \in \mathbb{R}^J \,|\, \mathbf{D}^t\mathbf{z} + \mathbf{e}_i \in \mathbb{R}_+^M,\, \mathbf{v}^t\mathbf{z} \le 0\}}{\operatorname{argmax}} U_i(\mathbf{D}^t\mathbf{z} + \mathbf{e}_i), i = 1, 2, ..., I;$

Market Clearing: $\sum_{i=1}^{I} \mathbf{z}_i = \mathbf{0}.$

Figure 5.1 illustrates a simple setting with two investors and two events. There is no arbitrage and the securities market is assumed to be complete such that, for given security prices, there is a unique event-price vector **p**. Since the securities market is complete we can without loss of generality treat the event-contingent transfers as marketable securities. Hence, each investor *i*'s transfers $\boldsymbol{\delta}_i$ constitute a portfolio of event-contingent securities, which must satisfy the $t = 0$ budget constraint $\mathbf{p}^t \boldsymbol{\delta}_i \leq 0$, i.e., each investor can make transfers along the line through his endowments with gradient **p**. The investors select their transfers to maximize their expected utility, which implies that an investor trades to the point where his expected utility gradient is proportional to the event-price vector. In Figure 5.1, the allocation $\{ \mathbf{c}_1, \mathbf{c}_2 \}$ is individually optimal, but the securities market does not clear, i.e., there is excess-demand of consumption in event y_1 while there is excess-supply of consumption in event y_2. In order to establish an equilibrium, the event-price vector, i.e., the slope of the budget constraint, must change so that the net transfers equal zero, which means that consumption in event y_1 must be relatively more expensive than in Figure 5.1.

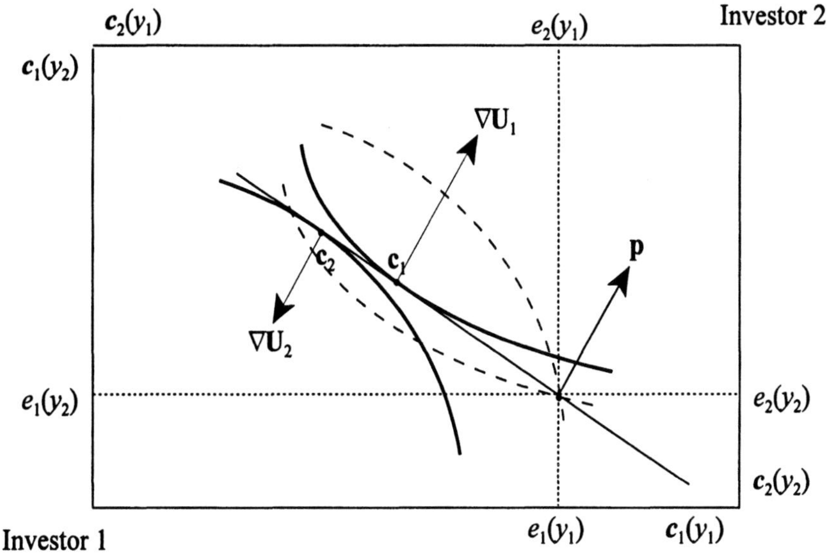

Figure 5.1: Dis-equilibrium in complete securities market with no arbitrage.

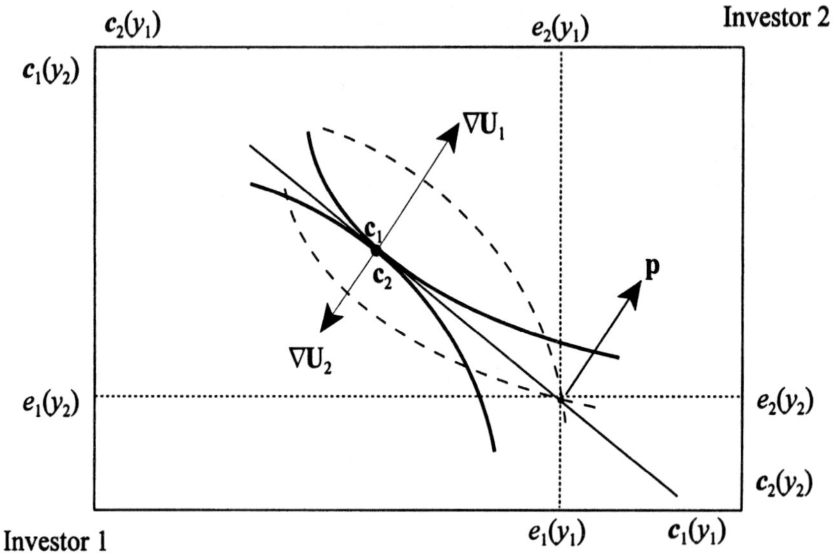

Figure 5.2: Equilibrium allocations with complete securities market.

Figure 5.2 illustrates an equilibrium in which the portfolio choices are individually optimal and the market clears. A key characteristic of the depicted equilibrium is that it is Pareto efficient. This follows from the facts that the aggregate consumption possibilities, $\mathbf{e}_1 + \mathbf{e}_2$, are fully allocated in each event and the allocation is such that the two investors' marginal rates of substitution between consumption in the two events are the same (see Proposition 4.1). The key assumption to get this result is that the market is complete.

Proposition 5.2 *The First Welfare Theorem*

If $\mathscr{E}$ is an equilibrium and the securities market is complete, then the equilibrium allocation of consumption is Pareto efficient.

Proof: Since $\mathscr{E}$ is an equilibrium and the securities market is complete, there is a unique event-price vector. Individual optimality, i.e., (5.8), implies that the state-prices are given by

$$p(y_m) = \frac{u_i'(c_i(y_m))\, \varphi_i(y_m) + \zeta_i(y_m)}{\lambda_i}, \quad m = 1, ..., M,$$

but these are the Borch first-order conditions for Pareto efficient risk sharing (see 4.14). Since market clearing implies that the aggregate consumption possibilities are precisely allocated in each event, the result now follows from the extension of Proposition 4.1 to include heterogeneous beliefs discussed in Section 4.1.3. **Q.E.D.**

In a partnership, efficient risk sharing is obtained by means of a sharing rule between the partners, whereas in a market setting efficient risk sharing is obtained by individually optimal trading in marketed securities. If the securities market is complete, there is enough flexibility in the marketed securities to obtain Pareto efficient risk sharing and, in particular, the properties of Pareto efficient risk sharing reported in Chapter 4 applies equally to equilibrium allocations in complete markets.

In a partnership, any Pareto efficient allocation can be obtained by assigning appropriate weights to the partners. This is not the case in a market setting, since the basis for the equilibrium is the investors' endowments. For example, no investor would trade to a consumption plan which gives him a lower expected utility than that of his endowments. This is illustrated in Figure 5.3.

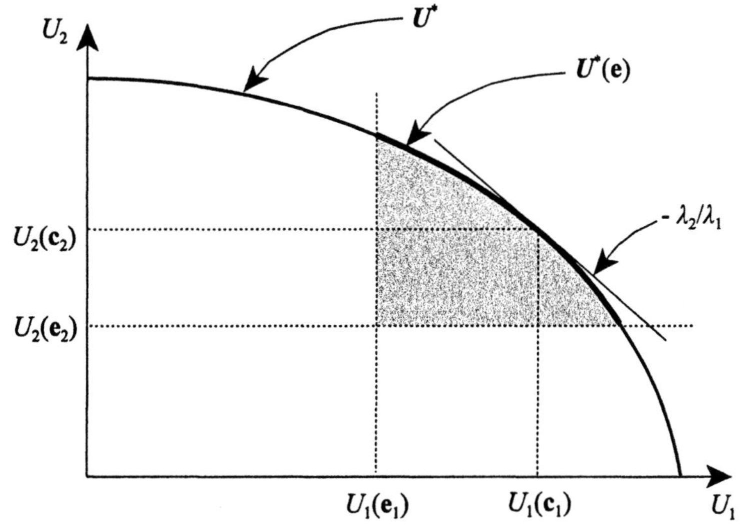

Figure 5.3: Pareto-efficient equilibrium allocations.

All allocations outside the shaded region will be blocked by at least one investor, i.e., equilibrium allocations must be in the shaded region (individual sovereignty). Hence, in a complete market, the equilibrium is on the frontier $\boldsymbol{U}^*(\mathbf{e})$. Again, given that the basis of trading is the investors' endowments, the equilibrium consumption plan is a unique point on that frontier (corresponding to the unique equilibrium allocation in Figure 5.2).[10] The slope of the frontier $\boldsymbol{U}^*(\mathbf{e})$ at the equilibrium point is the ratio of the multipliers of the investors' $t = 0$ budget-constraints, i.e., $-\lambda_2/\lambda_1$.

If the securities market is not complete, there may not be enough flexibility in dividends and prices to allow investors to trade to a point on the Pareto efficient frontier $\boldsymbol{U}^*(\mathbf{e})$. To illustrate this in the two-investor, two-event setting considered above, suppose there is only a single security available for trading with dividend $\mathbf{d} = (d(y_1), d(y_2))$ with $d(y_1) > 0$ and $d(y_2) < 0$. It follows from the investors' $t = 0$ budget constraints, i.e., $vz_i \leq 0$, that if investors are going to trade, the price of this security must equal zero.[11] Hence, the price of the security cannot adjust, and the investors can only trade to allocations along the line $\mathbf{d}z_i + \mathbf{e}_i$. This is illustrated in Figure 5.4.

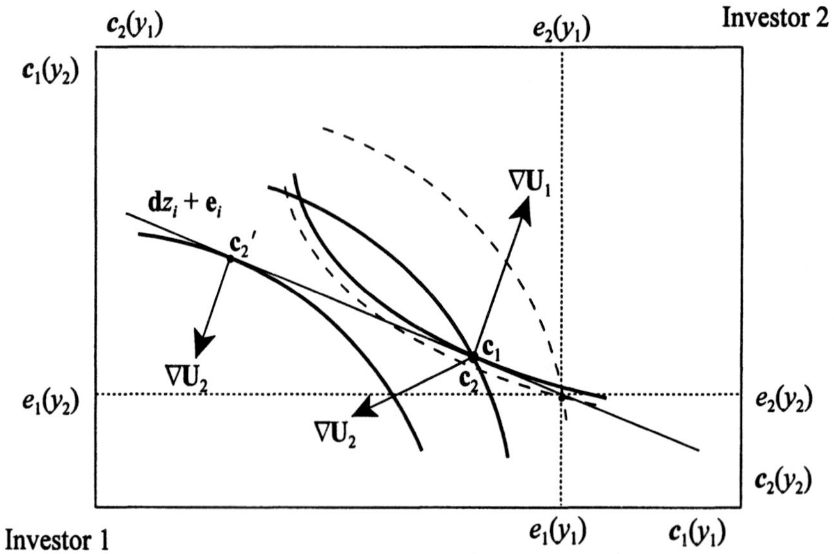

Figure 5.4: Non-existence of equilibrium in incomplete securities market.

---

[10] *The Second Welfare Theorem* states that in complete markets any Pareto optimal allocation can be obtained as an equilibrium with a suitable reallocation of endowments.

[11] If they trade, one must hold a long position while the other holds a short position to satisfy market clearing, and this can only satisfy the t=0 budget constraints for both investors if the price of the security is equal to zero. This leaves the question, whether there could exist a no-trade equilibrium. However, if the price of the security is positive, Investor 1 would take a short position to go to $\mathbf{c}_1$ (leaving slack in the t=0 budget constraint), while if the price is negative , Investor 2 would take a long position to go to $\mathbf{c}_2'$.

While there is market clearing for the allocation $\{\mathbf{c}_1,\mathbf{c}_2\}$ and both investors are better off than with their endowments, this allocation is not an equilibrium since $\mathbf{c}_2$ is not individually optimal for investor 2. The price of the security is zero, and he will seek to trade to $\mathbf{c}_2'$.

This simple example illustrates two points: in a complete market there exists an equilibrium under quite general conditions and it is Pareto efficient, while equilibria may not exist in incomplete markets and if an equilibrium does exist, it may not be Pareto efficient.[12] Of course, if endowments happen to be Pareto efficient, the endowment allocation is also an equilibrium allocation. In most of our analysis in this and the following chapters, we restrict our attention to complete markets (or, alternatively, markets that are sufficiently complete to allow efficient risk sharing). The following proposition summarizes some well known properties of complete markets.

Proposition 5.3 *Properties of Equilibria in Complete Markets*

Suppose the securities market is complete, investors have positive endowments, i.e., $\mathbf{e}_i > 0$, and infinite marginal utility of zero consumption, i.e., $u_i'(c_i) \to \infty$, as $c_i \downarrow 0$, and investors have strictly increasing and strictly concave utility functions.

(a) There exists an equilibrium with strictly positive consumption, $\mathbf{c}_i \in \mathbb{R}^M_{++}$, $i = 1, ..., I$, and it is Pareto efficient.

(b) There exists a unique equilibrium event-price vector $\mathbf{p}$ (up to a positive scalar transformation), and that event-price vector is proportional to the expected utility gradient for all investors, i.e., there exist positive constants $\lambda_1, ..., \lambda_I$ such that

$$p(y_m) = \frac{u_i'(c_i(y_m))\,\varphi_i(y_m)}{\lambda_i}, \quad m = 1, ..., M, \quad i = 1, ..., I. \tag{5.9}$$

Suppose beliefs are homogeneous and given by the probability function φ.

---

[12] In our example with two events, there is no equilibrium unless the complete market equilibrium happens to lie on the line $\mathbf{d}z + \mathbf{e}_i$. We can also note that if it was the case that $\mathbf{d} > 0$, then the endowment allocation would be an equilibrium (since there is nothing to exchange for something else). In fact, it can be shown under quite general conditions that there exists an equilibrium even if markets are incomplete, if there exists a portfolio $\mathbf{z}$ such that $\mathbf{D}^t\mathbf{z} > \mathbf{0}$. However, even if there exists an equilibrium in an incomplete market, that equilibrium may not be Pareto efficient. There is an extensive economics literature that deals with these issues (see, for example, Magill and Quinzii, 1996, for references).

(c) Individual consumption plans $\mathbf{c}_i$ are measurable with respect to aggregate consumption $\mathbf{x} = \Sigma_i \mathbf{e}_i$ and $c_i(x)$ is a strictly increasing function of x, $i = 1, ..., I$.

(d) Given the probability function φ, the valuation index q is measurable with respect to aggregate consumption and given by the "scarcity" of aggregate consumption as measured by the investors' marginal utility of consumption, i.e.,

$$q(y_m) = \frac{u_i'(c_i(y_m))}{\mathrm{E}[\, u_i'(c_i)\,]}$$

$$= \frac{u_i'(c_i(x(y_m)))}{\mathrm{E}[\, u_i'(c_i)\,]}, \quad m = 1, ..., M;\ i = 1, ..., I. \tag{5.10}$$

The completeness of the securities market and infinite marginal utility of zero consumption implies that no investor will choose a portfolio that ends up with zero consumption in some events – in a complete market, he can buy event-securities for those events at a finite cost while the marginal benefit is infinite at zero. Even though the securities market is complete, the equilibrium event-prices are not unique – we can always multiply all security prices by a positive constant without affecting the investors' $t = 0$ budget-constraints, $\mathbf{v}^t\mathbf{z}_i \le 0$. However, note that given the prices of the marketed securities, the implicit event-prices are unique. Condition (c) summarizes properties of efficient risk sharing with homogeneous beliefs (see Proposition 4.1). The identification of the valuation index follows directly from its definition and (5.9). Whereas the valuation index in incomplete markets with heterogeneous beliefs is almost a pure mathematical construct, it takes on economic substance with complete markets and homogeneous beliefs as the key measure of "scarcity" of consumption for valuing securities. Substituting (5.10) into (5.7) we get that

$$v_j = \beta\ \{\ \mathrm{E}[\, d_j\,] + \mathrm{Cov}[\, u_i'(c_i(x)), d_j\,]/\mathrm{E}[\, u_i'(c_i)\,]\ \},$$

$$j = 1, ..., J;\ i = 1, ..., I. \tag{5.11}$$

That is, the risk-adjustment is the covariance between the security's dividend and any investor's marginal utility of optimal consumption. Note that, if aggregate consumption x is high, optimal individual consumption is also high and, thus, marginal utility is low. Hence, if the dividend on a security is positively (negatively) correlated with aggregate consumption, the risk-adjustment is negative (positive). Of course, the intuition is that securities, that have their highest dividends when investors' optimal portfolios pay the least, are more valuable than securities that have their highest dividends when investors already have "enough." Value relation (5.11) is the fundamental consumption-based value relation equation in efficient markets with homogeneous beliefs. It is easily extended to multiple periods, and even to continuous time models with a continuum of events (in which it takes a particular simple form).[13]

5.4 EFFECTIVELY COMPLETE MARKETS

The analysis in the previous section established that a complete securities market is sufficient for an equilibrium to be Pareto efficient. However, note that the event y must describe any aspect of the state of the economy of relevance to dividends of securities (and in a multi-period setting any current information relevant for the prediction of future events). Consequently, the number of events is conceivably very large, and much larger than the number of marketed securities. Fortunately, the complete market assumption can be substituted by additional assumptions about preferences, beliefs, and the structure of dividends in order to yield effectively the same result. In this section we review two such approaches: invoke the conditions for linear risk sharing in partnerships; and use diversified portfolios to efficiently share diversifiable risks. We assume throughout the following analysis that the conditions are such that an equilibrium exists in an identical complete market economy.

5.4.1 Linear Risk Sharing

Proposition 4.3 establishes that if the members of a partnership have homogeneous beliefs and their preferences are represented by HARA utility functions with *identical risk cautiousness*, then any Pareto efficient partnership contract is linear, i.e., there exist parameters v_i and f_i such that $\mathbf{c}_i(x) = f_i + v_i x$, for all $i = 1,\ldots,n$, and $\Sigma_i v_i = 1$ and $\Sigma_i f_i = 0$ where x is the aggregate outcome to be shared between the n partners. The question is, what types of securities are needed in a securities market to achieve individual consumption allocations of this form, i.e., a constant plus a share of aggregate consumption. First, there has to be enough securities to "offset" the risks in the investors' endowments, i.e., $\mathbf{e}_i \in$ span $(\mathbf{D}^t)$, $i = 1, \ldots, I$. For example, that condition is directly satisfied if the endowments only consist of the investors' endowed portfolios $\bar{\mathbf{z}}_i$, i.e., $\mathbf{e}_i = \mathbf{D}^t\bar{\mathbf{z}}_i$. If investors also have uncertain personal consumption endowments $\bar{\mathbf{c}}_i$ (i.e., from sources other than endowed securities), there may be a need for marketable claims (such as insurance contracts) that can be used to offset those

[13] See, for example, Breeden (1979).

risks. Secondly, we need a riskless asset (or portfolio) to obtain the fixed component of the investors' efficient consumption.

As demonstrated in the following proposition, these two conditions imply that efficient consumption can be achieved by acquiring a portfolio that consists of three basic components. The first offsets the investor's personal endowment risk, while the second and third provide an efficient linear share of aggregate consumption.[14] In this analysis, we consider both the aggregate portfolio of (endowed) marketed securities and a "market portfolio" that encompasses the investors' personal consumption endowments. The former is $\mathbf{z}_m = \Sigma_i \bar{\mathbf{z}}_i$ and returns an aggregate dividend of $\mathbf{d}_m = \mathbf{D}^t\mathbf{z}_m$. The latter is denoted $\mathbf{z}_x$ and returns a dividend of $\mathbf{x} = \Sigma_i \mathbf{e}_i = \mathbf{d}_m + \Sigma_i \bar{\mathbf{c}}_i$. If there are no personal consumption endowments, then these two portfolios are equivalent.

Proposition 5.4

Suppose the investors have homogeneous beliefs and their preferences are represented by HARA utility functions with *identical risk cautiousness*.[15]

If there exists a riskless portfolio $\mathbf{z}_f$ (which pays dividend $\mathbf{d}_f = \mathbf{1}$) and $\bar{\mathbf{c}}_i \in$ span $(\mathbf{D}^t)$, $i = 1, ..., I$, then there is a Pareto efficient equilibrium, and the investors can be viewed as holding a portfolio consisting of three "funds:"

(a) A portfolio $\mathbf{z}_{ei}$ which, if sold, "undoes" personal consumption endowments, $\mathbf{D}^t\mathbf{z}_{ei} = \bar{\mathbf{c}}_i$;

(b) A share f_i of the riskless portfolio that pays dividend $f_i\mathbf{d}_f$;

(c) A share v_i of the market portfolio that pays dividend $v_i\mathbf{x}$.

Furthermore, the valuation index is independent of the distribution of initial endowments and is given by

$$q(x) = \frac{w_o'(x)}{\mathrm{E}[\, w_o'(x)\,]},$$

where $w_o(\cdot)$ is the partnership utility function with respect to aggregate consumption given in Table 4.2.

---

[14] We include the proof of this proposition in the text because it demonstrates, in a simple setting, the basic principle used in similar proofs in more complicated settings considered later.

[15] With HARA utility, the investors' consumption sets may include negative consumption, and efficient risk sharing may lead to negative consumption to some investors in some events (see Chapter 4). Consequently, in this setting, we also allow an equilibrium to include negative consumption if required.

Proof: Consider an augmented economy in which we have added a complete set of event-securities. We consider these securities as financial securities (which are in zero net-supply). By assumption, there is an equilibrium in the augmented economy, and it is Pareto efficient by Proposition 5.1. Let the equilibrium event-prices be $\mathbf{p}$, and the equilibrium consumption plans be $\mathbf{c}_i$, $i = 1, ..., I$. It follows from Proposition 4.3 that there are constants f_i and v_i such that

$$\mathbf{c}_i = f_i \mathbf{1} + v_i \mathbf{x}, \quad i = 1, ..., I,$$

where $\mathbf{1}$ is an M-dimensional vector with one's in all the coordinates, and $\mathbf{x} = \Sigma_i \mathbf{e}_i$ is the vector of event-contingent aggregate consumption. Furthermore, it follows from the assumption of strictly increasing utility and the budget constraints that

$$\mathbf{p}^t(\mathbf{c}_i - \mathbf{e}_i) = 0, \quad i = 1, ..., I. \tag{5.12}$$

We now want to show that all investors can implement their equilibrium consumption plans by trading in only the original securities and, that their portfolios of original securities satisfy the market clearing conditions in the original economy. That is, based on the equilibrium event-prices and consumption plans in the augmented economy, we construct an equilibrium in the original economy with the same consumption plans.

We start by assigning market prices to the original securities by the no-arbitrage condition in the augmented economy, i.e.,

$$\mathbf{v} = \mathbf{D}\mathbf{p}.$$

Denote the aggregate consumption endowments by

$$\bar{\mathbf{c}}_0 = \sum_{i=1}^{I} \bar{\mathbf{c}}_i.$$

Hence, the aggregate portfolio of securities $\mathbf{z}_m$ has dividend vector $\mathbf{d}_m \equiv \mathbf{x} - \bar{\mathbf{c}}_0$. Since $\bar{\mathbf{c}}_i \in$ span $(\mathbf{D}^t)$ for all i, there exists a portfolio $\mathbf{z}_{ei}$ such that $\mathbf{D}^t\mathbf{z}_{ei} = \bar{\mathbf{c}}_i$, and $\bar{\mathbf{c}}_0 \in$ span $(\mathbf{D}^t)$. This implies there exists a portfolio $\mathbf{z}_x = \mathbf{z}_m + \Sigma_i \mathbf{z}_{ei}$ with dividend $\mathbf{D}^t\mathbf{z}_x = \mathbf{x}$. Furthermore, since there is a riskless portfolio $\mathbf{z}_f$ with dividend vector $\mathbf{1}$, investor i's equilibrium consumption plan can be implemented by acquiring the portfolio (which is the desired portfolio minus a portfolio "undoing" the investor's endowments)

$$\mathbf{z}_i = f_i \mathbf{z}_f + v_i \mathbf{z}_x - (\mathbf{z}_{ei} + \bar{\mathbf{z}}_i),$$

with net dividend vector

$$\mathbf{D}^t\mathbf{z}_i = f_i\,\mathbf{1} + v_i\,\mathbf{x} - \mathbf{e}_i = \mathbf{c}_i - \mathbf{e}_i.$$

Of course, no arbitrage in the augmented economy implies that $\mathbf{v}^t\mathbf{z}_i = \mathbf{p}^t(\mathbf{c}_i - \mathbf{e}_i) = 0$ by (5.12). Thus, the investor's $t = 0$ budget constraint, $\mathbf{v}^t\mathbf{z}_i = 0$, and the $t = 1$ budget constraint for implementing $\mathbf{c}_i$, $\mathbf{c}_i = \mathbf{D}^t\mathbf{z}_i + \mathbf{e}_i$, are both satisfied. Furthermore, using that $\Sigma_i\, v_i = 1$ and $\Sigma_i\, f_i = 0$, the market clearing conditions are satisfied, i.e.,

$$\sum_{i=1}^{I} \mathbf{z}_i = \mathbf{z}_x - \sum_{i=1}^{I} (\mathbf{z}_{ei} + \bar{\mathbf{z}}_i) = 0,$$

where the last equality comes from the fact that

$$\sum_{i=1}^{I} \mathbf{e}_i = \mathbf{x} \quad \text{and, thus,} \quad \mathbf{z}_x = \sum_{i=1}^{I} (\mathbf{z}_{ei} + \bar{\mathbf{z}}_i).$$

Finally, given linear risk sharing, the valuation index is[16]

$$q(x) = \frac{w_i'(x)}{\mathrm{E}[\, w_i'(x)\,]}, \qquad i = 1, ..., I,$$

where $w_i(x) \equiv u_i(c(x))$. Since risk sharing is efficient, $w_i(\cdot)$ is a positive linear transformation of the partnership utility function (see Proposition 4.4 and Table 4.2). The partnership utility function depends only on the preference parameters of the investors and, thus, the valuation index is independent of the investors' endowments (or, equivalently, the utility weights in the optimal risk sharing problem). **Q.E.D.**

The key point of this proposition is that efficient risk sharing can be obtained in an incomplete market setting provided there is "enough" flexibility in the marketed securities to implement efficient consumption plans. In this particular

---

[16] Whenever the securities market is sufficiently complete to achieve an efficient equilibrium, we can construct a "representative agent" and express the valuation index in terms of his utility function defined on aggregate consumption. The "representative utility function" is given by a weighted sum of the investors' individual utility functions where the weights are the inverse of the multipliers for the investors' budget constraints. Thus, in general, the valuation index will depend on the distribution of endowments among investors. The assumptions made in the proposition provide an interesting exception.

case with linear risk sharing, the market portfolio and the riskless asset play key roles. If there are no personal consumption endowments, investors can restrict their portfolio choice to these two "funds" – in this case, Proposition 5.4 is commonly referred to as a "two-fund separation theorem."

The latter part of the proposition is commonly known as the "aggregation theorem" (see Rubinstein, 1974, and Brennan and Kraus, 1978).[17] In general, the valuation index and, thus, the equilibrium prices of securities, depend on all the fundamentals of the economy, i.e., beliefs, preferences, and endowments. However, with linear risk sharing, equilibrium prices do not depend on how the endowments are distributed among investors, and this provides the basis for asset pricing models in terms of exogenous parameters of the economy.

5.4.2 Diversifiable Risks

Condition (c) in Proposition 5.3 establishes that if beliefs are homogeneous, then Pareto efficient individual consumption plans are measurable with respect to aggregate consumption. That is, if aggregate consumption $\boldsymbol{x}(y)$ is the same in any two events y' and y'', then any investor consumes the same in the two events, $\boldsymbol{c}_i(y') = \boldsymbol{c}_i(y'')$. Hence, we may not need a complete market to facilitate a Pareto efficient allocation of consumption – the securities only have to facilitate an allocation which is measurable with respect to aggregate consumption. To achieve this (without adding further assumptions on endowments, preferences, and beliefs), the securities market must have marketed securities that can "offset" endowment risks, and securities that allow an efficient sharing of aggregate consumption risks.

Pricing on the Basis of Aggregate Consumption

Let Γ denote the coarsest partition of the set of events Y such that aggregate consumption is measurable with respect to that partition. With a slight abuse of notation we let $\gamma \in \Gamma$ denote the subset of events y that result in the aggregate consumption level γ, i.e., $\gamma = \{ y \in Y \,|\, \boldsymbol{x}(y) = \gamma \}$, $\gamma \in \Gamma$. The key to an efficient sharing of aggregate consumption is the existence of marketed securities that allow each investor to implement any financially feasible consumption plan *which is Γ-measurable.* To this end, define an aggregate consumption (AC)-security for the aggregate consumption event $\gamma \in \Gamma$ as a security with a dividend of one in all events $y \in Y$ with aggregate consumption level γ, and a dividend of zero in all other events, i.e.,

[17] We only present the sufficiency part of the theorem, but linear risk sharing is, in fact, also a necessary condition for aggregation (see Brennan and Kraus, 1978).

$$d_\gamma(y) = \begin{cases} 1 & \text{if } y \in \gamma, \\ 0 & \text{otherwise.} \end{cases}$$

Note that this security can be considered as a portfolio of the event-securities for events $y \in \gamma$, i.e.,

$$\mathbf{d}_\gamma = \sum_{y \in \gamma} \mathbf{d}_y,$$

and, consequently, for given event-prices the price of the AC-security for the event γ is

$$p(\gamma) = \sum_{y \in \gamma} p(y). \tag{5.13}$$

Proposition 5.5

Suppose the investors have homogeneous beliefs. If $\mathbf{e}_i \in$ span $(\mathbf{D}^t)$, $i = 1, ..., I$, and $\mathbf{d}_\gamma \in$ span $(\mathbf{D}^t)$, $\forall\, \gamma \in \Gamma$, then there is a Pareto efficient equilibrium,[18] and the event-prices are given by

$$p(y) = p(\gamma)\varphi(y|\gamma), \quad \text{for } y \in \gamma,\ \gamma \in \Gamma. \tag{5.14}$$

The proof follows the same principles as the proof of Proposition 5.4. With a complete set of event-securities we know from Proposition 5.3 that Pareto efficient individual consumption plans are Γ-measurable, i.e., we can write individual consumption as functions of γ, $c_i = \boldsymbol{c}_i(\gamma)$. Since $\mathbf{d}_\gamma \in$ span $(\mathbf{D}^t)$, $\forall\, \gamma \in \Gamma$, we can create a complete set of AC-securities as portfolios $\mathbf{z}_\gamma$ of the marketed securities. Hence, investor i's consumption plan can be implemented by acquiring a portfolio $\mathbf{z}_{ci}$ of AC-securities with portfolio weights $\boldsymbol{c}_i(\gamma)$, i.e.,

$$\mathbf{z}_{ci} = \sum_{\gamma \in \Gamma} \boldsymbol{c}_i(\gamma)\, \mathbf{z}_\gamma, \quad \mathbf{c}_i = \sum_{\gamma \in \Gamma} \boldsymbol{c}_i(\gamma)\, \mathbf{d}_\gamma, \quad i = 1, ..., I.$$

[18] Amershi (1985) extends this result to settings in which investors may have heterogeneous beliefs about the aggregate consumption events γ, but conditional on γ, they have homogeneous beliefs about events $y \in \gamma$. In this setting, efficient risk sharing may require side-bets on the aggregate consumption events (and these side-bets are facilitated by the AC-securities), but they do not want to take unnecessary risk within those events. Note that even though efficient consumption plans are Γ-measurable, they may not be monotonic functions of aggregate consumption.

Similarly, since $\mathbf{e}_i \in \text{span}(\mathbf{D}^t)$, $i = 1, ..., I$, there exist a portfolio $\mathbf{z}_{ei}$ which can be sold to "undo" the investor's endowments,

$$\mathbf{e}_i = \mathbf{D}^t\mathbf{z}_{ei}, \quad i = 1, ..., I,$$

and it follows from no arbitrage in the otherwise identical complete market that

$$\mathbf{v}^t(\mathbf{z}_{ci} - \mathbf{z}_{ei}) = \mathbf{p}^t(\mathbf{c}_i - \mathbf{e}_i) = 0, \quad i = 1, ..., I.$$

Hence, efficient consumption plans can be implemented by trading in the marketed securities **D**.

Note that even though the equilibrium is efficient, the event-prices are not unique if the market is not complete. However, the valuation index as a function of aggregate consumption given by

$$q(\gamma) = \frac{u_i'(c_i(\gamma))}{\mathrm{E}[\,u_i'(c_i)\,]}$$

is unique, and using (5.9) we may define "unique" event-prices by

$$\begin{aligned} p(y) &= \beta\, q(\gamma)\varphi(y), \\ &= \beta\, q(\gamma)\varphi(y|\gamma)\varphi(\gamma), \quad \text{for } y \in \gamma,\, \gamma \in \Gamma. \end{aligned} \tag{5.15}$$

We generally use these prices if beliefs are homogeneous and the equilibrium is efficient. Using (5.13) the price of the AC-security for γ is

$$p(\gamma) = \sum_{y \in \gamma} \beta\, q(\gamma)\varphi(y|\gamma)\varphi(\gamma) = \beta\, q(\gamma)\varphi(\gamma)$$

and, thus, the event-prices are given as in (5.14). Inserting (5.14) into the no-arbitrage condition (5.2), the prices of securities are given by

$$v_j = \sum_{y \in Y} d_j(y)p(\gamma)\,\varphi(y|\gamma) = \sum_{\gamma \in \Gamma} \mathrm{E}[d_j|\gamma]\,p(\gamma), \quad j = 1, 2, ..., J. \tag{5.16}$$

Hence, conditional on the aggregate consumption events, the dividends are evaluated by their conditional expected value, i.e., there is no risk-adjustment for events y within any given aggregate consumption event γ. That is, the prices of securities are as if investors are risk neutral with respect to which event occurs within aggregate consumption events. The risk-adjustment in the risk-neutral probabilities are the same for all events within any given aggregate consumption event,

$$\hat{\varphi}(y) = \varphi(y)\, q(\gamma), \quad y \in \gamma, \gamma \in \Gamma, \tag{5.17}$$

since the valuation index is Γ-measurable. Hence, the risk-adjusted probabilities are high (low) when aggregate consumption is low (high).

Of course, these pricing relations follow from the fact that the investors' optimal portfolio choice is such that their consumption plans do not vary with events within an aggregate consumption event. The idea is that the dividend of individual securities may vary with basic events y within an aggregate consumption event γ but the aggregate is the same. By holding "well-diversified portfolios" investors can eliminate the risk associated with the dividend of individual securities, and only take risk associated with variations in aggregate consumption – the risk associated with events $y \in \gamma$ is diversifiable, while the risk associated with aggregate consumption events $\gamma \in \Gamma$ is non-diversifiable.

The key to obtaining an efficient sharing of aggregate consumption risk is that investors can choose portfolios that "undo" their endowment risk[19] and then provide any desired consumption plan that varies with aggregate consumption. In the analysis that follows we assume that "undoing" endowment risk is not an issue by assuming, for simplicity, that investors have no consumption endowments, i.e., their endowments consist of their endowed portfolio of marketed claims, $\mathbf{e}_i = \mathbf{D}^t\bar{\mathbf{z}}_i$, such that $\mathbf{e}_i \in$ span $(\mathbf{D}^t)$, $i = 1, ..., I$, is trivially satisfied. We then focus on the use of sufficiently-varied set of well-diversified portfolios in what Feltham and Christensen (1988) call a quasi-complete market.[20]

Quasi-complete Markets

If two events produce the same level of aggregate consumption (e.g., $y', y'' \in \gamma$) but produce different dividends for some securities ($d_j(y') \neq d_j(y'')$, for some

[19] In general, with consumption endowment risks, an efficient risk sharing requires that investors can "insure" those risks, for example, through insurance contracts. Christensen, Graversen, and Miltersen (2000) consider insurance contracts in a general continuous-time framework with homogeneous beliefs and time-additive preferences.

[20] An alternative approach (see Breeden and Litzenberger, 1978) is to assume that there is a complete set of call options on aggregate consumption. A call option with exercise price k provides a Γ-measurable dividend of the form

$$d^k(\gamma) = \max \{ 0, \gamma - k \},$$

and the market is complete with respect to Γ if aggregate consumption can take N different values $\gamma_1, ..., \gamma_N$ and there are N options with exercise prices $k_1 = \gamma_1, ..., k_N = \gamma_N$.

j), the dividends of the securities must be stochastically dependent. We can, for example, think of the events $y \in \gamma$ as describing the "allocation" of the aggregate dividend "pie" among the firms in the economy, whereas the aggregate dividend (consumption) levels $\gamma \in \Gamma$ depict the "size of the pie." The size of the aggregate dividend pie allocated to the firms equals the size of the aggregate consumption pie distributed to investors, and the "firm-allocation" risks can be avoided by investors if they hold an appropriate market portfolio.

Observe that investing in market portfolios generating dividends that only vary with aggregate consumption is a form of risk avoidance through diversification – the "firm-allocation" risk is fully diversifiable. However, the spirit of the "gains to diversification" is generally viewed as occurring when there are independent variations in the firms' dividends which virtually "cancel out" in a portfolio in which investors hold small fractions of each of a large number of firms (see, for example, Samuelson, 1967, and Ross, 1976). We now explore this type of diversification.

In this setting, the events that influence the payments made by a particular firm are viewed as consisting of two types: economy-wide and firm-specific. Economy-wide events influence the payments made by many firms, whereas firm-specific events influence the payments made by only one firm. The existence of the latter type of events precludes the possibility of achieving market "completeness" unless there are a large variety of claims associated with each firm. However, diversification provides a potential means of dealing with firm-specific events. To facilitate our analysis, we make the following simplifying assumptions:

(*i*) the set of marketed securities consists only of ownership claims to a set of J firms (each firm issues only one type of claim);

(*ii*) endowments consist of marketed securities, i.e., $\mathbf{e}_i = \mathbf{D}^t \bar{\mathbf{z}}_i$.

We expand the definition of an event $y \in Y$ and let $y \equiv (y_e, \{ y_j \}_{j=1,\dots,J})$, where y is the "full" description of the event, y_e represents *economy-wide* events, and y_j represents *firm-specific* events that influence the dividends of firm j. The set of possible events is $Y \equiv Y_e \times Y_1 \times \dots \times Y_J$. Referring to y_j as firm-specific is justified by assuming that the following relations hold.

Definition *Economy-wide and Firm-specific Events*

If $y = (y_e, \{ y_j \}_{j=1,\dots,J})$, then y_e represents *economy-wide* events, and y_j represents *firm-specific* events for firm j, if the following conditions hold:

(a) the dividends for firm j depend only on y_e and y_j, i.e.,

$$d_j(y) = d_j(y_e, y_j), \quad \forall j = 1, \dots, J, y \in Y;$$

(b) beliefs about firm-specific events are conditionally independent, i.e.,

$$\varphi(y) = \varphi(y_e) \prod_{j=1}^{J} \varphi(y_j|y_e), \quad \forall\, y \in Y.$$

The independence of the firm-specific events is a rather strong assumption and, to some extent, is stronger than is required for the results that follow. That is, we could allow some dependence among firms. On the other hand, the above formulation is always possible in that one can always treat all events as economy-wide events, i.e., $Y_e = Y$, and thereby trivially satisfy the above conditions. That, of course, merely returns us to the preceding analyses.

The "size" of the economy is important in dealing with non-trivial firm-specific risk. We assume it is large. If the economy is large, then the independence of the firm-specific events implies that these events have little impact on aggregate consumption. Only economy-wide events significantly influence aggregate consumption. More formally, given suitable regularity and considering a sequence of economies in which J is increasing, the strong law of large numbers for independent random variables implies that[21]

$$\text{Prob}\left[\left\{y \in Y \,\middle|\, \lim_{J\to\infty} \left|\frac{1}{J}\sum_{j=1}^{J} \alpha_{oj}[d_j(y_e,y_j) - \bar{d}_j(y_e)]\right| \to 0\right\} \,\middle|\, y_e\right] = 1, \quad \forall\, y_e \in Y_e,$$

where

$$\bar{d}_j(y_e) \equiv \sum_{y_j \in Y_j} d_j(y_e,y_j)\, \varphi(y_j|y_e), \quad j = 1, ..., J,$$

and α_{oj}, $j = 1,..., J$, are arbitrary finite constants. That is, as the economy becomes infinitely large, the average difference between a weighted sum of realized firm dividends and expected firm dividends (for a given economy-wide event) is equal to zero with probability one – the random variations due to firm-specific events offset each other.

The above fact led Berninghaus (1977) to propose an alternative concept of Pareto efficiency for large economies.[22] We term this *quasi-efficiency*, which has as its key ingredient the concept of quasi-feasible consumption plans (compare to the definition of sharing rule feasibility in Chapter 4).

---

[21] See, for example, Berninghaus (1977).

[22] Berninghaus (1977) extends a similar analysis by Malinvaud (1972), who only considered firm-specific risks. Other papers that examine the impact of firm-specific risks include Malinvaud (1973) and Caspi (1974, 1978).

Definition *Quasi-feasibility*

Consumption plan **c** is *quasi-feasible* if

(a) $c_i(y) \in C_i, \quad \forall\, i = 1, \ldots, I,\; y \in Y;$

(b) $\Sigma_i\, \bar{c}_i(y_e) = \bar{x}(y_e), \quad \forall\, y_e \in Y_e,$

where $\bar{c}_i(y_e) \equiv \Sigma_y\, c_i(y)\, \varphi(y|y_e)$ and $\bar{x}(y_e) \equiv \Sigma_y\, x(y)\, \varphi(y|y_e)$.

The key difference between the definition of feasible consumption plans in Chapter 4 and quasi-feasibility is that in the latter the "supply-demand" restriction only has to hold in expectation conditional on the economy-wide events.[23]

Definition *Quasi-efficiency*

A consumption plan **c** is *quasi-efficient* if

(a) **c** is *quasi-feasible*; and

(b) there does not exist an alternative quasi-feasible consumption plan $\mathbf{c}'$ such that $U_i(\mathbf{c}_i') \geq U(\mathbf{c}_i)$, $i = 1, \ldots, I$, with at least one strict inequality.

Now consider the feasibility of implementing a quasi-efficient consumption plan through the trading of firm ownership. Firm dividends are influenced by firm-specific events and, hence, completeness does not hold. However, diversification may be a viable approach to efficiently sharing risks if the economy is large and there is sufficient flexibility to efficiently share the risks associated with variations in expected aggregate consumption. To illustrate this approach, consider an economy in which there are $N \times J$ firms and $N \times I$ investors, with N representing the size of the economy and with J and I representing the different types of firms and investors, respectively (there are N of each type).[24]

The dividends paid by firms are influenced by economy-wide and firm-specific events. As before, the firm-specific events are independently distributed, conditional on the economy-wide events. The key difference is that now, for any type j, the firm-specific events for all firms of a given type are independently and identically distributed. Let $d_{jn}(y_e, y_{jn})$ represent the dividend of the nth type j claim given economy-wide event y_e and firm-specific event y_{jn}. Now

---

[23] The reason is that even though the strong law of large numbers implies that the average dividend is independent of firm-specific events in the limit, total dividends are not. That is, even though investors hold well-diversified portfolios with dividends independent of firm-specific events, their total dividend aggregated across investors will depend on those events.

[24] There need not be identical firms and individuals for the following result to go through, but it is easier to satisfy both the flexibility and diversifiability requirements using this approach.

consider a well-diversified portfolio consisting of z_j / N units of each type j claim, $\forall j$.[25] The strong law of large numbers establishes that for a sequence of economies,

$$\text{Prob}\left[\left\{y \in Y \,\middle|\, \lim_{N \to \infty} \left| \frac{1}{N} \sum_{j=1}^{J} z_j \sum_{n=1}^{N} [d_{jn}(y_e, y_{jn}) - \bar{d}_j(y_e)] \right| \to 0 \right\} \,\middle|\, y_e \right] = 1,$$
$$\forall\, y_e \in Y_e, \tag{5.18}$$

where

$$\bar{d}_j(y_e) \equiv \sum_{y_{jn} \in Y_{jn}} d_{jn}(y_e, y_{jn})\, \varphi(y_{jn} | y_e).$$

That is, in a sufficiently large economy, a well-diversified portfolio will, with probability one, have a dividend at date $t = 1$ that is equal to its expected dividend given the economy-wide event. The effects of variations in dividends are diversified away.

Now consider the flexibility required to efficiently share the risks associated with variations in aggregate consumption due to the economy-wide events.

Definition:[26] *Quasi-complete market*

A set of $J \times N$ claims constitute a *quasi-complete market* (QCM) if the economy is large and the *expected dividend matrix*

$$\bar{\mathbf{D}} \equiv [\ \bar{d}_j(y_e)\ ]_{J \times |Y_e|},$$

has a rank equal to the number of economy-wide events.

A quasi-complete market has a sufficient variety of well-diversified investment portfolios to permit an investor to implement a quasi-efficient consumption plan.[27]

---

[25] If each type j firm has the same price, it is clear that if a risk-averse consumer choose to hold a total of z_j units of the type j claims, then he would choose to spread those z_j units evenly over the N type j firms.

[26] The term quasi-complete is taken from Leland (1978).

[27] The arguments used to establish this proposition follow primarily from Berninghaus (1977). Similar arguments are used by Ross (1976, 1977) in his arbitrage theory of asset pricing. Application of this approach is also found in Feltham and Christensen (1988).

Proposition 5.6

Suppose the investors have homogeneous beliefs. If $\mathbf{e}_i \in$ span $(\mathbf{D}^{\mathrm{t}})$, $i = 1, ..., I$, and the set of $J \times N$ claims constitute a *quasi-complete market*, then there is a quasi-efficient equilibrium, and the event-prices are given by

$$p(y) = p(y_e) \prod_{j=1}^{J} \prod_{n=1}^{N} \varphi(y_{jn}|y_e), \quad \text{for } y \in Y. \tag{5.19}$$

Proof: Consider an artificial economy with no firm-specific events, J securities with dividend matrix $\bar{\mathbf{D}}$, and I investors. In that economy, there is a Pareto-efficient equilibrium $\mathscr{E} \equiv \{ \mathbf{z}_1, ..., \mathbf{z}_I; v_1, ..., v_J \}$ with event prices $p(y_e)$, $y_e \in Y_e$. For all investors of type i, let their investors' portfolio choices in the economy with firm-specific risks be $z_{ijn} = z_{ij}/N$ units of each firm of type j. Since there is market clearing in the artificial economy, i.e., $\sum_i z_{ij} = 0$, $\forall j$, there is also market clearing in the economy with firm-specific risks. Furthermore, if we define event-prices by (5.19), the prices of firms of type j is

$$v_{jn} = \sum_{j \in J} \mathrm{E}[\, d_{jn} \,|\, y_e \,]\, p(y_e)$$

and, thus, the portfolios are budget-feasible at $t = 0$. It follows from (5.18) that with probability one, any investor of type i has the same consumption plan as investor i in the artificial economy. Note that these consumption plans are quasi-feasible, since $\sum_i \mathbf{c}_i(y_e) = \bar{\mathbf{x}}(y_e)$. Since $\mathbf{z}_i$ is optimal for investor i in the artificial economy, the defined portfolios for investors of type i in the economy with firm-specific risk are also individually optimal given the structure of the event-prices in (5.19) (i.e., firm-specific variations in dividends are priced as fair gambles and, thus, any strictly risk-averse investor will restrict his portfolio choice to well diversified portfolios). **Q.E.D.**

Figure 5.5 illustrates the role of diversification and quasi-completeness. There are two possible economy-wide events, y_e^1 and y_e^2, and two types of firms. There are two possible firm-specific events for each firm of each type. Let N denote the number of firms of each type. The first part of Figure 5.5 presents the events and dividends at $t = 1$ for the case where $N = 1$ (i.e., there is one firm of each type). In this case there are eight possible events and the availability of only two tradeable claims is insufficient to permit investors to implement a Pareto-efficient consumption plan. However, the expected dividends for the two firms for the two economy-wide events provide a matrix of expected dividends,

Y	y_1	y_2	y_3	y_4	y_5	y_6	y_7	y_8
Y_e	y_e^1	y_e^1	y_e^1	y_e^1	y_e^2	y_e^2	y_e^2	y_e^2
Y_1	y_1^1	y_1^1	y_1^2	y_1^2	y_1^1	y_1^1	y_1^2	y_1^2
Y_2	y_2^1	y_2^2	y_2^1	y_2^2	y_2^1	y_2^2	y_2^1	y_2^2
$\mathbf{d}_1(y)$	50	50	60	60	70	70	80	80
$\mathbf{d}_2(y)$	20	60	20	60	60	90	60	90
$\varphi(y)$	0.24	0.24	0.1	0.1	0.1	0.12	0.1	0.12

Y_e	y_e^1	y_e^2
$\varphi(y_e)$	.60	.40
$\varphi(y_1^1 \mid y_e) = 1 - \varphi(y_1^2 \mid y_e)$	.80	.50
$\varphi(y_2^1 \mid y_e) = 1 - \varphi(y_2^2 \mid y_e)$	.50	.40
$\bar{\mathbf{d}}_1(y_e)$	5240	7578
$\bar{\mathbf{d}}_2(y_e)$		

$$\text{Prob}\left[\left\{ y \in Y \,\middle|\, \left| \frac{1}{N} \sum_{n=1}^{N} \mathbf{d}_{1n}(y_e) - \bar{\mathbf{d}}_1(y_e) \right| \leq \varepsilon \right\} \,\middle|\, y_e = y_e^1 \right]$$

	$\varepsilon = 0.1$	$\varepsilon = 1.0$
$N =$ 1	.0000	.0000
10	.3020	.7718
100	.2919	.9916
1000	.5935	.9999
10000	.9876	.9999

Figure 5.5: Quasi-complete markets.

$$\bar{\mathbf{D}} = \begin{bmatrix} 52 & 75 \\ 40 & 78 \end{bmatrix},$$

which has rank two. Therefore, consumers can implement a quasi-efficient consumption plan by holding diversified portfolios of the two types of firms if N is sufficiently large.

The set Y contains $2 \cdot 2^{2N}$ possible events. If N is large, many states result in average dividends, for each type of firm, that are very close to the expected values contained in $\bar{\mathbf{D}}$. The probability that the difference for a given type of firm is less than ε is depicted in Figure 5.5 for firm type 1 and economy-wide event y_e^1. It becomes closer and closer to 1 as N increases.

The key to achieving quasi-efficiency is that the securities market spans the set of dividend vectors that only depend on the economy-wide events.[28] The preceding analysis assumes this is accomplished by trading well-diversified portfolios of ownership claims of firms. Alternatively, the investors could trade claims that pay dividends contingent on an index measuring "average" aggregate consumption.[29]

5.5 IMPACT OF PUBLIC INFORMATION

In the preceding analysis the information system is fixed so that investors do not receive any information prior to trading at $t = 0$, but do receive information at $t = 1$. That is, the information system at date t is η_t: $S \to Y_t$, where $Y_0 = \{S\}$ and Y_1 is some non-trivial partition of S such that the security dividends and the investors' endowments are Y_1-measurable. In this section, we consider the impact of varying the public information system $\boldsymbol{\eta} = (\eta_0, \eta_1)$ represented by the sets of signals Y_t^η, $t = 0, 1$. The sets of signals are partitions on the set of states and, to reflect that investors "do not forget what they have learned so far," we assume Y_1^η is at least as fine a partition of S as Y_0^η, i.e., for any $y_1 \in Y_1^\eta$ there exists $y_0 \in Y_0^\eta$ such that $y_1 \subseteq y_0$. We refer to η_1 as *ex post* information and η_0 as *ex ante* information.

---

[28] Of course, if multiple economy-wide events provide the same expected aggregate consumption conditional on the economy-wide events, those events do not have to be "spanned."

[29] Aggregate consumption varies with firm-specific events no matter how large N is, but, for example, an index of the form $x(y)/N$ does not.

5.5.1 *Ex Post* Information

Assume, as in the preceding analysis, that investors have no information prior to trading at $t = 0$, i.e., $Y_0^\eta = \{S\}$, and that investors receive *ex post* information η_1. Initially, we ask whether more *ex post* information can lead to more efficient consumption plans without worrying about the implementation of those consumption plans. Hence, we focus directly on the transfers $\delta_i = c_i - e_i$.

The following definition specifies the conditions that must be satisfied for a set of transfers to be consistent with the *ex post* information, and feasible with respect to other characteristics of the setting.

Definition η_1*-Consistent Transfers*

The set of functions $\Delta \equiv \{ \delta_i: S \rightarrow \mathbb{R}, i = 1, ..., I \}$ is η_1-consistent if it satisfies the following conditions.

(a) Individual feasibility: $e_i(s) + \delta_i(s) \in C_i, \quad \forall\, i, s.$

(b) Aggregate feasibility: $\Sigma_i\, \delta_i(s) \le 0, \quad \forall\, s.$

(c) Individual sovereignty: $U_i(\mathbf{e}_i + \boldsymbol{\delta}_i) \ge U_i(\mathbf{e}_i), \quad \forall\, i.$

(d) Public information measurability: δ_i is Y_1^η-measurable $\forall\, i.$

The definition of η_1-consistent transfers parallels the definition of feasible consumption plans in Chapter 4, except that transfers are restricted to leave no one worse off (see Figure 5.3). The key restriction for the analysis in this section is that transfers have to be measurable with respect to the public information system. Note that endowments are not restricted to be Y_1^η-measurable, so that investors may have private information about their endowments at $t = 1$.

Within the set of η_1-consistent transfers there is a subset that is Pareto efficient, given η_1.

Definition η_1*-Efficient Transfers*

The set of functions $\Delta \equiv \{ \delta_i: S \rightarrow \mathbb{R}, i = 1, ..., I \}$ is η_1-efficient if

(a) Δ is η_1-consistent,

(b) there does not exist an alternative η_1-consistent transfer Δ' such that

$$U_i(\mathbf{e}_i + \boldsymbol{\delta}_i') \ge U_i(\mathbf{e}_i + \boldsymbol{\delta}_i), \quad \forall\, i,$$

with at least one strict inequality.

To compare public *ex post* information systems, we adopt an efficiency perspective and define information system η_1 to be as efficient as η_1' if for every η_1'-efficient transfer there exists a η_1-consistent transfer that is Pareto preferred.

Definition *Information System Efficiency*

Information system η_1 is *as efficient as (more efficient than)* η_1' if for every η_1'-efficient transfer Δ' there exists an η_1-consistent transfer Δ that is (strictly) Pareto preferred to Δ', i.e.,

$$U_i(\mathbf{e}_i+\boldsymbol{\delta}_i) \geq U_i(\mathbf{e}_i+\boldsymbol{\delta}_i'), \quad \forall\, i,$$

(with at least one strict inequality).

In general, the efficiency of one information system relative to another depends on endowments, preferences, and beliefs. As in Chapter 3 we seek general statements that are independent of the choice problem based on the relative informativeness of the information systems. Since the information systems are represented as partitions on S, i.e., they are noiseless information systems relative to S, informativeness can be compared based on the partitions they induce on S.

Definition *Informativeness*

Information system η_1 is *as (more) informative as (than)* η_1' if Y_1^η is at least as fine a (a finer) partition of S as (than) $Y_1^{\eta'}$.

If information system η_1 is as informative as η_1', then any η_1'-efficient transfer Δ' is η_1-consistent and, thus, we get the following result (compare to Proposition 3.7).

Proposition 5.7

Information system η_1 is as efficient as η_1' if η_1 is as informative as η_1'.

The above relations are depicted in Figure 5.6. Suppose η_1 is more informative than η_1'. The set of η_1'-consistent expected utility levels, $\boldsymbol{U}(\eta_1')$, is a subset of the η_1-consistent expected utility levels, $\boldsymbol{U}(\eta_1)$. Hence, the set of η_1-efficient expected utility levels, $\boldsymbol{U}^*(\eta_1)$, is never below the set of η_1'-efficient expected utility levels, $\boldsymbol{U}^*(\eta_1')$. The expected utility levels associated with four transfer arrangements are depicted; all four are η_1-consistent, but only the first and second are η_1'-consistent. The first transfer yields $\mathbf{U}^1$ which is neither η_1- nor η_1'-efficient, and the second yields $\mathbf{U}^2$ which is η_1'-efficient and strictly Pareto preferred to $\mathbf{U}^1$. The third yields $\mathbf{U}^3$ which is strictly Pareto preferred to $\mathbf{U}^1$, but is not η_1-efficient and is not Pareto comparable to $\mathbf{U}^2$. The fourth provides $\mathbf{U}^4$ and is both η_1-efficient and strictly Pareto preferred to $\mathbf{U}^2$. Proposition 5.7 guarantees the existence of some $\mathbf{U}^4 \in U(\eta_1)$ that is at least weakly Pareto preferred to $\mathbf{U}^2 \in U(\eta_1')$.

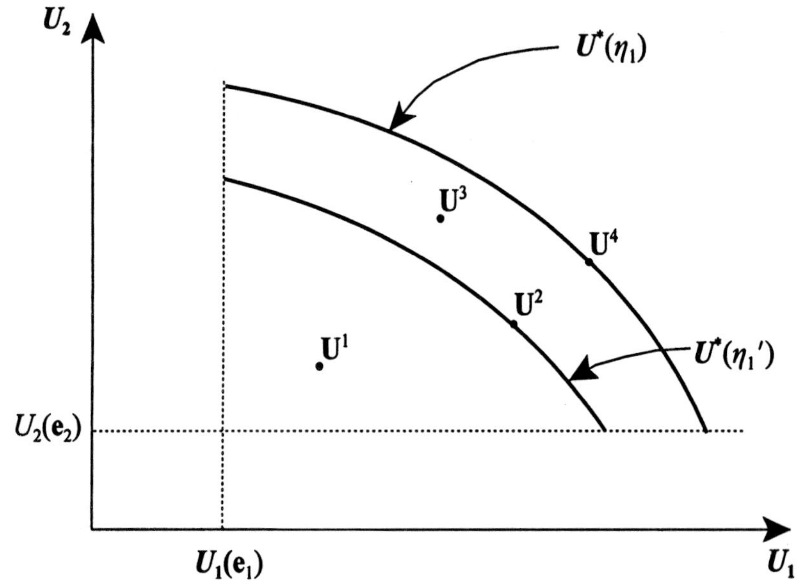

Figure 5.6: η_1- and η_1'-consistent transfers.

Proposition 5.7 relies on the fact that any additional information in η_1 compared with η_1' can be "ignored" when making transfers between investors and, thus, the additional information has no impact on the investors' expected utility. Another question is whether the additional information can lead to strict gains, for example, does the perfect information system η_1^p lead to more efficient transfers than the "null" information system, η_1^o ? The answer is probably yes. The null information system does not allow any risk sharing between investors, since transfers must be η_1^o-measurable, whereas perfect information allows investors to efficiently share all risks. The following proposition establishes conditions under which more information has no value.

Proposition 5.8

Suppose η_1 is a more informative information system than η_1'. The additional information in η_1 has no value, i.e., any η_1-efficient transfer is η_1'-consistent, if

(a) endowments are η_1'-measurable, and

(b) investors have homogeneous beliefs.

Proof: The proof follows from our prior analysis of efficient risk sharing. If endowments are η_1'-measurable, then aggregate consumption is also η_1'-measurable. This implies that η_1' is at least as fine a partition on S as the partition generated by aggregate consumption, Γ. It follows from Proposition 5.3 that with homogeneous beliefs an efficient consumption plan with information system η_1 is Γ-measurable and, hence, the transfers $\boldsymbol{\delta}_i(s) = \boldsymbol{c}_i(s) - e_i(s)$ are also η_1'-measurable for all i. That is, any η_1-efficient transfer is also η_1'-consistent.
Q.E.D.

If beliefs are homogeneous, investors efficiently consume the same amount within each aggregate consumption event $y \in \Gamma$ irrespectively of the information system, and if their endowments are η_1'-measurable, there is enough public information with η_1' to facilitate transfers that achieve this result – any additional information cannot be used to improve risk sharing between investors. Hence, necessary conditions for additional public information to be strictly valuable are that endowments are not measurable with respect to the less informative system or that investors have heterogeneous beliefs (or both).

If endowments are not η_1'-measurable, there is not enough information in η_1' to facilitate transfers that achieve Γ-measurable consumption plans.[30] That is, investors must retain some uninsurable endowment risk not related to variations in aggregate consumption. If the additional information in η_1 allows investors to share some (or all) of that risk, then the additional information is valuable, i.e., η_1 is more efficient than η_1'.

If beliefs are heterogeneous, more information provides additional opportunities for side-betting (see Section 4.1.3). For example, suppose endowments are Γ-measurable, and that η_1' only provides the information generated by aggregate consumption, i.e., $Y_1^{\eta'} = \Gamma$. Suppose there exist two signals y^1 and y^2 from η_1 within the same aggregate consumption $y \in \Gamma$ for which there exist (at least) two investors with different relative probabilities for the two events. Then an efficient consumption plan with η_1 is such that (see 4.15)

$$\frac{u_i'(\boldsymbol{c}_i(y^1))}{u_i'(\boldsymbol{c}_i(y^2))} = \frac{\mu(y^1)/\varphi_i(y^1)}{\mu(y^2)/\varphi_i(y^2)}$$

and, thus, each of the investors do not efficiently consume the same amount in both events. Hence, the additional information in η_1 is valuable.

The analysis in this section has considered the impact of public *ex post* information on efficient transfers (or consumption plans) without considering the implementation of those transfers through trading of marketed securities.

---

[30] Note that Γ is at least as coarse a partition of S as $Y_1^{\eta'}$.

Additional public *ex post* information has no value in a market setting unless additional securities are introduced that facilitate transfers based on that information – the feasible transfers in a market setting is determined by the "span" of the marketed securities. Any equilibrium based on η_1' is also an equilibrium with a more informative *ex post* information system η_1 given the same marketed securities.[31]

On the other hand, if the set of marketed securities are expanded, such that the securities market is complete relative to η_1, then Proposition 5.2 implies that the equilibrium transfers are η_1-efficient and, thus, the equilibrium transfers may be more efficient than the equilibrium transfers with η_1'. However, note that even though "efficiency" may be improved with η_1 if beliefs are heterogeneous or endowments are not η_1'-measurable, the additional information may make some investors worse off and others better off (but not everyone worse off). The additional information changes the structure of the event-prices and, thus, the value at $t = 0$ of the investors' individual endowments (i.e., their initial wealth) may decrease or increase (see, for example, Hakansson, Kunkel and Ohlson, 1982).

5.5.2 *Ex Ante* Information

Ex ante information is released before the investors trade, whereas *ex post* information is released after they trade. In this section we take the *ex post* information system η_1 as fixed. If endowments are η_1-efficient, then there will be no trading, no matter what *ex ante* system is used. However, if endowments are not η_1-efficient, then trading can facilitate investor risk sharing. More *ex post* information never leads to less efficient equilibrium transfers (although some investors may be worse off and others better off). On the other hand, an information structure that releases information about future events prior to trading at $t = 0$, *can make everyone worse off from the perspective of the investors' expected utility levels prior to the release of the ex ante information.*

This is commonly referred to as the *information risk problem* (see, e.g., Hirshleifer, 1971). It arises when investors cannot efficiently share their risks before receiving information.

To explore this issue more formally, fix η_1 as the *ex post* information system and let η_0^o be the "null" *ex ante* system, i.e., $Y_0^o = \{S\}$, with $\boldsymbol{\eta}' = (\eta_0^o, \eta_1)$. Now consider an alternative *ex ante* system η_0 that gives a non-trivial partition of S no finer than the *ex post* system η_1, and let $\boldsymbol{\eta} = (\eta_0, \eta_1)$. Furthermore, let $\mathscr{E}(\boldsymbol{\eta}')$ and $\mathscr{E}(\boldsymbol{\eta})$ denote equilibria for the two information systems.

[31] Note that in pure-exchange setting the dividends $d_j(s)$ are independent of the information system.

Proposition 5.9

If the equilibrium $\mathscr{E}(\boldsymbol{\eta}')$ is η_1-efficient, then there is no equilibrium $\mathscr{E}(\boldsymbol{\eta})$ that makes all investors at least as well off and at least one investor strictly better off.

If the securities market is complete, the equilibrium $\mathscr{E}(\boldsymbol{\eta}')$ is η_1-efficient and, thus, more *ex ante* information cannot lead to a strict Pareto improvement. On the other hand, more *ex ante* information can preclude risk sharing possibilities by precluding trading prior to the release of the information. To illustrate, consider an economy with two states which are revealed at $t = 1$ by η_1, i.e., $Y_1 = \{\{ s_1 \}, \{ s_2 \}\}$, and two investors, A and B, who have homogeneous beliefs and the following endowments:

$$\mathbf{e}_A = \{ 20, 40 \}, \quad \mathbf{e}_B = \{ 30, 10 \}.$$

Note that aggregate consumption is the same in the two states, and suppose there are two distinct marketed securities. Since beliefs are homogeneous, trading in the two securities based on no information at $t = 0$ results in riskless equilibrium consumption plans for both investors, and both investors are better off with their equilibrium consumption plans than their endowments. On the other hand, if the state is revealed prior to trading at $t = 0$, there is no basis for trading – both investors have to stick with their endowments. That is, both investors are worse off if the state is revealed before they can share the risk associated with which state is going to occur. Although more complicated, other examples can be constructed in which some investors are better off while others are worse off in equilibria with more *ex ante* information than the "null" information.

5.6 Concluding Remarks

In this chapter we have examined a basic single-period model of efficient risk sharing in competitive capital markets. We have established market value relations of risky securities under three increasingly restrictive assumptions, no arbitrage, individual optimality, and market equilibrium. Market completeness was emphasized as the means of achieving efficient risk sharing. We considered additional assumptions on preferences, beliefs and the structure of dividends that facilitate an effectively complete market. In particular, we introduced the distinction between firm-specific and economy-wide risks and identified diversification as a means of overcoming the market incompleteness created by firm-specific events. We also briefly considered the impact of public information and distinguished between *ex post* and *ex ante* information. Basically, *ex post* information in addition to dividends is of no value if beliefs are homogeneous and endowments are insurable. On the other hand, *ex ante* information may make everyone worse off because it may eliminate an efficient sharing of the risks, i.e., the information risk problem. Obviously, in a multi-period model *ex post* information for one period is *ex ante* information for the following periods. However, the basic insights apply to multi-period settings as well. Having fully understood these issues in the simple setting of a single-period model is an excellent starting point for the examination of similar issues in the more realistic setting of multi-period models, which we consider next.

REFERENCES

Amershi, A. H. (1985) "A Complete Analysis of Full Pareto Efficiency in Financial Markets for Arbitrary Preferences," *Journal of Finance* 40, 1235-1243.

Berninghaus, S. (1977) "Individual and Collective Risks in Large Economies," *Journal of Economic Theory* 15, 279-294.

Breeden, D., and R. Litzenberger. (1978) "Prices of State Contingent Claims Implicit in Options Prices," *Journal of Business* 51, 621-652.

Breeden, D. (1979) "An Intertemporal Asset Pricing Model with Stochastic consumption and Investment Opportunities," *Journal of Financial Economics* 7, 265-296.

Brennan, M., and A. Kraus. (1978) "Necessary Conditions for Aggregation in Securities Markets," *Journal of Quantitative and Financial Analysis* 13, 407-418.

Caspi, Y. (1974) "Optimal Allocation of Risk in a Market with Many Traders," in J. Dreze (ed.) *Allocation under Uncertainty: Equilibrium and Optimality*. New York: Macmillan.

Caspi, Y. (1978) "A Limit Theorem on the Core of an Economy with Individual Risks," *Review of Economic Studies* 45, 267-271.

Cass, D., and J. E. Stiglitz. (1970) "The Structure of Investor Preferences and Asset Returns, and Separability in Portfolio Allocation: A Contribution to the Pure Theory of Mutual Funds," *Journal of Economic Theory* 8, 122-160.

Christensen, P. O., S. E. Graversen, and K. R. Miltersen. (2000) "Dynamic Spanning in the Consumption Based Capital Asset Pricing Model," *European Finance Review* 4, 129-156.

Duffie, D. (1996) *Dynamic Asset Pricing Theory*, Princeton University Press, Princeton, New Jersey.

Feltham, G. A., and P. O. Christensen. (1988) "Firm-Specific Information and Efficient Resource Allocation," *Contemporary Accounting Research* 5, 133-169.

Hakansson, N. H. (1970) "Optimal Investment and Consumption Strategies under Risk for a Class of Utility Functions," *Econometrica* 38, 587-607.

Hakansson, N. H. (1977) "The Superfund: Efficient Paths toward Efficient Capital Markets in Large and Small Countries." in H. Levy and M. Sarnat (eds.), *Financial Decision Making under Uncertainty*. New York: Academic Press.

Hakansson, N. H., J. G. Kunkel, and J. A. Ohlson. (1982) "Sufficient and Necessary Conditions for Information to have Social Value in Pure Exchange," *Journal of Finance* 37, 1169-1181.

Hirshleifer, J. (1971) "The Private and Social Value of Information and the Reward to Inventive Activity," *American Economic Review* 61, 561-574.

Huang, C.-F., and R. H. Litzenberger. (1988) *Foundations for Financial Economics*. New York: North-Holland.

Leland, H. (1978) "Information, Managerial Choice and Stockholder Unanimity," *Review of Economic Studies* 45, 527-534.

Magill, M., and M. Quinzii. (1996) *Theory of Incomplete Markets*. Massachusetts: The MIT Press.

Malinvaud, E. (1972) "The Allocation of Individual Risk in Large Markets," *Econometrica* 40, 414-429.

Malinvaud, E. (1973) "Markets for an Exchange Economy with Individual Risk," *Econometrica* 41, 383-410.

Samuelson, P. A. (1967) "General Proof That Diversification Pays," *Journal of Financial and Quantitative Analysis* 2, 1-13.

Ross, S. (1976) "The Arbitrage Theory of Capital Asset Pricing," *Journal of Economic Theory* 15, 341-359.

Ross, S. (1977) "Return, Risk, and Arbitrage," in I. Friend and J. L. Bicksler (eds.) *Risk and Return in Finance*. Massachusetts: Ballinger.

Ross, S. (1978) "Mutual Fund Separation in Financial Theory: The Separating Distributions," *Journal of Economic Theory* 17, 254-286.

Rubinstein, M. (1974) "An Aggregation Theorem for Securities Markets," *Journal of Financial Economics* 1, 225-244.

CHAPTER 6

ARBITRAGE AND RISK SHARING IN MULTI-PERIOD MARKETS

This chapter extends the single period analysis in the prior chapter to a setting with multiple consumption dates and sequential trading of long-lived securities. The information system publicly reports a signal at each date. It is taken as given in this chapter, whereas in Chapter 7 we explore the impact of varying the public information system. Both Chapters 6 and 7 continue to examine pure exchange settings, i.e., production choice is exogenous and independent of the information system. However, in Chapter 8 we consider settings with endogenous production choices.

In the single-period models considered in prior chapters the information typically pertains to what is known by the investors (or the decision maker) at a given point in time, either before or after decisions are made. In a multi-period setting we must specify what is known to investors at different dates, i.e., how information evolves over time. Dividends, security prices, portfolio and consumption decisions must all be consistent with available information at different dates. Anticipating the future sequence of date-event contingent dividends and prices, the investors' portfolio problem is not just a matter of choosing a portfolio of securities, but rather choosing *portfolio and consumption plans* that specify the optimal portfolio and consumption for each possible event at each future date. Hence, dynamic trading of long-lived securities becomes a key issue. We establish the market value implications of no arbitrage for dynamic trading strategies in multi-period settings. These market value relations will be the basis for the examination of the relation between accounting information and market values of equity in Chapters 9 and 10. In addition, we examine efficient risk sharing with dynamic trading strategies, and in a similar vein as in Chapter 5 we provide conditions on preferences, beliefs, and the structure of dividends that facilitates an effectively dynamically complete market.

6.1 MARKET VALUE IMPLICATIONS OF NO ARBITRAGE IN MULTI-PERIOD SETTINGS

6.1.1 Basic Elements of the Multi-period Model

Our model of a multi-period economy has a finite horizon with the following dates:

$t = 0$, – the initial trading/information date;

$t = 1, 2, ..., T\text{-}1$, – subsequent trading/information/dividend/consumption dates;

$t = T$, – terminal information/dividend/consumption date.

As before, the probability spaces for the I investors are $\{ S, \Xi, P_i \}$, $i = 1, ..., I$, with a finite state space S and we assume for simplicity that $P_i(s) > 0$ for all i and all states $s \in S$.

A key characteristic of multi-period markets is how information evolves through time. Prior to trading and consumption at date t, information system η_t generates a public signal, i.e., η_t: $S \rightarrow Y_t$ where Y_t represents the set of signals as well as the corresponding partition on the state space S. Investors have "perfect recall" such that the sequence of partitions $\mathbf{Y} = \{ Y_0, Y_1, ..., Y_T \}$ is such that Y_t is at least as fine a partition of S as Y_{t-1}, $t = 1, ..., T$.[1]

Figure 6.1 illustrates a sequence of partitions in a four-date economy. At $t = 0$, there is no information about which one of the possible twelve states is the true state, i.e., $Y_0^\eta = \{S\}$. At subsequent dates, as more information is received, the set of possible states becomes smaller and smaller, i.e., $S \supseteq y_1 \supseteq ... \supseteq y_T \ni s$. Hence, given the information at date t, the investors' posterior beliefs for future events (assuming homogeneous beliefs) are

$$\varphi(y_\tau | y_t) = \begin{cases} \dfrac{\varphi(y_\tau)}{\varphi(y_t)} & \text{if } y_\tau \subseteq y_t \\ 0 & \text{otherwise.} \end{cases} \qquad \text{for all } \tau > t$$

[1] For notational simplicity we suppress the partitions' dependence on the information system η.

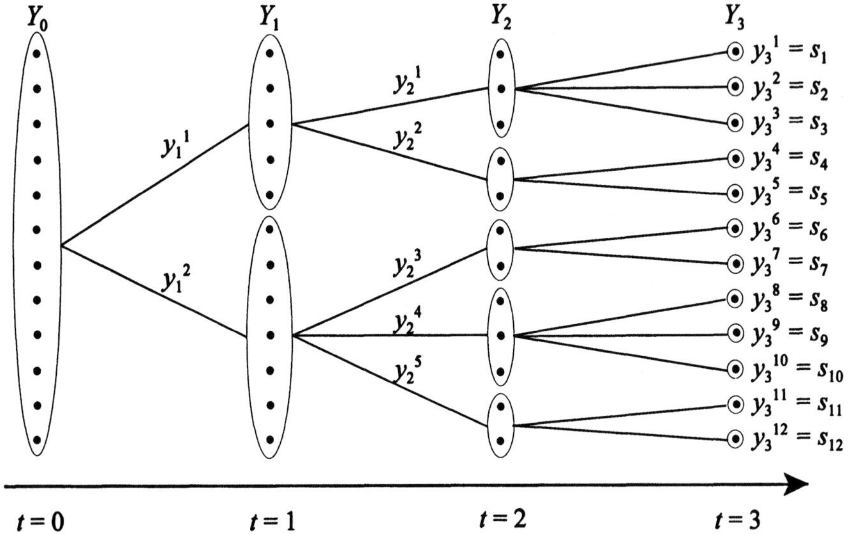

Figure 6.1: Sequence of partitions in a four-date economy.

Consistency requires that any publicly observable sequence of events, such as dividends or market values, must be measurable with respect to the public information system. Such a sequence of events is termed an *adapted (stochastic) process*. More formally, a sequence of random variables $\mathbf{X} = \{ X_0, X_1, ..., X_T \}$ is an adapted process with respect to $\mathbf{Y}$ if the random variable X_t is measurable with respect to Y_t, i.e., $X_t(s') = X_t(s'')$ for all $s', s'' \in y_t$, and, thus, we write it as a function of y_t, i.e., $X_t = X_t(y_t)$. Each of the J marketed securities is a claim to an adapted dividend process $\mathbf{d}_j$ with $d_{jt} = d_{jt}(y_t)$ denoting the dividend paid by security j at date t, $t = 0, 1, ..., T$. Similarly, each security has an adapted security-price process $\mathbf{v}_j$ where $v_{jt} = v_{jt}(y_t)$ is the *ex-dividend* security price at date $t = 0, 1, ..., T$ with $v_{jT} \equiv 0$. Hence, at each date the security pays its dividend d_{jt}, and is subsequently available for trading at its *ex-dividend* price v_{jt}. The cum-dividend price is denoted $V_{jt} = v_{jt} + d_{jt}$. The (vector) processes for dividends and security prices of the J marketed securities are denoted $\mathbf{d} = \{ \mathbf{d}_1, ..., \mathbf{d}_J \}$ and $\mathbf{v} = \{ \mathbf{v}_1, ..., \mathbf{v}_J \}$, respectively.

A portfolio plan is an adapted (vector) process $\mathbf{z}$ with $z_{jt} = z_{jt}(y_t)$ denoting the number of units held of security j after trading at date $t = 0, 1, ..., T$. The dividend process $\mathbf{d}^\mathbf{z}$ generated by the portfolio plan $\mathbf{z}$ is given by (a date-event-contingent relation)

$$d_t^\mathbf{z} = (\mathbf{v}_t + \mathbf{d}_t)^t \mathbf{z}_{t-1} - \mathbf{v}_t^t \mathbf{z}_t, \quad t = 0, 1, ..., T, \quad \mathbf{z}_{-1} \equiv \mathbf{0}.$$

That is, the cum-dividend price of the portfolio acquired at t - 1 minus the ex-dividend price of the portfolio acquired at t. We assume that no dividends are paid by any security at the initial date $t = 0$, i.e., $d_{j0} = 0$, $\forall j$. However, the dividend process of a portfolio plan has a non-zero dividend at the initial date if $d_0^{\mathbf{z}} = - \mathbf{v}_0^{\mathrm{t}}\mathbf{z}_0 \neq 0$.

6.1.2 No Arbitrage in Multi-period Markets

As in the single-period setting, an arbitrage opportunity is a portfolio plan that generates non-negative pay-offs in all events at all dates and strictly positive pay-offs in some events at some dates. That is, the dividend process of an arbitrage opportunity is a non-negative, non-zero process, $\mathbf{d}^{\mathbf{z}} > \mathbf{0}$.

Proposition 6.1[2]

There is no arbitrage if, and only if, there is a strictly increasing linear function $F: L \rightarrow \mathbb{R}$ such that $F(\mathbf{d}^{\mathbf{z}}) = 0$ for any portfolio plan $\mathbf{z}$, where L is the space of processes adapted to $\mathbf{Y}$ (which we treat as implicit). That is, there exists a *strictly positive* adapted event-price process $\mathbf{p}$ such that

$$d_0^{\mathbf{z}} p_0 + \sum_{t=1}^{T} \sum_{y_t \in Y_t} d_t^{\mathbf{z}}(y_t)\, p_t(y_t) = 0, \quad \forall\, \mathbf{z} \in L. \tag{6.1}$$

Clearly, the constant $p_0 > 0$ can be chosen arbitrarily. If we let $p_0 = 1$, and note that $d_0^{\mathbf{z}} = - \mathbf{v}_0^{\mathrm{t}}\mathbf{z}_0$, the initial value of any portfolio plan is equal to the dividends it generates times the corresponding date-event prices, i.e.,

$$\mathbf{v}_0^{\mathrm{t}}\mathbf{z}_0 = \sum_{t=1}^{T} \sum_{y_t \in Y_t} d_t^{\mathbf{z}}(y_t)\, p_t(y_t). \tag{6.2}$$

Furthermore, if we take the portfolio plan to be a "buy-and-hold strategy" in security j, the initial price of that security is given as its dividend process times the corresponding date-event prices, i.e.,

$$v_{j0} = \sum_{t=1}^{T} \sum_{y_t \in Y_t} d_{jt}(y_t)\, p_t(y_t). \tag{6.3}$$

---

[2] Although somewhat more complicated, the proof is essentially the same as for Proposition 5.1 using Stiemke's Lemma (see, for example, Duffie 1996, 2B, for a direct proof).

Hence, security prices are determined in a fashion similar to the single-period setting, i.e., the summation over *dates and events* of the dividends times the event-prices. The event-price $p_t(y_t)$ is the implicit price at $t = 0$ of acquiring a claim to an additional unit of account (e.g., consumption) at date t if event y_t occurs, i.e., the price of an *implicit date-event security* for y_t.

Of course, no arbitrage for general multi-period portfolio plans implies that there is no arbitrage in the periods between any two subsequent trading dates (or any other two trading dates). Assume that y_t is observed at date t. The possible events at the following date are the set of events $y_{t+1} \subseteq y_t$, and the pay-offs of the securities are the *cum-dividend* security prices at t+1. Proposition 5.1 implies that there is no arbitrage in the period from t to t+1 if, and only if, there are strictly positive event-prices $p_{t+1,t}(y_{t+1}|y_t)$ for $y_{t+1} \subseteq y_t$ such that[3]

$$v_{jt}(y_t) = \sum_{y_{t+1} \subseteq y_t} V_{jt+1}(y_{t+1})\, p_{t+1,t}(y_{t+1}|y_t), \quad j = 1, 2, \ldots, J. \tag{6.4}$$

where $$p_{t+1,t}(y_{t+1}|y_t) = \frac{p_{t+1}(y_{t+1})}{p_t(y_t)}, \qquad y_{t+1} \subseteq y_t.$$

Similarly, by using "buy-and-hold" portfolio plans between date t and T, we get that no arbitrage implies there are strictly positive date-event prices such that

$$v_{jt}(y_t) = \sum_{\tau = t+1}^{T} \sum_{y_\tau \subseteq y_t} d_{j\tau}(y_\tau)\, p_{\tau t}(y_\tau|y_t), \quad j = 1, 2, \ldots, J. \tag{6.5}$$

where $$p_{\tau t}(y_\tau|y_t) = \frac{p_\tau(y_\tau)}{p_t(y_t)}, \qquad \forall\, y_\tau \subseteq y_t,\ \tau > t.$$

The event-price $p_{\tau t}(y_\tau|y_t)$ can be interpreted as the price at date t given event y_t of a security that pays one unit of account at date $\tau > t$ if event $y_\tau \subseteq y_t$ occurs and nothing otherwise. Of course, given y_t at date t, the prices of date-event securities for events "not following" y_t (i.e., $y_\tau \not\subseteq y_t$, $\tau > t$) equal zero.

Dynamically Complete Markets

In the single-period setting, the securities market is defined to be complete if the marketed securities span all pay-off vectors. In that setting, there is only a

---

[3] This follows from the fact that

$$- v_{jt}(y_t)\, p_t(y_t) + \sum_{y_{t+1} \subseteq y_t} V_{jt+1}(y_{t+1})\, p_{t+1}(y_{t+1}) = 0.$$

single trading date, and any event-contingent pay-off vector at $t = 1$ can be obtained as a portfolio of the marketed securities. Establishing "completeness" in a multi-period setting is a more complex issue since implementing a given date-event contingent pay-off process may be accomplished by a sequence of trades.

However, before considering the use of a sequence of trades, we consider a setting in which the market is sufficiently complete to implement any date-event contingent pay-off process with one round of trading at $t = 0$. This is obviously the case if the set of marketed securities includes *date-event securities* for all events at all dates. In this case, any dividend process $\mathbf{d}$ can be obtained by acquiring a portfolio at $t = 0$ with $d_t(y_t)$ units of the date-event security for y_t, $y_t \in Y_t$, $t = 1, ..., T$.

Definition *Complete Multi-period Securities Market*

The multi-period securities market is said to be complete if the set of marketed securities includes date-event securities for all events at all dates.

In a complete multi-period securities market there is no need for trading at subsequent trading dates in order to generate a given dividend process. However, if the multi-period securities market is not complete, for example, if it only includes securities with payments at several dates and events, it may still be possible to implement any adapted dividend process by dynamically trading "long-lived" securities at subsequent trading dates. We refer to such a market as being dynamically complete.

Definition *Dynamically Complete Securities Market*

The securities market is said to be dynamically complete if for any adapted process $\mathbf{X}$ in L there exists a portfolio plan $\mathbf{z}$ which generates dividend process $d_t^{\mathbf{z}}(y_t) = X_t(y_t)$, $y_t \in Y_t$, $t = 1, ..., T$.[4]

For any trading date t and event $y_t \in Y_t$, let $M_t(y_t)$ denote the number of possible events at date t+1, i.e., the number of events $y_{t+1} \subseteq y_t$.[5] Furthermore, let $\mathbf{V}_{t+1}(y_t)$ denote the pay-off matrix of securities for the following period,

$$\mathbf{V}_{t+1}(y_t) \equiv \left[V_{jt+1}(y_{t+1}) \right]_{J \times M_t(y_t)},$$

[4] Note that the portfolio plan is flexible with respect to the values of X_t that can be generated for $t \geq 1$, but the value of X_0 for any plan is constrained by no-arbitrage condition (6.1), which establishes the initial "cost" of the plan.

[5] That is, the number of branches leaving the information set y_t (see Figure 6.1).

i.e., it is the $J \times M_t(y_t)$ matrix of *cum-dividend* security prices at t+1. If this matrix has rank $M_t(y_t)$, then any pay-off vector at t+1 in $\mathbb{R}^{M_t(y_t)}$ can be generated by selecting an appropriate portfolio at date t, given event y_t. Furthermore, if this condition holds for all t and y_t, then, for each adapted process **X** in L, there exists a portfolio plan **z** with dividend process $d_t^{\mathbf{z}}(y_t) = X_t(y_t)$, $y_t \in Y_t$, $t = 1, ..., T$. To see this, for each $y_{t+1} \subseteq y_t$, let $w_{t+1}^{\mathbf{X}}(y_{t+1})$ denote the wealth required at date t+1 to provide $X_{t+1}(y_{t+1})$ and acquire the portfolio $\mathbf{z}_{t+1}^{\mathbf{X}}(y_{t+1})$ which will be used to implement $X_\tau(y_\tau)$, $y_\tau \subseteq y_{t+1}$, $\tau > t+1$, i.e.,

$$w_{t+1}^{\mathbf{X}}(y_{t+1}) = X_{t+1}(y_{t+1}) + \sum_{j=1}^{J} v_{jt+1}(y_{t+1})\, z_{jt+1}^{\mathbf{X}}(y_{t+1}), \tag{6.6}$$

and let $\mathbf{w}_{t+1}^{\mathbf{X}}(y_t)$ denote the corresponding $M_t(y_t) \times 1$ wealth vector. Note that the required wealth is equal to the "current dividend," $X_{t+1}(y_{t+1})$, plus the ex-dividend value of a portfolio generating the "future dividends," X_τ, $\tau > t+1$. Since the pay-off matrix $\mathbf{V}_{t+1}(y_t)$ has rank $M_t(y_t)$, there exists a portfolio $\mathbf{z}_t^{\mathbf{X}}(y_t)$ at t and y_t such that

$$\mathbf{V}_{t+1}(y_t)^{\mathrm{t}}\, \mathbf{z}_t^{\mathbf{X}}(y_t) = \mathbf{w}_{t+1}^{\mathbf{X}}(y_t). \tag{6.7}$$

Hence, starting at T-1, the portfolio plan that generates the dividend process $X_t(y_t)$, $y_t \in Y_t$, $t = 1, ..., T$ can be constructed by backward substitution into (6.6) and (6.7), and its price at $t = 0$ is $\mathbf{v}_0^{\mathrm{t}}\mathbf{z}_0^{\mathbf{X}}$.

On the other hand, if the rank of the pay-off matrix is less than $M_t(y_t)$ for some t and y_t, there clearly exist adapted processes such that there are no portfolios at t and y_t that solve (6.7), i.e., there are dividend processes that cannot be implemented by trading in the marketed securities.

Proposition 6.2

The securities market is dynamically complete if, and only if, for each trading date $t = 0, 1, ..., T$-1, and each event $y_t \in Y_t$ the pay-off matrix $\mathbf{V}_{t+1}(y_t)$ has rank $M_t(y_t)$.

Let the *spanning number M* denote the maximum number of events following a prior event, i.e.,

$$M = \max_{t,\, y_t} \{\, M_t(y_t) \,\}.$$

Note that the securities market can only be dynamically complete if the number of securities J is greater than or equal to the spanning number M. In addition, the J securities must be sufficiently distinct that the pay-off matrix between any two dates has rank $M_t(y_t)$.

In a complete multi-period market, the date-event securities are traded directly. However, while not traded directly, any given date-event dividend can be generated by appropriate trading in a dynamically complete market. That is, for any *date-event dividend* security $\mathbf{d}^{y_t}$ such that

$$d_{t'}^{y_t}(y') = \begin{cases} 1 & \text{if } t' = t \text{ and } y' = y_t, \\ 0 & \text{otherwise,} \end{cases}$$

there exists a portfolio plan $\mathbf{z}^{y_t}$ that yields $\mathbf{d}^{y_t}$. Furthermore, the value of the initial portfolio based on the *unique* no-arbitrage prices equals the date-event price at $t = 0$, i.e.,

$$\mathbf{v}_0{}^t\mathbf{z}_0^{y_t} = p_t(y_t).$$

6.1.3 Alternative Representations of No-arbitrage Prices

As in the single-period model, no-arbitrage prices can be represented as the discounted, risk-adjusted expected dividends, where the risk adjustments are based on either risk-neutral probabilities or covariances of dividends with a valuation index. We again consider both approaches.

Risk-neutral Probabilities Based on the Prices of Zero-coupon Bonds
In the single-period setting we normalized the event-prices by the current price of the riskless asset (a zero-coupon bond) and obtained risk-neutral probabilities such that the price of any security could be determined as the discounted expected dividends using those probabilities. We can do essentially the same thing in the multi-period setting using the current prices of a sequence of zero-coupon bonds maturing at each future date.

Assume the set of marketed securities includes a zero-coupon bond for each date t which pays one unit of account in all events at date t (and nothing at any other date). Let $\beta_{\tau t}(y_t)$ denote the price at date t given event y_t of a zero-coupon bond maturing at date $\tau > t$, and let $R_{\tau t}(y_t)$ denote the corresponding return, i.e., $R_{\tau t}(y_t) = (\beta_{\tau t}(y_t))^{-1}$. The no-arbitrage relation (6.1) implies that

$$1 - \sum_{y_t \in Y_t} R_{t0}\, p_t(y_t) = 0.$$

Hence, we can define "risk-neutral" probabilities for date t by

$$\hat{\varphi}_{t0}(y_t) \equiv R_{t0}\, p_t(y_t), \quad t = 0, \ldots, T. \tag{6.8}$$

These probabilities are strictly positive, and they sum to one over all events for each date t, i.e., they satisfy the conditions for a probability distribution for events at date t.

The risk-neutral probabilities in (6.8) imply that the event prices can be expressed as

$$p_t(y_t) = \beta_{t0}\,\hat{\varphi}_{t0}(y_t),$$

which, when substituted into (6.3), yield

$$v_{j0} = \sum_{t=1}^{T} \beta_{t0}\,\hat{\mathrm{E}}_{t0}[d_{jt}]. \tag{6.9}$$

Hence, we again obtain an expression in which the market value of a security is expressed as the risk-adjusted expected dividend for each date t, discounted at the riskless interest rate from the initial date to t (i.e., the zero-coupon rate at $t = 0$ for maturity date t).

Now consider the market price at some date $t > 0$, given event y_t. The price of the zero-coupon bond maturing at date τ has now become $\beta_{\tau t}(y_t)$, and we can construct a set of conditional risk-neutral probabilities using the new zero-coupon prices:

$$\hat{\varphi}_{\tau t}(y_\tau | y_t) \equiv \begin{cases} R_{\tau t}(y_t)\, p_{\tau t}(y_\tau | y_t) & \text{if } y_\tau \subseteq y_t, \\ 0 & \text{otherwise,} \end{cases} \tag{6.11}$$

where

$$R_{\tau t}(y_t) = \frac{1}{\sum_{y_\tau \subseteq y_t} p_{\tau t}(y_\tau | y_t)}.$$

These risk-neutral probabilities are strictly positive and sum to one over all events at date $\tau > t$ and, thus, they satisfy the conditions for a conditional probability distribution given event y_t at date t.

The risk-neutral probabilities in (6.11) imply that the event-prices can be expressed as

$$p_{\tau t}(y_\tau | y_t) = \beta_{\tau t}(y_t)\,\hat{\varphi}_{\tau t}(y_\tau | y_t),$$

which, when substituted into (6.5), yields

$$v_{jt}(y_t) = \sum_{\tau=t+1}^{T} \beta_{\tau t}(y_t)\, \hat{\mathrm{E}}_{\tau t}[d_{j\tau}|y_t]. \tag{6.12}$$

That is, at any date, security prices are determined as their risk-adjusted expected dividends discounted at the zero-coupon rates given the information at that date. The risk-adjusted expectation is taken with respect to the conditional risk-neutral probabilities based on the zero-coupon prices at that date.

While (6.12) is very useful and correct, one must be careful to use the new bond prices to compute the new risk-neutral probabilities when moving from one date to the next. In particular, one cannot, in general, apply Bayes' rule to the prior risk-neutral probabilities to obtain the conditional risk-neutral probabilities. To see the inconsistency between the two approaches, we compute the difference between the risk-neutral probability in (6.11) and the result of applying Bayes' rule to beliefs at date t given event y_t with respect to $y_\tau \subseteq y_t$, $\tau > t$:[6]

$$\hat{\varphi}_{\tau t}(y_\tau|y_t) - \hat{\varphi}_{\tau 0}(y_\tau)/\hat{\varphi}_{t0}(y_t) = R_{\tau t}(y_t)\, p_{\tau t}(y_\tau|y_t) - R_{\tau 0}\, p_\tau(y_\tau)/[R_{t0}\, p_t(y_t)]$$

$$= p_{\tau t}(y_\tau|y_t)[R_{\tau t}(y_t) - R_{\tau 0}/R_{t0}].$$

This implies that the two approaches are only equivalent if the event-contingent riskless return between dates t and τ (i.e., $R_{\tau t}(y_t)$) is independent of y_t, and equal to the forward return (i.e., $R_{\tau 0}/R_{t0}$) for the same period as of date $t = 0$. Since, in general, interest rates are stochastic, the above difference is not, in general, equal to zero.

We use value relation (6.12) extensively in Chapter 9 in our analysis of the relation between market values of equity and accounting numbers – the lack of "time-consistency" of the risk-neutral probabilities is not a problem! However, for completeness, in Appendix 6A, we consider the use of the cumulative return on a bank account as deflator in determining risk-neutral probabilities. While the bank fixes the one-period interest rate at the start of each period, the interest rate, in general, changes from period to period depending on the realized events.

---

[6] An alternative approach to demonstrating the "time-inconsistency" of risk-neutral probabilities based on zero-coupon bonds is to demonstrate that

$$\hat{\varphi}_{t0}(y_t) \neq \sum_{y_{t+1} \subseteq y_t} \hat{\varphi}_{t+1,0}(y_{t+1}).$$

As can be shown, the inequality holds if interest rates are stochastic.

The use of the bank account has the virtue of yielding risk-neutral probabilities that are time-consistent, but has the drawback of using stochastic discount factors.

Multi-period Valuation Index

We now examine the use of the covariance of dividends with a value index as a means of risk-adjusting expected dividends. As with risk-neutral probabilities, we use the current prices of a sequence of zero-coupon bonds as deflators.

Similar to the single-period setting, there is a Riesz representation for linear functions of adapted processes.

Lemma *Riesz Representation Theorem*

Assume the function F: $L \to \mathbb{R}$ is linear and let $\boldsymbol{\varphi} = \{ \varphi(y_t) \}$ be a strictly positive probability vector (or, more precisely, a sequence of probability vectors defined over the sequence of possible events in **Y**). Then there is a unique $\boldsymbol{\pi}$ in L, such that

$$F(\mathbf{X}) = \mathrm{E}\left(\sum_{t=0}^{T} \pi_t(y_t) X_t(y_t) \right)$$

$$= \sum_{t=0}^{T} \sum_{y_t \in Y_t} \varphi(y_t) \pi_t(y_t) X_t(y_t) \quad \text{for all } \mathbf{X} \in L.$$

Moreover, F is strictly increasing if, and only if, $\boldsymbol{\pi}$ is strictly positive.

Based on no-arbitrage condition (6.1), the *Riesz representation* $\boldsymbol{\pi}$ of the linear function F is given by

$$\pi_t(y_t) = \frac{p_t(y_t)}{\varphi(y_t)}, \quad y_t \in Y_t,\ t = 0, 1, ..., T.$$

Proposition 6.1 immediately implies the following result.

Corollary

There is no arbitrage with prices **v** and dividends **d** if, and only if, there exists a strictly positive *event-price deflator* $\boldsymbol{\pi}$ such that

$$v_{jt}(y_t) = \sum_{\tau=t+1}^{T} \mathrm{E}\left[\pi_{\tau t} d_{j\tau} | y_t\right], \quad j = 1, ..., J,\ y_t \in Y_t,\ t = 0, 1, ..., T\text{-}1, \quad (6.13)$$

for any strictly positive probability vector $\boldsymbol{\varphi}$, where $\pi_{\tau t}(y_\tau|y_t) \equiv \pi_\tau(y_\tau)/\pi_t(y_t)$ for $y_\tau \subseteq y_t$.

The multi-period valuation index is obtained by normalizing the event-price deflator by the prices of zero-coupon bonds at date t, i.e.,

$$q_{\tau t}(y_\tau|y_t) \equiv \pi_{\tau t}(y_\tau|y_t)/\beta_{\tau t}(y_t)$$

$$= p_{\tau t}(y_\tau|y_t)/[\beta_{\tau t}(y_t)\ \varphi(y_\tau|y_t)]$$

$$= \frac{\hat{\varphi}_{\tau t}(y_\tau|y_t)}{\varphi(y_\tau|y_t)}, \quad y_\tau \subseteq y_t \in Y_t, \tau > t = 0, 1, ..., T\text{-}1. \tag{6.14}$$

Note that, as in the single-period setting, the expected value of the valuation index is equal to one for any subsequent date, i.e.,

$$\mathrm{E}[q_{\tau t}|\, y_t\,] = 1, \quad \forall\, y_t \in Y_t, \tau > t.$$

Hence, the prices of securities are also determined by the following relation,

$$v_{jt}(y_t) = \sum_{\tau=t+1}^{T} \beta_{\tau t}(y_t)\left\{\mathrm{E}\big[d_{j\tau}|y_t\big] + \mathrm{Cov}\big[d_{j\tau}, q_{\tau t}|y_t\big]\right\}, \tag{6.15}$$

$$j = 1, ..., J, y_t \in Y_t, t = 0, 1, ..., T\text{-}1.$$

When we investigate the relation between market values of equity and accounting numbers in Chapter 9, we make extensive use of the no-arbitrage relations between current security prices and future dividends derived above. The "missing link" between dividends and accounting numbers is the so called *Clean Surplus Relation.*

6.2 OPTIMAL PORTFOLIO PLANS

Investors are characterized by an adapted process of strictly positive endowments $\mathbf{e}_i = \{\, \mathbf{e}_{i1}, ..., \mathbf{e}_{iT} \,\} \in L_{++}$ in units of consumption at dates $t = 1, ..., T$, their event beliefs $\varphi_i(y_t)$, and a strictly increasing and strictly concave utility function u_i defined on non-negative adapted consumption processes $\mathbf{c}_i = \{\, \mathbf{c}_{i1}, ..., \mathbf{c}_{iT} \,\} \in L_+$. We initially examine the relation between prices and preferences in a setting with general preferences, and then consider settings in which preferences are time-additive.

General Preferences

As in the single-period setting, endowments may consist of the dividends from an endowed portfolio $\bar{\mathbf{z}}_i$,[7] as well as consumption endowments from other sources, $\bar{\mathbf{c}}_i$, such as compensation contracts and non-marketed assets, i.e.,

$$\mathbf{e}_i = \mathbf{d}^{\bar{\mathbf{z}}_i} + \bar{\mathbf{c}}_i.$$

An investor can make transfers of consumption $\boldsymbol{\delta}_i$ between the different dates and events by holding his endowed portfolio and implementing a separate portfolio plan $\mathbf{z}_i$ with dividend process $\mathbf{d}^{\mathbf{z}_i} = \boldsymbol{\delta}_i$, where

$$d_t^{\mathbf{z}_i} = \mathbf{V}_t^{\mathrm{t}}\mathbf{z}_{i,t-1} - \mathbf{v}_t^{\mathrm{t}}\mathbf{z}_{it}, \quad t = 0, 1, ..., T, \mathbf{z}_{i,-1} \equiv \mathbf{0},$$

are the date-event-contingent transfers such that he gets the date-event contingent consumption process $\mathbf{c}_{it} = \boldsymbol{\delta}_{it} + \mathbf{e}_{it}$, $t = 1, ..., T$. Since he has no wealth at $t = 0$, he must sell securities to buy securities and the price at $t = 0$ of any such portfolio plan must be non-positive, i.e., $d_0^{\mathbf{z}_i} \le 0$. Hence, investor i faces the following sequence of budget constraints,

$$d_0^{\mathbf{z}_i} = -\sum_{j=1}^{J} v_{j0}\, z_{ij0} \le 0, \tag{6.16a}$$

$$c_{it}(y_t) = d_t^{\mathbf{z}_i}(y_t) + e_{it}(y_t), \quad \forall\, y_t \in Y_t, t = 1, ..., T, \tag{6.16b}$$

where $$d_t^{\mathbf{z}_i}(y_t) = \sum_{j=1}^{J} V_{jt}(y_t)\, z_{ij,t-1}(y_{t-1}) - \sum_{j=1}^{J} v_{jt}(y_t)\, z_{ijt}(y_t).$$

We can therefore represent investor i's feasible consumption set (given his endowments, and the prices and dividends of marketed securities) as

$$C_i(\mathbf{e}_i, \mathbf{v}, \mathbf{d}) \equiv \left\{ \mathbf{c}_i \mid \mathbf{c}_i = \mathbf{d}^{\mathbf{z}} + \mathbf{e}_i \in L_+, \text{ where } \mathbf{v}_0^{\mathrm{t}}\mathbf{z}_0 \le 0 \right\}.$$

Observe that this consumption set consists of consumption plans that are non-negative and consistent with the information system (i.e., belongs to L_+) and can be implemented by a financially feasible portfolio plan (i.e., there exists a portfolio plan $\mathbf{z}$ with $\mathbf{v}_0^{\mathrm{t}}\mathbf{z}_0 \le 0$ such that $\mathbf{d}^{\mathbf{z}} = \mathbf{c}_i - \mathbf{e}_i$).

Investor i's decision problem can be formulated as follows.

---

[7] The endowed portfolio is expressed as $\bar{\mathbf{z}}_i$. It can be viewed as a plan consisting of an initial portfolio $\bar{\mathbf{z}}_{i0}$ that is held to date T, so that $\bar{\mathbf{z}}_{it}(y_t) = \bar{\mathbf{z}}_{i0}$, $\forall\, y_t \in Y_t$, $t = 1, ..., T$-1.

***Investor i's optimal portfolio choice problem*:**

$$\underset{\mathbf{c}_i \in C_i(\mathbf{e}_i,\mathbf{v},\mathbf{d})}{\text{maximize}} \; U_i(\mathbf{c}_i) = \underset{\mathbf{z}_i \in \{\mathbf{z} \in L^J \mid \mathbf{d}^{\mathbf{z}} + \mathbf{e}_i \in L_+, \, \mathbf{v}_0^t \mathbf{z}_0 \le 0\}}{\text{maximize}} \; U_i(\mathbf{d}^{\mathbf{z}_i} + \mathbf{e}_i).$$

where $U_i(\mathbf{c}_i)$ is the investor's expected utility, i.e.,

$$U_i(\mathbf{c}_i) = \sum_{y_T \in Y_T} u_i(\mathbf{c}_i(y_T))\, \varphi_i(y_T),$$

and $\mathbf{c}_i(y_T)$ denotes an entire "consumption path" (i.e., the sequence of consumption along the branches of the event tree that result in y_T). Assume for simplicity that there is a strictly interior optimal solution for the investor's optimal consumption plan (implying that there is no arbitrage and that the non-negativity constraints on consumption are not binding). The optimal portfolio plan is in that case a solution to the first-order condition for the following Lagrangian

$$\mathcal{L}_i = \sum_{y_T \in Y_T} u_i(\mathbf{c}_i(y_T))\, \varphi_i(y_T) - \lambda_i \sum_{j=1}^{J} z_{ij0}\, v_{j0},$$

where λ_i is the multiplier on the $t = 0$ budget constraint and $\mathbf{c}_i(y_T)$ is a function of the portfolio plan (see (6.16b)). *Ceteris paribus*, a marginal change in the number of shares of firm j acquired at date t given event y_t decreases the consumption at date t and increases the pay-off at date $t + 1$. Hence, the first-order conditions for an optimal investment in security j at $t = 0$ and at $t > 0$ given event y_t are[8]

[8] There is no consumption at $t = 0$, but the multiplier on the initial budget constraint establishes the marginal value of relaxing that constraint. The first-order conditions for subsequent periods follow from the fact that the first derivative with respect to $z_{ijt}(y_t)$ is

$$\sum_{y_T \subseteq y_t} \left[u_{ic_{t+1}}(\mathbf{c}_i(y_T))\, V_{j,t+1}(y_T) - u_{ic_t}(\mathbf{c}_i(y_T))\, v_{j,t}(y_T) \right] \varphi_i(y_T) = 0.$$

Furthermore, while the price functions at date t+1 vary with $y_{t+1} \subseteq y_t$, the price functions at date t do not, and

$$\varphi_i(y_T | y_t) = \varphi_i(y_T) \left[\sum_{y_T \subseteq y_t} \varphi_i(y_T) \right]^{-1}.$$

$$v_{j0} = \frac{1}{\lambda_i} \mathrm{E}_i[u_{ic_1}(\mathbf{c}_i(y_T))\, V_{j1}(y_1)], \quad j = 1, 2, ..., J, \tag{6.17a}$$

$$v_{jt}(y_t) = \frac{\mathrm{E}_i[u_{ic_{t+1}}(\mathbf{c}_i(y_T))\, V_{j,t+1}(y_{t+1}) \,|\, y_t]}{\mathrm{E}_i[u_{ic_t}(\mathbf{c}_i(y_T))|y_t]}, \quad j = 1, 2, ..., J, \tag{6.17b}$$

where u_{ic_t} is investor i's marginal utility with respect to a change in consumption at date t.

Observe that, since y_{t+1} reveals y_t, (6.17) can be expressed as

$$v_{j0} = \sum_{y_1 \in Y_1} \frac{1}{\lambda_i} \mathrm{E}_i[u_{ic_1}(\mathbf{c}_i(y_T))|y_1]\, V_{j1}(y_1)\, \varphi_i(y_1), \tag{6.18a}$$

$$v_{jt}(y_t) = \sum_{y_{t+1} \subseteq y_t} \frac{\mathrm{E}_i[u_{ic_{t+1}}(\mathbf{c}_i(y_T)) \,|\, y_{t+1}]}{\mathrm{E}_i[u_{ic_t}(\mathbf{c}_i(y_T))|y_t]} V_{jt+1}(y_{t+1})\, \varphi_i(y_{t+1}|y_t). \tag{6.18b}$$

Comparing no-arbitrage condition (6.4) to (6.18) establishes that the no-arbitrage prices between two adjacent dates, with optimal investment decisions, can be represented as

$$p_{t+1,t}(y_{t+1}|y_t) \equiv \begin{cases} \dfrac{1}{\lambda_i} \mathrm{E}_i[u_{ic_1}(\mathbf{c}_i(y_T))|y_1]\varphi_i(y_1) & y_1 \in Y_1,\ t = 0, \\[2ex] \dfrac{\mathrm{E}_i[u_{ic_{t+1}}(\mathbf{c}_i(y_T)) \,|\, y_{t+1}]}{\mathrm{E}_i[u_{ic_t}(\mathbf{c}_i(y_T))|y_t]} \varphi_i(y_{t+1}|y_t) & y_{t+1} \subseteq y_t,\ t > 0. \end{cases}$$

That is, the event-contingent prices between two dates reflect the change in expected marginal utilities and the related conditional probability. They can then be used to define a date-event price process **p** using

$$p_t(y_t) \equiv \prod_{\tau=0}^{t-1} p_{\tau+1,\tau}(y_{\tau+1}|y_\tau) = \frac{1}{\lambda_i} \mathrm{E}_i[u_{ic_t}(\mathbf{c}_i(y_T)) \,|\, y_t]\varphi_i(y_t).$$

Hence, no-arbitrage condition (6.3), with optimal investment decisions, implies

$$v_{j0} = \sum_{t=1}^{T} \sum_{y_t \in Y_t} d_{jt}(y_t) \frac{1}{\lambda_i} \mathrm{E}_i[u_{ic_t}(\mathbf{c}_i(y_T)) \,|\, y_t]\varphi_i(y_t).$$

Time-additive Preferences

With the general specification of the utility function defined on adapted consumption processes, the marginal utility of an additional unit of consumption at date t depends on past consumption as well as on future consumption, i.e., it depends on the entire "consumption path." While this is useful in some applications (e.g., in order to describe "habit formation"), most of our subsequent analysis will assume that investors have preferences that are represented by time-additive utility functions.

Definition *Time-additive Utility Functions (Preferences)*

The utility function u_i: $L_+ \to \mathbb{R}$ is time-additive if there exist "date utility functions" u_{it}: $\mathbb{R}_+ \to \mathbb{R}$ for each date such that for any non-negative consumption path $\mathbf{c}(y_T) \in L_+$

$$u_i(\mathbf{c}(y_T)) = \sum_{t=1}^{T} u_{it}(c_t(y_T)).$$

With time-additive preferences, the marginal utility of an additional unit of consumption at date t only depends on the consumption level at that date, hence, the date-event prices for any two subsequent dates depend only on the ratio of marginal utilities at the two dates and the conditional probability distribution for the latter date, i.e.,

$$p_{t+1,t}(y_{t+1}|y_t) \equiv \frac{u'_{it+1}(c_{it+1}(y_{t+1}))\, \varphi_i(y_{t+1}|y_t)}{u'_{it}(c_{it}(y_t))}, \quad y_{t+1} \subseteq y_t.$$

More generally, if there is a strictly interior optimal consumption plan for the investor's portfolio choice problem, there are date-event prices given y_t at date t for events $y_\tau \subseteq y_t$ at date τ,

$$p_{\tau t}(y_\tau|y_t) \equiv \frac{u'_{i\tau}(c_{i\tau}(y_\tau))\, \varphi_i(y_\tau|y_t)}{u'_{it}(c_{it}(y_t))}, \quad y_\tau \subseteq y_t, \ \tau > t = 0, ..., T\text{-}1. \qquad (6.19)$$

Risk-neutral Probabilities and Valuation Indices

With time-additive preferences and optimal investment decisions, the price at date t of a zero-coupon bond maturing at date τ can be expressed as

$$\beta_{\tau t}(y_t) = \frac{\mathrm{E}_i[u'_{i\tau}(c_{i\tau})|y_t]}{u'_{it}(c_{it}(y_t))},$$

and from (6.11) and (6.19) the risk-neutral probabilities based on the zero-coupon bonds are

$$\hat{\varphi}_{\tau t}(y_\tau | y_t) \equiv \begin{cases} \dfrac{u'_{i\tau}(c_{i\tau}(y_\tau))\, \varphi_i(y_\tau | y_t)}{\mathrm{E}_i[u'_{i\tau}(c_{i\tau}) | y_t]} & \text{if } y_\tau \subseteq y_t, \\ 0 & \text{otherwise.} \end{cases} \tag{6.20}$$

Inserting (6.20) into (6.14), we get the following multi-period valuation index,

$$q_{\tau t}(y_\tau | y_t) \equiv \frac{u'_{i\tau}(c_{i\tau}(y_\tau))}{\mathrm{E}_i[u'_{i\tau}(c_{i\tau}) | y_t]} \qquad \text{if } y_\tau \subseteq y_t. \tag{6.21}$$

Hence, as in the single-period setting the valuation index is a measure of "the scarcity" of optimal consumption for investor i. In general, each investor has his own valuation index, partly because the defined date-event prices are investor specific if the market is not dynamically complete, and partly because the valuation index is defined with respect to investor specific beliefs. If the market is dynamically complete (such that all the date-event securities can be replicated by a portfolio plan), then the date-event prices as well as the prices of zero-coupon bonds are unique and common to all investors. Since the risk-neutral probabilities are equal to the date-event prices multiplied by the returns on the corresponding zero-coupon bonds, those probabilities are also unique and common to all investors. However, the valuation index is equal to the ratio of the risk-neutral probability and the investor's subjective probability and, thus, the valuation index varies between investors if, and only if, they have heterogeneous beliefs.

6.3 EQUILIBRIUM AND EFFICIENT RISK SHARING

An equilibrium in the multi-period securities market is a collection of investor portfolio plans and security price processes, $\mathscr{E} \equiv \{ \mathbf{z}_1, \ldots, \mathbf{z}_I; \mathbf{v}_1, \ldots, \mathbf{v}_J \}$, such that, given security prices, the investors' portfolio plans are individually optimal, and such that the securities market "clears" at each event at each date. Hence, an equilibrium can be characterized as satisfying the following two sets of conditions:

Individual Optimality: $\mathbf{z}_i \in \underset{\mathbf{z}_i \in \{\mathbf{z} \in L^J | \mathbf{d}^{\mathbf{z}} + \mathbf{e}_i \in L_+, \mathbf{v}_0^t \mathbf{z}_0 \leq 0\}}{\text{argmax}} U_i(\mathbf{d}^{\mathbf{z}_i} + \mathbf{e}_i),\ i = 1, 2, ..., I;$

Market Clearing: $\sum_{i=1}^{I} \mathbf{z}_{it}(y_t) = \mathbf{0}, \quad \forall\, y_t \in Y_t,\ t = 0, ..., T\text{-}1.$

We refer to an equilibrium in a multi-period securities market as a *Radner sequential equilibrium* (RS-equilibrium), cf. Radner (1972, 1982), to explicitly recognize that investors must trade sequentially to implement their consumption plans. As a point of reference, we also consider an Arrow/Debreu equilibrium (AD-equilibrium) for an otherwise identical economy in which a complete set of date-event securities are marketed, i.e., a complete multi-period securities market. In that setting, investors can acquire any financially feasible consumption plan at $t = 0$ without any need for subsequent trading.

The concept of Pareto efficiency in single-period settings extends in an immediate fashion to multi-period settings, i.e., the consumption plans are Pareto efficient if, and only if, there are no other feasible consumption plans that make at least one investor strictly better off while leaving other investors no worse off. *The First Welfare Theorem* also generalizes to multi-period settings as it only requires strictly increasing preferences.

Proposition 6.3 *The First Welfare Theorem*

If $\mathscr{E}$ is an RS-equilibrium and the securities market is dynamically complete, then the equilibrium allocation of consumption is Pareto efficient.

Proof: Let $\mathbf{c}$ be the equilibrium consumption plan, and assume there is another feasible consumption plan $\mathbf{c}'$ which is strictly Pareto preferred to $\mathbf{c}$, i.e.,

$$U_i(\mathbf{c}_i') \geq U_i(\mathbf{c}_i), \quad i = 1, ..., I,$$

$$\exists \text{ some investor } h\text{: } U_h(\mathbf{c}_h') > U_h(\mathbf{c}_h).$$

Since $\mathscr{E}$ is an equilibrium and the securities market is dynamically complete, there is a unique strictly positive date-event price process. Moreover, since the investors' utility functions are strictly increasing, the price at the initial trading date of the dividend process of the portfolio plan $\mathbf{z}_i$ must be equal to zero for any investor i, i.e.,

$$\mathbf{v}_0^t \mathbf{z}_{i0} = \sum_{t=1}^{T} \sum_{y_t \in Y_t} [c_{it}(y_t) - e_{it}(y_t)]\, p_t(y_t) = 0.$$

Hence,

$$\sum_{t=1}^{T}\sum_{y_t\in Y_t} c_{it}(y_t)\,p_t(y_t) = \sum_{t=1}^{T}\sum_{y_t\in Y_t} e_{it}(y_t)\,p_t(y_t), \quad i = 1, \ldots, I.$$

The equilibrium portfolio plan **c** is individually optimal and, hence, it must be the case that

$$\sum_{t=1}^{T}\sum_{y_t\in Y_t} c'_{it}(y_t)\,p_t(y_t) \geq \sum_{t=1}^{T}\sum_{y_t\in Y_t} c_{it}(y_t)\,p_t(y_t), \quad i = 1, \ldots, I,$$

$$\sum_{t=1}^{T}\sum_{y_t\in Y_t} c'_{ht}(y_t)\,p_t(y_t) > \sum_{t=1}^{T}\sum_{y_t\in Y_t} c_{ht}(y_t)\,p_t(y_t).$$

Aggregating across investors implies

$$\sum_{i=1}^{I}\sum_{t=1}^{T}\sum_{y_t\in Y_t} c'_{it}(y_t)\,p_t(y_t) > \sum_{i=1}^{I}\sum_{t=1}^{T}\sum_{y_t\in Y_t} c_{it}(y_t)\,p_t(y_t)$$

$$= \sum_{i=1}^{I}\sum_{t=1}^{T}\sum_{y_t\in Y_t} e_{it}(y_t)\,p_t(y_t),$$

However, since the date-event price process is positive, this contradicts feasibility of the consumption plan $\mathbf{c}'$, i.e.,

$$\sum_{i=1}^{I} c'_{it}(y_t) \leq \sum_{i=1}^{I} e_{it}(y_t). \qquad \textbf{Q.E.D.}$$

In a dynamically complete market, the investors can implement any financially feasible consumption plan. That is, if for a given consumption plan there is another strictly Pareto preferred consumption plan, there is also enough flexibility in the marketed securities to trade from the former to the latter. Hence, an equilibrium must be Pareto efficient.

The existence of an equilibrium is a more subtle issue in multi-period settings than single-period settings. In the single-period setting, there is an equilibrium under the "usual conditions" on preferences and endowments, if the securities market is complete (see Proposition 5.3), i.e., if the exogenously given pay-off matrix has rank equal to the number of events. In a multi-period setting, the securities market is dynamically complete if, and only if, for each trading date $t = 0, 1, ..., T - 1$, and each event $y_t \in Y_t$ the pay-off matrix $\mathbf{V}_{t+1}(y_t)$ has rank equal to the number of events at $t + 1$ following y_t. Hence, dynamic completeness depends on the endogenously determined security prices.[9] However, if we expand the marketed securities with date-event securities for each event at each date, i.e., we have a complete multi-period securities market, the same approach as in the single-period setting can be applied (since there is no need for trading subsequent to the initial trading date). Secondly, if there is an AD-equilibrium in the augmented economy, and the cum-dividend prices of the original securities determined by the unique date-event prices provide a dynamically complete market, then there is an RS-equilibrium in the original economy and there is no need to trade in the date-event securities.

Proposition 6.4

Assume investors have positive endowments, infinite marginal utility of zero consumption at any date, and strictly increasing and strictly concave utility functions.

(a) There is an AD-equilibrium in an augmented economy with a complete set of date-event securities with a strictly positive equilibrium consumption plan $\mathbf{c}$ and a unique strictly positive date-event price process $\mathbf{p}$ (up to a strictly positive numeraire transformation).

(b) If the cum-dividend prices of the original securities determined by

$$V_{jt}(y_t) = d_{jt}(y_t) + \sum_{\tau=t+1}^{T} \sum_{y_\tau \subseteq y_t} d_{j\tau}(y_\tau)\, p_{\tau t}(y_\tau | y_t), \quad j = 1, 2, ..., J,$$

provide a dynamically complete securities market, then there is an RS-equilibrium in the original economy with consumption plan $\mathbf{c}$ and date-event prices $\mathbf{p}$.

Of course, the problem is that, in general, it is impossible to see from the exogenously specified dividend processes of marketed securities whether the securities market is dynamically complete – it depends on the date-event prices which in turn depend on endowments, preferences and beliefs.

The following proposition summarizes properties of Pareto efficient equilibria with homogeneous beliefs and time-additive preferences.

---

[9] Kreps (1982) demonstrates that if the number of long-lived securities is at least equal to the spanning number M, then the securities market is generic dynamically complete if the securities can be viewed as a random draw from the set of all possible securities that pay dividends conditioned on the set of events.

Proposition 6.5 *Properties of Pareto Efficient Equilibria*
Let $\mathscr{E}$ be an RS-equilibrium with a dynamically complete securities market. Assume investors have homogeneous beliefs $\boldsymbol{\varphi}$, positive endowments, time-additive preferences, infinite marginal utilities of zero consumption at any date, i.e., $u_{it}'(c_{it}) \to \infty$, as $c_{it} \downarrow 0$, and the date-utility functions u_{it} are strictly increasing and strictly concave.

(a) There is a unique, strictly positive date-event price process $\mathbf{p}$ (up to a strictly positive numeraire transformation) which is proportional to the expected utility gradient for all investors, i.e., there exist positive constants $\lambda_1, ..., \lambda_I$ such that

$$p(y_t) = \frac{u_{it}'(\boldsymbol{c}_{it}(y_t))\,\varphi(y_t)}{\lambda_i}, \quad \forall\, i, \forall\, y_t \in Y_t, t = 1, ..., T. \tag{6.22}$$

$$p_{\tau t}(y_\tau | y_t) = \frac{u_{i\tau}'(\boldsymbol{c}_{i\tau}(y_\tau))\,\varphi(y_\tau | y_t)}{u_{it}'(\boldsymbol{c}_{it}(y_t))}, \quad \forall\, i, \forall\, y_\tau \subseteq y_t, \tau > t. \tag{6.23}$$

(b) There is a unique set of risk-neutral probabilities based on zero-coupon bonds,

$$\hat{\varphi}_{\tau t}(y_\tau | y_t) \equiv \begin{cases} R_{\tau t}(y_t)\, p_{\tau t}(y_\tau | y_t) & \text{if } y_\tau \subseteq y_t, \\ 0 & \text{otherwise.} \end{cases} \tag{6.24}$$

(c) Individual consumption plans are measurable with respect to aggregate consumption at each date, i.e., $\boldsymbol{c}_{it}(y_t) = \boldsymbol{c}_{it}(y_t')$ if $\boldsymbol{x}_t(y_t) = \boldsymbol{x}_t(y_t')$ where $\mathbf{x}_t = \Sigma_i\, \mathbf{e}_{it}$, and $\boldsymbol{c}_{it}(x_t)$ is a strictly increasing function of x_t, $i = 1, ..., I$.

(d) Given the probability function $\boldsymbol{\varphi}$, the multi-period valuation index $\mathbf{q}$ based on zero-coupon bonds is measurable with respect to aggregate consumption at each date and given by the "scarcity" of aggregate consumption as measured by the investors' marginal utility of consumption, i.e.,

$$\begin{aligned} q_{\tau t}(y_\tau | y_t) &= \frac{u_{i\tau}'(\boldsymbol{c}_{i\tau}(y_\tau))}{\mathrm{E}[u_{i\tau}'(c_{i\tau}) | y_t]} \\ &= \frac{u_{i\tau}'(\boldsymbol{c}_{i\tau}(x_\tau(y_\tau)))}{\mathrm{E}[u_{i\tau}'(c_{i\tau}) | y_t]} \quad \text{if } y_\tau \subseteq y_t, \tau > t. \end{aligned} \tag{6.25}$$

A dynamically complete securities market and no arbitrage imply that the date-event prices and the risk-neutral probabilities based on zero-coupon bonds are "unique." Individual optimality of equilibrium portfolio plans imply that the vector of date-event prices at $t = 0$ is proportional to each investor's expected utility gradient, which in the case of time-additive preferences simplifies to (6.22). With time-additive preferences, Pareto efficiency of the equilibrium consumption plans implies that the allocation of aggregate consumption at each date must be Pareto efficient. Hence, given homogeneous beliefs, the measurability of individual consumption plans with respect to aggregate consumption at each date follows from the equivalent result in single-period settings (see Proposition 5.3(c)). The definition of the multi-period valuation index (6.14) combined with (6.23) and (c) imply (6.25). Hence, if future aggregate consumption is the same in two events y_τ and y_τ', then the valuation index is also the same for those events given the current information y_t, i.e., $q_{\tau t}(y_\tau|y_t) = q_{\tau t}(y_\tau'|y_t)$. Moreover, the multi-period valuation index is unique and by condition (c), it is strictly decreasing in aggregate consumption at date τ.

6.4 EFFECTIVELY DYNAMICALLY COMPLETE MARKETS

As in the single-period setting, completeness (even dynamic completeness) may not be necessary to ensure a Pareto efficient equilibrium if we impose additional conditions on endowments, preferences and beliefs. As in the single-period setting we review two such cases, both with homogeneous beliefs and time-additive preferences: (a) linear risk sharing and (b) diversifiable risk. In this analysis, we generally assume that there is an AD-equilibrium for an otherwise identical economy augmented with a complete set of date-event securities.

6.4.1 Linear Risk Sharing

Time-additive preferences, homogeneous beliefs, and HARA date-utility functions with identical risk cautiousness imply that, for any Pareto efficient consumption plan, individual consumption at any date is a linear function of aggregate consumption at that date.

Note from Table 4.1 that the parameters in the linear function only depend on the preference parameters and the weights attached to each agent in the efficient risk sharing problem (corresponding to the inverse of the Lagrange multiplier for the $t = 0$ budget constraint in the investors' portfolio choice problems). Hence, there are parameters v_{it} and f_{it} for each date such that $\mathbf{c}_{it}(x_t) = f_{it} + v_{it}x_t$, for all $i = 1,..., I$, and $\Sigma_i\, v_{it} = 1$ and $\Sigma_i\, f_{it} = 0$ for each $t = 1, ..., T$.

If there are zero-coupon bonds for all dates, the fixed components of consumption, f_{it}, can be achieved by investing in a portfolio of those bonds at $t = 0$, with no further trading needed. Furthermore, if the fractions v_{it} are the same for all t, i.e., $v_{it} = v_i$, then buying the fraction v_i of the market portfolio at $t = 0$, and holding it until date T, will provide the Pareto efficient share of aggregate consumption for all dates since the dividend on the market portfolio is the aggregate consumption at each date.

On the other hand, if the Pareto efficient fractions v_{it} differ across dates, then acquiring the fraction v_{it} of the market portfolio at t-1 will provide dividends at date t equal to efficient consumption, but it will not equal the total pay-off from the portfolio plan due to differences in the market value of the portfolio sold and the portfolio acquired, i.e., the total pay-off is

$$v_{it}(v_t^m + x_t) - v_{i,t+1}v_t^m = v_{it}x_t + (v_{it} - v_{i,t+1})v_t^m,$$

where v_t^m represents the ex-dividend market value of the market portfolio at date t. Hence, even though individual consumption at any date is a linear function of aggregate consumption at each date, those consumption plans cannot, in general, be implemented by a portfolio plan consisting of zero-coupon bonds and the market portfolio.

Proposition 6.6

Let $\mathscr{E}$ be a Pareto efficient equilibrium and assume the investors have homogeneous beliefs and time-additive preferences represented by HARA utility functions with identical risk cautiousness. Then there are parameters v_{it} and f_{it} such that

$$c_{it}(x_t) = f_{it} + v_{it}x_t, \quad i = 1, ..., I,$$

$$\Sigma_i v_{it} = 1 \text{ and } \Sigma_i f_{it} = 0, \quad t = 1, ..., T.$$

Each investor's fraction of aggregate consumption v_{it} is the same for all dates, i.e., $v_{it} = v_i$, if, and only if, one of the following conditions hold for all $i = 1, ..., I$ and for all $t = 1, ..., T$:

(a) $u_{it}(c_{it}) = -\beta_{it}^P \exp[-c_{it}/\rho_i]$, $\quad \beta_{it}^P > 0, \rho_i > 0;$

(b) $u_{it}(c_{it}) = \beta_t^P \ln(c_{it} + b_{it})$, $\quad \beta_t^P > 0, c_{it} + b_{it} > 0;$

(c) $u_{it}(c_{it}) = \beta_t^P \dfrac{1}{a-1}[ac_{it} + b_{it}]^{\frac{a-1}{a}}$, $\quad \beta_t^P > 0, a \neq 0, 1, ac_{it} + b_{it} > 0.$

The proof is almost identical to the proof in the single-period setting (see Proposition 4.3). The only difference is that the weight assigned to investor i's date t expected utility, λ_{it}, is the weight λ_i assigned to his total expected utility times the investor's personal discount factor, i.e.,

$$\lambda_{it} = \lambda_i \beta_{it}^{P}.$$

Using these weights in Table 4.1 provides the conditions (a) - (c). Recall that in the exponential utility function case v_{it} is given by

$$v_{it} = \frac{\rho_{it}}{\rho_{ot}},$$

where ρ_{ot} is the aggregate risk tolerance at date t, and, therefore, independent of the weight λ_{it}. Hence, the fraction of aggregate consumption is the same at all dates, if the risk tolerances are the same at all dates even though the investors may have heterogeneous personal discount factors. In the two other cases, i.e., $a_t \neq 0$, the fraction v_{it} depends on the weights λ_{it}, i.e.,

$$v_{it} = \frac{\lambda_{it}^{a_t}}{\sum_i \lambda_{it}^{a_t}},$$

implying that the investors must have homogeneous discount rates and the same risk cautiousness across periods for the fractions of aggregate consumption to be the same for all dates.

Proposition 6.7

Assume the investors have homogeneous beliefs and time-additive preferences which are represented by HARA date-utility functions with identical risk cautiousness satisfying either one of the conditions (a) - (c) in Proposition 6.6.

If there are zero-coupon bonds with all maturities and consumption endowments $\bar{c}_{it}$ are non-stochastic, then there is a Pareto efficient equilibrium, and the investors can be viewed as having portfolio plans consisting of the following three elements:

(a) A fixed portfolio of zero-coupon bonds to "undo" personal consumption endowments, i.e., with payments $\bar{c}_{it}$ for all i and $t = 1, ..., T$.

(b) A fixed portfolio of zero-coupon bonds with payments f_{it} for all i and $t = 1, ..., T$.

(c) A constant share v_i of the market portfolio that pays dividend $v_i x_t$ for all i and $t = 1, ..., T$.

The key for this result is that, under the assumed conditions, there is no need for trading subsequent to the initial trading date $t = 0$. Hence, if there is an AD-equilibrium, the equilibrium consumption plan can be implemented without subsequent trading and, therefore, the implementability of the equilibrium consumption plans does not depend on the date-event price process. On the other hand, if consumption endowments are stochastic, more securities may be needed to eliminate these personal risks and in that case, the equilibrium date-event price process determines whether this is possible.

6.4.2 Diversifiable Risks

Condition (c) in Proposition 6.5 establishes that if beliefs are homogeneous and preferences are time-additive, then Pareto efficient individual consumption plans are measurable with respect to aggregate consumption at each date. That is, any investor's consumption plan may be written as a function of aggregate consumption, $c_{it} = \boldsymbol{c}_{it}(x_t)$. Hence, we may not need a dynamically complete market to implement a Pareto efficient allocation of consumption – the securities only have to facilitate consumption plans that are measurable with respect to aggregate consumption.

Efficiently Sharing Aggregate Consumption

Let Γ_τ denote the coarsest partition of the set of events Y_τ such that aggregate consumption at date τ is measurable with respect to that partition. Let $\gamma_\tau \in \Gamma_\tau$ denote the subset of events y_τ that result in the aggregate consumption level γ_τ, i.e., $\gamma_\tau = \{ y_\tau \in Y_\tau \,|\, \boldsymbol{x}_\tau(y_\tau) = \gamma_\tau \}$, $\gamma_\tau \in \Gamma_\tau$, $\tau = 1, ..., T$. The key to an efficient sharing of aggregate consumption risks is the existence of marketed securities that allow each investor to implement any financially feasible consumption plan that is Γ_τ-measurable for all $\tau = 1, ..., T$. As in the single-period setting, define an AC_τ-security for the aggregate consumption event $\gamma_\tau \in \Gamma_\tau$ as a security with a pay-off of one at date τ in all events $y_\tau \in Y_\tau$ with aggregate consumption level γ_τ, and a pay-off of zero in all other events at date τ and at all other dates, i.e.,

$$d_{\gamma_\tau, t}(y_t) = \begin{cases} 1 & \text{if } t = \tau \text{ and } y_t \in \gamma_\tau, \\ 0 & \text{otherwise.} \end{cases}$$

This security can be considered to be a portfolio of the date-event securities for events $y_\tau \in \gamma_\tau$ and, hence, given the information y_t at date $t < \tau$ its price is

$$p_{\tau t}(\gamma_\tau|y_t) = \sum_{y_\tau \in \gamma_\tau} p_{\tau t}(y_\tau|y_t).$$

Proposition 6.8

Assume investors have time-additive preferences and homogeneous beliefs.

(a) For any Pareto efficient equilibrium there are date-event prices given by

$$p_{\tau t}(y_\tau|y_t) = p_{\tau t}(\gamma_\tau|y_t)\, \varphi(y_\tau|\gamma_\tau), \quad \text{for } y_t \supseteq y_\tau \in \gamma_\tau,\ \gamma_\tau \in \Gamma_\tau, \tag{6.26}$$

where

$$p_{\tau t}(\gamma_\tau|y_t) = \beta_{\tau t}(y_t)\, q_{\tau t}(\gamma_\tau|y_t)\, \varphi(\gamma_\tau|y_t). \tag{6.27}$$

(b) If investors have non-stochastic consumption endowments and there is a complete set of contingent claims on aggregate consumption (e.g., a complete set of call options on aggregate consumption for each date), then there is a Pareto efficient RS-equilibrium.

Condition (a) follows from Proposition 6.5. Note that the date-event prices have two components: the conditional probability of the event y_τ given the level of aggregate consumption, $y_\tau \in \gamma_\tau$, and the AC_τ-price for that level of aggregate consumption. Hence, no-arbitrage condition (6.5) implies that the prices of marketed securities is given as the summation of their conditional expected dividends given the level of aggregate consumption times the corresponding implicit AC_τ-prices, i.e.,

$$v_{jt}(y_t) = \sum_{\tau=t+1}^{T} \sum_{\gamma_\tau \in \Gamma_\tau} \mathrm{E}\left[d_{j\tau}|\gamma_\tau, y_t\right] p_{\tau t}(\gamma_\tau|y_t).$$

That is, the pricing of securities is *as if* the investors are risk-neutral with respect to variations in dividends for given levels of aggregate consumption. Of course, this is due to the fact that the investors' equilibrium consumption plans are independent of those variations – they are eliminated by diversification.

The implicit AC_τ-prices have three components. The first component is the discount factor (i.e., the current price of a zero-coupon bond),

$$\beta_{\tau t}(y_t) = \frac{\mathrm{E}[u_{i\tau}'(c_{i\tau})|y_t]}{u_{it}'(c_{it}(\gamma_t))}, \tag{6.28}$$

measuring the conditional expected "scarcity of future consumption" relative to the "scarcity of current consumption." The second component is the "scarcity of future consumption" for aggregate consumption level γ_τ,

$$q_{\tau t}(\gamma_\tau | y_t) = \frac{u'_{i\tau}(c_{i\tau}(\gamma_\tau))}{\mathrm{E}[u'_{i\tau}(c_{i\tau}) | y_t]}, \tag{6.29}$$

and, finally, the third component is the conditional probability of aggregate consumption level γ_τ given the current information y_t.

If investors have non-stochastic consumption endowments and there is a complete set of contingent claims on aggregate consumption, then investors can acquire any financially feasible consumption plan at $t = 0$ which is measurable with respect to aggregate consumption at any date. Hence, no subsequent trading is needed and, thus, implementability of Pareto efficient consumption plans does not depend on the date-event prices in an AD-equilibrium. Hence, if there is an AD-equilibrium, then there is also an RS-equilibrium.

While a complete set of contingent claims on aggregate consumption (and non-stochastic consumption endowments) ensures there is an RS-equilibrium (if there is an AD-equilibrium), many fewer securities are needed, in general, to implement a Pareto efficient RS-equilibrium with dynamic trading. The key is to recognize the structure of the implicit AC_τ-prices in (6.27).

For simplicity, we assume that investors have non-stochastic consumption endowments. Let a Pareto efficient equilibrium $\mathscr{E}$ be given, and let $\boldsymbol{\zeta}_i$ denote the dividends on the portfolio plan that generates investor i's equilibrium consumption plan, i.e., $\boldsymbol{\zeta}_i = \mathbf{c}_i - \bar{\mathbf{c}}_i$. Note that $\zeta_{i\tau}$ is Γ_τ-measurable for all $\tau = 1, ..., T$, i.e., $\zeta_{i\tau} = \zeta_{i\tau}(\gamma_\tau)$. Hence, the cum-dividend value of the portfolio plan given y_t at date t is

$$\begin{aligned} w^{\zeta}_{it}(y_t) &= \zeta_{it}(\gamma_t) + \sum_{\tau=t+1}^{T} \sum_{\gamma_\tau \in \Gamma_\tau} \zeta_{i\tau}(\gamma_\tau)\, p_{\tau t}(\gamma_\tau | y_t) \\ &= \zeta_{it}(\gamma_t) + \sum_{\tau=t+1}^{T} \beta_{\tau t}(y_t) \sum_{\gamma_\tau \in \Gamma_\tau} \zeta_{i\tau}(\gamma_\tau)\, q_{\tau t}(\gamma_\tau | y_t)\, \varphi(\gamma_\tau | y_t). \end{aligned} \tag{6.30}$$

Note that even though the dividend at date t is Γ_t-measurable, the ex-dividend value of the portfolio plan is not Γ_t-measurable, in general; it depends on the zero-coupon bond prices, the valuation index, and the conditional probabilities for future aggregate consumption.

Definition *Minimal Aggregate Consumption Statistic*
The statistic Ψ_t, $t = 1, ..., T$, is a minimal aggregate consumption statistic (*MAC*-statistic) if it is the coarsest partition of Y_t that defines a sufficient statistic with respect to

(a) aggregate consumption for each date, i.e.,

$$x_t(y_t) = x_t(\psi_t), \quad \forall\, y_t \subseteq \psi_t \in \Psi_t,\ t = 1, ..., T;$$

(b) conditional probabilities of future aggregate consumption, i.e.,

$$\varphi(\gamma_\tau|y_t) = \varphi(\gamma_\tau|\psi_t), \quad \forall\, y_t \subseteq \psi_t \in \Psi_t,\ \gamma_\tau \in \Gamma_\tau,\ \tau > t = 1, ..., T.$$

Note that an *MAC*-statistic is at least as fine a partition of Y_t as is Γ_t. The partition Γ_t only distinguishes between events that have different aggregate consumption levels at date *t*, whereas the *MAC*-statistic also distinguishes between events that have different conditional probabilities for future levels of aggregate consumption levels.

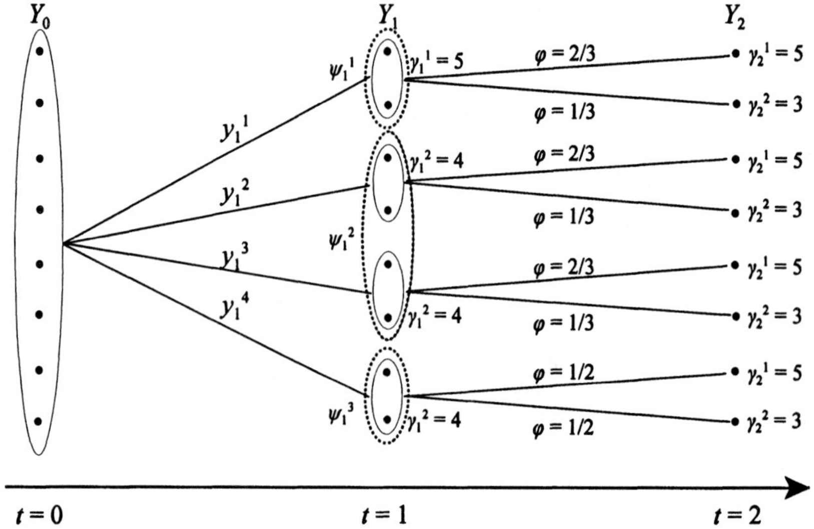

Figure 6.2: *MAC*-statistics and Γ-partitions in a three-date economy.

Figure 6.2 illustrates the difference between the two partitions in a three-date economy. The Γ-partitions at the two dates are $\Gamma_1 = \{\{y_1^1\}, \{y_1^2, y_1^3, y_1^4\}\}$, and $\Gamma_2 = \{\{y_2^1, y_2^3, y_2^5, y_2^7\}, \{y_2^2, y_2^4, y_2^6, y_2^8\}\}$, whereas the *MAC*-statistic at $t=1$, i.e., Ψ_1, also distinguishes between $\{y_1^2, y_1^3\}$ and $\{y_1^4\}$ because the conditional probability distribution for aggregate consumption at $t=2$ differs between those two sets of events. However, both current aggregate consumption and the conditional probability distribution for aggregate consumption at $t = 2$ are the same for y_1^2 and y_1^3 and, thus, the *MAC*-statistic at $t = 1$ does not distinguish between these two events.

The key characteristic of the *MAC*-statistic is that for events $y_t, y_t' \in \psi_t$ at date t, the current prices of zero-coupon bonds, the valuation index, and the conditional probability distributions for future aggregate consumption are all the same for the two events (see (6.28) and (6.29)). Hence, the investors' portfolio wealth given by (6.30) is Ψ_t-measurable.

Proposition 6.9

If $\mathscr{E}$ is a Pareto efficient equilibrium, and investors have time-additive preferences, homogeneous expectations and non-stochastic consumption endowments, then the equilibrium portfolio wealth for any investor at any date t is Ψ_t-measurable.

Note that the current prices of zero-coupon bonds given in (6.28) are increasing in the level of current aggregate consumption γ_t (since $c_{it}(\gamma_t)$ is an increasing function of γ_t). This reflects the fact that if current consumption is less scarce, the market is more willing to save, thereby driving down the current interest rate – which increases the price of bonds. For example, in Figure 6.2, the riskless discount factor is higher for y_1^1 than for y_1^2 and y_1^3 even though the conditional probability distributions for future aggregate consumption are the same for these three events. Hence, the ex-dividend portfolio wealth must also be higher for y_1^1 than for y_1^2 and y_1^3.

The conditional probability distribution for future aggregate consumption affects both the prices of zero-coupon bonds, and the valuation index, even though current aggregate consumption may be the same. That is, the portfolio wealth is (except in specific cases) different for y_1^4 and $\{y_1^2, y_1^3\}$.[10] However,

---

[10] If the investors have log-preferences, i.e., $u_{it}(c_{it}) = \beta_{it}^P \ln(c_{it})$, and no consumption endowments, i.e., $\zeta_{it} = c_{it}$, then the ex-dividend portfolio wealth is independent of the conditional probability distribution of future aggregate consumption,

$$\sum_{\tau=t+1}^{T} \sum_{\gamma_\tau \in \Gamma_\tau} \zeta_{i\tau}(\gamma_\tau) p_{\tau t}(\gamma_\tau | y_t) = \sum_{\tau=t+1}^{T} \sum_{\gamma_\tau \in \Gamma_\tau} c_{i\tau}(\gamma_\tau) \frac{\beta_{i\tau}^P c_{it}(\gamma_t)}{\beta_{it}^P c_{i\tau}(\gamma_\tau)} \varphi(\gamma_\tau | y_t)$$

$$= \frac{c_{it}(\gamma_t)}{\beta_{it}^P} \sum_{\tau=t+1}^{T} \beta_{i\tau}^P .$$

Hence, for this utility function, the cum-dividend wealth at any date t is Γ_t-measurable, i.e.,

(continued...)

the dividend, as well as the ex-dividend portfolio wealth, are the same for y_1^2 and y_1^3.

A dynamically complete securities market requires at least as many sufficiently distinct marketed securities as the spanning number, i.e., the maximum number of events following a prior event (e.g., in Figure 6.2 there must be at least four securities). However, since the investors' portfolio wealth need only be measurable with respect to the *MAC*-statistic, an efficient RS-equilibrium may be implemented with fewer securities (e.g., only three sufficiently distinct securities are required in Figure 6.2).

Definition *Dynamically MAC-Complete Securities Market*

The securities market is said to be dynamically *MAC*-complete if for each $\boldsymbol{\Psi}$-measurable process $\mathbf{X}$, there exists a portfolio plan $\mathbf{z}$ with cum-dividend value process $\mathbf{X}$, i.e., $V_t^{\mathbf{z}}(y_t) = X_t(\psi_t)$, $\forall\, y_t \subseteq \psi_t \in \Psi_t$, $t = 1, ..., T$.

There are two components to a dynamically *MAC*-complete securities market. First, there is a diversification requirement. That is, it should be possible to acquire "well diversified" portfolios that have the same cum-dividend values for all events within an element of the *MAC*-statistic (for example, the portfolios acquired at $t = 0$ in Figure 6.2 must have the same cum-dividend values at $t = 1$ for both y_1^2 and y_1^3). Note that contingent claims on aggregate consumption by construction have this property. Secondly, there should be enough sufficiently distinct "well diversified" portfolios to implement any $\boldsymbol{\Psi}$-measurable cum-dividend-value process.

Proposition 6.10

The securities market is effectively dynamically complete if, and only if, for each trading date $t = 1, ..., T$, and each event y_t, any $M_t(y_t)$-dimensional pay-off vector $\mathbf{X}_{t+1}$ with Ψ_{t+1}-measurable pay-offs is in the span of the pay-off matrix $\mathbf{V}_{t+1}(y_t)$, i.e.,

$$\mathbf{X}_{t+1} \in \text{span}\{\ \mathbf{V}_{t+1}(y_t)\ \},\quad X_{t+1}(y_{t+1}) = X_{t+1}(\psi_{t+1}),\ \forall\, y_{t+1} \subseteq \psi_{t+1} \in \Psi_{t+1}.$$

The following proposition demonstrates that a dynamically *MAC*-complete securities market has enough flexibility in the pay-offs of the marketed securities to implement Pareto efficient consumption plans.[11]

---

[10] (...continued)
investors do not "hedge" against information about future consumption possibilities. These preferences are, therefore, referred to as "myopic" preferences.

[11] The assumption that consumption endowments are non-stochastic is crucial here. If these endowments are influenced by personal risks, personalized insurance contracts must be intro-
(continued...)

Proposition 6.11

Assume investors have time-additive preferences, homogeneous beliefs, and non-stochastic consumption endowments, and that there is an AD-equilibrium with consumption plan **c** and date-event prices **p**. If the cum-dividend prices of the marketed securities determined by

$$V_{jt}(y_t) = d_{jt}(y_t) + \sum_{\tau=t+1}^{T} \sum_{y_\tau \subseteq y_t} d_{j\tau}(y_\tau)\, p_{\tau t}(y_\tau | y_t), \quad j = 1, 2, ..., J,$$

provide a dynamically *MAC*-complete securities market, then there is a Pareto efficient RS-equilibrium with consumption plan **c** and date-event prices **p**.

Contingent claims on aggregate consumption have Γ_t-measurable dividends and, thus, their market value at any date *t* is Ψ_t-measurable. Hence, they are "natural candidates" to facilitate a dynamically *MAC*-complete securities market. For example, if the aggregate consumption process is a Markov process, i.e., the conditional probability distribution of future aggregate consumption only depends on the current level of aggregate consumption, then $\mathbf{\Psi} = \mathbf{\Gamma}$. In this case, a sequence of a complete set of one-period call options on aggregate consumption is sufficient for a dynamically *MAC*-complete securities market. However, more generally, "long-lived" contingent claims on aggregate consumption are needed to facilitate optimal "insurance" against shifts in future consumption/investment possibilities.

Diversified Portfolios

As in the single-period setting, diversification of firm-specific risk and a sufficiently distinct set of well-diversified portfolios of firm shares is another, or complementary, means to achieve an effectively dynamically complete securities market. As in the single-period setting we expand the definition of an event $y_t \in Y_t$ and let $y_t \equiv (y_{et}, \{y_{jt}\}_{j=1,...,J})$, where y_t is the "full" description of the event at date *t*, y_{et} represents *economy-wide* events, and y_{jt} represents *firm-specific* events that influence the dividends of firm *j*.

Definition *Economy-wide and Firm-specific Events*

For each date t = 1, ..., T, if $y_t = (y_{et}, \{y_{jt}\}_{j=1,...,J})$, then y_{et} represents *economy-wide* events, and y_{jt} represents *firm-specific* events for firm *j*, if the following conditions hold:

---

[11] (...continued)
duced if Pareto efficiency is to be achieved (see Christensen, Graversen, and Miltersen 2000).

(a) the dividends at date t for firm j depend only on y_{et} and y_{jt}, i.e.,

$$d_{jt}(y_t) = d_{jt}(y_{et}, y_{jt}), \quad \forall j = 1, ..., J, y_t \in Y_t;$$

(b) beliefs about firm-specific events are conditionally independent, i.e.,

$$\varphi(y_t) = \varphi(y_{et}) \prod_{j=1}^{J} \varphi(y_{jt}|y_{et}), \quad \forall y_t \in Y_t.$$

(c) firm-specific information provides no additional information about future economy-wide events, i.e.,

$$\varphi(y_{e\tau}|y_t) = \varphi(y_{e\tau}|y_{et}), \quad \forall y_{e\tau} \in Y_{e\tau}, y_t \in Y_t, \tau > t.$$

Compared to the single-period setting, the additional condition is (c), which requires that current firm-specific information for one firm not only provides no additional information about any other firms, but also no additional information about future economy-wide events given the current economy-wide events.

The definition of quasi-feasibility and quasi-efficiency in the single-period setting extends in an immediate fashion to the multi-period setting and is therefore not repeated here.

Now consider the feasibility of implementing a quasi-efficient consumption plan through the dynamic trading of firm ownership. Consider, as in the single-period setting, an economy in which there are $N \times J$ firms and $N \times I$ investors, with N representing the size of the economy and with J and I representing the different types of firms and investors, respectively. Let $d_{jnt}(y_{et}, y_{jnt})$ represent the dividend at date t of the nth type j claim given economy-wide event y_{et} and firm-specific event y_{jnt}. The strong law of large numbers establishes that for a sequence of economies in which N increases, the dividend at date t of a well-diversified portfolio consisting of z_j/N units of each type j claim is equal to its expected dividend given the economy-wide event at date t with probability one, i.e.,

$$\text{Prob}\left[\left\{y_t \in Y_t \,\middle|\, \lim_{N\to\infty} \left|\frac{1}{N}\sum_{j=1}^{J} z_j \sum_{n=1}^{N} [d_{jnt}(y_{et}, y_{jnt}) - \bar{d}_{jt}(y_{et})]\right| \to 0\right\} \,\middle|\, y_{et}\right] = 1,$$

$$\forall y_{et} \in Y_{et},$$

where

$$\bar{d}_{jt}(y_{et}) \equiv \sum_{y_{jnt} \in Y_{jnt}} d_{jnt}(y_{et}, y_{jnt})\, \varphi(y_{jnt}|y_{et}).$$

In a quasi-efficient equilibrium, the date-event prices for the economy-wide events are also independent of current firm-specific information, since that information does not affect the beliefs about future economy-wide events given the current economy-wide information. Since aggregate consumption only depends on the economy-wide events, the definition of quasi-efficiency and Proposition 6.8(a) imply the following result.

Proposition 6.12

Assume the investors have time-additive preferences and homogeneous beliefs. For any quasi-efficient equilibrium there are date-event prices given by

$$p_{\tau t}(y_\tau|y_t) = p_{\tau t}(y_{e\tau}|y_{et}) \prod_{j=1}^{J} \prod_{n=1}^{N} \varphi(y_{jn\tau}|y_{e\tau}, y_{jnt}), \quad \forall\, y_t, y_\tau, y_{et} \supseteq y_{e\tau}, \tag{6.31}$$

where

$$p_{\tau t}(y_{e\tau}|y_{et}) = \beta_{\tau t}(y_{et})\, q^R_{\tau t}(y_{e\tau}|y_{et})\, \varphi(y_{e\tau}|y_{et}). \tag{6.32}$$

Furthermore, given y_t at any date t, the market prices of claims,

$$v_{jnt}(y_t) = v_{jnt}(y_{et}, y_{jnt}) = \sum_{\tau=t+1}^{T} \sum_{y_{e\tau} \in Y_{e\tau}} \mathrm{E}\left[d_{jn\tau}|y_{e\tau}, y_{jnt}\right] p_{\tau t}(y_{e\tau}|y_{et}), \tag{6.33}$$

are conditionally independent given the economy-wide event y_{et}.

Note that the structure of the date-event prices in (6.31) implies that the cum- and ex-dividend prices of claims only depend on the economy-wide event and the firm-specific event for that claim (see (6.33)). Hence, the cum- (ex-) dividend price at date t of a well-diversified portfolio consisting of z_j/N units of each type j claim is equal to its expected cum- (ex-) dividend price given the economy-wide event with probability one, i.e.,

$$\text{Prob}\left[\left\{y_t \in Y_t \,\Big|\, \lim_{N\to\infty}\Big|\frac{1}{N}\sum_{j=1}^{J} z_j \sum_{n=1}^{N} [V_{jnt}(y_{et}, y_{jnt}) - \bar{V}_{jt}(y_{et})]\Big| \to 0\right\} \Big|\, y_{et}\right] = 1,$$

$$\forall\, y_{et} \in Y_{et},$$

where

$$\bar{V}_{jt}(y_{et}) \equiv \sum_{y_{jnt} \in Y_{jnt}} V_{jnt}(y_{et}, y_{jnt})\, \varphi(y_{jnt} | y_{et}),$$

with a similar result for the ex-dividend values of well-diversified portfolios.

Definition *Dynamically Quasi-complete Market*
A set of $J \times N$ claims constitutes a *dynamically quasi-complete market* (DQCM) if the economy is large and the *expected price matrices,*

$$\bar{\mathbf{V}}_t(y_{et-1}) \equiv [\ \bar{V}_{jt}(y_{et})\ ]_{J \times M_{t-1}(y_{et-1})},$$

have rank $M_{t-1}(y_{et-1})$, for all $t = 1, \ldots, T$, and $y_{et-1} \in Y_{e,\,t-1}$, where $M_{t-1}(y_{et-1})$ is the number of economy-wide events following y_{et-1}.

A dynamically quasi-complete market has a sufficient variety of well-diversified portfolios to permit an investor to implement a quasi-efficient consumption plan.

Proposition 6.13
Assume investors have time-additive preferences, homogeneous beliefs, and non-stochastic consumption endowments. If the economy is large and the securities market is dynamically quasi-complete, then there is a quasi-efficient RS-equilibrium and the date-event prices are given by (6.31).

The key characteristics of a dynamically quasi-complete securities market are that investors restrict their portfolio plans to well-diversified portfolios to eliminate the impact of firm-specific events, and the available well-diversified portfolios are such that they constitute a dynamically complete securities market in terms of the economy-wide events. Of course, if more than one economy-wide event results in the same level of aggregate consumption, the required number and diversity of well-diversified portfolios can be reduced along the lines of a dynamically *MAC*-complete securities market.

6.5 Concluding Remarks

In this chapter we have examined the basic multi-period model of efficient risk sharing in a competitive capital market. The dynamics of the public information system was stressed, and as in Chapter 5 we have established market value relations of risky securities under three increasingly restrictive assumptions, no arbitrage, individual optimality, and market equilibrium. Dynamically complete markets were emphasized as the means to achieve efficient risk sharing. We also considered additional assumptions on preferences, beliefs and the structure of dividends that facilitate an effectively dynamically complete market. In particular, we extended the distinction between firm-specific and economy-wide information and identified dynamic trading of well-diversified portfolios as the means to overcome the market incompleteness created by firm-specific events.

APPENDIX 6A: RISK-NEUTRAL PROBABILITIES BASED ON THE RETURN ON A BANK ACCOUNT

In the text we use the prices of a sequence of zero-coupon bonds as deflators in obtaining risk-neutral probabilities. More generally, we can use any *strictly positive* adapted process ζ to deflate prices as follows. No-arbitrage condition (6.1) is equivalent to

$$[d_0^{\mathbf{z}}/\zeta_0]\, p_0^{\zeta} + \sum_{t=1}^{T} \sum_{y_t \in Y_t} [d_t^{\mathbf{z}}(y_t)/\zeta_t(y_t)]\, p_t^{\zeta}(y_t) = 0, \quad \forall\, \mathbf{z} \in L,$$

where $p_t^{\zeta}(y_t) \equiv p_t(y_t)\,\zeta_t(y_t)$, $\forall\, y_t \in Y_t$, $t = 0, ..., T$. That is, we can normalize all dividends and security prices with the *deflator* ζ, if we adjust the date-event prices accordingly. Observe that the date-event prices $p_t^{\zeta}(y_t)$ are strictly positive. Hence, there is no arbitrage if, and only if, there is no arbitrage for the deflated dividends and security prices.

The zero-coupon bonds have the feature that the deflator is independent of the future event, i.e., $\zeta_t(y_t) = R_{t0}$ for all y_t, but it yields conditional risk-neutral probabilities prices that are not time-consistent. We now examine the impact of using the cumulative return on a bank account as a deflator.

If one dollar is deposited at $t = 0$ in an *accumulating* bank account, then the balance in the account at date t given event y_t is

$$A_{t0}(y_t) = \prod_{\tau=0}^{t-1} R_{\tau+1,\tau}(y_t), \quad t = 1, ..., T, \;\; A_0 = 1,$$

where $R_{\tau+1,\tau}(y_t)$ is the return on the account from τ to $\tau+1 \le t$ given event $y_\tau \supseteq y_t$. We assume that the process $\mathbf{A}$ is strictly positive (i.e., the one-period interest rates are all greater than minus 100%). The no-arbitrage condition (6.1) with $p_0 = 1$ implies that

$$1 = \sum_{y_t \in Y_t} A_{t0}(y_t)\, p_t(y_t).$$

Hence, we can define "risk-neutral" probabilities by

$$\hat{\varphi}_t^A(y_t) \equiv A_{t0}(y_t)\, p_t(y_t), \quad t = 0, ..., T, \tag{6A.1}$$

where the "*A*" superscript indicates that the bank account return is used as the deflator. These probabilities are strictly positive, and they sum to one over all events for each date *t*.

Observe that the inverse of $A_{t0}(y_t)$ can be interpreted as a sequence of stochastic discount factors, i.e.,

$$A_{t0}^{-1}(y_t) = \prod_{\tau=0}^{t-1} \beta_{\tau+1,\tau}(y_t), \tag{6A.2}$$

where $\beta_{\tau+1,\tau}(y_t) = R_{\tau+1,\tau}(y_t)^{-1}$ is the one-period riskless discount factor between τ to $\tau+1 \le t$ given event $y_\tau \supseteq y_t$. Further observe that (6A.1) implies the event prices can be expressed as

$$p_t(y_t) = A_{t0}^{-1}(y_t)\, \hat{\varphi}_{t0}^A(y_t),$$

which, when substituted into (6.3), yields

$$v_{j0} = \sum_{t=1}^{T} \hat{\mathrm{E}}_{t0}^A[A_{t0}^{-1} d_{jt}]. \tag{6A.3}$$

Hence, we again obtain an expression in which the market value of a security is expressed as the risk-adjusted expected dividend for each date *t*, discounted using riskless interest rates. However, in this setting the discount factor is a composite of a sequence of discount factors based on the possible sequences of stochastic spot one-period interests rates.

This approach can be extended to the value relation at $t > 0$. No-arbitrage condition (6.5) implies

$$1 = \sum_{y_\tau \subseteq y_t} A_{\tau t}(y_\tau|y_t) p_{\tau t}(y_\tau|y_t),$$

where $A_{\tau t}(y_\tau|y_t) = A_{\tau 0}(y_\tau)/A_{t0}(y_t)$ is the cumulative return at date τ given y_τ from a dollar invested in the bank account at date $t < \tau$ given event $y_t \supseteq y_\tau$. Hence, we can define the conditional risk-neutral probability as

$$\hat{\varphi}_{\tau t}^A(y_\tau|y_t) \equiv A_{\tau t}(y_\tau|y_t) p_{\tau t}(y_\tau|y_t), \tag{6A.4}$$

and then substitute $p_{\tau t}(y_\tau|y_t) = A_{\tau t}^{-1}(y_\tau|y_t)\, \hat{\varphi}_{\tau t}^{A}(y_\tau|y_t)$ into (6.5) to obtain

$$v_{jt}(y_t) = \sum_{\tau=t+1}^{T} \hat{\mathrm{E}}_{\tau t}^{A}[d_{j\tau} A_{\tau t}^{-1} | y_t]. \tag{6A.5}$$

We now demonstrate that the risk-neutral probabilities defined in (6A.4) satisfy Bayes' rule, i.e., they are "time-consistent." To see this consistency, we compute the difference between the risk-neutral probability in (6A.4) and the result of applying Bayes' rule to beliefs at date t given event y_t with respect to $y_\tau \subseteq y_t$, $\tau > t$:

$$\hat{\varphi}_{\tau t}^{A}(y_\tau|y_t) - \hat{\varphi}_{\tau 0}^{A}(y_\tau)/\hat{\varphi}_{t0}^{A}(y_t)$$

$$= A_{\tau t}(y_\tau|y_t)p_{\tau t}(y_\tau|y_t) - A_{\tau 0}(y_\tau)\, p_\tau(y_\tau)/[A_{t0}(y_t)\, p_t(y_t)]$$

$$= p_{\tau t}(y_\tau|y_t)[A_{\tau t}(y_\tau|y_t) - A_{\tau 0}(y_\tau)/A_{t0}(y_t)] = 0.$$

REFERENCES

Berninghaus, S. (1977) "Individual and Collective Risks in Large Economies," *Journal of Economic Theory* 15, 279-294.

Caspi, Y. (1974) "Optimal Allocation of Risk in a Market with Many Traders," in J. Dreze(ed.) *Allocation under Uncertainty: Equilibrium and Optimality*, Macmillan, New York, 89-97.

Caspi, Y. (1974) "A Limit Theorem on the Core of an Economy with Individual Risks," *Review of Economic Studies* 41, 267-271.

Christensen, P. O., S. E. Graversen, and K. R. Miltersen. (2000) "Dynamic Spanning in the Consumption Based Capital Asset Pricing Model," *European Finance Review* 4, 129-156.

Debreu, G. (1959) *Theory of Value*, Yale University Press, New Heaven.

Duffie, D. (1996) *Dynamic Asset Pricing Theory*, Princeton University Press, Princeton, New Jersey.

Feltham, G. A. (1985) "The Impact of Public Information in Sequential Markets," Working Paper, The University of British Columbia, Vancouver.

Feltham, G. A., and P. O. Christensen. (1988) "Firm-Specific Information and Efficient Resource Allocation," *Contemporary Accounting Research* 5, 133-169.

Hakansson, N. H. (1970) "Optimal Investment and Consumption Strategies under Risk for a Class of Utility Functions," *Econometrica* 38, 587-607.

Hakansson, N. H. (1977) "The Superfund: Efficient Paths toward Efficient Capital Markets in Large and Small Countries." in H. Levy and M. Sarnat (eds.), *Financial Decision Making under Uncertainty*, Academic Press, New York, 165-201.

Huang, C.-F., and R. H. Litzenberger (1988) *Foundations for Financial Economics*, North-Holland, New York.

Kreps, D. (1982) "Multi-period Securities and the Efficient Allocation of Risk: A Comment on the Black-Scholes Option Pricing Model," in J. J. McCall (ed.), *The Economics of Information and Uncertainty*, Chicago: University of Chicago Press.

Malinvaud, E. (1972) "The Allocation of Individual Risk in Large Markets," *Econometrica* 40, 414-429.

Malinvaud, E. (1973) "Markets for an Exchange Economy with Individual Risk," *Econometrica* 41, 383-410.

Radner, R. (1972) "Existence of Equilibrium of Plans, Prices, and Price Expectations in a Sequence of Markets," *Econometrica* 40, 289-303.

Radner, R. (1982) "Equilibria under Uncertainty," in K. J. Arrow and M.D. Intriligator (eds.) *Handbook in Mathematical Economics: Volume II*, Amsterdam: North-Holland, 923-1006.

CHAPTER 7

PUBLIC INFORMATION IN MULTI-PERIOD MARKETS

Chapter 6 extends the single period analysis in Chapter 5 to a setting with multiple consumption dates and sequential trading of long-lived securities. This provides greater scope for exploring the impact of public information.

The analysis in Section 5.5 establishes, in a single-period setting, that a more informative public information system has no value (in terms of efficiency) if beliefs are homogeneous and endowments are measurable with respect to the less informative information system (see Propositions 5.8 and 5.9). Hence, more information is only valuable if it provides more opportunities for side-betting based on heterogeneous beliefs or insurance of endowment risks. In a market setting, more *ex post* information is weakly Pareto preferred, but more *ex ante* information may be detrimental to the insurance of endowment risks through trading. However, in a multi-period setting *ex post* information for one period is *ex ante* information for the next and, thus, the joint evolution of information and trading/insurance opportunities becomes important. These issues are examined in Sections 7.1 and 7.2.

In addition to examining information system changes on investor welfare we consider, in Sections 7.3 and 7.4, the impact of signals and information system changes on prices and trades. Prices and trades are readily observable, whereas beliefs and preferences are not. Hence, it is useful to understand the relation between signals, prices, and investor beliefs, and the relations between information systems, prices, and investor preferences. For example, there is a large empirical literature in accounting and finance, investigating the relation between the release of, for example, accounting information and stock prices. Like prices, trades are readily observable, but trading is more closely linked to consumption plans. Therefore, an examination of the relation between trades and signals may reveal whether particular signals influence consumption and, hence, investor preferences. The same may also apply to the relation between trades and information system changes.

In Section 7.5 we consider a simple parametric model in which investors have exponential utility and dividends are normally distributed. The investors' expected utility takes a simple form in this setting (see Proposition 2.7). It facilitates comparative static analysis examining the impact of differences in risk aversion, risk, and information precision on investor welfare and market prices. In this analysis all information is publicly reported, but the analysis is extended in Chapter 11 to consider settings in which there is both public and private information.

7.1 EFFICIENCY OF INFORMATION SYSTEMS

Let $\boldsymbol{\eta} \equiv \{ \eta_1, ..., \eta_T \}$ denote an information system for the multi-period economy with corresponding partitions on the state space $\mathbf{Y}^\eta \equiv \{ Y_1^\eta, ..., Y_T^\eta \}$ (we suppress the information at $t = 0$ in the notation since we assume throughout that the investors have no information at that date, i.e., $Y_0^\eta = \{S\}$). The definitions of consistent transfers, efficiency, and informativeness in the multi-period economy are similar to those in the single-period setting.

Definition $\boldsymbol{\eta}$-*Consistent Transfers*
The set of functions $\Delta \equiv \{ \delta_{it}: S \to \mathbb{R}, i = 1, ..., I; t = 1, ..., T \}$ is $\boldsymbol{\eta}$-consistent if it satisfies the following conditions.

(a) Individual feasibility: $e_{it}(s) + \delta_{it}(s) \in C_i, \quad \forall\, i, s; t = 1, ...,T.$

(b) Aggregate feasibility: $\Sigma_i\, \delta_{it}(s) \leq 0, \quad \forall\, s; t = 1, ..., T.$

(c) Individual sovereignty: $U_i(\mathbf{e}_i+\boldsymbol{\delta}_i) \geq U_i(\mathbf{e}_i), \quad \forall\, i.$

(d) Public information measurability: δ_{it} is Y_t^η-measurable, $\forall\, i; t = 1, ..., T.$

Definition $\boldsymbol{\eta}$-*Efficient Transfers*
The set of functions $\Delta \equiv \{ \delta_{it}: S \to \mathbb{R}, i = 1, ..., I; t = 1, ..., T \}$ is $\boldsymbol{\eta}$-efficient if the following conditions are satisfied.

(a) Δ is $\boldsymbol{\eta}$-consistent.

(b) There does not exist an alternative $\boldsymbol{\eta}$-consistent transfer Δ' such that

$$U_i(\mathbf{e}_i+\boldsymbol{\delta}_i') \geq U_i(\mathbf{e}_i+\boldsymbol{\delta}_i), \quad \forall\, i,$$

with at least one strict inequality.

Definition *Efficiency of Information Systems*

Information system η is *as efficient as (more efficient than)* η' if for every η'-efficient transfer Δ' there exists an η-consistent transfer Δ that is (strictly) Pareto preferred to Δ', i.e.,

$$U_i(\mathbf{e}_i+\boldsymbol{\delta}_i) \geq U_i(\mathbf{e}_i+\boldsymbol{\delta}_i'), \quad \forall\, i,$$

(with at least one strict inequality).

Definition *Informativeness*

Information system η is *as informative as* η' if Y_t^η is at least as fine a partition of S as $Y_t^{\eta'}$ for all $t = 1, ..., T$. Information system η is *more informative than* η' if η is *as informative as* η' and Y_t^η is a finer partition of S than $Y_t^{\eta'}$ for some t.

Note that in a multi-period setting, a more informative system may reveal information earlier without changing the information at the final date T. Figure 7.1 illustrates two information systems in a two-period setting. Clearly, η is more informative than η', and there are two sources of this: η distinguishes between the first two states at the final date, and if the true state is either one of the last two states, then η reveals the true state at date $t = 1$ whereas η' does not report that information until the final date.

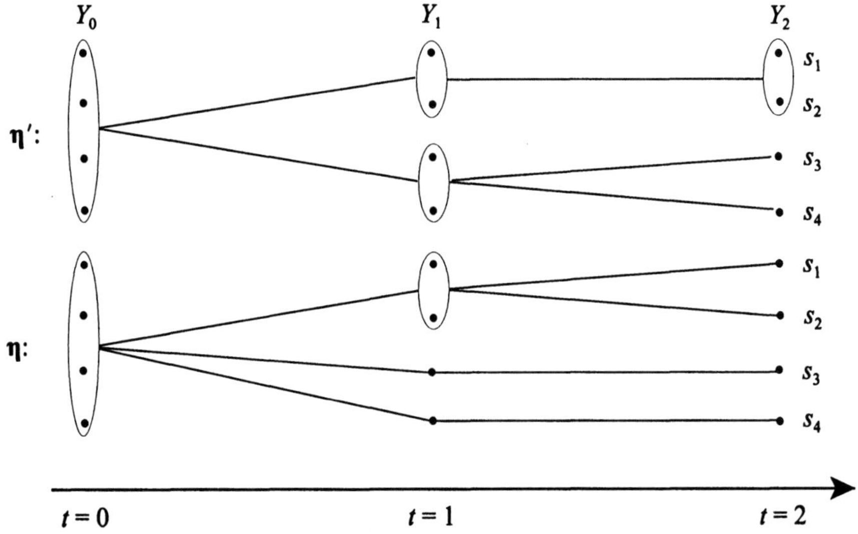

Figure 7.1: Two information systems in a two-period economy.

We let $\boldsymbol{\eta}' \equiv \{ \eta_1', ..., \eta_T' \}$ represent the existing information system and consider a change to $\boldsymbol{\eta} \equiv \{ \eta_1, ..., \eta_T \}$. As in the single-period setting, if $\boldsymbol{\eta}$ is as informative as $\boldsymbol{\eta}'$, then any $\boldsymbol{\eta}'$-efficient transfer Δ' is $\boldsymbol{\eta}$-consistent and, thus, we get the similar result as in Proposition 5.7.

Proposition 7.1

Information system $\boldsymbol{\eta}$ is as efficient as $\boldsymbol{\eta}'$ if $\boldsymbol{\eta}$ is as informative as $\boldsymbol{\eta}'$.

In single-period settings more information is only valuable if it provides more opportunities for side-betting or better insurance of endowment risks. In multi-period settings the efficiency of the inter-temporal allocation of consumption is an additional potential source of value of more information. The following result provides a multi-period equivalent to Proposition 5.8.[1]

Proposition 7.2

Assume $\boldsymbol{\eta}$ is a more informative system than $\boldsymbol{\eta}'$. The additional information in $\boldsymbol{\eta}$ has no value, i.e., any $\boldsymbol{\eta}$-efficient transfer is $\boldsymbol{\eta}'$-consistent, if

(a) endowments are $\boldsymbol{\eta}'$-measurable,

(b) investors have homogeneous beliefs, and

(c) investors have time-additive preferences.

With homogeneous beliefs and time-additive preferences, investors efficiently consume the same amount within each aggregate consumption event $y_t \in \Gamma_t$ at each date irrespectively of the information system (see Proposition 6.5(c)). There is enough public information to achieve this result if endowments are $\boldsymbol{\eta}'$-measurable, since time-additivity removes the possibility of gains from better coordination of consumption across dates. However, if preferences are *not* time-additive or endowments are *not* $\boldsymbol{\eta}'$-measurable, then a more informative system may permit the implementation of a more preferred transfer arrangement. This is illustrated by numerical examples in Appendix 7A.

Corollary

Assume $\boldsymbol{\eta}$ is a more informative system than $\boldsymbol{\eta}'$. If transfer arrangement Δ' is $\boldsymbol{\eta}'$-efficient, then a strictly preferred transfer arrangement Δ that is $\boldsymbol{\eta}$-

---

[1] This proposition and the following corollary are similar to the results for two-period models found in Ohlson and Buckman (1981) and Hakansson, Kunkel, and Ohlson (1982). Implicit in this proposition is the assumption that endowments are fixed. Chapter 8 considers the impact of production choice (which allows investors to influence their endowments).

consistent can only exist if at least one of the three following conditions are satisfied:

(a) endowments are *not* $\boldsymbol{\eta}'$*-measurable,*

(b) investors have *heterogeneous beliefs*, or

(c) preferences are *not time-additive.*

The corollary establishes that, if beliefs are homogeneous and preferences are time-additive, changing to a more informative system can only provide the basis for a preferred transfer arrangement if endowments are not measurable with respect to the less informative system. Of course, even if endowments are not $\boldsymbol{\eta}'$-measurable, $\boldsymbol{\eta}$ more informative than $\boldsymbol{\eta}'$ does not imply that $\boldsymbol{\eta}$ is more efficient than $\boldsymbol{\eta}'$. The more relevant question is whether $\boldsymbol{\eta}$ is more endowment informative than $\boldsymbol{\eta}'$.

Definition *Insurance Relevance*

Let $\boldsymbol{\Omega} \equiv (\Omega_1, ..., \Omega_T)$, where Ω_t is a partition of S. $\boldsymbol{\Omega}$ is *insurance relevant* with respect to the investors' endowments if, for all $t = 1, ..., T$:

(a) $\forall\, \omega_t \in \Omega_t$: $e_{it}(s') = e_{it}(s'') = e_{it}(\omega_t)$, $\quad \forall\, s', s'' \in \omega_t$ and $i = 1, ..., I$;

(b) for each distinct $\omega_t', \omega_t'' \in \Omega_t$, $\exists\, i$ with $e_{it}(\omega_t') \neq e_{it}(\omega_t'')$.

Definition *Insurance Informativeness*

Let $\boldsymbol{\Omega}$ be insurance relevant with respect to the investors' endowments, and assume investors have homogeneous beliefs. Information system $\boldsymbol{\eta}$ is *more insurance informative than* $\boldsymbol{\eta}'$ if, for all $t = 1, ..., T$, there exists a probability function $b(y_t'|y_t)$, $\forall\, y_t' \in Y_t^{\eta'}$ and $y_t \in Y_t^{\eta}$, such that

$$\varphi(y_t'|\omega_t) = \sum_{y_t \in Y_t} b(y_t'|y_t)\, \varphi(y_t|\omega_t), \qquad \forall\, \omega_t \in \Omega_t,$$

and there does not exist a probability function $b(y_t|y_t')$ such that the converse is true.

Observe that if endowments are $\boldsymbol{\eta}'$-measurable, then $\boldsymbol{\eta}$ cannot be more insurance informative than $\boldsymbol{\eta}'$ (even if it is more informative). Also observe that $\boldsymbol{\eta}$ more insurance informative than $\boldsymbol{\eta}'$ does not imply that $\boldsymbol{\eta}$ is more informative than $\boldsymbol{\eta}'$ (compare to the discussion of informativeness in Chapter 3).

Proposition 7.3

If beliefs are homogeneous and preferences are time-additive, then $\boldsymbol{\eta}$ more efficient than $\boldsymbol{\eta}'$ implies that $\boldsymbol{\eta}$ is more insurance informative than $\boldsymbol{\eta}'$ with respect to the investors' endowments.

The preceding analysis establishes that homogeneity of investor beliefs and time-additivity of preferences are powerful assumptions in a multi-date consumption setting. Under these assumptions the efficiency of an information system depends entirely on the extent to which it provides the basis for efficient risk sharing at each date, on a date-by-date basis. An information system that reports insurance relevant events earlier than the dates at which they apply is no more efficient than a system that reports those events at the dates the endowments are received. On the other hand, if investor preferences are not time-additive, then early reporting of insurance relevant events can improve efficiency by permitting improved sharing of consumption across dates. In most of the subsequent analyses we assume time-additive preferences, in the belief that the use of accounting information to efficiently share consumption across dates is of relatively minor importance.

7.2 IMPACT OF PUBLIC INFORMATION IN SECURITIES MARKETS

Propositions 7.1, 7.2, and 7.3 establish that a more informative system need not make any investor worse off and specify conditions that are necessary for a Pareto improvement to occur. Those results focus on what is feasible given complete control of the transfers that are implemented. We now examine how investors are affected by a change from a less informative to a more informative system given that the transfers are determined by trading in a competitive securities market.

Consider a change from information system $\boldsymbol{\eta}'$ to $\boldsymbol{\eta}$, where the latter is more informative. Initially assume that there is a complete set of date-event securities for both information systems, i.e., the marketed securities constitute a complete multi-period securities market. As already noted, the key in this type of market is that there is no need to trade subsequent to the initial trading date $t = 0$.

Definition

Endowments $\mathbf{e}$ are $\boldsymbol{\eta}'$-efficient if transfers $\Delta' = \mathbf{0}$ are $\boldsymbol{\eta}'$-efficient.

Proposition 7.4

Assume $\boldsymbol{\eta}$ is more informative than $\boldsymbol{\eta}'$, and let $\mathscr{E}(\boldsymbol{\eta}')$ denote an AD-equilibrium for $\boldsymbol{\eta}'$ with consumption plan $\mathbf{c}'$.

(a) If endowments **e** are $\boldsymbol{\eta}'$-efficient, then there exists an AD-equilibrium $\mathscr{E}(\boldsymbol{\eta})$ with consumption plan **c** such that **c** is weakly Pareto preferred to $\mathbf{c}'$.

(b) If beliefs are homogeneous, utility functions are time-additive, and endowments are $\boldsymbol{\eta}'$-measurable, then there exists an AD-equilibrium $\mathscr{E}(\boldsymbol{\eta})$ with consumption plan $\mathbf{c}'$ in which the date-event prices with $\boldsymbol{\eta}$ are given by

$$p_t(y_t) = p_t'(y_t')\,\varphi(y_t|y_t'), \quad \forall\, y_t \subseteq y_t' \in Y_t^{\eta'}.$$

Part (a) can be viewed as applying to a setting in which investors first trade on the basis of $\boldsymbol{\eta}'$ and then there is an announced change to $\boldsymbol{\eta}$. No one will be made worse off by such an announcement since investors now have efficient "endowments" with respect to $\boldsymbol{\eta}'$ and can always refuse to trade after the announcement. On the other hand, if such trading has not taken place, then the change may make some investors worse off and others better off (but not everyone worse off). The reason is that the structure of the date-event prices changes and, thus, the value at $t = 0$ of the investors' individual endowments may decrease or increase.

Part (b) is a setting in which $\boldsymbol{\eta}'$ provides sufficient information to efficiently share aggregate risks, and the investors' wealth at $t = 0$ are given by

$$\sum_{t=1}^{T} \sum_{\gamma_t \in \Gamma_t} \mathrm{E}[e_{it}|\gamma_t]\, p_t(\gamma_t).$$

Since endowments are $\boldsymbol{\eta}'$-measurable, the more informative system cannot provide a basis for improved risk sharing (given homogeneous beliefs and time-additive preferences). System $\boldsymbol{\eta}$ may provide information about aggregate consumption or personal endowments earlier than $\boldsymbol{\eta}'$, but consumption plan $\mathbf{c}'$ continues to be an equilibrium – the additional information is "useless." More specifically, while the additional information expands the events that are priced, the gambles associated with the additional information are fairly priced. Hence, investors have no incentive to bet on this information, and the stated prices induce the same initial wealth distribution, transfers, and consumption plans.

The results for complete multi-period securities markets in Proposition 7.4 can be extended to effectively dynamically complete markets. In this setting, we assume for simplicity that the endowments consist of ownership of marketed securities, i.e. $\bar{\mathbf{c}} = \mathbf{0}$.

Definition

Ownership endowments $\bar{\mathbf{z}}_{i0}$ are $\boldsymbol{\eta}'$-efficient if $\mathbf{c}'$ is $\boldsymbol{\eta}'$-efficient when $c_{it}'(y_t) = \mathbf{d}_t(y_t)\,\bar{\mathbf{z}}_{i0}$, $\forall\, i, t, y_t$.

Proposition 7.5

Assume $\boldsymbol{\eta}$ is more informative than $\boldsymbol{\eta}'$. Let $\mathscr{E}(\boldsymbol{\eta}')$ denote an RS-equilibrium for $\boldsymbol{\eta}'$ with consumption plan $\mathbf{c}'$, and assume that there are sufficient marketed securities to implement an $\boldsymbol{\eta}$-efficient consumption plan as an RS-equilibrium.

(a) If endowments are $\boldsymbol{\eta}'$-efficient, then there exists an RS-equilibrium $\mathscr{E}(\boldsymbol{\eta})$ with consumption plan $\mathbf{c}$ such that $\mathbf{c}$ is weakly Pareto preferred to $\mathbf{c}'$.

(b) If beliefs are homogeneous, utility functions are time-additive, and endowments are $\boldsymbol{\eta}'$-measurable, then there exists an RS-equilibrium $\mathscr{E}(\boldsymbol{\eta})$ with consumption plan $\mathbf{c}'$.

A key point to recognize is that in a dynamic trading context, trading at $t = 0$ is not sufficient to result in a portfolio that will lead to no trading at subsequent dates. Hence, the assumption of $\boldsymbol{\eta}'$-efficient endowments in (a) is a much more restrictive assumption than the corresponding assumption in Proposition 7.4(a).

The time period of our analysis, $t = 0, 1, ..., T$, can be viewed as a subset of a longer time horizon over which some information system $\boldsymbol{\eta}'$ has been in effect. In that case, an investor's endowed portfolio at $t = 0$ is the portfolio he acquired at the last trading date. If investors believe that $\boldsymbol{\eta}'$ will continue to be the information system, there will be no trading at $t = 0$ since no additional information is released at that date (and there is no consumption taking place). Now consider two types of changes to a more informative system $\boldsymbol{\eta}$.

Announcement of a System Change at t = 0

This can be viewed as a representation of the date at which investors become aware that a regulatory body, such as the SEC, FASB or ASC, will be requiring firms to change their reporting practices such that previously unreported information will be reported in the future (or information will become publicly known earlier). The following results can be established (and some are established by the above propositions).

(a) It is possible for some investors to be made worse off, but not everyone (when it is assumed that there are sufficient marketed securities to implement an $\boldsymbol{\eta}$-efficient consumption plan as an RS-equilibrium).

(b) It is possible for no one to be made worse off, and some might be made better off. This result is assured if prior trading has resulted in $\boldsymbol{\eta}'$-efficient "endowments" at $t = 0$. Observe that the lack of trading at $t = 0$ with $\boldsymbol{\eta}'$ does not imply that the endowments are $\boldsymbol{\eta}'$-efficient – there may need to be trading at $t = 1, ..., T\text{-}1$ in order to implement consumption plan $\mathbf{c}'$. However, there are special cases in which no future trading will occur if the existing system is continued and, hence, the unanticipated change to a more informative system will not make any investor worse-off. The following are three such special cases.

(*i*) The marketed securities constitute a complete multi-period securities market (cf. Proposition 7.4). As we noted earlier, there need not be any subsequent trading in an AD-equilibrium.

(*ii*) The economy has two periods, the dividends and endowments at $t = 1$ are known at $t = 0$, $\boldsymbol{\eta}'$ reports no information at $t = 1$, and prior trading has resulted in equilibrium endowments. This is a very special case, but it is one that received considerable attention in the literature.[2]

(*iii*) Investors have homogeneous beliefs and preferences that are represented by time-additive HARA utility functions which result in linear risk sharing with risky portfolios that have the same mix from period to period. In addition, there are zero-coupon bonds with all maturities (or some equivalent marketed securities), so that there is no need for further trading (see Proposition 6.7).

Release of Unanticipated Information at t = 1

In this case, the arrival of unanticipated information at $t = 1$ conveys to investors that there has been a change in the information system. Some or even all of the investors can be made worse-off.

The release of information creates risks. If there are sufficient marketed securities, then that risk can be efficiently shared as long as trading takes place prior to its release. If such trading has not taken place prior to release of the information, then the investors must bear that risk themselves. For example, assume that it is known that some event, such as an earthquake in your city, may or may not occur, but if it does, it will occur two years from now. People in your city plan to buy earthquake insurance if they own a home, but they have no need to buy it until next year. Unknown to everyone, a scientist has been

---

[2] For example, this condition is assumed in much of Ohlson and Buckman (1981) and in Hakansson, Kunkel, and Ohlson (1982).

working on a method to predict earthquakes and this is suddenly revealed by his announcement that your city will be hit by a devastating earthquake in two years. All those who had not purchased earthquake insurance prior to the scientist's announcement would be made worse off by the shift to a more informative system.

Incompleteness Due to Too Much Information

The preceding analysis has focused on settings in which there are sufficient marketed securities to implement an η-efficient consumption plan as an RS-equilibrium. However, the information system may also affect the possibility of implementing efficient consumption plans as an RS-equilibrium through dynamic trading. To illustrate, consider the three information systems depicted in Figure 7.2, where η' is more informative than η'', and η is more informative than η', and assume there are only two sufficiently distinct "long-lived" marketed securities.

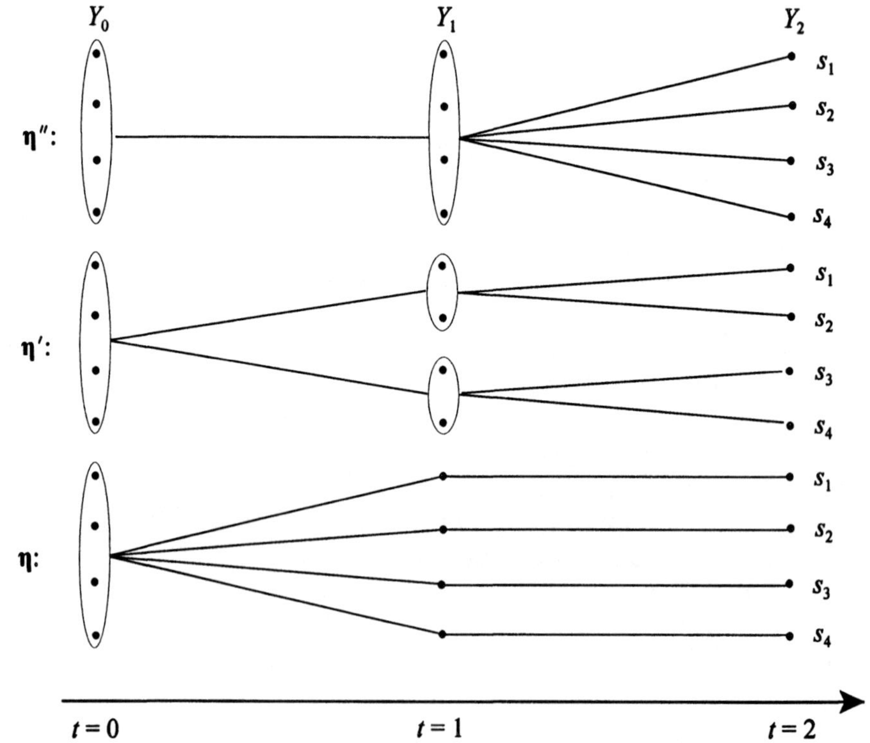

Figure 7.2: Three information systems in a two-period economy.

A change from the least informative η'' to the more informative η' makes the market dynamically complete and, thus, facilitates η'-efficient consumption plans, whereas η''-efficient equilibrium consumption plans are not guaranteed with η''. Hence, the additional intermediate information at $t = 1$ with η' may make everyone better off – it facilitates trading strategies in the two securities that enable investors to efficiently share the risk associated with the four states. However, even more information at $t = 1$, as with the most informative system, η may leave everyone worse off than with η' since the uncertainty is resolved "too fast" in order for the investors to efficiently share the risk associated with the four signals (states) at $t = 1$. This suggests that dynamically completeness is most likely to occur if information is released at an "even rate" (such that the spanning number of the information system is as low as possible).

7.3 INFORMATION AND PRICES

This section examines the impact of signals and information system changes on prices. Prices are readily observable, whereas beliefs and preferences are not. Hence, it is useful to understand the relation between signals, prices, and investor beliefs, and the relations between information systems, prices, and investor preferences. For example, there is a large empirical literature in accounting and finance, investigating the relation between the release of, for example, accounting information and stock prices.

First consider the *impact of signals on prices*. The impact of the signal y_t on prices can be "measured" by the change between the cum-dividend price at date t, $V_{jt}(y_t)$, and the ex-dividend price at date t - 1, $v_{jt-1}(y_{t-1})$, $y_{t-1} \supseteq y_t$. However, in making this comparison we must recognize that the "numeraire" on which these prices are based is likely to differ between the two dates.

In our model, the numeraire is current consumption, i.e., security prices at date t are expressed in terms of consumption units at that date. To remove the effect of the change in the numeraire between two dates we define the pre- and post-information prices as follows.

Definition

The *pre-information price* for security j at date t given signal y_{t-1} is

$$\vec{V}_{jt}(y_{t-1}) \equiv v_{jt-1}(y_{t-1})\, R_{t-1,\,t}(y_{t-1}),$$

where $R_{t-1,\,t}(y_{t-1})$ is the one-period riskless return from one unit invested at date t - 1 given signal y_{t-1}. The *post-information price* is the cum-dividend price $V_{jt}(y_t)$.

The following proposition establishes two basic characteristics of the relation between pre- and post-information prices.

Proposition 7.6

The following price relations hold for any RS-equilibrium $\mathscr{E}(\boldsymbol{\eta})$.

(a) The basic price relation for all securities j, $y_{t-1} \in Y_{t-1}$, $t = 1, ..., T$, is

$$\vec{V}_{jt}(y_{t-1}) = \hat{\mathrm{E}}_{t,t-1}[V_{jt} \,|\, y_{t-1}].$$

(b) If no new information is released at date t, then there is no change in prices, i.e., if $y_t = y_{t-1}$, then

$$\vec{V}_{jt}(y_{t-1}) = V_{jt}(y_t) \quad \forall j.$$

If there are no arbitrage opportunities, then pre-information prices are always equal to the *risk-adjusted* expected post-information prices (see (6.12)). However, note that the risk-neutral probabilities depend not only on investor beliefs but also on preferences and the "scarcity of consumption." If there is no new information, no arbitrage implies that pre-information prices must equal the post-information prices.

Given homogeneous beliefs and time-additive preferences, $\boldsymbol{\eta}$-efficient consumption varies only with aggregate consumption at each date and, hence, information about future aggregate consumption plays an interesting role in determining price relations.

Proposition 7.7[3]

If beliefs are homogeneous and preferences are time-additive, RS-equilibrium $\mathscr{E}(\boldsymbol{\eta})$ is $\boldsymbol{\eta}$-efficient, and the date t - 1 signal y_{t-1} reveals the level of aggregate consumption γ_t for date t, then the pre-information price equals the *expected* post-information price, i.e., if $y_{t-1} \subseteq \gamma_t$, then

$$\vec{V}_{jt}(y_{t-1}) = \mathrm{E}[V_{jt} \,|\, y_{t-1}].$$

[3] This is similar to propositions found in Ohlson and Buckman (1981) and Ohlson (1984). They analyze two-period models and compare the prices at t=1 for two systems that differ as to the information reported at t=1 (one reports more than the other). If the two systems result in the same $\boldsymbol{\eta}$-efficient consumption plans (and, hence, the additional information is of "no value"), then the prices with the coarser system are equal to the expected prices with the finer system. Furthermore, the variances of the prices with the finer system are greater than the variances of the prices with the coarser system. Of course, as the authors point out, the empirical implications of these results are limited by the fact that we cannot observe the prices under two different systems, except in experimental economies.

With homogeneous beliefs and time-additive preferences, the risk-adjustment of the probabilities depends only on the "scarcity of consumption," i.e., the valuation index at date t, and if that is known at date t - 1, the pre-information price is equal to the expected post-information price using the investors' "true probabilities."

The preceding analysis assumes that the signals are generated by a given information system – a system known to investors at the time they make their pre-signal trades. Now consider the impact on prices of an announced change in the information system. We assume that the announcement is made after pre-signal trades have taken place on the basis of the old system, but before any signals are received or consumption takes place. The date of this announcement is, without loss of generality, $t = 0$.

Efficient RS-equilibria have close links to the implicit date-event prices and both consumption plans and market prices of marketed securities (see Propositions 6.4 and 6.5). These linkages result in the following proposition.

Proposition 7.8

If there are sufficient marketed securities to achieve efficiency with both $\boldsymbol{\eta}'$ and $\boldsymbol{\eta}$, then the pre- and post-announcement prices for a change from $\boldsymbol{\eta}'$ to $\boldsymbol{\eta}$ are equal if $\boldsymbol{\eta}'$ and $\boldsymbol{\eta}$ result in the same consumption plans, i.e., price changes imply that at least some investors have changed their consumption plans.

Pre- and post-announcement prices only differ if $\boldsymbol{\eta}'$ and $\boldsymbol{\eta}$ result in different consumption plans. Hence, price changes imply that at least some investors prefer one system to the other, although the direction of that preference cannot be assessed from those changes. Of course, if $\boldsymbol{\eta}$ is more informative than $\boldsymbol{\eta}'$, then price changes imply that at least some investors prefer $\boldsymbol{\eta}$ to $\boldsymbol{\eta}'$.[4]

The preceding analysis has assumed that a change in information system is announced before information is received and consumption has taken place and, hence, is represented as a change at date $t = 0$. In some contexts, particularly when firms make changes in their reporting systems, the announcement of an information system change takes place at the same time as signals from the new system are released. This is represented as an *unanticipated change* at $t = 1$ and it *can have a negative impact on all investors*, if they have not efficiently shared

[4] A zero price change will occur if investors are indifferent between the two systems, but a zero change does not always imply indifference. For example, if individuals have time-additive logarithmic utility functions with $\beta_{it}^P = \beta_t^P$ and heterogeneous beliefs, a change in information system will not change the $t = 0$ prices of existing securities even though consumption plans may change to take advantage of additional side-betting opportunities. This appears to be a special case. In most other situations a change in consumption plans is accompanied by a change in prices.

their risks prior to the receipt of unanticipated information. If the securities acquired at $t = 0$ are such that there will be no further trading if $\boldsymbol{\eta}'$ is implemented, then an unanticipated change to a more informative system $\boldsymbol{\eta}$ will not make any investor worse off (since each investor can always refuse to trade). Problems arise when consumption plans are to be implemented with trades after $t = 0$.

7.4 INFORMATION AND TRADES

This section examines the impact of signals and information system changes on market trades. Like prices, trades are readily observable, but trading is more closely linked to consumption plans. As Ohlson and others stress,[5] *different consumption plans require different trades.* Therefore, an examination of the relation between trades and signals *may* reveal whether particular signals influence consumption and, hence, investor preferences. The same may also apply to the relation between trades and information system changes.

An investor has two basic reasons for trading. First, he will trade at any date t at which his endowment plus dividends do not equal his planned consumption for that period. Second, if, at date t, the portfolio acquired at $t - 1$ does not have the desired signal-contingent date $t + 1$ investment wealth, then trading will occur at date t.

In examining the *trade/consumption/signal relations,* a basic question is whether the impact of signals on consumption is coincident with their impact on trades. Trades and consumption are signal-contingent at time t if $\mathbf{z}_{it}(y_t)$ and $c_{it}(y_t)$ depend on $y_t \in Y_t$ in some non-trivial way. The following proposition establishes that the link between these two signal-contingencies is rather weak.

Proposition 7.9

Signal-contingent consumption at date t neither (a) implies nor (b) is implied by signal-contingent trades at date t.

The fact that *signal-contingent consumption does not imply contemporaneous signal-contingent trades* is most clearly illustrated by an economy in which there is a complete set of date-event securities. In that special case all trading can take place at $t = 0$ and, hence, there need be no trading at date t even though there may be signal-contingent consumption at that date. Part (a) is also illustrated by the lack of trading at date T even though consumption obviously varies with the event-contingent dividends at that date and there is no trading at that date in any single-good economy. An implication of part (a) is that,

---

[5] See, for example, Ohlson and Buckman (1981) and Lev and Ohlson (1982).

while consumption at date t may be signal-contingent, the trades used to implement that contingency may occur at an earlier date.

The fact that *signal-contingent trades do not imply contemporaneous signal-contingent consumption* can be illustrated by an economy with homogeneous beliefs, time-additive preferences, and no uncertainty about the level of aggregate consumption. In that setting, efficient consumption plans do not depend on the signals, but investors may have to trade dynamically in order to eliminate the risks in their endowments.

Now consider *trade/consumption/information system relations*. Assume that a change from $\boldsymbol{\eta}'$ to $\boldsymbol{\eta}$ is announced at $t = 0$ and the endowments reflect prior trading on the basis of $\boldsymbol{\eta}'$, i.e., if $\boldsymbol{\eta}'$ is implemented there will be no trading at $t = 0$. It is difficult to make general statements about the relations between the change in information system, changes in consumption plans, and trading. There is, however, a set of circumstances under which trading does imply a change in consumption plans.

Proposition 7.10

If no trading is required to implement the consumption plans for $\boldsymbol{\eta}'$ (i.e., equilibrium endowments), then trading on or after the announced change to $\boldsymbol{\eta}$ implies that investors have changed their consumption plans and have been made better off by the change.

The "no trading" condition can be satisfied if there has been a prior round of trading of a complete set of date-event securities. It can also be satisfied by a prior round of trading in many of the two-period economies examined in the literature.[6] However, it is not satisfied in more general multi-period economies in which a dynamic trading strategy is required to implement optimal consumption plans.

---

[6] See, for example, Ohlson and Buckman (1981) and Hakansson, Kunkel, and Ohlson (1982). The two-period economies examined in these papers have direct trading of $t = 1$ consumption at $t = 0$ and no uncertainty about the dividends to be paid at $t = 1$. Endowments are assumed to be such that there is no trading at $t = 0$ or $t = 1$ if no information is released at $t = 1$. Under these conditions, the release of information at $t = 1$ does not induce trading at either $t = 0$ or $t = 1$ unless the information induces a change in consumption plans. This cannot occur unless there are heterogeneous beliefs, non-additive preferences, or insufficient marketed securities to efficiently share risks.

7.5 EXPONENTIAL UTILITY AND NORMALLY DISTRIBUTED DIVIDENDS

In Sections 2.6 and 3.4.1, we demonstrate that assuming exponential utility with normally distributed beliefs provides a model in which a decision maker's expected utility takes a simple form. As a consequence, the model lends itself to comparative static analysis examining the impact of differences in risk aversion, risk, and information precision. In this section we extend this type of model to a single consumption date setting in which I investors trade shares in J firms in a competitive capital market. All information is publicly reported, whereas in Chapter 11 the analysis is extended to consider settings in which there is both public and private investor information.

7.5.1 Investor Portfolio Choice

We examine a single consumption date model in which the I investors are endowed at $t = 0$ with a portfolio of marketed securities, potentially receive public reports at $t=1$, and are paid terminal dividends by the marketed securities at $t = 2$. Trading of the marketed securities can take place at $t = 0$ and $t = 1$, but consumption only takes place at $t = 2$. We initially assume there is no public report at $t = 1$, so that there is only one round of trading (which can be at either $t = 0$ or $t = 1$). We then examine the impact of a public report at $t = 1$, with two rounds of trading.

The Investors' Beliefs and Preferences

There are $J + 1$ marketed claims consisting of a zero-coupon bond that pays one unit of consumption at $t = 2$ and is in zero net supply, and the shares in J firms for which the net supplies are $\mathbf{Z} = (Z_1, ..., Z_J)^t$. Investor i has no consumption endowments but is endowed with a portfolio of firm shares, represented by $\bar{\mathbf{z}}_i = (\bar{z}_{i1},...,\bar{z}_{iJ})^t$.[7] For notational simplicity, we now let $\mathbf{z}_{it}$ and z_{it0} represent investor i's portfolio of shares and units held of the zero-coupon bond after trading at date t, respectively.[8] Hence, the market clearing conditions at date t are

[7] The endowment could include holdings of the zero-coupon bond, but that would have essentially no effect on the results and so, for simplicity, we assume the endowments of bonds are all zero.

[8] In the preceding analysis, $\mathbf{z}_{it}$ represented the *difference* in the portfolio as a result of trading at date t.

$$\sum_{i=1}^{I} z_{it0} = 0, \quad \sum_{i=1}^{I} \mathbf{z}_{it} = \mathbf{Z} \equiv \sum_{i=1}^{I} \bar{\mathbf{z}}_i .$$

We initially assume there is no information reported at $t = 1$, so there is only one round of trading and we omit the time subscript from the traded portfolio.

Instead of expressing dividends at date $t = 2$ as functions of uncertain events at that date, the dividends per share paid by the J firms are represented by a vector of random variables $\mathbf{d} = (d_1, ..., d_J)^t$. Investor i's prior dividend beliefs are normally distributed, represented by $\mathbf{d} \sim \mathrm{N}(\mathbf{m}_i, \mathbf{\Sigma}_i)$, where $\mathbf{m}_i$ is a $J\times1$ vector of expected dividends per share and $\mathbf{\Sigma}_i = [\ \sigma_{ijk}\ ]_{J\times J}$ is investor i's $J\times J$ covariance matrix.

Investor i's consumption at $t = 2$ is denoted c_i and he has exponential utility with respect to consumption, i.e., $u_i(c_i) = -\exp[-\ r_i\ c_i]$, where r_i is his risk aversion. Investor i's consumption at $t = 2$ depends on the investment portfolio he owns at $t = 2$ and the dividends paid at $t = 2$, i.e., $c_i = z_{i0} + \mathbf{z}_i^t\mathbf{d}$. Hence, c_i is normally distributed with prior mean $z_{i0} + \mathbf{z}_i^t\mathbf{m}_i$ and variance $\mathbf{z}_i^t\mathbf{\Sigma}_i\mathbf{z}_i$.

Given exponential utility and normally distributed consumption, we know from Proposition 2.7 that investor i's expected utility given beliefs $(\mathbf{m}_i, \mathbf{\Sigma}_i)$ and portfolio $(z_{i0}, \mathbf{z}_i)$ is

$$\mathrm{E}[u_i(z_{i0} + \mathbf{z}_i^t\mathbf{d}) \,|\, \mathbf{m}_i, \mathbf{\Sigma}_i] = -\exp[-\ r_i\, CE_i(\mathbf{m}_i, \mathbf{\Sigma}_i, z_{i0}, \mathbf{z}_i)],$$

where his certainty equivalent CE_i is

$$CE_i(\mathbf{m}_i, \mathbf{\Sigma}_i, z_{i0}, \mathbf{z}_i) = z_{i0} + \mathbf{z}_i^t\mathbf{m}_i - \tfrac{1}{2}\, r_i \mathbf{z}_i^t\mathbf{\Sigma}_i\mathbf{z}_i. \tag{7.1}$$

Optimal Investment Portfolio

Given that there is a single consumption date, we can, without loss of generality, set the price of the zero-coupon bond equal to one, i.e. the shares are priced relative to that bond. The prices per share for the J firms are represented by the $J\times1$ vector $\mathbf{v}$ (we omit the time subscript when there is no information at $t = 1$ since there is only one round of trading).

Each investor i selects the portfolio that maximizes his certainty equivalent subject to a budget constraint that reflects the market prices $\mathbf{v}$:

$$z_{i0} + \mathbf{z}_i^t\mathbf{v} \le \bar{\mathbf{z}}_i^t\mathbf{v}. \tag{7.2}$$

Since an investor always prefers more to less, the budget constraint is binding and $z_{i0} = (\bar{\mathbf{z}}_i - \mathbf{z}_i)^t\mathbf{v}$. Hence, the investor's portfolio choice can be expressed as an unconstrained optimization problem of the form

$$CE_i^*(\mathbf{m}_i, \boldsymbol{\Sigma}_i, \mathbf{v}) = \underset{\mathbf{z}_i}{\text{maximize}}\ \mathbf{z}_i^t(\mathbf{m}_i - \mathbf{v}) - \tfrac{1}{2}\, r_i \mathbf{z}_i^t \boldsymbol{\Sigma}_i \mathbf{z}_i + \bar{\mathbf{z}}_i^t \mathbf{v}. \tag{7.3}$$

The first-order condition from this optimization problem yields the following optimal portfolio choice:

$$\mathbf{z}_i^* = \frac{1}{r_i}\mathbf{H}_i(\mathbf{m}_i - \mathbf{v}), \tag{7.4}$$

where $\mathbf{H}_i = \boldsymbol{\Sigma}_i^{-1}$ is the precision matrix for investor *i*'s beliefs.

Observe that the characterization of the optimal portfolio choice in (7.4) for a single firm setting (i.e., $J = 1$) yields the following intuitively appealing relations. Investor *i*'s demand for the firm's shares is:

(a) decreasing in his risk aversion (r_i);

(b) increasing in the precision of his belief ($h_i = 1/\sigma_i^2$);

(c) increasing in his expected dividend (m_i);

(d) independent of his wealth ($\bar{z}_i v$);

(e) decreasing in the price of the firm's shares (v).

7.5.2 Equilibrium Prices and Investment Portfolios

We now use the investors' demand function in (7.4) with market clearing to derive the equilibrium price functions. These prices are then used in the demand functions to characterize the investors' equilibrium investment portfolios.

Equilibrium Prices

In equilibrium, the demand for the firms' shares must equal the supply. Hence, using the demand function in (7.4), the price vector $\mathbf{v}$ must be such that

$$\sum_{i=1}^{I} \frac{1}{r_i}\mathbf{H}_i(\mathbf{m}_i - \mathbf{v}) = \mathbf{Z}. \tag{7.5}$$

Solving for $\mathbf{v}$ yields

$$\mathbf{v} = \varsigma_o^{-1}\left[\sum_{i=1}^{I} \varsigma_i \mathbf{m}_i - \mathbf{Z}\right], \tag{7.6}$$

$$\varsigma_i \equiv \frac{1}{r_i}\mathbf{H}_i, \quad \varsigma_o \equiv \sum_{i=1}^{I} \varsigma_i .$$

That is, the market prices are a "weighted average" of the mean beliefs of each investor minus an aggregate risk premium adjustment. The weight given to investor *i*'s prior mean increases with his risk tolerance (i.e., the inverse of his risk aversion) and the precision of his beliefs, and the aggregate risk premium is the number of shares outstanding multiplied by the inverse of the sum of each investor's risk tolerance times the precision of his beliefs.

If the investors have homogeneous beliefs, i.e., $\mathbf{m}_i = \mathbf{m}$ and $\boldsymbol{\Sigma}_i = \boldsymbol{\Sigma}$, then

$$\mathbf{v} = \mathbf{m} - r_o \boldsymbol{\Sigma}\mathbf{Z}, \tag{7.7}$$

where r_o is a measure of the investors' "aggregate risk aversion,"

$$r_o \equiv \left[\sum_{i=1}^{I} \frac{1}{r_i}\right]^{-1},$$

i.e., the inverse of the sum of the investors' risk tolerances. Observe that if the investors have identical risk aversion r, then $r_o = r/I$, so that it decreases as the number of investors increases.

In the homogeneous beliefs case with a single firm, the equilibrium price (7.7) is:

(a) increasing in the expected dividend (m);

(b) increasing in aggregate risk tolerance (i.e., decreasing in r_o);

(c) increasing in the precision of beliefs (i.e., decreasing in σ^2);

(d) decreasing in the supply of shares (Z).

In the limit, there is no risk premium and $v = m$ if either aggregate risk aversion r_o or belief uncertainty σ^2 goes to zero.

In the multiple firm case with homogeneous beliefs, the expression $\boldsymbol{\Sigma}\mathbf{Z}$ is a $J\times 1$ vector of the covariances of each firm's dividends with the aggregate dividend from the market portfolio, i.e. $d_o = \mathbf{d}^t\mathbf{Z}$ (which equals aggregate consumption). In particular, the market value per share for firm j is

$$v_j = m_j - r_o \sum_{k=1}^{J} \sigma_{jk} Z_k = m_j - r_o \sigma_{jo}, \tag{7.8}$$

where $\sigma_{jo} = \text{Cov}[d_j, d_o]$. Hence, the size of the risk premium deducted from the firm's expected dividend is a function of the covariance of the firm's dividend per share with aggregate consumption as well as the investors' aggregate risk aversion.

The market value, and expected dividend for the market portfolio are represented by $v_o = \mathbf{v}^t\mathbf{Z}$ and $m_o = \mathbf{m}^t\mathbf{Z}$, and the variance of the aggregate dividend is $\sigma_o^2 = \text{Cov}[d_1, d_o]Z_1 + \ldots + \text{Cov}[d_J, d_o]Z_J$. Multiplying both sides of (7.8) by Z_j, summing over all firms, and rearranging terms, establishes that

$$r_o = \frac{1}{\sigma_o^2}[m_o - v_o] = h_o\,[m_o - v_o]. \tag{7.9}$$

Substituting (7.9) into (7.8) yields the classical CAPM pricing model (in levels):

$$v_j = m_j - \beta_j[m_o - v_o], \tag{7.10}$$

where $\beta_j \equiv h_o \sigma_{jo}$.

Equilibrium Investment Portfolios

In order to determine the equilibrium investment portfolio for investor i we substitute the equilibrium price (7.6) into the investors' demand function (7.4). With heterogeneous beliefs, the result is

$$\mathbf{z}_i^* = \varsigma_i \left\{ \mathbf{m}_i - \varsigma_o^{-1} \left[\sum_{i=1}^{I} \varsigma_i \mathbf{m}_i - \mathbf{Z} \right] \right\}. \tag{7.11}$$

In the homogeneous beliefs case this simplifies to

$$\mathbf{z}_i^* = \frac{r_o}{r_i}\mathbf{Z}. \tag{7.12}$$

That is, each investor holds a fixed fraction of each firm's shares, and the fraction equals the ratio of the investor's risk tolerance ($1/r_i$) relative to the aggregate risk tolerance of all investors ($1/r_o$). Recall that we saw this result in our earlier discussion of efficient risk sharing when all partners have exponential utility and homogeneous beliefs (even if the beliefs are not normally distributed). See Table 4.1.

We have made very little comment on the investors' holdings of the zero-coupon bond. This is because each investor will always invest any excess funds in bonds or he will sell (i.e., go short in) bonds if the value of his endowed portfolio is less than his optimal share of the market portfolio, i.e., $z_{i0} = (\bar{\mathbf{z}}_i - \mathbf{z}_i^*)^t\mathbf{v}$. Since the aggregate number of endowed shares equals the aggregate number of acquired shares, it follows that

$$\sum_{i=1}^{I} z_{i0} = \sum_{i=1}^{I} (\bar{\mathbf{z}}_i - \mathbf{z}_i^*)^t\mathbf{v} = 0.$$

Hence, the market for zero-coupon bonds clears.[9]

7.5.3 Impact of Public Information

Assume now that at $t = 1$, an information system η generates an $M\times 1$ vector of reports $\mathbf{y}$. We assume that $\mathbf{y}$ and $\mathbf{d}$ are jointly normally distributed, and we represent the posterior beliefs with respect to $\mathbf{d}$ given $\mathbf{y}$ as $\mathbf{d} \sim N(\mathbf{m}_i(\mathbf{y}), \mathbf{\Sigma}_i(\eta))$. That is, the posterior mean depends on the specific reports received, whereas the posterior covariance matrix depends on the information system but not the specific reports. The prior distribution with respect to the posterior mean $\mathbf{m}_i(\mathbf{y})$ is normally distributed with mean $\mathbf{m}_i$ and covariance matrix $\mathbf{\Sigma}_{mi}(\eta)$, where the latter depends on the information system, but the former does not. The derivation of posterior beliefs in this setting is described in Section 3.1.3 (where one can view $\boldsymbol{\omega}$ as representing the dividend vector $\mathbf{d}$). Observe that the prior covariance matrix is equal to the sum of the posterior covariance matrix plus the prior covariance matrix with respect to the mean (which is often called the pre-posterior covariance matrix), i.e., $\mathbf{\Sigma}_i = \mathbf{\Sigma}_i(\eta) + \mathbf{\Sigma}_{mi}(\eta)$. That relation reflects the fact that $\mathbf{d} - \mathbf{m}_i(\mathbf{y})$ and $\mathbf{m}_i(\mathbf{y})$ are uncorrelated, and η serves to affect the division of the prior uncertainty into the posterior and pre-posterior covariance, where the latter increases and the former decreases as the informativeness of η increases.

In the homogeneous belief setting, (7.7) implies that the price vector at $t = 1$ is

$$\mathbf{v}_1(\mathbf{y}) = \mathbf{m}(\mathbf{y}) - r_o\mathbf{\Sigma}(\eta)\mathbf{Z} \tag{7.13}$$

---

[9] Of course, this is just *Walras' Law.*

Observe that given the price vector $\mathbf{v}_0$ and portfolio choice $\mathbf{z}_{i0}$ at $t = 0$, the price vector $\mathbf{v}_1(\mathbf{y})$ and portfolio decision $\mathbf{z}_{i1}(\mathbf{y})$ at $t = 1$, and dividend vector $\mathbf{d}$ at $t = 2$, investor i's consumption will be

$$c_i = \mathbf{z}_{i1}(\mathbf{y})^t [\mathbf{d} - \mathbf{v}_1(\mathbf{y})] + \mathbf{z}_{i0}{}^t [\mathbf{v}_1(\mathbf{y}) - \mathbf{v}_0] + \bar{\mathbf{z}}_i^t \mathbf{v}_0, \tag{7.14}$$

where $[\bar{\mathbf{z}}_i^t - \mathbf{z}_{i0}{}^t]\mathbf{v}_0$ is invested in the zero-coupon bond at $t = 0$, and an additional amount $[\mathbf{z}_{i0}{}^t - \mathbf{z}_{i1}(\mathbf{y})^t]\mathbf{v}_1(\mathbf{y})$ is invested at $t = 1$. Observe that $\mathbf{v}_1(\mathbf{y})$ is characterized by (7.13) and $\mathbf{z}_{i1}(\mathbf{y})$ is characterized by (7.12), so that

$$c_i = \frac{r_o}{r_i} \mathbf{Z}^t [\mathbf{d} - \mathbf{m}(\mathbf{y}) + r_o \boldsymbol{\Sigma}(\eta)\mathbf{Z}] + \mathbf{z}_{i0}{}^t [\mathbf{m}(\mathbf{y}) - r_o \boldsymbol{\Sigma}(\eta)\mathbf{Z} - \mathbf{v}_0] + \bar{\mathbf{z}}_i^t \mathbf{v}_0. \tag{7.14'}$$

Hence, at $t = 0$, investor i's belief about his consumption is normally distributed, with expectation and variance

$$\mathrm{E}[c_i | \mathbf{z}_{i0}, \eta] = \frac{r_o}{r_i} \mathbf{Z}^t [r_o \boldsymbol{\Sigma}(\eta)\mathbf{Z}] + \mathbf{z}_{i0}{}^t [\mathbf{m} - r_o \boldsymbol{\Sigma}(\eta)\mathbf{Z} - \mathbf{v}_0] + \bar{\mathbf{z}}_i^t \mathbf{v}_0, \tag{7.15a}$$

$$\mathrm{Var}[c_i | \mathbf{z}_{i0}, \eta] = \left[\frac{r_o}{r_i}\right]^2 \mathbf{Z}^t \boldsymbol{\Sigma}(\eta)\mathbf{Z} + \mathbf{z}_{i0}{}^t \boldsymbol{\Sigma}_m(\eta)\mathbf{z}_{i0}. \tag{7.15b}$$

Investor i selects $\mathbf{z}_{i0}$ so as to maximize his certainty equivalent:

$$CE_i(\mathbf{z}_{i0}, \eta) = \mathrm{E}[c_i | \mathbf{z}_{i0}, \eta] - \tfrac{1}{2} r_i \, \mathrm{Var}[c_i | \mathbf{z}_{i0}, \eta]. \tag{7.16}$$

Differentiating (7.16) with respect to $\mathbf{z}_{i0}$ yields first-order condition

$$\mathbf{z}_{i0} = \frac{1}{r_i} \mathbf{H}_m(\eta) [\mathbf{m} - r_o \boldsymbol{\Sigma}(\eta)\mathbf{Z} - \mathbf{v}_0], \tag{7.17}$$

where $\mathbf{H}_m(\eta) = \boldsymbol{\Sigma}_m(\eta)^{-1}$. Summing (7.17) over the I investors, setting the sum equal to $\mathbf{Z}$, and solving for the equilibrium price yields

$$\mathbf{v}_0 = \mathbf{m} - r_o \boldsymbol{\Sigma}\mathbf{Z}. \tag{7.18}$$

The optimal equilibrium portfolio is then obtained by substituting (7.18) into (7.17) – the result is the same as (7.12). That is, at $t = 0$, each investor acquires a share of the market portfolio equal to the ratio of his risk tolerance to the aggregate risk tolerance of all investors, and does not change that portfolio at

$t = 1$, although the prices will change depending on the signal $\mathbf{y}$. Of course, this is due to the fact that this model satisfies the conditions for linear risk sharing with constant fractions of aggregate output (see Proposition 6.6).

The change in the prices for a given signal and the variance of the change in prices are:

$$\Delta\mathbf{v}(\mathbf{y}) \equiv \mathbf{v}_1(\mathbf{y}) - \mathbf{v}_0 = \mathbf{m}(\mathbf{y}) - \mathbf{m} + r_o(\boldsymbol{\Sigma} - \boldsymbol{\Sigma}(\eta))\mathbf{Z}, \tag{7.19a}$$

$$\mathrm{Var}[\Delta\mathbf{v}(\mathbf{y})] = \mathrm{Var}[\mathbf{m}(\mathbf{y})] = \boldsymbol{\Sigma} - \boldsymbol{\Sigma}(\eta). \tag{7.19b}$$

Consider the single firm setting in which the prior beliefs are $d \sim \mathrm{N}(m,\sigma^2)$, the posterior beliefs are $d \sim \mathrm{N}(m(\mathbf{y}),\sigma^2(\eta))$, and the pre-posterior beliefs are $m(\mathbf{y}) \sim \mathrm{N}(m,\sigma_m^{\ 2})$, with $\sigma^2(\eta) = \sigma^2 - \sigma_m^{\ 2}(\eta)$. Applying these in (7.19) establishes the following.

(a) Increasing the information precision, represented by an increase in $\sigma_m^{\ 2}(\eta)$, decreases the posterior variance $\sigma^2(\eta)$ if σ^2 is held constant, and thereby increases the market price for a given signal $\mathbf{y}$ and increases the price variance.

(b) A signal $\mathbf{y}$ results in a price increase if $m(\mathbf{y}) > m$, or if $m(\mathbf{y})$ is only slightly less than m. The price decreases if $m(\mathbf{y})$ is sufficiently smaller than m to offset the reduction in the risk premium.

(c) Increasing aggregate risk aversion (r_o) reduces all prices and reduces the price change due to a change in the risk premium. It has no impact on the variance of the price change.

7.6 Concluding Remarks

In this chapter we have examined the impact of information system changes in competitive capital markets within a multi-period pure exchange setting. To be honest, for an accountant, the results are disappointing! A more informative system can only be strictly Pareto preferred to a less informative system if either one of the following conditions are satisfied, (a) endowments are not insurable with the less informative system, (b) investors have heterogeneous beliefs, and (c) preferences are not time-additive. However, none of these conditions seem to be key sources of value for publicly reported accounting information.

Understanding the impact of changing the information system requires care in identifying the timing of the announced change and the amount of information released at any one date. An unanticipated release of more information, due to an unannounced change in the information system, can make all investors worse off, due to the information risk problem. On the other hand, an announced information system change that will only affect future information can improve risk sharing or be detrimental to it. The key is whether the number of tradeable securities is limited and whether the change in the system "smooths" the amount of information released at any given date. Efficient risk sharing may not be implementable if "too much" information will be released at some dates.

Prices change when value-relevant information is released, but prices may not change when an information system change is announced. However, if efficient risk sharing is implementable with both systems, then price changes following the announced system change imply that at least some investors are made better off.

Dynamic trading may be required to implement optimal consumption plans. Nonetheless, a change in trading induced by a change in the information system does not imply that consumption plans have changed. It may merely reflect a change in the trades used to implement the desired consumption plan.

We considered a simple parametric model in which investors have exponential utility and dividends are normally distributed. Comparative static analysis was used to examine the impact of differences in risk aversion, risk, and information precision on investor welfare and market prices. While all information is publicly reported in this chapter, we use this model extensively in Chapter 11, where we consider settings in which there are both public and private information.

APPENDIX 7A: VALUE OF ADDITIONAL INFORMATION

Proposition 7.2 establishes that more information has no value if endowments are measurable with respect to the less informative system, beliefs are homogeneous, and investors have time-additive preferences. This appendix illustrates how more information can be valuable if one of the three conditions is not fulfilled. To keep things as simple as possible we consider a two-period model with two investors, two states, and the information systems shown in Figure 7A.1. The less informative system η' reveals the state at $t = 2$, while the more informative system η reveals the state already at $t = 1$.

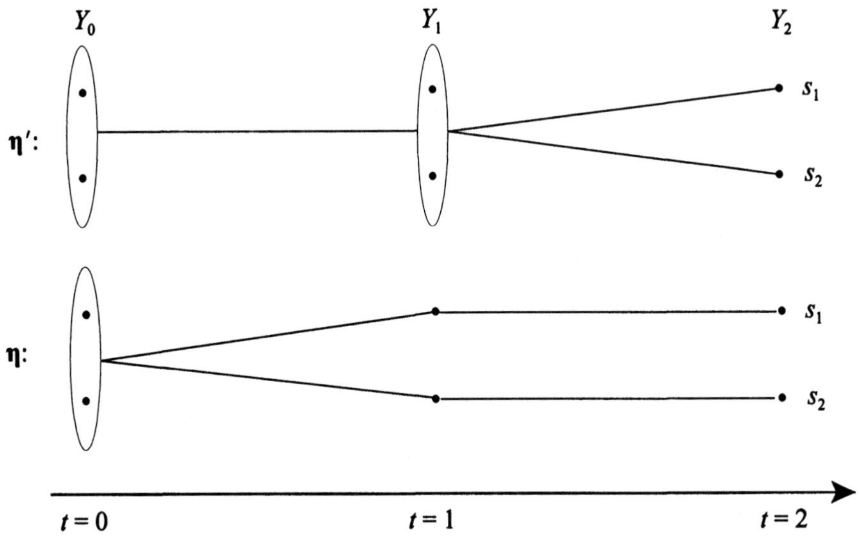

Figure 7A.1: Two information systems in a two-period economy.

(i): Homogeneous Beliefs, Time-Additive Preferences, and η′-Measurable Endowments

Beliefs: $\varphi_i(s_1) = .8;\quad \varphi_i(s_2) = .2;\qquad i = 1, 2.$

Preferences: $u_1(\mathbf{c}_1) = \ln(c_{11}) + \ln(c_{12}),\qquad c_{1t} > 0,$
$u_2(\mathbf{c}_2) = \ln(1+c_{21}) + \ln(1+c_{22}),\quad c_{2t} > -1.$

Endowments:

		$t = 1$		$t = 2$	
		$i = 1$	$i = 2$	$i = 1$	$i = 2$
$e_{it}(s)$, $i = 1,2$:	$s = s_1$	1.00	5.00	6.00	2.00
	$s = s_2$	1.00	5.00	2.00	2.00
$x_t(s)$:	$s = s_1$	6.00		8.00	
	$s = s_2$	6.00		4.00	
$U_i(\mathbf{e}_i)$, $i = 1,2$		$U_1(\mathbf{e}_1) = 1.572$		$U_2(\mathbf{e}_2) = 2.890$	

Of course, in this setting the additional information in $\boldsymbol{\eta}$ has no value since conditions (a) - (c) in Proposition 7.2 are satisfied:

$\boldsymbol{\eta}'$*- and* $\boldsymbol{\eta}$*-Efficient Consumption Plans* ($\lambda_2/\lambda_1 = 1.5$):

		$t = 1$		$t = 2$	
		$i = 1$	$i = 2$	$i = 1$	$i = 2$
$\mathbf{c}_{it}(s)$, $i = 1,2$:	$s = s_1$ $s = s_2$	2.80 2.80	3.20 3.20	3.60 2.00	4.40 2.00
$U_i(\mathbf{c}_i)$, $i = 1,2$		$U_1(\mathbf{c}_1) = 2.193$		$U_2(\mathbf{c}_2) = 3.004$	

Note that both investors efficiently consume the same amount for both states at $t = 1$ (since aggregate consumption is the same for both states), while their efficient second-period consumption plans are increasing in aggregate consumption. Note also that due to investor 2's higher risk tolerance, he takes more of the aggregate second-period risk than investor 1.

(*ii*): Homogeneous Beliefs, Time-Additive Preferences, and Endowments Not $\boldsymbol{\eta}'$-Measurable

Beliefs and preferences: as in (*i*).

Endowments:

		$t = 1$		$t = 2$	
		$i = 1$	$i = 2$	$i = 1$	$i = 2$
$e_{it}(s)$, $i = 1,2$:	$s = s_1$ $s = s_2$	1.25 0.00	4.75 6.00	6.00 2.00	2.00 2.00
$x_t(s)$:	$s = s_1$ $s = s_2$	6.00 6.00		8.00 4.00	
$U_i(\mathbf{e}_i)$, $i = 1,2$		$U_1(\mathbf{e}_1) =$ n.a.		$U_2(\mathbf{e}_2) = 2.887$	

While the $\boldsymbol{\eta}$-efficient consumption plans are the same as in the setting (*i*) (for all sets of weights λ_i), those consumption plans are not feasible with $\boldsymbol{\eta}'$ as they require transfers at $t = 1$ that are not $\boldsymbol{\eta}'$-measurable.

$\boldsymbol{\eta}'$*-Efficient Consumption Plans* ($\lambda_2/\lambda_1 = 1.5$):

		$t = 1$		$t = 2$	
		$i = 1$	$i = 2$	$i = 1$	$i = 2$
$\mathbf{c}_{it}(s)$, $i = 1,2$:	$s = s_1$ $s = s_2$	3.10 1.85	2.90 4.15	3.60 2.00	4.40 2.00
$U_i(\mathbf{c}_i)$, $i = 1,2$		$U_1(\mathbf{c}_1) = 2.192$		$U_2(\mathbf{c}_2) = 2.985$	

With $\boldsymbol{\eta}'$ the transfer at $t = 1$ must be the same for both states. The efficient transfer at $t = 1$ is a transfer of 1.85 from investor 2 to investor 1. Compared to the setting in (*i*), both investors are worse off with $\boldsymbol{\eta}'$ than with $\boldsymbol{\eta}$ (and $\lambda_2/\lambda_1 = 1.5$ in both cases), i.e., $\boldsymbol{\eta}$ facilitates a Pareto preferred allocation compared to the efficient allocation with $\boldsymbol{\eta}'$.

(*iii*): Homogeneous Beliefs, Non-additive Preferences, and $\boldsymbol{\eta}'$-Measurable Endowments

Beliefs and endowments: as in (*i*).

Preferences: $u_1(\mathbf{c}_1) = \ln(c_{11}) + \ln(c_{12})$, $c_{1t} > 0$,
$u_2(\mathbf{c}_2) = \ln(1+c_{21}) \ln(1+c_{22})$, $c_{2t} > 0$.

$\boldsymbol{\eta}'$*-Efficient Consumption Plans* ($\lambda_2/\lambda_1 = 0.995$):

		$t = 1$		$t = 2$	
		$i = 1$	$i = 2$	$i = 1$	$i = 2$
$\mathbf{c}_{it}(s)$, $i = 1,2$:	$s = s_1$ $s = s_2$	2.75 2.75	3.25 3.25	3.69 2.05	4.31 1.95
$U_i(\mathbf{c}_i)$, $i = 1,2$		$U_1(\mathbf{c}_1) = 2.200$		$U_2(\mathbf{c}_2) = 2.245$	

Note again that efficient second-period consumption plans are increasing in aggregate consumption.

η-*Efficient Consumption Plans* (λ_2/λ_1 = 1.000):

		$t = 1$		$t = 2$	
		$i = 1$	$i = 2$	$i = 1$	$i = 2$
$c_{it}(s)$, $i = 1,2$:	$s = s_1$ $s = s_2$	2.61 3.45	3.39 2.55	3.63 2.21	4.37 1.79
$U_i(\mathbf{c}_i)$, $i = 1,2$		$U_1(\mathbf{c}_1) = 2.206$		$U_2(\mathbf{c}_2) = 2.249$	

Note that in this setting, efficient first-period consumption plans vary with the state even though beliefs are homogeneous and aggregate consumption is the same for the two states. Due to investor 2's non-additive utility function, he prefers to smooth his consumption over the two dates for each state. Hence, efficient consumption plans give investor 2 "high" consumption at both dates for the "good second-period aggregate consumption state," s_1. Since aggregate first-period consumption is the same for both states, investor 1 gets "low" first-period consumption for s_1 (although he gets "high" second-period consumption for that state). The information system **η** facilitates efficient consumption smoothing over the two dates for investor 2, while this is not possible with **η**′ and, thus, both investors can be made better off with **η** than with **η**′.

(*iv*): **Heterogeneous Beliefs, Time-Additive Preferences, and η′-Measurable Endowments**

Beliefs: $\varphi_1(s_1) = .8$; $\varphi_1(s_2) = .2$;
$\varphi_2(s_1) = .6$; $\varphi_2(s_2) = .4$.

Preferences and endowments: as in (*i*).

η'-*Efficient Consumption Plans* $(\lambda_2/\lambda_1 = 1.5)$:

	$t = 1$		$t = 2$	
	$i = 1$	$i = 2$	$i = 1$	$i = 2$
$c_{it}(s)$, $i = 1,2$: $s = s_1$ $s = s_2$	2.80 2.80	3.20 3.20	4.24 1.25	3.76 2.75
$U_i(\mathbf{c}_i)$, $i = 1,2$	$U_1(\mathbf{c}_1) = 2.229$		$U_2(\mathbf{c}_2) = 2.901$	

Compared to the setting in (*i*), investor 1 efficiently takes much more of the second-period aggregate risk, since he attaches a higher probability to the "good aggregate consumption state" s_1 than does investor 2.

η-*Efficient Consumption Plans* $(\lambda_2/\lambda_1 = 1.5)$:

	$t = 1$		$t = 2$	
	$i = 1$	$i = 2$	$i = 1$	$i = 2$
$c_{it}(s)$, $i = 1,2$: $s = s_1$ $s = s_2$	3.29 1.75	2.71 4.25	4.24 1.25	3.76 2.75
$U_i(\mathbf{c}_i)$, $i = 1,2$	$U_1(\mathbf{c}_1) = 2.265$		$U_2(\mathbf{c}_2) = 2.914$	

With the information system η', the two investors cannot "side-bet" on the occurrence of the state in the first period. On the other hand, η facilitates side-betting on the occurrence of the state in both periods, and this facilitates a Pareto preferred allocation.

REFERENCES

Feltham, G. A. (1985) "The Impact of Public Information in Sequential Markets," Working Paper, The University of British Columbia, Vancouver.

Feltham, G. A., and P. O. Christensen. (1988) "Firm-Specific Information and Efficient Resource Allocation," *Contemporary Accounting Research* 5, 133-169.

Hakansson, N. H., J. G. Kunkel, and J. A. Ohlson. (1982) "Sufficient and Necessary Conditions for Information to have Social Value in Pure Exchange," *Journal of Finance* 37, 1169-1181.

Hirshleifer, J. (1971) "The Private and Social Value of Information and the Reward to Inventive Activity, *American Economic Review* 61, 561-574.

Lev, B., and J. Ohlson. (1982) "Market-Based Empirical Research in Accounting: A Review, Interpretation, and Extension," *Journal of Accounting Research* 20, 249-322.

Ohlson, J. (1984) "The Structure of Asset Prices and Socially Useless/Useful Information," *Journal of Finance* 39, 1417-1435.

Ohlson, J., and G. Buckman. (1981) "Towards a Theory of Financial Accounting. Welfare and Public Information," *Journal of Accounting Research* 19, 399-433.

CHAPTER 8

PRODUCTION CHOICE IN EFFICIENT MARKETS

In the pure exchange models considered in Chapters 5, 6, and 7, the dividends associated with each marketed security are taken as given. The sequence of event-contingent dividends paid by a firm can be viewed as representing that firm's production plan *and* its dividend (financing) policy. In this chapter we explicitly consider the choice of production plans.

The scope for public reporting to have value is limited in pure exchange settings. Additional public information is only valuable to investors if it facilitates better insurance of personally endowed consumption risks, more side-betting due to heterogeneous beliefs, or improved coordination of consumption across periods due to non-time-additive preferences. None of the above seem to be key sources of value for publicly reported accounting information. If there are production choices, then there is more scope for information to have value – it may facilitate more efficient use of the economy's resources. In particular, as in the settings of Chapters 2, 3, and 4, more information reduces the uncertainty about the future consequences of current actions and, thus, can help make better production choices. If efficient risk sharing is ensured, a change to a more informative system is generally valuable to investors.

Public reporting of accounting information involves reporting to investors what managers already know. The production choices are made by managers and, therefore, it is valuable that managers get more information to help make better production choices. But, is it important that this information be reported to investors? In the pure exchange setting we introduced the distinction between economy-wide and firm-specific events. In the production setting, we consider information about both economy-wide and firm-specific events, and allow for the possibility that managers might have firm-specific information that is not known by investors.

To focus on production choice, we assume that each firm finances its production plan through its equityholders. That is, all investment of the consumption good in production at date t is provided by the pre-dividend owners of the firm's equity at that date and any consumption good generated by the production activity at date t is distributed to the pre-dividend equityholders. Any financial claims are written directly between investors and serve to facilitate efficient sharing of aggregate consumption. We assume that this efficiency is achieved, but that is not the focus of this chapter. Hence, for simplicity we do not make explicit mention of the financial claims but focus on the equity claims for each firm. Hence, a firm's production plan is represented as the sequence of dividends on its equity claim.

In Sections 8.1, 8.2, and 8.3 we examine a general equilibrium model of a multi-period production economy in which the information available for implementing a production plan is the same as that available to investors. We establish that more public information is generally valuable, and that efficient production plans are achieved if managers maximize the market value of their firms' production plans, taking the implicit date-event prices as given.

In Section 8.4 we consider efficient production choice in a two-period setting in which the firm's owners invest funds at $t = 1$ and obtain outputs at $t = 2$. Efficient risk sharing is obtained by trading at $t = 0$ and $t = 1$. We impose additional structure on the production opportunities, and we introduce the distinction between economy-wide and firm-specific information in a production setting. Furthermore, for each of these types of information we distinguish between windfall and productivity information. Windfall information affects beliefs about future outputs that are not related to the amount invested at $t = 1$, whereas productivity information pertains to both the level of outputs and the marginal productivity of current investments. While firm-specific windfall information affects the beliefs about the dividends on individual ownership claims, it does not affect beliefs about the dividends on well-diversified portfolios. Economy-wide windfall information does not affect the returns on invested capital, but it does affect beliefs about future aggregate consumption, and that may lead to a change in current aggregate investments. Productivity information is clearly useful for making better production choices. However, it may not be important that managers report firm-specific productivity information to well-diversified investors, if the investors rationally anticipate that the managers have the information and choose the current investments so as to maximize *the intrinsic value* of their firms' current and future dividends.

8.1 PRODUCTION ALTERNATIVES AND EFFICIENCY

In this section we begin by examining the representation of production alternatives and the determination of efficient production plans consistent with the public information system. There is a set of investors I, and a set of firms J, each with a single equity claim. For simplicity, but with a slight abuse of notation, we use I and J to refer, respectively, to both the set of investors and firms and the number of investors and firms, i.e., the cardinality of the corresponding set. The pattern of dividends (operating cash flows) generated by a firm depends on its production plans, and the feasible set of production plans depends on the information structure. In most of our analysis we assume that the information available for implementing a production plan is the same as that available to investors, i.e., production plans are based on the public information system η represented by an increasing sequence of partitions of the state space S, i.e., $\mathbf{Y} = \{ Y_1, ..., Y_T \}$, where Y_t is at least as fine a partition of S as Y_{t-1}, $t = 1, ..., T$.[1] A production plan for firm j is an adapted[2] dividend process $\mathbf{d}_j = \{ d_{j1}, ..., d_{jT} \}$ with $d_{jt} = d_{jt}(y_t)$ denoting the dividend paid by security j at date t, $t = 1, ..., T$. The production plan for the economy is denoted $\mathbf{d} \equiv \{ \mathbf{d}_1, ..., \mathbf{d}_J \}$.

The set of production plans that can be implemented by firm j with information structure η is denoted $D_j(\eta)$. The set of total production possibilities is

$$D_o(\eta) = \{ \mathbf{d}_o \mid \mathbf{d}_o = \textstyle\sum_{j \in J} \mathbf{d}_j, \ \mathbf{d}_j \in D_j(\eta) \text{ for all } j \in J \}.$$

The production sets for all firms $j \in J$ and all information structures have the following properties.

Definition *Feasible Production Alternatives*

The production alternatives in the economy are characterized by the following assumptions. For all firms $j \in J$, $D_j(\eta)$ is closed, convex, permits zero production, requires $\mathbf{d}_j$ to be η-measurable, and if η is more informative than η', then $D_j(\eta') \subseteq D_j(\eta)$. In addition, the set of total production possibilities for all firms $D_o(\eta)$, is irreversible and permits free disposal.

For an elaboration of these assumptions see, for example, Debreu (1959). They require the production alternatives to be well-behaved. For example, the convexity condition requires production to be perfectly divisible with non-increasing returns to scale, and the irreversibility condition ensures that there is no "free production" (inputs are required to achieve outputs). The measurability condition ensures that any plan that is feasible with η' is also feasible with η. Observe that we have implicitly assumed that *production choices do not affect the events that are revealed by the information system*, i.e., there is no "learning" from production.

We assume investor i's endowments consist of his initial claims to ownership of the J assets plus direct endowments of the consumption good at each date. Investor i's initial claim to the ownership of firm j is $\bar{z}_{ij}$ and his date-event contingent consumption endowment is $\bar{\mathbf{c}}_i$. We express individual ownership as a fraction of the total ownership, so that $Z_j \equiv \sum_{i \in I} \bar{z}_{ij} = 1$. Hence, the maximum aggregate date-event contingent consumption for a *given* production plan is

---

[1] We assume throughout that investors have no information at the initial trading date $t = 0$, i.e., $Y_0 = \{ S \}$.

[2] See Chapter 6 for a discussion of the nature of an adapted process with respect to a given sequence of publicly reported events in $\mathbf{Y}$ (which are reported by information system η).

$$\mathbf{x} = \sum_{i\in I} \bar{\mathbf{c}}_i + \mathbf{d}_o.$$

With fixed production, i.e., in a pure exchange economy, aggregate consumption equals the fixed aggregate endowment **x**. Now, however, it depends on the production plans that are chosen by firms. Therefore, we now have a set of possible aggregate consumption levels, denoted

$$C_o(\boldsymbol{\eta}) = \{ \mathbf{c}_o \mid \mathbf{c}_o \le \sum_{i\in I} \bar{\mathbf{c}}_i + \mathbf{d}_o, \mathbf{d}_o \in D_o(\boldsymbol{\eta}) \}.$$

This expands the set of possible individual consumption plans (ignoring the distribution of endowments), which is denoted

$$C(\boldsymbol{\eta}) = \{ \mathbf{c} \mid \sum_{i\in I} \mathbf{c}_i \le \mathbf{c}_o, \mathbf{c}_i \in C_i(\boldsymbol{\eta}), \mathbf{c}_o \in C_o(\boldsymbol{\eta}) \},$$

where $C_i(\boldsymbol{\eta})$ is the set of non-negative consumption plans that are $\boldsymbol{\eta}$-measurable.

$\boldsymbol{\eta}$-efficient consumption plans are now specified relative to the set $C(\boldsymbol{\eta})$, recognizing that there is an opportunity to select both the production plan and the consumption plan. That is, while consumption plan **c** may be $\boldsymbol{\eta}$-efficient given aggregate production plan $\mathbf{d}_o$, it may not be $\boldsymbol{\eta}$-efficient when there is production choice. That is, there may exist an alternative production plan $\mathbf{d}_o'$ that permits the selection of another consumption plan $\mathbf{c}'$ that is Pareto preferred to **c**. Hence, $\boldsymbol{\eta}$-efficiency must consider the consumption plans that are feasible given all possible production plans – that set of alternatives is represented by $C(\boldsymbol{\eta})$.

Definition $\boldsymbol{\eta}$-*Efficient Consumption/Production Plans*

The consumption/production plan $(\mathbf{c}^*,\mathbf{d}^*)$ is $\boldsymbol{\eta}$-efficient if, and only if, there is no other consumption plan $\mathbf{c} \in C(\boldsymbol{\eta})$ that is strictly Pareto preferred to $\mathbf{c}^*$.

Observe that investor preferences do not directly depend on the production plans – they are only interested in what they get to consume. Given the above assumption about the production alternatives and the "usual" assumptions for preferences and beliefs, the consumption/production plan $(\mathbf{c}^*,\mathbf{d}^*)$ is $\boldsymbol{\eta}$-efficient if, and only if, it is a solution to the "central planner's" decision problem for some set of positive weights $\{ \lambda_i \}_{i\in I}$.

***Central Planner's Consumption/Production Problem*:**

$$\underset{\mathbf{c},\,\mathbf{c}_o}{\text{maximize}} \quad \sum_{i=1}^{I} \lambda_i\, U_i(\mathbf{c}_i), \tag{8.1a}$$

$$\text{subject to} \quad \sum_{i=1}^{I} c_{it}(y_t) \le c_{ot}(y_t), \qquad \forall\, t,\, y_t \in Y_t, \tag{8.1b}$$

$$\mathbf{c}_i \in C_i(\boldsymbol{\eta}), \quad \forall\, i \in I, \quad \mathbf{c}_o \in C_o(\boldsymbol{\eta}). \tag{8.1c}$$

Note that the central planner chooses the aggregate consumption plan, $\mathbf{c}_o$, consistent with the production alternatives, i.e., $\mathbf{c}_o \in C_o(\boldsymbol{\eta})$, and how the aggregate consumption possibilities are distributed among investors. Hence, for any given $\boldsymbol{\eta}$-efficient consumption plan there is a production plan that sustains it. Therefore, the conditions that characterize an $\boldsymbol{\eta}$-efficient consumption plan for a fixed production plan are also necessary conditions (but not sufficient) for a consumption plan to be $\boldsymbol{\eta}$-efficient when there is production choice. For example, if investors have homogeneous beliefs and time-additive preferences, the Lagrangian for the central planner's decision problem (for a fixed production plan and interior consumption plans) is

$$\mathcal{L} = \sum_{i=1}^{I} \lambda_i \sum_{t=1}^{T} \sum_{y_t \in Y_t} u_{it}(c_{it}(y_t))\, \varphi(y_t) - \sum_{t=1}^{T} \sum_{y_t \in Y_t} \mu_t(y_t) \left[\sum_{i=1}^{I} c_{it}(y_t) - x_t(y_t) \right].$$

Hence, the following are necessary conditions for consumption/production plan $(\mathbf{c}^*, \mathbf{d}^*)$ to be $\boldsymbol{\eta}$-efficient (compare to Proposition 4.1, and note that time-additive preferences imply that risk sharing is efficient, if, and only if, it is efficient on a date-by-date basis – as reflected in the characterization of an efficient equilibrium in Proposition 6.5):

(a) There exist positive weights λ_i, $\forall\, i \in I$, Lagrange multipliers $\mu_t(y_t)$, $\forall\, y_t \in Y_t$, $t = 1, \ldots, T$, such that

$$u_{it}'(c_{it}^*(y_t))\, \varphi(y_t) = \mu_t(y_t)/\lambda_i, \quad \forall\, i \in I,\, y_t \in Y_t,\, t = 1, \ldots, T. \tag{8.2}$$

(b) Aggregate consumption equals the *available* aggregate consumption possibilities:

$$\textstyle\sum_{i \in I} \mathbf{c}_i^* = \mathbf{c}_o^* = \sum_{i \in I} \bar{\mathbf{c}}_i + \mathbf{d}_o^*. \tag{8.3}$$

These conditions ensure that the consumption plan is efficient given the production plan, but they do not ensure that the production plan is efficient. That efficiency is ensured if the aggregate production plan satisfies the following condition.

$$\mathbf{d}_o^* \in \underset{\mathbf{d}_o \in D_o(\boldsymbol{\eta})}{\text{argmax}} \sum_{t=1}^{T} \sum_{y_t \in Y_t} \mu_t(y_t) d_{ot}(y_t). \tag{8.4}$$

The proof follows from the concavity of utility functions, the convexity of the consumption possibility set $\boldsymbol{C}(\boldsymbol{\eta})$, and noting that the Lagrange multiplier $\mu_t(y_t)$ is the "value" of a marginal increase in the aggregate amount of the single good available for consumption for event y_t at date t. The nature of $\boldsymbol{\eta}$-efficient production is depicted in Figure 8.1 in a setting with a single investor, a single period, and two states. The endowment point (at which aggregate production is zero) is on the frontier of the feasible consumption set and production permits total consumption in one event to increase by decreasing the total consumption in the other. The efficient production plan occurs at the point where the investor's indifference curve is tangent to the frontier of the set of alternative aggregate dividends (the slope of the tangency is - $\mu(y_1)/\mu(y_2)$).

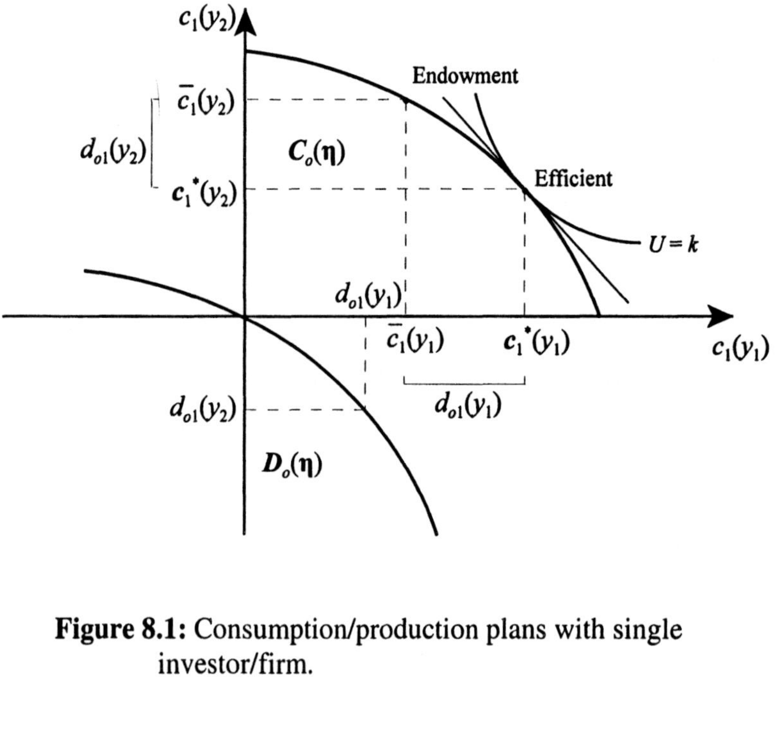

Figure 8.1: Consumption/production plans with single investor/firm.

8.2 EFFICIENT PRODUCTION CHOICE WITH PRIVATE OWNERSHIP

Once we remove the "planner" and move to a market economy, the aggregate production plan is determined by the plans selected for the individual firms. An important question is: *Who chooses the production plan that each firm implements and what criterion does that person use in making that choice?*

In this chapter we ignore the preferences of firm management and assume that they do whatever they are instructed to do. They are *automatons*. The key preferences are those of the endowed owners of the firms. What criterion do they want the managers to use in choosing production plans?

8.2.1 Complete Multi-period Securities Markets

The answer is straightforward if the economy trades a complete set of date-event securities. Endowments consist of the dividends from the endowed portfolio $\bar{\mathbf{z}}_i$, and consumption endowments $\bar{\mathbf{c}}_i$, i.e.,

$$\mathbf{e}_i = \mathbf{d}^{\bar{\mathbf{z}}_i} + \bar{\mathbf{c}}_i.$$

In that setting, the endowed owners want management to select the production plan that maximizes the current market value of the firm's dividends, since that maximizes the market value of their endowments (given the date-event prices). Hence, in an economy with production choice, an AD-equilibrium is defined as follows.

Definition *AD-equilibrium in Production Economy*
An equilibrium $\mathscr{E}(\eta) \equiv \{\mathbf{c}; \mathbf{d}; \mathbf{p}\}$ constitute an *AD-equilibrium* if

(a) For each investor i, the transfer $\boldsymbol{\delta}_i = \mathbf{c}_i - \mathbf{e}_i$ is a solution to investor i's decision problem:

$$\underset{\mathbf{c}_i \in C_i(\eta)}{\text{maximize}} \; U_i(\mathbf{c}_i) \quad \text{subject to} \quad \boldsymbol{\delta}_i \cdot \mathbf{p} \leq 0;$$

where $\mathbf{p}$ is the date-event price process (and "·" denotes "multiplication and summation over all dates and events").

(b) For each firm j, the production plan $\mathbf{d}_j$ is a solution to firm j's decision problem:

$$\underset{\mathbf{d}_j \in D_j(\eta)}{\text{maximize}} \ \mathbf{d}_j \cdot \mathbf{p}$$

(c) Market clearing: $\sum_{i\in I} \mathbf{c}_i = \sum_{i\in I} \bar{\mathbf{c}}_i + \sum_{j\in J} \mathbf{d}_j$.

Observe that, as in the pure exchange setting, the investors do not trade their endowed ownership of firms but merely trade direct claims to consumption. Given the availability of a complete set of date-event securities, there is no need to trade firm ownership. Given the "standard assumptions" on preferences and the stated assumptions for available production alternatives, the maximization of firm value results in an η-efficient consumption/production plan. Note that the beliefs of the manager are immaterial – he is a "price taker" with respect to the date-event prices. That is, given the date-event prices, he does not need any information about the investors' endowments, beliefs, or preferences in order to determine to the efficient production plan. Moreover, all investors with non-negative endowed ownership of the firm will unanimously support the choice of an efficient production plan, since it maximizes the value of their endowed ownership given the date-event prices.

There are two basic questions: (a) Does an equilibrium exist?, and (b) Is an AD-equilibrium η-efficient? The answer to both questions is yes, if the elements of the economy satisfy the standard assumptions.[3]

In Figure 8.1 of a single investor and a single firm we can depict the market economy by drawing a budget constraint for the investor with a slope given by the relative prices. The budget constraint will pass through the η-efficient point (which is the equilibrium consumption and production plan) and will be tangent to both the investor's indifference curve and the firm's production frontier.

8.2.2 Dynamically Complete Securities Markets

As in the pure exchange setting, one of the problems with the above model is that it assumes the existence of a complete set of date-event securities that we

---

[3] For example, Debreu (1959, pp. 83-84) proves the existence of an equilibrium assuming:

(a) Lower bound on the aggregate consumption set.
(b) Consumption set for each investor closed and convex.
(c) Non-satiation.
(d) Continuity of preferences.
(e) Convexity of preferences.
(f) Aggregate production set closed and convex and with a non-empty intersection with the aggregate consumption set net of endowment.
(g) "Positive" endowment of each "commodity."
(h) Zero production is possible.
(i) Intersection of aggregate consumption and production sets is bounded.

do not observe in the "real world" and it does not create any need to trade ownership claims (which we do observe being traded). A more realistic approach is to assume that not all event-contingent trades are feasible because of the cost of creating and trading securities. Instead, trading takes place with a set of firm ownership claims, and possibly an exogenously specified set of financial claims.

The relevant equilibrium concept is the Radner Sequential (RS) equilibrium. However, we must now specify the nature of equilibrium production choice in this economy. Observe that in the AD-equilibrium there are competitively determined prices for consumption at each date for each possible event. The manager uses those market determined prices to calculate the market value of each of his possible production plans and then selects the plan with the highest market value. In a sequential market the calculation of the market value of alternative production plans is problematic. It is now difficult to treat the manager as a price taker since the only observed prices are current consumption and the claims that are traded. Since he is determining the character of one of those claims, he is determining its price. In some sense, the manager is in a "monopoly" position with respect to one of the goods being traded in the market.

Radner (1972, 1982) avoids the potential problems of a "monopolist" making decisions in an otherwise competitive market by assuming that the manager selects his production plan according to some exogenous, well-behaved criterion that is known to investors. Following Radner we assume:

> The production plan for each firm is feasible (i.e., $\mathbf{d}_j \in \boldsymbol{D}_j(\boldsymbol{\eta})$) and is selected by the manager in accordance with a criterion that is known by investors.

A key result from Radner (see Feltham and Christensen (FC), 1988) is the following.

Proposition 8.1 (FC, Prop. 6)

If $\mathscr{E}(\boldsymbol{\eta}) = \{\mathbf{z}; \mathbf{d}; \mathbf{v}\}$ is an $\boldsymbol{\eta}$-efficient RS-equilibrium, then there exists an AD-equilibrium $\mathscr{E}(\boldsymbol{\eta}) = \{\mathbf{c}; \mathbf{d}; \mathbf{p}\}$ for the same economy (augmented with a complete set of AD-securities) such that:

(a) The two equilibria have the same consumption and production plans.

(b) The prices of the marketed securities in the RS-equilibrium are consistent with the date-event prices in the AD-equilibrium, i.e.,

$$v_{jt}(y_t) = \sum_{\tau=t+1}^{T} \sum_{y_\tau \subset y_t} d_{j\tau}(y_\tau)\, p_{\tau t}(y_\tau | y_t), \quad j = 1, 2, ..., J.$$

where $$p_{\tau t}(y_\tau|y_t) = \frac{p_\tau(y_\tau)}{p_t(y_t)}, \qquad \forall\, y_\tau \subseteq y_t,\ \tau > t.$$

(c) The production plan selected by each manager in the RS-equilibrium maximizes the current cum-dividend market value of his firm.

That is, if the manager takes the *implicit* date-event prices as given and maximizes the cum-dividend market value of his firm computed by using these prices, then those choices are consistent with the achievement of η-efficiency. Problems arise when the sequential equilibrium is not η-efficient, i.e., markets are not effectively dynamically complete. There is an extensive literature dealing with this setting (see, for example, Magill and Quinzii, 1996), but we limit our analysis to settings in which markets are sufficiently complete to permit η-efficient consumption/production plans.

8.3 IMPACT OF PUBLIC INFORMATION

FC consider the impact of changes in the information system in an economy with production choice. The introduction of production choice does not change the basic result regarding a change to a more informative system in a pure exchange economy.

Proposition 8.2

If information structure η is more informative than η', then for any consumption plan $\mathbf{c}' \in C(\eta')$ there exists a plan $\mathbf{c} \in C(\eta)$ that is weakly Pareto preferred.

That is, there is no need for anyone to be worse off with the more informative system. The key to extending this result to the production choice setting is that $D_j(\eta') \subseteq D_j(\eta)$, for all $j \in J$, i.e., the production choices expand if η is more informative than η'.

With *fixed production* we established that the following conditions are sufficient for the set of η-efficient consumption plans to be identical for all information systems η that are more informative than a given information system η' (see Proposition 7.2): endowments are η'-measurable; investors have homogeneous beliefs; and investors have time-additive utility functions. In the analysis that follows, these conditions are taken as given. Hence, any benefits from a more informative system will *not* come from better insurance, additional side-betting or from a better inter-temporal allocation of an existing pattern of aggregate consumption. The benefits will come from using information to obtain a more preferred pattern of aggregate consumption. That was not possible with fixed production, but it may be possible if there is production choice.

Proposition 8.3

If information system $\boldsymbol{\eta}$ is more informative than $\boldsymbol{\eta}'$, then for any consumption plan $\mathbf{c}' \in C(\boldsymbol{\eta}')$ there *may* exist a consumption plan $\mathbf{c} \in C(\boldsymbol{\eta})$ that is strictly Pareto preferred to $\mathbf{c}'$ even if investor preferences are time-additive, their beliefs are homogeneous, and their endowments are $\boldsymbol{\eta}'$-measurable.

It is relatively straightforward to generate examples to prove this proposition. Observe, however, that having more information does not necessarily provide a basis for Pareto preferred consumption plans. The key issue is whether the information permits the implementation of preferred production plans.

Corollary

Suppose investor preferences are time-additive, their beliefs are homogeneous, and their endowments are $\boldsymbol{\eta}'$-measurable, and let $(\mathbf{c},\mathbf{d})$ be an $\boldsymbol{\eta}$-efficient consumption/production plan. If $\boldsymbol{\eta}$ is more informative than $\boldsymbol{\eta}'$ and the production plan $\mathbf{d}$ is $\boldsymbol{\eta}'$-measurable, then the consumption plan $\mathbf{c}$ is $\boldsymbol{\eta}'$-measurable (and $\boldsymbol{\eta}'$-efficient) given $\mathbf{d}$.

That is, a necessary condition for a change in the information system to result in a Pareto improvement is that it results in a change in production plans.

In a market setting, we obtain essentially the same results as we obtained under pure exchange (see Propositions 7.4 and 7.5 and the following discussion).

Proposition 8.4

Suppose $\boldsymbol{\eta}$ is more informative than $\boldsymbol{\eta}'$. Let $\mathscr{E}(\boldsymbol{\eta}')$ denote an RS-equilibrium for $\boldsymbol{\eta}'$ with consumption/production plan $(\mathbf{c}',\mathbf{d}')$, and assume that there are sufficient marketed securities to implement an $\boldsymbol{\eta}$-efficient consumption plan as an RS-equilibrium.

(a) If endowments are positive and $\boldsymbol{\eta}'$-efficient, then there is an RS-equilibrium $\mathscr{E}(\boldsymbol{\eta}')$ in which no trading occurs, i.e., $\mathbf{z}' = \mathbf{0}$, and there exists an RS-equilibrium $\mathscr{E}(\boldsymbol{\eta}) = \{\mathbf{z};\ \mathbf{d};\ \mathbf{v}\}$ where $\mathbf{c}$ is weakly Pareto preferred to $\mathbf{c}'$.

(b) If the endowments are not $\boldsymbol{\eta}'$-efficient, then the equilibrium consumption plans $\mathbf{c}$ and $\mathbf{c}'$ may be Pareto non-comparable or $\mathbf{c}$ may be weakly Pareto preferred to $\mathbf{c}'$, but $\mathbf{c}'$ cannot be strictly Pareto preferred to $\mathbf{c}$.

In a pure exchange setting, (a) is straightforward since in that setting an investor can always choose to hold his existing portfolio and it will provide him with the same consumption plan as he would have obtained with $\boldsymbol{\eta}'$. However, in the production setting the no trading strategy does not imply that there is no change in the consumption plan. If firms change their production plans, then that will change the dividends that investors receive from an existing portfolio. The proof that this does not make investors worse off is an extension of the proof in Kunkel (1982). Kunkel points out that owning a share of a firm does not guarantee one a certain pattern of consumption across dates and events if information causes the implicit date-event prices to change and this induces value maximizing firms to change their production plans. However, $\boldsymbol{\eta}$-efficiency is sufficient for there to be equality across investors of the implicit prices for consumption in each date/event (i.e., the same marginal rates of substitution). Consequently, investors will assign the same value to changes in firms' production plans and no investors can be made worse off by additional information. The proof is by contradiction. Suppose investor i is made worse off, i.e.,

$$U_i(\mathbf{c}_i') > U_i(\mathbf{c}_i).$$

If that is the case, then it must be that $\mathbf{c}_i'$ is not financially feasible given the implicit date-event prices $\mathbf{p}$ with $\boldsymbol{\eta}$, i.e.,

$$\mathbf{c}_i \cdot \mathbf{p} < \mathbf{c}_i' \cdot \mathbf{p} = [\bar{\mathbf{c}}_i + \textstyle\sum_{j\in J} \bar{z}_{ij} \mathbf{d}_j'] \cdot \mathbf{p}.$$

On the other hand, the budget constraint $\boldsymbol{\delta}_i \cdot \mathbf{p} = 0$, implies that the value of investor i's consumption plan equals the value of his endowment

$$\mathbf{c}_i \cdot \mathbf{p} = [\bar{\mathbf{c}}_i + \textstyle\sum_{j\in J} \bar{z}_{ij} \mathbf{d}_j] \cdot \mathbf{p}.$$

The latter two then imply that

$$\textstyle\sum_{j\in J} \bar{z}_{ij} (\mathbf{d}_j \cdot \mathbf{p}) < \textstyle\sum_{j\in J} \bar{z}_{ij} (\mathbf{d}_j' \cdot \mathbf{p}).$$

Value maximization by the managers implies that

$$\mathbf{d}_j' \cdot \mathbf{p} \le \mathbf{d}_j \cdot \mathbf{p}, \quad \forall j \in J.$$

The last two inequalities are inconsistent given positive endowments, i.e., $\bar{z}_{ij} \ge 0, \forall\, i \in I, j \in J$.

On the other hand, if endowments are not $\boldsymbol{\eta}'$-efficient, then the change to a more informative system may make some investors worse off and others better off (but not everyone worse off). As opposed to the pure exchange setting, some investors may be worse off due to changes in the production plan even if investor preferences are time-additive, their beliefs are homogeneous, and their endowments are $\boldsymbol{\eta}'$-measurable.

8.4 EFFICIENT PRODUCTION CHOICE IN TWO-PERIOD ECONOMIES

In this section we consider a two-period model in which the firms' owners invest funds at $t = 1$ and obtain outputs at $t = 2$.

8.4.1 Basic Two-period Model

The owners of firm j invest $-\, d_{j1}$ at $t = 1$ and receive d_{j2} at $t = 2$. The production function is

$$d_{j2} = f_j(s,d_{j1}), \quad \text{with } f_j(s,0) = 0,\ \partial f_j(s,d_{j1})/\partial d_{j1} < 0 \text{ and } \partial^2 f_j(s,d_{j1})/\partial d_{j1}^{\,2} > 0.$$

There is always free disposal, so that f_j defines the maximum dividend that can be paid – of course, it will not be optimal to dispose of any of the operating cash flows that are generated.

The null information system $\boldsymbol{\eta}^o$ provides no information at $t = 1$, but reveals the state s at $t = 2$, i.e., $y_1^{\,o} = \{S\}$ and $y_2^{\,o} = s \in S$. Under $\boldsymbol{\eta}^o$, consumption and production at $t = 1$ are independent of the state, i.e., c_{i1} and d_{j1} are constants.

Investors are assumed to have homogeneous beliefs, time-additive preferences, and fixed strictly positive consumption endowments at $t = 1$ and zero consumption endowments at $t = 2$, i.e., $\bar{c}_{i1} > 0$ and $\bar{c}_{i2} = 0$ for all $s \in S$. Investors are endowed with ownership in the J firms and can trade at both $t = 0$ and $t = 1$. If there is no information at $t = 1$, then investors need only trade at that date (trading at $t = 0$ is redundant).

Investor i's consumption at $t = 2$ depends on his net ownership portfolio after trading at $t = 1$,

$$c_{i2}(s) = \textstyle\sum_{j \in J} z_{ij1}\, d_{j2}(s).$$

The cum-dividend market values of the J claims are denoted $\mathbf{V}_t = (V_{1t},...,V_{Jt})^{\text{t}}$, and the ex-dividend market prices are $\mathbf{v}_t = (v_{1t},...,v_{Jt})^{\text{t}}$.

With the null information system, investor i's decision problem at $t = 1$ is to select a consumption/investment plan $(c_{i1},\mathbf{z}_{i1})$ so as to maximize his expected utility (if the equity claims are not sufficient to achieve efficient allocation of consumption, then we can introduce financial claims to "complete the market"):

$$\underset{c_{i1},\, \mathbf{z}_{i1}}{\text{maximize}} \quad U_i(c_{i1},\mathbf{z}_{i1}) \equiv u_{i1}(c_{i1}) + \sum_{s \in S} u_{i2}(\textstyle\sum_{j\in J} z_{ij1}\, d_{j2}(s))\, \varphi(s),$$

$$\text{subject to} \quad c_{i1} \le \bar{c}_{i1} + \textstyle\sum_{j\in J} \bar{z}_{ij} d_{j1} + \sum_{j\in J} [\bar{z}_{ij} - z_{ij1}] v_{j1}.$$

The production plans are a solution to the following market value maximization problem:

$$\underset{d_{j1} \le 0}{\text{maximize}} \quad d_{j1} + \sum_{s \in S} f_j(s,d_{j1})\, p(s).$$

where $p_1(S) = 1$ and $p_2(s) = p(s)$ are the implicit date-event prices associated with the $\boldsymbol{\eta}^o$-efficient consumption/production plan. The optimal production plan and equilibrium prices are characterized by

$$\sum_{s \in S} p(s)\, \frac{\partial f_j(s,d_{j1})}{\partial d_{j1}} = -1, \qquad p(s) = \frac{\varphi(s)\, u_{i2}'(c_{i2}(s))}{u_{i1}'(c_{i1})}, \text{ for all } i.$$

8.4.2 Impact of Additional Information

Now consider an information system $\boldsymbol{\eta}$ that reveals $y_1 = y \in Y$ at $t = 1$ and $y_2 = s \in S$ at $t = 2$. In this case, any $\boldsymbol{\eta}$-efficient consumption/production plan is a solution to the following risk sharing/production problem for a set of positive utility weights $\{\lambda_i\}$:

$$\underset{\mathbf{c},\, \mathbf{d}_1}{\text{maximize}} \quad \textstyle\sum_{i\in I} \lambda_i\, U_i(\mathbf{c}_i),$$

$$\text{subject to} \quad \textstyle\sum_{i\in I} c_{i1}(y) = \sum_{i\in I} \bar{c}_{i1} + \sum_{j\in J} d_{j1}(y), \quad \forall\, y \in Y,$$

$$\textstyle\sum_{i\in I} c_{i2}(s) = \sum_{j\in J} f_j(s,d_{j1}(y)), \quad \forall\, s \in y,\, y \in Y.$$

The first-order conditions imply that the $\boldsymbol{\eta}$-efficient production plan is such that

$$\mu_1(y) + \sum_{s \in y} \mu_2(s)\, \frac{\partial f_j(s,d_{j1}(y))}{\partial d_{j1}} = 0, \quad \forall\, y \in Y, j \in J,$$

where $\mu_1(\cdot)$ and $\mu_2(\cdot)$ are the Lagrange multipliers for the $t = 1$ and $t = 2$ budget constraints, respectively. In this context, information structure $\boldsymbol{\eta}$ has value (relative to $\boldsymbol{\eta}^o$) if the information permits identification of firms that will be relatively more productive. An extreme example is one in which $J = S$ and firm $j = s$ only produces a positive output in state s. With no information at $t = 1$, it will be optimal to invest some positive amount in all firms. However, if signal y is received at $t = 1$, then it will be optimal to invest positive amounts in only those firms that provide positive output in states $s \in y$ and to invest zero in all firms that only produce output in states $s \notin y$.

In order to gain insights into the conditions under which information has value, we compare the null information system $\boldsymbol{\eta}^o$ to another system $\boldsymbol{\eta}$. Given time-additive preferences and homogeneous beliefs, the following relation must hold among the multipliers if no change is made in the production plan (based on the first order conditions for the investors's consumption at $t = 1$ and $t = 2$):

$$\frac{\mu_1(y)}{\varphi(y)} = \mu_1^o, \qquad \frac{\mu_2(s)}{\varphi(s)} = \frac{\mu_2^o(s)}{\varphi(s)},$$

where $\mu_1{}^o$ and $\mu_2{}^o(\cdot)$ are the Lagrange multipliers in the risk sharing/production problem for information system $\boldsymbol{\eta}^o$. Now consider whether the $\boldsymbol{\eta}^o$-efficient production plan $\mathbf{d}_1{}^o$ is optimal with $\boldsymbol{\eta}$ by examining the first-order condition for the optimal investment level in each firm. These conditions require that

$$\mu_1{}^o + \sum_{s \in S} \mu_2^o(s) \frac{\partial f_j(s, d_{j1}^o)}{\partial d_{j1}} = 0, \quad \forall\, j \in J.$$

If $\mathbf{d}_1{}^o$ continues to be optimal with $\boldsymbol{\eta}$, the following condition must hold:

$$\mu_1(y) + \sum_{s \in y} \mu_2(s) \frac{\partial f_j(s, d_{j1}^o)}{\partial d_{j1}} = 0, \quad \forall\, y \in Y, j \in J.$$

Using the equalities established above, these two conditions can both hold if, and only if,

$$\sum_{s \in y} \frac{\mu_2^o(s)}{\varphi(s)} \frac{\partial f_j(s, d_{j1}^o)}{\partial d_{j1}}$$

is independent of y for all firms $j \in J$.

8.4.3 Production Choice in a Dynamically Quasi-complete Market

We now consider efficient production choice in dynamically quasi-complete market with both economy-wide and firm-specific events (see Sections 5.4.2 and 6.4.2). The definition of an event $y_t \in Y_t$ is expanded, i.e., $y_t \equiv (y_{et}, \{y_{jt}\}_{j=1,...,J})$, where y_t is the "full" description of the event at date t, y_{et} represents *economy-wide* events that influence the dividends of several firms, and y_{jt} represents *firm-specific* events that influence the dividends of firm j. The beliefs about firm-specific events are independent conditional on the economy-wide event, and firm-specific information provides no additional information about future economy-wide events. We consider an economy in which there are $N \times J$ firms and $N \times I$ investors, with N representing the size of the economy and with J and I representing the different types of firms and investors, respectively. Letting the number of each type N approach infinity, the strong law of large numbers implies that the firm-specific events have no impact on aggregate consumption. Hence, the key to achieving quasi-efficiency in this economy is a sufficiently varied set of well-diversified portfolios with dividends and market values only depending on the economy-wide event. Focusing on a representative firm of type j, Proposition 6.12 demonstrates that the following structure of the date-event prices obtains for a quasi-efficient equilibrium:

$$p_t(y_{et}, y_{jt}) = p_t(y_{et})\, \varphi(y_{jt}),$$

$$p_{\tau t}(y_{e\tau}, y_{j\tau} | y_t) = p_{\tau t}(y_{e\tau} | y_{et})\, \varphi(y_{j\tau} | y_{et}, y_{jt}).$$

The motivation for these price relations is that the "scarcity of aggregate consumption" only depends on the economy-wide events. The output of firm j is very small relative to the total output in the market and variations in its output due to variations in its firm-specific events are "offset" in a well-diversified portfolio by firm-specific variations in the outputs of all the other firms of the same type.

Observe that if there are production alternatives (e.g., the manager of firm j chooses d_{j1}), then we achieve Pareto-efficiency if the manager selects his production plan so as to maximize the market value of his firm given the date-event prices. Hence, with $\boldsymbol{\eta}^o$, the firm's objective is to maximize

$$v_{j0} = V_{j1} = d_{j1} + \sum_{s_e \in S_e} \sum_{s_j \in S_j} f_j(s_e, s_j, d_{j1})\, p_2(s_e)\, \varphi(s_j | s_e)$$

$$= d_{j1} + \sum_{s_e \in S_e} \bar{f}_j(s_e, d_{j1})\, p_2(s_e).$$

8.4.4 Information and Firm Value in a Dynamically Quasi-complete Market

Now consider information system $\boldsymbol{\eta}$, which reports information $y \in Y$ at $t = 1$. This information can consist of both economic-wide and firm-specific information. In a quasi-complete market the firm-specific information may not influence consumption plans, but it can influence both the production plans and the market value of a particular firm. Observe that, with $\boldsymbol{\eta}$, the cum-dividend market value of the firm at $t = 1$ is

$$V_{j1}(y_e,y_j) = d_{j1}(y_e,y_j) + \sum_{s_e \in S_e} \sum_{s_j \in S_j} f_j(s_e, s_j, d_{j1}(y_e,y_j))\, p_{21}(s_e|y_e)\, \varphi(s_j|s_e,y_j)$$

$$= d_{j1}(y_e,y_j) + \sum_{s_e \in S_e} \bar{f}_j(s_e, y_j, d_{j1}(y_e,y_j))\, p_{21}(s_e|y_e). \tag{8.5}$$

The firm-specific information at $t = 1$, y_j, enters into this expression in two places: it can change the inputs used and it can change the expected return (even if there is no change in input). Hence, prices are influenced by the release of firm-specific information as well as by economy-wide information, even if firm-specific information does not influence the consumption plans of investors who hold well-diversified portfolios.

8.4.5 The Value of Windfall and Productivity Information

We assume that beliefs are homogeneous and preferences are time-additive. Therefore, information has value if, and only if, it induces changes in production plans that result in changes in the expected aggregate dividends at either $t = 1$ or $t = 2$ (contingent on y_e and s_e). That is, the basic prices $p_2(s_e)$ versus $p_{21}(s_e|y_e)$ induce different action choices.

In order to obtain insight into this we introduce the concept of *windfall* and *productivity* events at both the economy and firm-specific levels.

Definition *Windfall and Productivity Events*

θ and θ_j constitute windfall events and ξ and ξ_j constitute productivity events if $s_e = (\theta,\xi)$ and $s_j = (\theta_j,\xi_j)$ such that

(a) $\varphi(s_e,s_j) = \varphi(\theta)\varphi(\xi)\varphi(\theta_j|\theta)\varphi(\xi_j|\xi)$, – independence

(b) $f_j(s_e,s_j,d_{j1}) = g_j(\theta,\theta_j) + h_j(\xi,\xi_j,d_{j1})$, – separable production impact

(c) ξ and ξ_j influence both the level and slope of $h_j(\cdot)$.

Proposition 8.5 (FC, Prop. 5)

Given homogeneous beliefs, time-additive preferences, equilibrium non-negative endowments (with respect to $\boldsymbol{\eta}^o$), sufficient claims to achieve either $\boldsymbol{\eta}^o$- or $\boldsymbol{\eta}$-efficiency, market value maximization by managers, and a sufficiently varied set of alternative actions, the following types of information have *value* (in the sense that there exists a Pareto-preferred consumption/ production plan) in a production economy:

(a) information about *economy-wide windfall events* (θ).

(b) information about *economy-wide productivity events* (ξ).

(c) information about *firm-specific productivity events* (ξ_j).

However, information about firm-specific windfall events (θ_j) does *not* have value.

Proof: Managers select the production level d_{j1} so as to maximize

$$(\boldsymbol{\eta}^o): \quad d_{j1} + \textstyle\sum_\xi \bar{h}_j(\xi, d_{j1})\, p_2(\xi),$$

$$(\boldsymbol{\eta}): \quad d_{j1} + \textstyle\sum_\xi \bar{h}_j(\xi, y_j, d_{j1})\, p_{21}(\xi|y_e), \qquad \forall\, y_j \in Y_j,\ y_e \in Y_e,$$

where

$$\bar{h}_j(\xi, y_j, d_{j1}) = \textstyle\sum_{\xi_j} h_j(\xi, \xi_j, d_{j1})\, \varphi(\xi_j|\xi, y_j),$$

$$p_2(\xi) = \textstyle\sum_\theta p_2(\theta, \xi), \quad p_{21}(\xi|y_e) = \textstyle\sum_\theta p_{21}(\theta, \xi|y_e).$$

The prices are assumed to be sufficiently varied that the two decisions differ if there is a change in either the basic prices (i.e., $p_2(\xi) \neq p_{21}(\xi|y_e)$), or the expected state-contingent output (i.e., $\bar{h}_j(\xi, d_{j1}) \neq \bar{h}_j(\xi, y_j, d_{j1})$).

The firm-specific and economy-wide productivity information both have a direct impact on $\bar{h}_j(\cdot)$. However, the effect of the economy-wide productivity information is more pervasive since it changes the beliefs that are implicit in $p_{21}(\xi|y_e)$ and, hence, changes the prices used in valuing production alternatives.

On the other hand, while the firm-specific and economy-wide windfall information have no direct impact on $\bar{h}_j(\cdot)$, the latter has an impact on $p_{21}(\xi|y_e)$ *if* the expected aggregate consumption associated with ξ is changed. Firm-specific windfall information for the various firms "cancel each other out" leaving no change in beliefs about aggregate output. However, it is influenced by economy-wide windfall information since the economy-wide windfall events affect aggregate consumption.

To establish the latter, consider the impact of perfect information about the economy-wide windfall events, i.e., $y_e = \theta$. Observe that there are no changes in the production plans only if

$$p_2(\xi) = p_{21}(\xi | y_e), \quad \forall\, \xi.$$

If there are no changes in production plans, then there should be no change in the event-contingent consumption plans. That will occur only if

$$p_2(s_e)/\varphi(s_e) = p_{21}(s_e | \theta)/\varphi(\xi), \quad \forall\, s_e \in \{ s_e |\ s_e = (\theta,\xi), \text{ for some } \xi \},$$

since $\varphi(s_e | \theta) = \varphi(\xi)$. However, that would imply that $p_2(s_e) = p_2(\xi)\, \varphi(\theta)$, which would only occur if θ has no impact on aggregate output. **Q.E.D.**

8.4.6 Optimal Behavior when Managers have Private Firm-specific Information

The preceding analysis assumes that all information is reported to investors. An interesting alternative is to assume that while the economy-wide information y_e is publicly reported, the firm-specific information y_j is known only to the manager of firm j (although it is common knowledge that managers receive that information). We assume the managers continue to be automatons acting in the best interests of investors, but the interesting question is whether there is any benefit from having them report their private firm-specific information to investors.

Observe that if y_j is not reported, then the firm will be over- or under-valued, depending on whether y_j is "bad" or "good" news. However, *it is not essential for that information to be reported in order to achieve η-efficiency.* To achieve η-efficiency we require the following basic ingredients:

(a) Managers select production plans so as to maximize the "intrinsic" value of the firm as computed using (8.5). Observe that this is accomplished if the managers compute the expected dividends in each state s_e using y_e and y_j, not just the publicly reported y_e, and the basic prices $p_{21}(s_e | y_e)$. Hence, if $p_{21}(\cdot)$ is the same as it would be if all information y was publicly reported instead of just y_e, then the production plans would be the same in both cases.

(b) Given the management behavior in (a), there exist well-diversified portfolios such that the expected state-contingent (s_e) dividends based on y_e are the same as they would be based on y. That is, diversification can effectively remove the uncertainty investors have about both the managers' production decisions (conditioned on firm-specific information) and the firm-specific events that will influence the outcomes of those decisions.

(c) Investors select consumption plans on the basis of the basic prices $p_{21}(s_e|y_e)$ and implement those plans by trading diversified portfolios of the type assumed in (b). The market values of those portfolios are based on y_e, but are the same as if y was reported.

(d) The equilibrium economy-wide event-prices $p_{21}(s_e|y_e)$, which underlie the market values of the firms, are the same as would occur if y was reported instead of just y_e.

The equivalence of the "fundamental" prices under the two reporting regimes is stated as an assumption, but it is a condition whose existence is assured by the first three assumptions. That is, the demand and supply for expected state-contingent consumption is the same in both reporting regimes and, hence, they have the same equilibrium prices.

8.5 CONCLUDING REMARKS

In this chapter we have examined the impact of information system changes on efficient production choices. As in the single decision maker and partnership settings, more information helps make better production choices, i.e., it facilitates more efficient use of the resources in the economy. Productivity information is valuable whether it pertains to economy-wide events or firm-specific events. However, windfall information is only valuable if it pertains to economy-wide events. This is the good news!

Most accounting research implicitly (or explicitly) assumes that publicly reported accounting information is firm-specific. There are other types of typically more timely public reports on "the-state-of-the-economy." The bad news is that there is no benefit to mandating managers to report their private firm-specific information to investors if the investors trade well-diversified portfolios in a competitive market in which they all receive the same information (and they have homogeneous beliefs, as well as time-additive preferences). That is, while reporting firm-specific information may appear to facilitate the investors' investment decisions (because it influences market prices), the investors gain no benefit from that information whether it pertains to windfall or productivity information.

Given these results, one may question whether it is worthwhile for accounting researchers to study general equilibrium models of competitive markets. Obviously, we feel that it is. It is important for accounting researchers to understand the nature of these results so that we do not use arguments for the value of accounting information that are incorrect. For example, establishing that accounting reports or earnings forecasts affect prices establishes that the report or forecast influences investors' beliefs, but it does not establish that reporting this information to investors makes them better off.

General equilibrium models are essential for understanding the implications of the investors' opportunity to trade claims, particularly in contexts in which there are both diversifiable and non-diversifiable risks. In Parts C and D of this volume, and in the second volume, we consider partial equilibrium models of settings in which markets are not perfectly competitive, due, for example, to private investor information, imperfect competition in product markets, and incentive issues for managers. In those settings there is greater scope for financial reporting to investors to have value. Partial equilibrium models are used for tractability reasons. However, their appropriateness depends on how well they reflect the prices that would result from a general equilibrium model. Understanding general equilibrium prices and investor welfare in a perfectly competitive market is useful for understanding prices and investor welfare in imperfectly competitive markets.

For example, the agency literature commonly assumes a risk-neutral principal without any further justification. That assumption can be justified in a general equilibrium setting if the contractible information is viewed as pertaining to firm-specific events, and the principal is viewed as a partnership of investors who hold a diversified portfolio of firms. On the other hand, if there are both firm-specific and economy-wide risks, the latter type of risk must be recognized when we specify the principal's utility function.

Before closing this chapter it should be noted that we assumed a very simple financial structure for the firm. Each firm has a single ownership claim, and any need for funding is provided by the pre-dividend owners of the firm's equity. Efficient production choices are obtained by maximizing the market (or intrinsic) value of the dividends to the equityholders (using the date-event prices), and the equityholders unanimously support that objective. However, if the firm has issued both equity and debt, care must be taken in specifying the manager's decision criterion in making production decisions. Does he maximize the value of the firm's equity or the value of the firm (i.e., the value of the equity plus the debt)?

Ex post (i.e., after the debt has been issued), the equityholders will prefer that the manager select the production choices that maximize the value of the equity, possibly at the expense of the debtholders. However, the debtholders will anticipate those choices when they invest in the debt, i.e., they will be "price protected." Consequently, *ex ante* (i.e., before the debt is issued) the equityholders will want to convince the potential investors in the firm's debt that the manager will select the production choices that will maximize the value of the firm. In this chapter we assume the manager exogenously acts in the best interests of the equityholders, and if that criterion is specified *ex ante*, then the manager will maximize the value of the firm.

In Volume II we explicitly consider management incentives, but not in a context with debt. However, the incentive contracting approach could be extended to consider debt. A key issue is whether the manager's incentive contract is signed before or after the debt contract is signed. Furthermore, we can view debt covenants as implicitly part of the manager's contract, in that debt covenants constrain the manager's actions. Ideally, the manager is motivated (possibly using constraints) to maximize the value of the firm. Of course, achieving that motivation may be difficult. These issues have been extensively examined in the corporate finance literature, but have received only limited examination in the accounting literature.[4]

Finally, while finding the production plan that maximizes the current value of the firm is a simple idea, conceptually, it may be a tremendous task in reality. Recall that a production plan specifies the investments or dis-investments for all possible events at all future dates. The "real options" literature in corporate finance typically assumes a particular (simple) information dynamics, and then uses techniques from the theory on dynamic programming or on optimal exercise of American options to simultaneously derive the optimal production plan as well as the current value of the firm. Applying this approach may prove useful in obtaining additional insights into the role of information in dynamic production settings.

REFERENCES

Debreu, G. (1959) *Theory of Value*, New Heaven: Yale University Press.

Begley, J., and G. A. Feltham. (1999) "An Empirical Examination of the Relation between Debt Contracts and Management Incentives," *Journal of Accounting and Economics* 27, 229-259.

Feltham, G. A., and P. O. Christensen. (1988) "Firm-Specific Information and Efficient Resource Allocation," *Contemporary Accounting Research* 5, 133-169.

Kunkel, J. G. (1982) "Sufficient Conditions for Public Information to have Social Value in a Production and Exchange Economy," *Journal of Finance* 37, 1005-1013.

---

[4] Begley and Feltham (1999) discuss these issues in the context of an empirical study that considers both debt covenants and share ownership by managers.

Magill, M., and M. Quinzii. (1996) *Theory of Incomplete Markets*, Massachusetts: The MIT Press.

Radner, R. (1972) "Existence of Equilibrium of Plans, Prices, and Price Expectations in a Sequence of Markets," *Econometrica* 40, 289-303.

Radner, R. (1982) "Equilibria under Uncertainty," in K. J. Arrow and M. D. Intriligator (eds.), *Handbook in Mathematical Economics: Volume II*, Amsterdam: North-Holland, 923-1006.

CHAPTER 9

RELATION BETWEEN MARKET VALUES AND FUTURE ACCOUNTING NUMBERS

In the preceding chapters, the value of a marketed security is represented as the net present value of risk-adjusted expected dividends. The expectations change with the information received by investors, and accounting reports could be a source of that information. Furthermore, even if accounting reports are not the source, accounting numbers may be used in representing investor information. However, the representations used in prior chapters are abstract and provide little direct insight as to how accounting numbers relate to market values.

We now explore the theoretical relation between accounting numbers and market values. Dividends represent a firm's distribution of value to its equity-holders, whereas accounting income is a representation of the firm's generation of value. The discounted dividend model focuses on the *anticipated distribution of value*. However, as we establish in this chapter, forecasted accounting numbers can be used to represent current market values in terms of the *anticipated generation of value*. The "value distribution" and "value generation" approaches are equivalent – one is the dual of the other. However, the "value generation" approach allows us to link forecasts of accounting numbers, which are common in practice, to market values.

The "value generation" approach distinguishes between value that has already been recorded (the book value of equity) and "above-normal" income (which we call residual income) that is expected to be recorded in the future, which explains the difference between the current market and book values of equity. The "value generation" approach allows us to ignore the firm's dividend policy if the classical Modigliani-Miller conditions are satisfied and the non-operating (which we call financial) assets are marked-to-market. Under these conditions we can focus on the valuation of operating assets, and the predicted residual operating income is independent of the timing of a firm's distribution of value (assuming the dividend policy does not affect the value-enhancing activities undertaken by the firm).

In this chapter, we continue to use the same abstract representation of information as was used in the preceding chapters. However, this analysis provides a foundation for Chapter 10, in which we explore the relation between market values and accounting representations of *current value-relevant* information. The key is that if one represents the value-relevant forecasts in terms of accounting numbers and one has beliefs about the stochastic relation between past, current, and future accounting numbers, then one can use past and current accounting numbers in representing the current value-relevant information.

Chapters 9 and 10 are designed to help us understand the theoretical relations between market values and accounting numbers in a public information, pure exchange setting. The analysis is fully consistent with the fundamental theories of finance. The focus is on accounting representations of forecasts and information. Different representations do not lead to different economic consequences. Therefore, the analyses in these two chapters do not provide direct guidance as to how we should "do" accounting – there are few, if any, normative statements in Chapters 9 and 10. Nonetheless, we believe that a clear understanding of the relations explored in these two chapters provide theoretical insights that will prove useful in future theoretical and empirical accounting research.

We begin, in Section 9.1, by demonstrating that the no-arbitrage, discounted dividend model developed in Chapter 6 can be transformed into a no-arbitrage, discounted residual income model, where residual income is the difference between accounting income minus a capital charge based on start-of-period book value. The equivalency of the two approaches holds under very general assumptions and any accounting rules that satisfy what is called the "clean surplus relation."

The basic discounted residual income model is extended in Section 9.2 to consider separately the value of operating and financial assets (net of financial debt) under the Modigliani-Miller assumptions that imply dividend policy irrelevance. We then invoke mark-to-market accounting for financial assets, which permits us to focus on predictions of residual operating income (or "free" operating cash flows) in characterizing the value of the firm's operations. These predictions are independent of the dividend policy.

It is impractical to explicitly forecast dividends, residual income, residual operating income, or "free" operating cash flows for the entire anticipated life of the firm. Hence, there is practical interest in using explicit forecasts for a limited horizon (e.g., three to five years), and then making a truncation adjustment. In Section 9.3 we discuss the nature of the truncation adjustments required to maintain equivalency of the alternative approaches.

Throughout our analysis we adopt a *proprietorship theory* perspective.[1] That is, we assume the objective is to characterize the relation between accounting numbers and the market value of the current common equity outstanding

[1] Ohlson (2000) refers to the "proprietorship theory" perspective of accounting, and strongly argues that this theory should be adopted in setting GAAP. Some implications of that theory for accounting are examined in Section 9.4, which considers the impact of the anticipated issuance of new equity.

(the firm's residual claims). Other claims (including debt and preferred shares) may exist, but we treat them as financial debt and assume they are marked-to-market. Furthermore, we initially assume that there are a fixed number of common shares outstanding and that the dividend number (d_{jt}) represents the cash dividends distributed to the owners of those shares (if d_{jt} is negative, it represents cash invested by the owners of those shares). In Section 9.4 we consider the issuance of new equity and contingent claims to equity (e.g., convertible debt or executive stock options). Under proprietorship theory, contingent equity claims are treated as debt until shares are issued, and care must be taken in defining "clean surplus accounting."

For simplicity, much of our analysis assumes there are no taxes. However, taxes do exist and are significant. In Appendix 9A we demonstrate that care must be taken in defining the accounting numbers and discount rates when there are taxes.

9.1 NO-ARBITRAGE ACCOUNTING-VALUE RELATIONS

Before deriving the no-arbitrage accounting-value relations, we direct the reader's attention to the no-arbitrage dividend-value relations in Chapter 6. The basic model for the *ex*-dividend value of firm j's common equity at date t given event y_t, denoted $v_{jt}(y_t)$, is given by (6.5). Observe that it is based on the date-event-contingent dividends and prices, i.e., $d_{j\tau}(y_\tau)$ and $p_{\tau t}(y_\tau | y_t)$. We refer to this *dividend-value relation* as DVR.

We now shift from focusing on the future distribution of value (as represented by dividends) to the future generation of value (as represented by accounting numbers). As in the dividend-value relation we focus on the market value of common equity. The accounting system reports both the book value of common equity and the net income attributable to common equity. We permit the existence of pure debt, but for the purposes of the discussion in this section we preclude the existence of contingent claims to common equity (e.g., convertible debt). If there are preferred shares, then we implicitly treat them as debt. Most of the following discussion is based on the analysis in Feltham and Ohlson (1999) (FO99).

9.1.1 Clean Surplus Relation

Dividends are the net distribution of value to the common equityholders. We drop the subscript j and focus on a specific firm. Hence, $d_t(y_t)$ represents the dividends paid at date t in event y_t. The two basic accounting numbers are $bv_t(y_t)$ and $ni_t(y_t)$, which represent the book value of common equity at date t and the net income attributable to common equity (e.g., after deducting preferred dividends) for the period ending at date t, given event y_t. The book value of common equity is the difference between the firm's assets and liabilities, which in the distant past was called the owners' "surplus." An accounting system that classified all changes in the "surplus" as either exchanges of cash between the firm and its owners (represented by net dividends in our setting) or an element of net income, was deemed to satisfy the "clean surplus relation." For example, this precluded direct write-offs of assets to surplus. Later this was called the "all-inclusive income" concept, and more recently has been referred to as the "comprehensive income" concept. Following Ohlson (1995) and Feltham and Ohlson (1995), we use the term "clean surplus," in part because we do not want the concept to be encumbered with issues that have been raised in the literature with respect to how the "all-inclusive" or "comprehensive" income concepts should be implemented.

More precisely, the clean surplus relation implies that the accounting system is such that the change in book value of common equity (i.e., surplus) between any two dates equals net income minus net dividends:

$$bv_\tau(y_\tau) = bv_{\tau-1}(y_{\tau-1}) + ni_\tau(y_\tau) - d_\tau(y_\tau), \quad \forall\, y_\tau \subseteq y_{\tau-1} \in Y_{\tau-1},\ \tau = 1,...,T. \quad \text{(CSR)}$$

Furthermore, if the firm ceases to exist at date T, so that $v_T(y_T) = 0$, it follows that the clean surplus relation also implies that adjustments are made through net income (e.g., write-off of worthless assets) to set the book value equal to zero, i.e., $bv_T(y_T) = 0$.

Observe that, at any given date $t = 0, ..., T$ and for any terminal event $y_T \subseteq y_t$, the total of all future dividends equals the current book value plus the total of all future net income, i.e.,

$$\sum_{\tau=t+1}^{T} d_\tau(y_T) = bv_t(y_t) + \sum_{\tau=t+1}^{T} ni_\tau(y_T), \tag{9.1}$$

for all accounting rules that satisfy the clean surplus relation CSR, where $d_\tau(y_T) = d_\tau(y_\tau)$ and $ni_\tau(y_T) = ni_\tau(y_\tau)$ for $y_\tau \supseteq y_T$.[2] Over the entire life of the firm (and for every "path" through the "tree" of events), beginning with a book value of zero, the total dividends equal the total net income.

Observe that *if* changing from one clean surplus accounting policy to another has no "real" effect (i.e., the date-event-contingent dividends are unchanged), then the change in accounting policy only affects the timing of the reported net income but not its total.

---

[2] That is, the dividend and net income numbers are those that occur at each event on the "path" through the event "tree" that terminates at y_T.

9.1.2 Accounting-value Relation

A key element in the accounting-value relation introduced below is what Ohlson (1995) (Oh95) and Feltham and Ohlson (1995) (FO95) called "abnormal earnings," but what is more commonly referred to as "residual income." We adopt the latter term and define it to equal the net income minus a capital charge, which equals the riskless start-of-period interest rate times start-of-period book value, i.e.,

$$ri_\tau(y_\tau) \equiv ni_\tau(y_\tau) - \imath_{\tau-1}(y_{\tau-1})bv_{\tau-1}(y_{\tau-1}), \quad \forall\ y_{\tau-1} \supseteq y_\tau \in Y_\tau,\ \tau = 1,...,T,$$

where

$$\imath_{\tau-1}(y_{\tau-1}) \equiv \beta_{\tau,\tau-1}(y_{\tau-1})^{-1} - 1 \tag{9.2a}$$

is the riskless one-period spot interest rate at date τ-1 given event $y_{\tau-1}$ and

$$\beta_{\tau,\tau-1}(y_{\tau-1}) = \sum_{y_\tau \subseteq y_{\tau-1}} p_{\tau,\tau-1}(y_\tau | y_{\tau-1}) \tag{9.2b}$$

is the corresponding spot price of a one-period discount bond.

Observe that residual income can be interpreted as the accumulation of value in excess of the "normal" return as measured by the riskless interest rate times start-of-period book value. Obviously, this measure depends on the firm's accounting policy. Nonetheless, the following accounting-value relation holds for all accounting policies that satisfy CSR. Fundamentally, this relation states that one can assess market value either by pricing future date-event-contingent distributions of value (i.e., net dividends) or by pricing current book value plus future date-event-contingent accumulations of value in excess of "normal" returns on book value (i.e., residual income). We include the proof of the following proposition since it is not immediately obvious that this accounting-value relation holds.

Proposition 9.1 (F099, Prop. 1)

No arbitrage and CSR are sufficient for the following *accounting-value relation* (AVR) to hold:

$$v_t(y_t) = bv_t(y_t) + \sum_{\tau=t+1}^{T} \sum_{y_\tau \subseteq y_t} ri_\tau(y_\tau)\, p_{\tau t}(y_\tau | y_t), \tag{9.3}$$

$$\forall\ y_t \in Y_t,\ t = 0,1,...,T\text{-}1,$$

where $p_{\tau t}(y_\tau | y_t)$ is the no-arbitrage event-price used in (6.5).

Proof: The accounting numbers are assumed to be η-measurable (i.e., they are consistent with the information that is common knowledge to investors) and $d_\tau(y_T)$, $bv_\tau(y_T)$, and $ni_\tau(y_T)$ represent the amounts for event $y_\tau \supseteq y_T$ at date $\tau = 1,...,T$. Observe that CSR implies

$$d_\tau(y_\tau) = ni_\tau(y_\tau) + bv_{\tau-1}(y_\tau) - bv_\tau(y_\tau), \quad \forall\, y_\tau \subseteq y_t,\ \tau = t+1,...,T, \tag{9.4}$$

where $bv_{\tau-1}(y_\tau) \equiv bv_{\tau-1}(y_{\tau-1})$, $y_{\tau-1} \supseteq y_\tau$. Substitute (9.4) into (6.5):

$$v_t(y_t) = \sum_{\tau=t+1}^{T} \sum_{y_\tau \subseteq y_t} [ni_\tau(y_\tau) + bv_{\tau-1}(y_\tau) - bv_\tau(y_\tau)]\, p_{\tau t}(y_\tau|y_t). \tag{9.5}$$

Observe that, since $bv_{\tau-1}(y_\tau) = bv_{\tau-1}(y_{\tau-1})$, $\forall\, y_\tau \subseteq y_{\tau-1}$, and $bv_T(y_T) = 0$, $\forall\, y_T \in Y_T$,

$$-\sum_{\tau=t+1}^{T} \sum_{y_\tau \subseteq y_t} bv_\tau(y_\tau)\, p_{\tau t}(y_\tau|y_t) = bv_t(y_t) - \sum_{\tau=t+1}^{T} \sum_{y_{\tau-1} \subseteq y_t} bv_{\tau-1}(y_{\tau-1})\, p_{\tau-1,t}(y_{\tau-1}|y_t).$$

Substituting this expression into (9.5), and using (9.2) plus the fact that $p_{\tau,\tau-1}(y_\tau|y_{\tau-1}) = p_{\tau t}(y_\tau|y_t)/p_{\tau-1,t}(y_{\tau-1}|y_t)$ yields (9.3). **Q.E.D.**

Of particular note is the fact that the accounting-value relation (9.3) is based on the current book value and forecasted residual income, and is not based on forecasted accounting income *per se*. Total dividends equal total accounting income (under clean surplus), but except under a "full payout" dividend policy (in which dividends equal accounting income), the net present value of the two streams are not likely to be equal. Including current book value and a capital charge for the book value at the start of each period serves to ensure that the (6.5) and (9.3) are always equivalent. For example, consider a shift of one dollar of income from period τ to period τ-1 (without a change in dividend policy) in a setting in which there is no new information (i.e., $y_\tau = y_t$, for all $\tau > t$). This results in a one dollar increase in the book value of equity at the start of period τ. Hence, the change in NPV is equal to

$$p_{\tau-1,t} - p_{\tau t}\,[1 + \imath_{\tau-1}] = 0.$$

That is, the increase in value from reporting income one period earlier is precisely offset by the increased capital charge in the second period.

Another significant aspect of accounting-value relation (9.3) is that the capital charge used in measuring residual income is the riskless one-period spot interest rate. That is, there is no use of a risk-adjusted cost of capital. Instead, the risk adjustment is implicit in the event prices that are applied to the net residual income. In the following section, we consider alternative representations of the accounting-value relation that highlight the use of riskless discount factors and capital charges in combination with risk-adjusted expected residual income.

9.1.3 Alternative Accounting-value Relations

Accounting-value relation (9.3) is very general, requiring only a limited set of assumptions. The date-event prices reflect the investors' beliefs and preferences, and are precisely the same as those used in dividend-value relation (6.5). Hence, we can develop equivalent representations using risk-neutral probabilities (see (6.11) and (6.12)) or a valuation index (see (6.14) and (6.15)). Now, instead of discounting risk-adjusted expected dividends at the zero-coupon bond rate, we discount the risk-adjusted expected residual income.

Proposition 9.2

No arbitrage and CSR are sufficient for the following alternative accounting-value relations to hold:

$$v_t(y_t) = bv_t(y_t) + \sum_{\tau=t+1}^{T} \beta_{\tau t}(y_t)\, \hat{\mathrm{E}}[ri_\tau|y_t], \quad \forall\, y_t \in Y_t,\ t = 0,1,\ldots,T\text{-}1, \tag{9.6a}$$

$$= bv_t(y_t) + \sum_{\tau=t+1}^{T} \beta_{\tau t}(y_t)\Big\{ \mathrm{E}[ri_\tau|y_t] + \mathrm{Cov}[ri_\tau, q_{\tau t}|y_t] \Big\}, \tag{9.6b}$$

$$\forall\, y_t \in Y_t,\ t = 0,1,\ldots,T\text{-}1,$$

where the expectation $\hat{\mathrm{E}}[ri_\tau|y_t]$ is derived using the same risk-neutral probability function $\hat{\varphi}_{\tau t}$ as in (6.11)[3] and the expectation E and covariance Cov are derived using the same probability function $\varphi_{\tau t}$ and valuation index $q_{\tau t}$ as in (6.14).

The no-arbitrage assumption provides the foundation for accounting-value relations (9.3) and (9.6), but it does not provide direct insights into the nature of risk adjustments that are made. However, if investors have time-additive preferences and homogeneous beliefs, and the equilibrium is Pareto efficient,

[3] For simplicity of notation we drop the subscripts on the risk-neutral expectation operator referring to the zero-coupon bonds used as numeraires. In this chapter we use these numeraires throughout so there should be no confusion as to which risk-neutral probabilities we are using.

then the risk-neutral probabilities and valuation index are the same as in (6.24) and (6.25). In that setting, the valuation index is a decreasing function of aggregate consumption, so that the risk adjustment in (9.6b) is negative if residual income is positively correlated with aggregate consumption. The greater the correlation, the larger the risk adjustment.

Risk aversion and random variations in aggregate consumption create the need for risk adjustments in valuation, and they also induce stochastic interest rates. Loosely speaking, the spot interest rate reflects the concavity of the investors' utility functions (since the marginal utilities decrease with increased consumption) plus the difference between current aggregate consumption and expectations about next period's aggregate consumption. The book value of equity represents the value that has been invested and generated (as recorded by the accounting system) and not distributed. The higher the current interest rate (reflecting greater scarcity of consumption today relative to next period), the greater the normal return from that retention and therefore the greater the capital charge in computing residual income.

In much of the analysis in Chapter 10, we assume (as do Ohlson 1995, and Feltham and Ohlson 1995, 1996) that the dividend-value model can be expressed as

$$v_t(y_t) = \sum_{\tau=t+1}^{T} \beta^{\tau-t}\mathrm{E}[d_\tau|y_t], \tag{9.7a}$$

so that the corresponding accounting-value model is

$$v_t(y_t) = bv_t(y_t) + \sum_{\tau=t+1}^{T} \beta^{\tau-t}\mathrm{E}[ri_\tau|y_t], \tag{9.7b}$$

where $\beta = (1 + \imath)^{-1}$, $ri_\tau = ni_\tau - \imath bv_{\tau-1}$, and $\imath$ is the spot interest rate for each date and event. That is, investors are effectively risk neutral with homogeneous beliefs, and the spot interest rates are constant. The "risk-neutrality" assumption can be interpreted as assuming that either some investors are risk neutral (so that they absorb all risk and their marginal utilities in any given period are independent of their consumption levels) or investors hold well-diversified portfolios and all risks are firm-specific (so that aggregate consumption is not stochastic). These are unrealistic assumptions. Nonetheless, if risk aversion and stochastic interest rates are not important in the issues being examined, then these assumptions can be useful since they significantly simplify the analysis.

Empirical research has frequently used models based on (9.7). Obviously, risk aversion and aggregate risk have a significant impact on observed prices. The common approach for adjusting for risk in empirical research is to replace the riskless interest rate $\imath$ with a so-called "risk-adjusted cost of capital" $\hat{\imath}$ =

$(1+\imath)(1+\zeta) - 1$, where ζ is the risk premium. A disquieting aspect of this approach is that it assumes the risk adjustment to expected dividends or residual income grows multiplicatively, whereas (9.6b) implies it grows additively with the covariance between the dividend and the valuation index. To illustrate this point, assume a constant interest rate and let $\pi_\tau(y_t) = \mathrm{E}[ri_\tau|y_t] - \hat{\mathrm{E}}[ri_\tau|y_t]$ represent the residual income risk adjustment. Expression (9.6b) implies that $\pi_\tau(y_t) = - \mathrm{Cov}[ri_\tau, q_{\tau t}|y_t]$, with a negative covariance for most firms. Now consider (9.7b) with $\hat{\beta} = (1+\hat{r})^{-1}$ and $\hat{ri}_\tau = ni_\tau - \hat{r}\, bv_{\tau-1}$, so that

$$\pi_\tau(y_t) = \mathrm{E}[ri_\tau|y_t] - \mathrm{E}[\hat{ri}_\tau|y_t]/(1+\zeta)^{\tau-t}.$$

Whether the latter is a reasonable approximation of the former is an open question, but they clearly have different forms. The former is independent of the expected residual income – only its covariations with aggregate consumption matter, whereas the latter is proportional to the expectation. Furthermore, the capital charge used in computing residual income differs.[4]

An interesting aspect of accounting-value relations (9.3) and (9.6) is that the firm's accounting policy can affect the forecasted date-event-contingent residual income, the risk-adjusted expected residual income for each date, and the covariance between residual income and the valuation index q for each date. Nonetheless, changing the accounting policy does not change the market value $v_t(y_t)$, as long as the accounting policy does not have any economic consequences (e.g., tax effects). Changing the accounting policy so that more value is recognized in one period will always result in the recognition of less value in some other periods, and the effects are precisely offsetting if the clean surplus relation is satisfied. These results may be surprising, but the results are fundamentally mathematical and do not depend on the use of "proper" accounting, e.g., accounting that reflects changes in economic value.

To give some intuition why the above relations hold, we observe that the book value and date-event-contingent residual income constitute a viable revised sequence of date-event-contingent dividends provided the firm can, at each date, borrow or save for one period at the riskless spot rate and the change in dividends does not have economic consequences. In particular, assume the firm borrows $bv_t(y_t)$ at date t and pays this out as an immediate dividend. At date t+1, some event $y_{t+1} \subseteq y_t$ occurs, the firm repays $[1 + \imath_t(y_t)]bv_t(y_t)$ using the original dividend $d_{t+1}(y_{t+1})$, borrows $bv_{t+1}(y_{t+1}) = bv_t(y_t) + ni_{t+1}(y_{t+1}) - d_{t+1}(y_{t+1})$, and pays a revised dividend of $ri_{t+1}(y_{t+1}) = ni_{t+1}(y_{t+1}) - \imath_t(y_t)bv_t(y_t)$.

[4] If the risk-adjusted cost of capital $\hat{r}$ is used in (9.7a), then (9.7b) will yield the same answer if the risk-adjusted cost of capital is used in defining residual income. That is, both approximations yield the same answer.

While the preceding discussion is based on a change in dividend policy that has no economic effect, that is merely for expositional purposes. The results in this section do not require that there be dividend policy irrelevance. Only the no-arbitrage condition is required for (6.5), while Propositions 9.1 and 9.2 merely add the clean surplus relation.

9.2 SEPARATION OF FINANCIAL AND OPERATING ACTIVITIES

The accounting-value relation focuses on the forecasted generation of value, as measured by residual income. While residual income can be influenced by both operating and financial activities, the primary source of value, in excess of the cash invested, comes from the opportunity to undertake positive net present value (NPV) operating projects. The firm's dividend policy affects how those projects are financed, but need not affect which projects are undertaken.

While we need not assume dividend policy irrelevance in the preceding section, it is a useful assumption for the following discussion. In particular, it allows us to separate the valuation of the firm's operating activities from the impact of the firm's financial activities. We further simplify the analysis by assuming the financial assets (net of financial liabilities) are marked-to-market, so that the expected residual income attributable to the firm's financial activities equals zero. That is, while the book value of common equity includes both financial and operating assets, the risk-adjusted expected residual income includes only residual operating income.

Modigliani and Miller (1958) and Miller and Modigliani (1961) (jointly referred to as MM) derived well-known theorems on the irrelevancy of a firm's financial structure and dividend policy to its value. While there has been considerable research into various factors that can cause dividend policy irrelevance not to hold, it is useful to consider the conditions under which irrelevance holds and their implications for accounting valuation models. The following *MM-conditions* capture the spirit of MM's assumptions:

(a) If a firm requires funds to invest in a project or pay dividends, then it can costlessly obtain those funds at the market rate. Similarly, if it has excess funds it can costlessly invest those funds at the market rate.

(b) A firm's future date-event-contingent investments and disinvestments that have non-zero NPV are known and independent of the zero NPV investments and disinvestments (or borrowing) that can be used to vary dividends.

(c) Owners are indifferent between whether a firm invests funds at the market rate or pays dividends and permits the owners to personally invest those funds. They can costlessly vary their holdings of the asset and can borrow/lend on personal account.

Observe that condition (b) is satisfied if all positive NPV investments are assumed to be undertaken no matter what the dividend policy. The dividend policy only influences the firm's borrowing and investment activities at the market rate. These conditions require, for example, that there are no differences in the tax treatment of interest expense and dividends paid, and there are no dead-weight costs incurred if the firm goes bankrupt (it can be reorganized to continue any operations that have value).

Ohlson often makes reference to a bank account. It is the epitome of a financial asset that is marked-to-market. The balance in the account is both its market and book value. The income for the next period is equal to the current book value times the current interest rate, so that the residual income will equal zero. The planned withdrawals (the dividend policy) do not affect its current value, and if a dollar is paid out now, then both its market and book values decrease by a dollar. Investments in marketable securities are similar, except that the realized return is stochastic. This implies that the realized residual income can be positive or negative, but of importance for our analysis is the fact that the risk-adjusted expected residual income from these investments equals zero. For simplicity, we assume that financial debt (a negative financial asset) is marked-to-market, so that its risk-adjusted expected residual income equals zero.

9.2.1 Accounting Relations

We now divide the firm's accounts into financial and operating accounts as follows:

$$bv_t(y_t) = fa_t(y_t) + oa_t(y_t) \tag{9.8a}$$

$$ni_t(y_t) = fi_t(y_t) + oi_t(y_t). \tag{9.8b}$$

where

$fa_t(y_t)$ = book value of financial assets at date t given event y_t (this is negative if the firm's debt exceeds its investment in financial assets, such as marketable securities);

$oa_t(y_t)$ = book value of operating assets at date t given event y_t;

$fi_t(y_t)$ = financial income for period t given event y_t;

$oi_t(y_t)$ = operating income for period t given event y_t.

The distinction between operating and financial income is inherently arbitrary. However, we assume the distinction is such that the accounting for financing activities satisfies the following conditions.

Financial Asset Relation (FAR): All transfers to the common equity-holders are made through the financial assets, and these assets are further influenced by financial income and the ("free") cash flows from operations, which are denoted $oc_t(y_t)$:

$$fa_t(y_t) = fa_{t-1}(y_{t-1}) + fi_t(y_t) + oc_t(y_t) - d_t(y_t). \qquad \text{(FAR)}$$

Financial Assets Marked-to-Market (FAM): The risk-adjusted expected financial income equals the riskless spot interest rate times the opening book value of the financial assets:

$$\hat{\mathrm{E}}[fi_t | y_{t-1}] = \imath_{t-1}(y_{t-1})\, fa_{t-1}(y_{t-1}). \qquad \text{(FAM)}$$

The FAR relation is a component of the clean surplus relation (the other component is introduced below) and is not very restrictive. The FAM relation, on the other hand, is very restrictive. It implies that we assume all assets and liabilities included in fa_t are recorded at their current market values. The financial income equals the increase in market value (adjusted for deposits and withdrawals) and, given equilibrium prices, the expected increase (adjusted for risk) equals the riskless interest rate times the current market value.

While we describe the transfer between the operating and financing activities as "free" operating cash flows, it is not essential that the transfer be in the form of cash. For example, we could treat accounts receivable as either an operating or a financial asset. If it is an operating asset, then the transfer to the financing activities is in the form of the cash received from customers. However, if it is a financial asset, then the transfer is recorded at the "value" of the receivables (so that FAR and FAM are satisfied) and any difference between the amount collected and the value at date of transfer is part of financial income. That is, oc_t must be cash or "cash equivalents." Of course, this can be negative, representing the amount "invested" in operations.

We do not assume operating assets are marked-to-market. In fact, we do not view that as even reasonable for most operating assets, since their value comes from their synergistic use, not their disposal. However, we do assume that the accounting for operating activities is consistent with the clean surplus relation (CSR). Given (9.8) and financial asset relation FAR, it follows that CSR is only satisfied if the following operating asset relation holds.

> ***Operating Asset Relation (OAR):*** The operating assets are increased by operating earnings and reduced by the free operating cash flows transferred to the financial assets:
>
> $$oa_t(y_t) = oa_{t-1}(y_{t-1}) + oi_t(y_t) - oc_t(y_t). \qquad \text{(OAR)}$$

Observe that, given (9.8), any two of CSR, FAR and OAR implies the third.

9.2.2 Operating Income-value Relation

The book value of the financial assets is assumed to equal their market value, but, in general, the book value of the operating assets does not equal their market value. We now develop an accounting-value relation for the operating assets, which can be combined with the book value of the financial assets to determine the market value of the firm's common equity.

We begin by dividing residual income into its financial and operating components, i.e.,

$$ri_t(y_t) = rfi_t(y_t) + roi_t(y_t),$$

where

$$rfi_t(y_t) \equiv fi_t(y_t) - \imath_{t-1}(y_{t-1})fa_{t-1}(y_{t-1})$$

$$roi_t(y_t) = oi_t(y_t) - \imath_{t-1}(y_{t-1})oa_{t-1}(y_{t-1}),$$

with $y_{t-1} \supseteq y_t$. If we assume FAM holds, then it follows that

$$\hat{\mathrm{E}}[rfi_t | y_{t-1}] = 0.$$

This provides the *operating income-value relation*. In this relation, the market value of the firm's common equity equals the book value of its financial assets (which are marked-to-market) and the market value of its operating assets (which equals the book value of the operating assets plus the discounted risk-adjusted expected residual operating income). As in the dividend- and accounting-value relations, the risk-adjusted expected residual operating income can be expressed in terms of either the risk-neutral probabilities $\hat{\varphi}_{\tau t}$ or an adjustment for the covariance between the residual operating income and the valuation index $q_{\tau t}$, as defined in (6.11) and (6.14), respectively.

Proposition 9.3 (FO99, Prop. 4)

No arbitrage, FAR, FAM, and OAR are sufficient for the following *operating income-value relations* (OVR) to hold:

$$v_t(y_t) = bv_t(y_t) + \sum_{\tau=t+1}^{T} \sum_{y_\tau \subseteq y_t} roi_\tau(y_\tau)\, p_{\tau t}(y_\tau | y_t), \tag{9.9a}$$

$$= bv_t(y_t) + \sum_{\tau=t+1}^{T} \beta_{\tau t}(y_t)\, \hat{\mathrm{E}}[roi_\tau | y_t], \tag{9.9b}$$

$$= bv_t(y_t) + \sum_{\tau=t+1}^{T} \beta_{\tau t}(y_t) \Big\{ \mathrm{E}[roi_\tau | y_t] + \mathrm{Cov}[roi_\tau, q_{\tau t} | y_t] \Big\}, \tag{9.9c}$$

$$\forall\, y_t \in Y_t,\ t = 0,1,...,T\text{-}1.$$

While the market value of the financial assets is often equal to the sum of the disposal values of individual financial assets, the market value of the operating assets generally exceeds the sum of the disposal values of the individual operating assets (unless it is optimal for the firm to dispose of its operating assets). Individual operating assets are purchased and then used in combination (e.g., projects) to generate a return. The acquisition price of an operating asset is often capitalized (thereby increasing book value) and then expensed over its use (thereby decreasing both book value and operating income). The aggregate market value of the operating assets *in use* exceeds the current book value if the NPV of expected risk-adjusted future residual operating income (generated by the use of the assets) is positive.

9.2.3 Operating Cash Flow-value Relation

In the finance literature, discussions of the value of a firm's operating assets usually focus on the future cash flows from operations. While that is not the focus in this book, we briefly connect our results to the operating cash flow model by observing that cash flow accounting for operations can be viewed as a special case of clean surplus accounting. In particular, under cash flow accounting, $oa_\tau(y_\tau) = 0$ and $oi_\tau(y_\tau) = oc_\tau(y_\tau)$ for all y_τ and τ. This trivially satisfies OAR, which leads to the following operating cash flow-value relations.

Proposition 9.4 (FO99, Prop. 3)

No arbitrage, FAR and FAM are sufficient for the following *operating cash flow-value relations* (CVR) to hold:

$$v_t(y_t) = fa_t(y_t) + \sum_{\tau=t+1}^{T} \sum_{y_\tau \subseteq y_t} oc_\tau(y_\tau)\, p_{\tau t}(y_\tau | y_t), \tag{9.10a}$$

$$= fa_t(y_t) + \sum_{\tau=t+1}^{T} \beta_{\tau t}(y_t)\, \hat{\mathrm{E}}[oc_\tau | y_t], \tag{9.10b}$$

$$= fa_t(y_t) + \sum_{\tau=t+1}^{T} \beta_{\tau t}(y_t) \Big\{ \mathrm{E}[oc_\tau | y_t] + \mathrm{Cov}[oc_\tau, q_{\tau t} | y_t] \Big\}, \tag{9.10c}$$

$$\forall\, y_t \in Y_t,\ t = 0,1,\ldots,T\text{-}1.$$

Hence, we can view the value of the common equity as the sum of the value of the financial assets (which will be negative if there is substantial debt financing) and the value of the operating assets, where the latter is equal to the net present value (using the zero-coupon discount rates at date t) of the risk-adjusted expected operating cash flows. The risk adjustments used here are again the same as those that applied to the dividends given the no-arbitrage relation.

9.3 TRUNCATED FORECASTS

Implementation of the value relations developed above requires forecasts of dividends, residual income, residual operating income, or operating cash flows for the entire anticipated life of the firm. Practical implementation obviously requires some form of simplification, and the simplifications may lead to differences in the results provided by the various models. In Chapter 10 we consider infinite horizon models based on simple dynamics of the operating cash flows and residual income. An alternative approach is to develop explicit forecasts for a limited horizon, e.g., two to five years, and then make a truncation adjustment. A truncated sequence of forecasts can yield the same result as a sequence for the entire life of the firm provided an appropriate adjustment is made for the terminal value at the end of the truncated sequence.

Penman (1997) and Ohlson and Zhang (1998) discuss valuation based on truncated forecasts and terminal value in settings with a constant "cost of capital." In this subsection we briefly identify the appropriate terminal adjustment for each of the models considered above. Observe that in each case the "truncated model" yields the same result as the "full model," and the truncation adjustment would be the same if we used event-prices, risk-neutral probabilities, or the valuation index. In the following proposition, we allow for non-constant, stochastic interest rates and make risk adjustments using risk-neutral probabilities.

Proposition 9.5

Assume no arbitrage and let $\check{T} < T$ represent the truncation date.

(a) Dividend model:

$$v_t(y_t) = \sum_{\tau=t+1}^{\check{T}} \beta_{\tau t}(y_t)\,\hat{\mathrm{E}}[d_\tau|y_t] + \beta_{\check{T}t}(y_t)\;\hat{\mathrm{E}}[v_{\check{T}}\,|\,y_t]. \tag{9.11a}$$

(b) Residual income model (with CSR):

$$v_t(y_t) = bv_t(y_t) + \sum_{\tau=t+1}^{\check{T}} \beta_{\tau t}(y_t)\,\hat{\mathrm{E}}[ri_\tau|y_t] + \beta_{\check{T}t}(y_t)\,\hat{\mathrm{E}}[v_{\check{T}} - bv_{\check{T}}\,|\,y_t]. \tag{9.11b}$$

(c) Residual operating income model (with FAR, FAM, and OAR):

$$v_t(y_t) = bv_t(y_t) + \sum_{\tau=t+1}^{\check{T}} \beta_{\tau t}(y_t)\,\hat{\mathrm{E}}[roi_\tau|y_t] + \beta_{\check{T}t}(y_t)\,\hat{\mathrm{E}}[v_{\check{T}} - bv_{\check{T}}\,|\,y_t]. \tag{9.11c}$$

(d) Operating cash flow model (with FAR and FAM):

$$v_t(y_t) = fa_t(y_t) + \sum_{\tau=t+1}^{\check{T}} \beta_{\tau t}(y_t)\,\hat{\mathrm{E}}[oc_\tau|y_t] + \beta_{\check{T}t}(y_t)\,\hat{\mathrm{E}}[v_{\check{T}} - fa_{\check{T}}\,|\,y_t]. \tag{9.11d}$$

The terminal value required for the dividend model is the risk-adjusted expected market value at $\check{T}$, whereas in the residual income model it is the risk-adjusted expected difference between the market and book values at $\check{T}$. The residual operating income model has the same terminal value, but since financial assets are marked-to-market we can view this as the risk-adjusted expected difference between the market and book values of the operating assets. Finally, the terminal value for the operating cash flow model can be viewed as the risk-adjusted expected market value of the operating assets.

Some, such as Penman (1997), have felt that the residual income model has the advantage of requiring the estimate of a smaller terminal value. However, as emphasized by Lundholm and O'Keefe (2001a), this may not be a substantive argument since the models inherently contain the same components. They are merely presented differently. See Penman (2001) and Lundholm and O'Keefe (2001b) for a subsequent exchange of arguments on this issue.

9.4 ANTICIPATED EQUITY TRANSACTIONS[5]

We have adopted a proprietorship theory perspective, which leads us to focus on the value of the shares held by the current equityholders. To facilitate the discussion in the preceding sections, we assumed that no new equity will be issued in the future. Hence, all future net dividends will go directly to (or, if negative, be received from) the current equityholders or anyone who buys their equity. Furthermore, the clean surplus relation implies that the only anticipated changes in the book value of a firm's equity consists of exchanges of cash between the firm and its existing equityholders and net income.

We now consider the anticipated issuance of new equity. This has little impact on our analysis if the new equity is expected to be issued for cash at the market price per share at the time of issuance. The cash received from the new equityholders can be treated as a negative dividend, without distinguishing between whether the cash comes from old or new equityholders. In addition, in the dividend-value relation (such as (6.5)) no distinction is made between dividends paid to old or new equityholders. The new equity is merely a means of financing the firm's operating investments. Hence, if we assume dividend policy irrelevance and financial assets are marked-to-market, then the risk-adjusted expected residual income and the residual operating income are independent of the issuance of new equity for cash. All the accounting-value relations discussed above still hold.

Similarly, stock repurchase at the current market price is the same as the payment of a dividend, even though only some equityholders receive cash. Stock dividends and stock splits are assumed to have no effect other than to change the number of shares representing the equityholders' ownership of the firm.

The applicability of the accounting-value relations is potentially more problematic if shares are not issued for cash. Examples of other types of new equity transactions include:

- issuance of new equity for non-monetary assets;
- issuance of new equity for shares in another firm;
- issuance of new equity to employees (for past or future services);
- issuance and exercise of detachable stock warrants or convertible debt;
- issuance and exercise of employee stock options.

---

[5] The discussion in this section is based on an unpublished working paper by Feltham (1996).

The following discussion identifies accounting rules that permit the accounting-value relations to continue to hold in these settings. We view these rules as specifying "clean surplus accounting" for new equity transactions.

9.4.1 Pure- Versus Mixed-equity Concepts

In defining "clean surplus accounting" we must first specify what we want to include in common equity at any given date. That is, we must specify the equity claims we want to value using the accounting valuation model introduced below. We consider two distinct equity concepts. Under a proprietorship theory perspective, the current common equity at any date consists of the shares currently outstanding, i.e., the shares to which common dividends are paid if a dividend is declared and is payable to equityholders of record on that date. We refer to this as the "pure-equity" concept, and we let v_t^p denote the market value of the common shares currently outstanding.

The second concept views the current common equity at any date as consisting of the shares to which current dividends would be paid, *plus* claims to common equity that might be exercised in the future. The latter are typically contingent claims which give the claimant the right (i.e., option) to exchange a specified amount of cash (or some other asset or claim, such as convertible debt) for equity at some future date (or range of dates). We refer to this as the "mixed-equity" concept, and we let v_t^m denote the aggregate market value of the currently outstanding common shares and contingent claims to common shares that have not yet been exercised. The mixed-equity concept often underlies U.S. GAAP, but it is somewhat disturbing because it can result in significantly different accounting for contingent claims to equity and contingent claims to cash, even though the effect of the two types of claims may be essentially the same.[6]

The two equity concepts lead us to specify two clean surplus accounting concepts: super-clean and mixed. If the accounting is "super-clean", then the accounting valuation model introduced below characterizes the market value of the "pure" equity at all dates. If the accounting is "mixed", then the accounting

---

[6] The classic example is the accounting for employee stock options and the accounting for stock appreciation rights. These are effectively equivalent forms of compensation (ignoring tax issues) if the firm buys shares from the market to provide the employee with the necessary shares if he exercises his options. In particular, in both cases there is no change in the shares outstanding and the firm pays out cash equal to the difference between the market price and the exercise price on the exercise date. If stock appreciation rights are used, the cash paid out is reported as a compensation expense and there is no direct change in equity. However, if employee stock options are used, with GAAP as recommended in SFAS 123, the total compensation expense equals the *ex ante* value of the options at the contract date and the net cash paid out at the exercise date is treated as a direct change in equity (the share repurchase is similar to a dividend).

valuation model characterizes the market value of the "mixed" equity. Obviously, if the accounting concept is inconsistent with the equity concept, then there will be dates at which the accounting valuation model does not provide the desired value. Furthermore, U.S. GAAP permits the use of what we call dirty-surplus accounting, which can make the accounting valuation model inapplicable for either equity concept at some dates. We now make these concepts more precise.

9.4.2 Accounting Valuation Model

In Proposition 9.1 we establish that accounting-value relation (9.3) characterizes the relation between the current market value, book value, and future date-event-contingent residual income. This relation is based on dividend-value relation (6.5) and the clean surplus relation (CSR) under the assumption that there will be no new equity and the only transactions between the firm and investors will be the net dividends paid to common equityholders.

If new equity is issued, then there will be direct changes to common equity other than net income and dividends paid. We now expand the accounting to encompass these other direct equity transactions. We continue to let bv_t and ni_t refer to the book value of common equity and the net income attributable to common equity, and $ri_t = ni_t - \iota_{t-1} bv_{t-1}$ is the residual income. Equity transactions are divided into two components (we drop explicit reference to the events y_t whenever this is not likely to cause confusion):

d_t = cash dividends paid to the common equityholders of record at date t,

δ_t = increase in common equity recorded at date t in conjunction with the issuance of "new" equity.

In this setting, the basic accounting relation is

$$bv_t = bv_{t-1} + ni_t - d_t + \delta_t, \tag{9.12}$$

with $bv_T = 0$. This relation is similar to the clean surplus relation, CSR, but issues arise as to whether the accounting procedures used to jointly determine ni_t and δ_t can be viewed as satisfying the clean surplus relation. Merely satisfying (9.12) is not sufficient. This is the focus of the following discussion.

We now introduce an estimate of the value of common equity based on the accounting valuation model, for a given event y_t at date t:

$$v_t^\delta(y_t) \equiv bv_t(y_t) + \sum_{\tau=t+1}^{T} \sum_{y_\tau \subset y_t} ri_\tau(y_\tau)\, p_{\tau t}(y_\tau | y_t). \tag{9.13}$$

Observe that v_t^δ has a superscript "δ". This is to indicate that the estimated value is based on the date-event-contingent residual income as calculated using the accounting rules that jointly determine ni_t and δ_t.

The following relation follows directly from (9.12), without requiring the accounting for equity transactions to satisfy the clean surplus relation.

Lemma (F96, Prop. 1)[7]

Accounting relation (9.12) and accounting valuation model (9.13) imply

$$v_t^\delta(y_t) = \sum_{\tau=t+1}^{T} \sum_{y_\tau \subseteq y_t} [d_\tau(y_\tau) - \delta_\tau(y_\tau)]\, p_{\tau t}(y_\tau | y_t), \quad \forall\, y_t \in Y_t,\ t = 0,1,...,T\text{-}1. \quad (9.14)$$

This lemma establishes Proposition 9.1 if there is no new equity, i.e., $\delta_t(y_t) = 0$. However, $v_t^\delta(y_t)$ may not equal the market value of the common equity if new equity is expected to be issued.

9.4.3 Accounting for the Issuance of New Equity

In the following analysis we recognize that there are often multiple dates associated with equity transactions. We allow for two such dates. The first, termed the *contract date*, is the date at which the "old" common equityholders make a contract with the potential "new" common equityholders. For example, this is the date at which convertible debt, stock warrants, or employee stock options are issued by the firm. The second, termed the *exercise date*, is the date at which new shares are issued to the new common equityholders. The contract and exercise date are the same in simple transactions such as the issuance of new shares for cash. However, in contingent contracts, such as those associated with convertible debt, stock warrants, and employee stock options, the exercise date is later than the contract date. Furthermore, in contingent contracts the timing may depend on the events that occur, and exercise may not ever take place (i.e., the contract may expire before the events are sufficiently favorable to induce the potential "buyer" to exercise his right to "buy").

To simplify the discussion, we assume there is a fixed date $\tau = c$ at which investors believe the firm *may* issue a fixed or contingent claim to equity, and there is a fixed date $\tau = e \geq c$ at which the claim *may* be exercised. We refer to the contract as a contingent claim to equity. The events that result in the exercise of the contingent claim are denoted Y_e^n and the events that do not result in the exercise of that claim are denoted Y_e^o, with $Y_e^n \cup Y_e^o = Y_e$.

---

[7] The proof is essentially the same as the proof of Proposition 9.1.

The total number of shares outstanding at date τ is denoted N_τ. Prior to the exercise date, $N_\tau = N_\tau^o$, which represents the number of shares held by the old (pre-existing) equityholders. If the contingent claim is not exercised, then the number of shares outstanding does not change. However, if the claim is exercised (i.e., $y_e \in Y_e^n$), then $N_\tau = N_\tau^o + N_\tau^n$, for $\tau \geq e$, where N_τ^n is the number of new shares issued.

The total cash dividends paid to all equityholders of record at date τ is denoted d_τ. These dividends all go to the old equityholders prior to the exercise date and after the exercise date if the claim expires. However, the dividend is split between the old and new equityholders after the exercise date if the claim is exercised. We let $d_\tau^o = d_\tau N_\tau^o / N_\tau$ and $d_\tau^n = d_\tau N_\tau^n / N_\tau$ for $\tau \geq e$ and $y_\tau \in Y_e^n$.

Dividends are the only cash flows between the firm and the old equityholders. However, there are other cash flows between the firm and those who acquire equity claims. Let κ_t represent the net non-dividend cash flows between the firm and those who acquire claims to new equity. For example, in the case of a detachable warrant, κ_c is the cash paid for the claim at date c and κ_e is the exercise price paid at date e (contingent on the events that occur). In the case of convertible debt, κ_c is the price paid for the claim at date c and $-\kappa_\tau$ is the interest paid to the debtholders at dates $\tau > c$ (which is equal to zero after date e if the debt is converted to equity).

We now formally define super-clean and mixed surplus accounting.

(1) ***Super-clean Surplus Accounting:***[8] The accounting for the issuance of new equity is defined to be "super-clean" if an equity transaction is only recorded when the equity is issued and the amount recorded equals the market value of the equity issued, i.e., $\delta_c(y_c) = 0$, $\delta_e(y_e) = 0$ if $y_e \in Y_e^o$, and

$$\delta_e(y_e) = v_e^n(y_e) = \sum_{\tau=e+1}^{T} \beta_{\tau e}(y_e)\, \hat{E}[d_\tau^n(y_\tau) | y_e], \quad \text{if } y_e \in Y_e^n.$$

(2) ***Mixed Surplus Accounting:*** If the non-dividend cash flow between the firm and the new equity claimants only occurs at the contract and exercise dates (where either could equal zero), then the accounting is defined to be "mixed" if an initial equity transaction is recorded at the contract date at the *ex ante* market value of the claim, i.e.,

$$\delta_c(y_c) = \beta_{ec}(y_c)\, \hat{E}[v_e^n(y_e) - \kappa_e(y_e) | y_c],$$

---

[8] This term is used by Feltham (1996), but the adoption of essentially the same concept in GAAP is also supported by Ohlson (2000).

and a second equity transaction is recorded at the exercise date at the exercise price, i.e., $\delta_e(y_e) = \kappa_e(y_e)$.

If the accounting is not super-clean or mixed, then it is dirty. Dirty surplus accounting can take many forms. One common form is to only record an equity transaction at the exercise date, but at an amount not equal to the market value of the equity issued, i.e., $\delta_c(y_c) = 0$, $\delta_e(y_e) = 0$ if $y_e \in Y_e^o$, and

$$\delta_e(y_e) \neq v_e^n(y_e), \quad \text{if } y_e \in Y_e^n.$$

Super-clean, mixed, and dirty surplus accounting procedures are quite different, yet each is found among the procedures allowed under GAAP. To illustrate this point, we consider several types of equity transactions. In discussing these accounting procedures it is important to note that the timing at which gains or losses are recorded is immaterial (this does not affect "cleanliness"), it is the timing and amount of recorded direct change in equity that is important.

(a) ***Issuance of New Equity for Non-monetary Goods or Services***: Most issuance of new equity is for cash, with no contingency. In that case, the contract and exercise date are synonymous and super-clean accounting is used, provided the selling price is equal to the current market price. The accounting for the issuance of equity in return for non-monetary goods and services is also super-clean if the transaction is recorded at the market value of the equity issued (irrespective of the perceived value of the goods and services received). For example, U.S. GAAP requires that employee stock grants be recorded at the market value of the stock issued and, hence, the accounting is super-clean.

(b) ***Mergers and Acquisitions.*** The accounting for the issuance of new equity to acquire ownership of another firm's shares is dirty if "pooling" is used (i.e., the new equity is recorded at the book value of the acquired firm's equity), whereas it is super-clean if the transaction is treated as a "purchase" (i.e., the new equity is recorded at the market value of the new equity issued).

(c) ***Detachable Stock Warrants:*** Stock warrants are issued for cash at the contract date. In return, the investors receive call options that give an option-holder the right to purchase additional stock prior to some future date at an exercise price specified at the contract date. U.S. GAAP specifies mixed surplus accounting for detachable stock warrants. That is, the issuance of warrants is treated as an equity transaction, whereas super-clean surplus accounting would require that the issuance of warrants be treated as a debt transaction.

(d) ***Convertible Debt:*** U.S. GAAP does not record an equity transaction when convertible debt is issued, although some authors have called for identification of an equity component. Consequently, GAAP is either super-clean or dirty. The issue is whether the new equity issued at the conversion date is recorded at the book value of the debt at that date (which would be dirty surplus accounting) or at the market value of the equity issued (which would be super-clean surplus accounting).

(e) ***Employee Stock Options:*** Employee stock options are similar to warrants, except they are issued at the contract date in return for an employee's past, current, or future services. U.S. GAAP permits the use of the "intrinsic value method" for employee stock options. This is dirty surplus accounting in which there is no compensation expense (if the exercise price equals the market price at the contract date) and $\delta_e(y_e)$ equals the cash received, i.e., the exercise price). However, SFAS 123 recommends (but does not require) the "fair value method." This is similar to the mixed surplus approach under which the total compensation expense equals the "value" of the option at the contract date (but is allocated over the employee's term of service)[9] and $\delta_e(y_e)$ equals the exercise price. Under super-clean surplus accounting, the net compensation expense equals the difference between the market value and the exercise price at the exercise date, and $\delta_e(y_e)$ equals the market price of the stock at the exercise date.

Earlier we introduced two concepts of current equity. Under the ***pure-equity*** concept, only the shares outstanding are included in current equity, and $v_t^P(y_t)$ represents their value at date t given event y_t. Only the "old" equity is outstanding prior to the exercise date, and the market value of the "old" equity equals the value of the dividends that will be received by those equityholders:

$$v_t^P(y_t) \equiv \sum_{\tau=t+1}^{T} \beta_{\tau t}(y_t)\, \hat{\mathrm{E}}[d_\tau^o(y_\tau)|y_t], \quad \forall\, y_t \in Y_t,\ t = 0,1,...,e\text{-}1. \qquad (9.15a)$$

At and after the exercise date, only the old equity is outstanding if the claim is not exercised, but both the old and new equity are outstanding if the claim is exercised. In either case, the equity outstanding will receive all future dividends:

---

[9] As we have defined mixed surplus accounting, an equity transaction is recorded at the contract date at the value of the options granted. The debit can be to "prepaid compensation," an asset account which is deducted from net income over the employee's term of service. However, under SFAS 123, while the value of the options granted is identified at the contract date, there need be no change in the book value of equity at that date. Instead, the compensation expense is offset by an increase in contributed capital when the expense is recorded.

$$v_t^p(y_t) \equiv \sum_{\tau=t+1}^{T} \beta_{\tau t}(y_t)\, \hat{E}[d_\tau(y_\tau)|y_t], \quad \forall\, y_t \in Y_t,\ t = e,e+1,...,T. \quad (9.15b)$$

If future claims to equity are detachable (e.g., warrants), then the ***mixed-equity*** measure of current equity includes both the common equity currently outstanding plus claims to the future issuance of common equity, and $v_t^m(y_t)$ represents their aggregate value. Prior to the contract date and after the exercise date, there are no future claims outstanding, and $v_t^m(y_t) = v_t^p(y_t)$, as specified in (9.15). However, between the contract and exercise date the value of mixed-equity is

$$v_t^m(y_t) \equiv \sum_{\tau=t+1}^{T} \beta_{\tau t}(y_t)\, \hat{E}[d_\tau(y_\tau)|y_t] - \beta_{et}(y_t)\hat{E}[\kappa_e(y_e)|y_t], \quad (9.16)$$

$$\forall\, y_t \in Y_t,\ t = c,c+1,...,e\text{-}1.$$

The accounting for new equity claims will influence the predicted residual income and book values. See, for example, the earlier discussion of dirty, mixed, and super-clean surplus accounting for employee stock options.

The following proposition establishes that the accounting-based valuation $v_t^\delta(y_t)$, see (9.13), equals the market value of the firm's common equity if the accounting matches the equity concept under either the pure- or mixed-equity measures. (In this analysis, we let $v_e^n(y_e) = \kappa_e(y_e) = 0$ if $y_e \in Y_e^o$, i.e., the claim to new equity has no value and does not result in any cash flow if the claim is not exercised.)

Proposition 9.6 (F96, Prop. 2)

Assume no arbitrage and (9.12) hold.

(a) Under the *pure-equity* measure and *super-clean* surplus accounting,

$$v_t^p(y_t) = v_t^\delta(y_t), \quad \forall\, y_t \in Y_t,\ t = 0,1,...,T\text{-}1.$$

(b) Under the *mixed-equity* measure and *mixed* surplus accounting,

$$v_t^m(y_t) = v_t^\delta(y_t), \quad \forall\, y_t \in Y_t,\ t = 0,1,...,T\text{-}1.$$

Using inconsistent equity and accounting concepts can result in an incorrect value. For example, under the *pure-equity* measure and *mixed* surplus accounting,[10]

$$v_t^P(y_t) = v_t^\delta(y_t), \quad \forall\, y_t \in Y_t,\ t = 0,1,\ldots c\text{-}1, e, e+1, \ldots, T\text{-}1,$$

$$v_t^P(y_t) \begin{Bmatrix} < \\ = \end{Bmatrix} v_t^\delta(y_t), \quad \text{if } \hat{\mathrm{E}}[v_e^n(y_e) - \kappa_e(y_e) | y_t] \begin{Bmatrix} > \\ = \end{Bmatrix} 0,$$

$$\forall\, y_t \in Y_t,\ t = c, c+1, \ldots, e\text{-}1.$$

In addition, dirty surplus accounting will result in an incorrect value with either equity concept. For example, under the *pure-equity* measure and *dirty* surplus accounting (with $\delta_c(y_c) = 0$, $\delta_e(y_e) = 0$ if $y_e \in Y_e^o$, and $\delta_e(y_e) = \kappa_e(y_e)$ if $y_e \in Y_e^n$),

$$v_t^P(y_t) = v_t^\delta(y_t), \quad \forall\, y_t \in Y_t,\ t = e, e+1, \ldots, T\text{-}1.$$

$$v_t^P(y_t) \begin{Bmatrix} < \\ = \end{Bmatrix} v_t^\delta(y_t), \quad \text{if } \hat{\mathrm{E}}[v_e^n(y_e) - \kappa_e(y_e) | y_t] \begin{Bmatrix} > \\ = \end{Bmatrix} 0,$$

$$\forall\, y_t \in Y_t,\ t = 0, 1, \ldots, e\text{-}1.$$

Similarly, under the *mixed-equity* measure and *dirty* surplus accounting,

$$v_t^m(y_t) = v_t^\delta(y_t), \quad \forall\, y_t \in Y_t,\ t = c, c+1, \ldots, T\text{-}1.$$

$$v_t^m(y_t) \begin{Bmatrix} < \\ = \end{Bmatrix} v_t^\delta(y_t), \quad \text{if } \hat{\mathrm{E}}[v_e^n(y_e) - \kappa_e(y_e) | y_t] \begin{Bmatrix} > \\ = \end{Bmatrix} 0,$$

$$\forall\, y_t \in Y_t,\ t = 0, 1, \ldots, c\text{-}1.$$

Observe that while the accounting procedures used in the past influence the current and future accounting numbers, they do not influence the applicability of the accounting-value relation. However, the accounting procedures used in predicting future residual income do influence its applicability. For example, in the three settings considered above, v_t^δ overstates the value of equity if there is a positive probability that the accounting procedures will fail to fully recognize the cost of the new equity that will be issued.

---

[10] The second part of this statement follows from the fact that the value of the new equity, $v_e^n(y_e)$, is greater than or equal to the exercise price, $\kappa_e(y_e)$, at date e for all events in which exercise occurs, $y_e \in Y_e^n$.

9.4.4 Treating Contingent Claims as Debt

To further illustrate the implications of super-clean surplus accounting, we return to the setting in which we assume dividend policy irrelevance and divide the firm's activities into financing and operating activities. To keep the discussion relatively simple, we initially examine detachable stock warrants, and then consider employee stock options.

Under super-clean surplus accounting, warrants are recorded as debt from the contract date until the exercise date, at which time they either expire or are exercised. Assuming net financial assets are marked-to-market (FAM), and assuming the warrants are the only financial asset (debt in this case) provide further structure to the discussion.

The market value of the warrants from the contract date to the exercise date can be expressed as

$$v_t^w(y_t) = \beta_{et}(y_t) \sum_{y_e \in Y_e^n} \hat{\mathrm{E}}[v_e^n(y_e) - \kappa_e(y_e)|y_t], \quad \forall\, y_t \in Y_t,\ t = c, c+1, ..., e.$$

That is, the market value of the warrants equals the discounted risk-adjusted expected difference between the market price of new shares issued and the exercise price paid, for those events in which exercise takes place. Let $-fa_t(y_t)$ represent the book value of the warrants for $y_t \in Y_t$, $t = c, c+1, ..., e-1$. The warrants are recorded as debt at the contract date and we assume the selling price κ_c is equal to the market value of the warrants, so that

$$fa_c(y_c) = -\kappa_c(y_c) = -v_c^w(y_c).$$

Under FAM, the book value of the warrants equals their market values and under FAR the financial income equals the change in market values, i.e.,

$$fi_t(y_t) = fa_t(y_t) - fa_{t-1}(y_{t-1}) = v_{t-1}^w(y_{t-1}) - v_t^w(y_t), \quad \forall\, y_t \subseteq y_{t-1} \in Y_{t-1},\ t = c+1, ..., e.$$

The financial income (to the old equityholders) is positive (negative) if the warrants decrease (increase) in value. The residual financial income is $rfi_t = fi_t - \imath_{t-1} fa_{t-1}$, and it is straightforward to show that FAM is satisfied by these accounting procedures, i.e.,

$$\hat{\mathrm{E}}[rfi_{t+1}|y_t] = 0, \quad \forall\, y_t \in Y_t,\ t = c, c+1, ..., e-1.$$

Observe that at the exercise date, the book value of the warrants, $-fa_e(y_e) = v_e^w(y_e)$, equals zero if the warrants are not exercised (i.e., $y_e \in Y_e^o$), and equals $v_e^n(y_e) - \kappa_e(y_e) > 0$ if they are exercised (i.e., $y_e \in Y_e^n$). In the latter case, upon exercise, the book value of the warrants and cash paid increase the book value of equity by a total of $v_e^n(y_e)$.

Employee stock options are similar to warrants, except that instead of paying cash $\kappa_c(y_c)$ at the contract date, the employee provides labor to operations. There is more than one way to implement super-clean surplus accounting for options. One is to adopt an approach similar to the approach for warrants. Under that approach the "market value" of the options at the contract date[11] is recorded as debt, with a corresponding "transfer" to the operating assets, i.e.,

$$fa_c = fa_{c-1} + oc_c - d_c - v_c^o,$$

$$oa_c = oa_{c-1} + oi_c - oc_c + v_c^o,$$

where v_c^o is the value of the options. The initial value of the options is ultimately recognized as a reduction of operating income, and financial income is ultimately increased by v_c^o if the options are not exercised, or decreased by $v_e^n - \kappa_e - v_c^o$ if they are exercised.

Another approach is to treat the options as an operating liability (a negative operating asset that can be accrued in a variety of ways) and, if the options are exercised at date e, increase operating assets by $v_e^n - \kappa_e$ (i.e., remove the operating liability), financial assets by κ_e, and book value of equity by v_e^n. If the options are not exercised, then the total compensation expense associated with the options is zero, whereas the total compensation expense equals $v_e^n - \kappa_e$ if they are exercised.

The preceding discussion focuses on the use of residual operating income in valuing equity. Recall that using operating cash flows can be interpreted as a special case of the residual operating income model (e.g., CVR is equivalent to OVR if cash accounting is used for operating assets). The analysis in this section implies that if one is using CVR in a setting in which the firm is expected to issue, or has issued, options in return for operating labor, then one *must* treat options as affecting future operating cash flows. For example, the parallel to the second approach described above is to include $\kappa_e - v_e^n$ in the operating cash flows at date e.

---

[11] The term "market value" is in quotes here because its meaning is narrowly defined. The option is not traded, and the value of interest is not the market value that would result if it was made a traded option. As is well-known, the dates and events at which an investor would choose to exercise a traded option differs from the choices that would be made by an employee holding an non-traded option (due to risk aversion and lack of diversification). The value of interest is the market value of a claim that would yield the same cash flows between the owner and the firm as the non-traded employee stock option.

9.4.5 Per-share Calculations

Super-clean surplus accounting treats contingent claims to equity as debt (or an operating liability), whereas GAAP frequently treats the issuance of such claims as an equity transaction. The GAAP treatment leads to the calculation of "fully diluted" earnings-per-share (EPS) in an attempt to recognize the possible impact of contingent claims on the value of the current equityholders' shares. While this approach has some logical consistency, the usual procedures for computing the "fully diluted" EPS fail to adequately reflect the uncertain number of shares that will be issued in the future. Furthermore, it is not clear why one wants to focus on EPS in the first place, since the link between earnings and the value of a unit of stock is at best unclear.

We have established a clear link between the market value of current equity and two types of accounting numbers, i.e., the book values of current equity and risk-adjusted expectations about future residual income. If there is a link between current and future residual income (which we explore in Chapter 10), then that suggests that instead of considering EPS we should consider the book-value-per-share (BVPS) and residual-income-per-share (RIPS). As the following discussion illustrates, this approach has the advantage of permitting us to ignore the diluting effects of the future issuance of equity *if* we have mark-to-market accounting for the contingent claims associated with the issuance of future equity.[12]

To illustrate, again consider the setting in which warrants issued at date c are treated as financial debt (which is the only financial asset), and are recorded at their market value from the contract date to the exercise date. Assume the accounting for operating assets is such that the following linear relation holds:

$$ov_t = oa_t + \pi roi_t,$$

where ov_t is the market value of operating assets. The book value, residual income, and market value per share before and after the warrants are exercised are:

[12] If we do not have mark-to-market accounting, the diluting effects of those claims are handled by recognizing their effect on future residual financial income.

before exercise	after exercise
$\bar{bv}_e^o = \frac{1}{N_e^o}[fa_e + oa_e],$	$\bar{bv}_e = \frac{1}{N_e}[\kappa_e + oa_e],$
$\bar{roi}_e^o = \frac{1}{N_e^o} roi_e,$	$\bar{roi}_e = \frac{1}{N_e} roi_e,$
$\bar{v}_e^o = \bar{bv}_e^o + \pi\,\bar{roi}_e^o,$	$\bar{v}_e = \bar{bv}_e + \pi\,\bar{roi}_e,$

where

$$fa_e = \kappa_e - v_e^n, \qquad v_e^n = \frac{N_e^n}{N_e} v_e.$$

Observe that exercise of the warrants results in an increase in total book value, i.e., $bv_e = bv_e^o + v_e^n = oa + \kappa_e > oa + fa_e$. The increase in total book value is sufficient to more than offset the increase in the total number of shares, so that the book value per share increases. Furthermore, as the following demonstrates, this latter increase precisely offsets the decrease in residual income per share:

$$\bar{v}_e = \frac{1}{N_e}[bv_e + \pi\, roi_e] = \frac{1}{N_e}[bv_e^o + v_e^n + \pi\, roi_e]$$

$$= \frac{1}{N_e}[bv_e^o + N_e^n \bar{v}_e^o + \pi\, roi_e] = \frac{1}{N_e}\left[bv_e^o + \frac{N_e^n}{N_e^o}(bv_e^o + \pi\, roi_e) + \pi\, roi_e\right]$$

$$= \frac{1}{N_e^o}[bv_e^o + \pi\, roi_e] = \bar{v}_e^o.$$

9.5 CONCLUDING REMARKS

This chapter has examined accounting-value relations that relate the current market value of common equity to its current book value plus forecasts of future residual income. These accounting-value relations are based on the no-arbitrage assumption that underlies the dividend-value relations developed in Chapter 6, plus an assumption that the forecasted income (used to compute forecasted residual income) satisfies the clean surplus relation. Observe that this latter condition does not require that the current book value be determined using clean surplus accounting. The key assumption is that all future effects on market value are reflected in the expected income numbers used in computing expected residual income.

The basic model does not assume dividend policy irrelevance. However, separation of the book value of equity into operating assets and financial assets (net of financial liabilities) is particularly useful if the MM conditions for dividend policy irrelevance are satisfied and financial assets are marked-to-market. Under those conditions, the difference between the market and book values of common equity can be represented as the NPV of the risk-adjusted expected residual operating income. This approach is used in Chapter 10, where we explore the relation of the current market value of common equity to its current book value and its current residual income (or accounting income).

Taxes generally result in violation of the MM assumptions underlying dividend policy irrelevance, as do dead-weight bankruptcy costs. The basic accounting valuation model can be applied even if there are taxes and a possibility of bankruptcy. Appendix 9A provides insights into the adaptation of the model to explicitly consider potential tax effects.

APPENDIX 9A: TAX EFFECTS

The assumption that there are no taxes simplifies the discussion, but it is not realistic. The impact of taxes on value relations is a complex issue and, until recently, has received limited attention in the accounting literature. Part of the complexity arises from the differences in tax rates among the individuals and institutions that may acquire the firm's equity and debt. These differences raise issues as to which tax rates influence the market price (i.e., who is the "marginal investor" and what do we mean by arbitrage-free prices). Furthermore, there is a question as to the extent of trading by investors, since trading results in capital gains and losses, which tends to create another layer of taxes.[13]

The analysis in this appendix is not designed to be comprehensive, but to merely illustrate how the introduction of taxes can influence value relations. In our initial analysis we consider the fact that distributions of earnings are taxable in the hands of investors, whereas distributions of contributed capital are not. Then we consider the fact that interest payments are tax deductible for the firm, whereas dividend payments are not. Throughout this analysis we assume there is a single tax clientele for which no arbitrage holds.[14]

---

[13] See Collins and Kemsley (2000) for a discussion of the potential impact of capital gains taxes.

[14] If investors have different tax rates and dividends, interest, and capital gains are taxed differently, then there are no arbitrage-free prices under quite general conditions due to "tax-arbitrage." Restrictions on short-selling (i.e., negative positions) can eliminate tax-arbitrage. In (continued...)

9A.1 Distribution of Earnings and Contributed Capital

In the following discussion we set aside the tax issues associated with debt and consider an all-equity firm, i.e., there are no financial assets. Harris and Kemsley (1999) introduce taxes into the "residual income model" by recognizing that a distribution of earnings is taxed in the hands of investors, whereas a distribution of contributed capital is not. This differential tax effect implies that investors value a dollar of dividends more highly if it is a distribution of contributed capital rather than a distribution of earnings. We expand our model to reflect this distinction. Let $d_t = d_{et} + d_{ct}$, where d_{et} is a taxable distribution of earnings and d_{ct} is a non-taxable distribution of contributed capital. (The latter could be negative, in which case it represents the issuance of new equity.) If investors are taxed on dividends received at the rate χ_d and the implicit prices (including the riskless discount factors) are expressed in terms of dollars available for consumption (i.e., after-tax dollars), then the dividend-value relation is

$$v_t(y_t) = \sum_{\tau=t+1}^{T} \beta_{\tau t}(y_t)\, \hat{\mathrm{E}}[d_{ct} + (1-\chi_d)d_{et} \,|\, y_t].$$

The book value of equity is divided into contributed capital, bv_{ct}, and retained earnings, bv_{et}, and the latter is increased by the firm's after-tax net income, ni_t, so that the clean surplus relation is

$$bv_t = bv_{ct} + bv_{et}, \quad bv_{ct} = bv_{ct-1} - d_{ct}, \quad bv_{et} = bv_{et-1} + ni_t - d_{et}. \qquad (\text{CSR}^{\chi})$$

Observe that after-tax dividends $d_{ct} + (1 - \chi_d)d_{et}$ can be expressed as $(1 - \chi_d)d_t + \chi_d d_{ct}$. Using the previously established relation of d_t to bv_t and ri_t leads to the following value relation (an extension of Propositions 9.1 and 9.2):[15]

[14] (...continued)
that setting, investors invest in different types of securities depending on their tax rates and the composition of the pay-off, i.e., the tax-clientele effect. We assume there is a single type of investor with no restrictions on short-selling, such that the relative prices of securities are arbitrage-free on an after-tax basis for that type of investor.

[15] This relation, while stated slightly differently, is equivalent to Harris and Kemsley's (1999) expression (3). Hanlon *et al.* (2001) has an expression similar to ours.

$$v_t(y_t) = (1 - \chi_d)\left[bv_t + \sum_{\tau=t+1}^{T} \beta_{\tau t}(y_t)\,\hat{E}[ri_\tau|y_t]\right]$$
$$+ \chi_d\left[bv_{ct} - \sum_{\tau=t+1}^{T} \beta_{\tau t}(y_t)\,\hat{E}[\iota_{\tau-1} bv_{c\tau-1}|y_t]\right]. \qquad (9A.1)$$

This relation is essentially the same as accounting-value relation (9.6a) except that the firm's value is restated to reflect the taxes the investors will have to pay when the income is distributed. If there is no contributed capital, then (9.6a) is merely multiplied by one minus the tax rate on dividend income (since all distributions will be taxed). However, if there is current or anticipated contributed capital, then adjustments must be made to reflect the fact that the distribution of contributed capital is not taxed. Of course, delaying that benefit by retaining the contributed capital in the firm results in an implicit cost, and the cost will offset the benefit if distribution of the contributed capital is expected to be deferred indefinitely.[16]

We have assumed that there are no financial assets, so that dividends equal the cash flow from operations. Treating the firm's operating decisions as exogenous, it follows that the total dividends paid are exogenous. However, we can consider the impact of changing the dividend mix. Observe that the total future distribution of contributed capital must equal bv_{ct} and the total future distribution of earnings must equal bv_{et} plus the total future net income.

Consider the impact of the following simple change in dividend policy on the cum-dividend value of the firm's equity, which equals $v_t + d_{ct} + (1 - \chi_d)d_{et}$. Assume a dollar of dividends from contributed capital is paid one period earlier, while a dollar of dividends from retained earnings is paid one period later. That is, d_{ct} and d_{et+1}, $\forall\, y_{t+1} \subseteq y_t$, are each increased by one dollar, while d_{et} and d_{ct+1}, $\forall\, y_{t+1} \subseteq y_t$, are each decreased by one dollar. From (9A.1) it follows that

$$\Delta(v_t + d_{ct} + (1 - \chi_d)d_{et}) = 1 - (1 - \chi_d) - \beta_{t+1,t}(y_t)[1 - (1 - \chi_d)]$$
$$= [1 - \beta_{t+1,t}(y_t)]\chi_d > 0.$$

Hence, it is optimal to distribute the contributed capital prior to distributing earnings. The key here is that delaying the distribution of earnings delays the

---

[16] For example, the second line of (9A.1) equals zero with risk neutrality and a constant interest rate if $d_{c\tau} = 0$, $\forall\, \tau > t$, and $T \to \infty$, since $bv_{c\tau-1} = bv_{ct}$, $\forall\, \tau > t$, and

$$\sum_{\tau=t+1}^{\infty} \beta^{\tau-t}\iota = 1.$$

date at which the tax is paid by investors. Of course, while there are mechanisms for distributing capital, such as share repurchases,[17] firms are largely restricted from distributing capital before distributing earnings.

9A.2 Differential Taxes on Dividends and Interest

We now introduce financial debt (a negative financial asset). Interest payments are tax deductible for the firm, whereas dividend payments are not. However, both interest and dividends received are taxed as income to investors (unless the dividend is a distribution of contributed capital). Assume that the firm's taxable income equals its accounting income,[18] and that the firm's tax rate is χ_f. Also assume that the investors' tax rate on interest income is χ_i and their tax rate on dividend income (except for the distribution of contributed capital) is χ_d.[19]

Again assume the implicit prices are expressed in after-tax dollars and consider borrowing for a single period. The investors must pay taxes on their interest income, so that no arbitrage implies that the interest rate charged to the firm is $\iota_t(y_t)/(1 - \chi_i)$. Consequently, if the firm borrows $-fa_t$ at date t, it repays $-fa_t(1 + \iota_t(y_t)/(1 - \chi_i))$ at date t+1, and the reported financial expense at date t+1 is $-fi_{t+1} = -fa_t\, \iota_t(y_t)/(1 - \chi_i)$.

The firm's before-tax operating income is oi_t and its before-tax interest expense is $-fi_t$, so that the after-tax net income is $ni_t = (1 - \chi_f)[oi_t + fi_t]$. Let oc_t represent the before-tax operating cash flows and let oa_t represent operating assets. Taxes are excluded from the operating accounting relation so that it is again expressed as

$$oa_t = oa_{t-1} + oi_t - oc_t. \tag{OAR}$$

However, taxes are a key element of the financial accounting relation, which is expressed as

$$fa_t = fa_{t-1} + (1 - \chi_f)fi_t + oc_t - \chi_f oi_t - d_t\,. \tag{FAR$^\chi$}$$

[17] Share repurchases are a mechanism for distributing contributed capital and for distributing earnings at the capital gains tax rate instead of the dividend income tax rate, which often differ.

[18] See Amir *et al.* (2000) for a discussion of deferred taxes in the context of the residual income model. Deferred taxes potentially arise in settings in which the timing of taxable income differs from the timing of reported accounting income.

[19] Some countries, such as the U.S., have the same tax rate for interest and dividend income, but many others have different tax rates. For example, a dividend tax credit is used in Canada to mitigate the "double taxation" associated with firm operating income that is distributed to investors as dividends instead of as interest.

The book value of equity again consists of contributed capital and retained earnings, so that

$$bv_t = bv_{ct} + bv_{et} = oa_t + fa_t.$$

Accounting-value relation (9A.1) continues to hold, with

$$ri_t = roi_t + rfi_t,$$

$$roi_t = (1 - \chi_f)oi_t - \imath_{t-1}\, oa_{t-1},$$

$$rfi_t = (1 - \chi_f)fi_t - \imath_{t-1}\, fa_{t-1}.$$

Mark-to-market accounting for financial assets and the no-arbitrage interest rate on debt imply

$$rfi_t = (\chi_i - \chi_f)fa_{t-1}\, \imath_{t-1} /(1 - \chi_i).$$

Hence, the residual financial income equals zero if, and only if, the firm's tax rate equals the investors' tax rate on interest income. If $\chi_f >$ (<) χ_i, then there will be positive (negative) goodwill associated with debt. If the two tax rates are equal, then with respect to tax effects, the equityholders are indifferent between financing with debt or retained earnings.

To illustrate the impact of the tax rates on the choice of dividend policy, consider the impact of borrowing a dollar at date t to distribute it as a dividend from retained earnings. The repayment of the debt plus interest (net of taxes) at t+1 will reduce the dividend from retained earnings at that date (and will have no further impact on future dividends). The impact of this change in dividend policy on the cum-dividend value of the firm is

$$\Delta(v_t + d_{ct} + (1 - \chi_d)d_{et}) = (1 - \chi_d)\{1 - \beta_{t+1,t}\, [1 + (1 - \chi_f)\, \imath_t /(1 - \chi_i)]\}$$

$$= (1 - \chi_d)\beta_{t+1,t}\, [\chi_f - \chi_i]\, \imath_t /(1 - \chi_i).$$

Hence, this change in dividend policy is irrelevant if $\chi_f = \chi_i$, but is desirable if $\chi_f > \chi_i$. That is, it is optimal to borrow to pay dividends if income is taxed more highly within the firm than as interest income in the hands of investors. In this setting, a benefit accrues to the equityholders because the total taxes paid by the firm and investors are reduced by issuing debt and debt is valued on an after-tax basis. Interestingly, the tax rate on dividends does not affect this preference – it only affects the magnitude of the equityholders' after-tax return of the tax advantage from issuing debt.

We have established that paying dividends from contributed capital is preferred to paying dividends from retained earnings, and that borrowing to pay dividends from retained earnings has no cost or benefit if $\chi_f = \chi_i$. Therefore, it is not surprising that financing operations by issuing debt is preferred to issuing new equity (a negative dividend from contributed capital that is not tax deductible at the time of the investment). To illustrate, consider a firm with no capital which undertakes a one-period project that requires $-oc_t$ dollars of capital at date t and will produce oc_{t+1} dollars of cash flow at date t+1. The taxable operating income at date t+1 is $oi_{t+1} = oc_{t+1} + oc_t$. If debt financing is used, $d_{ct} = d_{ct+1} = 0$, $fa_t = oc_t$, $fi_{t+1} = oc_t\, \imath_t /(1 - \chi_i)$, $d_{et+1} = (1 - \chi_f)[fi_{t+1} + oi_{t+1}] = (1 - \chi_f)[oc_{t+1} + (1 + \imath_t /(1 - \chi_i))\, oc_t]$, and the *cum-dividend* value of the firm is

$$V_t(\text{debt}) = \beta_{t+1,t}\,(1 - \chi_d)(1 - \chi_f)[oc_{t+1} + (1 + \imath_t /(1 - \chi_i))\, oc_t].$$

On the other hand, if equity financing is used, then $d_{ct} = oc_t$, $d_{ct+1} = -\, oc_t$, $d_{et+1} = (1 - \chi_f)oi_{t+1}$, and the *cum-dividend* value of the firm is

$$V_t(\text{equity}) = oc_t + \beta_{t+1,t}\{-\, oc_t + (1 - \chi_d)(1 - \chi_f)[oc_{t+1} + oc_t]\}.$$

If $\chi_f = \chi_i$, then

$$V_t(\text{debt}) - V_t(\text{equity}) = -\, \beta_{t+1,t}\, \chi_d\, \imath_t\, oc_t \geq 0.$$

Hence, debt financing is strictly preferred to new equity financing if investors pay taxes on dividend income (and the firm and investors have the same tax rate on interest expenses and income).

Obviously, while firms frequently use some debt financing, there is always some equity. This issue has received considerable attention in the finance literature and will not be explored in this book. It suffices to say that issues of control, moral hazard, bankruptcy, etc. make it optimal for firms' to use a mixture of debt and equity. To simplify the discussion and focus on the issues of interest, we ignore taxes in the subsequent analysis, despite their potential importance in valuation.

REFERENCES

Amir, E., M. Kirschenheiter, and K. Willard. (2000) "The Aggregation and Valuation of Deferred Taxes," Working Paper, Columbia University.

Collins, J. H., and D. Kemsley. (2000) "Capital Gains and Dividend Taxes in Firm Valuation: Evidence of Triple Taxation," *The Accounting Review* 75, 405-427.

Feltham, G. A. (1996) "Valuation, Clean Surplus Accounting, and Anticipated Equity Transactions," Working Paper, University of British Columbia.

Feltham, G. A., and J. A. Ohlson. (1995) "Valuation and Clean Surplus Accounting for Operating and Financial Activities," *Contemporary Accounting Research* 11, 689-731.

Feltham, G. A., and J. A. Ohlson. (1996) "Uncertainty Resolution and the Theory of Depreciation Measurement," *Journal of Accounting Research* 34, 209-234.

Feltham, G. A., and J. A. Ohlson. (1999) "Residual Earnings Valuation With Risk and Stochastic Interest Rates," *The Accounting Review* 74, 165-183.

Hanlon, M., J. Myers, and T. Shevlin. (2001) "Dividend Taxes and Firm Valuation: A Re-Examination," Working Paper, University of Washington.

Harris, T. S., and D. Kemsley. (1999) "Dividend Taxation in Firm Valuation: New Evidence," *Journal of Accounting Research* 37, 275-291.

Lundholm, R., and T. O'Keefe. (2001a) "Reconciling Value Estimates from the Discounted Cash Flow Value Model and the Residual Income Model," *Contemporary Accounting Research* 18, 311-335.

Lundholm, R., and T. O'Keefe. (2001b) "On Comparing Cash Flow and Accrual Accounting Models for Use in Equity Valuation: A Response to Penman 2001," *Contemporary Accounting Research* 18, 693-696.

Miller, M. H., and F. Modigliani. (1961) "Dividend Policy, Growth and the Valuation of Shares," *Journal of Business* 34, 411-433.

Modigliani, F., and M. H. Miller. (1958) "The Cost of Capital, Corporation Finance and the Theory of Investment," *American Economic Review* 48, 655-659.

Ohlson, J. A. (1990) "A Synthesis of Security Valuation Theory and the Role of Dividends, Cash Flows, and Earnings," *Contemporary Accounting Research* 6, 648-676.

Ohlson, J. A. (1995) "Earnings, Book Values, and Dividends in Equity Valuation," *Contemporary Accounting Research* 11, 661-687.

Ohlson, J. A. (2000) "Prescriptions for Improved Financial Reporting," Working Paper, New York University.

Ohlson, J. A. (2001) "Earnings, Book Values, and Dividends in Equity Valuation: An Empirical Perspective," *Contemporary Accounting Research* (forthcoming).

Ohlson, J. A., and X.-J. Zhang. (1998) "Accrual Accounting and Equity Valuation," *Journal of Accounting Research* 36, 85- 111.

Ohlson, J. A., and X.-J. Zhang. (1999) "On the Theory of Forecast Horizon in Equity Valuation," *Journal of Accounting Research* 37, 437-449.

Penman, S. H. (1997) "A Synthesis of Equity Valuation Techniques and the Terminal Value Calculation for the Dividend Discount Model," *Review of Accounting Studies* 2, 303-323.

Penman, S. H. (2001) "On Comparing Cash Flow and Accrual Accounting Models for Use in Equity Valuation: A Response to Lundholm and O'Keefe," *Contemporary Accounting Research* 18, 681-692.

CHAPTER 10

RELATION BETWEEN MARKET VALUES AND CONTEMPORANEOUS ACCOUNTING NUMBERS

There is a broad interest in the relation between the market value of a firm's common equity and the accounting numbers reported by the firm. For example, virtually every business school has a course in financial statement analysis for valuation purposes, and both investors and analysts consider the information in accounting reports when making investment decisions or recommendations. Furthermore, there are a large number of empirical studies in which accounting researchers examine this relation. We do not try to summarize or provide specific references to this literature, but we note that there is a significant subset of this research that seeks to understand how market values relate to contemporaneous accounting numbers.[1] In some cases, the studies assume that, or explore whether, the accounting reports are a source of investor information, whereas in other studies the accounting numbers are merely viewed as representations of investor information.

In this chapter, we are not concerned with the source of the investors' information, only the use of accounting numbers in representing investor information. Accounting policies influence the relation because they affect the representation, but we have no criteria for selecting one representation over another. That is, our analysis merely describes the representational effects of accounting policies – there are no normative statements with respect to what the accounting policies should be.

While accounting empiricists are likely to be more interested in this chapter than in Chapter 9, this chapter is less fundamental and requires the introduction of many more assumptions, which constrain the applicability of the results. Our primary objective in this chapter is to help accounting researchers develop their skills in modeling the factors that are likely to affect the relation between market values and accounting numbers. It is not practical, or even feasible, to construct a general model. Instead, we focus on particular types of economic forces and

---

[1] For recent discussions of many of these types of papers see Holthausen and Watts (2001), Barth, Beaver, and Landsmen (2001), Kothari (2001), and Lee (2001).

how economic events are recorded by the accounting system. Pragmatic issues dictate that we develop parsimonious models that are conjectured to capture the key forces of interest in a particular study. All of the models presented in this chapter should be viewed as illustrative. We encourage accounting researchers (including empiricists) to develop their own models, focusing on the key factors they are exploring.

Throughout this chapter we assume dividend policy irrelevance and represent the market value of the firm's equity as the sum of the value of its financial and operating assets. Financial assets are assumed to be marked-to-market, whereas the operating assets are not. This allows us to ignore the firm's dividend policy and focus on the relation of the market value of the operating assets to representations of the investors' information. This focus reflects our belief that the key role of accounting income (or residual income) in valuation pertains to operating assets, not to financial assets (including financial debt).

As implied by accounting-value relations (9.9) and operating cash flow-value relations (9.10), the value of a firm's operating assets can be represented as the book value of the operating assets plus the NPV of risk-adjusted expected residual operating income or the NPV of risk-adjusted expected operating cash flows.

The key to representing the investors' current value-relevant information is to identify their beliefs about the stochastic relation between past and future flows. Our basic approach is to consider a specific setting in which we posit a set of information dynamics that are assumed to represent investor beliefs. Then we derive the implied relation between the market value of the firm's operating assets and representations of the investors' information. While one can write the information dynamics directly in terms of accounting numbers, as in Ohlson (1995) (Oh95) and Feltham and Ohlson (1995) (FO95), we prefer the approach in Feltham and Ohlson (1996) (FO96).

The direct approach treats the accounting numbers as being generated by a black box, so that it is difficult to examine the impact of accounting policies on the relation between market values and accounting numbers. The FO96 approach, on the other hand, begins with a dynamic model of economic events in which operating cash flows play a central role. In this basic model, there is no direct use of accounting numbers in representing the investors' information. Accounting policies are introduced and applied to the basic model to yield a model in which accounting numbers are used in representing the investors' value-relevant information. Accounting policies can be varied to determine their impact on the relation of market values to contemporaneous accounting numbers in the setting being modeled.

While the valuation models developed in Chapter 9 assume the anticipated life of the firm is finite, the models developed in this chapter assume the anticipated life of the firm is infinite.[2] This allows us to use what are commonly called stationary Markovian models in which the firm's market value is expressed as a time-independent function of a parsimonious representation of the investors' information.

We simplify our discussion by focusing on linear information dynamics, which yield linear value functions. This is common in the literature, and is appealing to empiricists who typically employ linear regression to estimate the parameters of the value function. However, the linearity assumption is not essential, and cannot reflect some phenomena, such as real option effects or firm's adaptive behavior when operations become unprofitable. There have been some non-linear models in the accounting literature, but they are few in number.[3] We anticipate that there will more extensive use of non-linear models in the future.

Our focus on simple linear models limits our representation of market risk. Following the work of Garman and Ohlson (1980) (GO), we illustrate how market risk can be represented and still maintain the linear structure. However, in most of our illustrations we assume risk neutrality (or, equivalently, that the risks are firm-specific and investors are well-diversified). Furthermore, we assume throughout this chapter that the one-period spot interest rates are constant. Empiricists often use Oh05 or FO95 as the motivation for their regression models, but assume that the discount factor is based on a "risk-adjusted cost of capital." As discussed in Chapter 9, this is an *ad hoc* approach to recognizing market risk. In all our illustrations the discount factor is based on the riskless interest rate, as is the capital charge used in determining residual operating income. This applies even in the settings in which we illustrate the impact of market risk.

Section 10.1 describes a set of assumptions that GO establish are sufficient for the existence of a stationary model in which the market value of equity is expressed as a linear function of an n-dimensional statistic representing the investors' information. The basic no-arbitrage conditions that underlie the GO model are the same as in Chapter 9. The stochastic linear information dynamics, which describe investor beliefs about the inter-period relation between statistics, are a key ingredient in deriving the linear relation between market value and the current statistic. GO assume the statistic includes the current dividend, and we illustrate the application of their model by providing a simple example in which dividends are assumed to be auto-regressive. The example illustrates how market risk can be represented and still maintain linearity.

---

[2] Of course, with infinitely lived firms, we must impose transversality conditions that ensure the value of the firm is finite.

[3] See, for example, Yee (2000) and G. Zhang (2000).

While the GO model focuses on information about future dividends, we demonstrate that the model can be readily adapted to focus on information about future residual income. In addition, as in Chapter 9, we assume dividend policy irrelevance and introduce the separation of financial and operating assets, with mark-to-market accounting for financial assets. In this setting the financial dynamics are immaterial, and the linear information dynamics focus on either operating cash flows or residual operating income.

Sections 10.2 and 10.3 provide several examples in which we begin with information dynamics for the operating cash flows and then use accounting numbers in representing the investors' information. This approach allows us to explore how the underlying dynamics and accounting policies affect the relation between the market value of a firm's operating assets and the accounting numbers used in representing the investors' current information. Throughout this analysis we assume the accounting policies affect the representation of the investors' information, but do not affect what the investors know.

The model examined in Section 10.2 is similar to the model in FO96. Cash is invested in a productive asset that generates a persistent, but decaying, stream of net cash receipts. The current cash investments are the primary information about future investments, which may grow over time. The accounting system capitalizes and then depreciates the investments in the operating asset. In the basic model (Section 10.2.1), the value of the operating asset can be expressed as the book value of the operating asset plus multiples of the current residual operating income, the current cash investment, and the start-of-period book value of the operating asset. The current cash investment can be omitted if future investments are expected to have zero NPV, and the start-of-period book value can be omitted if the depreciation rate is the same as the decay rate in cash receipts. Positive NPV investments and aggressive depreciation are two sources of accounting conservatism, which is defined to occur if, in the long run, market value is expected to exceed book value. The basic model assumes risk neutrality, but we conclude Section 10.2.1 with an illustration of how market risk is impounded in the value relation through the use of risk-adjusted coefficients. We also demonstrate that using a risk-adjusted depreciation rate can result in a simple value relation, but also be a source of accounting conservatism.

Section 10.2.2 introduces "other" investor information about the persistence of the cash receipts from past investments and growth in future investments. Accounting accruals can "efficiently" impound this information into the accounting numbers such that the firm's market value equals its book value plus a multiple of its residual operating income. However, this is unlikely, particularly if the firm invests in positive NPV projects.

The existence of "other" information that is not efficiently impounded in the firm's accounting numbers and is not readily observable by researchers creates problems for empiricists. Section 10.2.3 examines the use of analysts' forecasts as a means of inferring the investors' "other" information. The existence of information about both the persistence of cash receipts and growth in positive NPV investments is demonstrated to imply that regression models using one- and two-period-ahead residual income forecasts will place a large positive weight on the latter and a large negative weight on the former.

Section 10.3 modifies the basic capital investment model to examine how other factors affect the relation between market values and accounting numbers. Section 10.3.1 demonstrates that transitory earnings should be omitted from the current residual income (for valuation purposes), since they do not persist into the future. Transitory investments, on the other hand, should not be omitted, but should be considered separately because of their differential effect on beliefs about future investments.

Section 10.3.2 introduces a lag between sales and cash receipts, with "other" information about bad debts. This provides a natural role for accounts receivable, adjusted for an allowance of bad debts, and demonstrates how the associated accounting policy influences the relation between market values and accounting numbers. The analysis also illustrates the impact of treating accounts receivable as a financial asset instead of an operating asset.

Finally, Section 10.3.3 considers research and development (R&D) expenditures, which are a major source of conservatism in accounting. This model has a two-period lag between an R&D expenditure and the initial receipts from that expenditure. In the intervening period, the firm has investments in productive assets which are required to implement the R&D findings. The R&D expenditures are expensed immediately, whereas the investments in productive assets are capitalized and then depreciated. The value relation does not capitalize the R&D, but does use the available information to fully reflect the value of future cash receipts and productive investments generated from prior R&D and the net value of future R&D investments.

Section 10.4 provides some concluding remarks.

10.1 SOME BASICS OF DYNAMIC MODELS

In this section we identify some general aspects of developing dynamic models, and formulate a general linear dynamic model.

10.1.1 Stationary Dividend-value Relation

The discussion in this section follows the dividend-value relation approach of Garman and Ohlson (1980) (GO). Their first four assumptions are effectively the same as those that underlie the no-arbitrage dividend-value relations developed in Chapter 6.

A1. *Perfect Markets:* There are no transaction costs or restrictions on short sales.

A2. *Concordant Expectations:* All investors agree on the current event, the set of possible future events, and the prices and dividends that will obtain for any given event at each date.

A3. *Arbitrage-Free Economy:* There are no arbitrage opportunities.

A4. *Riskless Asset:* There exists a riskless asset that can be traded at each date.

These assumptions yield dividend-value relation (6.15), which we can restate as

$$v_t(y_t) = \beta_{t+1,t}(y_t)\{\mathrm{E}[d_{t+1} + v_{t+1}|y_t] + \mathrm{Cov}[d_{t+1} + v_{t+1}, q_{t+1}|y_t]\}. \qquad (10.1)$$

This form focuses on the relation between the current market value and risk-adjusted expectations with respect to next period's dividend and market value.

As noted in Chapter 9, dividend-value relation (10.1) does not require the investors' beliefs to be homogeneous, but that is not precluded. GO assume the investors' event beliefs are homogeneous.

A5. *Homogeneous Beliefs*: For any given current event, all investors assign the same probability to each future event.

A key aspect of the GO model is to assume $y_t \in Y_t$ (the event representation of the investors' cumulative information at date t) can be replaced with a statistic $\psi_t \in \Psi_t$ (a partial description of the investors' information at date t) that has the following characteristics.

A6. *Markovian Environment:* The statistic ψ_t used to describe the event at each date t is sufficiently complete that the current dividend and the probability of the statistic for the next period depends only on ψ_t. That is, if g_t: $Y_t \rightarrow \Psi_t$ is the function characterizing the statistic, then $d_t(y_t') = d_t(y_t'')$ and $\varphi(\psi_{t+1}|y_t') = \varphi(\psi_{t+1}|y_t'')$ if $g_t(y_t') = g_t(y_t'')$.

A7. *Stationarity:* The market value of the firm's equity and its dividends depend only on the statistic describing the event and not on time. Hence, given A2, the dividend and ex-dividend market value at date t can be expressed as $d(\psi_t)$ and $v(\psi_t)$, respectively. Similarly, the one-period riskless spot rate and the one-period riskless discount factor can be expressed as $\iota(\psi_t)$ and $\beta(\psi_t)$, respectively. Furthermore, the set of possible statistics is independent of t, i.e., $\psi_t \in \Psi$.

The Markovian environment assumption can always be satisfied by using a sufficiently detailed statistic to describe an event. However, the development of tractable models requires the setting to be such that this condition is satisfied by relatively simple statistics. That will be the case in the models that follow. Stationarity is a key simplifying assumption.

The following proposition restates dividend-value relation (10.1). The only difference is that we replace events with the statistics and drop the date subscripts on the value, dividend, and valuation index functions (due to the stationarity assumption).

Proposition 10.1 (GO, Theorem 1)
Assumptions A1-A7 imply that there exists a dvaluation index $q(\psi_{t+1})$ such that the valuation function $v(\psi_t)$ satisfies:[4]

$$v(\psi_t) = \beta(\psi_t)\ \{\mathrm{E}[d(\psi_{t+1}) + v(\psi_{t+1})|\psi_t] \\ + \mathrm{Cov}[d(\psi_{t+1}) + v(\psi_{t+1}), q(\psi_{t+1})|\psi_t]\}. \quad (10.2)$$

10.1.2 A General Linear Dividend Valuation Model

GO and Ohlson (1990) discuss several specific forms of the process by which either dividends or returns are generated. These specific forms are used to develop specific valuation models. Among the most interesting are those that are based on the following relatively strong assumptions introduced by GO.

A8. The statistic is an n-dimensional vector of random variables, $\boldsymbol{\psi}_t = (\psi_{t1},...,\psi_{tn})'$, with $\psi_{t1} = d_t$ representing the net dividend paid to the equityholders at date t.

A9. The dynamics are described by a general linear process of the form:

$$\tilde{\boldsymbol{\psi}}_{t+1} = [\,\boldsymbol{\Omega} + \tilde{\boldsymbol{\Theta}}_{t+1}\,]\boldsymbol{\psi}_t + \boldsymbol{\kappa} + \tilde{\boldsymbol{\varepsilon}}_{t+1}, \quad (10.3)$$

where

[4] We define q slightly differently than GO. In our setting the expected value of q equals one, whereas in GO it equals β.

$\mathbf{\Omega} = [\omega_{ij}]$ = an nxn matrix of "variable" coefficients,

$\tilde{\mathbf{\Theta}}_{t+1} = [\, \tilde{\theta}_{ijt+1}]$ = an nxn matrix of random "variable" coefficients,

$\boldsymbol{\kappa} = [\, \kappa_i \,]$ = an nx1 vector of "fixed" coefficients,

$\tilde{\boldsymbol{\varepsilon}}_{t+1} = [\, \tilde{\varepsilon}_{it+1}]$ = an nx1 vector of random "fixed" coefficients.

The random variables $\tilde{\theta}_{ijt+1}$ and $\tilde{\varepsilon}_{it+1}$ have zero means, and can be correlated with distributions that depend on ψ_t.[5]

A10. The riskless interest rate is independent of ψ_t, i.e., $\imath = \imath(\psi_t)$, $\forall\, \psi_t \in \mathbf{\Psi}$, and the corresponding discount factor is $\beta = [1+\imath]^{-1}$.

A11. The covariances between the valuation index q and the random variables are independent of ψ_t, i.e., $\forall\, \psi_t \in \mathbf{\Psi}$,

$$\mathrm{Cov}[\tilde{\theta}_{ijt+1}, \tilde{q}_{t+1} \,|\, \psi_t] \equiv -\,\sigma_{\theta ij},$$

$$\mathrm{Cov}[\, \tilde{\varepsilon}_{it+1}, \tilde{q}_{t+1} \,|\, \psi_t] \equiv -\,\sigma_{\varepsilon i}.$$

GO then demonstrate that these assumptions result in a linear value function.

Proposition 10.2 (GO, Theorem 2)
Under assumptions A1-A11, there exist constants $\boldsymbol{\pi} = (\pi_0, \pi_1, \ldots, \pi_n)^t$ such that:

$$v(\psi_t) = \pi_0 + \sum_{i=1}^{n} \pi_i \psi_{ti}. \tag{10.4}$$

Linear value function (10.4) is the solution to (10.2) using the assumed linear dynamics (10.3). The Markovian environment allows us to express the firm's market value at date t as a function of the statistic ψ_t. The linearity of that function depends crucially on the fact that the dynamics are assumed to be linear, the interest rate is assumed to be constant, and the effect of market risk

[5] While the random variables at date t+1 can be correlated with distributions that depend on ψ_t, they cannot be correlated with the random variables at date t except through their effect on ψ_t. That is, any inter-temporal correlations must be explicitly modeled.

takes the form assumed in A11.[6] The stationarity assumption (which includes the fact that the parameters $\mathbf{\Omega}$, $\boldsymbol{\kappa}$, $\sigma_{\theta ij}$, and $\sigma_{\varepsilon i}$ are time independent) then implies that the value function coefficients are independent of the valuation date.

Of course, the statistic $\boldsymbol{\psi}_t$ can include elements that are given zero weight. For example, π_i will equal zero if $\mathrm{E}[d_\tau|\boldsymbol{\psi}_t]$ and $\mathrm{Cov}[d_\tau,q_\tau|\boldsymbol{\psi}_t]$ are independent of ψ_{ti} for all $\tau > t$. This suggests a criteria for deciding which information is "value-relevant." However, one must be careful in making such inferences because the weights may not be unique for a given vector $\boldsymbol{\psi}_t$, and the vector used as a sufficient statistic to represent the event y_t is never unique. If there are multiple solutions, then some solutions may assign zero weights to ψ_{ti}, while others assign non-zero weights. And even if all solutions assign zero weights to π_i for a given vector $\boldsymbol{\psi}_t$, there is still a possibility that changing other elements of the vector can result in an alternative sufficient statistic in which π_i is non-zero.

10.1.3 A Simple Auto-regressive Dividend Model

To illustrate the derivation of (10.4), we consider a simple setting in which the linear dividend dynamics are auto-regressive.[7] That is, we assume dividends follow a simple random walk, with both multiplicative and additive random variations in dividends. These random variations play two roles. First, they introduce uncertainty such that the current dividend provides new information about future dividends. Second, the correlation of these random variations with the valuation index introduces adjustments for market risk.

In this model, we assume the current dividend and valuation index are the only elements in the statistic (i.e., $n = 2$ and $\psi_t = (d_t, q_t)$), and the linear dynamics are

$$\tilde{d}_{t+1} = [\omega + \tilde{\theta}_{d,t+1}]d_t + \tilde{\varepsilon}_{d,t+1},$$

$$\tilde{q}_{t+1} = \tilde{\varepsilon}_{q,t+1}.$$

Consistent with A11, the covariances with the valuation index q are assumed to be

[6] Assumption A10 holds if there is at least one risk-neutral investor, and all risk-neutral investors have preferences characterized by constant marginal rates of substitution from one period to next. However, the basic theory in Chapters 6 and 9 suggest that market risk is likely to result in stochastic interest rates. Nonetheless, we follow GO and assume a constant interest rate even if there is market risk, since that significantly simplifies the analysis.

[7] This example was introduced by Rubinstein (1976) and has been used by Ohlson (1979) and GO.

$$\mathrm{Cov}[\tilde{\theta}_{d,t+1}, \tilde{q}_{t+1} | \psi_t] = \mathrm{Cov}[\tilde{\theta}_{d,t+1}, \tilde{\varepsilon}_{q,t+1} | \psi_t] = -\sigma_\theta,$$

$$\mathrm{Cov}[\tilde{\varepsilon}_{d,t+1}, \tilde{q}_{t+1} | \psi_t] = \mathrm{Cov}[\tilde{\varepsilon}_{d,t+1}, \tilde{\varepsilon}_{q,t+1} | \psi_t] = -\sigma_\varepsilon.$$

We now derive the coefficients of the linear value function[8]

$$v(d_t) = \pi_0 + \pi_1 d_t.$$

Proposition 10.2 establishes that the value function is linear, and we can substitute it into dividend-value relation (10.2) to obtain

$$\pi_0 + \pi_1 d_t = \beta\{ [\omega d_t + (\pi_0 + \pi_1 \omega d_t)] - [\sigma_\theta\, d_t + \sigma_\varepsilon + \pi_1(\sigma_\theta d_t + \sigma_\varepsilon)] \}.$$

The terms *not* containing d_t imply[9]

$$\pi_0 = \beta\, [\pi_0 - \sigma_\varepsilon(1 + \pi_1)]\,, \tag{10.5a}$$

while the terms containing d_t imply

$$\pi_1 = \beta\{\omega + \pi_1\omega - \sigma_\theta - \pi_1\sigma_\theta\}. \tag{10.5b}$$

This gives us two linear equations in two unknowns. Solving (10.5) for π_0 and π_1 establishes that

$$\pi_0 = -\frac{1}{\iota}\frac{R}{R - (\omega - \sigma_\theta)}\sigma_\varepsilon\,, \tag{10.6a}$$

$$\pi_1 = \frac{\omega - \sigma_\theta}{R - (\omega - \sigma_\theta)}, \tag{10.6b}$$

where $R = \beta^{-1} = 1 + \iota$. Hence, the current market value is a linear function of current dividends, with a negative intercept π_0 if there is additive systematic risk with $\sigma_\varepsilon > 0$. The multiple of current dividends is a discounted, "risk-adjusted"

[8] The current valuation index q_t is omitted because the assumed dynamics imply the current index provides no information about future dividends and valuation indices.

[9] The general principle used here is to "match coefficients." This principle is applicable (not only for linear functions) whenever the n-dimensional statistic ψ_t can take on any value in an n-dimensional subset of $\mathbb{R}^n$.

growth term.[10] Observe that risk neutrality (i.e., $\sigma_\theta = \sigma_\varepsilon = 0$) implies $\pi_0 = 0$ and $\pi_1 = \omega/(R - \omega)$.

The dividend dynamics are specified using the "true" probabilities. However, we could equivalently state the dividend dynamics using the risk-neutral probabilities. Observe that $\mathrm{E}[\tilde{\theta}_{d,t+1}|\psi_t] = \mathrm{E}[\tilde{\varepsilon}_{d,t+1}|\psi_t] = 0$ whereas $\hat{\mathrm{E}}[\tilde{\theta}_{d,t+1}|\psi_t] = -\sigma_\theta$ and $\hat{\mathrm{E}}[\tilde{\varepsilon}_{d,t+1}|\psi_t] = -\sigma_\varepsilon$.[11] Hence, if we let

$$\tilde{\theta}^q_{d,t+1} \equiv \tilde{\theta}_{d,t+1} + \sigma_\theta, \quad \tilde{\varepsilon}^q_{d,t+1} \equiv \tilde{\varepsilon}_{d,t+1} + \sigma_\varepsilon, \quad \tilde{q}^q_{t+1} \equiv 1,$$

we can express the dynamics in terms of a risk-adjusted growth term $\omega - \sigma_\theta$ and a risk-adjusted intercept $-\sigma_\varepsilon$, i.e.,

$$\tilde{d}_{t+1} = [\omega - \sigma_\theta + \tilde{\theta}^q_{d,t+1}]d_t - \sigma_\varepsilon + \tilde{\varepsilon}^q_{d,t+1},$$

$$\hat{\mathrm{E}}[\tilde{d}_{t+1}|\psi_t] = [\omega - \sigma_\theta]d_t - \sigma_\varepsilon,$$

$$\hat{\mathrm{Cov}}[\tilde{\theta}^q_{d,t+1}, \tilde{q}^q_{t+1}|\psi_t] = \hat{\mathrm{Cov}}[\tilde{\varepsilon}^q_{d,t+1}, \tilde{q}^q_{t+1}|\psi_t] = 0.$$

This provides exactly the same intercept and multiple on current dividends as in (10.6).

The two approaches are equivalent not only in this simple example but also for general information dynamics. In most of the literature on linear information dynamics it is assumed that investors are risk neutral. According to the latter approach we may interpret the results in that literature as applicable to settings with risk aversion by assuming that the information dynamics are stated for the risk-neutral probabilities. The problem, of course, is that the parameters in the information dynamics with risk-neutral probabilities cannot be empirically estimated using time-series data for the information variables – only the parameters under the "true" probabilities can be estimated in this way. However, a procedure commonly followed in the finance literature is to use market prices

---

[10] GO point out that in this example, if $\sigma_\varepsilon = 0$, then the model is equivalent to the expected dividend-capitalization model:

$$v_t = \sum_{\tau=t+1}^{\infty} \hat{R}^{t-\tau}\mathrm{E}[\tilde{d}_\tau|d_t],$$

where $\hat{R} - 1 = R\omega/(\omega - \sigma_\theta) - 1$ is the "risk-adjusted cost-of-capital."

[11] This follows from the fact that the valuation index is the ratio of the (conditional) risk-neutral probabilities to the "true" probabilities (see Chapter 5), e.g.,

$$\mathrm{Cov}[\tilde{\theta}_{t+1}, \tilde{q}_{t+1}|\psi_t] = \mathrm{E}[\tilde{\theta}_{t+1}\tilde{q}_{t+1}|\psi_t] = \mathrm{E}[\tilde{\theta}_{t+1}\frac{\hat{\varphi}_{t+1}}{\varphi_{t+1}}|\psi_t] = \hat{\mathrm{E}}[\tilde{\theta}_{t+1}|\psi_t].$$

of tradable claims depending on the same information variables to "back out" the parameters in the risk-neutral process assuming that the valuation model is correct. In most of the analysis in this chapter we assume investors are risk neutral, but bear in mind that the results also hold with risk aversion provided the information dynamics are stated under the risk-neutral probabilities.

Observe that the risk-neutral probability approach does not involve an adjustment to the discount factor. We continue to discount using the riskless interest rate – *not a risk-adjusted cost of capital.*[12]

10.1.4 Stationary Accounting-value Relations

The statistic in dividend-value relation (10.2) can include accounting numbers, so that (10.2) can be used to identify the relation between market values and contemporaneous accounting numbers. However, in the subsequent analysis in this chapter, it is useful to use the accounting-value relations developed in Chapter 9 as the foundation for our stationary accounting-based valuation models.

Residual Income Model

We know from Chapter 9 that, instead of discounting the risk-adjusted expected dividends, we can express the market value of equity as the current book value plus the NPV of the risk-adjusted expected residual income. The GO model can be readily adapted to use this accounting approach by replacing dividends with the current book value of equity (*bv*) and current residual income (*ri*) in the Markovian environment and stationarity assumptions. There then exists a value function $v(\psi_t)$ such that[13]

$$v(\psi_t) = bv(\psi_t) + \beta(\psi_t)\{\,\mathrm{E}[ri(\psi_{t+1}) + v(\psi_{t+1}) - bv(\psi_{t+1})\,|\,\psi_t]$$

$$+ \mathrm{Cov}[ri(\psi_{t+1}) + v(\psi_{t+1}) - bv(\psi_{t+1}),\, q(\psi_{t+1})\,|\,\psi_t]\,\}. \qquad (10.7)$$

---

[12] Ang and Liu (2001) extend the analysis to settings with both risk aversion and stochastic interest rates. They demonstrate that there is a linear relation between market value and accounting numbers if the stochastic interest rates are uncorrelated with the accounting variables. However, the relation is non-linear if the accounting variables are correlated with the interest rates.

[13] This relation can be viewed as a corollary to Proposition 10.1 since (10.7) can be derived directly from (10.2) based on the fact that the clean surplus relation implies

$$\beta(\psi_t)d(\psi_{t+1}) = \beta(\psi_t)[bv(\psi_t) + ni(\psi_{t+1}) - bv(\psi_{t+1})]$$

$$= bv(\psi_t) + \beta(\psi_t)[\,ni(\psi_{t+1}) - \imath(\psi_t)bv(\psi_t) - bv(\psi_{t+1})].$$

Also observe that (10.7) is similar to the truncated value relation (9.11b) with $\check{T} = t+1$.

If we also modify assumption A8, so that bv_t and ri_t are elements of the statistic ψ_t, then we can use (10.3) and (10.7) to derive the parameters of the value function (10.4). To illustrate, we consider another simple example. We assume risk neutrality (so that the valuation index q is a constant equal to one) and the statistic consists of the current book value and current residual income, i.e., $\psi_t = (bv_t, ri_t)$. To keep the model very simple, we adopt Oh95's assumption that residual income is auto-regressive, i.e., the current book value has no effect on investors' beliefs about future residual income. This makes the book value dynamics irrelevant, but, for completeness, we include book value dynamics similar to FO95. In particular, we assume

$$\tilde{ri}_{t+1} = \omega_{rr} ri_t + \tilde{\varepsilon}_{r,t+1}, \qquad (10.8a)$$

$$\tilde{bv}_{t+1} = \omega_{bb} bv_t + \tilde{\varepsilon}_{b,t+1}, \qquad (10.8b)$$

where $\omega_{rr} \in (0,1)$ is the persistence in residual income and $\omega_{bb} \in (0,R)$ is one plus the expected growth rate in book value.

From Proposition 10.2, the general form of the linear value function is

$$v(\psi_t) = \pi_0 + \pi_{bv} bv_t + \pi_{ri} ri_t. \qquad (10.9)$$

Using (10.8) and (10.9) in (10.7) yields

$$\pi_0 + \pi_{bv} bv_t + \pi_{ri} ri_t = bv_t + \beta\, [\omega_{rr} ri_t + \pi_0 + \pi_{ri}\omega_{rr} ri_t + (\pi_{bv} - 1)\omega_{bb} bv_t].$$

Collecting the constant, book value, and residual income terms yields the following three equations in three unknowns:

$$\pi_0 = \beta \pi_0,$$

$$\pi_{bv} = 1 + \beta\, (\pi_{bv} - 1)\omega_{bb},$$

$$\pi_{ri} = \beta\, [\omega_{rr} + \pi_{ri}\omega_{rr}].$$

Hence, $\pi_0 = 0$, $\pi_{bv} = 1$, and $\pi_{ri} = \omega_{rr}/(R - \omega_{rr})$, so that

$$v(\psi_t) = bv_t + \frac{\omega_{rr}}{R - \omega_{rr}} ri_t. \qquad (10.10)$$

Oh95 demonstrates that (10.10) can be used to restate the value function in terms of current book value, current net income, and current dividends. This is accomplished by using the fact that $ri_t \equiv ni_t - \iota bv_{t-1}$ and the clean surplus relation $bv_{t-1} = bv_t + d_t - ni_t$ in (10.10) to obtain

$$v_t = (1 - k)bv_t + k(\xi\, ni_t - d_t), \qquad (10.11)$$

where $k = \iota\pi_{ri}$ and $\xi \equiv R/\iota$.

Value relation (10.11) has received much attention in the empirical literature because of its simplicity and the fact that it can be viewed as the weighted average of two basic value models. The first is based on book value, which will, in the limit, receive a weight of one if $\omega_{rr} \rightarrow 0$, i.e., there is no persistence in the residual income. This is the case if we have mark-to-market accounting, such as in the case of a portfolio of marketable securities – the random "excess" return is not persistent. The second is based on net income, with an adjustment for current dividends. The dividend adjustment merely reflects the fact that the cum-dividend value, $v_t + d_t$, is a multiple of net income, $\xi\, ni_t$, if, in the limit, $\omega_{rr} \rightarrow 1$.

It is perhaps surprising that the growth in book value is irrelevant in (10.10) and (10.11). The key to this aspect of those results is that the dynamics in (10.8) imply the accounting is such that the expected future residual income is independent of the current book value. The difference between the current market and book values is attributable to the NPV of the expected future residual income, and (10.8) implies that those expectations depend only on the current residual income, i.e., residual income is auto-regressive. This value relation, from Oh95, has been widely used in empirical research, but it holds only under some very strong assumptions about the firm's accounting policies. We provide more insight into this in subsequent sections.

Separation of Financial and Operating Assets

If we assume dividend policy irrelevance and mark-to-market accounting for financial assets, then we do not need to model the dynamics that determine future financial assets or future financial income. That is, the model can focus on the dynamics that determine the market value of the operating assets. This can be based on the dynamics for operating cash flows by expressing the Markovian environment and stationarity assumptions in terms of time-independent functions for operating cash flows (*oc*) and market value of operating assets (*vo*). In that case, there exists an operating asset value function that satisfies[14]

[14] Relation (10.12) can be viewed as a corollary to Proposition 10.1 – the operating assets are merely a specific asset to which (10.2) can be applied, and for which the operating cash flows represent the dividends "paid" by that asset.

$$v(fa_{t,}\psi_t) = fa_t + vo(\psi_t) = fa_t + \beta(\psi_t)\{\,\mathrm{E}[oc(\psi_{t+1}) + vo(\psi_{t+1})\ |\psi_t]$$

$$+ \mathrm{Cov}[oc(\psi_{t+1}) + vo(\psi_{t+1}), q(\psi_{t+1})|\psi_t]\,\}. \quad (10.12)$$

Alternatively, the Markovian environment and stationarity assumptions can be expressed in terms of the book value of the operating assets (*oa*), residual operating income (*roi*), and market value of operating assets (*vo*). In that case, if we assume OAR (i.e., $oa_{t+1} = oa_t + oi_{t+1} - oc_{t+1}$), then there exists an operating asset value function that satisfies[15]

$$v(fa_{t,}\psi_t) = fa_t + vo(\psi_t)$$

$$= fa_t + oa_t(\psi_t) + \beta(\psi_t)\{\,\mathrm{E}[roi(\psi_{t+1}) + vo(\psi_{t+1}) - oa(\psi_{t+1})|\psi_t]$$

$$+ \mathrm{Cov}[roi(\psi_{t+1}) + vo(\psi_{t+1}) - oa(\psi_{t+1}), q(\psi_{t+1})|\psi_t]\,\}. \quad (10.13)$$

In the subsequent discussion in this chapter we focus on the operating asset value function. We typically begin by assuming there exist dynamics that satisfy A9 for which the operating cash flows oc_t is one of the elements of the statistic ψ_t (or, equivalently, the components of oc_t are elements of ψ_t). We then use (10.3) and (10.12) to derive a linear value function of the form

$$v(fa_t, \psi_t) = fa_t + \pi_0 + \sum_{i=1}^{n} \pi_i \psi_{ti}. \quad (10.14)$$

In this initial model, we assume the investors' information is represented by a statistic that does not contain accounting numbers *per se*. This then allows us to introduce accounting policies which generate accounting numbers that are used to generate an alternative representation of the investors' information. The accounting-based statistic is represented by ψ_t^a and the revised linear value function is expressed as

$$v(fa_t, \psi_t^a) = fa_t + \alpha_0 + \sum_{i=1}^{N} \alpha_i \psi_{ti}^a, \quad (10.15)$$

where N is the number of elements in ψ_t^a.

---

[15] Again, relation (10.13) is a corollary to Proposition 10.1, for reasons similar to (10.7) and (10.12).

Observe that value function (10.15) can be derived by specifying the dynamics for the accounting-based statistic ψ_t^a (assuming it includes oa_t and roi_t) and then using (10.3) with (10.13). However, in some examples, it is straightforward to obtain (10.15) from (10.14).

10.2 A CAPITAL INVESTMENT MODEL

We now explore a capital investment model introduced by (FO96). A key feature of this analysis is that in the basic model the statistic representing investor information does not involve accounting numbers. However, we develop alternative statistics that involve accounting numbers based on explicit accounting policies.

In Section 10.2.1, the statistic for the basic model consists of cash receipts from operations and cash investments in operating assets. The role of accounting numbers is limited here, but we still obtain useful insights into the impact of conservative accounting in a setting in which there is growth in investment opportunities. Section 10.2.2 introduces "other" investor information about future persistence of cash receipts and future growth in investment opportunities. This expands the potential role of accounting numbers in that they can parsimoniously impound the "other" information. Generally accepted accounting policies do not produce accounting numbers that fully reflect the investors' "other" information. In Section 10.2.3 we consider the use of analysts' earnings forecasts as a means of inferring the "other" investor information not reflected in the current accounting numbers.

Throughout this section we assume dividend policy irrelevancy, separation of financial and operating activities, and mark-to-market accounting for financial assets. The market value of the firm's equity is expressed as the sum of the market value of the financial assets plus a linear value function for the operating assets. The statistic includes either the operating cash flow or the book value of operating assets and the residual operating income, so that the value function is derived from either (10.12) or (10.13), as represented by (10.14) or (10.15). The impact of market risk is illustrated at the end of Section 10.2.1. However, to focus on the impact of accounting policies, we generally assume risk neutrality (i.e., either the valuation index q_t is a constant, or investors are well-diversified and the random variables in the information dynamics are not correlated with the valuation index).

10.2.1 Capital Investment and Depreciation

The model in this section is a simplified version of the FO96 model.

The Basic Cash Flow Dynamics

As in FO96, we assume the "free" operating cash flows have two components: cash receipts from operations, cr_t, and cash investments, ci_t. The cash investments depend on the investment opportunities at any given date, and we assume current investments are the only relevant information about future investments. Cash receipts represent the difference between the receipts and expenditures that vary with sales resulting from implementation of past investment opportunities. Current cash receipts are the only relevant information about future cash receipts from past investments, whereas current investments are the only relevant information about future cash receipts from current and future investments. These relations are depicted by the following linear information dynamics (LID1):[16]

$$\tilde{cr}_{t+1} = \omega_{rr} cr_t + \omega_{ri} ci_t + \tilde{\varepsilon}_{rt+1}, \qquad \text{(LID1a)}$$

$$\tilde{ci}_{t+1} = \omega_{ii} ci_t + \tilde{\varepsilon}_{it+1}, \qquad \text{(LID1b)}$$

where $\omega_{rr} \in (0,1)$ is the persistence in the cash receipts from prior investments, $\omega_{ri} > 0$ is the expected cash receipts in period t+1 from a dollar invested at date t, and $\omega_{ii} \in [0,R)$ is one plus the expected growth (or decay, if negative) in investment opportunities. Applying operating cash flow-value relation (10.12), with risk neutrality, yields the following value function.

Proposition 10.3 (FO96, Prop. 1)

Risk neutrality, a constant interest rate, LID1, and (10.12) imply

$$v_t = fa_t + \pi_{cr} cr_t + \pi_{ci} ci_t, \qquad (10.16)$$

where

$$\pi_{cr} \equiv \Phi_r \omega_{rr}, \qquad \Phi_r \equiv [R - \omega_{rr}]^{-1},$$

$$\pi_{ci} \equiv R\lambda\Phi_i + 1, \qquad \Phi_i \equiv [R - \omega_{ii}]^{-1}, \qquad \lambda \equiv \Phi_r \omega_{ri} - 1.$$

A proof is provided in Appendix 10A – it is similar to the approach used to derive value function (10.10), but based on (10.12) instead of (10.7).

We assume the NPV of a dollar of investment is non-negative, and allow for it to be either zero or strictly positive. The valuation model is particularly simple if all investments have zero NPV.

---

[16] We refer to this as LID1 since it is our initial linear information dynamics and we will introduce alternative dynamics in subsequent sections.

Corollary

If $\Phi_r\omega_{ri} = 1$, then $v_t = fa_t + \Phi_r\omega_{rr}cr_t + ci_t$.

That is, in the zero NPV setting, value is attributable to expected cash receipts that are still to be generated as a result of prior investments ($\Phi_r\omega_{rr}cr_t$) plus the amount invested in the current period (ci_t).

An Accounting Model with Depreciation of Capital Investments

In our simple capital investment model, the financial assets, cash receipts, and cash investments constitute a sufficient statistic for the investors' information. There is no need for (accrual) accounting information. Nonetheless, it is instructive to consider an accounting representation of the same information. In this simple setting, we treat the cash receipts as net revenue of the period, capitalize investments, and then depreciate those investments. Furthermore, the accounting policy is such that the depreciation expense in period t is a fixed fraction $1\text{-}\delta$ of the date t-1 book value of plant & equipment (pe_{t-1}), which is the only operating asset in this setting, i.e., $dep_t = (1\text{-}\delta)pe_{t-1}$. Hence, the accounting relations for operating activities are:

$$oa_t = pe_t = pe_{t-1} + ci_t - dep_t = \delta pe_{t-1} + ci_t,$$

$$oi_t = cr_t - dep_t = cr_t - (1\text{-}\delta)pe_{t-1},$$

$$roi_t = cr_t - (R\text{-}\delta)pe_{t-1}.$$

Observe that while ω_{rr} is the persistent rate for the cash receipts, δ is the persistence rate for the book value of plant & equipment (and for the depreciation and capital charge based on that book value). If the accounting policy parameter δ equals ω_{rr}, then all components of residual income persist at the same rate, but if they are not equal, then cr_t and $(R\text{-}\delta)pe_{t-1}$ persist at different rates. As illustrated by the following proposition, the choice of δ significantly affects the relation between market values and accounting numbers.

Proposition 10.4 (FO96, Prop. 2)

Risk neutrality, a constant interest rate, LID1, (10.13), and declining balance depreciation at rate $1\text{-}\delta$ imply

$$v_t = fa_t + pe_t + \alpha_{roi}roi_t + \alpha_{pe}pe_{t-1} + \alpha_{ci}ci_t, \tag{10.17}$$

where

$$\alpha_{roi} \equiv \Phi_r\omega_{rr}, \quad \alpha_{pe} \equiv R\Phi_r(\omega_{rr} - \delta), \quad \alpha_{ci} \equiv \lambda R\Phi_i.$$

An approach similar to the proof of Proposition 10.3 can be used here and in developing the accounting-value relations in the remainder of this chapter. Appendix 10A describes the key elements of the proof of (10.17), but we leave subsequent proofs to the reader.

Observe that α_{roi} is the same as π_{cr} in the cash flow model. This weight is assigned to the residual operating income, and it reflects the persistence of the operating cash receipts from prior investments. This rate of persistence also applies to the depreciation expense plus capital charge if $\delta = \omega_{rr}$, in which case $\alpha_{pe} = 0$ and the start-of-period book value is irrelevant. However, if $\delta \neq \omega_{rr}$, then an adjustment must be made for the fact that the weight applied to residual income is "not correct" for all its components. This leads to an adjustment of $\alpha_{pe} pe_{t-1}$.

This latter adjustment can be avoided if a "line-item" approach is adopted with respect to residual operating income. In this simple model there are two components of residual operating income that can persist at different rates: the cash receipts and the depreciation expense plus capital charge. Separating these two components yields the following "line-item" model:

$$v_t = fa_t + pe_t + \{\alpha_{cr} cr_t - \alpha_{dep}[dep_t + \imath pe_{t-1}]\} + \alpha_{ci} ci_t, \qquad (10.17')$$

where $\alpha_{cr} \equiv \alpha_{roi}$, $\alpha_{dep} \equiv \Phi_\delta \delta$, and $\Phi_\delta \equiv [1 + \imath - \delta]^{-1}$. The weight assigned to the depreciation expense plus capital charge reflects that their persistence depends on the depreciation parameter δ. Of course α_{dep} is the same as α_{cr} if $\delta = \omega_{rr}$, in which case the components of residual operating income can be aggregated.

The weight assigned to the capital investment can be expressed as

$$\alpha_{ci} = \Phi_r \omega_{ri} + \lambda \Phi_i \omega_{ii} - 1 = \pi_{ci} - 1,$$

which is the same weight as in the cash flow model except for the deduction of ci_t, which is already included in pe_t. This weight equals zero if $\lambda = 0$, which occurs if these are zero NPV investments.

The preceding comments make it obvious that the value relation is simplified if the depreciation rate corresponds to the decay rate for the cash receipts, and all investments are zero NPV. In this simple case, the market value of equity is equal to the sum of the book value of equity plus a multiple of current residual operating income.[17]

---

[17] As we discuss in Section 10.2.2, Ohlson and Zhang (1998) define the accounting to be "efficient" if the market value can be expressed as book value plus a multiple of residual income.

Corollary

If $\delta = \omega_{rr}$ and $\lambda = 0$, then

$$v_t = fa_t + pe_t + \alpha_{roi} roi_t = fa_t + (1 - k)pe_t + k[\xi\, oi_t - oc_t], \qquad (10.18)$$

where $k = \iota\, \alpha_{roi}$ and $\xi = R/\iota$.

Observe that (10.18) is similar to the value relations for the simple autoregressive model from Oh95 that is described in Section 10.1.4 (see expressions (10.10) and (10.11)). A key difference is that in (10.18) the book value of equity is separated into its financial and operating components, and the residual financial income is ignored because it is not persistent. To obtain full equivalence of this basic FO96 model with the basic Oh95 model requires investment of the financial assets in the riskless asset (so that the realized residual financial income equals zero), as well as requiring investments to have zero NPV and a depreciation rate equal to the decay rate in operating cash flows from prior investments. This illustrates the strong assumptions implicit in the Oh95 model.

Conservative Accounting

Now consider how the accounting policy affects the relation between the market and book value of the firm's operating assets. We take as given that the accounting system capitalizes investment expenditures and makes no attempt to reflect information about future positive NPV investments in the current book value of the operating assets. Therefore, unless the firm only invests in zero NPV investments, it follows that the book value will tend to be less than the market value. Furthermore, the book value of past investments equals the original investment minus cumulative depreciation, and no attempt is made to adjust the book value for changes in market value due to random variations in the cash receipts generated by those investments. These variations may be positive or negative, implying that even if the investments have zero NPV *ex ante*, the current market value can be either greater or less than current book value. Furthermore, if the depreciation rate exceeds the decay rate in cash receipts, the current book value of prior investments will tend to be less than their market value. The following discussion examines these relations more formally.

The difference between current market value and current book value is referred to as unrecorded goodwill, and it is entirely attributable to the discounted expected residual operating income. For example, if residual income is autoregressive (which occurs if $\delta = \omega_{rr}$ and $\lambda = 0$), then

$$gw_t \equiv v_t - bv_t = \Phi_r \omega_{rr} roi_t.$$

At any date t, random variations in cash receipts will result in non-zero residual income. However, if residual income is auto-regressive, the expected goodwill at date $t+\tau$, $\tau = 1,2,...$ will be

$$\mathrm{E}[gw_{t+\tau}|\psi_t] = \Phi_r \omega_{rr}^{\tau+1} roi_t.$$

Obviously, given a persistence rate ω_{rr} between zero and one, it follows that in the limit, as τ goes to infinity, the expected goodwill goes to zero. As in FO95 and FO96, we refer to accounting policies that have this property as being *unbiased.* On the other hand, accounting policies are defined to be *conservative* if they are expected to persistently result in positive goodwill (i.e., book value less than market value):

$$\lim_{\tau \to \infty} \mathrm{E}[gw_{t+\tau}|\psi_t] > 0.$$

In our risk-neutral capital investment setting, two factors determine whether the accounting is conservative. First, the accounting is conservative if the depreciation rate is greater than the decay rate in cash receipts. Second, since we have assumed that investment opportunities are ignored by the accounting system until an investment is made, it follows that the accounting is conservative if current and future investments are expected to have positive NPV.

Proposition 10.5 (FO96, Prop. 3)

Assume risk neutrality, a constant interest rate, LID1, (10.13), and declining balance depreciation at rate 1-δ.

(a) If *both* $\delta = \omega_{rr}$ *and* $\lambda = 0$, then $\mathrm{E}[gw_{t+\tau}|\psi_t] \to 0$, as $\tau \to \infty$.

(b) If *either* $\delta < \omega_{rr}$ *or* $\lambda > 0$, then $\mathrm{E}[gw_{t+\tau}|\psi_t] > 0$, as $\tau \to \infty$.

The reader should keep in mind that conservative accounting implies that "on average" market value exceeds book value, but for any given firm in any given period the reverse may occur. Further observe that, while growth may affect the magnitude of the goodwill if accounting is conservative, growth is not essential for the occurrence of conservatism.

We now explore some relations that more fundamentally reflect the interactive effect of conservatism and growth. In particular, we consider the relation between economic income and reported net income, and the relation between the cum-dividend market value and reported net income. With mark-to-market accounting, the reported net income equals economic income, i.e., $ni_t = v_t + d_t - v_{t-1}$. If there is no uncertainty, then mark-to-market accounting also yields the following relation between the cum-dividend market value and net income (see

FO95):[18] $v_t + d_t = \xi\, ni_t$, where $\xi \equiv R/\iota$. Of course, while the "price/earnings" ratio is a constant ξ under certainty, that is not the case under uncertainty. However, both economic income $v_t + d_t - v_{t-1}$ and the ratio ξ serve as useful benchmarks in characterizing the effects of unbiased versus conservative accounting for expectations far into the future. As the following proposition demonstrates, the existence of growth in investment opportunities ($\omega_{ii} > 1$) plays an important role in characterizing the impact of accounting conservatism.[19]

Proposition 10.6 (FO96, Prop. 4)

Assume risk neutrality, a constant interest rate, LID1, (10.13), and declining balance depreciation at rate $1\text{-}\delta$.

(a) If there is *either no growth* ($\omega_{ii} = 1$) *or unbiased accounting* ($\lambda = 0$ and $\delta = \omega_{rr}$), then

$$E[v_{t+\tau} + d_{t+\tau} - v_{t+\tau-1} - ni_{t+\tau} | \psi_t] \to 0, \quad \text{as } \tau \to \infty,$$

$$E[v_{t+\tau} + d_{t+\tau} - \xi\, ni_{t+\tau} | \psi_t] \to 0, \quad \text{as } \tau \to \infty.$$

(b) If there are *both growth* ($\omega_{ii} > 1$) *and conservative accounting* ($\lambda > 0$ or $\delta < \omega_{rr}$), then

$$E[v_{t+\tau} + d_{t+\tau} - v_{t+\tau-1} - ni_{t+\tau} | \psi_t] > 0, \quad \text{as } \tau \to \infty,$$

$$E[v_{t+\tau} + d_{t+\tau} - \xi\, ni_{t+\tau} | \psi_t] > 0, \quad \text{as } \tau \to \infty.$$

Interestingly, conservative accounting (by definition) results in a positive spread between market and book value of equity whether or not there is positive growth. However, unless there is growth, conservative accounting does not affect the "average" relation between economic and reported income, or the relation between the cum-dividend value of equity and reported income. This follows because, with zero growth, the differences between the expected market and book values are the essentially the same for dates $t+\tau$-1 and $t+\tau$ if τ is large.

Impact of Market Risk

While we assume risk neutrality in our subsequent examples, it is useful to illustrate the impact of market risk on the accounting-value relation by examining

[18] With mark-to-market accounting and certainty, $ni_t = \iota v_{t-1}$ and $v_t + d_t = Rv_{t-1}$. Using the first to obtain $v_{t-1} = ni_t/\iota$ and substituting into the second yield $v_t + d_t = Rni_t/\iota$.

[19] Zhang (2000a) obtains similar results without being specific about the information dynamics and the source of the accounting conservatism.

its effect in our basic capital investment model.[20] Similar to A11, we assume the noise terms in LID1 take the following form:[21]

$$\tilde{\varepsilon}_{rt+1} = \tilde{\theta}_{rr} cr_t + \tilde{\theta}_{ri} ci_t,$$

$$\tilde{\varepsilon}_{it+1} = \tilde{\theta}_{ii} ci_t,$$

with Cov[$\tilde{\varepsilon}_{rt+1}$, $\tilde{q}_{t+1}$] = - [$\sigma_{rr}\, cr_t + \sigma_{ri}\, ci_t$] and Cov[$\tilde{\varepsilon}_{it+1}$, $\tilde{q}_{t+1}$] = - $\sigma_{ii}\, ci_t$. Let $\hat{\omega}_{rr} \equiv \omega_{rr} - \sigma_{rr}$, $\hat{\omega}_{ri} \equiv \omega_{ri} - \sigma_{ri}$, and $\hat{\omega}_{ii} \equiv \omega_{ii} - \sigma_{ii}$ denote the risk-adjusted coefficients for the linear cash flow dynamics using the risk-neutral probabilities with $\tilde{q}^q_{t+1} \equiv 1$. Now applying (10.13) yields the following risk-adjusted accounting-value relation:

$$v_t = fa_t + pe_t + \hat{\alpha}_{roi} roi_t + \hat{\alpha}_{pe} pe_{t-1} + \hat{\alpha}_{ci} ci_t, \tag{10.19}$$

where $\hat{\alpha}_{roi} = \hat{\Phi}_r \hat{\omega}_{rr}$, $\hat{\alpha}_{ci} = \hat{\lambda} R \hat{\Phi}_i$, $\hat{\alpha}_{pe} = R\hat{\Phi}_r(\hat{\omega}_{rr} - \delta)$, $\hat{\Phi}_r \equiv [R - \hat{\omega}_{rr}]^{-1}$, $\hat{\Phi}_i \equiv [R - \hat{\omega}_{ii}]^{-1}$, and $\hat{\lambda} \equiv \hat{\Phi}_r \hat{\omega}_{ri} - 1$. That is, the value relation is the same as (10.17) except that all the coefficients are risk-adjusted.

Not surprisingly, the multiple $\hat{\alpha}_{roi}$ applied to the residual operating income is a decreasing function of the risk adjustment σ_{rr} for the persistence parameter. Furthermore, the depreciation rate 1 - δ required to set $\hat{\alpha}_{pe}$ equal to zero is the risk-adjusted decay rate in cash receipts, 1 - ω_{rr} + σ_{rr}, which is an increasing function of σ_{rr}. The multiple $\hat{\alpha}_{ci}$ applied to current cash investments is a decreasing function of the risk adjustment σ_{ii} for the growth in future investments if the multiple is postive. However, the sign of the cash investment multiple depends on the risk-adjusted NPV of a dollar of investment, $\hat{\lambda}$, which is a decreasing function of the risk adjustments in both the persistence of the cash receipts (for $\hat{\omega}_{ri} > 0$) and the initial cash receipts from a dollar invested, i.e., σ_{rr} and σ_{ri}.[22]

---

[20] Some of the following insights are similar to Ohlson (1999b).

[21] Recall that the noise terms have zero mean, but their distributions can depend on the statistic for the preceding period. In this example, we assume the distributions are such that the noise can be interpreted as noise in the linear dynamic coefficients, as opposed to being additive noise *per se*.

[22] One cannot use a risk adjusted cost-of-capital to derive the value of the operating assets. There are effectively two sets of risky assets here. The first consists of the prior investments for which the risk is associated with random variations in the persistence of the future cash receipts from those investments. The second consists of current and future investments for which there is risk with respect to the magnitude of the future investment opportunities and then risk with respect to both the initial and subsequent cash receipts.

If the depreciation rate is risk-adjusted (i.e., $\delta = \hat{\omega}_{rr}$), and future investments have a risk-adjusted expected NPV of zero ($\hat{\lambda} = 0$), then we obtain a result similar to the Corollary to Proposition 10.4:

$$v_t = fa_t + pe_t + \hat{\alpha}_{roi} roi_t = fa_t + (1 - \hat{k})pe_t + \hat{k}[\xi\, ni_t - d_t], \qquad (10.20)$$

where $\hat{k} = \imath \hat{\alpha}_{roi}$. Observe that, while the residual operating income coefficient and the depreciation rate are risk-adjusted, we still use the riskless interest rate $\imath$ in measuring residual income. Also, the multiple $\xi = R/\imath$ on net income in the "weighted average" model is based on the riskless interest rate, whereas the weight $\hat{k}$ on the net income decreases and the weight $1 - \hat{k}$ on book value increases as the persistence risk σ_{rr} increases.

Given the risk-adjusted depreciation rate and zero NPV investments, unrecorded goodwill is a multiple of residual operating income,

$$gw_t = \hat{\alpha}_{roi} roi_t.$$

However, in this setting, that does not imply the accounting is unbiased, since the residual operating income is not auto-regressive. In particular,

$$\mathrm{E}[roi_{t+1} | \psi_t] = \omega_{rr} roi_t + (R - \delta)(\omega_{rr} - \delta)pe_{t-1} + [\omega_{ri} - (R - \delta)]ci_t$$

with $\omega_{rr} - \delta = \sigma_{rr}$ and $\omega_{ri} - (R - \delta) = \sigma_{ri}$. Hence, while the roi_t term may be positive or negative, the pe_{t-1} and ci_t terms are positive if σ_{rr} and σ_{ri} are positive (e.g., the firm's cash receipts are positively correlated with aggregate consumption in the economy). Extending the expectation to $roi_{t+\tau}$, and assuming $\omega_{ii} \in [1,R)$, yield[23]

$$\mathrm{E}[roi_{t+\tau} | \psi_t] = \omega_{rr}^{\tau} roi_t + (R - \delta)(\omega_{rr}^{\tau} - \delta^{\tau})pe_{t-1}$$

$$+ \left[\omega_{ri}\frac{\omega_{ii}^{\tau} - \omega_{rr}^{\tau}}{\omega_{ii} - \omega_{rr}} - (R - \delta)\frac{\omega_{ii}^{\tau} - \delta^{\tau}}{\omega_{ii} - \delta}\right] ci_t > 0, \qquad \text{as } \tau \to \infty.$$

Hence, if the firm's investments are expected to remain constant or grow, then *risk-adjusted depreciation results in conservative accounting*, even with zero NPV investments.

---

[23] The terms associated with roi_t and pe_{t-1} go to zero in the limit, while the term associated with ci_t is positive given $\omega_{ii} \geq 1$, $\delta < \omega_{rr} \in (0,1)$, and $\omega_{ri} > R - \delta$.

10.2.2 Information and Accounting Accruals

The cash flow model in Section 10.2.1 provides little scope for accounting numbers to play a significant role in representing investor information. We now expand that scope by introducing "other" information that may be communicated by management through accounting accruals. The other information consists of two types: persistence of cash receipts from prior investments and growth in future investments. We introduce a working capital accrual to reflect the former, and can potentially use the book value of plant and equipment to reflect the latter. Of course, the investment information is irrelevant if the firm invests in zero NPV projects.

In linear information dynamics LID1 there are two types of cash flows, and ε_{rt+1} and ε_{it+1} represent the random changes in cash receipts and cash investments, respectively. FO96 consider a model in which investors have partial knowledge of that change when the current cash flows are announced, and Begley and Feltham (2002) (BF) use a slightly extended version of that model to generate hypotheses with respect to the relation between market values, current accounting numbers, and earnings forecasts. The following discussion uses the BF model to discuss issues explored in FO96 and BF. For a somewhat more general examination of some of these issues, see Ohlson and Zhang (1998) (OZ98).

The Basic Model with "Other" Information

In this model, at date t, the investors have information with respect to the random changes in cash receipts and cash investments between date t and t+1. This information is represented by υ_{rt} and υ_{it}, which we assume have been scaled (without loss of generality) so that they represent shifts in the expected changes in cash flows. The unanticipated changes in these cash flows are again represented by ε_{rt+1} and ε_{it+1}. As in BF (and FO95) we allow υ_{rt} and υ_{it} to be correlated across dates, and let $\varepsilon_{\upsilon rt+1}$ and $\varepsilon_{\upsilon it+1}$ represent the random variations in that information. More specifically, the linear information dynamics are

$$\tilde{cr}_{t+1} = \omega_{rr}cr_t + \omega_{ri}ci_t + \upsilon_{rt} + \tilde{\varepsilon}_{rt+1}, \tag{LID2a}$$

$$\tilde{ci}_{t+1} = \omega_{ii}ci_t + \upsilon_{it} + \tilde{\varepsilon}_{it+1}, \tag{LID2b}$$

$$\tilde{\upsilon}_{rt+1} = \omega_{\upsilon r}\upsilon_{rt} + \tilde{\varepsilon}_{\upsilon rt+1}, \tag{LID2c}$$

$$\tilde{\upsilon}_{it+1} = \omega_{\upsilon i}\upsilon_{it} + \tilde{\varepsilon}_{\upsilon it+1}. \tag{LID2d}$$

Given risk neutrality, a constant interest rate, LID2, and (10.12) the value relation based on the current cash flow and "other" information is

$$v_t = fa_t + \pi_{cr}cr_t + \pi_{ci}ci_t + \pi_{\upsilon r}\upsilon_{rt} + \pi_{\upsilon i}\upsilon_{it}, \tag{10.21}$$

where π_{cr} and π_{ci} are the same as in (10.16), while

$$\pi_{\upsilon r} \equiv R\Phi_r\Phi_{\upsilon r}, \qquad \Phi_{\upsilon r} \equiv [R - \omega_{\upsilon r}]^{-1},$$

$$\pi_{\upsilon i} \equiv R\lambda\Phi_i\Phi_{\upsilon i}, \qquad \Phi_{\upsilon i} \equiv [R - \omega_{\upsilon i}]^{-1}.$$

This is an extension of (10.16) and, as in the basic model, we can restate the value relation in terms of accounting numbers simply by capitalizing the new investment and depreciating the operating asset balance at some rate 1- δ. This is done by BF, who obtain the following result:

$$v_t = fa_t + pe_t + \alpha_{roi}roi_t + \alpha_{pe}pe_{t-1} + \alpha_{ci}ci_t + \alpha_{\upsilon r}\upsilon_{rt} + \alpha_{\upsilon i}\upsilon_{it}, \tag{10.22}$$

where α_{roi}, α_{pe}, and α_{ci} are the same as in (10.17), while $\alpha_{\upsilon r} = \pi_{\upsilon r}$ and $\alpha_{\upsilon i} = \pi_{\upsilon i}$ from (10.21).

Accruals Based on Cash Flows and "Other" Information

OZ98 consider a more general set of accounting policies in which the accruals are potentially based on both the cash flows and the "other" information. Adapting their approach to our setting, we assume there are two operating assets: working capital (denoted by wc_t) and plant & equipment (denoted by pe_t). The relation of these assets to the cash flows and "other" information is characterized by six accounting policy parameters. The capitalization parameters, ζ_{wc} and ζ_{pe}, specify the fraction of cash receipts and investments that are treated as assets, so that $(1+\zeta_{wc})cr_t$ is revenue and $(1-\zeta_{pe})ci_t$ is an expense. The income recognition parameters, ξ_{wc} and ξ_{pe}, specify the fraction of other information variables that are treated as assets (balanced by increases in net income). The accrual reversal parameters δ_{wc} and δ_{pe} specify the fraction of the two assets that are carried forward to the next period, while 1-δ_{wc} and 1-δ_{pe} increase the corresponding revenues and expenses. More specifically,

$$oa_t = wc_t + pe_t,$$

$$wc_t = \zeta_{wc}cr_t + \delta_{wc}wc_{t-1} + \xi_{wc}\upsilon_{rt}, \qquad pe_t = \zeta_{pe}ci_t + \delta_{pe}pe_{t-1} + \xi_{pe}\upsilon_{it},$$

$$oi_t = (1 + \zeta_{wc})cr_t - (1 - \delta_{wc})wc_{t-1} + \xi_{wc}\upsilon_{rt} - [(1 - \zeta_{pe})ci_t + (1 - \delta_{pe})pe_{t-1} - \xi_{pe}\upsilon_{it}].$$

If υ_{rt} pertains to future sales and υ_{it} pertains to future investment opportunities, then traditional accounting policies will ignore this "other" information in setting current accruals, i.e., $\xi_{wc} = \xi_{pe} = 0$. Furthermore, in this simple example, revenue will equal cash receipts so that there is no working capital, i.e., $\zeta_{wc} = 0$ and δ_{wc} is immaterial. If cash investments are capitalized, then $\zeta_{pe} = 1$ and $1 - \delta_{pe}$ is the depreciation rate. With these policies, $wc_t = 0$, $pe_t = ci_t + \delta_{pe} pe_{t-1}$, and $oi_t = cr_t - (1 - \delta_{pe})pe_{t-1}$, which results in value relation (10.22).

On the other hand, if υ_{rt} is associated with sales orders that have been filled but for which the cash flow has not yet taken place, then traditional accounting policies will use this information in determining current revenue. To illustrate this case, assume cash receipts are credited directly to income, i.e., $\zeta_{wc} = 0$, and assume the revenue recognition and accrual reversal parameters, ξ_{wc} and δ_{wc}, are non-zero. Hence, the accounting numbers are $wc_t = \delta_{wc} wc_{t-1} + \xi_{wc}\upsilon_{rt}$, $pe_t = ci_t + \delta_{pe} pe_{t-1}$, and $oi_t = cr_t - (1 - \delta_{wc})wc_{t-1} + \xi_{wc}\upsilon_{rt} - (1 - \delta_{pe})pe_{t-1}$. These numbers and LID2 yield the following accounting-value relation:

$$v_t = fa_t + wc_t + pe_t + \alpha_{roi} roi_t + \alpha_{pe} pe_{t-1} + \alpha_{ci} ci_t + \alpha_{\upsilon i}\upsilon_{it}$$

$$+ \alpha_{wc} wc_{t-1} + \alpha_{\upsilon r}\upsilon_{rt}, \qquad (10.23)$$

where α_{roi}, α_{pe}, α_{ci}, and $\alpha_{\upsilon i}$ are the same as in (10.22), while

$$\alpha_{wc} = R\Phi_r(\omega_{rr} - \delta_{wc}),$$

$$\alpha_{\upsilon r} = R\Phi_r\Phi_{\upsilon r}[1 - (R - \omega_{\upsilon r})\xi_{wc}].$$

"Efficient" Accounting

Accounting-value relation (10.23) is potentially more complex than (10.22) since the former allows for a broader set of accounting policies. However, those policies can also be used to simplify (10.23). To explore this, we follow OZ98 who define accounting to be "efficient" if the policies are such that value can be expressed as book value plus a multiple of residual income, i.e., the "other" information can be ignored and we obtain the simple Oh95 model illustrated in (10.10). We modify that definition slightly, since we assume any random variations in financial income are entirely transitory (given that financial assets are marked-to-market), while random variations in residual operating income may persist. That is, only the accounting policies that pertain to operating assets are of interest.

Definition

Accounting policies are "efficient" if $v_t = bv_t + \alpha_{roi} roi_t$.

The standard accounting treatment of capital investments, i.e., $\zeta_{pe} = 1$, $\xi_{pe} = 0$, is not efficient unless investments have zero NPV, i.e., $\lambda = 0$. The following proposition takes that setting as given and identifies "efficient" accounting with respect to the "other" cash receipts information, assuming $\zeta_{wc} = 0$.

Proposition 10.7

Assume mark-to-market accounting for financial assets, risk neutrality, a constant interest rate, LID2, (10.13), $\lambda = 0$, $\zeta_{pe} = 1$, and $\zeta_{wc} = \xi_{pe} = 0$. The accounting policy is "efficient" if, and only if, $\delta_{pe} = \delta_{wc} = \omega_{rr}$ and $\xi_{wc} = \Phi_{\upsilon r}$.

Observe that to achieve "efficiency," the start-of-period book value of the two operating assets, working capital and plant & equipment, must reverse (i.e., depreciate) at the same rate as the decay in cash receipts from prior investments, $1 - \omega_{rr}$. This ensures that the residual operating income parameter, α_{roi}, applies to all three of these components of residual operating income. There is a fourth component of current residual income, $\xi_{wc}\upsilon_{rt}$, and this is also included in wc_t. From (10.23), we observe that the impact of υ_{rt} on market value is $\alpha_{\upsilon r}\upsilon_{rt}$. Hence, to achieve the desired result by including $\xi_{wc}\upsilon_{rt}$ in residual income and working capital, we require $\xi_{wc} = \alpha_{\upsilon r}/[1 + \alpha_{roi}] = \Phi_{\upsilon r}$. Observe that if the "other" information is not correlated across periods (i.e., $\omega_{\upsilon r} = 0$), then $\xi_{wc} = \beta$ is "efficient", which is the result obtained by FO96 (see the corollary to their Proposition 5).

The preceding analysis takes $\zeta_{wc} = 0$ as exogenous, and it is this fact that leads to $\alpha_{roi} = \Phi_r\omega_{rr}$ and $\delta_{pe} = \delta_{wc} = \omega_{rr}$. The more general accounting setting considered by OZ98 permits them to identify a class of "efficient" accounting policies, with α_{roi} as an arbitrary parameter.[24] The following applies their result to our basic model.

Proposition 10.8 (OZ98, Prop. 1)

Assume mark-to-market accounting for financial assets, risk neutrality, a constant interest rate, LID2, and (10.13). For each $\alpha_{roi} > 0$, the accounting policy is "efficient" if

$$\delta_{wc} = \delta_{pe} = R\alpha_{roi}\Xi,$$

$$\zeta_{wc} = [\pi_{cr} - \alpha_{roi}]\Xi, \qquad \zeta_{pe} = [\pi_{ci} + \alpha_{roi}]\Xi,$$

$$\xi_{wc} = \pi_{\upsilon r}\Xi, \qquad \xi_{pe} = \pi_{\upsilon i}\Xi,$$

where $\Xi \equiv [1 + \alpha_{roi}]^{-1}$.

OZ98 point out the following implications of this proposition. First, the accrual reversal and depreciation rates (i.e., $1 - \delta_{wc}$ and $1 - \delta_{pe}$) must be decreased if α_{roi} is increased.

---

[24] That is, there is one degree of freedom, in that any one parameter can be selected arbitrarily and then there is a unique solution for the other parameters.

Second, the standard treatment of cash investments (i.e., $\zeta_{pe} = 1$) occurs if, and only if, $\pi_{ci} = 1$, which implies that the NPV is zero, i.e., $\lambda = 0$. If $\lambda > 0$, then $\pi_{ci} > 1$ and $\zeta_{pe} > 1$. That is, achieving efficient accounting in a setting with positive NPV investments requires capitalization of an amount in excess of the initial investment. Since this is inconsistent with most accounting policies, "efficient" accounting is unlikely to be achieved unless investments have zero NPV.

Third, the standard treatment of cash receipts (i.e., $\zeta_{wc} = 0$) occurs if, and only if, $\alpha_{roi} = \pi_{cr}$, which implies that the persistence in the operating assets equals the persistence in the cash receipts (i.e., $\delta_{wc} = \delta_{pe} = \omega_{rr}$). This is, of course, the setting considered in Proposition 10.7.

The preceding analysis assumes that, while accruals influence the relation between market values and accounting numbers, accruals do not influence the firm's market value. That is, if other information is not revealed by accruals, then investors obtain the information from other sources. Feltham and Pae (FP) (2000) demonstrate how the model can be used to examine the impact of accruals on market prices under the assumption that the accruals imperfectly reflect private management information and the investors have no other source of this information. FP treat management's accrual process as exogenous. Ideally, the management's disclosure decisions would be endogenously determined.

10.2.3 Inferring Information from Analysts' Forecasts

Numerous empirical studies in accounting have used the linear models of Oh95, FO95, or FO96 as the basis for exploring the relation between market values and contemporaneous accounting numbers. Most focus on book value and residual income (or net income). However, it is highly unlikely that the accounting systems are "efficient", i.e., a firm's market value is likely to also depend on information beyond that represented by current book value and residual operating income. Some of the additional investor information that affects market value may be readily obtained from public sources. For example, the start-of-period book value of plant and equipment (pe_{t-1}) and current investments in plant and equipment (ci_t), which are used in value relation (10.22), can be obtained from the firm's financial reports. However, it may be difficult to identify and measure "other" information, such as υ_{rt} and υ_{it} in (10.22).

Empirical studies that ignore "other" information may have correlated omitted variables problems in interpreting the coefficients for the accounting variables. This led Ohlson (2001) (Oh01) to propose the use of analysts' forecasts as a means of inferring "other" investor information, under the assumption that analysts know what investors know and this knowledge is reflected in their forecasts. Oh01 uses the simple Oh95 model discussed earlier. It assumes unbiased accounting, so that the "other" information pertains solely to the persistence of residual income (or net income) from prior investments. Hence, Oh01 need only use a one-period-ahead earnings forecast to infer the investors' "other"information. The fact that the Oh95 model assumes unbiased accounting implies there is no role for information about growth. This led Liu and Ohlson (2000) (LO) to apply the same approach to the FO95 model. Their model includes value relevant "other" information about both persistence in cash flows from prior investments and growth in operating assets, which LO infer from one-period-ahead forecasts of earnings and operating assets.

Begley and Feltham (2002) (BF) provide a general discussion of how a researcher can infer unobservable information from observable forecasts (assuming the forecasts impound the unobservable information). They then apply it to the use of one- and two-period-ahead earnings forecasts to infer investor information about the "other" persistence and growth information as depicted in LID2. BF also provide empirical research based on their theoretical analysis, while Dechow *et al.* (2000) provide empirical research based on Oh01 and LO.

We report some of the general discussion from BF, and then apply it to the LID2 model in the preceding section.

A General Model of Inferring Unobservable Information from Forecasts

Consider a value relation in which $\psi_t = (\mathbf{X}_t^{\mathrm{t}}, \mathbf{Y}_t^{\mathrm{t}})$ represents the investors' information at date t, where $\mathbf{X}_t$ is an $m\times 1$ vector of publicly observable variables and $\mathbf{Y}_t$ is an $n\times 1$ vector of variables that are known by investors but not directly observable by a researcher.[25] The value relation based on the investors' information is

$$v_t = \mathbf{A}_x^{\mathrm{t}}\mathbf{X}_t + \mathbf{A}_\upsilon^{\mathrm{t}}\mathbf{Y}_t, \tag{10.24}$$

where $\mathbf{A}_x$ and $\mathbf{A}_\upsilon$ are $m\times 1$ and $n\times 1$ vectors of time-independent valuation parameters.

The lack of direct observability of $\mathbf{Y}_t$ creates problems in estimating (10.24) from publicly reported data. However, we assume that there exists a vector of k forecasts at date t, represented by the $k\times 1$ vector $\mathbf{F}_t$, that are influenced by $\mathbf{Y}_t$, as well as $\mathbf{X}_t$. In particular,

$$\mathbf{F}_t = \mathbf{\Theta}_x\mathbf{X}_t + \mathbf{\Theta}_\upsilon\mathbf{Y}_t, \tag{10.25}$$

where $\mathbf{\Theta}_x$ and $\mathbf{\Theta}_\upsilon$ are $k\times m$ and $k\times n$ matrices of forecast model parameter. In stating these relations we assume $\mathbf{X}_t$ contains all observable variables relevant

[25] Observe that superscript "t" should not be confused with the subscript "t". The former refers to the transpose of a matrix or vector, while the latter refers to the date.

to both (10.24) and (10.25), which may include observable information relevant to one but not the other.

As in BF, we assume that $\mathbf{Y}_t$ can be inferred from $\mathbf{F}_t$ and $\mathbf{X}_t$. If $\mathbf{\Theta}_\upsilon$ has rank n and $k = n$, then $\mathbf{\Theta}_\upsilon^{-1}$ exists and[26]

$$\mathbf{Y}_t = \mathbf{\Theta}_\upsilon^{-1}[\mathbf{F}_t - \mathbf{\Theta}_x\mathbf{X}_t]. \tag{10.26}$$

Substituting (10.26) into (10.24) yields a value relation strictly in terms of observable data:

$$v_t = \hat{\mathbf{A}}_x^{\mathrm{t}}\mathbf{X}_t + \hat{\mathbf{A}}_f^{\mathrm{t}}\mathbf{F}_t, \tag{10.27}$$

where

$$\hat{\mathbf{A}}_x^{\mathrm{t}} = \mathbf{A}_x^{\mathrm{t}} - \mathbf{A}_\upsilon^{\mathrm{t}}\mathbf{\Theta}_\upsilon^{-1}\mathbf{\Theta}_x,$$

$$\hat{\mathbf{A}}_f^{\mathrm{t}} = \mathbf{A}_\upsilon^{\mathrm{t}}\mathbf{\Theta}_\upsilon^{-1}.$$

Using Forecasts in the Capital Investment Model

We now illustrate the above analysis by applying it to the LID2 version of the capital investment model, which is examined in Section 10.2.2. The linear information dynamics contain two types of "other" information. One type, υ_{rt}, pertains to random variations in the persistence in cash receipts from current and prior investments, and the other, υ_{it}, pertains to random variations in the growth of capital investments. For purposes of the following analysis, we assume that these two types of "other" information do not influence accounting accruals (i.e., $\zeta_{wc} = \xi_{wc} = \xi_{pe} = 0$) and are not directly observable by researchers.[27] However, as in BF, one- and two-period-ahead residual operating income forecasts are observable, denoted f_{1t} and f_{2t}.

We assume the forecasts equal the expected one- and two-period-ahead residual operating income based on $\psi_t = (\mathbf{X}_t^{\mathrm{t}}, \mathbf{Y}_t^{\mathrm{t}})$, where $\mathbf{X}_t = (fa_t, pe_t, roi_t, pe_{t-1}, ci_t)^{\mathrm{t}}$ and $\mathbf{Y}_t = (\upsilon_{rt}, \upsilon_{it})^{\mathrm{t}}$. Hence, applying (10.25) yields

---

[26] More generally, if $\mathbf{\Theta}_\upsilon$ has rank $k \geq n$, then

$$\mathbf{Y}_t = (\mathbf{\Theta}_\upsilon^{\mathrm{t}}\mathbf{\Theta}_\upsilon)^{-1}\mathbf{\Theta}_\upsilon^{\mathrm{t}}[\mathbf{F}_t - \mathbf{\Theta}_x\mathbf{X}_t],$$

$$\hat{\mathbf{A}}_x^{\mathrm{t}} = \mathbf{A}_x^{\mathrm{t}} - \mathbf{A}_\upsilon^{\mathrm{t}}(\mathbf{\Theta}_\upsilon^{\mathrm{t}}\mathbf{\Theta}_\upsilon)^{-1}\mathbf{\Theta}_\upsilon^{\mathrm{t}}\mathbf{\Theta}_x,$$

$$\hat{\mathbf{A}}_f^{\mathrm{t}} = \mathbf{A}_\upsilon^{\mathrm{t}}(\mathbf{\Theta}_\upsilon^{\mathrm{t}}\mathbf{\Theta}_\upsilon)^{-1}\mathbf{\Theta}_\upsilon^{\mathrm{t}}.$$

[27] We also assume $\zeta_{wc} = 0$, which implies δ_{wc} is immaterial. Investments are capitalized (i.e., $\zeta_{pe} = 1$) and depreciated at the rate of $1 - \delta_{pe}$, with $\delta_{pe} \in (0, \omega_{rr}]$.

$$f_{1t} = \mathrm{E}[roi_{t+1}] = \theta_{roi}^{\,1}\, roi_t + \theta_{pe}^{\,1}\, pe_{t-1} + \theta_{ci}^{\,1}\, ci_t + \theta_{\upsilon r}^{\,1}\, \upsilon_{rt}, \tag{10.28a}$$

$$f_{2t} = \mathrm{E}[roi_{t+2}] = \theta_{roi}^{\,2}\, roi_t + \theta_{pe}^{\,2}\, pe_{t-1} + \theta_{ci}^{\,2}\, ci_t + \theta_{\upsilon r}^{\,2}\, \upsilon_{rt} + \theta_{\upsilon i}^{\,2}\, \upsilon_{it}, \tag{10.28b}$$

where

$$\theta_{roi}^{\,1} = \omega_{rr}, \qquad \theta_{roi}^{\,2} = \omega_{rr}^{\,2},$$

$$\theta_{pe}^{\,1} = (R - \delta_{pe})(\omega_{rr} - \delta_{pe}), \qquad \theta_{pe}^{\,2} = (R - \delta_{pe})(\omega_{rr}^{\,2} - \delta_{pe}^{\,2}),$$

$$\theta_{ci}^{\,1} = \omega_{ri} - (R - \delta_{pe}), \qquad \theta_{ci}^{\,2} = \omega_{ri}(\omega_{rr} + \omega_{ii}) - (R - \delta_{pe})(\delta_{pe} + \omega_{ii}),$$

$$\theta_{\upsilon r}^{\,1} = 1, \qquad \theta_{\upsilon r}^{\,2} = \omega_{rr} + \omega_{\upsilon r},$$

$$\theta_{\upsilon i}^{\,2} = \omega_{ri} - (R - \delta_{pe}).$$

Observe that in this setting $k = n = 2$, and υ_{it} does not impact the one-period-ahead forecast, but does impact the two-period-ahead forecast (assuming $\omega_{ri} \neq R - \delta_{pe}$). This simplifies the inferences from the forecasts as follows:

$$\boldsymbol{\Theta}_{\upsilon}^{-1} = \begin{bmatrix} 1 & 0 \\ -\theta_{\upsilon r}^{\,2}/\theta_{\upsilon i}^{\,2} & 1/\theta_{\upsilon i}^{\,2} \end{bmatrix},$$

$$\upsilon_{rt} = f_{1t} - [\theta_{roi}^{\,1}\, roi_t + \theta_{pe}^{\,1}\, pe_{t-1} + \theta_{ci}^{\,1}\, ci_t], \tag{10.29a}$$

$$\upsilon_{it} = \{\, f_{2t} - [\theta_{roi}^{\,2}\, roi_t + \theta_{pe}^{\,2}\, pe_{t-1} + \theta_{ci}^{\,2}\, ci_t + \theta_{\upsilon r}^{\,2}\, \upsilon_{rt}]\,\}/\theta_{\upsilon i}^{\,2}. \tag{10.29b}$$

We now complete the process by substituting (10.29) into (10.22) to obtain a specific version of accounting-value relation (10.27):

$$v_t = fa_t + pe_t + \hat{\alpha}_{roi} roi_t + \hat{\alpha}_{pe} pe_{t-1} + \hat{\alpha}_{ci} ci_t + \hat{\alpha}_{f1} f_{1t} + \hat{\alpha}_{f2} f_{2t}, \tag{10.30}$$

where

$$\hat{\alpha}_{roi} = \alpha_{roi} - [\hat{\alpha}_{f1}\theta_{roi}^{\,1} + \hat{\alpha}_{f2}\theta_{roi}^{\,2}], \qquad \hat{\alpha}_{f1} = \alpha_{\upsilon r} - \hat{\alpha}_{f2}\theta_{\upsilon r}^{\,2},$$

$$\hat{\alpha}_{pe} = \alpha_{pe} - [\hat{\alpha}_{f1}\theta_{pe}^{\,1} + \hat{\alpha}_{f2}\theta_{pe}^{\,2}], \qquad \hat{\alpha}_{f2} = \alpha_{\upsilon i}/\theta_{\upsilon i}^{\,2},$$

$$\hat{\alpha}_{ci} = \alpha_{ci} - [\hat{\alpha}_{f1}\theta_{ci}^{\,1} + \hat{\alpha}_{f2}\theta_{ci}^{\,2}].$$

The basic linear dynamics are simple, but the coefficients for the observable data are complex functions of the information dynamics parameters ω_{rr}, ω_{ri}, ω_{ii},

$\omega_{\upsilon r}$, and $\omega_{\upsilon i}$, and the accounting policy parameter δ_{pe}. Hence, determining the signs of some of the coefficients of accounting-value relation (10.30) is complex. BF explore this using both theoretical and numerical analysis. We restrict our comments to some basic theoretical analysis.

Focusing on Forecasts

The most significant theoretical effect, and one that is consistent with the empirical results in BF, pertains to the differential effect of persistence and growth. The coefficient for the two-period-ahead forecast ($\hat{\alpha}_{f2}$) is large and positive, while the coefficient for the one-period-ahead forecast ($\hat{\alpha}_{f1}$) is large and negative. This result is seen most sharply if the depreciation rate is unbiased, the "other"information is independent across periods, and investments have positive NPV.

Proposition 10.9 (BF Prop. 1)

In value relation (10.30), if $\delta_{pe} = \omega_{rr}$, $\omega_{\upsilon r} = \omega_{\upsilon i} = 0$,[28] and $\lambda > 0$ then

$$\hat{\alpha}_{roi} = \hat{\alpha}_{pe} = \hat{\alpha}_{ci} = 0,$$

$$\hat{\alpha}_{f1} = \Phi_r[1 - \Phi_i\omega_{rr}], \qquad \hat{\alpha}_{f2} = \Phi_r\Phi_i > 0. \tag{10.31}$$

The coefficient for the one-period-ahead forecast, $\hat{\alpha}_{f1}$, is negative if the persistence rate ω_{rr} is greater than the difference between the interest rate $\imath$ and the growth rate $\omega_{ii} - 1$, which seems highly likely.

To understand this result it is useful to consider the following representation of the one-, two-, and three-period ahead forecasts:

$$f_{1t} = \omega_{rr}\, roi_t + \upsilon_{rt} + [\omega_{ri} - (R - \omega_{rr})]\; ci_t, \tag{10.32a}$$

$$f_{2t} = \omega_{rr} f_{1t} + [\omega_{ri} - (R - \omega_{rr})][\omega_{ii} ci_t + \upsilon_{it}], \tag{10.32b}$$

$$\begin{aligned} f_{3t} &= \omega_{rr}^2 f_{1t} + (\omega_{rr} + \omega_{ii})[\omega_{ri} - (R - \omega_{rr})][\omega_{ii} ci_t + \upsilon_{it}] \\ &= (\omega_{rr} + \omega_{ii}) f_{2t} - \omega_{ii}\omega_{rr} f_{1t}. \end{aligned} \tag{10.32c}$$

In (10.32c), the positive weight of $\omega_{rr} + \omega_{ii}$ on f_{2t} reflects the desired weight on the one-period-ahead investment forecast $\omega_{ii} ci_t + \upsilon_{it}$. However, from (10.32b) we see that this implicitly places a weight of $(\omega_{rr} + \omega_{ii})\omega_{rr}$ on f_{1t}, whereas the desired weight is only ω_{rr}^2. Hence, a negative adjustment of $- \omega_{ii}\omega_{rr}$ must be

---

[28] Current residual operating income is redundant information if $\omega_{\upsilon r} = 0$, even if $\omega_{\upsilon i} \neq 0$, but both parameters must equal zero for current investments to be redundant information.

made. A similar phenomenon occurs in value relation (10.30) since f_{1t} and f_{2t} are used both directly and in predicting the residual income for periods beyond t+2. The key point is that f_{2t} is the only source of information about υ_{it}, which has a much larger effect on value than on the two-period-ahead forecast. Hence, $\hat{\alpha}_{f2}$ is large and positive, and this implicitly puts too much weight on f_{1t}, thereby requiring a large negative adjustment.

The above result depends significantly on the existence of "other" information about both the persistence of residual income from prior investments and the growth in positive NPV investments. Several empirical studies have focused on expressing value in terms of forecasts, with a truncation adjustment that assumes either a perpetuity or constant rate of growth applied to the last forecast.[29] That is, they assume

$$v_t = \beta f_{1t} + \beta^2 f_{2t} + \beta^2 \frac{1+g}{\iota - g} f_{2t} = \beta f_{1t} + \beta \frac{1}{\iota - g} f_{2t}, \tag{10.33}$$

where g is the anticipated growth rate in residual income beyond $t = 2$. Observe that the coefficients in (10.31), under the conditions assumed in Proposition 10.9, are equivalent to the coefficients in (10.33) if there is no persistence in cash receipts (i.e., $\omega_{rr} = 0$), and the growth in residual income stems from the growth in positive NPV investments (i.e., $g = \omega_{ii} - 1$).

Using Both Current Accounting Numbers and Forecasts

From (10.32a) we see that both f_{1t} and roi_t are required to identify υ_{rt}, but in the setting considered in Proposition 10.9 it is only necessary to infer $\omega_{rr} roi_t + \upsilon_{rt}$. Similarly, from (10.32b) we see that f_{1t}, f_{2t}, and ci_t are required to infer υ_{it}, but it is only necessary to infer $\omega_{ii} ci_t + \upsilon_{it}$. Hence, the current accounting numbers roi_t and ci_t are irrelevant given f_{1t} and f_{2t}. However, inferring υ_{rt} and υ_{it} can be necessary if depreciation is conservative or the other information is correlated across periods. For example, BF demonstrate (see their Proposition 2) that if $\delta_{pe} < \omega_{rr}$ and $\omega_{\upsilon i} = \omega_{\upsilon r} = 0$, then $\hat{\alpha}_{roi} = 0$ and $\hat{\alpha}_{ci} < 0$. Furthermore (see their Proposition 3), if $\delta_{pe} = \omega_{rr}$, $\omega_{\upsilon i} = 0$, and $\omega_{\upsilon r} \neq 0$, then sign $\{\hat{\alpha}_{roi}\}$ = sign $\{\hat{\alpha}_{ci}\}$ = sign $\{\omega_{\upsilon r}\}$.

In summary, the forecast coefficients in value relation (10.30) reflect their dual roles. If all forecasts were available, then the coefficients for the one- and two-period-ahead forecasts would be β and β^2, respectively. However, with only two forecasts, their coefficients (and those assigned to roi_t, ci_t, and pe_{t-1}) must also reflect their use in predicting the present value of the expected residual income values for periods three and beyond. In all settings (except under extremely conservative depreciation), the weight on the two-period-ahead fore-

[29] See, for example, Frankel and Lee (1998) and Lee *et al.* (1999).

cast is large and positive, whereas the weight on the one-period-ahead forecast is generally large and negative. This is consistent with BF's empirical results for most industries.

10.3 OTHER FACTORS INFLUENCING ACCOUNTING-VALUE RELATIONS

The discussion in Section 10.2 is based on the linear dynamics in LID1 and their extension to include "other" information in LID2. In this section we modify the basic linear information dynamics so that we can illustrate other factors that influence the relation between market values and current accounting numbers. These include transitory earnings and investments, accounts receivable and bad debts, and research and development expenditures. Obviously, the factors we consider are not exhaustive, but hopefully they will help readers to understand how they can extend the models considered here to reflect issues of interest to them.

10.3.1 Transitory Earnings and Investments

Empirical researchers often use net income before extraordinary items in examining the relation between market values and contemporaneous residual income (or net income). Many apologize for using this measure because it violates the clean surplus assumption. However, their apology is unnecessary. The key role of the clean surplus assumption pertains to forecasts (as emphasized in Chapter 9). This section demonstrates that, if a component of current residual income will not persist (i.e., it is transitory), then it should be given zero weight in the value relation. This can be done by either adopting a line-item approach in which the transitory component of residual income is given zero weight (i.e., omitting it), or by using the net residual income and then introducing an adjustment that removes the effect of the transitory component.

In the basic linear information dynamics LID1, cash receipts and cash investments are assumed to persist from one period to the next, subject to some decay or growth rate and random variations. We now consider a simple setting in which cash receipts and investment opportunities both consist of persistent and transitory components. The basic valuation result is that the transitory cash receipts are ignored, while transitory investments have a positive but significantly smaller impact than do persistent investment opportunities. Some of the insights presented here are developed in Ohlson's (1999a) discussion of transitory earnings.

In this setting we let pr_t and pi_t represent the persistent cash receipts and investments, respectively. The dynamics of these persistent components are similar to the cash receipts and investments in LID1. However, in this setting the cash receipts and investments also contain transitory components, υ_{rt} and υ_{it}, which only affect the current cash flows – they do not persist or grow. More specifically, the linear information dynamics in this setting are represented by[30]

$$\tilde{cr}_{t+1} = \tilde{pr}_{t+1} + \tilde{\upsilon}_{rt+1}, \tag{LID3a}$$

$$\tilde{pr}_{t+1} = \omega_{rr} pr_t + \omega_{ri} ci_t + \tilde{\varepsilon}_{rt+1}, \tag{LID3b}$$

$$\tilde{ci}_{t+1} = \tilde{pi}_{t+1} + \tilde{\upsilon}_{it+1}, \tag{LID3c}$$

$$\tilde{pi}_{t+1} = \omega_{ii} pi_t + \tilde{\varepsilon}_{it+1}. \tag{LID3d}$$

We could develop an operating cash flow value relation, as in Proposition 10.3, but we go directly to the accounting-value relation. We assume that all cash receipts are treated as current revenue, and all cash investments are capitalized (and then depreciated using the declining balance method).

Proposition 10.10

Assume mark-to-market accounting for financial assets, risk neutrality, a constant interest rate, LID3, (10.13), and declining balance depreciation at rate 1-δ imply

$$v_t = fa_t + pe_t + \alpha_{roi}[roi_t - \upsilon_{rt}] + \alpha_{pe} pe_{t-1} + \alpha_{ci}[ci_t - \upsilon_{it}] + \alpha_{\upsilon i}\upsilon_{it}, \tag{10.34}$$

where α_{roi}, α_{pe}, and α_{ci} are the same as in Proposition 10.4, and $\alpha_{\upsilon i} = \lambda$.

The transitory cash receipts are removed from the current residual income because they do not affect beliefs about future residual income. The transitory cash investments are also removed from current cash investments because they do not affect beliefs about future investments. However, the transitory cash investments are included separately so as to recognize the NPV of those investments.

---

30 We could also represent this model as a special case of LID2. To see this, observe that LID3 can be written as:

$$\tilde{cr}_{t+1} = \omega_{rr} cr_t + \omega_{ri} ci_t - \omega_{rr}\upsilon_{rt} + [\tilde{\varepsilon}_{rt+1} + \tilde{\varepsilon}_{\upsilon rt+1}],$$

$$\tilde{ci}_{t+1} = \omega_{ii} ci_t - \omega_{ii}\upsilon_{it} + [\tilde{\varepsilon}_{it+1} + \tilde{\varepsilon}_{\upsilon it+1}],$$

$$\tilde{\upsilon}_{rt+1} = \tilde{\varepsilon}_{\upsilon rt+1}, \quad \tilde{\upsilon}_{it+1} = \tilde{\varepsilon}_{\upsilon it+1}.$$

A line-item approach provides the following accounting-value relation:

$$v_t = fa_t + pe_t + \{\alpha_{cr} pr_t - \alpha_{dep}[dep_t + \iota pe_{t-1}]\} + \alpha_{ci} pi_t + \alpha_{\upsilon i} \upsilon_{it}. \quad (10.34')$$

Observe that in this case, υ_{rt} is omitted because it is given zero weight, whereas υ_{it} is included because it influences beliefs about future cash receipts.

If investments have zero NPV ($\lambda = 0$), and there is unbiased depreciation ($\delta = \omega_{rr}$), then we obtain

$$v_t = fa_t + pe_t + \alpha_{roi}[roi_t - \upsilon_{rt}].$$

This is essentially the case considered by Ohlson (1999a). The transitory cash receipts are removed (irrelevant) because they do not affect beliefs about future cash receipts, and transitory cash investments are irrelevant because the NPV of those investments is zero. Implicitly, Ohlson assumes unbiased accounting and then considers a somewhat more complex set of possible relations among the two components of net income. The second component is deemed to be transitory if the relations are such that the current second component is irrelevant in (i) forecasting the second component of next period, (ii) forecasting the first component in the next period, and (iii) in determining the current market price. Ohlson establishes that any two of these attributes implies the third.

Ohlson also points out that while the current transitory component is irrelevant in determining the current market value, it is relevant in determining the current return. The key here is that the return focuses on changes and the transitory component is reflected in the change in book and market values. More specifically, let $ret_t \equiv [v_t + d_t]/v_{t-1} - R$ denote the unanticipated return for period t and let $fi_t = \iota fa_{t-1} + \varepsilon_{ft}$ represent the financial income for period t. Consequently, if investments have zero NPV, i.e., $\lambda = 0$, then

$$ret_t = [\varepsilon_{ft} + \upsilon_{rt} + (1 + \alpha_{roi})\varepsilon_{rt}]/v_{t-1}.$$

There are both financial and operating transitory components in net income, ε_{ft} and υ_{rt}. Both have a one-to-one effect on the current return. The persistent random component of operating income, ε_{rt}, on the other hand, has both a one-to-one current effect and a forecast effect of α_{roi}.

Extending this to the setting with positive NPV investments, i.e., $\lambda > 0$, yields

$$ret_t = [\varepsilon_{ft} + \upsilon_{rt} + (1 + \alpha_{roi})\varepsilon_{rt} + \lambda\upsilon_{it} + \lambda(1 + \Phi_i\omega_{ii})\varepsilon_{it}]/v_{t-1}.$$

Neither of the random changes in investments, υ_{it} and ε_{it}, affect current income, but both affect the unanticipated return. The transitory investment increases the market value by λ (the NPV of that investment), whereas the persistent component has a direct NPV effect of λ plus a forecast effect of $\lambda\Phi_i\omega_{ii}$.

10.3.2 Receivables and Bad Debt Expense

In the capital investment model considered to this point in the chapter, there is a one-period lag between cash investments and the initial net cash receipts generated by investment. In this and the subsequent section, we consider models in which there is a two-period lag. In this section, the additional lag is attributable to a one-period delay in net cash receipts relative to sales, which begin one period after investment. The model is similar to that examined in Feltham and Pae (2000).

The sales at date t can be viewed as another form of "other" information, and are denoted by υ_{st}. The sales at date t are treated as an accounting transaction, i.e., net revenue is recognized at date t even though the cash has not yet been received. This results in an accounting accrual, which we refer to as accounts receivable. The model recognizes that not all receivables are collected, and there may be "other" information about that collection.

As with the other models in Sections 10.2 and 10.3, the model examined here is designed to illustrate how one can formulate linear information dynamics that yield insights into the relation between market values and accounting numbers. Receivables are interesting because they can be viewed as either operating or financial assets, particularly if management activity has little impact on the cash collected once the receivables are created.

A Cash Flow Model with Sales and Lagged Cash Receipts

We treat receivables as operating assets and assume that all financial assets are marked-to-market. A key difference between the following linear information dynamics and LID1 is that there is a one-period lag between sales and cash receipts, and it is the sales that persist rather than the cash receipts *per se*. We refer to the difference between the amount sold and the cash received as bad debts, and include "other" information about those bad debts, denoted υ_{bt}. The basic linear information dynamics are:[31]

$$\tilde{\upsilon}_{st+1} = \omega_{ss}\upsilon_{st} + \omega_{si}ci_t + \tilde{\varepsilon}_{st+1} \qquad \text{(LID4a)}$$

$$\tilde{cr}_{t+1} = \omega_{rs}\upsilon_{st} - \upsilon_{bt} + \tilde{\varepsilon}_{rt+1}, \qquad \text{(LID4b)}$$

[31] For simplicity, we omit "other" cash investment information and assume that the "other" bad debt information is not correlated across time. We also assume that all receivables are either collected in the following period or never collected. It is relatively straightforward to extend the model to encompass more general relations in each of these areas.

$$\tilde{ci}_{t+1} = \omega_{ii} ci_t + \tilde{\varepsilon}_{it+1}, \tag{LID4c}$$

$$\tilde{\upsilon}_{bt+1} = \tilde{\varepsilon}_{bt+1} \tag{LID4d}$$

where $\omega_{ss} \in (0,1)$ is the persistence in sales from prior investments, $\omega_{si} > 0$ is the expected incremental sales in period t+1 per dollar invested at date t, $\omega_{rs} \in (0,1)$ is the expected incremental net cash receipts in period t+1 per dollar of sales in period t, and $\omega_{ii} \in [0,R)$ is one plus the expected growth (or decay, if $\omega_{ii} < 1$) in investment opportunities. We assume υ_{st} is measured in dollars, and $1 - \omega_{rs}$ is the *a priori* expected bad debts expressed as a fraction of the amount sold. The expected bad debts from the sales at date t given the "other" bad debt information at date t equal $(1 - \omega_{rs})\upsilon_{st} + \upsilon_{bt}$.

Applying (10.13) to LID4 yields the following value relation.

Proposition 10.11

Mark-to-market accounting for financial assets, risk neutrality, a constant interest rate, LID4, and (10.13) imply

$$v_t = fa_t + \pi_s \upsilon_{st} + \pi_{ci} ci_t + \pi_b \upsilon_{bt}, \tag{10.35}$$

where

$$\pi_s \equiv \Phi_s \omega_{rs}, \qquad \Phi_s \equiv [R - \omega_{ss}]^{-1},$$

$$\pi_{ci} \equiv R\lambda\Phi_i + 1, \qquad \Phi_i \equiv [R - \omega_{ii}]^{-1}, \qquad \lambda \equiv \beta\Phi_s\omega_{rs}\omega_{si} - 1,$$

$$\pi_b \equiv -\beta.$$

Comparing (10.35) to (10.16) reveals the following key differences. First, sales replace cash receipts since it is sales that persist, not the cash receipts *per se*. Second, the NPV per unit of investment, λ, is slightly more complex since the cash receipts lag sales by one period (resulting in the inclusion of the discount factor β), and we must include the expected receipts per sales dollar, ω_{rs}. The bad debt information is included at its NPV, given a one-period lag in its cash effect.

An Accounting Model with Receivables and Bad Debt Expense

The accounting for capital investments is the same as in the basic capital investment model. The lag between sales and net cash receipts now introduces the possibility of recognizing net revenue at the date of sale rather than at the date the net cash is received. We let ar_t denote the accounts receivable at date t, net of the allowance for bad debts, and we let bde_t represent the bad debt expense for period t.

The general form of the operating accounting numbers are as follows:

$$oa_t = ar_t + pe_t, \qquad oi_t = rev_t - bde_t - dep_t,$$

$$ar_t = ar_{t-1} + rev_t - cr_t - bde_t, \qquad pe_t = pe_{t-1} + ci_t - dep_t,$$

where rev_t is the revenue recognized in period t, dep_t is the depreciation expense for period t, and bde_t is the bad debt expense recognized in period t.

We again assume cash investments are capitalized and then depreciated at the declining balance rate of $1 - \delta_{pe}$. In this model, we assume the revenue recognized equals sales, i.e., $rev_t = \upsilon_{st}$. The accounting policy of interest is characterized by two bad debt allowance parameters, δ_s and δ_b. The first, δ_s, represents one minus the fraction of current sales recognized as a current bad debt, while the second, δ_b, represents the fraction of υ_{bt} recognized as a current bad debt expense. The bad debt expense also includes the actual bad debts from last period's sales minus last period's bad debt allowance. Hence,

$$ar_t = \delta_s \upsilon_{st} - \delta_b \upsilon_{bt}, \qquad pe_t = \delta_{pe} pe_{t-1} + ci_t,$$

$$bde_t = (1 - \delta_s)\upsilon_{st} + \delta_b \upsilon_{bt} + ar_{t-1} - cr_t, \qquad dep_t = (1 - \delta_{pe})pe_{t-1}.$$

Observe that, in this setting, residual operating income takes the following form:

$$roi_t \equiv oi_t - \iota\, oa_{t-1} = \delta_s \upsilon_{st} + (cr_t - Rar_{t-1}) - \delta_b \upsilon_{bt} - (R - \delta_{pe})pe_{t-1}.$$

Of particular note is the fact that roi_t is influenced by $cr_t - Rar_{t-1}$, which is a transitory effect, i.e., it is uninformative about the residual income in subsequent periods, given υ_{st} and υ_{bt}.

The following proposition characterizes the accounting-value relation given LID4 and the preceding accounting policies.

Proposition 10.12

Mark-to-market accounting for financial assets, risk neutrality, a constant interest rate, LID4, (10.13), declining balance depreciation at rate $1-\delta_{pe}$, and bad debt allowance parameters δ_s and δ_b imply

$$v_t = fa_t + ar_t + pe_t + \alpha_{roi}[roi_t - (cr_t - Rar_{t-1})]$$

$$+ \alpha_{\upsilon b} \upsilon_{bt} + \alpha_{pe} pe_{t-1} + \alpha_{ci} ci_t, \qquad (10.36)$$

where

$$\alpha_{roi} \equiv \Phi_s[\omega_{ss} + \delta_s^{-1}\omega_{rs} - R], \qquad \alpha_{\upsilon b} \equiv [\alpha_{roi} + 1]\delta_b - \beta,$$

$$\alpha_{pe} \equiv \alpha_{roi}[R - \delta_{pe}] - \delta_{pe}, \qquad \alpha_{ci} \equiv \lambda R \Phi_i.$$

Observe that in this representation of the accounting-value relation, the transitory component of residual income, $cr_t - Rar_{t-1}$, is removed before applying the multiplier α_{roi}. No other adjustments need be made for cr_t and Rar_{t-1} since they have no effect on beliefs about future residual income, irrespective of the accounting policies.

There are three possible sources of accounting bias in this model, and unbiasedness is achieved if, and only if, $\delta_s = \beta\omega_{rs}$, $\delta_{pe} = R\alpha_{roi}[1 + \alpha_{roi}]^{-1}$, and $\lambda = 0$. The sales revenue recognition parameter δ_s is adjusted for both the expected bad debts and the one-period lag in cash receipts and results in $\alpha_{roi} = \alpha^*_{roi} \equiv \Phi_s\omega_{ss}$, which depends only on the persistence in sales. The depreciation parameter δ_{pe} is such that $\alpha_{pe} = 0$ and, if $\delta_s = \beta\omega_{rs}$, then unbiased accounting requires $\delta_{pe} = \omega_{ss}$, as in the earlier models. As before, $\lambda = 0$ implies that current and future investments have zero NPV.

The "other" bad debt information parameter δ_b does not affect biasedness (since this information has zero mean). If no accounting adjustment is made for this information (i.e., $\delta_b = 0$), then $\alpha_{\upsilon r} = -\beta$, reflecting the fact that υ_{rt} represents the revenue that will not be collected next period. On the other hand, $\delta_b = \beta\,[1 + \alpha_{roi}]^{-1}$ yields $\alpha_{\upsilon b} = 0$, reflecting the fact that δ_b has two effects – it is a reduction in the book value of accounts receivable (which is given a weight of one) and it is a reduction in residual operating income (which is given a weight of α_{roi}). Another possibility is to set $\delta_b = \beta$, i.e., fully recognize the NPV of the bad debt information in the current accounts receivable and current residual operating income. This results in $\alpha_{\upsilon b} = \beta\alpha_{roi}$ and $cr_t - Rar_{t-1} = \varepsilon_{rt}$, i.e., a value adjustment must be made for the bad debt information, but the full reversal of the start-of-period accounts receivable is truly transitory. We use the last approach in the following corollary.

Corollary

If $\delta_s = \beta\omega_{rs}$, $\delta_b = \beta$, $\delta_{pe} = \omega_{ss}$, and $\lambda = 0$, then

$$v_t = fa_t + ar_t + pe_t + \alpha^*_{roi}(roi_t - \varepsilon_{rt} + \beta\upsilon_{rt}). \tag{10.37}$$

Observe that in this setting, unbiased accounting is not "efficient", since we must remove the transitory components of current residual income, $\varepsilon_{rt} - \beta\upsilon_{rt}$, before applying the multiplier α^*_{roi}. As discussed in OZ98, the adjustment for ε_{rt} could be avoided by capitalizing the transitory cash flow at the rate $\zeta_{\varepsilon r} = -\beta\omega_{ss}$ and reversing the resulting accrual at the rate $1 - \delta_{\varepsilon r} = 1 - \omega_{ss}$. Of course, this approach is not representative of traditional accounting policies.

The above analysis has treated the accounts receivable as an operating asset. However, we could treat it as a financial asset. In that case, mark-to-market accounting for financial assets is obtained by letting the operating revenue equal the NPV of the expected cash receipts from the accounts receivable, i.e., $ar_t = \beta[\omega_{rs}\upsilon_{st} - \upsilon_{bt}]$, and transferring this amount to financial assets. Financial income would include $cr_t - ar_{t-1}$ and the expected residual financial income would equal zero. Observe that with ε_{rt} now a component of residual financial income, the accounting for operating assets would be "efficient" if $\delta_{pe} = \omega_{ss}$ and $\lambda = 0$.

As before, the accounting is conservative if the depreciation rate exceeds the decay rate in sales ($\delta_{pe} < \omega_{ss}$) or if the current and future capital investments have positive NPV ($\lambda > 0$). With respect to revenue recognition, the accounting is biased if $\delta_s \neq \beta\omega_{rs}$. Interestingly, in this case *the bias adjustment in the accounting-value relation is made through the parameters* as specified in (10.36), not by including other variables as in the case of conservatism with respect to investments. For example, the accounting is "aggressive" if the revenue recognized equals the expected cash receipts from actual sales (i.e., $\delta_s = \omega_{rs}$ and $\delta_b = 1$), and the residual income parameter is reduced, i.e., $\alpha_{roi} = \Phi_s[\omega_{ss} + 1 - R] < \alpha^*_{roi} \equiv \Phi_s\omega_{ss}$.

10.3.3 Research and Development

Perhaps the most widely recognized form of extreme conservatism in accounting is the immediate expensing of expenditures on research and development (R&D). We can introduce immediate expensing of investments into our basic capital investment model by using a depreciation rate of $1-\delta = 1$, but that results in cash accounting and fails to reflect the fact that most firms which invest in R&D also invest in assets that are not immediately expensed. In this section, we consider a simple model in which investments in R&D are depicted as generating opportunities that will require investment in production facilities which will then generate revenues.[32]

There are two types of cash investments: rd_t represents the investment in R&D, and ci_t represents investments in production facilities. We assume expected R&D activities grow at the rate $\omega_{dd} - 1$, while investment opportunities in production facilities grow (decay, if negative) at the rate $\omega_{ii} - 1$. A dollar of investment in R&D is expected to generate ω_{id} dollars of investment opportunities in production facilities (e.g., property, plant, equipment) in the following period, and each dollar invested in production facilities is expected to generate ω_{ri} dollars of cash receipts in the subsequent period (there is no lag in

[32] The model is essentially the same as the R&D model in an appendix in an earlier version of Begley and Feltham (2002). Zhang (2000b) uses a similar model in his exploration of conservative accounting.

cash receipts in this model). The expected cash receipts from prior investments will persist at the rate ω_{rr}. More specifically, the operating information dynamics are as follows:

$$cr_{t+1} = \omega_{rr}\, cr_t + \omega_{ri}\, ci_t + \varepsilon_{rt+1}, \tag{LID5a}$$

$$ci_{t+1} = \omega_{ii}\, ci_t + \omega_{id}\, rd_t + \varepsilon_{it+1}, \tag{LID5b}$$

$$rd_{t+1} = \omega_{dd}\, rd_t + \varepsilon_{dt+1}. \tag{LID5c}$$

We could readily include "other" information about the cash receipts from prior investments, the productive investment opportunities from prior R&D, and new R&D investment opportunities. However, we keep the model simple so that we can focus on the effect of conservative accounting for R&D expenditures.

The investment in R&D is expensed immediately, while the investment in production facilities is depreciated at the rate 1- δ.[33] Hence, the basic accounting relations for operating activities are as follows:

$$oi_t = cr_t - rd_t - (1\text{-}\delta)pe_{t\text{-}1},$$

$$pe_t = \delta pe_{t\text{-}1} + ci_t,$$

$$roi_t = oi_t - \imath\, pe_{t\text{-}1}.$$

Proposition 10.13

Mark-to-market accounting for financial assets, risk neutrality, a constant interest rate, LID5, (10.13), immediate expensing of R&D, and declining balance depreciation for production investments at rate 1-δ imply

$$v_t = fa_t + pe_t + \alpha_{roi}\, roi_t + \alpha_{pe} pe_{t\text{-}1} + \alpha_{ci}\, ci_t + \alpha_{rd}\, rd_t, \tag{10.38}$$

where α_{roi} and α_{pe} are the same as in (10.17), while

$$\alpha_{ci} = R\Phi_i\lambda_i, \qquad \Phi_i = [R - \omega_{ii}]^{-1}, \qquad \lambda_i = \Phi_r\omega_{ri} - 1,$$

$$\alpha_{rd} = (\alpha_{roi} + 1) + R\Phi_d\lambda_d, \qquad \Phi_d = [R - \omega_{dd}]^{-1}, \qquad \lambda_d = \Phi_i\lambda_i\omega_{id} - 1.$$

We assume the NPV of a dollar invested in R&D, denoted λ_d, is non-negative. Hence, the NPV of a dollar invested in production facilities, denoted λ_i, *must be*

---

[33] Zhang (2000b) considers a more general set of accounting rules in his analysis of a similar R&D model.

positive. Therefore, given that the NPV of the future production opportunities generated by R&D are not recorded when the R&D results are known, it follows that *the accounting for production investments is inherently conservative.*

The expressions for residual income, start-of-period book value of production facilities, and the current investments in production facilities are all essentially the same as in the basic capital investment model. The key difference is the adjustment for the conservatism associated with R&D. There are two aspects of that conservatism. The first is the fact that roi_t has been reduced by rd_t even though that investment is expected to produce future benefits. The first two terms of α_{rd} adjust for that conservatism by first adding back the reduction in value associated with residual operating income (i.e., $\alpha_{roi} rd_t$) and also adding the cost of the investment (i.e., $1 rd_t$). That, of course, is sufficient if the R&D investments have zero NPV (i.e., $\lambda_d = 0$). However, the third term is required if a dollar of investment in R&D has a positive NPV. If there is zero expected growth in R&D, then the third term is equal to $\xi\lambda_d rd_t$ (where $\xi \equiv R/\imath$), reflecting the NPV of the perpetuity of future R&D projects. On the other hand, if there is growth, then the expression $R\Phi_d\lambda_d rd_t$ reflects the NPV of the future stream of R&D projects given the current level of R&D.

As in other models, there is an equivalent value relation that uses line-items from the accounting statements. In this case, the line-item model is

$$v_t = fa_t + pe_t + \{\alpha_{cr}\, cr_t - \alpha_{dep}[dep_t + \imath pe_{t-1}]\} + \alpha_{ci} ci_t + \alpha_{rd}'\, rd_t, \quad (10.38')$$

where α_{cr}, α_{dep}, and α_{ci} are the same as in (10.17′) and $\alpha_{rd}' = \alpha_{rd} - \alpha_{roi} = 1 + R\Phi_d\lambda_d$. The key here is that we now omit R&D from the residual income line items and apply a coefficient that reflects the current R&D investment plus the NPV of the current and future R&D investments. The last term reflects the fact that the only information about future R&D investments is current R&D investments. In this model, there is no information to be communicated by amortizing R&D instead of expensing it immediately. However, one must adjust for the fact that such expensing does "contaminate" the information communicated by current residual income.

10.4 CONCLUDING REMARKS

In Chapter 9 we examined some basic theory regarding the relation between current market values and forecasts of future accounting numbers. In this chapter we demonstrate how models of information dynamics can be used to develop insights into the relation between current market values and current accounting numbers. In these models we generally describe the information dynamics in terms of operating cash flows and "other" information, and then introduce accounting policies to develop the resulting accounting numbers. We use this approach because we want to illustrate how one can construct models that provide insights into the impact of varying specific accounting policies on the relation between current market values and current accounting numbers.

We restrict our analysis to linear models on the grounds that they are the predominant models in the current literature, they are relatively simple to analyze, and they produce intuitively appealing insights. Of course, while these insights may apply to many firms, they are not likely to apply to firms who face financial difficulties or invest heavily in real options. Non-linear models are required in these cases.

We identify accounting policies that yield what OZ98 call "efficient accounting," i.e., market value can be expressed as a function of book value and residual operating income. However, accounting policies based on GAAP seldom yield "efficient accounting," and we do not argue that they should. Instead, the key issue is to identify the information in addition to aggregate book value and the net residual operating income that is required to represent what investors know.

In our examples, we emphasize the distinction between the value of the firm's equity attributable to prior investments (i.e., assets-in-place at the start of the current period) and the value attributable to current and future investment opportunities. The latter equals zero if the investors believe that the firm will invest in zero NPV projects, but it is positive if they believe the firm will have the opportunity to invest in positive NPV projects. If investments are only recorded at their cost when the investment takes place (as is common under GAAP), then the accounting will not be "efficient." Any model of value will have to include a representation of the investors' information about future positive NPV projects. In our examples we assume the information consists of the current level of investment (because that level is expected to persist, and possibly grow), plus "other" information about future investments.

The current market value attributable to prior investments can be expressed as the current book value of the prior investments plus the NPV of expected residual operating income generated by those investments. The accounting is "efficient" if the latter can be expressed as a multiple of the current residual income. However, that effectively assumes the accounting is such that all components of residual income persist at the same rate. For example, the depreciation rate applied to the book value of plant and equipment must equal the decay rate in the sales generated by prior investments. Our examples illustrate the nature of the information that must be included in the accounting-value relation to adjust for differences in persistence, and how that information depends on the firm's accounting policies. We also illustrate a line-item approach in which different multiples are applied to the components of residual operating income.

The line-item approach is particularly useful if some elements of the current residual income are transitory. Since these elements are uninformative about future residual income (by definition), they can be excluded from current residual operating income in representing the investors' value-relevant information. Of course, any information about future transitory components is value-relevant. Hence, the assumption of clean surplus accounting that underlies the residual income valuation model does not imply that the market value is a function of the current residual income. What is important is that, if we determine the current market value by discounting expected future residual income, then expected residual income must satisfy the clean surplus relation – we must not omit anything of value.

Most of our examples assume investors are risk neutral with respect to the random variations in the firm's cash flows. However, the basic GO assumptions allow for the inclusion of market risk in a manner that permits retention of a linear structure. At the end of Section 10.2.1, we demonstrate the impact of market risk in the basic capital investment model from FO96. The key result is that if the model coefficients are random and co-vary with the valuation index, then the valuation model parameters will be based on risk-adjusted coefficients. This implies, for example, that the weight placed on current residual income will be less than the weight implied by its statistical persistence.

Throughout the analysis in this chapter we have assumed, as in Chapters 5, 6, 7, and 9, that all investors have the same information. In Chapters 11 and 12 we consider rational expectations models in which some investors have more information than others. Kwon (2001) integrates the theoretical analysis in this chapter and Chapter 12, and we examine an extended version of Kwon's model in Section 12.2.2. In our model, some investors observe "other" information about cash receipts and investments, and the price reflects the uninformed market-maker's rational expectations about the value implications of the investors' "other" information based on publicly observed trading volume.

APPENDIX 10A: PROOFS

Proof of Proposition 10.3

Let $vo(\psi_t)$ represent the market value of the operating assets given statistic $\psi_t = (cr_t, ci_t)$. Risk neutrality, a constant interest rate, (10.12), and LID1 imply

$$vo(\psi_t) = \beta\, \mathrm{E}[cr_{t+1} - ci_{t+1} + vo(\psi_{t+1}) \,|\, \psi_t].$$

Conjecture that the value function is linear, $vo(\psi_t) = \pi_{cr} cr_t + \pi_{ci} ci_t$, and substitute into the above, using $\mathrm{E}[cr_{t+1} | \psi_t] = \omega_{rr} cr_t + \omega_{ri} ci_t$ and $\mathrm{E}[ci_{t+1} | \psi_t] = \omega_{ii} ci_t$:

$$\pi_{cr} cr_t + \pi_{ci} ci_t = \beta\, [\omega_{rr} cr_t + \omega_{ri} ci_t - \omega_{ii} ci_t + \pi_{cr}(\omega_{rr} cr_t + \omega_{ri} ci_t) + \pi_{ci}\omega_{ii} ci_t].$$

Collect terms associated with cr_t and with ci_t to form two equations in two unknowns:

$$\pi_{cr} = \beta\,[\omega_{rr} + \pi_{cr}\omega_{rr}],$$

$$\pi_{ci} = \beta\,[\omega_{ri} - \omega_{ii} + \pi_{cr}\omega_{ri} + \pi_{ci}\omega_{ii}].$$

Solving for π_{cr} and π_{ci} yields (10.16). **Q.E.D.**

Proof of Proposition 10.4

Given separation of financial and operating assets, with financial assets marked-to-market, unrecorded goodwill can be expressed as $gw_t \equiv v_t - bv_t = vo_t - pe_t$. With risk neutrality, (10.13) then implies

$$gw_t = \beta\,\mathrm{E}[roi_{t+1} + gw_{t+1}]. \tag{10A.1}$$

Now conjecture that the value of the operating assets is a linear function of pe_t, roi_t, pe_{t-1}, and ci_t, for all t, with zero intercept and a coefficient of one on pe_t. Hence, we can express goodwill as

$$gw_t = \alpha_{roi}roi_t + \alpha_{pe}pe_{t-1} + \alpha_{ci}ci_t, \quad \forall\, t. \tag{10A.2}$$

Substitute (10A.2) into (10A.1), and then substitute in $roi_t = cr_t - (R - \delta)pe_{t-1}$, $\mathrm{E}[roi_{t+1}] = \omega_{rr}cr_t + \omega_{ri}ci_t - (R - \delta)pe_t$, $pe_t = \delta pe_{t-1} + ci_t$, and $\mathrm{E}[ci_{t+1}] = \omega_{ii}ci_t$. This results in an equation expressed in terms of variables cr_t, pe_{t-1}, and ci_t, and coefficients α_{roi}, α_{ci}, and α_{pe}. Collecting the terms associated with each of the three variables yields three equations in three unknowns:

$$\alpha_{roi} = \beta\omega_{rr}(1 + \alpha_{roi}),$$

$$-(R - \delta)\alpha_{roi} + \alpha_{pe} = \beta\{-(R - \delta)\delta(1 + \alpha_{roi}) + \delta\alpha_{pe}\},$$

$$\alpha_{ci} = \beta\{(\omega_{ri} - (R - \delta))(1 + \alpha_{roi}) + \alpha_{pe} + \omega_{ii}\alpha_{ci}\}.$$

Solving this system of equations yields (10.17). **Q.E.D.**

REFERENCES

Ang, A., and J. Liu. (2001) "A General Affine Earnings Valuation Model," *Review of Accounting Studies* 6, 397-425.

Barth, M. E., W. H. Beaver, and W. R. Landsmen. (2001) "The Relevance of the Value Relevance Literature for Financial Accounting Standard Setting: Another View," *Journal of Accounting and Economics* 31, 77-104.

Begley, J., and G. A. Feltham. (2002) "The Relation Between Market Values, Earnings Forecasts, and Reported Earnings," *Contemporary Accounting Research* 19,1-48.

Dechow, P., R. Sloan, and A. Sweeney. (2000) "An Empirical Assessment of the Residual Income Valuation Model," *Journal of Accounting and Economics* 26, 1-34.

Feltham, G. A., and J. A. Ohlson. (1995) "Valuation and Clean Surplus Accounting for Operating and Financial Activities," *Contemporary Accounting Research* 11, 689-731.

Feltham, G. A., and J. A. Ohlson. (1996) "Uncertainty Resolution and the Theory of Depreciation Measurement," *Journal of Accounting Research* 34, 209-234.

Feltham, G. A., and J. Pae. (2000) "Analysis of the Impact of Accounting Accruals on Earnings Uncertainty and Response Coefficients," *Journal of Accounting, Auditing & Finance* 15, 199-224.

Frankel, R., and C. M. C. Lee. (1998) "Comparing the Accuracy and Explainability of Dividend, Free Cash Flow and Abnormal Earnings Equity Valuation Models," *Journal of Accounting and Economics* 25, 283-319.

Garman, M. B., and J. A. Ohlson. (1980) "Information and the Sequential Valuation of Assets in Arbitrage-Free Economies," *Journal of Accounting Research* 18, 420-440.

Gode, D., and J. A. Ohlson. (2000) "P-E Multiples and Changing Interest Rates," Working Paper, New York University.

Holthausen, R. W., and R. L. Watts. (2001) "The Relevance of the Value-Relevance Literature for Financial Accounting Standard Setting," *Journal of Accounting and Economics* 31, 3-75.

Kothari, S. P. (2001) "Capital Market Research in Accounting," *Journal of Accounting and Economics* 31, 105-231.

Kwon, Y. K. (2001) "Book Value, Residual Earnings, and Equilibrium Firm Value with Asymmetric Information," *Review of Accounting Studies* 6, 387-395.

Lee, C. M. C. (2001) "Market Efficiency and Accounting Research: A Discussion of 'Capital Market Research in Accounting,' by S. P. Kothari," *Journal of Accounting and Economics* 31, 233-253.

Lee, C. M. C., J. Myers, and B. Swaminathan. (1999) "What is the Intrinsic Value of the Dow?" *Journal of Finance* 54, 1693-1741.

Liu, J., and J. A. Ohlson. (2000) "The Feltham-Ohlson (1995) Model: Empirical Implications," *Journal of Accounting, Auditing & Finance* 15, 321-331.

Ohlson, J. A. (1979) "Risk, Return, Security-Valuation and the Stochastic Behavior of Security Prices," *Journal of Financial and Quantitative Analysis* 14, 317-336.

Ohlson, J. A. (1990) "A Synthesis of Security Valuation Theory and the Role of Dividends, Cash Flows, and Earnings," *Contemporary Accounting Research* 6, 648-676.

Ohlson, J. A. (1995) "Earnings, Book Values, and Dividends in Equity Valuation," *Contemporary Accounting Research* 11, 661-687.

Ohlson, J. A. (1999a) "On Transitory Earnings," *Review of Accounting Studies* 4, 145-162

Ohlson, J. A. (1999b) "Conservative Accounting and Risk," Working Paper, New York University.

Ohlson, J. A. (2001) "Earnings, Book Values, and Dividends in Equity Valuation: An Empirical Perspective," *Contemporary Accounting Research* 18, 107-120.

Ohlson, J. A., and X.-J. Zhang. (1998) "Accrual Accounting and Equity Valuation," *Journal of Accounting Research* 36, 85-111.

Rubinstein, M. (1976) "The Valuation of Uncertain Income Streams and the Pricing of Options," *Bell Journal of Economics* 7, 407-425.

Yee, K. K. (2000) "Opportunities Knocking: Residual Income Valuation of an Adaptive Firm," *Journal of Accounting, Auditing & Finance* 15, 225-270.

Zhang, G. (2000) "Accounting Information, Capital Investment Decisions, and Equity Valuation: Theory and Empirical Implications," *Journal of Accounting Research* 38, 271-295.

Zhang, X.-J. (2000a) "Conservative Accounting and Equity Valuation," *Journal of Accounting and Economics* 29, 125-149.

Zhang, X-J. (2000b) "Conservatism, Growth, and the Analysis of Line Items in Earnings Forecasting and Equity Valuation," Working Paper, University of California at Berkeley.

PART C

PRIVATE INVESTOR INFORMATION IN EQUITY MARKETS

CHAPTER 11

IMPACT OF PRIVATE INVESTOR INFORMATION IN EQUITY MARKETS

Part B (Chapters 5 through 10) considers the impact of public information in competitive capital markets in which all investors receive the same information and are price takers. Part C (Chapters 11 and 12) considers the impact of private investor information and non-price taking behavior. Why are we interested in private investor information? As accounting researchers we are not interested in private information *per se*, but we have a particular interest in the interactive effect of public reports and private investor information. For example, it is widely recognized that investors often know much of the information content in an accounting report before it is released. One reason for this is that investors may have acquired that information privately before it is released. The major gain from private information comes from going long or short in a firm's shares immediately before the release of a public report that causes the price to increase or decrease (and then reversing the position after the information is impounded in the price). Thus, intuitively, one expects investor demand for private information to increase immediately prior to an anticipated public report. Hence, a key question is how the informativeness of the accounting system affects the prior acquisition of private information. In addition, the timely release of earnings forecasts and other management information may reduce the incremental informativeness of a private signal and, thus, reduce the incentive to acquire the private signal. This type of analysis allows us to examine the relation between public reporting and private information acquisition, price changes, price informativeness, and trading volume.

If some investors know more about the future events than is publicly reported, they will obviously use that information (in addition to the public information) to determine their optimal demands for individual securities. Hence, the aggregate demand for individual securities and, thus, the market clearing prices, depend on the investors' private information (as well as on the publicly reported information). Rational investors realize that there is a dependence between private investor information and equilibrium prices. In other words, rational investors will use the equilibrium prices as a signal about the other investors' private information. Hence, the equilibrium concept must recognize that the equilibrium prices of securities themselves are a source of information that affects the investors' demand for individual securities. Equilibria that reflect attempts by investors to infer other investors' information from the equilibrium prices are termed *rational expectations equilibria.*

A key question is how much of the private information can be inferred from equilibrium prices. In turn, the informativeness of equilibrium prices affects the investors' incentives to acquire private information themselves. Consequently, we examine both the formation of equilibrium security prices and the equilibrium private information acquisition. The informativeness of equilibrium prices depends on how aggressively investors react to their private information, i.e., price informativeness and trading volume are closely related. This analysis ties into the empirical accounting literature examining the relation between, for example, earnings announcements and trading volume.

We consider two basic types of rational expectations models. In this chapter we assume the rational investors are risk-averse price takers. Most of the analysis further assumes investors have the same constant risk aversion. The investors can decide to acquire a common private signal at a certain cost. Investors deciding not to acquire the signal, i.e., the uninformed investors, imperfectly infer the common private signal from the price. The price-taking assumption implies that the informed investors ignore the impact of their trades on the information conveyed to uninformed investors through the resulting price. This is a reasonable assumption in settings in which many competing investors become informed and their individual actions have a relatively small impact on the price. However, in some settings there are relatively few investors who become informed (e.g., insiders), and they may well restrain their trades so as to partially "hide" their private information while still making a profit from its use in their trades. This latter type of analyses is examined in Chapter 12.

Section 11.1 examines some basic equilibrium issues in settings in which prices reveal private investor information, while Section 11.2 reviews the basic Grossman and Stiglitz (1980) model in which there is no public information, other than dividends. We extend this model in Sections 11.3 and 11.4 to examine the impact of public reports in the presence of private information acquisition.

In Section 11.3 the public report is released prior to investors acquiring private information. Increasing the informativeness of the public report about the final dividend is likely to reduce the incremental informativeness of the private signal and, thus, the advantage of acquiring the private signal is reduced. Hence, the equilibrium fraction of investors acquiring the signal is also reduced implying that the equilibrium price will be less informative about the private signal. That is, the increased informativeness of the public report may be offset by the reduced informativeness of the price.

Section 11.4 considers a setting in which the public report is released subsequent to investors acquiring private information. In this setting, increasing the informativeness of the public report increases the advantage of privately acquiring information about the forthcoming public information, resulting in a more informative equilibrium price prior to the release of the public report. On the other hand, the price reaction to the public report when it is released may be reduced. Hence, in this setting, there is a negative relation between the informativeness of the public report and price reaction to the release of the report. If the additional information in the public report cannot be privately accessed, the impact of increased informativeness of the public report is opposite. This highlights the fact that it is important to clearly specify how the informativeness of the public report is related to the informativeness of the private signal when making comparative statics of the impact of increasing the informativeness of a public report.

11.1 REVELATION OF PRIVATE INVESTOR INFORMATION THROUGH PRICES

In this section we consider single-trading-date models with the following elements. The investors begin with homogeneous beliefs at $t = 0$. At least some investors receive private information at $t = 1$, which results in trading by all investors. Terminal dividends are paid to the holders of the traded securities at $t = 2$. Consumption occurs at $t = 2$, and the models can also allow for consumption and production choice at $t = 1$.

11.1.1 Unsophisticated Versus Fully Informed Equilibria

Our first step is to consider competitive market equilibria. We assume investors are "unsophisticated" in that they trade on the basis of their personal beliefs and ignore the possibility that they may be trading with investors who have different (and, possibly, "better") information.

A Basic Model

In our basic model, there are I investors who trade the shares of a single firm that will pay a terminal dividend d at $t = 2$ (as well as a zero-coupon bond that has a price of 1 at $t = 1$, pays one unit of consumption at $t = 2$, and has a net supply of zero).[1] At $t = 0$, the investors have homogeneous beliefs represented by a normal distribution $d \sim N(m_0, \sigma_0^2)$. At $t = 1$ each investor potentially receives a private signal $\mathbf{y}_i$ (possibly a vector), and investor i's posterior belief based on his private signal is $d \sim N(m_{i1}(\mathbf{y}_i), \sigma_{i1}^2)$. An investor's posterior mean

[1] Note that this implies that we are using the price of the zero-coupon bond as numeraire, i.e., the price of the risky security at $t = 1$ is stated in terms of units of the zero-coupon bond and not in terms of consumption units. This allows us to omit any discounting from the analysis.

varies with the private signal received and is an important characteristic of that signal. Investor i's pre-posterior belief with respect to his posterior mean is $m_{i1} \sim N(m_0, \sigma_{mi}^2)$, with $\sigma_{mi}^2 = \sigma_0^2 - \sigma_{i1}^2$. If investor i does not receive a private signal, then $m_{i1} = m_0$ and $\sigma_{i1}^2 = \sigma_0^2$. The information received by all investors is represented by $\mathbf{y}_o = (\mathbf{y}_1, ..., \mathbf{y}_I)^t$.

Investor i's preference for consumption c_i at $t = 2$, is represented by an exponential utility function $u_i(c_i) = -\exp[-r_i c_i]$, where r_i represents investor i's risk aversion. Assume that investor i is endowed at $t = 0$ with the ownership of $\hat{z}_{i0} = (r_o/r_i)Z$ shares, where Z is the total number of shares outstanding and r_o is "aggregate risk aversion," i.e.,

$$r_o = \left[\sum_{i=1}^{I} \frac{1}{r_i} \right]^{-1}.$$

Hence, the endowments are an equilibrium allocation of shares if the investors' beliefs are homogeneous so that $z_{i0} = \hat{z}_{i0}$ (see (7.12)).

Let v_1 represent the market price of the firm's shares at $t = 1$. If the investors are "unsophisticated" and trade only on the posterior beliefs given their own private signals, then investor i's demand for the firm's shares is[2]

$$z_{i1} = \varsigma_{i1}[m_{i1} - v_1], \tag{11.1}$$

where $\varsigma_{1i} = 1/(r_i \sigma_{1i}^2)$ is the product of the investor's risk tolerance $(1/r_i)$ and the posterior precision of his beliefs $(1/\sigma_{i1}^2)$. In equilibrium, the sum of the investors' demands must equal the supply, Z. Hence, summing (11.1) over i, setting the sum equal to Z, and solving for v_1, yields the unsophisticated equilibrium price

$$v_1^u(\mathbf{y}_o) = \bar{m}^u(\mathbf{y}_o) - \frac{1}{\varsigma_{o1}} Z, \tag{11.2}$$

where $\bar{m}^u(\mathbf{y}_o)$ is the following weighted average of the investors' posterior means:

$$\bar{m}^u(\mathbf{y}_o) = \frac{1}{\varsigma_{o1}} \sum_{i=1}^{I} \varsigma_{i1} m_{i1}(\mathbf{y}_i), \quad \varsigma_{o1} = \sum_{i=1}^{I} \varsigma_{i1}.$$

[2] See (7.4) for the derivation of the investors' demand in this setting.

A Common Private Signal Model

So far we have made no assumptions about the relations among the investors' private signals. If they all receive the same signal ($\mathbf{y}_i = \mathbf{y}\ \forall\ i$), then they have homogeneous beliefs at $t = 1$ ($d \sim N(m_1(\mathbf{y}),\sigma_1^2)$), and (11.2) simplifies to

$$v_1(\mathbf{y}) = m_1(\mathbf{y}) - r_o\sigma_1^2 Z. \tag{11.3}$$

Observe that the fully informed price $v_1(\mathbf{y})$ is monotonically increasing in $m_1(\mathbf{y})$, so that the posterior mean generated by the investors' private signal, i.e., $m_1(\mathbf{y})$ can be inferred from the price v_1.

What happens if a set I_y of investors are informed about a signal $\mathbf{y}$, while the remaining set I_u are uninformed? In that setting, (11.2) becomes

$$v^u(\mathbf{y},\lambda) = \frac{\lambda h_1 m_1(\mathbf{y}) + (1-\lambda)h_0 m_0 - r_o Z}{\lambda h_1 + (1-\lambda)h_0} \tag{11.4}$$

where $h_1 = 1/\sigma_1^2$ and $h_0 = 1/\sigma_0^2$ are the precisions of the informed and uninformed investors' beliefs at $t = 1$, respectively, and λ is the fraction of the aggregate risk tolerance attributable to the informed investors, i.e.,

$$\lambda = \frac{r_o}{r_y}, \qquad r_y = \left[\sum_{i\in I_y} \frac{1}{r_i}\right]^{-1}.$$

In this setting, the unsophisticated equilibrium price $v^u(\mathbf{y},\lambda)$ is monotonically increasing in $m_1(\mathbf{y})$. Hence, after trading to an unsophisticated equilibrium at $t = 1$, the uninformed investors will be able to infer $m_1(\mathbf{y})$ from $v^u(\mathbf{y},\lambda)$. If they realize this, and if another round of trading takes place, their demand for the firm's shares will change, and the fully informed equilibrium price $v_1(\mathbf{y})$ (see (11.3)) will occur.

A troublesome aspect of this sequence of events is that the uninformed investors lose money by trading with the informed investors. Based on the informed posterior mean m_1, the value of the shares is $v_1(\mathbf{y})$. However, in the first round of trading, each uninformed investor i either bought $z_{i1} - z_{i0} > 0$ shares for a price $v^u(\mathbf{y},\lambda) > v_1(\mathbf{y})$ and then sold the shares back for $v_1(\mathbf{y})$, or he sold $z_{i0} - z_{i1}$ shares for a price $v^u(\mathbf{y},\lambda) < v_1(\mathbf{y})$ and then bought the shares back for $v_1(\mathbf{y})$. Hence, if an uninformed investor is "sophisticated" he will refuse to trade if he knows that some investors are informed, even though he does not know the signal they have received.

Instead of refusing to trade, a rational (sophisticated) uninformed investor might seek to infer the informed investors' private signal from the process that yields the equilibrium price. If that is possible, then the fully informed equilibrium price (11.3) would be achieved in the first round of trading.

What happens if the informed investors are only informed if they incur an information cost κ? If the uninformed are unsophisticated, then the informed investors gain by trading with the uninformed, and this gain may be sufficient to cover the information cost. However, as pointed out by Grossman and Stiglitz (1980), if the uninformed are rational and able to infer the private signal from the equilibrium process, then investors will have no incentive to incur the information cost κ and no one will be informed. On the other hand, if every investor believes that no investor has acquired information, then an investor could gain by secretly acquiring the private signal **y** and trading on it (he would be effectively trading with unsophisticated investors). Of course, the uninformed investors could refuse to trade, but the "bottom line" is that there is effectively no equilibrium in a setting in which private information is costly and uninformed investors can infer the informed investors' private signal from the equilibrium price. This line of argument has been termed *the information paradox.*

A Diverse Private Signals Model

From (11.2) we observe that the unsophisticated equilibrium price reveals the fully informed posterior mean if, and only if, $m_1(\mathbf{y}_o)$ is a monotonic function of $\bar{m}^u(\mathbf{y}_o)$. In general, that will not be the case, particularly given that $m_1(\mathbf{y}_o)$ depends only on the investors' beliefs, whereas $\bar{m}^u(\mathbf{y}_o)$ depends on both their beliefs and their risk aversion. Of course, if all investors have the same risk aversion (i.e., $r_i = r$, $\forall\, i$), then the average unsophisticated posterior mean reflects the relative precision of the investors' posterior beliefs:

$$\bar{m}^u(\mathbf{y}_o) = \frac{1}{h_{o1}} \sum_{i=1}^{I} h_{i1} m_{i1}, \quad h_{o1} = \sum_{i=1}^{I} h_{i1}.$$

Whether $\bar{m}^u(\mathbf{y}_o)$ reveals $m_1(\mathbf{y}_o)$ depends on the information system. Consider, for example, a setting in which investor i's posterior belief is based on a signal $y_i \sim \mathrm{N}(d,\sigma_{yi}^2)$, $\forall\, i$, that is a noisy measure of the terminal dividend, and assume the noise is independent across investors. In this setting, $m_{i1} = \sigma_{i1}^2[h_0 m_0 + h_{yi} y_i]$, where $\sigma_{i1}^2 = [h_0 + h_{yi}]^{-1}$ is investor i's posterior variance and $h_{yi} = 1/\sigma_{yi}^2$ is the precision of his signal. Furthermore, the fully informed posterior mean and variance are

$$m_1(\mathbf{y}_o) = \sigma_{1y_o}^2 \left[h_0 m_0 + \sum_{i=1}^{I} h_{yi} y_i \right] = \sigma_{1y_o}^2 \left[(1 - I) h_0 m_0 + h_{o1}\, \bar{m}^u(\mathbf{y}_o) \right], \quad (11.5a)$$

$$\sigma^2_{1y_o} = \left[h_0 + \sum_{i=1}^{I} h_{yi} \right]^{-1}. \tag{11.5b}$$

Consequently, $m_1(\mathbf{y}_o)$ is a linear function of $\bar{m}^u(\mathbf{y}_o)$.

Throughout this chapter we focus on models in which dividends and information are normally distributed and investors either have exponential utility functions or are risk neutral. This focus reflects the nature of the models that have been considered in the accounting literature. However, the reader should be aware that in the finance and economics literature there are papers that consider general preferences and general state beliefs. Grossman (1981) provides a foundational paper in this literature, and its main elements are summarized in Appendix 11A. A key result is that if the market is complete, then the fully informed equilibrium prices reveal a sufficient statistic for the investors' information so that investors trading on that information achieve a fully informed equilibrium.

Market Efficiency

A market is defined to be efficient with respect to the private signals from a particular information system if prices act as if everyone knows the information.[3] While the unsophisticated equilibrium prices may well reveal a sufficient statistic for the investors' information, that does not imply that the unsophisticated equilibrium prices are the same as the fully informed equilibrium prices. For example, in the common private signal model examined above, the unsophisticated equilibrium price in (11.4) does not equal the fully informed equilibrium price in (11.3) except in the knife-edge case in which $m_1(\mathbf{y}) = m_0$.

As demonstrated by Easley and Jarrow (1983), this lack of efficiency in an unsophisticated equilibrium is pervasive.

Proposition 11.1 (Easley and Jarrow 1983)

The prices in an unsophisticated equilibrium are not efficient (except for a negligible subset of prior beliefs).

We do not examine the technical details of this proposition, but merely state it here to confirm what we saw in our examples. Rational investors have incentives to infer what other investors have observed by considering the prices at which they are willing to trade and this affects the prices at which they do trade.

---

[3] Note that this is a different concept than efficiency of consumption allocation.

11.1.2 Rational Expectations Equilibria

Equilibria that reflect attempts by investors to infer other investors' information from the price process are termed "rational expectations equilibria." A key issue in these equilibria is the extent to which private information is revealed by the price process. There have been two broad types of analyses. First, the initial analyses in this area generally assumed that private information is the only random factor affecting prices. The key result from this work is that, except in knife-edge cases, the price process fully reveals a sufficient statistic for the investors' information. The resulting equilibrium is referred to as a *fully revealing rational expectations equilibrium.*

As illustrated in Section 11.1.1, the existence of a fully revealing rational expectations equilibrium implies that investors have no incentive to expend resources acquiring private information since there are no gains to acquiring this information in our pure exchange setting. However, in the real world, investors clearly expend resources trying to acquire private information. This implies that they believe they will be able to trade on this information without fully revealing it in the trading process. Some research has been done in which the details of the price formation process are considered, and while the price process ultimately reveals the information, there are gains from moving first.[4] While this may be a realistic approach to the issue, the more common approach in the literature is to assume investors infer information from prices in a simultaneous equilibrium process. However, there is some unobservable, exogenous random factor that influences the price and precludes investors from fully inferring the information acquired by other investors. The equilibria in these settings are referred to as *noisy rational expectations equilibria.*

Admati (1991) provides a useful overview of some of the rational expectations literature. This includes a summary of the work by Grossman (illustrated by Grossman and Stiglitz, 1980, which we use extensively in this chapter, and Grossman, 1981, which we briefly summarize in Appendix 11A). She also gives a broad perspective of a variety of research that stems from this foundational work. In this chapter, we focus on work that has been of interest to accounting researchers. In the accounting literature, Verrecchia (1993) provides an insightful, short perspective on rational expectations research that helps us understand the impact of information (private and public) on the variability of market prices and trading volume.

Within this literature there are three basic types of models. The GS type model follows from the model in Grossman and Stiglitz (1980). This type assumes investors are identically risk-averse price takers who can acquire a common private signal and the uninformed investors imperfectly infer the

---

[4] See, for example, Bray (1981).

common private signal from the price. The HV type model follows from the models in Hellwig (1980) and Verrecchia (1982). This type assumes investors are differentially risk-averse price takers who can acquire differentially precise private signals and make imperfect inferences about the other investors' information from the price. The Kyle (1985) type model assumes investors are risk neutral, the uninformed investor (the market-maker) sets the market price based on the total number of shares sold, and the informed investors act strategically in that they recognize that the size of their orders will influence the uninformed investor's inference about their information.

The GS and HV type models obtain similar results since both assume investors are risk-averse price takers. Several papers in the accounting literature use HV type models, but we focus on the GS type models because they tend to be less complex. However, we make reference to some of the related work that uses the HV model. The risk neutrality of investors makes the Kyle type model relatively simple to use, and provides somewhat different results because of its focus on trading volume and strategic trading by the informed investors. Hence, in Chapter 12 we examine some Kyle type models that consider the interaction between public and private information.

11.1.3 Expected Utility from Competitive Acquisition of Risk

The lack of demand for private information acquisition in a fully revealing rational expectations equilibrium has led to models that introduce "noise" into prices, i.e., an exogenous, unobservable source of uncertainty that causes prices to vary in addition to the variations induced by private information. The primary approach for accomplishing this has been to assume the supply of the risky asset (Z) is exogenously random. Some papers have assumed this is a result of random endowments of the rational investors. Unfortunately, the random endowments approach implies that investors are not able to efficiently share their risks before information is released (leading to the well known information risk problem identified by Hirshleifer, 1971). An alternative approach, and the one we use, is to assume the rational investors have fixed endowments but they buy (or sell) shares supplied (or acquired) by "liquidity traders" who trade for reasons that are independent of the price and the information acquired by the rational investors. Unfortunately, the preferences of the liquidity traders are unmodelled, making it impossible to examine social welfare issues. Nevertheless, this type of model serves to provide a simple means of introducing noise into the price process, and thereby permit examination of the interactive effect of public and private information on private information acquisition, as well as the response of prices and trading volume to the two types of information.

Before considering noisy rational expectations equilibria with private information, we briefly discuss the impact of random variations in the supply of the firm's shares in a public information setting. This will help us understand some basic economic forces in the private information models.

We return to the setting in Section 11.1.1 in which there are I rational investors with exponential utility and a single firm that pays a normally distributed dividend $d \sim N(m_0,\sigma_0^2)$ at $t = 2$. For simplicity, we assume the rational investors have zero endowments at $t = 0$ (i.e., initially, all shares are held by liquidity traders) and the supply of shares by the liquidity traders at $t = 1$ is normally distributed with $Z_\ell \sim N(0,\sigma_Z^2)$.[5] That is, Z_ℓ is the number of shares the liquidity traders wish to sell at $t = 1$ and, in equilibrium, all of these shares are purchased by the rational investors. (A negative Z_ℓ represents purchases by the liquidity traders and short-sales by the rational investors.)

Assume all rational investors receive the same signal **y**. Their common posterior dividend belief is represented by $d \sim N(m_1(\mathbf{y}),\sigma_1^2)$ and their pre-posterior belief about the posterior mean is represented by $m_1 \sim N(m_0,\sigma_m^2)$, with $\sigma_m^2 = \sigma_0^2 - \sigma_1^2$. The fully informed equilibrium price for a given posterior mean m_1 and a given supply of shares Z_ℓ is stated in (11.3), and investor i's equilibrium demand for shares is $z_i = (r_o/r_i)Z_\ell$. Observe that the number of shares acquired varies with the supply Z_ℓ, but it is independent of the signal **y**. However, the signal influences the price of the shares.

Investor i's posterior equilibrium expected utility, given signal **y** and shares Z_ℓ, is

$$U_{i1}(\mathbf{y},Z_\ell) = \mathrm{E}[- \exp[- r_i(r_o/r_i)Z_\ell(d - v_1(\mathbf{y}))] \,|\mathbf{y},Z_\ell] = - \exp[- ½r_o^2Z_\ell^2\sigma_1^2]. \quad (11.6)$$

If the supply of shares is zero, then investor i's expected utility is - exp[0] = -1. Hence, he effectively earns an "excess" risk premium of $½r_oZ_\ell^2\sigma_1^2$ to absorb his efficient fraction of the firm's shares put into the market by the liquidity traders. This premium is positive whether the liquidity traders wish to buy or sell shares.

If the liquidity traders could make "take it or leave it" offers to the rational investors, the price offered would be $v_1^\dagger(\mathbf{y}) = m_1(\mathbf{y}) - ½r_oZ_\ell\sigma_1^2$, since that would be sufficient to compensate the rational investors for the risk they are taking by acquiring Z_ℓ given **y**.[6] However, we assume the liquidity traders must dispose of their shares in a competitive market and $v_1^\dagger(\mathbf{y})$ would not clear the market (since the investors in a competitive market can acquire whatever fraction they prefer). That is, the competitive market leads to a risk premium twice the cost of the risk to the rational investors (compare the competitive market price in (11.3) to $v_1^\dagger(\mathbf{y})$).

---

[5] Assuming zero endowments and zero expected supply simplifies the analysis without substantially influencing the results.

[6] That is, the price at which the partnership of rational investors would be indifferent to the trade.

Observe that $U_{i1}(\mathbf{y},Z_\ell)$ is independent of **y** but increasing in σ_1^2, and achieves its maximum if **y** is uninformative, i.e., $\sigma_1^2 = \sigma_0^2$ and $\sigma_m^2 = 0$. That is, the rational investors would prefer to have no information released before they absorb the liquidity trades, since that will maximize the "excess" risk premium they can earn.

Further observe that $U_{i1}(\mathbf{y},Z_\ell)$ is increasing in the absolute value of Z_ℓ. That is, the more shares the liquidity traders want to buy or sell, the greater is the "excess" risk premium the rational investors earn. We assume that Z_ℓ is normally distributed and, hence, investor i's expected utility at $t = 0$ is[7]

$$U_{i0} = \mathrm{E}[-\exp[-\tfrac{1}{2}r_o^2 Z_\ell^2 \sigma_1^2]] = -\sqrt{\frac{1}{1 + r_o^2 \sigma_Z^2 \sigma_1^2}}.$$

Therefore, a rational investor's expected utility is increasing in the aggregate risk aversion of the rational investors (r_o), his posterior uncertainty about dividends (σ_1^2), and the variability in the number of shares bought or sold by the liquidity traders (σ_Z^2). Of course, the benefits to the rational investors come at the expense of the liquidity traders.

11.2 ACQUISITION OF PRIVATE INFORMATION BY PRICE-TAKING INVESTORS

In this section we review the basic GS model in which dividends are the only public information. In the following two sections we extend the analysis to explore information settings in which (a) public reports are released prior to the acquisition of private information, and (b) public reports are released subsequent to the acquisition of private information, respectively.

The Basic GS Model

The basic GS model is essentially the common private signal model introduced in Section 11.1.1, but with the assumption that all rational investors have the same risk aversion. The key characteristics of the model are as follows.

- There is a single firm that pays a risky dividend $d = m_0 + \varepsilon$, where ε is the random component with prior normal distribution $\varepsilon \sim N(0,\sigma_0^2)$.

---

[7] See Appendix 3A for the general derivation of the expected value of an exponential-quadratic function of a normally distributed random variable.

- There are I rational investors each with exponential utility and risk aversion r (so that the aggregate risk aversion is $r_o = r/I$).

- There is a signal **y** (e.g., a vector representing the elements of a privately available financial report) that can be acquired by investor i at a cost κ_i, for all i. The fraction of the rational investors who acquire the signal is denoted λ.

- To simplify the discussion, but without loss of generality, we represent the informed investors' signal **y** with $y_i = \mathrm{E}[\varepsilon|\mathbf{y}]$, i.e., the informed investors' posterior mean with respect to the random component of the dividend. An informed investor's pre-posterior belief (i.e., his prior belief about the posterior mean) is $y_i \sim \mathrm{N}(0,\sigma_{yi}^2)$ and his posterior random dividend belief given **y** is $\boldsymbol{\varepsilon} \sim \mathrm{N}(y_i,\sigma_{i1}^2)$.

- The rational investors have zero endowed shares at $t = 0$, but at $t = 1$ they absorb $Z_\ell \sim \mathrm{N}(0,\sigma_Z^2)$ shares sold by liquidity traders. We express this supply in terms of the average number of shares per rational investor, i.e. $z_\ell = Z_\ell/I$, $z_\ell \sim \mathrm{N}(0,\sigma_z^2)$, and $\sigma_Z^2 = I^2\sigma_z^2$.[8]

- The informed investors are price takers, i.e., they do not consider the impact of their trades on the information revealed by the price.

The basic sequence of events for the informed investors are depicted in Figure 11.1. Observe that $\sigma_0^2 = \sigma_{yi}^2 + \sigma_{i1}^2$.

11.2.1 Exogenous Set of Informed Investors

We initially solve for the equilibrium price and investments taking the fraction λ of informed investors as given. Then we solve for the equilibrium set of informed investors. Observe that since all investors have the same risk aversion, the fraction informed λ is the fraction of aggregate risk aversion attributable to informed investors.

[8] GS do not consider liquidity trades and, instead, assume the rational investors' endowments are random. They permit the mean of those endowments to be non-zero, but many papers make the zero mean assumption.

Figure 11.1
Sequence of Events in the Basic GS Model

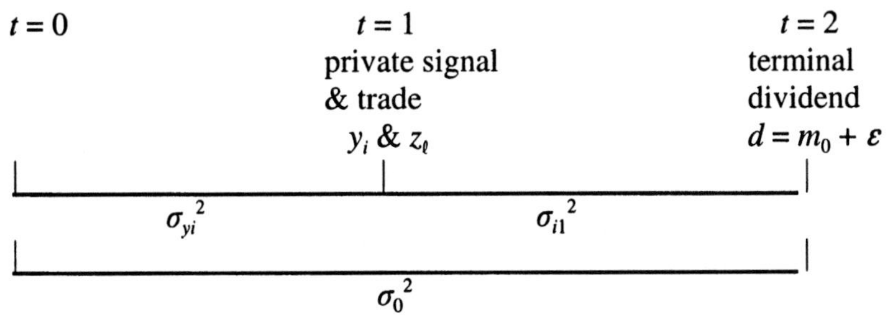

The uninformed investors do not know the private signal **y** and hold posterior beliefs based on the inferences they can make from the equilibrium price v_1. To derive the uninformed posterior beliefs we assume the uninformed investors conjecture that the equilibrium price is a linear function of the informed posterior mean y_i and the random supply of shares z_ℓ, i.e., there exist parameters π_y and π_z such that

$$v_1(y_i,z_\ell) = m_0 + \pi_y y_i - \pi_z z_\ell. \tag{11.7}$$

The uninformed traders do not observe either y_i or z_ℓ, but they can infer the statistic

$$\psi = \frac{1}{\pi_y}[v_1 - m_0] = y_i - \frac{\pi_z}{\pi_y} z_\ell. \tag{11.8}$$

Observe that v_1 and ψ have the same information content with respect y_i, but ψ is an easier variable with which to work. Note that ψ is a mean-preserving spread of y_i created by the random supply of shares from liquidity traders, and this prevents the uninformed investors from perfectly inferring y_i from the price.

Under the assumed conditions, ε, y_i, and ψ (or v_1) are jointly normally distributed. In particular, see Table 11.1 for a specification of the prior mean and covariance matrix for these three variables, as well as the posterior mean and variance of ε given ψ.[9]

[9] See Section 3.1.3 for a general statement of conditional means for joint normally distributed variables. Observe that y_i is a sufficient statistic for (y_i,ψ) with respect to beliefs about ε.

Table 11.1
Rational Dividend Beliefs Based on Price

Prior mean and covariance matrix:

$$\begin{bmatrix} \varepsilon \\ y_i \\ \psi \end{bmatrix} \sim \mathrm{N}\left(\begin{bmatrix} 0 \\ 0 \\ 0 \end{bmatrix}, \begin{bmatrix} \sigma_0^2 & \sigma_{yi}^2 & \sigma_{yi}^2 \\ \sigma_{yi}^2 & \sigma_{yi}^2 & \sigma_{yi}^2 \\ \sigma_{yi}^2 & \sigma_{yi}^2 & \sigma_\psi^2 \end{bmatrix} \right), \qquad \sigma_\psi^2 = \sigma_{yi}^2 + \frac{\pi_z^2}{\pi_y^2}\sigma_z^2.$$

Posterior means and variances with respect to ε given y or ψ:

$$\mu_{i1}(\mathbf{y}) = y_i, \qquad \sigma_{i1}^2 = \sigma_0^2 - \sigma_{yi}^2,$$

$$\mu_{u1}(\psi) = \frac{\sigma_{yi}^2}{\sigma_\psi^2}\psi, \qquad \sigma_{u1}^2 = \sigma_0^2 - \frac{\sigma_{yi}^2}{\sigma_\psi^2}\sigma_{yi}^2.$$

The demand for shares by an informed investor given private signal y_i and price v_1 is (see (7.4))

$$z_i(y_i,v_1) = \frac{1}{r}h_{i1}[m_0 + y_i - v_1], \tag{11.9}$$

where $h_{i1} = 1/\sigma_{i1}^2$ is an informed investor's posterior precision with respect to ε and $\mathrm{E}[d|\mathbf{y}] = m_0 + y_i$ is his posterior mean with respect to the terminal dividend.

Similarly, the demand for shares by an uninformed investor given statistic ψ and price v_1 is

$$z_u(\psi,v_1) = \frac{1}{r}h_{u1}[m_0 + \mu_{u1}(\psi) - v_1], \tag{11.10}$$

where $h_{u1} = 1/\sigma_{u1}^2$ is an uninformed investor's posterior precision with respect to ε and $\mathrm{E}[d|\psi] = m_0 + \mu_{u1}(\psi)$ is his posterior mean (see Table 11.1).

Given that a fraction λ of rational investors are informed, market clearing requires the equilibrium price to be such that the supply from the liquidity traders equals the average demand from the informed and uninformed investors:

$$z_\ell = \lambda z_i(y_i, v_1) + (1-\lambda) z_u(\psi, v_1). \tag{11.11}$$

Substituting (11.9) and (11.10) into (11.11) and solving for v_1 yields

$$v_1 = m_0 + \frac{1}{\bar{h}_1}\,[\lambda h_{i1} y_i + (1-\lambda) h_{u1}\mu_{u1}(\psi) - r z_\ell], \tag{11.12}$$

where $\bar{h}_1 = \lambda h_{i1} + (1-\lambda) h_{u1}$ is the average posterior precision. Of course, h_{u1} and $\mu_{u1}(\psi)$ are functions of the parameters (π_y, π_z). The equilibrium parameters are characterized in the following proposition. We provide the proof in Appendix 11B as an illustration of how the parameters are derived in GS type models.

Proposition 11.2 (GS, Theorem 1)
The equilibrium price parameters in the basic GS model for $\lambda \in (0,1)$ are:

$$\pi_y = \frac{1}{\bar{h}_1}\left[\lambda h_{i1} + (1-\lambda) h_{u1}\frac{\sigma_{yi}^2}{\sigma_\psi^2}\right], \quad \pi_z = \frac{r}{\lambda h_{i1}}\pi_y \tag{11.13}$$

$$h_{u1} = \frac{\sigma_\psi^2}{\sigma_0^2\sigma_\psi^2 - \sigma_{yi}^4}, \quad \sigma_\psi^2 = \sigma_{yi}^2 + \frac{1}{\lambda^2} r^2 \sigma_{i1}^4 \sigma_z^2. \tag{11.14}$$

Observe that (11.13) implies that $\pi_y/\pi_z = \lambda h_{i1}/r$. Hence, the informed investors' private signal **y** has relatively more impact on the price than does the supply of shares z_ℓ if the fraction of informed investors (λ) is increased, the investors' risk aversion (r) is decreased, or the precision of the information (h_{i1}) is increased.

11.2.2 Endogenous Information Acquisition

Now consider information costs and assume that, in equilibrium, some rational investors choose to become informed, while the others do not.

Ex Ante Expected Utility
The terminal wealths of informed and uninformed investors, given the optimal investment decisions (11.9) and (11.10), are

$$w_i = z_i \Delta - \kappa_i = \frac{1}{r} h_{i1}[m_0 + y_i - v_1]\Delta - \kappa_i, \tag{11.15a}$$

$$w_u = z_u \Delta = \frac{1}{r} h_{u1}[m_0 + \mu_{u1}(\psi) - v_1]\Delta, \quad (11.15b)$$

where $\Delta \equiv d - v_1$ and (11.15a) reflects the fact that, to be informed, investor i must pay κ_i. Both expressions contain two random differences: the difference between the posterior mean and the price, and Δ, which is the difference between the terminal dividend and the price. The latter is the same for both types of investors, but the former depends on the information they receive at $t = 1$. Based on (11.7) and the relation between ε and y_i in Table (11.1), it follows that, from an *ex ante* perspective,

$$\mathrm{E}[\Delta] = \mathrm{E}[\varepsilon - (\pi_y y_i - \pi_z z_\ell)] = 0,$$

$$\sigma_\Delta^2 \equiv \mathrm{Var}[\Delta] = \mathrm{Var}[\varepsilon - (\pi_y y_i - \pi_z z_\ell)] = \sigma_0^2 + \pi_y^2 \sigma_{yi}^2 - 2\pi_y \sigma_{yi}^2 + \pi_z^2 \sigma_z^2.$$

The following proposition provides a simple representation of the *ex ante* expected utilities for the two types of investors given an exogenous fraction λ of the investors are informed. These expressions can be obtained by applying Proposition 3.1 in Admati and Pfleiderer (1987).[10] To highlight the role of the fraction informed, we explicitly recognize that σ_{u1}^2 and σ_Δ^2 are functions of λ.

Proposition 11.3 (Admati and Pfleiderer 1987, Prop. 3.1)
Given that a fraction λ of the investors are informed, the expected utilities for the informed and uninformed investors are:

$$U_{i0}(\lambda) = \mathrm{E}[-\exp[-rw_i]|\lambda] = -\frac{\sigma_{i1}}{\sigma_\Delta(\lambda)}\exp[r\kappa_i], \quad (11.16a)$$

$$U_{u0}(\lambda) = \mathrm{E}[-\exp[-rw_u]|\lambda] = -\frac{\sigma_{u1}(\lambda)}{\sigma_\Delta(\lambda)}. \quad (11.16b)$$

Equilibrium Set of Informed Investors
Now we consider the endogenous investors' information acquisition decisions. Let I_y represent the set of investors who choose to become informed and let $\lambda = |I_y|/I$ represent the fraction of investors in set I_y. The set of informed investors I_y is an equilibrium if no investor prefers to change his type. Assume the number of investors is sufficiently large that a change in type by one investor has a minuscule effect on the expected utilities in (11.16).

---

[10] The expressions can also be obtained by applying result (ii) in Appendix 3A. However, the application of the Admati and Pfleiderer proposition is straightforward.

Proposition 11.4

In the GS model, with a large number of rational investors and varied information costs, there exists a cost cut-off $\hat{\kappa}$ such that $\kappa_i \leq \hat{\kappa}$, $\forall\, i \in I_y$, where I_y is the equilibrium set of informed investors.

This result formalizes the intuition that if there are both informed and uninformed investors, the former will consist of those who have the lowest information acquisition costs.

To facilitate the characterization of the equilibrium, GS assume the cost $\kappa_i = \kappa$ for all investors and they treat the fraction of informed traders as a continuous variable. Hence, if the equilibrium set of informed investors does not consist of either no or all investors, then the equilibrium fraction informed is such that all investors are indifferent between being informed or uninformed. In characterizing this condition it is useful to consider the ratio of the *ex ante* expected utilities of the informed and uninformed investors. From (11.16) it is obvious that this takes the following simple form:

$$Q(\lambda) \equiv \frac{U_{i0}(\lambda)}{U_{u0}(\lambda)} = \exp[r\kappa]\,\frac{\sigma_{i1}}{\sigma_{u1}(\lambda)}. \tag{11.17}$$

The posterior uncertainty of the uninformed investors, $\sigma_{u1}(\lambda)$, is decreasing in λ.[11] Hence, $Q(\lambda)$ is an increasing function of λ, and GS obtain the following result, where λ^* is the equilibrium fraction informed (note that expected utilities are negative such that the gain from becoming informed decreases with λ).

Proposition 11.5 (GS, Theorem 3)

The following conditions hold in the GS model.

(a) If $Q(0) \geq 1$, then the cost of information is so high that $U_{i0}(0) \leq U_{u0}(0)$, implying $\lambda^* = 0$.

(b) If $Q(1) \leq 1$, then the cost of information is so low that $U_{i0}(1) \geq U_{u0}(1)$, implying $\lambda^* = 1$.

(c) If $Q(0) < 1 < Q(1)$, then there exists an equilibrium fraction $\lambda^* \in (0,1)$ such that $Q(\lambda^*) = 1$.

---

[11] From (11.14) and Table 11.1 we obtain:

$$\frac{d\sigma_\psi^2}{d\lambda} = -\frac{2}{\lambda^3} r^2 \sigma_{i1}^2 \sigma_z^2 < 0, \qquad \frac{d\sigma_{u1}^2}{d\lambda} = \frac{\sigma_{yi}^4}{\sigma_\psi^4}\frac{d\sigma_\psi^2}{d\lambda} < 0.$$

If case (c) holds, then we can characterize the equilibrium fraction informed by solving for $Q(\lambda^*) = 1$ using (11.14) and (11.17). The result is

$$\lambda^* = r\sigma_z\sigma_{i1}\sqrt{\frac{\sigma_{yi}^2 - K\sigma_{i1}^2}{K\sigma_{yi}^2}}, \tag{11.18}$$

where $K = \exp[2r\kappa] - 1$ is a transformed measure of the information cost.

The precisions of the informed and uninformed investors' posterior dividend beliefs are $h_{i1} = 1/\sigma_{i1}^2$ and $h_{u1} = 1/\sigma_{u1}^2$, respectively. If $\lambda < 1$, then $h_{u1} < h_{i1}$ and we can view the difference in precision as a measure of the informativeness of the price. Alternatively, we can follow GS and define price-informativeness as the squared correlation between the informed posterior mean y_i and the price. This takes a relatively simple form when based on the equilibrium fraction informed (see Appendix 11B for a proof).

Proposition 11.6 (GS, Eqs. 17 and 19)

If $\lambda^* \in (0,1)$, then the equilibrium price-informativeness in the basic GS model is

$$\text{Corr}^2(y_i, v_1) = 1 - K\frac{\sigma_{i1}^2}{\sigma_{yi}^2}. \tag{11.19}$$

Hence, the following comparative statics can be readily obtained by differentiating (11.19).

Proposition 11.7 (GS, Th. 4)

If $\lambda^* \in (0,1)$, then the equilibrium price-informativeness in the basic GS model is:

(a) increasing in signal-informativeness ($h_{i1} = 1/\sigma_{i1}^2$);

(b) decreasing in the information cost (κ);

(c) decreasing in investor risk aversion (r);

(d) unaffected by noise (σ_z^2).

Result (a) reflects the fact that increased signal-informativeness implies there is more information to be conveyed by price, and the informed investors trade more aggressively, so that their trades have a relatively larger impact on price. The reduced cost in (b) makes it more attractive for investors to become informed, and the increased trading on signal **y** has a relatively larger impact on price. In (c), a decrease in risk aversion induces the informed investors to trade more aggressively on the signal **y**, and thus they have a relatively larger impact on price. The impact of noise in (d) is more subtle. For a given fraction λ, more noise makes it more difficult to infer the informed posterior mean y_i from the price. However, that induces more investors to become informed and the larger number of investors trading on y_i precisely offsets the increased noise.

The last result is somewhat surprising, so it is useful to demonstrate that noise does not affect the precision of an uninformed investor's posterior belief, in equilibrium. First observe that h_{u1} in (11.14) is affected by σ_z only through σ_ψ^2, whereas σ_z affects the latter both directly and through its impact on λ^*. Hence, we first differentiate λ^* with respect to σ_z and then totally differentiate σ_ψ^2 in (11.14):

$$\frac{d\lambda^*}{d\sigma_z} = \frac{1}{\sigma_z}\lambda^* > 0,$$

$$\frac{d\sigma_\psi^2}{d\sigma_z} = r^2\sigma_{i1}^4\left[-\frac{2}{\lambda^{*3}}\frac{d\lambda^*}{d\sigma_z}\sigma_z^2 + \frac{2}{\lambda^{*2}}\sigma_z\right] = 0.$$

Since σ_z only impacts h_{u1} through σ_ψ^2, it follows that there is no effect.

Rational Investors "Shoot Themselves in the Foot"

If no investor are expected to become informed (i.e., $\lambda = 0$), then

$$v_1 = m_0 - r\sigma_0^2 z_\ell, \quad \sigma_\Delta^2 = \sigma_0^2 + r^2\sigma_0^4\sigma_z^2, \quad \sigma_{u1}^2 = \sigma_0^2,$$

and an investors' *ex ante* expected utility is

$$U_{u0}(0) = -\sqrt{\frac{1}{1 + r^2\sigma_0^2\sigma_z^2}}.$$

This is the maximum expected utility for the uninformed investor (i.e., $dU_{u0}(\lambda)/d\lambda < 0$). Consequently, $U_{u0}(0) > U_{u0}(\lambda^*) = U_{i0}(\lambda^*)$ if $\lambda^* > 0$. This implies that all investors are made worse off by low cost opportunities to acquire private information, if it is common knowledge that those opportunities exist. An important factor leading to this result is provided by the analysis in Section 11.1.3. In that analysis, we established that the rational investors' expected utilities are higher the more uncertainty they face, because that allows them to extract a larger "excess" risk premium from the liquidity traders.

Interestingly, despite that result, the above analysis establishes that some fraction of the rational investors will pay a cost κ to reduce their uncertainty if the cost is sufficiently small. Why? A key factor is that while the aggregate number of informed investors reduces the "excess" risk premium from the liquidity traders, the decision to become informed by any one investor does not affect that premium. Hence, an individual investor's decision to become informed is driven by his desire to obtain an informational advantage over those who do not become informed (or to avoid an informational disadvantage relative to those who do become informed). Of course, in equilibrium, the cost κ is just sufficient to offset the benefit of being informed, and in the GS model all investors are indifferent between being informed or uninformed. Hence, we can view the rational investors as effectively "shooting themselves in the foot" relative to what they could achieve if they coordinated their actions. That is, in their attempts to take advantage of each other, the *ex post* rational actions of the investors have reduced their advantage with respect to the liquidity traders. If they could collude and make binding commitments not to acquire private information, they would be better off doing so, and this would be better for them than having a regulator dictate that the signal **y** be publicly reported. Of course, the gain to the rational investors would be at the expense of the liquidity traders.

Diverse Private Signals Models

The analysis can be extended to consider settings in which the investors differ with respect to their risk aversion and investors receive individual specific private signals. We refer to these as HV models since Hellwig (1980) and Verrecchia (1982) are two of the first papers to adopt this approach. Hellwig derives the equilibrium demand and prices for a setting with a large number of rational investors in which each investor i receives a signal $y_i = d + \varsigma_i$, where ς_i is noise that is independent across investors and has exogenous precision h_i. A key feature of the equilibrium price is that it takes the following form:

$$v_1 = \pi_0 m_0 + \pi_d d - \pi_z z_\ell.$$

That is, due to the large number of investors with independent private signals, the price varies directly with the terminal dividend (since the average signal for all investors almost surely equals the dividend and this is a sufficient statistic for all the information). However, because the investors do not know each other's signals and only make imperfect inferences from the price, the price is also influenced by variations in the supply of shares from the liquidity traders.

Verrecchia (1982) extends the Hellwig model to include endogenous choice of the signal precision in a setting in which each investor's information cost is an increasing, convex function of the signal's precision. The analysis establishes that the signal precision chosen by investor i is a non-decreasing function of his risk tolerance (i.e., $1/r_i$) and prior dividend uncertainty, and a non-increasing function of his marginal cost of signal precision and a measure which Verrecchia refers to as the informativeness of the price. Loosely speaking, this informativeness measure equals the square of the investors' average risk tolerance times signal precision divided by the variance in the supply of shares from the liquidity traders.[12] Consequently, the signal precision chosen by an investor is a non-increasing function of the average risk tolerance and signal precision of the investors in the economy, and a non-decreasing function of the noise due to liquidity traders.

Holthausen and Verrecchia (HoV) (1990) use the HV model to explore price and volume effects of private information when there is a single round of trading. They treat the precision of the private signals as exogenous and assume investor i's private signal is $y_i = d + \varsigma_0 + \varsigma_i$, where ς_0 is noise that is common to all investors. They simplify their analysis by assuming all investors have the same risk tolerance and the same signal precision. The equilibrium price takes the following form:

$$v_1 = \pi_0 m_0 + \pi_{\bar{y}} \bar{y} - \pi_z z_\ell,$$

where $\bar{y} = d + \varsigma_0$. If there is no investor specific signal noise, i.e., all investors observe $\bar{y}$, then the trading volume is z_ℓ and the price parameters are such that $\pi_0 m_0 + \pi_{\bar{y}} \bar{y} = \mathrm{E}[d|\bar{y}]$ and $\pi_z = r\mathrm{Var}[d|\bar{y}]$. However, differences in investor information create additional trading and differences in prices.

HoV develop two measures, which they call *informedness* and *consensus*. The former equals the precision of an investor's posterior belief about d given y_i and v_1, while the latter is the correlation between $d - \mathrm{E}[d|y_i,v_1]$ and $d - \mathrm{E}[d|y_j,v_1]$ for any pair of investors i and j. They then establish that, holding informedness constant, increasing consensus results in a decrease in expected trading volume and an increase in the price variance. Furthermore, holding consensus constant, increasing informedness results in an increase in trading volume and an increase in the price variance.

Indjejikian (IND) (1991) can be interpreted as extending the model in HoV to consider the impact of endogenous information acquisition. IND interprets $\bar{y} = d + \varsigma_0$ as representing a public report that is difficult to understand, and then interprets investor i's private signal $y_i = d + \varsigma_0 + \varsigma_i$ as noisy information about the public report. The price function is the same as in HoV. There are two information choices in this model. At $t = 0$, the manager of the firm chooses (and publicly announces) the precision of the public report his firm will issue. At $t = 1$, each investor chooses the precision of his private signal with respect

---

[12] In Verrecchia's model, the larger this measure, the larger the weight investors give to the price in determining their posterior beliefs.

to the public report (i.e., $h_i = 1/\text{Var}[\varsigma_i]$) given the precision of the public report (i.e., $h_0 = 1/\text{Var}[\varsigma_0]$) and a convex cost function $\kappa(h_i)$. There are no liquidity traders in this model, since IND assumes the randomness of supply stems from randomness in the endowed shares of the rational investors. Hence, IND assumes the manager of the firm acts on the behalf of the investors and selects h_0 so as to maximize the investors' *ex ante* expected utility. The randomness of endowments implies that the investors do not have equilibrium endowments, and IND precludes any trading before information is acquired. From our analysis in Chapter 7, we know that each investor's *ex ante* expected utility is reduced if public information is released before they trade to an equilibrium and is unaffected by the release of public information after they have traded to an equilibrium (assuming production choice is fixed). Hence, in this model, the optimal precision of the public report is zero, so that it is totally uninformative and there is nothing the investors can learn by acquiring private information about the public report.

11.3 PUBLIC REPORTS AND THE CONCURRENT DEMAND FOR PRIVATE INFORMATION

In accounting, we are interested in private investor information for two reasons. First, the new information conveyed to the market by an accounting report is likely to be reduced by the prior acquisition of private information by investors. In that setting, which we examine in Section 11.4, the demand for (prior) private information is likely to increase as the precision of the public report increases. Second, the timely release of earnings forecasts and other management information may influence the incremental informativeness of a private signal. In this setting, which we examine here, the demand for (concurrent) private information decreases as the precision of the public report increases.

The Basic Model

Feltham and Wu (FW) (2000) extend the GS model to a setting in which all rational investors receive a public accounting report and informed investors (who choose to pay a cost κ) also receive a common private signal. FW assume the terminal dividend is influenced by the unobserved actions of a manager, and they develop their model as a means of examining the role of accounting reports and market prices in setting incentives for the manager. We defer discussion of the incentive model until Volume II and, in this section, we focus on the impact of public reports on the rational investors' equilibrium acquisition of private information.

As in the basic GS model, the firm's terminal dividend is expressed as $d = m_0 + \varepsilon$, where ε is a random variable for which investors hold normally distributed prior beliefs $\varepsilon \sim N(0,\sigma_0^2)$. The public report is represented by the posterior mean y_a that would result if an investor had no other information.[13] More specifically, the prior report belief is represented by $y_a \sim N(0,\sigma_{ya}^2)$ and the posterior belief given the public report is $\varepsilon|y_a \sim N(y_a,\sigma_{a1}^2)$, with $\sigma_{ya}^2 + \sigma_{a1}^2 = \sigma_0^2$. All investors who observe the private signal, also observe the public report. Hence, we can represent the private signal by the change in posterior mean generated by the private signal (relative to the posterior mean based on the public report). More specifically, the posterior random dividend belief given the public report and private signal is $\varepsilon|y_a,y_i \sim N(y_a + y_i,\sigma_{i1}^2)$, with $\sigma_{ai}^2 + \sigma_{i1}^2 = \sigma_{a1}^2$ and $y_i|y_a \sim N(0,\sigma_{ai}^2)$.

Figure 11.2
Sequence of Events in the FW Model

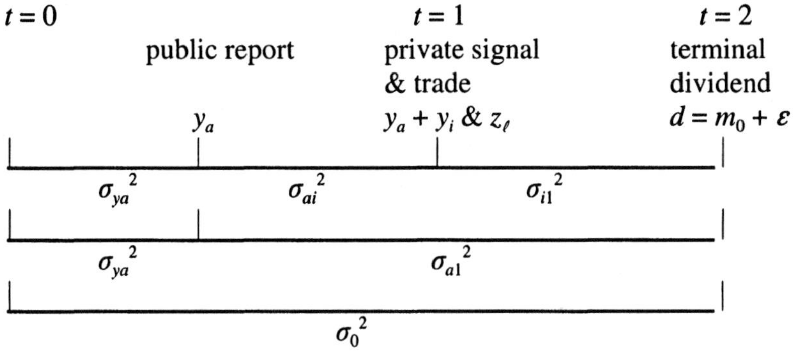

Equilibrium Price

The uninformed investors do not know y_i and hold a posterior belief based on y_a and the inferences they can make from the equilibrium price v_1. To derive the uninformed posterior belief we assume the uninformed investors conjecture that the equilibrium price is a linear function of y_a, y_i, and z_ℓ, i.e., there exist parameters π_a, π_i, and π_z such that

$$v_1(y_a,y_i,z_\ell) = m_0 + \pi_a y_a + \pi_i y_i - \pi_z z_\ell. \tag{11.20}$$

We again introduce the statistic

$$\psi = \frac{1}{\pi_i}[v_1 - m_0 - \pi_a y_a] = y_i - \frac{\pi_z}{\pi_i} z_\ell, \tag{11.21}$$

[13] Observe that the public report could be a vector $\mathbf{y}_a$, but the only aspect of that vector that is relevant is the posterior belief it generates.

which the uninformed investors can infer from the price and the public report.

The joint distribution for ε, y_a, y_i, and ψ, and the posterior beliefs, are summarized in Table 11.2.

Table 11.2
Rational Dividend Beliefs Based on Price and a Public Report

Prior mean and covariance matrix:

$$\begin{bmatrix} \varepsilon \\ y_a \\ y_i \\ \psi \end{bmatrix} \sim N\left(\begin{bmatrix} 0 \\ 0 \\ 0 \\ 0 \end{bmatrix}, \begin{bmatrix} \sigma_0^2 & \sigma_{ya}^2 & \sigma_{ai}^2 & \sigma_{ai}^2 \\ \sigma_{ya}^2 & \sigma_{ya}^2 & 0 & 0 \\ \sigma_{ai}^2 & 0 & \sigma_{ai}^2 & \sigma_{ai}^2 \\ \sigma_{ai}^2 & 0 & \sigma_{ai}^2 & \sigma_\psi^2 \end{bmatrix} \right), \qquad \sigma_\psi^2 = \sigma_{ai}^2 + \frac{\pi_z^2}{\pi_i^2}\sigma_z^2.$$

Posterior means and variances with respect to ε given y_a and either y_i or ψ:

$$\mu_{i1}(y_a,y_i) = y_a + y_i, \qquad \sigma_{i1}^2 = \sigma_{a1}^2 - \sigma_{ai}^2,$$

$$\mu_{u1}(y_a,\psi) = y_a + \frac{\sigma_{ai}^2}{\sigma_\psi^2}\psi, \qquad \sigma_{u1}^2 = \sigma_{a1}^2 - \frac{\sigma_{ai}^2}{\sigma_\psi^2}\sigma_{ai}^2.$$

Our representation of the public report and private signal differ from FW, but our models are equivalent. The advantage of our representation is that it results in a structure very similar to the structure we used in the basic GS model (e.g., compare Tables 11.1 and 11.2). Consequently, the analysis used for the basic GS model is readily extended to our public report model. For example, value relation (11.12) now becomes

$$v_1 = m_0 + y_a + \frac{1}{\bar{h}_1}[\lambda h_{i1} y_i + (1-\lambda) h_{u1} \hat{\mu}_{u1}(\psi) - r z_e], \tag{11.22}$$

where $\hat{\mu}_{u1}(\psi) = \mu_{u1}(\psi) - y_a$. This then leads to the following equilibrium price parameters.

Proposition 11.8 (FW, Prop. 3)

The equilibrium price parameters in the GS model with a public report for $\lambda \in (0,1)$ are:

$$\pi_a = 1, \qquad \pi_i = \frac{1}{\bar{h}_1}\left[\lambda h_{i1} + (1-\lambda)h_{u1}\frac{\sigma_{ai}^2}{\sigma_\psi^2}\right]^\circ, \qquad \pi_z = \frac{r}{\lambda h_{i1}}\pi_i, \quad (11.23)$$

$$h_{u1} = \frac{\sigma_\psi^2}{\sigma_{a1}^2\sigma_\psi^2 - \sigma_{ai}^4}, \qquad \sigma_\psi{}^2 = \frac{1}{\lambda^2}[\lambda^2\sigma_{ai}{}^2 + r^2\sigma_{i1}{}^4\sigma_z{}^2]. \quad (11.24)$$

Equilibrium Private Information Acquisition

Similarly, the expressions for the *ex ante* expected utility are the same as in (11.16), but with appropriate changes in $\sigma_\Delta(\lambda)$ and $\sigma_{u1}(\lambda)$. The latter is particularly important, since it plays a crucial role in specifying the equilibrium level of λ (see (11.17)). After making those changes, the equilibrium fraction informed in FW's public reporting setting, if $\lambda^* \in (0,1)$, is

$$\lambda^* = r\sigma_z\sigma_{i1}\sqrt{\frac{\sigma_{ai}^2 - K\sigma_{i1}^2}{K\sigma_{ai}^2}}. \quad (11.25)$$

This is structurally the same as (11.18), but with $\sigma_{ai}{}^2$ instead of $\sigma_{yi}{}^2$. Consequently, the comparative statics for the basic GS model in Proposition 11.7 also apply to the FW model (using our representation of information).

An interesting issue raised by the FW model is the impact of increasing the informativeness of the public report, $h_{a1} = 1/\sigma_{a1}{}^2$, holding $\sigma_{i1}{}^2$ fixed (i.e., the incremental uncertainty resolved by the private signal, $\sigma_{ai}{}^2$, is reduced). Differentiating (11.25) with respect to $\sigma_{a1}{}^2$ yields

$$\frac{d\lambda^*}{d\sigma_{a1}^2} = \frac{1}{2}r\sigma_z\sigma_{i1}\left[\frac{\sigma_{ai}^2 - K\sigma_{i1}^2}{K\sigma_{ai}^2}\right]^{-1/2}\frac{\sigma_{i1}^2}{\sigma_{ai}^4} > 0. \quad (11.26)$$

Hence, $d\lambda^*/dh_{a1} < 0$, which establishes that increasing the informativeness of the public report reduces the fraction of investors who become informed. This is not surprising, since increasing the informativeness of the public report reduces the incremental informativeness of the private signal, thereby making the latter less valuable.

Of course, in this setting the informativeness of the price about the private signal goes down, but the more interesting comparative static is with respect to the precision of an uninformed investor's posterior belief about the dividend, h_{u1}. The direct effect of an increased precision of the public report is a reduction in an uninformed investor's uncertainty about the dividend. However, there is an opposite indirect effect on the information that can be inferred from the price. When σ_{i1}^2 is fixed, there is less to be learned about the dividend from the private signal, and fewer investors acquire that private signal, both implying that the informativeness of the price about the dividend is reduced. Interestingly, the reduction in the information that can be inferred from the price precisely offsets the increased informativeness of the public report. To see this, substitute equilibrium conditions (11.23), (11.24), and (11.25) into the expression for σ_{u1}^2 in Table 2:

$$\sigma_{u1}^2 = (1 + K)\sigma_{i1}^2,$$

i.e., the precision of an uninformed investor's posterior belief about the dividend, h_{u1}, is independent of the precision of the public report, h_{a1}, when the informed investors' posterior uncertainty about the dividend, σ_{i1}^2, is fixed. On the other hand, if the public report does not affect the precision of the information in the private signal, i.e., σ_{ai}^2 is fixed while σ_{i1}^2 is reduced, then h_{u1} increases as the precision of the public report is increased. However, as in the basic GS model, this implies that the rational traders are made worse off *ex ante* since there is a smaller "excess" risk premium to be extracted from the liquidity traders. We can view the former setting as one in which the public report "pre-empts" the information that can be obtained by concurrent private information acquisition, while the latter setting can be viewed as one in which the public report and private signal reveal information with respect to independently distributed events.

The FW model can be used to examine issues that have been of interest in the accounting literature, such as characterizing the trading volume and price-variability around earnings announcements. For example, is increased precision of the public report associated with higher trading volume and more price-variability?

Trading Volume

There are three groups of traders: the liquidity traders, the rational informed investors, and the rational uninformed investors. Some are buyers and some are sellers. The liquidity traders sell Iz_ℓ shares, the informed investors buy $\lambda I z_i$ shares, and the uninformed investors buy $(1-\lambda)Iz_u$ shares. The total trading volume is measured as one half times the absolute number of shares bought or sold per rational investor, i.e.,

$$T = \tfrac{1}{2}\{\,|z_\ell| + \lambda|z_i| + (1-\lambda)|z_u|\,\}.$$

The demand functions for the rational investors are

$$z_i(y_a,y_i,v_1) = \frac{1}{r}h_{i1}[m_0 + y_a + y_i - v_1],$$

$$z_u(y_a,\psi,v_1) = \frac{1}{r}h_{u1}[m_0 + \mu_{u1}(y_a,\psi) - v_1].$$

These trades are normally distributed and, hence, the expected trading volume for a given fraction of informed investors $\lambda \in (0,1)$ is[14]

$$\mathrm{E}[T|\lambda] = \sqrt{\frac{1}{2\pi}}\left[\sigma_z + \lambda\sqrt{\mathrm{Var}[z_i]} + (1-\lambda)\sqrt{\mathrm{Var}[z_u]}\right]. \tag{11.27}$$

Based on price relation (11.22), the price parameters in (11.23), and the demand functions we obtain

$$\mathrm{Var}[z_{i1}] = \frac{h_{i1}^2}{r^2}(1-\pi_i)^2\sigma_{ai}^{\ 2} + \frac{1}{\lambda^2}\pi_i^{\ 2}\sigma_z^{\ 2},$$

$$\mathrm{Var}[z_{u1}] = \frac{h_{u1}^2}{r^2}\left(\frac{\sigma_{ai}^2}{\sigma_\psi^2} - \pi_i\right)^2\left(\sigma_{ai}^2 + \frac{r^2}{\lambda^2 h_{i1}^2}\sigma_z^2\right).$$

If either no investor or all investors are informed (i.e., $\lambda = 0$ or 1), then

$$\mathrm{E}[T|\lambda] = 2\sqrt{\frac{1}{2\pi}}\sigma_z.$$

This is the base level of trading induced by the liquidity traders – if the rational investors have the same information, they merely absorb those trades. However, if there are both informed and uninformed investors (i.e., $\lambda \in (0,1)$), then the informed investors will "take advantage" of the uninformed investors by taking speculative positions based on their private information at $t = 1$ and, thus, the trading volume with $\lambda \in (0,1)$ is higher than the base level.

One might ask: Why would the uninformed investors trade given that the informed investors are "taking advantage" of them? The answer is that both the informed and uninformed are obtaining "excess" risk premia from the liquidity traders, and there is a net positive gain to trading by the uninformed investors.

---

[14] We use the fact that for any normally distributed variable $x \sim \mathrm{N}(0,\sigma^2)$, $\mathrm{E}[|x|] = \sqrt{2/\pi}\,\sigma$.

Price-Variability

Let $\delta = v_1 - v_0$ represent the change in prices from $t = 0$ to $t = 1$, where v_0 is the market price at an initial round of trading. The *ex ante* variance in the price change for a given fraction informed, if $\lambda \in (0,1)$, is

$$\mathrm{Var}[\delta|\lambda] = \sigma_{ya}^2 + \pi_i^2\sigma_{ai}^2 + \frac{r^2\pi_i^2}{\lambda^2 h_{i1}^2}\sigma_z^2. \qquad (11.28)$$

The first pair of terms represent the price-variability due to changes in information, whereas the third term represents the price-variability due to variations in the risk premium induced by the randomness in the number of shares supplied by the liquidity traders.

If no investor is informed, then

$$\mathrm{Var}[\delta|\lambda = 0] = \sigma_{ya}^2 + \frac{r^2}{h_{a1}^2}\sigma_z^2,$$

whereas if all investors are informed, then

$$\mathrm{Var}[\delta|\lambda = 1] = \sigma_{ya}^2 + \sigma_{ai}^2 + \frac{r^2}{h_{i1}^2}\sigma_z^2.$$

Obviously, the price-variability due to changes in information is greater with $\lambda = 1$ than with $\lambda = 0$. However, the price-variability due to randomness in the supply of shares is lower with $\lambda = 1$ than with $\lambda = 0$, making the total parameter-dependent.

Comparative Statistics

Deriving the impact of increasing the informativeness of the public report on the expected trading volume and price-variability is excruciatingly cumbersome (calling, essentially, for substitution of the λ^* characterization into the noted expressions). However, we can illustrate this numerically for a given set of parameters. Figure 11.3 shows the equilibrium fraction informed, λ^*, the price-informativeness conditional on the public report, $\mathrm{Corr}^2(y_i,v_1|y_a)$, the expected trading volume, $\mathrm{E}[T|\lambda^*]$, and the price-variability, $\mathrm{Var}[\delta|\lambda^*]$, as a function of σ_{ya}^2. The precision of the informed investors' posterior beliefs h_{i1} is held constant as the precision of the public report increases. We consider two cases: low information costs, $\kappa_{low} = 550$, and high information costs, $\kappa_{high} = 3{,}500$.

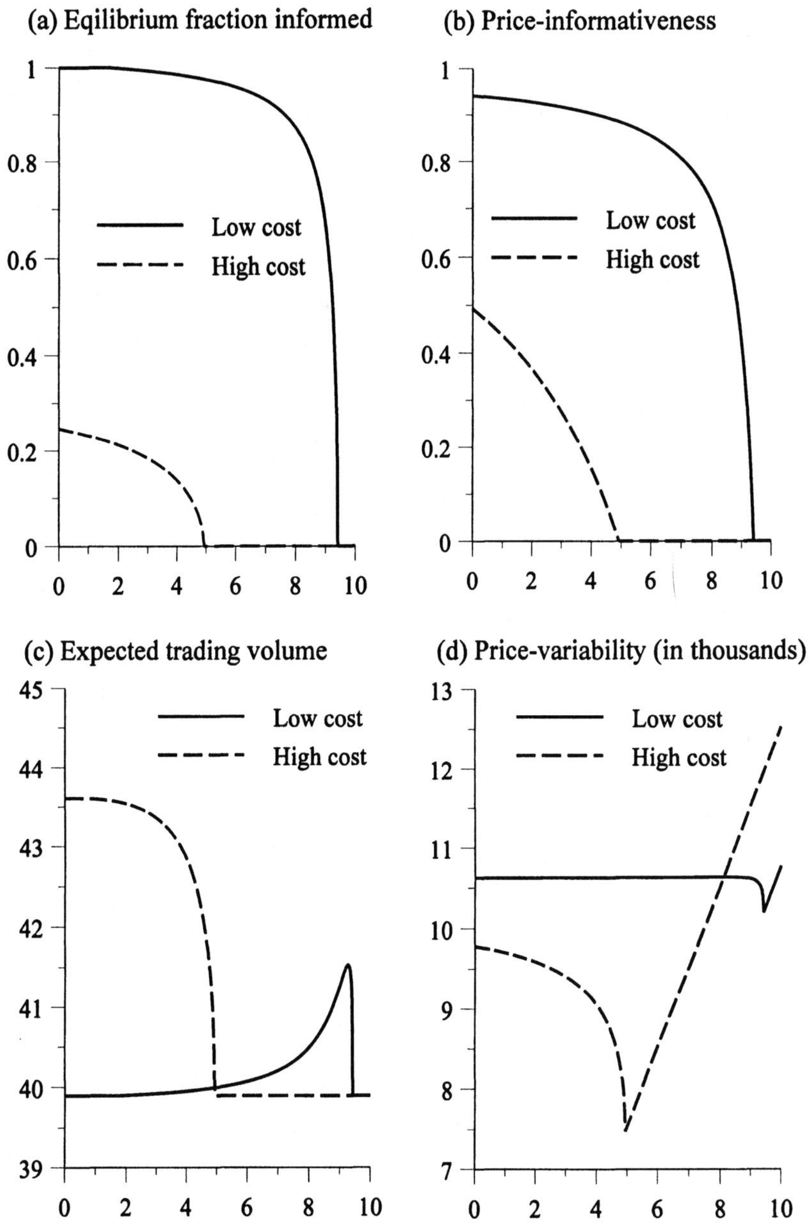

Figure 11.3. Summary statistics for varying information content of the public report. Horizontal axis = $\sigma_{ya}^2/1{,}000$. $\sigma_0^2 = 15{,}000$; $\sigma_{i1}^2 = 5{,}000$; $r = 0.0001$, $\kappa_{low} = 550$; $\kappa_{high} = 3{,}500$.

In both cases, increasing the informativeness of the public report reduces the equilibrium fraction of investors informed (as demonstrated in (11.26)) implying that the price-informativeness is also reduced. In the "low-cost" setting, λ^* = 1 when the informativeness of the public report is low (and, thus, the informativeness of the private signal is high), whereas $\lambda^* = 0$ in both settings when the informativeness of the public report is high.

The expected trading volume is at the base level induced by the liquidity traders when λ^* is either one or zero. In the "high-cost" setting the expected trading volume is decreasing in the informativeness of the public report, and it is substantially higher than in the "low-cost" setting for low informativeness of the public report. This is due to a "few" informed investors trading very aggressively on their highly informative private signal. In the "low-cost" setting, the relationship between the informativeness of the public report and the expected trading volume is non-monotonic.

Of course, if no investor is privately informed ($\lambda^* = 0$), increasing the informativeness of the public report increases the price-variability. On the other hand, if all investors are informed ($\lambda^* = 1$), changing the informativeness of the public report changes the source of the information but does not affect what each investor knows and there is no change in price-variability. In the intermediate cases, the impact on the price-variability depends on the change in the fraction of investors informed, and how aggressively those investors trade on their private information. Interestingly, the price-variability decreases in the informativeness of the public report in the "high-cost" setting for low informativeness of the public report.

Diverse Private Signals Model

The accounting literature contains several papers that extend the HV model to consider the impact of public information on private information acquisition in settings in which the rational investors acquire different private signals.

Lundholm (1988, 1991), which we refer to as LU88 and LU91, are two early papers that introduce public reports. LU88 assumes that, at $t = 1$, each investor observes a public signal $y_a = d + \varsigma_a$ and a private signal $y_i = d + \varsigma_i$, where ς_a and ς_i are random noise terms. He assumes $\text{Cov}[\varsigma_i,\varsigma_j] = 0$, for all i, j, $i \neq j$, but $\text{Cov}[\varsigma_a,\varsigma_i] = \sigma_{ai}$, for all i. The latter condition is interpreted as implying that the noise in each investor's private signal may impact the public report – which contains some additional noise as well. LU91, on the other hand, assumes each investor observes a public signal $y_a = d + \varsigma_a$ and possibly two private signals, where the kth signal takes the form $y_{ki} = d + \varsigma_{ki}$, where $\text{Cov}[\varsigma_a, \varsigma_{ki}] = \text{Cov}[\varsigma_{1i},\varsigma_{2j}] = 0$, for all i, j, and $\text{Corr}[\varsigma_{ki},\varsigma_{kj}] = \theta_k$, for all $i, j, i \neq j$. LU88 assumes the information received by each investor is exogenously determined, whereas LU91 assumes each private signal is costly and determines the endogenous acquisition decision. The information structures in these models are unusual,[15] so we do not summarize their results.

As in Indjejikian (IND) (1991) – which we briefly discuss at the end of Section 11.2, Bushman (BU) (1991) considers a setting in which the manager of the firm selects (at $t = 0$) the informativeness of a public signal (so as to maximize the *ex ante* expected utility of the randomly endowed investors). However, unlike IND, BU assumes the public signal y_a is understood by all investors, but they can choose to supplement it, at a cost κ, with a private signal y_i which has both common and investor specific noise terms that have fixed precision and are independent of the noise in the public report. That is, $y_a = d + \varsigma_a$ and $y_i = d + y_0 + \varsigma_i$, with $\text{Cov}[\varsigma_a,\varsigma_0] = \text{Cov}[\varsigma_a,\varsigma_i] = \text{Cov}[\varsigma_0,\varsigma_i] = \text{Cov}[\varsigma_i,\varsigma_j] = 0$, for all $i, j, i \neq j$. As in IND (and based on our analysis in Chapter 7), the investors' *ex ante* expected utility is maximized if all release of information prior to trading can be blocked. However, in the BU setting the precision of the public report equal to zero will not stop the investors from acquiring private information. They will effectively "shoot themselves in the foot" by expending funds to acquire personal information to take advantage of the other investors. The key is that, in equilibrium, personal information causes them all to be worse off due to both the information risk it creates and the cost of the information. Of course, a more informative public report will directly increase the information risk, but will induce the investors to be less willing to expend resources to acquire private information. Hence, the optimal level of public signal precision is context specific. The analysis in BU is further complicated because he assumes the private information is supplied by a monopolist who sets the price of his investor specific signals so as to maximize his profits.

11.4 PUBLIC REPORTS AND THE PRIOR DEMAND FOR PRIVATE INFORMATION

It is widely recognized that investors often know much of the information content in a public report before it is released. One reason for this is private information acquisition by investors. In fact, one intuitively expects investor demand for private information acquisition to increase immediately prior to an anticipated public report. The major gain from private information comes from going long or short in a firm's shares immediately before the release of a public report that causes the price to increase or decrease (and then reversing the position after the information is impounded in the price).

---

[15] It is not unreasonable to assume that the public and private signals are correlated, as in LU88, but the events that cause them to be correlated are likely to cause the private signals to be correlated across investors.

In this section we summarize Demski and Feltham's (DF) (1994) extension of the GS model to a setting in which there are two trading dates.[16] At $t = 1$ there is no public report, but liquidity traders have $z_{\ell 1}$ shares (per rational investor) they wish to sell and the rational investors can acquire a common private signal at a cost κ. At $t = 2$ there is no private signal available, but the liquidity traders change the number of shares they do not want to hold to $z_{\ell 2}$ (i.e., they sell $z_{\ell 2} - z_{\ell 1}$ additional shares) and the public (e.g., accounting) report is released. The firm pays a terminal dividend at $t = 3$.

The Basic Model

We again represent the terminal dividend as $d = m_0 + \varepsilon$, where $\varepsilon \sim N(0,\sigma_0^2)$ is the investors' prior belief. The private signal at $t = 1$ is informative about the public report at $t = 2$, and the latter is informative about ε. For simplicity, DF assume that the public report at $t = 2$ is a sufficient statistic for the private signal at $t = 1$, so that all investors have the same dividend beliefs at $t = 2$. Hence, we can represent the investors' information at $t = 2$ as y_a, where the posterior dividend belief is $\varepsilon | y_i, y_a \sim N(y_a, \sigma_{ad}^2)$. The private signal at $t = 1$ is represented as y_i, where the informed posterior report belief at $t = 1$ is $y_a | y_i \sim N(y_i, \sigma_{ia}^2)$. The above structure implies that the informed posterior random dividend belief at $t = 1$ is $\varepsilon | y_i \sim N(y_i, \sigma_{i1}^2)$, where $\sigma_{i1}^2 = \sigma_{ia}^2 + \sigma_{ad}^2$. The prior private signal and public report beliefs are $y_i \sim N(0,\sigma_{yi}^2)$ and $y_a \sim N(0,\sigma_{ya}^2)$, with $\sigma_0^2 = \sigma_{yi}^2 + \sigma_{i1}^2 = \sigma_{ya}^2 + \sigma_{ad}^2$ and $\sigma_{ya}^2 = \sigma_{yi}^2 + \sigma_{ia}^2$. These events and variances are depicted in Figure 11.3.

The above representation is such that we can view ε as consisting of three independent zero mean random variables y_i, ε_a, ε_d, with variances σ_{yi}^2, σ_{ia}^2, and σ_{ad}^2. These variables are such that $y_a = y_i + \varepsilon_a$, and $\varepsilon = y_i + \varepsilon_a + \varepsilon_d = y_a + \varepsilon_d$.

The supplies of shares by the liquidity traders at dates $t = 1,2$ are assumed to be identically and independently distributed with mean zero and variance σ_z^2 (DF permit the variance to differ across periods).

[16] Three pairs of authors simultaneously examined this setting. Kim and Verrecchia (1991) published the first paper using a model based on the Hellwig-Verrecchia diverse private signal model. DF and McNichols and Trueman (1994) were published in the same issue of the *Journal of Accounting and Economics*. Despite the later publication date, these authors had not seen the initial paper when they did their research. Interestingly, the three papers are extensions of three different rational expectations models and, therefore, yield different (but complementary) results. As noted in the text, the DF model is an extension of the GS common private signal model. In Chapter 12 we formally introduce the Kyle model and review McNichols and Trueman's extension to that model.

Figure 11.4
Sequence of Events in the DF Model

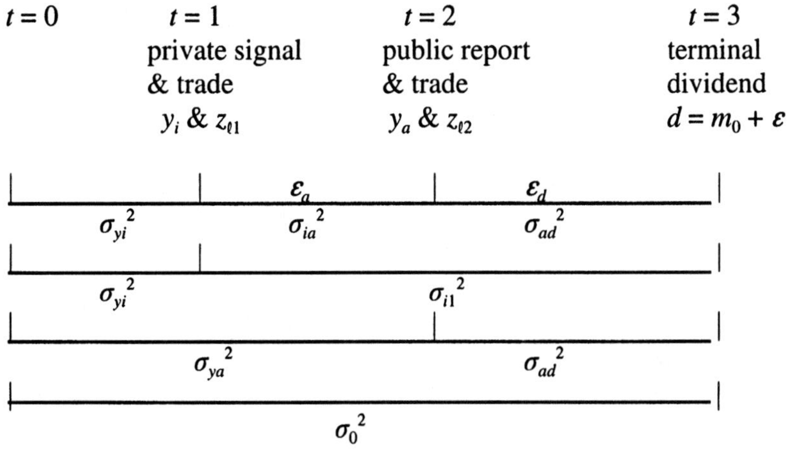

Equilibrium Demand and Prices

The assumption that all investors have the same beliefs at $t = 2$ implies that all investors will have the following demand for the risky asset based on the information provided by the accounting reports:

$$z_{a2} = \frac{1}{r\sigma_{ad}^2}[m_0 + y_a - v_2]. \tag{11.29}$$

Hence, given that demand must equal the supply $z_{\ell 2}$, the equilibrium price is

$$v_2 = m_0 + y_a - r\sigma_{ad}^2 z_{\ell 2}. \tag{11.30}$$

Of course, since investors have identical risk aversion and identical beliefs, they all have average holdings, i.e., $z_{a2} = z_{\ell 2}$.

The analysis of trading at $t = 1$ is more complex than in the basic GS model since both the informed and uninformed traders realize that they will trade again at $t = 2$. Using (11.29) and (11.30) provides the following characterization of informed and uninformed investors' terminal wealth given that they acquirer z_{i1} and z_{u1}, respectively, at $t = 1$:

$$w_i = z_{\ell 2} d + q_2 - \kappa = z_{\ell 2} d + (z_{i1} - z_{\ell 2})v_2 + q_1 - \kappa$$

$$= z_{\ell 2}(m_0 + y_i + \varepsilon_a + \varepsilon_d) + (z_{i1} - z_{\ell 2})[m_0 + y_i + \varepsilon_a - r\sigma_{ad}^2 z_{\ell 2}] - z_{i1}v_1 - \kappa, \quad (11.31a)$$

$$w_u = z_{\ell 2}(m_0 + y_i + \varepsilon_a + \varepsilon_d) + (z_{u1} - z_{\ell 2})[m_0 + y_i + \varepsilon_a - r\sigma_{ad}^2 z_{\ell 2}] - z_{u1}v_1, \quad (11.31b)$$

where q_t is the amount of the riskless claim held after trading at date t. Hence, an investor's terminal wealth is a function of four independent random variables $(y_i, \varepsilon_a, \varepsilon_d, z_{\ell 2})$. All investors have the same beliefs with respect to ε_a, ε_d and $z_{\ell 2}$, but at $t = 1$ the informed and uninformed investors differ in their beliefs with respect to y_i.

The informed investors know y_i at $t = 1$, but, as in the basic GS model, the uninformed investors imperfectly infer y_i from the equilibrium market price at $t = 1$. We assume they conjecture that the price takes the following form:

$$v_1(y_i, z_{\ell 1}) = m_0 + \pi_{yi} y_i - \pi_{z1} z_{\ell 1}, \quad (11.32)$$

and we again use the price statistic $\psi = y_i - (\pi_{z1} / \pi_{yi}) z_{\ell 1}$. Table 11.3 is very similar to Table 11.1, except that in this analysis our focus is on the informed and uninformed report beliefs (instead of the dividend beliefs) at $t = 1$.

Table 11.3
Rational Report Beliefs Based on Price

Prior mean and covariance matrix:

$$\begin{bmatrix} y_a \\ y_i \\ \psi \end{bmatrix} \sim \mathrm{N}\left(\begin{bmatrix} 0 \\ 0 \\ 0 \end{bmatrix}, \begin{bmatrix} \sigma_{ya}^2 & \sigma_{yi}^2 & \sigma_{yi}^2 \\ \sigma_{yi}^2 & \sigma_{yi}^2 & \sigma_{yi}^2 \\ \sigma_{yi}^2 & \sigma_{yi}^2 & \sigma_{\psi}^2 \end{bmatrix} \right), \qquad \sigma_{\psi}^2 = \sigma_{yi}^2 + \frac{\pi_{z1}^2}{\pi_{yi}^2}\sigma_z^2.$$

Posterior means and variances with respect to y_a given y_i or ψ:

$$\mu_{ia}(y_i) = y_i, \qquad \sigma_{ia}^2 = \sigma_{ya}^2 - \sigma_{yi}^2,$$

$$\mu_{ua}(\psi) = \frac{\sigma_{yi}^2}{\sigma_{\psi}^2}\psi, \qquad \sigma_{ua}^2 = \sigma_{ya}^2 - \frac{\sigma_{yi}^2}{\sigma_{\psi}^2}\sigma_{yi}^2.$$

The next step is to determine the investors' demand functions. An investor's terminal wealth (see (11.31)) is a quadratic function of three normally distributed random variables, so we use result (ii) from Appendix 3A to obtain the following demand functions (see Appendix 11B for proof).

Proposition 11.9 (DF, Prop. 2)
In the DF model with $\lambda \in (0,1)$, the demand functions at $t = 1$ for the two types of investors are

$$z_{i1} = \frac{1}{r\hat{\sigma}_{i1}^2}[m_0 + y_i - v_1], \quad \hat{\sigma}_{i1}^2 = \sigma_{ia}^2 + \sigma_{ad}^2\left[1 - \frac{1}{r^2\sigma_{ad}^2\sigma_z^2 + 1}\right], \tag{11.33a}$$

$$z_{u1} = \frac{1}{r\hat{\sigma}_{u1}^2}[m_0 + \mu_{ua}(\psi) - v_1], \; \hat{\sigma}_{u1}^2 = \sigma_{ua}^2 + \sigma_{ad}^2\left[1 - \frac{1}{r^2\sigma_{ad}^2\sigma_z^2 + 1}\right]. \tag{11.33b}$$

Observe that the demand functions are the same as in the basic GS model, except that the variance of the return from investing at $t = 1$ is more complex due to the anticipated trading at $t = 2$. For example, if an informed investor did not anticipate trading at $t = 2$, then his demand would reflect his uncertainty about the dividend as represented by $\sigma_{ia}^2 + \sigma_{ad}^2$. However, as reflected in (11.33), the variance is less when trading is anticipated. And, of course, the variance is higher for the uninformed investors, since they do not know y_i and imperfectly infer it from ψ.

In equilibrium, the average demand $\lambda z_{i1} + (1-\lambda)z_{u1}$ must equal the supply $z_{\ell 1}$. Using the demand functions in (11.33) and solving for the equilibrium price at $t = 1$ yields

$$v_1 = m_0 + \frac{1}{\hat{h}_1}[\lambda \hat{h}_{i1} y_i + (1-\lambda)\hat{h}_{u1}\mu_{ua}(\psi) - rz_{\ell 1}], \tag{11.34}$$

where $\hat{h}_{i1} = 1/\hat{\sigma}_{i1}^2$, $\hat{h}_{u1} = 1/\hat{\sigma}_{u1}^2$, and $\hat{h}_1 = \lambda\hat{h}_{i1} + (1-\lambda)\hat{h}_{u1}$. The approach used in Proposition 11.2 can be used here to determine the endogenous price function parameters given that the uninformed investors conjecture that price relation (11.32) holds. We state the result in a manner consistent with our earlier results, which differs in form, but not in substance, from the result in DF.

Proposition 11.10 (DF, Prop. 2)

The equilibrium price parameters in the basic DF model for $\lambda \in (0,1)$ are:

$$\pi_{yi} = \frac{1}{\hat{h}_1}\left[\lambda \hat{h}_{i1} + (1-\lambda)\hat{h}_{u1}\frac{\sigma_{yi}^2}{\sigma_\psi^2}\right], \qquad \pi_{z1} = \frac{r}{\lambda \hat{h}_{i1}}\pi_{yi}, \tag{11.35}$$

$$\hat{h}_{u1} = \frac{\sigma_\psi^2}{\sigma_0^2\sigma_\psi^2 - \sigma_{yi}^4}, \qquad \sigma_\psi^2 = \sigma_{yi}^2 + \frac{1}{\lambda^2}r^2\hat{\sigma}_{i1}^4\sigma_z^2. \tag{11.36}$$

Equilibrium Information Acquisition

As in the two previous GS models, the equilibrium fraction informed (λ) equals zero if the information cost κ is sufficiently large that no one wants to be informed, whereas $\lambda = 1$ if κ is sufficiently small that all investors want to be informed. Otherwise, the equilibrium fraction is such that the rational investors are indifferent between being informed or uninformed. Applying the same approach as in the basic GS model yields the following characterization of the equilibrium fraction informed.

Proposition 11.11 (DF, Prop. 3)

If the equilibrium fraction informed is between zero and one in the DF model, then

$$\lambda^* = r\sigma_z\hat{\sigma}_{i1}\sqrt{\frac{\sigma_{yi}^2 - K\hat{\sigma}_{i1}^2}{K\sigma_{yi}^2}}. \tag{11.37}$$

The structure of λ^* is the same as in (11.18), except that $\hat{\sigma}_{i1}^2$ replaces σ_{i1}^2, thereby reflecting the difference in the riskiness of the return when there is a second round of trading after the public report is received. Hence, the results from the basic GS model are readily extended to the DF model. However, the DF model raises some additional issues. For example, as in our analysis of the FW model in Section 11.3, DF explore the impact of various parameters on the trading volume and the variance of the change in prices when the public report is revealed at $t = 2$.

Trading Volume

Again, there are three groups of traders: the liquidity traders, the rational informed investors, and the rational uninformed investors. At $t = 2$, the liquidity traders sell $I(z_{\ell 2} - z_{\ell 1})$ shares, the informed investors buy $\lambda I(z_{i2} - z_{i1})$ shares, and the uninformed investors buy $(1-\lambda)I(z_{u2} - z_{u1})$ shares. The total trading volume is measured as one half times the absolute number of shares bought or sold per rational investor, i.e.,

$$T = \tfrac{1}{2}\{\,|z_{\ell 2} - z_{\ell 1}| + \lambda|z_{\ell 2} - z_{i1}| + (1-\lambda)|z_{\ell 2} - z_{u1}|\,\},$$

where we take advantage of the fact that $z_{i2} = z_{u2} = z_{\ell 2}$.

DF establish (see their Proposition 5) that the expected trading volume, for a given fraction informed λ, is

$$\mathrm{E}[T|\lambda] = \sqrt{\frac{1}{2\pi}}\left[\sqrt{2}\,\sigma_z + \lambda\sqrt{\sigma_z^2 + \mathrm{Var}[z_{i1}]} + (1-\lambda)\sqrt{\sigma_z^2 + \mathrm{Var}[z_{u1}]}\right]. \quad (11.38)$$

Based on price relation (11.32), the demand functions in (11.33), and the price parameters in (11.35), we obtain

$$\mathrm{Var}[z_{i1}] = \frac{\hat{h}_{i1}^2}{r^2}(1 - \pi_{yi})^2\sigma_{yi}^{\;2} + \frac{1}{\lambda^2}\pi_{yi}^{\;2}\sigma_z^{\;2},$$

$$\mathrm{Var}[z_{u1}] = \frac{\hat{h}_{u1}^2}{r^2}\left(\frac{\sigma_{yi}^2}{\sigma_\psi^2} - \pi_{yi}\right)^2\left(\sigma_{yi}^2 + \frac{r^2}{\lambda^2\hat{h}_{i1}^2}\sigma_z^2\right).$$

If either no investor or all investors are informed (i.e., $\lambda = 0$ or 1), then

$$\mathrm{E}[T|\lambda] = 2\sqrt{\frac{1}{2\pi}}\sigma_z,$$

which is the base level of trading induced by the liquidity traders. If there are both informed and uninformed investors (i.e., $\lambda \in (0,1)$), then the informed investors will, as in FW model, "take advantage" of the uninformed investors by taking speculative positions based on their private information at $t = 1$. This will increase the trading at $t = 2$ when they reverse their speculative positions.

Price-Variability

Let $\delta = v_2 - v_1$ represent the change in prices from $t = 1$ to $t = 2$. The *ex ante* variance in the price change for a given fraction informed, if $\lambda \in (0,1)$, is

$$\mathrm{Var}[\delta|\lambda] = \left[\sigma_{ia}^{\;2} + (1 - \pi_{yi})^2\sigma_{yi}^{\;2}\right] + r^2\left[\sigma_{ad}^{\;4} + \frac{1}{\lambda^2}\hat{\sigma}_{i1}^4\pi_{yi}^2\right]\sigma_z^2. \quad (11.39)$$

The first pair of terms represent the price-variability due to changes in information, whereas the second pair of terms represent the price-variability due to changes in the risk premium. The latter is due to the change in the number of shares supplied by the liquidity traders.

If no investor is informed, then

$$\text{Var}[\delta|\lambda = 0] = \sigma_{ia}^2 + \sigma_{yi}^2 + r^2\left[\sigma_{ad}^4 + \hat{\sigma}_{01}^4\right]\sigma_z^2,$$

$$\hat{\sigma}_{01}^2 \equiv \sigma_{yi}^2 + \hat{\sigma}_{i1}^2,$$

whereas if all investors are informed, then

$$\text{Var}[\delta|\lambda = 1] = \sigma_{ia}^2 + r^2\left[\sigma_{ad}^4 + \sigma_{i1}^4\right]\sigma_z^2.$$

Obviously, both sources of price-variability are greater with no investor informed ($\lambda = 0$) than with all investors informed ($\lambda = 1$). Hence, $\text{Var}[\delta|\lambda = 0] > \text{Var}[\delta|\lambda = 1]$ if $\sigma_{yi}^2 > 0$, which is consistent with the view that price-variability is greatest when there is a larger change in the investors' information.

Comparative Statics

DF consider the impact of three types of changes in the information structure. In all three cases the total uncertainty σ_0^2 is held constant, while one of its sub-components is increased and another is decreased. They obtain analytical results for some of their comparative statics, whereas others are based on numerical analyses that are presented in graphs (as in Figure 11.3). We restrict our discussion to a general description of their results. In interpreting these settings, we recommend that the reader refer to our Figure 11.4. All results are obtained treating the fraction informed as endogenous (i.e., λ^*).

(a) *Increased inaccessible public disclosure:* In their first setting, DF hold σ_{yi}^2 constant, increase σ_{ia}^2, and decrease σ_{ad}^2. This is interpreted as a setting in which the informativeness of the public report is increased, while holding the informativeness of the private signal constant. That is, the additional information content of the public report cannot be obtained in advance by an informed investor. The basic impact of this information change is that the price-informativeness at $t = 1$ decreases, the price-variability at $t = 2$ increases, and the expected trading volume at $t = 2$ decreases. The first follows from the fact that the increased post-report uncertainty causes the informed investors to trade less aggressively and thereby reveal less of their private signal through the price. The second occurs primarily because there is more new information at $t = 2$. The third occurs because of the reduced aggressiveness of the informed investors at $t = 1$ – resulting in less trading at $t = 2$ due to reduced reversal of speculative positions taken at $t = 1$.

(b) *Increased accessible public disclosure:* In their second setting, DF hold σ_{ia}^2 constant, increase σ_{yi}^2, and decrease σ_{ad}^2. This is interpreted as a setting in which the informativeness of the public report at $t = 2$ is increased (there is less uncertainty after the public report is released), but that additional information can be acquired at $t = 1$ by informed investors, so that the incremental informativeness of the public report is constant. The basic impact of this information change is that the price-informativeness at $t = 1$ increases, the price-variability at $t = 2$ decreases, and the expected trading volume at $t = 2$ increases.[17] Hence, the results are opposite to the first setting. The private signal removes a larger fraction of the uncertainty about the forthcoming public report, causing the informed investors to trade more aggressively at $t = 1$. This reduces the uninformed investors' uncertainty about the private signal at $t = 1$ and, hence, also results in less new information at $t = 2$. The more aggressive trading at $t = 1$, results in more trading volume at $t = 2$ due to the increased reversal of the speculative positions taken at $t = 1$.

(c) *Increased private information:* In their third setting, DF hold σ_{ad}^2 constant, increase σ_{yi}^2, and decrease σ_{ia}^2. This is interpreted as a setting in which informed investors acquire more information about the public report. This information change increases the price-informativeness at $t = 1$, decreases the price variance at $t = 2$, and increases the expected trading volume at $t = 2$. Hence, the results are the same as in the second setting, and the reasons for their occurrence are essentially the same. That is, the key factor is that with a more informative private signal, informed investors trade more aggressively at $t = 1$.

DF also describe how the equilibrium fraction informed is influenced by the above changes. This is of less empirical interest since it is difficult to obtain a good proxy for this variable. Furthermore, while the results for price-informativeness, price variance and expected trading volume are largely monotonic, this is not always the case for λ^*.

Diverse Private Signals Models

Papers by Grundy and McNichols (GM) (1989) and Kim and Verrecchia (KV91a, KV91b) (1991a, 1991b) extend the HV model to consider settings in which there are two rounds of trading, with diverse private information at the first round and the release of additional information to all investors at the second round.

---

[17] The results for price-informativeness, price-variability, and expected trading volume are generally monotonic in all three types of changes in information. However, for some extreme values the fraction informed is zero, so that, in the extreme range, price-informativeness is zero and the expected trading volume is constant at the base level.

GM initially introduce a second round of trading with no new information, except the price, at $t = 2$. At $t = 1$, each investor receives an investor-specific private signal $y_i = d + \varsigma_0 + \varsigma_i$, where ς_0 is signal noise common to all investors and ς_i is independent investor-specific noise. The economy is assumed to be large, so that we again have an equilibrium price at $t = 1$ of the form:

$$v_1 = \pi_{01}m_0 + \pi_{\bar{y}1}\,\bar{y} - \pi_{z1}\,z_{\ell 1},$$

where $\bar{y} = d + \varsigma_0$. The number of shares not held by the liquidity traders is assumed to remain constant, so that the second round price takes the same form, i.e., $z_{\ell 2} = z_{\ell 1}$ and

$$v_2 = \pi_{02}m_0 + \pi_{\bar{y}2}\,\bar{y} - \pi_{z2}\,z_{\ell 1}.$$

If $\pi_{\bar{y}1}/\pi_{z1} \neq \pi_{\bar{y}2}/\pi_{z2}$, then, at $t = 2$, there are two equations in two unknowns and the investors can infer $\bar{y}$ and $z_{\ell 1}$ from the prices. GM prove there is, what they call, a $\bar{y}$-revealing equilibrium, in which case $\pi_{02}m_0 + \pi_{\bar{y}2}\,\bar{y} = \mathrm{E}[d|\,\bar{y}]$ and $\pi_{z1} = r\mathrm{Var}[d|\,\bar{y}]$. However, they also prove there is a non-$\bar{y}$-revealing equilibrium in which $v_2 = v_1$, and v_1 is the same price as if there was only one round of trading.

GM extend their model by introducing a public report at $t = 2$. They assume that it takes the form $y_a = d + \varsigma_a$, where ς_a is independent of ς_i, all i, but may be correlated with ς_0. The form of the price at $t = 1$ is unchanged, but now the price at $t = 2$ takes the form

$$v_2 = \pi_{02}m_0 + \pi_{a2}\,y_a + \pi_{\bar{y}2}\,\bar{y} - \pi_{z2}\,z_{\ell 1}.$$

The model is similar to DF if $\mathrm{Cov}[\varsigma_a,\varsigma_0] = \mathrm{Var}[\varsigma_a]$, since that implies y_i equals y_a plus noise and y_a is a sufficient statistic for $(y_a,\bar{y})$ with respect to beliefs about d. In that case, $\pi_{\bar{y}2} = 0$. However, y_a is not a sufficient statistic and $\pi_{\bar{y}2} \neq 0$ if $\mathrm{Cov}[\varsigma_a,\varsigma_0] \neq \mathrm{Var}[\varsigma_a]$.

If y_a is not a sufficient statistic, then there is again an issue as to whether the equilibrium is $\bar{y}$-revealing or non-$\bar{y}$-revealing (which occurs if $\pi_{\bar{y}1}/\pi_{z1} = \pi_{\bar{y}2}/\pi_{z2}$). GM demonstrate that both are possible. Observe that this issue disappears if $z_{\ell 2}$ randomly differs from $z_{\ell 1}$. The assumption of equality of the supply across periods arises naturally in the GM model because they assume it is due to random investor endowments. DF, on the other hand, assume the random supply is due to liquidity traders, in which case it seems natural to assume the supply randomly changes across periods. Since randomness of supply is assumed merely as a convenient means to introduce noise into prices (recall our discussion in Section 11.1.2), it seems reasonable to adopt the DF approach. Interestingly, in the last section of their paper, GM briefly examine a model with a random change in supply.

KV91a analyze a setting that can be viewed as a special case of the settings considered by GM, but with endogenous acquisition of private information. At $t = 1$, each investor i acquires an investor-specific private signal $y_i = d + \zeta_i$ and, at $t = 2$, a public signal $y_a = d + \zeta_a$ is released. The noise in the investors' signals and the public signal are assumed to be independent, i.e., $\text{Cov}[\zeta_i,\zeta_j] = \text{Cov}[\zeta_i,\zeta_a] = 0$, for all $i, j, i \neq j$. Hence, like GM and unlike DF, the public report is not a sufficient statistic for the public and private signals.

Also, like GM and unlike DF, the supply of shares at $t = 2$ is assumed to equal the random supply at $t = 1$. There is no common component to the noise in the investor's signals. Hence, in a large economy, the KV91a equilibrium prices take the following form:

$$v_1 = \pi_{01}m_0 + \pi_{d1}d - \pi_{z1}z_{\ell 1},$$

$$v_2 = \pi_{02}m_0 + \pi_{a2}y_a + \pi_{d2}d - \pi_{z2}z_{\ell 1}.$$

Similar to GM, an issue arises as to whether the equilibrium is such that it is d-revealing or non-d-revealing at $t = 2$. Both types of equilibria exist, but KV91a focus on the one which is non-d-revealing (i.e., $\pi_{d1}/\pi_{z1} = \pi_{d2}/\pi_{z2}$). Again, as pointed out in KV91a, this issue would not arise if they assumed there was a random change in supply at $t = 2$.

The precisions of the public report and private signals are represented by $h_a = 1/\text{Var}[\zeta_a]$ and $h_i = 1/\text{Var}[\zeta_i]$, respectively. The investors are assumed to differ in their risk tolerances, so that they are motivated to choose different levels of precision. The degree of information asymmetry is represented by Q, which equals the weighted average of $|\bar{h} - h_i|$, where $\bar{h}$ is the weighted average precision of the private signals and the investors' choices are weighted by their risk tolerances. The precision of the investors' prior dividend beliefs is $H_0 = 1/\text{Var}[d]$, and the average precision of the investors' posterior dividend beliefs at $t = 1$ and 2 are represented by H_1 and H_2. The precision of the supply noise is denoted $h_z = 1/\text{Var}[z_{\ell 1}]$.

The cost of investor i's private signal is a linear function of h_i. KV91a provide a number of results with respect to the impact of model parameters on the endogenous levels of precision and information asymmetry. For example, the effects of changes in the precision of the public report are as follows.

- h_i, $\bar{h}$, H_1 and H_2 are the same whether there is no public report (i.e., $h_a = 0$) or the public report is perfect (i.e., $h_a \to \infty$).

- $\bar{h}$, H_1 and H_2 are greater for $h_a \in (0,\infty)$ than for $h_a = 0$ or $h_a \to \infty$.

- h_i is greater (less) for $h_a \in (0,\infty)$ than for $h_a = 0$ or $h_a \to \infty$ if $h_i > (<)\ \bar{h}$.

- $dQ/dh_a > (<)\ 0$ for $h_a < (>)\ H_1$.

That is, the anticipation of a more informative public report induces the acquisition of more precise private signals, on average. However, this can lead to more diversity since those who acquire less than the average (e.g., low risk tolerance) acquire less precise information, while those who acquire more than the average (e.g., high risk tolerance) acquire more precise information.

Some of the effects of changes in the precision of the investors' prior beliefs and the precision of the supply noise are as follows.

- $d\bar{h}/dh_0 = dh_i/dh_0 < 0$, $dH_1/dh_0 = dQ/dh_0 = 0$.

- $d\bar{h}/dh_z = dh_i/dh_z < 0$, $dH_1/dh_z = dQ/dh_z = 0$.

That is, as in DF, increased prior uncertainty and supply noise are offset by the acquisition of more precise private information by all investors. KV91a also demonstrate that an increase in the marginal information costs of all investors results in the acquisition of less precise information and less diversity of choice.

KV91a explore the impact of some model parameters on the expected trading volume and price-variability at $t = 2$. The expected trading volume and price-variability are both increasing in the prior uncertainty and the supply noise. An increase in the marginal cost of all investors will result in an increase in price-variability (since the public report has a more significant impact), but the impact on expected trading volume is ambiguous.

KV91b also examine trading volume and price-variability in a model with two trading dates. The information structure is, in one dimension, more general than the others we have discussed in that public reports are released at both trading dates. However, the KV91b model is less general in that the precision of the private information acquired at $t = 1$ is exogenous.

We represent the public signal at date t as y_{at}. The noise in the public reports and all the private signals are assumed to be independent. And, as in GM and KV91a, the supply of the risky asset is assumed not to change from one date to the next. Hence, in a large economy, the equilibrium prices take the form:

$$v_1 = \pi_{01} m_0 + \pi_{a1} y_{a1} + \pi_{d1} d - \pi_{z1} z_{\ell 1},$$

$$v_2 = \pi_{02} m_0 + \pi_{a1}{}^2 y_{a1} + \pi_{a2} y_{a2} + \pi_{d2} d - \pi_{z2} z_{\ell 1}.$$

The equilibrium issues raised in GM and KV91a arise here as well, and KV91b again assume the non-d-revealing equilibrium holds in their analysis.

The price change is separated into a *surprise* component (due to new information at $t = 2$) and a *noise* component (due to variations in $z_{\ell 1}$). Trading volume is shown to be proportional to the absolute change in price and a measure of differential precision of the investor's posterior beliefs at $t = 2$, so that trading volume also varies with surprise and noise. Comparative statics establish that price-variability and expected trading volume are increasing in the precision of the second public report, and decreasing in the precision of the first public report, the prior beliefs, and the private signals.

11.5 CONCLUDING REMARKS

In this chapter we have examined the interactive effect of public reports and private investor information. We have focused on the impact of informativeness of a public report on price informativeness, price variability, and trading volume. The identified relations provide insights that are potentially useful in explaining the relations observed in empirical studies.

In addition, these relations have been used in exploring the use of public reports and market prices in incentive contracts within settings in which the market price is influenced by both accounting reports and private investor information. In papers such as Bushman and Indjejikian (1993) and FW00, both the accounting report and the investors' private information are assumed to be useful for incentive contracting, but the latter is not contractible information. The stock price is contractible and reflects both the accounting report and the investors' private information. However, the price does not efficiently aggregate these two sources of information from an incentive contracting perspective. Hence, both the market price and the accounting report are used in an optimal contract. We explore these issues in Chapter 21 in Volume II.

Unfortunately, while the models described in this chapter, and in Chapter 12, can be used to describe the impact of changes in the informativeness of public reports, they cannot be used to make social welfare statements in this type of analysis because the preferences of the liquidity traders are not explicitly modeled. However, in the next chapter (Section 12.2.3), we describe a recent model by Zhang (2001) in which the informativeness of a public report at $t = 1$ is chosen at the time of an IPO ($t = 0$) by the firm's current owner. There is no private information at $t = 0$ and the IPO shares are purchased by liquidity traders. They are assumed to be risk neutral and anticipate being required to sell some random number of shares at the public reporting date. Commitment at $t = 0$ to a more informative public report at $t = 1$ will increase the IPO price. The current owner chooses the informativeness of the future public report so as to trade off the benefits of the price received relative to the cost of providing the public report.

We explore disclosure choice models in Part D (Chapters 13, 14, and 15). Those models generally focus on private management information, and do not consider private investor information. However, as discussed by Verrecchia

(2001, Section 4.2), combining the two types of models may provide a useful means of exploring the impact of disclosure policies on a firm's "information asymmetry component of the cost of capital."

APPENDIX 11A: PRIVATE INFORMATION IN A COMPLETE MARKET

The Basic Model

Grossman (1981) considers an event-contingent model in which trading takes place at $t = 1$ after investors receive private information about the event, and firms pay dividends at $t = 2$ that vary with the event. The set of possible private signals at $t = 1$ for the I investors is represented by $\mathbf{Y} = Y_1 \times \ldots \times Y_I$ and the set of possible dividend-relevant events at $t = 2$ is represented by Θ. Observe that Θ represents only those aspects of the state that affect the firms' terminal dividends (i.e., the outcome-relevant states) – this does not include all aspects of the state known by investors at $t = 2$. The likelihood of the vector of private signals $\mathbf{y}$ given the event θ is denoted $\varphi(\mathbf{y}|\theta)$ and the common prior event belief is $\varphi(\theta)$. Investor i only observes y_i, and his posterior belief given that private signal is $\varphi(\theta|y_i)$ – which is obtained by applying Bayes' theorem.

There is a set J of firms (with tradeable equity claims) and $\mathbf{D}$ represents the $|J| \times |\Theta|$ matrix of event-contingent firm dividends at $t = 2$ ($\mathbf{d}_j$ represents the jth row). There are no dividends at $t = 1$, only at $t = 2$, but every investor i is endowed with $\bar{c}_{i1}$ units of the consumption good at $t = 1$, which they can trade for equity claims. Investor i is also endowed with a portfolio of equity claims $\bar{\mathbf{z}}_i$.

Let $\mathbf{p}$ represent the vector of implicit event prices at $t = 1$ for event-contingent consumption at $t = 2$ and let $\mathbf{v}_1$ represent the vector of firm market values at $t = 1$, so that

$$\mathbf{v}_1 = \mathbf{D}\mathbf{p}.$$

Grossman permits production and assumes $\mathbf{d}_j$ is selected by the manager of firm j so as to maximize its market value v_{j1} at $t = 1$.

Unsophisticated Equilibrium

Each investor is assumed to have time-additive preferences and to make his consumption decision based strictly on his own information and the equilibrium event-contingent prices (but he ignores the information content of the prices). The market at $t = 1$ is assumed to be complete so that the investor can be represented as directly selecting consumption plan $\mathbf{c}_i = (c_{i1}, \mathbf{c}_{i2})$ at $t = 1$, where c_{i1} is current consumption and $\mathbf{c}_{i2}$ is the event-contingent consumption at $t = 2$.

The investor implements his consumption plan by selecting an appropriate investment portfolio. That is, in an unsophisticated equilibrium, investor i solves the following unsophisticated optimization problem.

$$U_i^u(y_i,\mathbf{p}) = \underset{\mathbf{c}_i}{\text{maximize}} \quad u_{i1}(c_{i1}) + \sum_{\theta \in \Theta} u_{i2}(c_{i2}(\theta))\, \varphi(\theta|y_i), \tag{11A.1a}$$

$$\text{subject to} \quad c_{i1} \geq 0,\, c_{i2}(\theta) \geq 0, \quad \forall\, \theta \in \Theta, \tag{11A.1b}$$

$$c_{i1} + \mathbf{c}_{i2}^{\mathrm{t}}\mathbf{p} \leq \bar{c}_{i1} + \bar{\mathbf{z}}_i^{\mathrm{t}}\mathbf{D}\mathbf{p}. \tag{11A.1c}$$

The equilibrium prices must be such that the market clears when investors make their individual choices, i.e.,

$$\sum_{i=1}^{I} [c_{i1} - \bar{c}_{i1}] = 0, \quad \sum_{i=1}^{I} c_{i2}(\theta) = \sum_{j \in J} d_j(\theta), \quad \forall\, \theta \in \Theta. \tag{11A.2}$$

Observe that each investor's consumption plan depends on the private signal that he receives. Hence, the equilibrium price depends on the private signals received by each investor.

Let $\mathbf{p}^u(\mathbf{y})$ represent the vector of unsophisticated equilibrium event prices induced by the vector of private signals $\mathbf{y}$ if each investor i trades strictly on the basis of his private signal y_i. Recall that in the homogeneous beliefs case, the equilibrium price for event θ depends on the aggregate supply of consumption in that event *and* the probability of the event. Now we have a different belief for each investor and $p^u(\theta|\mathbf{y})$ reflects the aggregate effect of the individual beliefs. For example, the implicit price will tend to be higher if many investors have received private signals that the event is likely to occur versus private signals that the event is unlikely to occur. Consequently, the vector $\mathbf{p}^u(\mathbf{y})$ provides *information to investor i about the private signals received by other investors.*

Rational Expectations Equilibria

In an unsophisticated equilibrium the belief in the investor's decision problem is not conditioned on the price vector $\mathbf{p}$. However, a price function (or possibly a mapping) $\mathbf{p}(\mathbf{y}) = \mathbf{p}$ does exist and, hence, investors have information that they are not using.

Consider a price function $\mathbf{p}^r(\mathbf{y})$: $\mathbf{Y} \to \mathbb{R}_+^{|\Theta|}$ such that for $\mathbf{p}^r(\mathbf{y}) = \mathbf{p}$ each investor i selects his consumption plan $\mathbf{c}_i$, conditional on y_i and $\mathbf{p}$ so as to solve

$$U_i^r(y_i,\mathbf{p}) = \underset{\mathbf{c}_i}{\text{maximize}} \quad u_{i1}(c_{i1}) + \sum_{\theta \in \Theta} u_{i2}(c_{i2}(\theta))\, \varphi(\theta|y_i,\mathbf{p}), \tag{11A.3}$$

subject to constraints (11A.1b) and (11A.1c). Furthermore, the price function is such that market clearing conditions (11A.2) are satisfied given that the dividends chosen by the managers maximize the market values of each firm. The key to the price function is the belief held by each investor i, which is denoted $\varphi(\theta|y_i,\mathbf{p})$. Each investor is assumed to know the joint distribution of $\tilde{\theta}$, $\tilde{y}_i$, and $\mathbf{p}^r(\tilde{\mathbf{y}})$, which are all random variables. He then observes $\mathbf{p}$ and y_i and derives his posterior belief about $\tilde{\theta}$, which he uses to select $\mathbf{c}_i$ (see (11A.3)). The decisions of all investors and firms must clear the market.

Observe that in a fully informed economy (in which all investors observe $\mathbf{y}$) the only aspect of $\mathbf{y}$ that is important is $\varphi(\theta|\mathbf{y})$. If any two sets of information produce the same posterior beliefs then they are for all practical purposes the same information. Therefore, we can view the fully informed equilibrium prices $\mathbf{p}^f(\mathbf{y})$ as a function of $\varphi(\cdot|\mathbf{y})$. There are $|\Theta|$ events whose probabilities sum to one and there are $|\Theta|$ relative prices (including the price of $t = 1$ consumption that we set to unity). Hence we can view $\mathbf{p}^f(\mathbf{y})$ as a function from $\mathbb{R}_+^{|\Theta|-1}$ to $\mathbb{R}_+^{|\Theta|}$. The key question is whether this function is invertible.

Proposition 11A.1 (Grossman 1981, Theorem 1)

Assume the investors are non-satiable and have strictly concave, differentiable, and time-additive preferences, that $\varphi(\theta|\mathbf{y}) > 0$ for all $\theta \in \Theta$ and $\mathbf{y} \in \mathbf{Y}$, and that maximizing $\mathbf{d}_j\mathbf{p}$, $\forall j$, defines a function (not a correspondence) of market prices. Let $\mathbf{y}'$ and $\mathbf{y}''$ denote two information vectors that produce different posterior beliefs. If there exists an investor i such that $\mathbf{c}_i(\mathbf{y}') \neq \mathbf{c}_i(\mathbf{y}'')$, then $\mathbf{p}^f(\mathbf{y}') \neq \mathbf{p}^f(\mathbf{y}'')$.

The proof is by contradiction. If the prices do not change then the firms will make the same production decisions and the aggregate event-contingent supply of the consumption good will be identical. If one investor wishes to change his consumption plan, then the sum of the others must change and the aggregate amount of their change must be in the opposite direction. That is impossible given that they hold homogeneous beliefs.

Proposition 11A.2 (Grossman 1981, Theorem 2)

Given the assumptions in Proposition 11A.1, the fully informed equilibrium prices $\mathbf{p}^f(\mathbf{y})$ can sustain a rational expectations equilibrium for the economy where investor i only observes y_i and $\mathbf{p}$.

The proof follows from the fact that if $\mathbf{p}^f(\cdot)$ is invertible, then the investors who maximize with respect to a belief function based on y_i and $\mathbf{p}$ will have the same demands as those who maximize with respect to a belief function based on $\mathbf{y}$. And if $\mathbf{p}_f(\cdot)$ is not invertible, then Grossman shows by contradiction that it is still a rational expectations equilibrium. This draws on Proposition 11A.1 in that if prices are the same for two private signals (beliefs), then the investors must select the same consumption plan given those private signals.

Proposition 11A.3 (Grossman 1981, Theorem 3)

Given a rational expectations equilibrium under the assumptions of Proposition 11A.2, there is no other feasible allocation (e.g., by a central planner) based on the information $\mathbf{y}$ that is Pareto superior.

Grossman makes the following additional remarks. First, the three propositions also hold in an economy with many goods per event. Second, time-additive preferences may not be necessary for the propositions to hold. Third, if markets are not complete, then there are counter examples to the existence of an equilibrium. However, these are knife-edge examples and Radner (1979) proves the generic existence of a rational expectations equilibrium (i.e., if $\mathbf{p}^f(\cdot)$ is not invertible for the given preferences then small changes in preferences result in a new function that is invertible). Fourth, there may be multiple rational expectations equilibria.

The complete markets assumption is key to the Grossman results. There is enough variability in event prices (a $|\Theta|$-dimensional space) to reveal all relevant aspects of the information, i.e., the posterior beliefs about the events (a ($|\Theta|$-1)-dimensional space). DeMarzo and Skiadas (1998) extend the analysis to what they call "quasi-complete" economies. An example is an economy with common prior beliefs and HARA utilities with identical risk cautiousness, i.e., the conditions for linear risk sharing considered in earlier chapters. In the fully informed economy, investors hold a fraction of the market portfolio and the basic structure of the event prices, i.e., the valuation index, is independent of the initial distribution of wealth (see Proposition 5.4). Hence, the same trades can be sustained in a rational expectations equilibrium in which investors only observe y_i and $\mathbf{p}$, and the investors do not want to deviate from those trades based on heterogeneous posterior beliefs as they realize that the other investors' only motive to take "side-bets" is to utilize their private information (see also the "no-trade theorem" by Milgrom and Stokey (1982), and Kreps (2001)).[18]

---

[18] In our analysis, there is no trade at the initial date $t = 0$ but investors have common prior beliefs. Milgrom and Stokey (1982) demonstrate in a single consumption date model that if there is an initial round of trading at $t = 0$ in a complete market (or the investors have equilibrium endowments), then there will be no trades at $t = 1$ in a rational expectations equilibrium in which investors only observe y_i and $\mathbf{p}$, and the investors' posterior beliefs are independent of their private signals. That is, any attempt to speculate on the basis of private information results in the information being impounded in prices eliminating profitable trades on the basis of that information. This holds even if investors have heterogeneous prior beliefs about the outcome-relevant events θ. However, conditional on the outcome-relevant events, the investors must have homogeneous beliefs about the events affecting the private information $\mathbf{y}$ but not outcomes.

(continued...)

APPENDIX 11B: PROOFS

Proof of Proposition 11.2
Observe that Table 11.1 and (11.8) imply

$$\mu_{u1} = \frac{\sigma_{yi}^2}{\sigma_\psi^2}\left(y_i - \frac{\pi_z}{\pi_y} z_\ell \right). \tag{11B.1}$$

Substituting (11B.1) into (11.12), and collecting terms, provides

$$v_1 = m_0 + \frac{1}{\bar{h}_1}\left\{\left[\lambda h_{i1} + (1-\lambda)h_{u1}\frac{\sigma_{yi}^2}{\sigma_\psi^2}\right] y_i - \left[(1-\lambda)h_{u1}\frac{\sigma_{yi}^2}{\sigma_\psi^2}\frac{\pi_z}{\pi_y} + r\right] z_\ell\right\}. \tag{11B.2}$$

Using conjecture (11.7) with (11B.2) implies

$$\pi_y = \frac{1}{\bar{h}_1}\left[\lambda h_{i1} + (1-\lambda)h_{u1}\frac{\sigma_{yi}^2}{\sigma_\psi^2}\right], \tag{11B.3a}$$

$$\pi_z = \frac{1}{\bar{h}_1}\left[(1-\lambda)h_{u1}\frac{\sigma_{yi}^2}{\sigma_\psi^2}\frac{\pi_z}{\pi_y} + r\right]. \tag{11B.3b}$$

Solving (11B.3b) for π_z, and substituting (11B.3a) for π_y in the denominator, provides

$$\pi_z = \frac{r\sigma_\psi^2 \pi_y}{\bar{h}_1 \sigma_\psi^2 \pi_y - (1-\lambda)h_{u1}\sigma_{yi}^2} = \frac{r}{\lambda h_{i1}}\pi_y. \tag{11B.4}$$

Hence, $\pi_z/\pi_y = r/[\lambda h_{i1}]$, which is used to specify σ_ψ^2 and h_{u1} from Table 11.1.

Q.E.D.

---

[18] (...continued)
Otherwise, there could be beneficial side-betting opportunities on the occurrence of the information.

Proof of Proposition 11.6

Using (11.18), the relations in Table 11.1, and $\pi_z/\pi_y = r\sigma_{i1}^2/\lambda$ from (11.13), establishes that the following relations hold in equilibrium if $\lambda^* \in (0,1)$:

$$\sigma_\psi^2 = \sigma_{yi}^2 + \left[\frac{r\sigma_{i1}^2}{\lambda^*}\right]^2 \sigma_z^2 = \frac{\sigma_{yi}^4}{\sigma_{yi}^2 - K\sigma_{i1}^2}, \qquad (11B.5a)$$

$$\sigma_{u1}^2 = \sigma_{i1}^2(1 + K), \qquad (11B.5b)$$

$$\bar{h}_1 = \frac{1 + K\lambda^*}{1 + K} h_{i1}. \qquad (11B.5c)$$

Substituting (11B.5) into the price parameter for y_i in (11.13) establishes that

$$\pi_y = 1 - \frac{1 - \lambda^*}{1 + K\lambda^*} \frac{K\sigma_{i1}^2}{\sigma_{yi}^2}. \qquad (11B.6)$$

Using (11B.6) and π_z in (11.13) yields

$$\mathrm{Var}[v_1] = \pi_y^2\sigma_{yi}^2 + \left[\frac{r\sigma_{i1}^2}{\lambda^*}\right]^2 \pi_y^2\sigma_z^2 = \pi_y^2\sigma_{yi}^2 \frac{\sigma_{yi}^2}{\sigma_{yi}^2 - K\sigma_{i1}^2},$$

$$\mathrm{Cov}[y_i, v_1] = \pi_y\sigma_{yi}^2,$$

$$\mathrm{Corr}^2[y_i, v_1] = \frac{\mathrm{Cov}^2[y_i, v_1]}{\sigma_{yi}^2 \mathrm{Var}[v_1]} = \frac{\sigma_{yi}^2 - K\sigma_{i1}^2}{\sigma_{yi}^2}. \qquad \text{Q.E.D.}$$

Proof of Proposition 11.9

We first express the elements an informed investor's beliefs and terminal wealth (see (11.31))

$$w_i = [z_{i1}(m_0 + y_i - v_1) - \kappa] + z_{i1}[\varepsilon_a - r\sigma_{ad}^2 z_{\ell 2}] + z_{\ell 2}[\varepsilon_d + r\sigma_{ad}^2 z_{\ell 2}],$$

in terms of the notation in Appendix 3A:

$$\mathbf{x} = [\varepsilon_a, \varepsilon_d, z_{\ell 2}]', \; f = [z_{i1}(m_0 + y_i - v_1) - \kappa], \; \mathbf{v} = [z_{i1}, 0, -r\sigma_{ad}^2 z_{i1}]', \; \boldsymbol{\mu} = [0, 0, 0]',$$

$$\mathbf{Q} = \begin{bmatrix} 0 & 0 & 0 \\ 0 & 0 & 1 \\ 0 & 1 & 2r\sigma_{ad}^2 \end{bmatrix}, \quad \mathbf{\Sigma} = \begin{bmatrix} \sigma_{ia}^2 & 0 & 0 \\ 0 & \sigma_{ad}^2 & 0 \\ 0 & 0 & \sigma_z^2 \end{bmatrix}, \quad \mathbf{H} = \begin{bmatrix} \sigma_{ia}^{-2} & 0 & 0 \\ 0 & \sigma_{ad}^{-2} & 0 \\ 0 & 0 & \sigma_z^{-2} \end{bmatrix}.$$

Hence, $r\mathbf{v} - \mathbf{H}\boldsymbol{\mu} = r\mathbf{v}$ and

$$r\mathbf{Q} + \mathbf{H} = \begin{bmatrix} \sigma_{ia}^{-2} & 0 & 0 \\ 0 & \sigma_{ad}^{-2} & r \\ 0 & r & 2r^2\sigma_{ad}^2 + \sigma_z^{-2} \end{bmatrix}.$$

From Appendix 3A we obtain

$$\mathrm{E}[u(w_i)|y_i,z_{i1},v_1] = -\ |\mathbf{H}|^{½}\ |r\mathbf{Q}+\mathbf{H}|^{-½} \exp[-\ rC(y_i,z_{i1},v_1)],$$

$$C(y_i,z_{i1},v_1) = f + \frac{1}{2r}\boldsymbol{\mu}^t\mathbf{H}\boldsymbol{\mu} - \frac{1}{2r}r\mathbf{v}^t(r\mathbf{Q} + \mathbf{H})^{-1}r\mathbf{v}$$

$$= z_{i1}(m_0 + y_i - v_1) - \kappa - ½\, r z_{i1}{}^2\hat{\sigma}_{i1}^2.$$

Differentiating $C(y_i,z_{i1},v_1)$ with respect to z_{i1} yields the informed demand function in (11.28) as the first-order condition for the investor's decision problem at $t = 1$.

The same approach can be used to obtain the demand function for an uninformed investor by deleting y_i, and replacing ε_{ia} and $\sigma_{ia}{}^2$ with y_a and $\sigma_{ua}{}^2$.

Q.E.D.

REFERENCES

Admati, A. R. (1991) "The Informational Role of Prices," *Journal of Monetary Economics* 28, 347-361.

Admati, A. R., and P. Pfleiderer. (1987) "Viable Allocations of Information in Financial Markets," *Journal of Economic Theory* 43, 76-115.

Bray, M. (1981) "Futures Trading, Rational Expectations, and the Efficient Market Hypothesis," *Econometrica* 49, 575-596.

Bushman, R. M. (1991) "Public Disclosure and the Structure of Private Information Markets," *Journal of Accounting Research* 29, 261-276.

Bushman, R. M., and R. J. Indjejikian. (1993) "Accounting Income, Stock Price, and Managerial Compensation," *Journal of Accounting and Economics* 16, 3-23.

DeMarzo, P., and C. Skiadas. (1998) "Aggregation, Determinacy, and Informational Efficiency for a Class of Economies with Asymmetric Information," *Journal of Economic Theory* 80, 123-152.

Demski, J. S., and G. A. Feltham. (1994) "Market Response to Financial Reports," *Journal of Accounting and Economics* 17, 3-40.

Easley, D., and R. A. Jarrow. (1983) "Consensus Beliefs Equilibrium and Market Efficiency," *Journal of Finance* 38, 903-911.

Feltham, G. A., and M. G. H. Wu. (2000) "Public Reports, Information Acquisition by Investors, and Management Incentives," *Review of Accounting Studies* 5, 155-190.

Grossman, S. J. (1981) "An Introduction to the Theory of Rations Expectations Under Asymmetric Information," *Review of Economic Studies* 48, 541-559.

Grossman, S. J., and J. E. Stiglitz. (1980) "On the Impossibility of Informationally Efficient Markets," *American Economic Review* 70, 393-408.

Grundy, B. D., and M. McNichols. (1989) "Trade and the Revelation of Information Through Prices and Direct Disclosure," *Review of Financial Studies* 2, 495-526.

Hellwig, M. (1980) "On the Aggregation of Information in Competitive Markets," *Journal of Economic Theory* 22, 477-498.

Hirshleifer, J. (1971) "The Private and Social Value of Information and the Reward to Inventive Activity," *American Economic Review* 61, 561-574.

Holthausen, R. W., and R. E. Verrecchia. (1990) "The Effect of Informedness and Consensus on Price and Volume Behavior," *The Accounting Review* 65, 191-208.

Indjejikian, R. J. (1991) "The Impact of Costly Information Interpretation on Firm Disclosure Decisions," *Journal of Accounting Research* 29, 277-301.

Kim, O., and R. E. Verrecchia. (1991a) "Market Reaction to Anticipated Announcements," *Journal of Financial Economics* 30, 273-309.

Kim, O., and R. E. Verrecchia. (1991b) "Trading Volume and Price Reactions to Public Announcements," *Journal of Accounting Research* 29, 302-321.

Kim, O., and R. E. Verrecchia. (1994) "Market Liquidity and Volume Around Earnings Announcements," *Journal of Accounting and Economics* 17, 41-67.

Kreps, T. (2001) "Endogenous Probabilities and the Information Revealed by Prices," *Journal of Mathematical Economics* 36, 1-18.

Kyle, A. S. (1985) "Continuous Auctions and Insider Trading," *Econometrica* 53, 1315-1335.

Kyle, A. S. (1989) "Informed Speculation with Imperfect Competition," *Review of Economic Studies* 56, 317-356.

Lundholm, R. J. (1988) "Price-Signal Relations in the Presence of Correlated Public and Private Information," *Journal of Accounting Research* 26, 107-118.

Lundholm, R. J. (1991) "Public Signals and the Equilibrium Allocation of Information," *Journal of Accounting Research* 29, 322-349.

McNichols, M., and B. Trueman. (1994) "Public Disclosure, Private Information Collection, and Short-Term Trading," *Journal of Accounting and Economics* 17, 69-94.

Milgrom, P., and N. Stokey. (1982) "Information, Trade, and Common Knowledge," *Journal of Economic Theory* 26, 17-27.

Radner, R. (1979) "Rational Expectations Equilibrium: Generic existence and the Information Revealed by Prices," *Econometrica* 47, 655-678.

Verrecchia, R. E. (1982) "Information Acquisition in a Noisy Rational Expectations Economy," *Econometrica* 50, 1415-1430.

Verrecchia, R. E. (1993) "How Do We Assess a Model of Price and Volume?" *The Accounting Review* 68, 870-873.

Verrecchia, R. E. (2001) "Essays on Disclosure," *Journal of Accounting and Economics* 32, 97-180.

Zhang, G. (2001) "Private Information Production, Public Disclosure, and the Cost of Capital: Theory and Implications," *Contemporary Accounting Research* 18, 363-384.

CHAPTER 12

STRATEGIC USE OF PRIVATE INVESTOR INFORMATION IN EQUITY MARKETS

In the GS (and HV) models examined in Chapter 11, the informed investors are assumed to act as price takers when they trade on their private information. The investors rationally anticipate the relation between the private information and the equilibrium price, but nonetheless they ignore the effect their trades will have on the information conveyed to uninformed investors through the resulting price. If there are many competing investors who become informed and their individual actions have a relatively small impact on the price, this is a reasonable assumption. Risk aversion plays a key role in these models as it determines how aggressively the informed investors react to their private information. In other settings there are only a few investors, such as insiders, who become informed. Even if they are risk neutral, they may well restrain their trades so as to partially "hide" their private information while still making a profit from its use in their trades.

Kyle (1985) introduced a model in which there is a privately informed rational investor, a rational market-maker, and liquidity traders. The informed investor and the liquidity traders place orders for shares with the market-maker, who sets the price so that he is expected to breakeven given his inferences about the informed investor's private information based on the total orders received.

The informed investor and the market-maker are risk neutral, and the informed investor acts strategically in that he anticipates the market-maker's rational inferences from the total orders received. The risk-neutrality assumption makes the model relatively simple to use, and provides somewhat different results because of its focus on trading volume and strategic trading by the informed investor. The following are key features of the basic Kyle model that differ from the basic GS model.

- All rational investors are risk neutral (so that risk premia play no role in this model).

- There is a single informed investor who selects his trading volume in anticipation of the resulting price, rather than acting as a price taker.

- There is a single uninformed investor, called the market-maker, who sets the price so that it equals the expected terminal dividend based on the information he has received.

- The market-maker imperfectly infers the informed investor's private signal from the net supply of shares (i.e., the shares sold by the liquidity traders minus the shares purchased by the informed investor).

- The market-maker absorbs the net supply of shares at a price equal to the expected terminal dividend.

While we assume that there is a single market-maker, he sets the price as if it was set competitively. That can be formally modeled, but it adds little to the insights of interest in this chapter. A key feature of the market-maker is that he is a rational investor, so his posterior beliefs are based on his rational anticipation of how the informed investor behaves. Furthermore, the informed investor rationally anticipates the inferences that will be made by the market-maker, and acts accordingly.

As in Chapter 11 we initially assume there are no public information, other than dividends, and then consider the impact of public reports prior and subsequent to private information acquisition.

12.1 THE BASIC STRATEGIC INVESTOR MODEL

The events as depicted in Figure 11.1 are also descriptive of the events in the basic Kyle model. There is a single firm that pays an uncertain dividend at $t = 2$, which is represented by $d = m_0 + \varepsilon$, where ε is a zero mean, normally distributed random variable. The investors' prior beliefs with respect to dividends, the private signal, and the liquidity trades are $\varepsilon \sim N(0,\sigma_0^2)$, $y_i \sim N(0,\sigma_{yi}^2)$, and $z_\ell \sim N(0,\sigma_z^2)$,[1] while the informed investor's posterior random dividend belief is $\varepsilon|y_i \sim N(y_i,\sigma_{i1}^2)$.

Consistency requires that $\sigma_0^2 = \sigma_{yi}^2 + \sigma_{i1}^2$, and we can interpreted either σ_{yi}^2 or $h_{i1} = 1/\sigma_{i1}^2$ as a measure of the informativeness of the private signal with respect to ε. We initially treat the informativeness as exogenous, and then as endogenous.

---

[1] In this setting, since there is a single rational investor, the average supply, denoted z_ℓ, equals the total supply, denoted Z_ℓ. We use z_ℓ.

12.1.1 Exogenous Informativeness of the Private Signal

As in our prior notation, the liquidity traders sell z_ℓ shares and the informed investor purchases (places an order for) z_i shares. The uninformed investor (i.e., the market-maker) observes the net supply $z_u = z_\ell - z_i$ and acquires those shares at a price per share of v_1. We ignore the information costs, so that the informed and uninformed investors' terminal wealths are

$$w_i = (d - v_1)z_i, \quad w_u = (d - v_1)z_u. \tag{12.1}$$

The informed investor knows that the uninformed investor will set the market price equal to the expected dividend based on the net supply, i.e.,

$$v_1 = m_0 + \mu_{u1}(z_u), \tag{12.2}$$

where $\mu_{u1}(z_u) = \mathrm{E}[\varepsilon | z_u]$ is the uninformed investor's posterior mean with respect to ε based on the net supply. Furthermore, we assume that the informed investor conjectures that the uninformed investor's posterior mean is proportional to the net demand (i.e., the negative of the net supply), which we express as

$$\mu_{u1}(z_u) = - bz_u. \tag{12.3}$$

Given that conjecture, the expected price resulting from an order of z_i units is

$$\mathrm{E}[v_1 | z_i] = m_0 + bz_i, \tag{12.4}$$

since $\mathrm{E}[z_\ell|z_i] = \mathrm{E}[z_\ell] = 0$. Hence, the informed investor's expected payoff given signal y_i is

$$U_{i1}(y_i,z_i) = [y_i - bz_i]z_i. \tag{12.5}$$

Differentiating (12.5) provides the first-order condition that characterizes the informed investor's demand function:

$$z_i(y_i) = \frac{1}{2b}y_i. \tag{12.6}$$

If the uninformed investor believes that (12.6) characterizes the informed investor's demand function (i.e., the informed investor holds conjecture (12.3)), then the uninformed investor's posterior mean will take the following form (see Section 3.1.3 for derivation of a posterior mean with normal distributions):

$$\mu_{u1}(z_u) = \frac{\text{Cov}[y_i,z_u]}{\text{Var}[z_u]} z_u = - \frac{\frac{1}{2b}\sigma_{yi}^2}{\frac{1}{4b^2}\sigma_{yi}^2 + \sigma_z^2} z_u. \tag{12.7}$$

In a rational expectations equilibrium, the uninformed investor's posterior belief (12.7) is consistent with the informed investor's conjecture (12.3). Hence,

$$b = \frac{\frac{1}{2b}\sigma_{yi}^2}{\frac{1}{4b^2}\sigma_{yi}^2 + \sigma_z^2} \Rightarrow b = \frac{\sigma_{yi}}{2\sigma_z}. \tag{12.8}$$

The following proposition summarizes the above analysis.[2]

Proposition 12.1 (Kyle 1985, Theorem 1)
The equilibrium demand and price functions in the basic Kyle model are:

$$z_i = \frac{\sigma_z}{\sigma_{yi}} y_i, \qquad v_1 = m_0 - \frac{\sigma_{yi}}{2\sigma_z} z_u. \tag{12.9}$$

In this setting, the GS measure of the informativeness of price is

$$\text{Corr}^2[y_i,v_1] = ½. \tag{12.10}$$

That is, the informativeness is independent of the noise created by the liquidity traders and of the variance of the private signal. This constancy occurs because the informed investor's demand increases with noise and decreases with private signal variance (see (12.9)), precisely so as to yield the same correlation between his information and the price. The same result holds if we consider a similar measure of the informativeness based on the net supply, i.e.,

$$\text{Corr}^2[y_i,z_u] = ½. \tag{12.11}$$

Of course, while the variance in the informed investor's private signal and the noisiness of the liquidity trades do not affect informativeness, they do affect the informed investors *ex ante* equilibrium expected payoff:

$$\text{E}[w_i] = ½\sigma_{yi}\sigma_z. \tag{12.12}$$

---

[2] Kyle seems to have made a slight error in stating b (his λ) in the theorem – he multiplies by 2 instead of dividing by 2. However, his analysis is correct.

That is, greater variability of y_i (which implies the private signal is more precise) and more noise result in a larger expected payoff for the informed investor. The uninformed investor is breaking even, so the informed investor's gain comes at the expense of the liquidity traders – they receive less than the expected dividend for the shares they sell.

Kyle (1985) extends his model to consider a sequence of trades by the informed investor, and Kyle (1989) extends the model to consider multiple informed traders. In the next section, we consider a model by Kim and Verrecchia (KV94) (1994) which has multiple informed investors in a setting with both a public report and a private signal.

12.1.2 Endogenous Informativeness of the Private Signal

There are two basic approaches to endogenizing private signal informativeness. One is to determine an equilibrium number of informed investors in a setting in which there are many investors who can acquire their own costly private signals. We consider that approach in Section 12.2.1, and in that setting we fix the informativeness of each signal and assume an investor only observes his private signal if he incurs a fixed information cost. The second approach is to hold the number of informed investors fixed and allow them to choose the informativeness of their signal, assuming the cost of the signal is increasing in its informativeness.

In this section, we consider a simple model based on the second approach. In particular, as in the basic model, we assume there is a single informed investor. The key difference is that now the informed investor chooses σ_{yi}^2 at a cost $\kappa(\sigma_{yi})$, where κ is strictly increasing ($\kappa' > 0$) and strictly convex ($\kappa'' > 0$), with $\kappa(0) = 0$, $\kappa'(0) = 0$ and $\kappa'(\infty) = \infty$.[3]

We assume the market-maker observes the informed investor's choice of σ_{yi} even though he does not observe y_i. Hence, the informed investor's *ex ante* expected utility from his private information is obtained from (12.12) and deducting the information cost, i.e.,[4]

$$U_{i0}(\sigma_{yi}^2) = \tfrac{1}{2}\sigma_{yi}\sigma_z - \kappa(\sigma_{yi}).$$

[3] Similar cost functions are found in several papers. For example, Zhang (2001) uses a similar cost function in a Kyle type model which includes both a public report and a private signal. The initial owner of the firm chooses the informativeness of the public report, while an informed investor chooses the incremental informativeness of his private signal.

[4] The analysis is more complex if the market-maker does not observe σ_{yi}. In that case, the market-maker sets the price based on his conjecture of σ_{yi} and the informed investor chooses the optimal level of σ_{yi} given the market-maker's conjecture. In a rational expectations equilibrium, the market-maker's conjecture will be such that it is the optimal choice of the informed investor given that conjecture.

Differentiating with respect to σ_{yi} provides the following characterization of the informed investor's optimal choice of private signal informativeness:

$$\kappa'(\sigma_{yi}) = ½\sigma_z.$$

Given the parametric structure of our model, the level of private signal informativeness is increasing in the noise introduced by liquidity traders, and is independent of the total uncertainty σ_0^2. The latter is, in part, a consequence of the assumption that all investors are risk neutral. All that matters is the cost of the uncertainty resolved by the private signal relative to the informed investor's ability to "hide" his information in the noise created by liquidity traders.

12.2 PUBLIC REPORTS AND THE CONCURRENT DEMAND FOR PRIVATE INFORMATION

The events described in Figure 11.2 can be interpreted as applying to the model considered here. That is, the model considers the simultaneous generation of a public report and acquisition of incremental private information. It can be viewed as a simplified version of the KV94 model (e.g., they consider multiple cash flow dates, whereas we consider a single terminal dividend date). Furthermore, we use a representation that is consistent with our preceding notation; it differs in form from the representation in the KV94 paper, but the two representations do not differ in substance.

KV94 describe their model as one in which a public report (e.g., an accounting report) is released which provides imperfect information about future cash flows (in our model, the terminal dividend). The noise in the report can be partially reduced if a rational investor acquires a private signal about that noise. The uninformed investor (i.e., the market-maker) receives the noisy public report and then imperfectly infers the informed investors' private signals about the noise from the net supply. This interpretation can be applied to our model, but the model applies to any setting in which investors can acquire incremental private information at the time of a public report.

12.2.1 Multiple Informed Investors

As in the KV94 model, we expand the basic Kyle model to consider multiple informed investors (*I*), as well as introducing a public report. We continue to have only one uninformed investor (the market-maker) who sets the market price.

The Basic Model

The investors' prior beliefs about the terminal dividend, public report, and private signal are $d = m_0 + \varepsilon$, $\varepsilon \sim N(0,\sigma_0^2)$, $y_a \sim N(0,\sigma_{ya}^2)$, and $y_i = N(0,\sigma_{yi}^2)$. The posterior random dividend belief given only the public report is $\varepsilon|y_a \sim N(y_a,\sigma_{a1}^2)$, with $\sigma_{a1}^2 < \sigma_0^2$, so that $\varepsilon_{ad} = \varepsilon - y_a \sim N(0,\sigma_{a1}^2)$ represents the prior belief about the noise in the public report.

Since rational investors (other than the market-maker) only trade if they become informed and the number of informed rational investors is endogenous in this analysis, it is not useful to describe the supply of shares from liquidity traders in terms of the average amount per active rational investor. Hence, we let Z_ℓ represent the total supply of shares from the liquidity traders and let $Z_\ell \sim N(0,\sigma_Z^2)$ represent the informed and uninformed rational investors' prior beliefs about that supply.

The private signals are informative about the noise in the public report, so that informed investor i's posterior random dividend belief, given both the public report y_a and his private signal y_i, is $\varepsilon|y_a,y_i \sim N(y_a+y_i,\sigma_{i1}^2)$, with $\sigma_{i1}^2 < \sigma_{a1}^2$ and $\mathrm{Cov}[y_a,y_i] = 0$. The prior belief about a private signal is $y_i \sim N(0,\sigma_{yi}^2)$, with $\sigma_{yi}^2 + \sigma_{i1}^2 = \sigma_{a1}^2$, $i = 1, ..., I$. While we retain the i subscript to reflect that it refers to an informed investor, we assume the informativeness of each private signal is the same, i.e., $\sigma_{yj}^2 = \sigma_{yi}^2$ and $\sigma_{j1}^2 = \sigma_{i1}^2$, for all $j = 1, ..., I$. The fact that the private signals are all informative about ε_{ad} implies that the private signals (as represented by the posterior mean) are likely to be correlated if they are informative. Of course, if the private signals are identical, then the correlation between pairs of private signals equals 1. We let $\rho \in [0,1]$ represent the correlation between pairs of private signals, so that the covariance is $\rho\sigma_{yi}^2$.[5] Observe that this structure implies that if investor i observes y_i, then his expectation with respect to y_j is

$$E[y_j|y_i] = \rho y_i. \tag{12.13}$$

The net supply is

$$z_u = Z_\ell - \sum_{i=1}^{I} z_i. \tag{12.14}$$

The uninformed investor bases his dividend expectations on the public report and the net supply, as represented by

[5] The perfect correlation case ($\rho = 1$) is one in which all investors receive the same private signal. The zero correlation case ($\rho = 0$) is one in which each investor is informed about a different component of ε_{ad}, which can only occur if $I\sigma_{yi}^2 \leq \sigma_{a1}^2$.

$$v_1 = m_0 + y_a + \mu_{u1}(z_u), \tag{12.15}$$

where $\mu_{u1}(z_u)$ is the uninformed posterior mean with respect to ε_{ad}. The informed investors conjecture that the uninformed investor's posterior mean with respect to ε_{ad} is proportional to the net supply, which we express as

$$\mu_{u1}(z_u) = - bz_u. \tag{12.16}$$

With multiple informed investors, each informed investor must also conjecture what the others will demand as a result of their private signals. Assume that the other investors' conjecture with respect to investor i's demand is represented by[6]

$$z_i(y_i) = \beta y_i. \tag{12.17}$$

Equilibrium Demand and Price

The informed investors must place their orders before observing the net supply (so the only information they have about the other investors' private signals is their own private signal). Hence, (12.13), (12.14), (12.15), (12.16), and (12.17) imply that investor i's expected price, given public report y_a, private signal y_i, and order quantity z_i, is

$$\mathrm{E}[v_1 | y_a, y_i, z_i] = m_0 + y_a + b[(I - 1)\beta\rho y_i + z_i], \tag{12.18}$$

where $(I - 1)\beta\rho y_i$ is investor i's expectations with respect to the orders placed by the other informed investors. Consequently, from (12.1), $\mathrm{E}[d | y_a, y_i] = m_0 + y_a + y_i$, and (12.18), investor i's expected payoff is

$$U_i(y_a, y_i, z_i) = \{y_i - b[(I - 1)\beta\rho y_i + z_i]\}z_i, \tag{12.19}$$

and his demand function is

$$z_i(y_i) = \frac{1}{2b}\,[1 - b(I - 1)\beta\rho]y_i. \tag{12.20}$$

In a rational expectations equilibrium, demand function (12.20) must be consistent with conjecture (12.17), which implies

[6] We could allow the conjecture to be a function of y_a and y_i, but, in our representation of information, the result would be that the demand is independent of y_a. Hence, we simplify the analysis by limiting the conjectured demand to be a function of y_i.

$$\beta = \frac{1}{2b}\,[1 - b(I - 1)\beta\rho\,] \quad \Rightarrow \quad \beta = \frac{1}{[2 + \rho(I-1)]\,b}. \tag{12.21}$$

If the uninformed investor believes that (12.17) characterizes each informed investor's demand function, then the uninformed posterior mean with respect to ε_{ad} will take the following form:

$$\mu_{u1}(z_u) = \frac{\mathrm{Cov}[\varepsilon_{ad}, z_u]}{\mathrm{Var}[z_u]}\, z_u = -\frac{\beta I \sigma_{yi}^2}{\beta^2 I[1 + \rho(I-1)]\sigma_{yi}^2 + \sigma_Z^2}\, z_u. \tag{12.22}$$

In a rational expectations equilibrium, the uninformed investor's posterior belief (12.22) is consistent with the informed investors' conjecture (12.16), which implies (after substituting (12.21) into (12.22)) that

$$b = \frac{I[2 + \rho(I-1)]\,b\sigma_{yi}^2}{I[1 + \rho(I-1)]\sigma_{yi}^2 + [2 + \rho(I-1)]^2 b^2 \sigma_Z^2}. \tag{12.23}$$

The solution to (12.23) and its implications are summarized in the following proposition.

Proposition 12.2

The equilibrium demand and price functions in our representation of the KV94 model are:

$$z_i = \beta y_i, \qquad \beta = \frac{1}{\sqrt{I}}\frac{\sigma_Z}{\sigma_{yi}}, \tag{12.24a}$$

$$v_1 = m_0 + y_a - b z_u, \qquad b = \frac{\sqrt{I}}{2 + \rho(I-1)}\frac{\sigma_{yi}}{\sigma_Z}. \tag{12.24b}$$

Equilibrium Information Acquisition

Now assume that there are a large number of potential investors who could become informed and enter the market. If a potential investor does not become informed, he refrains from trading – the only uninformed traders are the liquidity traders and the market-maker. Furthermore, while the market-maker does not observe the informed investors' private signals or the size of their orders, he does know how many have paid to be informed. The cost of becoming informed is κ, so that an informed investor's payoff is

$$w_i = (d - v_1)z_i - \kappa, \tag{12.25}$$

and his *ex ante* expected equilibrium payoff, given that I are informed, is

$$\begin{aligned} \mathrm{E}[w_i|I] &= \mathrm{E}\left[\left\{\varepsilon_{ad} - b\left(\beta\sum_{j=1}^{I} y_j - Z_\ell\right)\right\}\beta y_i\right] - \kappa \\ &= [1 - b\beta\{1 + (I - 1)\rho\}]\beta\sigma_{yi}^2 - \kappa \\ &= \frac{1}{2 + \rho(I-1)}\frac{1}{\sqrt{I}}\sigma_Z\sigma_{yi} - \kappa. \end{aligned} \tag{12.26}$$

Clearly, the payoff is decreasing in the number of informed investors. Hence, no investors become informed if a single informed investor has a negative expected payoff, i.e., if

$$\mathrm{E}[w_i|I = 1] = \tfrac{1}{2}\sigma_Z\sigma_{yi} - \kappa < 0. \tag{12.27}$$

On the other hand, if $\mathrm{E}[w_i|I = 1] > 0$, then the equilibrium number of informed investors is the number I^* such that $\mathrm{E}[w_i|I^*] > 0 > \mathrm{E}[w_i|I^* + 1]$. As in the GS model, KV94 (see their Proposition 1) ignore the fact that the number of informed investors is an integer and treat I as a continuous variable. Hence, I^* is such that $\mathrm{E}[w_i|I^*] = 0$. In our subsequent analysis we assume the parameters are such that $I^* > 1$, so that the correlation among private signals matters.

Setting (12.26) equal to zero and totally differentiating provides the following relations between the model parameters and the number of informed investors.

Proposition 12.3 (KV94, Prop. 1)
In the KV94 model, if $I^* > 1$, then the equilibrium number of informed investors is:

(a) independent of the informativeness of the public report (σ_{ya}^2);

(b) increasing in the incremental informativeness of the private signal (σ_{yi}^2);

(c) decreasing in the correlation of the informed investors' private signals (ρ);

(d) increasing in the liquidity trader noise (σ_Z^2);

(e) decreasing in the cost of the information (κ).

These results are all quite intuitive, except possibly result (a). The key here is that the parametric structure of our model is such that changing the informativeness of the public report does not change the incremental informativeness of the private signal. KV94 use an alternative parametric structure, and it is such that increasing the informativeness of the public report reduces the incremental informativeness of the private signal – so that our result (b) applies.

Trading Volume

The market-maker absorbs the net supply from the informed investors and the liquidity traders. However, the trading volume is more appropriately measured as the number of shares that change hands, which equals ½ of the total of the absolute number of shares bought and sold. Hence, the expected trading volume at the public report date, if there are $I > 1$ informed investors, is[7]

$$E[T|I] = \tfrac{1}{2}\, E\left[|Z_\ell| + \sum_{i=1}^{I} |z_i| + |z_u| \right]$$

$$= \sqrt{\frac{1}{2\pi}}\left[\sigma_Z + I\beta\sigma_{yi} + \sqrt{I[1+\rho(I-1)]\beta^2\sigma_{yi}^2 + \sigma_Z^2} \right]$$

$$= \sqrt{\frac{1}{2\pi}}\left[1 + \sqrt{I} + \sqrt{I[1+\rho(I-1)] + 1} \right]\sigma_Z. \qquad (12.28)$$

Obviously, for exogenous I, the expected trading volume is increasing in the number of informed investors, the correlation among their private signals, and variance in the noise trades. Letting I equal the equilibrium number of informed investors (I^*) yields the following comparative statics.

Proposition 12.4

In the KV94 model, if $I^* > 1$, then the equilibrium expected trading volume is:

(a) independent of the informativeness of the public report (σ_{ya}^2);

(b) increasing in the incremental informativeness of the private signal (σ_{yi}^2);

---

7 In the following expressions we use the fact that for any normally distributed variable $x \sim N(0,\sigma^2)$, $E[|x|] = \sqrt{2/\pi}\,\sigma$. From (12.24a) we obtain $Var[z_i] = \beta^2\sigma_{yi}^2$, and (12.14) then implies that $Var[z_u] = \sigma_Z^2 + I[1+\rho(I-1)]\beta^2\sigma_{yi}^2$.

(c) increasing in the liquidity trader noise (σ_Z^2);

(d) decreasing in the cost of the information (κ);

(e) increasing in the private signal correlation (ρ).

The results (a)-(d) follow directly from Proposition 12.3 and (12.28). The impact of the private signal correlation is complex since increasing ρ increases the expected trading volume for fixed I, but reduces I^*. However, direct computation shows that the former effect dominates the latter.

Price-Variability and Price-Informativeness

KV94 consider the change between the pre- and post-report prices, and compute the variance of that price change. In our simplified setting, the pre-report price equals m_0, since that is the expected dividend given no information. The equilibrium price and parameters, with I informed investors, are characterized by (12.24). Hence, the variance of the price change, if there are $I > 1$ informed investors, is

$$\begin{aligned} \text{Var}[v_1|I] &= \sigma_{ya}^2 + b^2\text{Var}[z_u|I] = \sigma_{ya}^2 + b^2[I[1+\rho(I-1)]\beta^2\sigma_{yi}^2 + \sigma_Z^2] \\ &= \sigma_{ya}^2 + \frac{I\sigma_{yi}^2}{[2+\rho(I-1)]}. \end{aligned} \tag{12.29}$$

Differentiating (12.29) with respect to σ_{ya}^2, σ_{yi}^2, and ρ establishes that, for a fixed number of informed investors $I > 1$, the price variance is increasing in the informativeness of the public report and the incremental informativeness of the private signals, and is decreasing in the correlation between private signals. Differentiating (12.29) with respect to I establishes that the price variance is increasing in the number of informed investors. These relations and Proposition 12.3 then imply the following comparative statics if we let I equal the equilibrium number of informed investors (I^*).

Proposition 12.5

In the KV94 model, if $I^* > 1$, then the price variance is:

(a) increasing in the informativeness of the public report (σ_{ya}^2);

(b) increasing in the incremental informativeness of the private signal (σ_{yi}^2);

(c) decreasing in the private signal correlation (ρ);

(d) increasing in the liquidity trader noise (σ_Z^2);

(e) decreasing in the cost of the information (κ).

The dividend uncertainty given only the public report is Var[$d|y_a$] = σ_{a1}^2. KV94 define the *informativeness of the price* to be the reduction in dividend uncertainty if one also knows the price, and an equilibrium number I^* of rational investors are informed, i.e., Var[$d|y_a$] - Var[$d|y_a,v_1,I^*$]. We can interpret their results as establishing that their measure of price-informativeness is increasing in the incremental informativeness of the private signal (σ_{yi}^2) and the noise created by liquidity traders (σ_Z^2), and decreasing in the correlation of the investors' private signals (ρ) and the cost of information (κ).

Recall that GS defined price-informativeness to be the square of the correlation between the investors' private signal and the price (see Proposition 11.6 and its application to the basic Kyle model in (12.10)). This measure is not directly applicable to the KV94 setting since there are multiple private signals (unless $\rho = 1$) and the number of private signals increases with the number of informed investors. Furthermore, the price is also influenced by the public report. However, we can use an approach similar to GS if we hold I fixed and consider the correlation between the posterior mean given all the investors' private signals ($\mathbf{y} = (y_1, ..., y_I)$) and market price, conditional on the public report. Observe that the fully-informed posterior mean with respect to ε_{ad} is

$$\mu_1(\mathbf{y}) = \frac{1}{1 + \rho(I - 1)} \sum_{i=1}^{I} y_i. \tag{12.30}$$

Hence, the price-informativeness with respect to the fully-informed posterior mean is

$$\text{Corr}^2(\mu_1, v_1 \text{-} y_a) = \frac{1 + \rho(I-1)}{2 + \rho(I-1)}.$$

As in the single informed investor case, the informativeness of the price is independent of the informativeness of the private signals and the noise created by liquidity traders. However, it is increasing in both the number of informed investors and the correlation of their private signals.

12.2.2 Private Investor Information in an Infinite Horizon, Residual Income Model

The preceding discussion assumes the firm only operates for one period and the public report is succinctly represented by the expected terminal dividend given that report. Kwon (2001) provides a brief note which expands the representation of the accounting information by applying the Kyle model to an infinite horizon, residual income model of the type considered in Chapter 10. We briefly consider a similar model.

The Accounting Policies and Informed Information Dynamics

As in Chapter 10, we assume the firm's accounting policies satisfy the clean surplus relation, so that the end-of-period book value (bv_t) equals the start-of-period book value (bv_{t-1}) plus the net income for the period (ni_t) minus the end-of-period dividend (d_t). The book value is divided into financial and operating assets, and the financial assets (fa_t) are carried at mark-to-market. We assume dividend policy irrelevance and a constant interest rate $\imath$ per period, so that the expected financial income (fi_t) equals $\imath fa_{t-1}$. The operating assets consist of plant & equipment (pe_t), so that the residual operating income is $roi_t = oi_t - \imath pe_{t-1}$, where oi_t is the operating income.

We further assume that a risk-neutral market-maker sets the market price equal to the discounted expected dividends based on the information available to him (represented by ψ_t). As established in Chapter 9, if the market value of the firm is equal to the discounted expected future dividends, financial assets are recorded at mark-to-market, and there is dividend policy irrelevance, then the market value can be equivalently expressed as (see (9.11c) for $\breve{T} = t + 1$)

$$v_t(\psi_t) = bv_t + \beta\, \mathrm{E}[roi_{t+1} + v_{t+1} - bv_{t+1} | \psi_t], \tag{12.31}$$

where $\beta = [1 + \imath]^{-1}$.

To explore the relation between market values and accounting numbers in a context in which informed investors have private information, we assume the following linear information dynamics represent the informed investors' information (this is the same as LID2 in Chapter 10 except that, for simplicity, we assume the private signals υ_{rt} and υ_{it} are not correlated across time):

$$\tilde{cr}_{t+1} = \omega_{rr} cr_t + \omega_{ri} ci_t + \upsilon_{rt} + \tilde{\varepsilon}_{rt+1}, \tag{12.32a}$$

$$\tilde{ci}_{t+1} = \omega_{ii} ci_t + \upsilon_{it} + \tilde{\varepsilon}_{it+1}, \tag{12.32b}$$

$$\tilde{\upsilon}_{rt+1} = \tilde{\varepsilon}_{\upsilon rt+1}, \tag{12.32c}$$

$$\tilde{\upsilon}_{it+1} = \tilde{\varepsilon}_{\upsilon it+1}, \tag{12.32d}$$

where cr_t and ci_t are the operating cash receipts and investments, υ_{rt} and υ_{it} are the informed investors' private information about next period's cash receipts and investment opportunities, and $(\tilde{\varepsilon}_{rt+1}, \tilde{\varepsilon}_{it+1}, \tilde{\varepsilon}_{\upsilon rt+1}, \tilde{\varepsilon}_{\upsilon it+1})$ are zero mean random variables. The parameters are such that $\omega_{rr} \in (0,1)$, $\omega_{ii} \in [1,R)$, where $R = \beta^{-1}$, and $\omega_{ri} > R - \omega_{rr}$, which ensures that each dollar invested has positive NPV (see Chapter 10 for a more extensive discussion of this type of model).

We assume cash receipts are treated as revenue of the period, while cash investments are capitalized and then depreciated at a declining balance rate of 1-δ. To simplify the discussion we assume $\delta = \omega_{rr}$. Hence, the operating income is $oi_t = cr_t - (1- \omega_{rr})pe_{t-1}$ and the operating assets are $pe_t = \omega_{rr}pe_{t-1}$.

The Uninformed and Fully-informed Accounting-value Relations

If the market-maker only observes the accounting numbers bv_t, roi_t, and ci_t, and believes that the informed investor is not trading, then we can use (10.17) to determine the following accounting-value relation:

$$v_t = bv_t + \alpha_{roi}\, roi_t + \alpha_{ci}\, ci_t, \tag{12.33a}$$

where $\alpha_{roi} = \Phi_r\omega_{rr}$ and $\alpha_{ci} = \lambda R\Phi_i$, with $\Phi_r = [R - \omega_{rr}]^{-1}$, $\lambda = \Phi_r\omega_{ri}$, and $\Phi_i = [R - \omega_{ii}]^{-1}$. However, if the market-maker knows υ_{rt} and υ_{it}, then we can use (10.23) to determine the following accounting-value relation:

$$v_t = bv_t + \alpha_{roi}\, roi_t + \alpha_{ci}\, ci_t + \alpha_{\upsilon r}\, \upsilon_{rt} + \alpha_{\upsilon i}\, \upsilon_{it}, \tag{12.33b}$$

where $\alpha_{\upsilon r} = \Phi_r$ and $\alpha_{\upsilon i} = \lambda\Phi_i$. Observe that $\alpha_{\upsilon r}$ – the coefficient for the private information about next period's residual income – reflects the fact that the residual income will persist at the rate ω_{rr}. Similarly, $\alpha_{\upsilon i}$ – the coefficient for the private information about next period's investment opportunities – reflects the fact that the investment opportunities will grow at the rate ω_{ii} - 1 and each dollar invested has an NPV of λ.

A Rational Expectations Accounting-value Relation

Now assume that the informed investors trade on the basis of their private information and the market-maker realizes that the net supply of shares he receives at date t equals a random supply $Z_{\ell t} \sim N(0,\sigma_Z^2)$ from the liquidity traders minus the demand z_{it} from each of the I informed investors. At date t the informed investors do not know υ_{rt+1} or υ_{it+1}, i.e., the private information they will have next period, and their expectations with respect to both types of information equal zero. On the other hand, they do know υ_{rt} and υ_{it} at date t, and they know this information will be fully impounded in the price at date t+1 (since they will be fully reflected in roi_{t+1} and ci_{t+1}).

To apply the Kyle model we assume $(\tilde{\varepsilon}_{rt+1}, \tilde{\varepsilon}_{it+1}, \tilde{\varepsilon}_{\upsilon rt+1}, \tilde{\varepsilon}_{\upsilon it+1})$ are normally distributed. Furthermore, for simplicity, we assume the variables are independently distributed with variances σ_{cr}^2, σ_{ci}^2, $\sigma_{\upsilon r}^2$, and $\sigma_{\upsilon i}^2$, respectively. The informed investors' private signal is represented by the difference between the fully-informed price (12.33b) and the uninformed price (12.33a), i.e.,

$$y_{it} = \alpha_{vr}\, v_{rt} + \alpha_{vi}\, v_{it}. \tag{12.34}$$

The expected value of y_{it} equals zero and its variance is

$$\sigma_{yi}^2 = \alpha_{vr}^2\sigma_{vr}^2 + \alpha_{vi}^2\sigma_{vi}^2. \tag{12.35}$$

As before, the market-maker conjectures that each informed investor *i* orders

$$z_{it} = \beta y_{it} \tag{12.36}$$

and the informed investors conjecture that the market-maker will set the current price equal to

$$v_t = bv_t + \alpha_{roi}\, roi_t + \alpha_{ci}\, ci_t - b\, z_{ut}, \tag{12.37}$$

where $z_{ut} = Z_{\ell t} - \Sigma_{i=1}^{I} z_{it}$. From Proposition 12.2 it follows that the equilibrium parameters, for a fixed number of informed investors I and perfectly correlated private signals ($\rho = 1$), are

$$\beta = \frac{1}{\sqrt{I}}\frac{\sigma_Z}{\sigma_{yi}}, \qquad b = \frac{\sqrt{I}}{I+1}\frac{\sigma_{yi}}{\sigma_Z}. \tag{12.38}$$

Observe that equilibrium accounting-value relation (12.37) is expressed as a linear function of current book value, current residual income, current cash investments, and the current net supply of shares traded. However, substituting (12.34), (12.35), (12.36), and (12.38) into (12.37) allows us to restate this relation as

$$v_t = bv_t + \alpha_{roi}\, roi_t + \alpha_{ci}\, ci_t + \frac{I}{I+1}[\alpha_{vr}\, v_{rt} + \alpha_{vi}\, v_{it}] - b\, Z_{\ell t}. \tag{12.35}$$

Hence, the liquidity trades result in random variations in the price and allow the informed investors to partially hide their private information. However, the private information becomes closer to being fully revealed as the number of informed investors increase, i.e., in the limit as $I \to \infty$, (12.35) $\to$ (12.33b).

12.2.3 Endogenous Informativeness of the Public Report

In the prior analysis in this chapter we have assumed that there is either no public report or its informativeness is exogenous. In this section we consider the endogenous choice of the informativeness of the public report in a model similar to Zhang (2001).

As in Section 12.1.2, we assume that there is a single informed investor and that investor endogenously chooses the informativeness of his private signal. We introduce a public report similar to the model in Section 12.2.1. The total uncertainty about the terminal dividend is σ_0^2, the uncertainty resolved by the public report y_a is σ_{ya}^2, and the incremental uncertainty resolved by the informed investor's private signal y_i is σ_{yi}^2. The variance of the noise created by liquidity traders is again σ_z^2. From Proposition 12.2, it follows that the equilibrium demand and price functions, given σ_{yi}^2 and σ_z^2, are

$$z_i = \frac{\sigma_z}{\sigma_{yi}} y_i, \quad v_1 = m_0 + y_a - \frac{1}{2}\frac{\sigma_{yi}}{\sigma_z} z_u. \tag{12.36}$$

A key assumption implicit in Zhang's model is that the marginal cost of the incremental informativeness of the private signal is increasing in the informativeness of the public report. That is, the more informative the public report, the more costly it is for the informed investor to obtain additional information. We capture this characteristic by assuming the cost of the private signal has the following specific functional form:

$$\kappa_i(\sigma_{ya},\sigma_{yi}) = \tfrac{1}{2}\, k_i\,(1 + \sigma_{ya})\sigma_{yi}^2,$$

where $k_i > 0$ is a private information cost parameter.[8] The informed investor knows σ_{ya} when he selects σ_{yi}, and his *ex ante* expected utility is (see 12.12)

$$U_{i0}(\sigma_{yi}|\sigma_{ya}) = \tfrac{1}{2}\sigma_{yi}\sigma_z - \tfrac{1}{2}\, k_i\,(1 + \sigma_{ya})\sigma_{yi}^2. \tag{12.37}$$

Differentiating (12.37) with respect to σ_{yi} provides the following characterization of the informed investor's choice of his private signal informativeness and his optimal expected utility:

$$\sigma_{yi} = \frac{1}{2k_i}\frac{\sigma_z}{1 + \sigma_{ya}}, \tag{12.38a}$$

$$U_{i0}(\sigma_{ya}) = \frac{1}{8k_i}\frac{\sigma_z^2}{1 + \sigma_{ya}}. \tag{12.38b}$$

[8] This cost function has the following key characteristics: $\partial\kappa_i/\partial\sigma_{yi} > 0$, $\partial\kappa_i/\partial\sigma_{ya} > 0$, $\partial^2\kappa_i/\partial\sigma_{yi}^2 > 0$, $\kappa_i(\sigma_{ya},0) = 0$, $\partial\kappa_i(\sigma_{ya},0)/\partial\sigma_{yi} = 0$, and $\partial\kappa_i(\sigma_{ya},\infty)/\partial\sigma_{yi} = \infty$.

Not surprisingly, both the choice of σ_{yi} and the informed investor's expected utility are increasing in the noise created by liquidity traders, decreasing in the information cost, and decreasing in the informativeness of the public report.

Zhang assumes the owner of the firm sells his shares in an initial public offering (IPO) at $t = 0$, and at the time of his IPO he makes a commitment with respect to the informativeness of the public report his firm will release at $t = 1$. We assume the cost of that report is

$$\kappa_a(\sigma_{ya}) = k_a \sigma_{ya}^2,$$

where k_a is a public disclosure cost parameter.[9] Zhang further assumes there are no informed investors acquiring the shares at $t = 0$, and the price is set such that an investor who believes he may be a liquidity trader at $t = 1$ expects to break-even. That is,

$$v_0(\sigma_{ya}) = m_0 - \frac{1}{8k_i}\frac{\sigma_z^2}{1 + \sigma_{ya}} - k_a \sigma_{ya}^2, \tag{12.39}$$

where the second term represents the loss in value due to having an informed investor in the market at $t = 1$ (which is the negative of the informed investor's gross benefit from being informed).

Differentiating (12.39) with respect to σ_{ya} provides the following characterization of the optimal level of public disclosure:

$$\frac{1}{8k_i}\frac{\sigma_z^2}{[1 + \sigma_{ya}]^2} = 2k_a \sigma_{ya}. \tag{12.40}$$

We obtain the following comparative statics from totally differentiating (12.40) and differentiating (12.39).

Proposition 12.6

In our representation of the Zhang (2001) model, the initial owner's choice of public report informativeness (σ_{ya}) is decreasing in both cost parameters (k_a and k_i), and is increasing in the noise due to liquidity traders (σ_z^2). The optimal IPO price (v_0) is decreasing in the public report cost (k_a) and the noise due to liquidity traders (σ_z^2), and is increasing in the private signal cost (k_i).

---

[9] This cost function has the following key characteristics: $\kappa_a' > 0$, $\kappa_a'' > 0$, $\kappa_a(0) = 0$, $\kappa_a'(0) = 0$, and $\kappa_a'(\infty) = \infty$.

Increasing the cost of public disclosure has an obvious direct effect in reducing the optimal level of public disclosure and the IPO price. On the other hand, the informed investor incurs the cost of private information, so that it does not directly affect the owner. However, increasing the private information cost decreases both the loss due to trading with the informed investor and the marginal benefit from reducing that loss by increasing the public report informativeness. So that increasing k_i has opposite effects on the optimal choice of σ_{ya} and on v_0. Conversely, increasing the noise due to liquidity traders increases both the loss due to trading with the informed investor and the marginal benefit from reducing that loss by increasing the public report informativeness. Hence, increasing σ_z^2 also has opposite effects on the optimal choice of σ_{ya} and on v_0.

Zhang interprets his results as pertaining to the "cost of capital" in an IPO. That cost consists of the loss due to trading with the informed investor and the cost of public disclosure. Due to the assumption that investors are risk neutral, there is no risk premium in this "cost of capital."

12.3 PUBLIC REPORTS AND THE PRIOR DEMAND FOR PRIVATE INFORMATION

As noted in Chapter 11, three papers have examined settings in which private information acquisition takes place prior to the anticipated issuance of a public report. In Section 11.4, we considered Demski and Feltham's (DF) (1994) GS type model, and briefly commented on Kim and Verrecchia's (1991) HV type model. In this section, we consider a model similar to McNichols and Trueman's (MT) (1994) Kyle type model.

The Basic Model

The basic elements of the DF model are depicted in Figure 11.3. We initially use those elements in a basic Kyle type model.

The key features of our basic Kyle type model are as follows. The prior uncertainty with respect to the terminal dividend at $t = 3$ is σ_0^2. An informed investor acquires a private signal at $t = 1$ and a public report is produced at $t = 2$. Following DF, we assume (whereas MT do not) that the public report is a sufficient statistic for the public report and private signal with respect to beliefs about the terminal dividend, and that it is represented by the posterior mean y_a ~$N(0,\sigma_{ya}^2)$. Due to the risk neutrality of the market-maker and the sufficiency of y_a, the market price at $t = 2$ is

$$v_2 = m_0 + y_a,$$

and the informed investor has no incentive to trade at that date. This stands in contrast to the DF model, in which an informed investor's risk aversion induces him to avoid unnecessary risk by reversing his speculative position once the informed and uninformed investors have homogeneous beliefs.

The private signal at $t = 1$ generates a posterior mean y_i with respect to the public report (and the terminal dividend). The prior private signal belief is $y_i \sim$ N$(0,\sigma_{yi}^2)$, and we interpret σ_{yi}^2 as the informativeness of the private signal. This informativeness measure pertains to the reduction in the prior uncertainty with respect to the public report (σ_{ya}^2) and the terminal dividend (σ_0^2), but it is the former reduction that is relevant here. The liquidity traders' supply of shares at $t = 1$ is $z_{\ell 1} \sim$ N$(0,\sigma_z^2)$ – the supply at $t = 2$ is immaterial in our basic model.

The informed investor's equilibrium demand and the market price at $t = 1$ are precisely the same as in Proposition 12.1, even though the informed investor's concern here is the price at which he can sell his shares at the public report date, rather than the terminal dividend. Hence,

$$z_{i1} = \frac{\sigma_{z1}}{\sigma_{yi}} y_i, \qquad v_1 = m_0 - \frac{\sigma_{yi}}{2\sigma_{z1}} z_{u1}. \tag{12.41}$$

where z_{i1} is the informed investor's demand for shares at $t = 1$ and $z_{u1} = z_{\ell 1} - z_{i1}$ is the net supply of shares observed by the market-maker.

If the informed investor chooses the informativeness of his private signal, and the cost of that informativeness is $\kappa(\sigma_{yi}) = ½k\sigma_{yi}^2$, then (see Section 12.1.2) his optimal choice of informativeness and expected utility is

$$\sigma_{yi}^* = \frac{1}{2k}\sigma_{z1}, \qquad U_{i0}^* = \frac{1}{8k}\sigma_{z1}^2.$$

That is, the informed investor's demand and expected utility are increasing in the noise created by liquidity traders and decreasing in the cost of private signal informativeness.

A More General Model

A key feature of the MT model is that the informed investor's posterior dividend belief at $t = 2$ depends on both the private and public information. That is, y_a is not a sufficient statistic for (y_i,y_a) with respect to beliefs about ε.

MT express the public report and private signal as being equal to the terminal dividend plus noise, where the noise in one may be correlated with the noise in the other. The scaling of signals is arbitrary and we scale the public report y_a so that it equals the expected random dividend ε given the public information, and we scale the private signal y_i so that it equals the expected public report given the private information. This was done in the DF model, but DF also assumed that y_a is a sufficient statistic for (y_i, y_a) with respect to beliefs about the random dividend ε. To encompass the MT setting, we allow for the possibility that the informed investor's posterior dividend belief at $t = 2$ may depend on both y_i and y_a. Table 12.1 provides the prior and posterior beliefs for this setting.

From Table 12.1 the posterior expected dividend at $t = 2$ is $E[d|y_i,y_a] = m_0 + \lambda_i y_i + \lambda_a y_a$. The special case in which y_a is a sufficient statistic (i.e., $\lambda_i = 0$) occurs if $\sigma_{\varepsilon i} = \sigma_{yi}^2$. On the other hand, if $\sigma_{yi}^2 < \sigma_{\varepsilon i} < \sigma_{ya}^2$, then both λ_i and λ_a are positive, whereas λ_i is negative if $\sigma_{\varepsilon i} < \sigma_{yi}^2$ and λ_a is negative if $\sigma_{ya}^2 < \sigma_{\varepsilon i}$.

MT assume the informed investor has a "short-term horizon" so that, at $t = 2$, he closes out any position he took at $t = 1$, i.e., $z_{i2} = - z_{i1}$, where z_{it} is the informed investor's demand at date t. MT also assume that, at $t = 2$, the liquidity traders buy back any shares they sold at $t = 1$, i.e., $z_{\ell 2} = - z_{\ell 1} \sim N(0,\sigma_z^2)$, where $z_{\ell t}$ is the supply of shares from the liquidity traders at date t. Consequently, the net supply of shares observed by the market-maker at the two dates are $z_{u2} = - z_{u1} = z_{i1} - z_{\ell 1}$ and, hence, the only new information at $t = 2$ is the public report y_a.

At $t = 1$, the market-maker observes the net supply of shares, and at $t = 2$ also observes the public report. The informed investor conjectures that the prices set by the market-maker will equal the expected dividends given the market-maker's information and, hence, are linear functions of these variables, i.e.,

$$v_1 = m_0 - b_{u1} z_{u1}, \tag{12.42a}$$

$$v_2 = m_0 + b_{a2} y_a - b_{u2} z_{u1}. \tag{12.42b}$$

When the informed investor places his order at $t = 1$ he knows y_i, and he selects z_{i1} so as to maximize his expected utility, based on the short-term profit:

$$\begin{aligned} U_{i1}(z_{i1},y_i) &= E[(v_2 - v_1)z_{i1}|y_i] \\ &= \{ b_{a2} E[y_a|y_i] + (b_{u1} - b_{u2}) E[z_{u1}|y_i,z_{i1}] \}z_{i1} \\ &= b_{a2} y_i z_{i1} - (b_{u1} - b_{u2}) z_{i1}^2. \end{aligned} \tag{12.43}$$

Differentiating (12.43) with respect to z_{i1} provides the following characterization of the informed investor's optimal demand at $t = 1$ (given the MT "short-term horizon" assumption):

$$z_{i1} = \beta y_i, \quad \beta = \frac{1}{2}\frac{b_{a2}}{b_{u1} - b_{u2}}. \tag{12.44}$$

Table 12.1
Prior and Posterior Beliefs with
a Private Signal and a Public Report

Prior Beliefs (with $\sigma_{yi}^2 < \sigma_{ya}^2 < \sigma_0^2$):

$$\begin{bmatrix} y_i \\ y_a \\ \varepsilon \end{bmatrix} \sim \mathrm{N}\left(\begin{bmatrix} 0 \\ 0 \\ 0 \end{bmatrix}, \begin{bmatrix} \sigma_{yi}^2 & \sigma_{yi}^2 & \sigma_{\varepsilon i} \\ \sigma_{yi}^2 & \sigma_{ya}^2 & \sigma_{ya}^2 \\ \sigma_{\varepsilon i} & \sigma_{ya}^2 & \sigma_0^2 \end{bmatrix} \right).$$

Informed Investor's Posterior Expectations at $t = 1$ and $t = 2$:

$$t = 1: \ \mathrm{E}[y_a|y_i] = y_i, \quad \mathrm{E}[\varepsilon|y_i] = \frac{\sigma_{\varepsilon i}}{\sigma_{yi}^2} y_i;$$

$$t = 2: \ \mathrm{E}[\varepsilon|y_i,y_a] = \lambda_i y_i + \lambda_a y_a, \quad \lambda_i = \frac{\sigma_{ya}^2(\sigma_{\varepsilon i} - \sigma_{yi}^2)}{\sigma_{yi}^2(\sigma_{ya}^2 - \sigma_{yi}^2)}, \quad \lambda_a = \frac{\sigma_{ya}^2 - \sigma_{\varepsilon i}}{\sigma_{ya}^2 - \sigma_{yi}^2}.$$

Market-maker's Posterior Dividend Beliefs at $t = 1$ and $t = 2$ (given $z_{i1} = \beta y_i$):

$$t = 1: \ \mathrm{E}[\varepsilon|z_{u1}] = - b_{u1} z_{u1},$$

$$t = 2: \ \mathrm{E}[\varepsilon|y_a,z_{u2}] = b_{a2} y_a + b_{u2} z_{u2},$$

where

$$b_{u1} = - \frac{\sigma_{\varepsilon u}}{\sigma_u^2}, \qquad b_{a2} = \frac{\sigma_{ya}^2\sigma_u^2 - \sigma_{\varepsilon u}\sigma_{au}}{\sigma_{ya}^2\sigma_u^2 - \sigma_{au}^2}, \qquad b_{u2} = - \frac{\sigma_{ya}^2(\sigma_{\varepsilon u} - \sigma_{au})}{\sigma_{ya}^2\sigma_u^2 - \sigma_{au}^2},$$

$$\sigma_u^2 \equiv \mathrm{Var}[z_{u1}] = \beta^2\sigma_{yi}^2 + \sigma_z^2, \qquad \sigma_{au} \equiv \mathrm{Cov}[y_a,z_{u1}] = - \beta\sigma_{yi}^2,$$

$$\sigma_{\varepsilon u} \equiv \mathrm{Cov}[\varepsilon,z_{u1}] = - \beta\sigma_{\varepsilon i}.$$

Observe that because of risk neutrality and the "short-term horizon," the informed investor is not directly concerned with the impact of his private signal on his posterior dividend belief. At $t = 1$, his only concern is the prediction of the price at $t = 2$. On the other hand, the prices set by the market-maker at both $t = 1$ and $t = 2$ are influenced by his beliefs about the terminal dividend and, hence, they depend on the market-maker's beliefs about the informed investor's private signal.

Table 12.1 derives the price function parameters b_{u1}, b_{a2}, and b_{u2} for a given demand function parameter β. Substituting those parameters into the expression for β in (12.44) and solving for β provides the following characterization of the equilibrium demand function parameter:

Proposition 12.7 (MT, Prop. 1)

Given our representation of the MT model, the equilibrium demand and price function parameters are:

$$\beta = \pm\frac{\sigma_z}{\sigma_{yi}}, \qquad b_{u1} = \pm\frac{1}{2}\frac{\sigma_{\varepsilon i}}{\sigma_{yi}\sigma_z}, \tag{12.45}$$

$$b_{a2} = \frac{2\sigma_{ya}^2 - \sigma_{\varepsilon i}}{2\sigma_{ya}^2 - \sigma_{yi}^2}, \qquad b_{u2} = \pm\frac{\sigma_{ya}^2(\sigma_{yi}^2 - \sigma_{\varepsilon i})}{\sigma_z\sigma_{yi}(2\sigma_{ya}^2 - \sigma_{yi}^2)},$$

where the unspecified signs are the same as the sign of b_{a2}.

We do not go through the details of the proof, but the approach used by MT is readily applied. The first step is to assume $\beta = \{\text{sign } b_{a2}\}\sigma_z/\sigma_{yi}$ and substitute this into the expressions for b_{u1}, b_{a2}, and b_{u2} in Table 12.1 to obtain the results in the proposition. The second step is to substitute the price function parameters in the proposition into (12.44) to demonstrate that $\beta = \{\text{sign } b_{a2}\}\sigma_z/\sigma_{yi}$ is optimal.[10]

Observe that the demand function is precisely the same as in the setting in which y_a is a sufficient statistic. This is because, with risk neutrality and the "short-term horizon," the informed investor is only concerned with the reduction in his uncertainty about the price at $t = 2$, relative to the noise created by the liquidity traders. However, the price parameters are more complicated because the market-maker sets prices on the basis of the expected dividends, and the private signal (which is imperfectly revealed by the net supply at $t = 1$) affects market-maker's dividend expectations at both $t = 1$ and $t = 2$.

[10] MT demonstrate that the second-order condition for the informed investor's decision problem requires (in our formulation) $b_{u2} > b_{u1}$. This condition is only satisfied if $\beta = \{\text{sign } b_{a2}\}\sigma_z/\sigma_{yi}$.

Comparative Statics

Substituting (12.44) into (12.43) and taking the expectation with respect to y_i provides the following general expression for the informed investor's expected utility from his short-term trading:

$$U_{i0} = \frac{1}{4}\frac{b_{a2}^2}{b_{u1} - b_{u2}}\sigma_{yi}^2. \tag{12.46}$$

Inserting the parameter values from Proposition 12.7 makes (12.46) a complex expression and, hence, the comparative statics for the informed investor's expected utility are complex.

Of course, the comparative statics are greatly simplified if $\sigma_{\varepsilon i} = \sigma_{yi}^2$, which returns us to the basic model (in which y_a is a sufficient statistic) and implies $b_{a2} = 1$, $b_{u2} = 0$, $b_{u1} = \sigma_{yi}/(2\sigma_z)$, and $U_{i0} = \frac{1}{2}\sigma_{yi}\sigma_z$. As in the basic model (with or without the public report), the informed investor's expected utility is increasing in the informativeness of his private signal (σ_{yi}) and the noise due to liquidity traders (σ_z). The existence of a public report and its informativeness (σ_{ya}) are irrelevant.

We leave the more complex comparative statics for the interested reader to work through. The results will differ somewhat from the comparative statics reported by MT since the parametric structures of our models differ. The interested reader is also referred to MT for analysis of endogenous private information acquisition in a setting in which the release of a public report at $t = 2$ only occurs with some positive probability. MT also provide analysis of the price reaction to the public report, which is similar to the DF analysis which we consider in Section 11.4.

In concluding this section we briefly comment on the MT's examination of long-term versus short-term profits. In the "long-term horizon" setting, the public report is immaterial because the informed investor is assumed to hold the shares he acquires at $t = 1$ until dividends are paid at $t = 3$. As already noted, the results will be precisely identical if y_a is a sufficient statistic, because in that setting the uncertainty resolved about the public report is precisely the same as the uncertainty resolved about the terminal dividend. However, this is not the case if $\sigma_{\varepsilon i} \neq \sigma_{yi}^2$. In that case, our scaling of y_i is no longer such that it equals the posterior expected random dividend – see $E[\varepsilon|y_i]$ in Table 12.1. To apply our basic model with no public report, we replace y_i with $\hat{y}_i = y_i\sigma_{\varepsilon i}/\sigma_{yi}^2$, which has a prior variance of $\hat{\sigma}_{yi}^2 = \sigma_{\varepsilon i}^2/\sigma_{yi}^2$. Hence, whether the private signal is more (or less) informative about the terminal dividend than the public report depends on whether $\sigma_{\varepsilon i} > (<) \sigma_{yi}^2$. See MT's Proposition 6 for proof that these conditions determine whether the informed investor prefers to close his position when the public report is released at $t = 2$ or hold the position until the terminal dividend is paid at $t = 3$.

12.4 CONCLUDING REMARKS

This chapter concludes our analysis of the interactive effect of public reports and private investor information. The analysis is descriptive in the sense that it examines the relation between public reports and market prices in the presence of private information acquisition. The analysis highlights the fact that these relations depend on the timing of the release of public reports relative to the acquisition of private information but, of course, private information can be acquired both prior and subsequent to the release of public reports. Hence, we have only pointed to partial effects that may occur in a more general setting.

We reiterate the fact that this analysis does not provide any social welfare statements about the desirability of public reporting. Furthermore, the analysis is performed within a pure exchange setting, and we know from our analysis in Part B that public reporting, other than the reporting of dividends, is largely of no social value when investors have homogeneous prior beliefs (as is the case in this part as well). Thus, from a social perspective, the potential value of public reporting lies in reducing the resources spent on acquiring socially useless private information. Moreover, as we saw in Chapter 11, more information at the date where the rational investors trade with the liquidity traders may actually make the rational investors worse off (to the benefit of the liquidity traders).[11]

Introducing production and incentive problems into the model may provide more scope for the social value of public reporting. The analysis in Chapter 8 establishes that it is important that managers have firm-specific information, but it is not important that they report that information publicly. However, in Chapters 14 and 15 we consider settings in which there are imperfect competition in the firms' product markets. Depending on the type of imperfect competition and the nature of the managers' information, public reporting of that information may be valuable. When we examine performance measurement in Volume II, public reporting is generally valuable, and the interactive effect of public reports and private investor information is a key issue when managers have stock-based incentive contracts (see Chapter 21).

REFERENCES

Demski, J. S., and G. A. Feltham. (1994) "Market Response to Financial Reports," *Journal of Accounting and Economics* 17, 3-40.

Dye, R. A. (2001) "An Evaluation of "Essays on Disclosure" and the Disclosure Literature in Accounting," *Journal of Accounting and Economics* 32, 181-235.

---

[11] See Dye (2001) for a critical perspective on the rational expectations literature in accounting.

Grossman, S. J., and J. E. Stiglitz. (1980) "On the Impossibility of Informationally Efficient Markets," *American Economic Review* 70, 393-408.

Kim, O., and R. E. Verrecchia. (1991) "Market Reaction to Anticipated Announcements," *Journal of Financial Economics* 30, 273-309.

Kim, O., and R. E. Verrecchia. (1994) "Market Liquidity and Volume Around Earnings Announcements," *Journal of Accounting and Economics* 17, 41-67.

Kyle, A. S. (1985) "Continuous Auctions and Insider Trading," *Econometrica* 53, 1315-1335.

Kyle, A. S. (1989) "Informed Speculation with Imperfect Competition," *Review of Economic Studies* 56, 317-356.

Kwon, Y. K. (2001) "Book Value, Residual Earnings, and Equilibrium Firm Value with Asymmetric Information," *Review of Accounting Studies* 6, 387-395.

McNichols, M., and B. Trueman. (1994) "Public Disclosure, Private Information Collection, and Short-Term Trading," *Journal of Accounting and Economics* 17, 69-94.

Zhang, G. (2001) "Private Information Production, Public Disclosure, and the Cost of Capital: Theory and Implications," *Contemporary Accounting Research* 18, 363-384.

PART D

DISCLOSURE OF PRIVATE OWNER INFORMATION IN EQUITY AND PRODUCT MARKETS

CHAPTER 13

DISCLOSURE OF PRIVATE INFORMATION BY AN UNDIVERSIFIED OWNER

In Chapter 7 we consider the impact of public information in an equity market under pure exchange. The firms' managers are ignored since their production decisions are assumed to be fixed, and they are assumed to play no role in determining the information publicly reported to investors. Investors, on the other hand, trade claims to implement their consumption plans and those trades, as well as the market prices of the traded claims, are endogenously determined. The public information system is exogenously specified, and the system specified may influence the investors' consumption plans. However, a key result from Chapter 7 is that an anticipated change in the public information system has no impact on the investors' consumption plans (and, hence, their expected utility) if they have homogeneous beliefs, time-additive preferences, and insurable consumption endowments. This result holds even though the trades used to implement the consumption plans, and the market prices, may be influenced by the information system.

Chapter 8 extends the analysis of exogenous public information to an equity market in which production decisions are endogenously determined. The focus is on Pareto efficient consumption/production plans, and it is demonstrated that Pareto efficiency is achieved with a sufficiently complete market of tradeable claims and the selection of the production plan for each firm that maximizes its market value. The analysis in Chapter 8 establishes that a more informative information system can be Pareto preferred due to improvements in the resulting production decisions (which result in changes in consumption plans). In particular, an information system is Pareto preferred if it is more informative about firm-specific or economy-wide events that influence the productivity of endogenous investments in firms or about economy-wide events that influence the firms' windfall gains or losses. Information about firm-specific windfall gains or losses have no benefit, even though they affect the market values of specific firms.

The analysis in Chapter 8 further demonstrates that, while reporting firm-specific productivity information to managers is Pareto preferred, achievement of Pareto efficiency does not require that firm-specific productivity information be reported to investors. There are three key features of the setting that yield this result. First, each manager is assumed to implement the production plan that maximizes the "intrinsic" market value of his firm, i.e., the market value it would have if investors knew what the manager knows. The managers' objectives are exogenously imposed – they are not endogenously determined by a contract between the manager and the firm's owners.

Second, the firms sell their outputs in perfectly competitive product markets. That is, each firm is sufficiently small that its output has no effect on output prices. All managers are assumed to have the same economy-wide (or industry-wide) information and their decisions would not be influenced by knowledge of the other managers' firm-specific information.

Third, the economy is large and firm-specific risks are diversifiable, so that all investors trade in well-diversified portfolios. The investors know that the managers have private firm-specific productivity or windfall information, and value their well-diversified portfolios accordingly. If the firm-specific information is not publicly reported, then some firms will be over-priced and others will be under-priced. However, well-diversified portfolios will be accurately priced, and the production and consumption plans will be Pareto efficient.

While Pareto efficiency can be achieved without publicly disclosing the managers' firm-specific information, investors are motivated to expend resources to acquire that information (or any other productivity or windfall information they can acquire) if their trades do not fully reveal their information to all other investors. This type of information acquisition is explored in Part C (Chapters 11 and 12). Sections 11.3 and 12.2 demonstrate that the release of more informative public reports can reduce the simultaneous acquisition of private management information. On the other hand, the analysis in Sections 11.4 and 12.3 demonstrate that the release of more informative public reports can increase the prior acquisition of private information.

In Part D (Chapters 13, 14, and 15), we examine some of the research that has considered the voluntary disclosure of private management information. Throughout Part D, either the owner is the manager or the manager is assumed to exogenously act in the best interests of his firm's owners. In this chapter, there is a single owner who seeks to share his firm-specific risks with (and possibly obtain investment capital from) well-diversified investors. In Chapters 14 and 15, the manager acts on behalf of well-diversified investors, possibly obtaining funds by issuing new equity to other well-diversified investors.

13.1 BASIC DISCLOSURE ISSUES

We assume managers exogenously act in the best interests of their firms' owners. These actions include the sale of equity after fully or partially disclosing their information at $t = 1$. Terminal dividends are distributed to the equity holders at $t = 2$. The market price at $t = 1$ can be described as being set by either the manager or the investors. To facilitate the application of game theoretic equilibrium concepts, we assume the manager (who moves first) specifies the market price in a "take it or leave it" public offer, and the investors either accept or reject the offer.

Our prior analyses of the impact of public reports have implicitly assumed that those reports are not voluntary (e.g., quarterly financial reports), and their information content cannot be (or, at least, is not) manipulated by management. We could consider the manipulation of those reports, but we focus on management reports that may or may not be issued. That is, with respect to the information considered in our analysis, a manager always has the option of not reporting anything.

A key issue in disclosure models is the believability of what a manager reports if he chooses to report. For example, if a manager's report takes the form of a dividend forecast that is claimed to be the expected dividend given his private information, there is an issue as to what investors rationally believe is the relation between the manager's "true" expectations and his forecast. Is it rational for him to report fully and truthfully?

Broadly speaking, there are four types of model assumptions with respect to the "truthfulness" issue. First, there are models in which it is assumed there is no mechanism by which a manager can assure investors as to the truthfulness of his report. If he has an incentive to lie, he will lie. Any incentive not to lie must stem endogenously from the effects of his report. In most of the settings we consider, there is effectively no disclosure if a manager is "free" to lie. However, in Chapter 14, we briefly consider "cheap talk" equilibria, in which truthful, but incomplete, disclosure is sustained by tensions created by the desire to tell "good news" to the capital market and "bad news" to competitors in the firm's product market.

Second, many models implicitly assume that while a manager can withhold information with impunity, he does not lie if he reports his information. Most papers do not model the specific reasons for not lying. However, some make reference to the threat of severe legal penalties if it is subsequently discovered that the manager has lied. A key issue here is whether this enforcement mechanism applies to all reports. In particular, does it apply to a report by the manager that he has no private information and is there a positive probability that this is the case? In Chapters 14 and 15 we consider models in which all signals are verifiable, and models in which the manager cannot verify that he has received a null (i.e., uninformative) signal.

Third, an early partial disclosure model by Verrecchia (1983) can be interpreted as one in which it is assumed the manager can pay an auditor to verify his report. As we shall see, the manager will incur this verification cost if, and only if, he does not have sufficiently bad news. An alternative interpretation of the Verrecchia model is that there is no cost of verifying the manager's disclosure, but any disclosure is subject to a cost due to the release of proprietary information, e.g., to the product market. Verrecchia did not explicitly model the product market, but there are a number of subsequent papers that do. We consider some in Chapters 14 and 15.

The fourth type of assumption is that there is no direct verification or enforcement mechanism, but the manager has some observable action he can take that is less costly to him if he has good news than if he has bad news. Models that make this type of assumption are generally referred to as signaling models, and are treated as being quite distinct from the so-called voluntary disclosure models. This distinction stems from the fact that the analysis of signaling models generally involves different analytical techniques than the other disclosure models. However, we believe it is useful to view signaling models as merely a particular type of disclosure model.

We examine settings in which the manager issues equity to the market and acts on behalf of the firm's current owners. It is a setting which can reasonably be characterized as a sequential game in which a privately informed player (the manager) moves first. Often, the term "game" is not used with respect to voluntary disclosure models, but it is used with respect to signaling models. Nonetheless, all of the voluntary disclosure models are implicitly games, and all involve an informed player who moves first.

It is important to distinguish between sequential games in which an informed player moves first from those in which one or more uninformed players move first, since the equilibrium issues differ significantly in the two settings. We focus on games in which the informed player moves first, and in this chapter the games involve risk sharing. There are related games in which competing risk-neutral players (e.g., insurance companies) offer risk sharing contracts to privately informed players who seek to share their firm-specific risk (e.g., managers seeking insurance). This type of game is sometimes referred to as a screening game.

In Volume II we consider settings in which a firm's well-diversified owners (or purchasers) offer a menu of contracts to a privately informed manager. This is part of the agency theory literature, and we assume the menu can be constructed so as to induce the manager to truthfully reveal his private information through the choice he makes from the menu. These are typically referred to as adverse selection games and the existence of an optimal menu of contracts that induce truthful reporting by the manager is an application of what is commonly referred to as the Revelation Principle (which we discuss in Volume II).

In games in which there is private pre-contract information, an issue naturally arises as to whether contracting can take place before any player acquires private information. We do not formally analyze this issue in this chapter, but note that a risk-averse player who seeks to share his risks with well-diversified investors will always prefer to sell his equity before he acquires private information, but that is often not possible. (See the discussion of information risk in Section 5.5.2.) Furthermore, our discussion of agency theory in Volume II extensively examines games in which contracts are offered to managers who will become privately informed and will be induced to truthfully reveal their private information.

The structure of the remainder of this chapter is as follows. Section 13.2 introduces some key game theoretic concepts that provide the basis for identifying plausible equilibrium strategies for the informed and uninformed players (e.g., the owner and investors, respectively). The informed player's strategy consists of signal-contingent choices of observable actions (e.g., contracts offered), whereas the uninformed players' strategies consist of their responses (e.g., accept or reject contracts) to each possible action. Equilibria are often sustained by threats of undesirable investor responses to off-equilibrium actions. The key issue is the identification of equilibria that are sustained by plausible threats, and the elimination of those that are sustained by implausible threats.

With the key game theoretic concepts in hand, we examine a series of disclosure games in which a privately informed, risk-averse owner seeks to share his risk, and possibly obtain capital from, well-diversified investors. Section 13.3 considers settings in which the owner's only means of communicating (signaling) his private information about the outcome from the investment is through the contract he offers investors. Two models are considered. In the model with finite numbers of signals and outcomes, a contract specifies outcome-contingent owner compensation, whereas in the model with continua of signals and outcomes, a contract specifies the fraction of the firm's equity that is retained by the owner. In both settings, the owner fully reveals his private information by retaining more risk the better is his information. In Sections 13.3.1 and 13.3.2, all risk is assumed to be firm-specific. Section 13.3.2 then explores the impact of market risk and of risk that is diversifiable by investors, but is correlated among a subset of firms and, hence, can be used by the undiversified owner to insure some of his retained risk.

In Section 13.4 we consider settings in which the owner can again use risk retention to signal his private information, but now he also has the option of issuing a verified report (e.g., an audited accounting report) that may perfectly or imperfectly reveal his private information at the time he offers a contract to the investors. If the report can perfectly and costlessly reveal all his signals, then the owner will report all signals and retain no risk. However, if some signals (e.g., a null signal) cannot be verified, then risk retention is used to reveal the non-verifiable signals and costless verified reports are used where possible. Furthermore, if a verified report is possible for all signals, but the report is costly, then risk retention will be used for the worst signals, whereas verified reports will be used for the best signals. A combination of a report and risk retention may be used to signal the owner's private information if the report imperfectly reveals that information. To be valuable, the imperfect report must be discriminating in the sense that only a subset of signals could possibly generate the report. The more discriminating the reporting system (e.g., the auditor), the more valuable it is. And that value increases with the amount of risk faced by the owner.

Section 13.5 briefly considers the value of verified reports that will not be generated until the end of the period. At the time of contracting the report is uncertain to both the owner and the investor. However, if the report will be informative about the owner's signal, then the owner is better off if the contract he offers makes his compensation contingent on both the forthcoming report and the outcome, rather than the outcome alone.

Section 13.6 considers a model in which the owner is privately informed about both his posterior mean and posterior variance with respect to the outcome. As a result, equity retention alone cannot be used to reveal his private information. The well-diversified investors are not directly concerned about the variance, but it affects the owner's cost of retaining risk. A second costly signal is introduced in the form of a report (e.g., an outcome forecast) for which the cost is decreasing in both the mean and variance (possibly reflecting the potential costs of litigation if the realized outcome is significantly less than the forecast).

Finally, Section 13.7 provides some brief concluding remarks.

13.2 EQUILIBRIA IN DISCLOSURE GAMES

We use the term "disclosure game" to refer to settings in which there is an informed player (referred to as IP) who moves first by taking an observable action (e.g., sending a message and offering a contract) and an uninformed player (referred to as UP) who then responds (e.g., accepts or rejects the contract). Many signaling games have this structure, but so do many voluntary disclosure models in the accounting literature. In this section we present a general formulation of a disclosure game and the nature of an equilibrium in that game.

IP receives a private signal $y \in Y$ at $t = 0$, and UP's prior distribution function with respect to those signals is $\Phi(y)$. At $t = 1$, IP selects an observable action $a \in A$, after which UP selects a response $\delta \in \Delta$. The expected utilities for the two players, given y, a, and δ, are $U_i(y,a,\delta)$ and $U_u(y,a,\delta)$.

IP's strategy, i.e., his action choice given his signal, is allowed to be mixed (i.e., random) and is represented by π_i: $A \times Y \rightarrow [0,1]$, where $\pi_i(a|y)$ is a conditional distribution function. Similarly, UP's strategy, i.e., his response given each observed action, is represented by π_u: $\Delta \times A \rightarrow [0,1]$, where $\pi_u(\delta|a)$ is a conditional distribution function. The sets of possible strategies for IP and UP are $\mathbf{\Pi}_i$ and $\mathbf{\Pi}_u$.

13.2.1 Sequential Equilibria

Each player makes a conjecture about the other player's strategy, and then makes a choice that is optimal given their conjecture. In a *Nash equilibrium*, the optimal action or response of one player is consistent with the conjecture of the other. That is, a pair of strategies $\pi^* = (\pi_i^*, \pi_u^*)$ is a Nash equilibrium if:[1]

$$\int_A \int_\Delta U_i(y,a,\delta)\, d\pi_u^*(\delta|a)\, d\pi_i^*(a|y)$$

$$\geq \int_A \int_\Delta U_i(y,a,\delta)\, d\pi_u^*(\delta|a)\, d\pi_i(a|y), \quad \forall\, \pi_i \in \mathbf{\Pi}_i,\ y \in Y, \tag{13.1a}$$

$$\int_Y \int_A \int_\Delta U_u(y,a,\delta)\, d\pi_u^*(\delta|a)\, d\pi_i^*(a|y)\, d\Phi(y)$$

$$\geq \int_Y \int_A \int_\Delta U_u(y,a,\delta)\, d\pi_u(\delta|a)\, d\pi_i^*(a|y)\, d\Phi(y), \quad \forall\, \pi_u \in \mathbf{\Pi}_u. \tag{13.1b}$$

Observe that (13.1a) reflects the fact that IP knows his signal y when he selects action a, so that there is a separate statement of optimal choice for each signal. UP knows a when he selects δ, but that is not explicitly reflected in (13.1b). However, we can restate (13.1b) by imposing the following sequential rationality requirement which is stated using Φ_u: $Y \times A \to [0,1]$, where $\Phi_u(y|a)$ is the posterior belief upon which UP's strategy π_u is based.

Definition *Sequential Equilibrium*

A Nash equilibrium in the disclosure game is a *sequential equilibrium* if there exists a belief Φ_u^* for UP such that:

(a) Bayes' theorem is applied if possible, i.e., if there exists some $y \in Y$ such that $d\pi_i^*(a|y) > 0$, then

---

[1] This is a game of incomplete information and the equilibrium is often referred to as a Bayesian or Bayesian Nash equilibrium. See Harsanyi (1967-68) for a key initial analysis of games of incomplete information. Various books on game theory provide more in depth reviews and analysis of these types of games, including signaling games. See, for example, Fudenberg and Tirole (1991).

$$\Phi_u^*(y|a) = \frac{\pi_i^*(a|y)\,\Phi(y)}{\int_Y \pi_i^*(a|y)\,d\Phi(y)}. \tag{13.2}$$

(b) UP's response is optimal given his equilibrium belief, i.e.,

$$\int_Y \int_\Delta U_u(y,a,\delta)\,d\pi_u^*(\delta|a)\,d\Phi_u^*(y|a)$$

$$\geq \int_Y \int_\Delta U_u(y,a,\delta)\,d\pi_u(\delta|a)\,d\Phi_u^*(y|a), \;\; \forall\, \pi_u \in \mathbf{\Pi}_u. \tag{13.1b'}$$

Bayes' theorem cannot be applied for any a such that $d\pi_i^*(a|y) = 0$ for all $y \in Y$. That is, sequential rationality does not impose any restrictions on UP's beliefs given off-equilibrium actions. As a result, some equilibria can be sustained by "threats" by UP to believe the worst if he observes an off-equilibrium action. Refinements of the sequential equilibrium requirements, which we consider in Section 13.2.3, constrain the off-equilibrium beliefs that can be used to sustain an equilibrium.

13.2.2 A Simple Risk-sharing Example

Before introducing refinements, we illustrate the preceding comments using a simple disclosure model in which IP is risk averse and seeks to insure the firm-specific risk of his wholly owned firm with UP, who is risk neutral (e.g., representing a set of well-diversified investors). It is Pareto efficient for UP to bear all the risk by, for example, buying the asset. However, UP knows IP has private information, and that IP will only sell the firm if the price provides a utility at least as great as his expected utility from retaining equity. As a result, if IP has either good news or bad news, and his only options are to sell or not sell the asset, then the equilibrium price equals the firm's value given bad news and IP does not sell if he has good news.[2]

Of course, an all or nothing sale of the firm may not be IP's only options. In our example, we assume IP can offer UP an outcome-contingent risk-sharing contract. This gives IP a mechanism for signaling (disclosing) his private information. There are many equilibria in this setting, but, as we demonstrate, the most plausible equilibrium signal-contingent contracts transfer all risk to UP if IP has bad news, and partially transfer risk if IP has good news.

---

[2] This is the classic "lemons" problem identified by Akerlof (1970).

Outcome-contingent Contracts

Effectively, the owner sells the firm's equity to the investors in return for an outcome-contingent contract $\boldsymbol{c}$: $D \rightarrow \mathbb{R}$, which specifies the amount IP will receive at $t = 2$, conditional on the dividend $d \in D$ paid by the firm at that date. Hence, IP's observable action at $t = 1$ is a contract, i.e., $a = \boldsymbol{c}$, and UP's response is to either accept ($\delta = 1$) or reject ($\delta = 0$) the offered contract. If the contract is accepted, then IP receives $\boldsymbol{c}(d)$ and UP receives $d - \boldsymbol{c}(d)$. If the contract is rejected, then IP receives d and UP receives zero.

The above description does not involve a direct statement by IP regarding his private signal. We could expand the action a to include both a message (e.g., forecasts in a prospectus) and the contract that is offered. However, the message would be irrelevant in this model – UP would form his posterior beliefs strictly based on the contract offered. In Chapters 14 and 15 we consider disclosure models in which IP's message plays a central role.

To keep our example as simple as possible, we assume there are only two possible dividends, $D = \{d_1, d_2\}$, with $d_1 < d_2$, and two possible signals, $Y = \{y_g, y_b\}$, where y_g is good news and y_b is bad news. The posterior probability that the terminal dividend will equal d_j, $j = 1,2$, given signal y_k, $k = g,b$, is φ_{jk}. Of course, the high outcome is more likely if IP has good news than if he has bad news, i.e., $\varphi_{2g} > \varphi_{2b}$. The prior probability that IP receives signal y_k is φ_k, $k = g,b$, and the prior probability that the terminal dividend will equal d_j, $j = 1,2$, is $\varphi_j = \varphi_{jg}\varphi_g + \varphi_{jb}\varphi_b$.

IP is strictly risk averse, and his utility for consumption $c \in \mathbb{R}$ is represented by $u(c)$, with $u'(c) > 0$ and $u''(c) < 0$. UP, on the other hand, is risk neutral and will only accept the contract if his expected net payoff is non-negative. Hence, IP's and UP's expected utilities given the acceptance of contract $a = (c_1, c_2)$ and signal y_k, $k = g,b$, are

$$U_i(y_k, a) = u(c_1)\varphi_{1k} + u(c_2)\varphi_{2k},$$

$$U_u(y_k, a) = [d_1 - c_1]\varphi_{1k} + [d_2 - c_2]\varphi_{2k},$$

provided IP's action leads UP to believe that IP's signal is y_k. If the contract does not reveal IP's signal (i.e., the contract offered is independent of the signal), then UP's expected utility (based on his prior beliefs) from contract $a = (c_1, c_2)$ is

$$U_u(Y, a) = [d_1 - c_1]\varphi_1 + [d_2 - c_2]\varphi_2.$$

We let $a^o = \boldsymbol{c}^o$ represent the null contract in which IP's consumption equals his firm's dividends (and UP's net payoff is zero). The figures used in this section depict a corner of an Edgeworth box in which UP has "deep pockets" and is better off the closer the contract is to the origin. IP is better off the further the contract is from the origin.

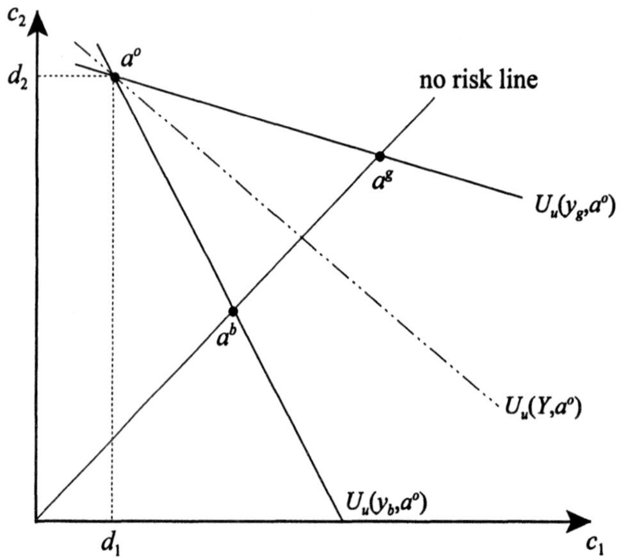

Figure 13.1: Investor's indifference curves.

Figure 13.1 depicts UP's indifference curves relative to $a^o = c^o$ for each of the beliefs he might hold. To the right of a^o, the indifference curve given good news is "above" the indifference curve given bad news, since the former assigns a higher probability to the high outcome. Furthermore, the indifference curve based on UP's prior beliefs lies between the two extremes and is a weighted average based on prior beliefs φ_g and φ_b. Hence, the closer φ_g is to one, the closer $U_u(Y,a^o)$ is to $U_u(y_g,a^o)$.

The "no risk line" is the set of contracts for which IP bears no risk – it is all borne by the risk-neutral UP. Contracts a^g and a^b represent the optimal signal-contingent, risk-sharing contracts (i.e., IP bears no risk) that are acceptable to UP.

Figure 13.2 depicts IP's indifference curves given his signal. Since he is strictly risk averse, his indifference curves are strictly convex.[3] Four contracts are depicted. Observe that IP strictly prefers a^1 to the null contract a^o (whether he has observed y_g or y_b), but it would be rejected by UP – no matter what he believes (since it lies above both $U_u(y_b,a^o)$ and $U_u(y_g,a^o)$). IP strictly prefers a^2 to a^o if he has observed y_b, but not if he has observed y_g. UP, on the other hand,

[3] Note that given the private signal, the slopes of the indifference curves for IP and UP are the same along the no risk line (and equal to - $\varphi_{2k}/\varphi_{1k}$).

has the reverse preferences. IP also prefers a^3 to a^o if he has observed y_b, but is indifferent between a^3 and a^o if he has observed y_g, whereas UP would reject (accept) a^3 if he believes IP has observed y_b (y_g).

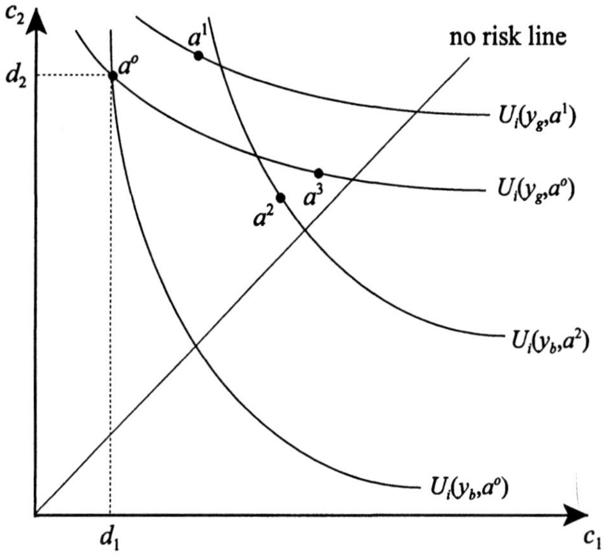

Figure 13.2: Owner's indifference curves.

Full-disclosure Equilibria

We focus on pure strategies and let $\pi_i = \boldsymbol{a} = (a_g,a_b)$, where $a_k = (c_{k1},c_{k2})$ represents the contract IP offers if he has observed y_k and c_{kj} is IP's consumption if the contract a_k is accepted and the dividend d_j is realized. An equilibrium is defined to be a full-disclosure (or separating) equilibrium if IP offers a different contract for each signal, i.e., $a_g \neq a_b$.

Figure 13.3 illustrates the optimal full-disclosure equilibrium from IP's perspective. In this setting, $a_b = a^b$, i.e., IP bears no risk if he observes (and reveals) that he has received bad news. On the other hand, IP bears risk if he has received good news. In Figure 13.3, a_g is the best contract, from the perspective of IP if he has good news, that would be accepted by UP (given good news) and would not be preferred to a^b by IP if he has bad news. Observe that a_g lies at the intersection of $U_i(y_b,a_b)$ and $U_u(y_g,a^o)$.

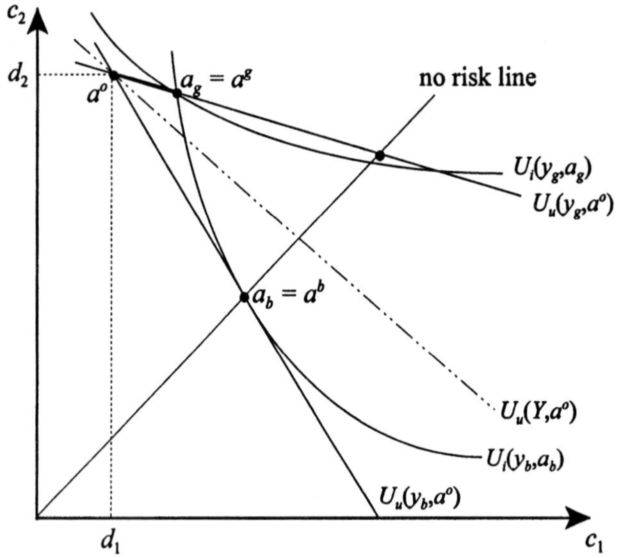

Figure 13.3: Full-disclosure equilibrium.

No-disclosure Equilibrium

In a no-disclosure (or pooling) equilibrium IP offers the same contract irrespective of his signal. To be acceptable to UP, such a contract must be on or below $U_u(Y,a^o)$. In Figure 13.3, the prior beliefs are assumed to be such that $U_u(Y,a^o)$ lies below $U_i(y_g,a_g)$. That implies that there is no single contract that is acceptable to UP and would be preferred by IP if he has good news. Nonetheless, if there is a contract a_Y that is acceptable to UP, i.e., $U_u(Y,a_Y) \geq U_u(Y,a^o)$, and is preferred by IP relative to the null contract if he has good news, i.e., $U_i(y_g,a_Y) \geq U_i(y_g,a^o)$, then there exists a sequential equilibrium in which a_Y is always offered. This may seem surprising, since IP would prefer a_g if he has observed y_g. However, a_g is an off-equilibrium contract in the no-disclosure equilibrium, and the equilibrium can be sustained if UP's off-equilibrium posterior probability $\varphi_u(y_b|a_g)$ is sufficiently large to induce UP to reject a_g.

While the off-equilibrium belief used to sustain the no-disclosure equilibrium in this setting is not precluded by the sequential rationality requirements, one may question whether this is a "plausible" belief. Or, stated differently, is it credible for UP to threaten to reject a_g if it is offered. It is this type of plausibility issue that has led to refinements in equilibrium requirements.

Before introducing some refinements, we introduce Figure 13.4. This is the same setting as in the previous three figures except that now we assume the prior probability of good news, i.e., $\varphi(y_g)$, is sufficiently high that $U_u(Y,a^o)$ intersects $U_i(y_g,a_g)$. This implies that there is a set of no-disclosure contracts that are acceptable to UP and preferred to a_g by IP irrespective of his information. The no-disclosure contract a_Y depicted in Figure 13.4 is the no-disclosure contract most preferred by IP if he has good news. In particular, at a_Y, IP's indifference curve given y_g is tangent to UP's indifference curve given Y. In this setting, $\boldsymbol{a} = (a_g, a_b)$ is still an equilibrium – the full-disclosure equilibrium most preferred by IP. However, IP strictly prefers the no-disclosure equilibrium a_Y to all full-disclosure equilibria.

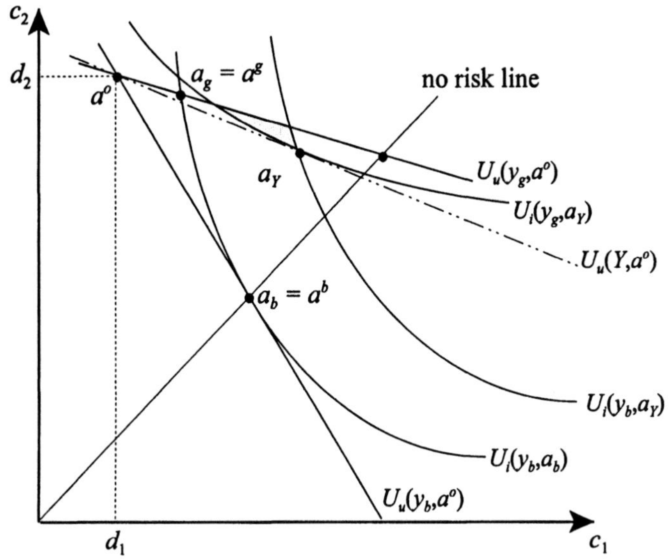

Figure 13.4: No-disclosure equilibrium.

13.2.3 Stable Equilibria

The requirements of a sequential equilibrium impose a degree of rationality on the players, but there are often multiple equilibria and, in some equilibria, UP's strategy involves non-credible threats. This has led to what are called "refinements" of the Nash equilibrium concept. We do not provide a general exploration of those refinements, but we do introduce some that are helpful in identifying the most plausible equilibria in a disclosure game.

Kohlberg and Mertens (KM) (1986) introduce the concept of stability in their seminal work on Nash equilibrium refinements for finite games (i.e., games in which the set of signals and the sets of alternative actions are finite). Determining which equilibria are stable is often difficult. However, Cho and Kreps (CK) (1987) and Banks and Sobel (BS) (1987) developed criteria that are readily applied to finite signaling games, and are necessary for stability. Furthermore, these refinements can be applied to signaling games, such as the disclosure games considered in this chapter, even if the informed player's set of possible private signals and set of possible contracts are not finite.[4] We first state and then illustrate the "intuitive stability criterion" introduced by CK.

The CK-criterion

Recall that $\pi_i \in \mathbf{\Pi}_i$ and $\pi_u \in \mathbf{\Pi}_u$ represent the sets of possible strategies for IP and UP. To simplify our discussion, we assume that, in equilibrium, IP plays a pure strategy, represented by $\boldsymbol{a}$: $Y \rightarrow A$, but it is useful to consider mixed strategies for UP. A sequential equilibrium is characterized by the players' strategies and UP's posterior signal beliefs, denoted by $\gamma^* = (\boldsymbol{a}^*, \pi_u^*, \Phi_u^*)$. The signal-contingent equilibrium expected utilities for IP are represented by

$$U_i^*(y) \equiv \int_{\Delta} U_i(y, \boldsymbol{a}^*(y), \delta)\, d\pi_u^*(\delta | \boldsymbol{a}^*(y)), \quad \forall\, y \in Y.$$

UP does not directly observe y, and he makes inferences based on the observed a. Let $\mathbf{\Phi}_a$ represent the set of all possible probability distribution functions defined over the set of signals Y, where the a subscript reminds us that this is a possible belief given a specific action. Let Y' denote a non-empty set of "possible" signals given a, i.e., $\Pr(Y'|a) = 1$ (and, thus, $\Pr(Y \backslash Y'|a) = 0$). Furthermore, let $\mathbf{\Phi}_a(Y') \subseteq \mathbf{\Phi}_a$ represent the set of all possible probability distribution functions defined over the subset of "possible signals" $Y' \subseteq Y$. Similarly, let $\mathbf{\Pi}_{ua}$ represent the set of possible responses (mixed strategies) by UP given action a and let $\mathbf{\Pi}_{ua}(\Phi_a)$ represent UP's set of *best responses* given that IP has taken action a and UP holds arbitrary belief $\Phi_a \in \mathbf{\Phi}_a$. That is,

$$\mathbf{\Pi}_{ua}(\Phi_a) \equiv \underset{\pi_{ua} \in \Pi_{ua}}{\text{argmax}} \int_Y \int_{\Delta} U_u(y, a, \delta)\, d\pi_{ua}(\delta)\, d\Phi_a(y),$$

and his set of best responses for all possible beliefs concentrated on a set of "possible signals" Y' is

$$\mathbf{\Pi}_{ua}(Y') = \{\, \pi_{ua} \mid \pi_{ua} \in \mathbf{\Pi}_{ua}(\Phi_a), \text{ for some } \Phi_a \in \mathbf{\Phi}_a(Y') \,\}.$$

Recall that in a sequential equilibrium, Bayes' theorem must be used to determine UP's posterior belief given any equilibrium action $a \in A_e^* \equiv \{\, a \mid a = \boldsymbol{a}^*(y), \text{ for some } y \in Y \,\}$. Hence, our focus is on the beliefs assigned to off-equilibrium actions $a \in A_o^* = A \backslash A_e^*$. For each off-equilibrium action $a \in A_o^*$, let

[4] Cho and Sobel (CS) (1990) apply the criteria from CK and BS to what they call monotonic signaling games. Our disclosure games are essentially (if not technically) monotonic, so that the CS results apply.

$Y^*(a)$ represent the set of signals for which IP would strictly prefer the equilibrium action $\boldsymbol{a}^*(y)$ instead of a, no matter how favorably UP responds (subject to requiring consistency with some belief by UP), i.e.,

$$Y^*(a) \equiv \left\{ y \mid U_i^*(y) > \underset{\pi_{ua} \in \boldsymbol{\Pi}_{ua}(Y)}{\text{maximize}} \int_{\Delta} U_i(y,a,\delta)\, d\pi_{ua}(\delta) \right\}.$$

Note that when UP observes an off-equilibrium action a, it is unreasonable for him to assign a positive probability to any signals in the set $Y^*(a)$. From IP's perspective, the off-equilibrium action is strictly dominated by the equilibrium actions for signals $y \in Y^*(a)$ no matter how favorably UP may respond, i.e., a is *equilibrium dominated* for $y \in Y^*(a)$. Hence, the only set that can reasonably be assigned positive probability is the set of signals for which IP would at least weakly prefer a to $\boldsymbol{a}^*(y)$ if UP were to respond favorably, which we denote $Y(a) \equiv Y \backslash Y^*(a)$. Consequently, in a "reasonable" sequential equilibrium, UP's beliefs given an off-equilibrium action a must be concentrated on the set $Y(a)$, i.e., $\Phi_a \in \boldsymbol{\Phi}_a(Y(a))$, if $Y(a)$ is not an empty set. The set $Y(a)$ is not empty if, and only if, the off-equilibrium action a is not equilibrium dominated for all signals $y \in Y$.

Now we come to the formal definition of the CK-criterion. It is in the form of a constraint. That is, a sequential equilibrium in the disclosure game is not stable if it fails the following criterion.

Definition *CK-criterion*

A sequential equilibrium $\gamma^* = (\boldsymbol{a}^*, \pi_u^*, \Phi_u^*)$ *fails* the *CK-criterion* if for any off-equilibrium action there is some signal for which IP would prefer the off-equilibrium action even if he received the worst "best response" from UP (given that UP's beliefs are restricted to $Y(a)$). That is, failure occurs if for some $a \in A_o^*$ there exists some signal $y \in Y(a)$ such that

$$U_i^*(y) < \underset{\pi_{ua} \in \boldsymbol{\Pi}_{ua}(Y(a))}{\text{mimimize}} \int_{\Delta} U_i(y,a,\delta)\, d\pi_{ua}(\delta).$$

Observe that this criterion still permits an equilibrium to be sustained by very pessimistic uninformed beliefs about the signal that induced IP to take an off-equilibrium action. However, those pessimistic beliefs are restricted to the set of signals for which IP would weakly prefer the off-equilibrium action if he could obtain the most favorable response from UP.

Application of the CK-criterion

We now return to our simple risk-sharing example. In that game, the action a is a dividend-contingent contract and δ is a simple accept/reject response in which rejection results in the null contract. Observe that UP's mixed strategy takes a particularly simple form which can be expressed as $\pi_u: A \rightarrow [0,1]$, where $\pi_u(a)$ is the probability of accepting $a \in A$ and $A = \mathbb{R}\times\mathbb{R}$ is the set of possible contracts. Let $y^* = (\boldsymbol{a}^*,\pi_u^*,\Phi_u^*)$ denote an equilibrium, and recall that $U_i(y,a) = U_i(y,a,\delta{=}1)$ and $U_u(y,a) = U_u(y,a,\delta{=}1)$. Also note that $U_i(y,a^o) = U_i(y,a,\delta{=}0)$ and $U_u(y,a,\delta{=}0) = 0$, for all y and a. Hence, the set of plausible signals that could result in off-equilibrium action a is

$$Y(a) \equiv \{\, y \mid U_i(y,a) \geq U_i(y,\boldsymbol{a}^*(y)),\ y \in Y \,\}.$$

In the initial statement of the example we assumed that there were only two possible outcomes and two possible signals. The following statement of the CK-criterion permits a more general set of outcomes and signals.

Definition

The equilibrium $(\boldsymbol{a}^*,\pi_u^*,\Phi_u^*)$ fails to satisfy the CK-criterion if, for any off-equilibrium contract a:

(a) $U_i(y,a) > U_i(y,\boldsymbol{a}^*(y))$, for *some* $y \in Y(a)$, and

(b) $U_u(y,a) \geq 0$, for *all* $y \in Y(a)$.

That is, we consider the set of signals $Y(a)$ for which IP would weakly prefer a to $\boldsymbol{a}^*(y)$ if accepted. Condition (a) then requires that there is some signal in $Y(a)$ for which IP has strict preference for a, while condition (b) requires that UP would be willing to accept that contract even if he thought IP had the "worst" possible signal in $Y(a)$.

Now consider Figure 13.3, which depicts an "optimal" full-disclosure equilibrium. In this setting, there are many other full-disclosure equilibria and, possibly, many no-disclosure equilibria. However, the full-disclosure equilibrium that is depicted in Figure 13.3 is the only equilibrium satisfying the CK-intuitive criterion.

To illustrate, consider an alternative full-disclosure equilibrium with $\boldsymbol{a}' = (a_g',a_b)$, where a_g' is on the short dark line between a^o and a_g. IP prefers a_g' to a_b and a^o if he has signal y_g, but prefers a_b if he has observed y_b. IP prefers a_g to a_g', but (a_g',a_b) can be sustained as a sequential equilibrium by UP's willingness to accept a_g' (since $U_u(y_g,a_g') = 0$) and his threat to reject a_g (or any contract "close to" it), claiming to believe that IP has observed y_b if he offers any of those contracts. However, the CK-criterion effectively states that the threatened belief is implausible, since it assigns a positive probability to y_b given a_g even though a_g is equilibrium dominated for y_b. In particular, there exists a contract a between a_g' and a_g that is acceptable to UP given y_g, and is such that IP prefers a to a_g' if he has observed y_g and prefers a_b to a if he has observed y_b.

Hence, $Y(a) = \{y_g\}$, $U_i(y_g,a) > U_i(y_g,a_g')$, and $U_u(y_g,a) \geq 0$, which means failure with respect to the CK-criterion.

Now consider the no-disclosure equilibrium in Figure 13.4. While IP strictly prefers the no-disclosure contract a_Y to the optimal full-disclosure equilibrium contracts (irrespective of his signal), the no-disclosure equilibrium does not satisfy the CK-criterion. To see this, consider a contract a in the shaded region above and to the left of a_Y. This contract is acceptable to UP if it is only offered given signal y_g and, if IP has observed y_g, he prefers a to a_Y, whereas he has the reverse preference if he has observed y_b. Hence, $Y(a) = \{y_g\}$, $U_i(y_g,a) > U_i(y_g,a_Y)$, and $U_u(y_g,a) \geq 0$, which means failure with respect to the CK-criterion.

One can then demonstrate that, as in Figure 13.3, only the optimal full-disclosure equilibrium satisfies the CK-criterion. This holds even though IP strictly prefers the no-disclosure equilibrium. The problem is that the threats required to sustain the no-disclosure equilibrium are not credible – any attempt to implement the no-disclosure equilibrium is subject to manipulation by IP if he has good news for any "reasonable" beliefs UP might hold.[5]

Other Refinements

We now consider an alternative formulation of the CK-criterion, and then extend this formulation to present some stronger refinements examined by CK and BS.

Recall that $\boldsymbol{\Pi}_{ua}(Y)$ represents the set of possible best responses to off-equilibrium action a given all possible posterior beliefs $\Phi_a \in \boldsymbol{\Phi}_a(Y)$. For a given equilibrium IP strategy $\boldsymbol{a}^*$, a given signal y, and a given off-equilibrium action $a \in A_o^*$, some of UP's best responses might strictly induce IP to select a instead of $\boldsymbol{a}^*(y)$, while other responses might make IP indifferent between a and $\boldsymbol{a}^*(y)$. We denote these two sets of responses as

$$\boldsymbol{\Pi}^+_{ua}(y) \equiv \left\{ \pi_{ua} \in \boldsymbol{\Pi}_{ua}(Y) \mid U_i^*(y) < \int_\Delta U_i(y,a,\delta)\, d\pi_{ua}(\delta) \right\},$$

$$\boldsymbol{\Pi}^0_{ua}(y) \equiv \left\{ \pi_{ua} \in \boldsymbol{\Pi}_{ua}(Y) \mid U_i^*(y) = \int_\Delta U_i(y,a,\delta)\, d\pi_{ua}(\delta) \right\}.$$

---

[5] Feltham and Hughes (1988) note that if IP with good news offers and gains acceptance of a contract a in the shaded region, then UP will reject a_Y. This would induce IP with bad news to also offer a, which would cause UP to lose money. They propose an alternative equilibrium refinement that sustains the no-disclosure equilibrium most preferred by IP with good news (if this is preferable to the optimal full-disclosure contract).

This raises a question as to the criteria we impose in identifying the most plausible equilibrium in settings in which there are multiple equilibria. Ultimately, this is an empirical question rather than one of merely applying economic rationality.

The CK-criterion can be restated using these sets as follows.

Definition *CK-criterion*

A sequential equilibrium $\gamma^* = (\mathbf{a}^*, \pi_u^*, \Phi_u^*)$ does not satisfy the CK-criterion *unless* for every off-equilibrium action $a \in A_o^*$, UP's posterior belief $d\Phi_u^*(y|a)$ equals zero (if possible), if

$$\{ \Pi_{ua}^{+}(y) \cup \Pi_{ua}^{0}(y) \} = \emptyset.$$

That is, UP cannot assign a positive probability to y if IP strictly prefers $\mathbf{a}^*(y)$ to a no matter what response UP makes to a, i.e., a is equilibrium dominated for y.

BS introduce what they call the divinity and universal divinity criterion. We refer to these as the D1- and D2-criteria and define them as follows.

Definition *Divinity and Universal Divinity*

Consider a sequential equilibrium $\gamma^* = (\mathbf{a}^*, \pi_u^*, \Phi_u^*)$.

(a) The D1-criterion is not satisfied *unless,* for every off-equilibrium action $a \in A_o^*$, UP's posterior belief $d\Phi_u(y|a)$ equals zero if there exists a signal y' such that

$$\{ \Pi_{ua}^{+}(y) \cup \Pi_{ua}^{0}(y) \} \subseteq \Pi_{ua}^{+}(y').$$

(b) The D2-criterion is not satisfied *unless,* for every off-equilibrium action $a \in A_o^*$, UP's posterior belief $d\Phi_u(y|a)$ equals zero if

$$\{ \Pi_{ua}^{+}(y) \cup \Pi_{ua}^{0}(y) \} \subseteq \bigcup_{\substack{y' \in Y \\ y' \neq y}} \Pi_{ua}^{+}(y').$$

That is, the D1-criterion does not allow UP to assign a positive probability to y if there is *some other* signal y' that *always* has a strict incentive to deviate whenever IP weakly prefers $\mathbf{a}^*(y)$ to a given y. The D2-criterion requires a zero probability if there is *any other* signal $y' \in Y$ that has a strict incentive to deviate whenever IP weakly prefers $\mathbf{a}^*(y)$ to a given y.

Finally, the most stringent refinement follows from the "Never Weak Best Response" (NWBR) critrion proposed by Kohlberg and Mertens (1986).

Definition *NWBR-criterion*

A sequential equilibrium $\gamma^* = (\boldsymbol{a}^*, \boldsymbol{\pi}_u^*, \Phi_u^*)$ does not satisfy the NWBR-criterion *unless* for every off-equilibrium action $a \in A_o^*$, UP's posterior belief $d\Phi_u^*(y|a)$ equals zero if

$$\boldsymbol{\Pi}^0_{ua}(y) \subseteq \bigcup_{\substack{y' \in Y \\ y' \neq y}} \boldsymbol{\Pi}^+_{ua}(y').$$

That is, UP cannot assign a positive probability to y if for any response that would make IP indifferent between $\boldsymbol{a}^*(y)$ and a, there is at least one other signal $y' \in Y$ for which that response would induce IP to strictly prefer $\boldsymbol{a}^*(y')$ to a.

In a disclosure game in which UP's only response is to accept or reject a contract offered by IP, the NWBR-criterion takes a simple form. With only two responses, we can let π_{ua} represent the probability of accepting contract a, so that the set of possible mixed responses is $\boldsymbol{\Pi}_{ua} = [0,1]$. If for any given action a, UP always strictly prefers to accept (reject), i.e., $U_u(y,a) >(<) 0, \forall y \in Y$, then UP's set of best responses is accept (reject) with certainty irrespective of his beliefs, i.e., $\boldsymbol{\Pi}_{ua}(Y) = \{1\}$ ($\boldsymbol{\Pi}_{ua}(Y) = \{0\}$). On the other hand, if there are some signals for which UP weakly prefers accept and other signals for which he weakly prefers reject, then his set of possible best responses equals the set of all possible responses, i.e., $\boldsymbol{\Pi}_{ua}(Y) = [0,1]$.

Now identify the set of off-equilibrium actions for which UP's set of possible best responses is [0,1], and for each action a in that set identify the set of signals for which IP strictly prefers a to $\boldsymbol{a}^*(y)$, i.e.,

$$A_o^{*+} \equiv \{ a \in A_o^* \mid U_i(y,a) > U_i(y,\boldsymbol{a}^*(y)), \text{ for some } y \in Y, \text{ and } \boldsymbol{\Pi}_{ua}(Y) = [0,1] \},$$

$$Y_a^{*+} \equiv \{ y \in Y \mid U_i(y,a) > U_i(y,\boldsymbol{a}^*(y)) \}, \quad \forall a \in A_o^{*+}.$$

For each signal in Y_a^{*+} there is a break-even probability of acceptance, which we represent as

$$\pi_{ua}^0(y) = \frac{U_i(y,a^*(y)) - U_i(y,a^o)}{U_i(y,a) - U_i(y,a^o)}, \quad \forall y \in Y_a^{*+},$$

i.e., this is the lowest probability of acceptance that would induce IP to offer a if he has observed y.

The next step is to identify the set of signals for which the break-even probability of acceptance is the smallest, i.e.,

$$Y_a^{*\pm} = \underset{y \in Y_a^{*+}}{\text{argmin}}\ \pi_{ua}^{0}(y).$$

The NWBR-criterion can then be stated as requiring $d\Phi_u^*(y|a)$ to equal zero for any $a \in A_o^{*+}$ and any signal $y \notin Y_a^{*\pm}$. That is, a positive probability can only be assigned to a signal that has the lowest break-even acceptance probability. Of course, the test of the equilibrium then becomes one of whether this belief will cause UP to accept or reject a.

To demonstrate the application of the NWBR-criterion, we revisit Figure 13.4. Consider the no-disclosure equilibrium in which IP offers a_Y given both signals. Again consider an off-equilibrium contract a in the shaded region above and to the left of a_Y. IP only prefers a to a_Y if he has observed y_g (not y_b), so that $Y_a^{*\pm} = Y_a^{*+} = \{y_g\}$. Hence, $\varphi_u^*(y_g|a)$ must equal one, which will induce UP to accept a, and this in turn will induce IP to offer a instead of a_Y. Consequently, the no-disclosure equilibrium a_Y does not satisfy the NWBR-criterion.

Now consider the full-disclosure equilibrium based on (a_g,a_b). In this case, $a = a_Y$ is an off-equilibrium contract. IP prefers a_Y to a_g and a_b if he has observed y_g and y_b, respectively, so that $Y_a^{*+} = Y$. For which signal is the break-even acceptance probability the smallest? It is apparent that IP has much more to gain by obtaining acceptance of a_Y if he has observed y_b than if he has observed y_g. Hence, $Y_a^{*\pm} = \{y_b\}$, and UP will reject a_Y with $\varphi_u^*(y_b|a_Y) = 1$. The NWBR-criterion is also satisfied for all other off-equilibrium actions and, hence, there is a full-disclosure equilibrium based on (a_g,a_b). In fact, this is the only equilibrium that satisfies the NWBR-criterion.

The NWBR-criterion result is not surprising since we obtained the same unique result with the weaker CK-criterion. In each of the following settings, the sequential equilibrium satisfying the CK-criterion is unique and also satisfies the D1-, D2-, and NWBR-criteria. Hence, we loosely refer to such an equilibrium as stable.

13.3 SIGNALING WITH OUTCOME-CONTINGENT CONTRACTS

In this section we consider a setting which we refer to as the *investment-disclosure game* with outcome-contingent contracts. In this game, a privately informed, risk-averse owner of a production technology seeks to acquire capital from and share risks with well-diversified investors. At $t = 1$, the owner of the production technology observes a private signal y that is informative about the outcome $d \in D$ that will result at $t = 2$ from an investment of $q > 0$ units of capital at $t = 1$. After observing the signal, the owner decides whether to undertake the investment and, if he does, he offers to sell the firm to well-diversified investors in return for q units of capital and an outcome-contingent contract c: $D \to \mathbb{R}$. If the contract is accepted, then the investment is undertaken, whereas it is not undertaken if the contract is rejected.

The investors' willingness to accept the offered contract depends on the terms of the contract and their posterior outcome beliefs after observing the terms. In Section 13.3.1, we assume the set of possible outcomes is finite and identify the outcome-contingent contracts in a stable sequential equilibrium. In Section 13.3.2, we assume the set of possible outcomes is infinite (i.e., the real line) and restrict the contracts to be linear (i.e., the owner retains some of the firm's equity). We then identify the linear contracts in a stable sequential equilibrium (given the linear restriction). There is full-disclosure in both settings, and the owner receives the maximum expected utility that he can obtain by fully disclosing his private information through outcome-contingent and linear contracts, respectively.

13.3.1 Outcome-contingent Contracts with Finite Sets of Outcomes and Signals

In this section, we consider a setting based on the model in Feltham and Hughes (FH) (1988). In this FH-model, the sets of possible terminal dividends $D = \{d_1, ..., d_m\}$ and signals $Y = \{y_1, ..., y_n\}$ are finite, with $d_1 < ... < d_m$ and $y_1 < ... < y_n$. The probability of dividend d, given the owner's signal y and the investment of q, is represented by $\varphi(d|y)$. As illustrated by our example in Section 13.2, the analysis is relatively straightforward if $m = n = 2$, but it can be quite complex if m and n exceed two. This complexity is significantly reduced if the following spanning condition is satisfied.[6]

Definition *Spanning Condition* (SC)

The spanning condition is satisfied if there exist two probability functions $\underline{\varphi}: D \to [0,1]$ and $\bar{\varphi}: D \to [0,1]$ such that

(a) the *monotone likelihood ratio property* is satisfied, i.e., for any pair of dividends $d^1 < d^2$,

$$\frac{\underline{\varphi}(d^1)}{\bar{\varphi}(d^1)} \geq \frac{\underline{\varphi}(d^2)}{\bar{\varphi}(d^2)}, \tag{13.3}$$

[6] This condition is introduced into the signaling literature by Feltham and Hughes (1988), and its use was suggested to them by Amin Amershi. A very similar condition was introduced earlier into the agency theory literature by Grossman and Hart (1983), and we examine it in that context in Chapter 17.

(b) the set of signals Y can be represented such that the owner's posterior dividend belief is

$$\varphi(d|y) = (1\text{-}y)\underline{\varphi}(d) + y\bar{\varphi}(d), \quad \forall\, d \in D,\, y \in Y = [0,1].$$

We know from Section 2.8 that the monotone likelihood ratio property implies that $\bar{\varphi}$ first-order stochastically dominates (*FS*-dominates) $\underline{\varphi}$. Hence, these two conditions imply that $\varphi(\cdot|y_{i'})$ *FS*-dominates $\varphi(\cdot|y_i)$ if $i < i'$, so that $y_{i'}$ is clearly better news than y_i.

In this section we assume all risks are firm-specific and express all values at $t = 1$ in terms of a zero-coupon bond that pays one unit at $t = 2$ and has a price of one at $t = 1$, i.e., the interest rate is zero. Hence, the *cum*-investment market value of the firm's equity at $t = 1$, given signal y and the investment of q, is

$$V(y) = \mathrm{E}[d|y] - q = \sum_{d \in D} d\,\varphi(d|y) - q. \tag{13.4}$$

Of course, it will not be optimal to invest q if the signal is such that the *cum*-investment value is negative. The set of signals for which the *cum*-investment value is positive is denoted

$$Y^* \equiv \{\, y \in Y \mid V(y) > 0 \,\}.$$

We assume the contract offered to investors is the only action by which the owner can convincingly disclose a signal $y \in Y^*$. The contract specifies outcome-contingent compensation that is to be paid to the owner at $t = 2$. More formally, we let $a = \boldsymbol{c}$, where $\boldsymbol{c}$: $D \rightarrow \mathbb{R}$ is the outcome-contingent compensation.

There is no consumption at $t = 1$ and the owner's utility for compensation at $t = 2$ is represented by the utility function $u(c)$, $c \in [\underline{c},\infty)$, which is increasing and strictly concave in c, i.e., $u'(c) > 0$ and $u''(c) < 0$. The owner is the informed player, and his expected utility from acceptance of contract $\boldsymbol{c}$ given signal y is

$$U_i(y,\boldsymbol{c}) \equiv \sum_{d \in D} u(\boldsymbol{c}(d))\,\varphi(d|y).$$

The well-diversified investors are uninformed players, and their aggregated expected net payoff from acquiring the firm given signal y is

$$U_u(y,\boldsymbol{c}) \equiv \sum_{d \in D} [d - \boldsymbol{c}(d) - q]\,\varphi(d|y).$$

Of course, the investors do not know y unless it is revealed by $\boldsymbol{c}$.

We let $\mathbf{c}$: $Y \to \mathbb{R}^n$ represent the owner's strategy conditional on the signal he observes and we let $\mathbf{c}_i = (c_{i1}, ..., c_{im})$, where $\mathbf{c}_i$ is the contract offered if the owner observes y_i and c_{ij} is the compensation received by the owner under contract $\mathbf{c}_i$ if d_j is realized at $t = 2$. Under the null contract, there is no investment and the owner receives $c^o \equiv 0$ (and there is no reported dividend). The owner's strategy is defined to provide full-disclosure if $\mathbf{c}_i = c^o$ for $y_i \in Y \backslash Y^*$ and $\mathbf{c}_i \neq \mathbf{c}_{i'}$ for $y_i \in Y^*$, $\forall\, y_{i'} \in Y, i' \neq i$. That is, the owner fully discloses all signals for which investing q has positive net value.

A Full-disclosure Equilibrium

The following proposition establishes that if we impose the CK-criterion then the only equilibrium is a full-disclosure equilibrium. Furthermore, it is the full disclosure equilibrium that maximizes the owner's expected utility given signal y, subject to the requirement that he would have no incentive to offer $\mathbf{c}_i$ if he has observed $y_{i'}$, $i' < i$.

Proposition 13.1 (Feltham and Hughes 1988, Prop. 9.1)

In the FH-model (i.e., the investment-disclosure game with contingent contracting, spanning (SC), and finite sets of dividends and signals), the only stable sequential equilibrium has the following characteristics:

(a) the investment is undertaken if, and only if, $y_i \in Y^*$;

(b) $\mathbf{c}_i = c^o$ if $y_i \notin Y^*$;

(c) $c_{1j} = V(y_1)$, $\forall\, j$, if $y_1 \in Y^*$;

(d) for each $y_i \in Y^*$, $i > 1$, there exist positive multipliers λ_i and μ_i such that

$$u'(c_{ij}) = \lambda_i \left[1 - \mu_i \frac{\varphi(d_j|y_{i-1})}{\varphi(d_j|y_i)} \right]^{-1}, \quad \forall\, j, \tag{13.5}$$

subject to $c_{ij} = \underline{c}$ if $u'(\underline{c})$ is greater than the right-hand-side.

Observe that if the investment is profitable even with the owner's worst signal, i.e., y_1, then the owner bears no risk if his signal is y_1. This is similar to the simple example in Section 13.2. However, we allow there to be one or more bad signals for which the investment is unprofitable. The equilibrium is such that the investment is not undertaken if the owner receives any of those signals. For any better signals, including the worst signal for which the investment is profitable, the equilibrium contract imposes risk on the owner and, the better the signal, the greater the risk.

The equilibrium contract for each profitable signal is characterized by the likelihood ratio for the signal received relative to the next worst signal. To illustrate the derivation of this result, assume the investment is profitable for all signals. In this case, if the owner observes y_1, we can interpret his no risk contract $\mathbf{c}_1$ as deriving from the sale of the firm to the investors for a fixed fee of $V(y_1)$, which he invests in zero coupon bonds. We now proceed by induction. Assume the optimal full-disclosure contracts $\mathbf{c}_1^*, ..., \mathbf{c}_{i-1}^*$ have been derived and determine the optimal full-disclosure contract given y_i. The owner's decision problem is as follows.

$$U_i(y_i,\mathbf{c}_i^*) = \underset{\mathbf{c}_i}{\text{maximize}} \quad U_i(y_i,\mathbf{c}_i)$$

$$\text{subject to} \quad U_u(y_i,\mathbf{c}_i) \geq 0,$$

$$U_i(y_k,\mathbf{c}_i) \leq U_i(y_k,\mathbf{c}_k^*), \qquad \forall\, k = 1, ..., i\text{-}1,$$

$$c_{ij} \geq \underline{c}, \qquad \forall\, j = 1, ..., m.$$

The first constraint is a *participation constraint* which requires the contract to be acceptable to the investors if they believe the owner has observed y_i. The second set of constraints are *full-disclosure* (or *truthtelling*) *constraints* which ensure that the contract is such that the owner does not have a strict incentive to offer that contract if he observes a signal worse than y_i. That is, an owner with signal y_i must offer a contract that owners with lower signals have no incentive to offer. The third set of constraints impose the exogenous lower bound on compensation. The Lagrangian for this decision problem (assuming, for simplicity, that we can drop the lower bound on compensation) is

$$\mathcal{L} = U_i(y_i,\mathbf{c}_i) + \lambda_i\, U_u(y_i,\mathbf{c}_i) - \sum_{k=1}^{i-1} \mu_{ik}\,[U_i(y_k,\mathbf{c}_i) - U_i(y_k,\mathbf{c}_k^*)], \tag{13.6}$$

Differentiating with respect to c_{ij} yields first-order condition

$$u'(c_{ij}) = \lambda_i \left[1 - \sum_{k=1}^{i-1} \mu_{ik} \frac{\varphi(d_j|y_k)}{\varphi(d_j|y_i)} \right]^{-1}. \tag{13.7}$$

This yields (13.5) if only the adjacent full-disclosure constraint is binding, i.e., if $\mu_i = \mu_{ii-1} > 0$ and $\mu_{i1} = ... = \mu_{ii-2} = 0$. This clearly holds for $i = 2$. To show that it holds for $i > 2$, consider a relaxed decision problem for the owner who has observed y_i in which we only include the full-disclosure constraint for $k = i$ -1, and let the optimal contract in this program be denoted $\hat{c}_i$. First, note that it must be the case that $\hat{\lambda}_i > 0$ since the owner has a strictly increasing utility function. Secondly, it must be the case that $\hat{\mu}_{ii-1} > 0$, i.e., $U_i(y_{i-1},\hat{c}_i) = U_i(y_{i-1},c_{i-1}^*)$. Otherwise, the contract $\hat{c}_i(d)$ is a constant, and a constant contract satisfying the participation constraint would be preferred to c_{i-1}^* by the owner with signal y_{i-1}. The spanning condition then implies that $\hat{c}_i(d)$ is increasing in d (since the likelihood-ratios are decreasing in d). If the owner with signals less than y_{i-1} does not have an incentive to offer $\hat{c}_i(d)$, then $\hat{c}_i(d)$ is also the optimal solution to the unrelaxed decision problem, i.e., $\hat{c}_i = c_i^*$ with $\hat{\mu}_{ii-1} = \mu_i$. Assume to the contrary that there is a signal $y_l < y_{i-1}$ such that

$$U_i(y_l,\hat{c}_i) > U_i(y_l,c_l^*). \tag{13.8}$$

The spanning condition implies that there exists a constant $w \in (0,1)$ such that

$$\begin{aligned} U_i(y_{i-1},\hat{c}_i) &= w\, U_i(y_i,\hat{c}_i) + (1\text{-}w)\, U_i(y_l,\hat{c}_i) \\ &> w\, U_i(y_i,\hat{c}_i) + (1\text{-}w)\, U_i(y_l,c_l^*) \\ &\geq w\, U_i(y_{i-1},\hat{c}_i) + (1\text{-}w)\, U_i(y_l,c_l^*), \end{aligned}$$

where the last inequality comes from the facts that $\hat{c}_i(d)$ is increasing in d and $\varphi(d|y_i)$ *FS*-dominates $\varphi(d|y_{i-1})$. However, this is inconsistent with $w \in (0,1)$ and (13.8).

13.3.2 Equity Retention with Normally Distributed Outcomes

In this section, we consider a setting based on Leland and Pyle's (LP) (1977) model of an initial public offering. In the LP-model, the owner uses linear contracts to disclose his private signal y with respect to the terminal dividend d. More specifically, the owner is described as disclosing his signal through equity retention – the better his signal the more equity he retains and the higher the price he obtains for the equity that he sells. Any difference between the amount obtained from the sale of equity and the capital required is either borrowed or invested by trading zero-coupon bonds at the risk-free interest rate (which we let equal zero).

Equity retention implicitly restricts the outcome-contingent contracts to be linear. As in many other settings examined in this book, linear contracts yield simple, yet interesting, results when they are combined with exponential utility and normally distributed outcomes. However, linear contracts are not as efficient as outcome-contingent contracts, such as those considered in the prior section. Appendix 13A characterizes efficient outcome-contingent compensation contracts in a setting with a continuum of signals and outcomes. The efficient full-disclosure contract given signal $y > q$ is strictly concave, not linear.

The Basic Model

We initially assume there is no market risk and investors are well-diversified, so that the market value of the firm's equity equals the expected terminal dividend (less any investments that are yet to be made). We assume the set of possible private signals is a bounded continuum, i.e., $Y = [\underline{y}, \bar{y}]$, with $y \in Y$ set equal to the owner's posterior mean with respect to the terminal dividend. The owner's posterior variance, denoted σ^2, is assumed to be independent of the signal, so that the owner's posterior distribution at $t = 1$ is $d|y \sim N(y,\sigma^2)$.

If $q < \underline{y}$, then it is optimal to undertake the investment for all signals, so that $Y^* = Y$. However, if $q > \underline{y}$, then there are some signals for which the investment is not profitable and $Y^* = [q, \bar{y}]$.

Unlike the model in the preceding section, we assume the owner personally finances any investment (which is again either 0 or q). If the owner decides to invest, then his publicly observable action consists of a promise to invest, his retained equity z, and the equity offer price v. If rejected, the owner does not invest, and his compensation is zero. If accepted, the owner immediately receives $(1-z)v$, borrows $q - (1-z)v$, and invests q in the firm. Hence, the owner's compensation function is

$$\boldsymbol{c}(d) = zd + (1-z)v - q. \tag{13.9a}$$

Since $\boldsymbol{c}(d)$ is a linear function of d (characterized by parameters z and v), and d is normally distributed (given signal y), it follows that the owner's compensation is normally distributed. More specifically,

$$c|y \sim N(zy + (1-z)v - q,\ z^2\sigma^2). \tag{13.9b}$$

The owner's utility function is exponential with risk aversion r and no lower bound on compensation, i.e., $u(c) = -\exp[-rc]$, $c \in (-\infty, +\infty)$.[7] With exponential utility and normally distributed compensation (see Section 2.6), the owner's expected utility given signal y and acceptance of contract $\boldsymbol{c} = (z,v)$ is

$$U_i(y,z,v) = -\exp[-r\,CE(y,z,v)], \tag{13.10a}$$

$$CE(y,z,v) = zy + (1-z)v - q - \tfrac{1}{2} r z^2\sigma^2. \tag{13.10b}$$

[7] The utility function could be defined with respect to the owner's terminal wealth w, which would equal his initial wealth plus current compensation c. However, since there is no wealth effect with exponential utility, the character of the results would be identical.

A Full-disclosure Equilibrium

The owner's strategy $\boldsymbol{a}$ specifies, for each signal $y \in Y$, whether he undertakes the investment q and, if undertaken, his retained equity $z \in Z = [0,1]$ and the offer price $v \in Y = [\underline{y}, \bar{y}]$. Let $Y^\dagger$ represent the set of signals for which the owner undertakes the investment, and let $\boldsymbol{z}$: $Y^\dagger \rightarrow Z$ and $\boldsymbol{v}$: $Y^\dagger \rightarrow Y$ represent the owner's retained equity levels and offer prices for those signals for which the investment is undertaken.

If the owner decides to undertake the investment, then the investors infer the owner's signal (his posterior mean) from his retained equity, and accept the contract as long as the offer price does not exceed the inferred expected dividend. Let $\boldsymbol{y}^\dagger: Z \rightarrow Y$ represent the investor's equilibrium inferences, which specifies the maximum offer price the investors will accept for each level of retained equity.

A stable sequential equilibrium, characterized by $(Y^\dagger, \boldsymbol{z}^\dagger, \boldsymbol{y}^\dagger)$, has the following characteristics. First, the investment is undertaken if, and only it is profitable, i.e., $Y^\dagger = Y^*$. Second, if the investment is undertaken, the retained equity reveals the owner's signal, i.e., $\boldsymbol{y}^\dagger(\boldsymbol{z}^\dagger(y)) = y$, $\forall\ y \in Y^\dagger$. Third, given the investor's inferences $\boldsymbol{y}^\dagger$, it is optimal for the owner to implement $Y^\dagger$ and $\boldsymbol{z}^\dagger$, i.e.,

(a) $\forall\, y \notin Y^*$: $\quad CE(y,z,\boldsymbol{y}^\dagger(z)) \leq 0, \quad \forall\, z \in Z,$

(b) $\forall\, y \in Y^*$: $\quad CE(y, \boldsymbol{z}^\dagger(y), y) \geq CE(y,z,\boldsymbol{y}^\dagger(z)), \quad \forall\, z \in Z.$

The next step is to characterize $\boldsymbol{z}^\dagger$ and $\boldsymbol{y}^\dagger$. This is accomplished by assuming that $\boldsymbol{y}^\dagger$ is a continuous function of z and is such that $CE(y,z,\boldsymbol{y}^\dagger(z))$ is a concave function of z with a unique maximum. Hence, the owner's choice of z given y is characterized by the owner's first-order condition,

$$CE_z + CE_v \boldsymbol{y}_z^\dagger = 0,$$

where the subscripts indicate first derivatives with respect to the indicated variables. More specifically, using (13.10b), this condition implies that, for all $y \in Y^*$, $\boldsymbol{z}^\dagger$ and $\boldsymbol{y}^\dagger$ must satisfy

$$y - \boldsymbol{y}^\dagger(z) + (1 - z)\boldsymbol{y}_z^\dagger(z) - rz\sigma^2 = 0, \quad \text{for } z = \boldsymbol{z}^\dagger(y). \tag{13.11a}$$

Now we recognize that, in a full-disclosure equilibrium, the investors correctly infer y from z, so that $\boldsymbol{y}^\dagger(z) = y$, for $z = \boldsymbol{z}^\dagger(y)$. Hence, (13.11a) becomes

$$(1 - z)\boldsymbol{y}_z^\dagger(z) = rz\sigma^2. \tag{13.11b}$$

This expression is a first-order differential equation, and we can solve for $\boldsymbol{y}^\dagger$ by dividing 1-z and then integrating both sides of the expression. This results in

$$y^\dagger(z) = -\, r\sigma^2\, [\ln(1\text{-}z) + z] + K, \tag{13.12a}$$

where K is a constant of integration. (You can check to see that this is correct by differentiating (13.12a) to obtain (13.11b).)

Each constant of integration K yields a full-disclosure equity retention strategy.[8] Obviously, the owner prefers to retain as little equity as possible (so as to shift as much firm-specific risk to the well-diversified investors as possible). Furthermore, the equilibrium is not stable unless this is the case. Consequently, the owner undertakes the investment and retains zero equity if he has observed the worst signal for which it is optimal to undertake the investment. That is, $z^\dagger(y) = 0$ if $y = \max\{\underline{y}, q\}$. This implies, from (13.12a), that $K = \max\{\underline{y}, q\}$. Hence, $z^\dagger(y)$ is such that

$$-\,[\ln(1\text{-}z^\dagger(y)) + z^\dagger(y)] = \frac{1}{r\sigma^2}[y - \max\{\underline{y}, q\}]. \tag{13.12b}$$

Observe that if $y < q$, then the owner has no incentive to offer $z = 0$, since $v = q$ and he receives no benefit from operating the firm. Also, he has even less incentive for selecting $z > 0$ than he does if $y = q$. Hence, the owner will not undertake the investment if $y < q$. (See LP Proposition I.)

Observe that (13.12b) implies that the owner's risk aversion and his posterior firm-specific risk influence the equilibrium level of equity retention for each signal. LP provide the following characterization.

Proposition 13.2 (LP, Prop. II)[9]

In the LP-model, an increase in either risk aversion r or firm-specific risk σ^2 reduces the owner's equilibrium equity retention $z^\dagger(y)$ for any signal $y > \max\{\underline{y}, q\}$.

Obviously, either $\underline{y}$ or q also influence the equilibrium equity retention. The impact of $\underline{y}$ is particularly interesting in that, if the investment is profitable given the worst possible signal, then increasing $\underline{y}$ reduces the equity retained. The

---

[8] To check the second-order condition, substitute (13.11b) and (13.12b) into (13.11a) to obtain the first derivative $y + r\sigma^2\, [\ln(1\text{-}z) + z] + K$. Then, differentiate with respect to z to obtain the second derivative $-r\sigma^2 z/(1\text{-}z) < 0$, for $z > 0$. Hence, the owner's decision problem given $y^\dagger$ is strictly concave, with a unique maximum.

[9] The proof is straightforward. Observe that (13.12b) can be expressed as $-[\ln(1\text{-}z) + z] = L$, where $L = (y - q)/(r\sigma^2)$. Totally differentiating (13.12b) yields $dz/dL = (1\text{-}z)/z > 0$. Hence, since increasing r or σ^2 reduces L, they also reduce z.

LP's Proposition III, which considers the comparative static for the owner's expected utility with respect to σ^2, contains an error – they should have taken total instead of partial derivatives, and this results in more complex relations. Note that, increasing the firm-specific risk σ^2 reduces the equilibrium equity retention $z^\dagger(y)$, but increasing σ^2 also increases the risk premium $\frac{1}{2} rz^2\sigma^2$ for a fixed z. The net effect depends on the specifics of the problem (see also Proposition 19.2).

implications of this result in assessing the value of a public report about y are explored in Section 13.6.

Proposition 13.3[10]

In the LP-model, an increase in max $\{\underline{y}, q\}$ reduces the owner's equilibrium equity retention $z^{\dagger}(y)$ for any signal $y > \max\{\underline{y}, q\}$. Furthermore, if $q > \underline{y}$, then an increase in the investment cost q increases the set of signals $[\underline{y}, q)$ for which the investment is not undertaken.

13.3.3 Correlated Outcomes among Firms

For simplicity, the above discussion assumes the firm's outcome is uncorrelated with the outcomes of all other firms, and there is no market risk. In this section we first consider the impact of market risk (i.e., variations in the aggregate outcome from all firms) that is correlated with the firm's outcome. Then we consider variations in outcomes that are diversifiable by investors, but are correlated among a subset of firms. There are two key points in this analysis. First, the correlation of a firm's outcome with the outcomes of other firms permits an undiversified owner to insure some of his risk by investing (long or short) in other firms. The remaining uninsured risk is partially shared with well-diversified investors through the sale of equity, with partial retention used to signal the owner's private firm-specific information. Second, market prices induce investors to efficiently share market risks. Hence, the owner, as an investor, shares in the market risk, i.e., efficiently invests directly or indirectly in the market portfolio.

Investing in the Market Portfolio

While we ignore market risk in our presentation of the basic LP-model, the original paper assumes the firm's outcome is correlated with the return on the market portfolio, and identifies the owner's optimal investment in the market portfolio. We now briefly consider the LP-model with market risk. The key point is that if there is market risk, then it is efficient for the owner (as a participant in the economy) to bear a share of the market risk equal to his risk tolerance divided by the aggregate risk tolerance of all investors in the economy. (See Section 7.5, equation (7.12).) If his firm's dividend is correlated with the aggregate consumption, then equity retention will impose some market risk on the owner, but this is not likely to be the efficient level. However, the owner can modify his market risk by investing (going long or short) in the market portfolio. As a result, the market risk has no direct impact on the owner's equity retention for disclosing firm-specific information. Of course, market risk affects

[10] The proof of Proposition 13.2 is readily extended to this proposition.

the value of the firm, which affects the owner's decision to invest. This has an effect on the equilibrium equity retention. Nonetheless, it is firm-specific risk that has the primary effect on the equity retained to disclose firm-specific information.

To introduce market risk we use the approach adopted by Christensen *et al.* (2002) and assume a dollar invested in the market portfolio yields a return of

$$R_o = \bar{R}_o + \varepsilon_o,$$

where $\varepsilon_o \sim N(0,\sigma_o^2)$ is the random variation in the market return.[11] The market portfolio is priced with respect to a zero-coupon bond which has a price of one at $t = 1$. Hence,

$$\bar{R}_o - 1 = r_o\sigma_o^2, \tag{13.13}$$

where r_o is a measure of the investors' aggregate risk aversion. The *ex*-investment market value of the firm's equity, given signal y and investment of q, is[12]

$$v(y) = E[d|y] - r_o\text{Cov}[d,\varepsilon_o|y]. \tag{13.14a}$$

We express the dividend as $d = y + \varepsilon_d$, where $\varepsilon_d = \varepsilon_i + \zeta\varepsilon_o$, $\varepsilon_i \sim N(0,\sigma_i^2)$ is the firm-specific variation in dividends, and $\text{Cov}[\varepsilon_i,\varepsilon_o] = 0$. Consequently, the owner's posterior belief about the firm's dividend, given the investment of q, is $d|y \sim N(y,\sigma^2)$, where $\sigma^2 = \sigma_i^2 + \zeta^2\sigma_o^2$ and $\text{Cov}[d,\varepsilon_o|y] = \zeta\sigma_o^2$. Consequently, this structure and (13.14a) imply

$$v(y) = y - r_o\zeta\sigma_o^2. \tag{13.14b}$$

The market covariance parameter ζ can be positive or negative.

Let z_o represent the owner's investment in the market portfolio. The owner can invest in the market portfolio even if he does not undertake the investment in his firm. In that case, his certainty equivalent (assuming he borrows z_o to invest in the market) is

[11] We assume the firm is "small" such that the owner's choice of equity retention does not affect the return on the market portfolio.

[12] As demonstrated in Section 7.5.2, this is the market price in an economy in which the terminal values of all firms are normally distributed, investors have exponential utility, and r_o is the normalized measure of the investors' aggregate risk aversion. More specifically, if v_j and d_j represent the market value and terminal dividend of firm j, and r_i is investor i's risk aversion, then $r_o = \sum_i r_i / v_o$, where $v_o = \sum_j v_j$. Furthermore, $R_o = d_o/v_o \sim N(\bar{R}_o,\sigma_o^2)$, where $d_o = \sum_j d_j$.

$$CE[z_o] = z_o[\bar{R}_o - 1] - ½rz_o^2\sigma_o^2. \quad (13.15)$$

Differentiating (13.15) with respect to z_o and substituting in (13.13) yields the following first-order condition:

$$z_o^* = [\bar{R}_o - 1]/(r\sigma_o^2) = r_o/r. \quad (13.16)$$

Hence, we obtain the standard result that, with exponential utility, the investor's efficient share of the market portfolio equals his risk tolerance r^{-1} divided by the investors' aggregate risk tolerance r_o^{-1}.

If the owner observes y and undertakes the investment with accepted contract $\boldsymbol{c} = (z,v)$ and investment portfolio z_o, then his certainty equivalent is

$$CE[y,z,v,z_o] = zy + (1-z)v - q + z_o[\bar{R}_o - 1]$$

$$- ½\, r[z^2(\sigma_i^2 + \zeta^2\sigma_o^2) + z_o^2\sigma_o^2 + 2zz_o\zeta\sigma_o^2]. \quad (13.17)$$

Differentiating (13.17) with respect to z_o and substituting in (13.13) yields the following first-order condition:

$$z_o^\dagger = z_o^* - z\zeta. \quad (13.18)$$

That is, the owner invests in the market portfolio so that the sum of direct holdings of the market portfolio ($z_o^\dagger$) plus his indirect share through his retained equity ($z\zeta$) equals his efficient share (z_o^*).

Substituting (13.18) into (13.17) yields the following certainty equivalent:

$$CE^\dagger[y,z,v] = z[y - r_o\zeta\sigma_o^2] + (1-z)v - q + z_o^* r_o\sigma_o^2$$

$$- ½\, r[z^2\sigma_i^2 + z_o^{*2}\sigma_o^2]. \quad (13.19)$$

The value of the firm's equity given y and investment of q is stated in (13.14b). This expression implies that the set of signals for which the owner invests q is $Y^* = [\max\{\underline{y}, q + r_o\zeta\sigma_o^2\}, \bar{y}]$. That is, to be profitable the expected dividend must exceed the sum of the cost of the investment plus the market risk premium. Furthermore, if the owner retains z units of equity and the investors infer the owner's private signal is $\boldsymbol{y}^\dagger(z)$, the maximum offer price the investors will accept is $\boldsymbol{y}^\dagger(z) - r_o\zeta\sigma_o^2$.

Applying the same approach as in the no market risk setting yields

$$\boldsymbol{y}^\dagger(z) = - r\sigma_i^2 [\ln(1-z) + z] + \max\{\underline{y}, q + r_o\zeta\sigma_o^2\}, \quad (13.20a)$$

$$-[\ln(1-z^\dagger(y)) + z^\dagger(y)] = \frac{1}{r\sigma_i^2}[y - \max\{\underline{y}, q + r_o\zeta\sigma_o^2\}]. \qquad (13.20b)$$

The form is the same as (13.12), but (13.20) highlights the difference in effect of firm-specific risk (σ_i^2) and market risk ($\zeta\sigma_o^2$). The latter is irrelevant if the investment has a market value greater than q given the worst possible signal.

Correlated Diversifiable Risk

Restricting the investment in other firms to a common fraction z_o (of the market portfolio) does not recognize the opportunity to use investments in other firms as a means of insuring diversifiable risks. From the investors' perspective, the key distinction is between diversifiable and non-diversifiable risks. The former are irrelevant, whereas the latter are reflected in the market price. However, from an undiversified owner's perspective, the key distinction is between insurable and uninsurable risks. As demonstrated above, an owner can insure the so called non-diversifiable risks implicit in his retained equity by adjusting his investment in the market portfolio. In addition, an owner may be able to offset some of the diversifiable risk implicit in his retained equity by investing (going long or short) in firms whose diversifiable risk is correlated with his firm's diversifiable risk (e.g., firms in the same industry).

Mayers (1972) provides a general analysis of the optimal investment strategy and equilibrium prices when investors hold portfolios of both non-tradeable (personally endowed) and tradeable claims. The optimal holding of tradeable claims consists of two portfolios. One is tailored to offset, as much as possible, the risks in his non-tradeable claims, while the other is his efficient share of the market portfolio. In our setting, retained equity is similar to a non-tradeable claim – it can be traded but the owner chooses not to do so as a means of signaling his private information.

To provide a simple illustration of this point, consider two firms, i and j, for which $d_k = y_k + \varepsilon_k + \zeta_{ko}\varepsilon_o$, $k = 1,2$, and for which the diversifiable risk is correlated, i.e., $\text{Cov}[\varepsilon_i,\varepsilon_j] = \sigma_{ij} \neq 0$. The equity retained by the owner of firm i is z_{ii} and his investments in firm j and in the market portfolio are z_{ij} and z_{io}, respectively. The market price of firm k given disclosure of signal y_k, $k = i, j$, is

$$v_k(y_k) = y_k - r_o\zeta_{ko}\sigma_o^2. \qquad (13.21)$$

Assuming the owners of firms i and j both undertake their investments (q_i and q_j), the certainty equivalent for the owner of firm i, given y_i, is

$$CE[y_i,z_{ii},v_i,z_{ij},z_{io}] = z_{ii}y_i + (1-z_{ii})v_i - q_i + z_{ij}[y_j - v_j] + z_{io}[\bar{R}_o-1]$$

$$- \tfrac{1}{2} r[z_{ii}^2(\sigma_i^2 + \zeta_{io}^2\sigma_o^2) + z_{ij}^2(\sigma_j^2 + \zeta_{jo}^2\sigma_o^2) + z_{io}^2\sigma_o^2 \qquad (13.22)$$

$$+ 2z_{ii}z_{ij}\sigma_{ij} + 2z_{ii}z_{io}\zeta_{io}\sigma_o^2 + 2z_{ij}z_{io}\zeta_{jo}\sigma_o^2 + 2z_{ii}z_{ij}\zeta_{io}\zeta_{jo}\sigma_o^2].$$

Substituting $y_j - v_j = r_o\zeta_{jo}\sigma_o^2$ from (13.21) and $\bar{R}_o - 1 = r_o\sigma_o^2$ from (13.13), and differentiating (13.22) with respect to z_{io} yields

$$z_{io}^{\dagger} = z_{io}^{*} - z_{ii}\zeta_{io} - z_{ij}\zeta_{jo}. \tag{13.23}$$

That is, the owner of firm *i* invests in the market portfolio so that the sum of his direct holding of the market portfolio ($z_{io}^{\dagger}$) plus his indirect share through his retained equity ($z_{ii}\zeta_{io}$) and through his investment in firm *j* ($z_{ij}\zeta_{jo}$) equals his efficient share (z_{io}^{*}).

Substituting (13.23) into (13.22) yields

$$CE^{\dagger}[y_i,z_{ii},v_i,z_{ij}] = z_{ii}[y_i - r_o\zeta_{io}\sigma_o^2] + (1-z_{ii})v_i - q_i + z_{io}^{*}r_o\sigma_o^2$$

$$- \tfrac{1}{2}\, r[z_{ii}^2\sigma_i^2 + z_{ij}^2\sigma_j^2 + 2z_{ii}z_{ij}\sigma_{ij} + z_{io}^{*2}\sigma_o^2]. \tag{13.24}$$

Hence, the market risk plays the same role with or without the correlation in the diversifiable risk for the two firms. That is, it merely affects the set of signals for which the investment has positive value. Now differentiate (13.24) with respect to z_{ij}, which yields the following first-order condition:

$$z_{ij}^{\dagger} = -\frac{\sigma_{ij}}{\sigma_j^2} z_{ii}. \tag{13.25}$$

That is, the investment in firm *j* is selected so as to reduce the diversifiable risk that is born by the owner if he retains some of his firm's equity. Owner *i*'s investment in firm *j* is zero if the diversifiable risks for the two firms are uncorrelated, or the owner does not retain any equity (e.g., $y_i \le \max\{\underline{y}_i, q + r_o\zeta_o\sigma_o^2\}$).

Substituting (13.25) into (13.24) yields

$$CE^{\ddagger}[y_i,z_{ii},v_i] = z_{ii}[y_i - r_o\zeta_{io}\sigma_o^2] + (1-z_{ii})v_i - q_i + z_{io}^{*}r_o\sigma_o^2$$

$$- \tfrac{1}{2}\, r[z_{ii}^2\hat{\sigma}_i^2 + z_{io}^{*2}\sigma_o^2], \tag{13.26}$$

where $\hat{\sigma}_i^2 \equiv \sigma_i^2 - \sigma_{ij}^2/\sigma_j^2$ is an adjusted measure of the firm-specific risk. It is this measure that is used to determine the equity retained to signal $y_i > \max\{\underline{y}_i, q + r_o\zeta_o\sigma_o^2\}$. Note that (13.26) is exactly the same as (13.19) except that the measure of firm-specific risk is reduced by the insurable part of that risk.

13.4 VERIFIED *EX ANTE* REPORTS

While risk retention can be used to fully reveal the owner's private information (if he is risk averse), that does not make verified reports, such as audited accounting reports, redundant. The value of a verified report arises from the fact that risk retention is costly to the owner and, hence, he may find it valuable to either use a verified report in place of risk retention or to reduce the risk retention necessary to fully reveal his information.

In this section we explore the impact of verified (e.g., audited) reports issued by the owner at $t = 1$ (*ex ante*). To simplify the analysis, we assume throughout this analysis that the firm's outcome is uncorrelated with the outcomes of other firms and there is no market risk. We consider settings in which the sets of outcomes and signals are finite (the FH-model) and settings in which the outcomes given the owner's private signal are normally distributed (the LP-model).

13.4.1 Perfect *Ex Ante* Reports

A verified report is defined to be *perfect* if it reveals the owner's signal. We assume that the owner can choose between issuing a truthful report or no-disclosure. More specifically, let m represent the owner's verified message (report) and let $M(y) = \{y, \emptyset\}$ represent the set of possible messages given signal y, where $m = \emptyset$ represents no disclosure. Hence, if the owner chooses to disclose, he must tell the truth, i.e., $m = y$, but he need not disclose his signal. Of course, in addition to the message choice, the owner must choose which contract to offer investors.

Costless Verification

The simplest case to consider is one in which a verified report of the owner's private signal is costless. In Section 13.3, we established that, without the verified report option, a risk-averse owner discloses his signal through the outcome-contingent contract he offers investors. He undertakes the investment if, and only if, it is profitable, i.e., $y \in Y^*$. Disclosing profitable signals through outcome-contingent contracts imposes risk on the owner (unless he has the worst possible signal), and risk is costly to the owner. Hence, if he has the option of disclosing his signal by issuing a costless verified report, he will do so. This result applies whether the set of possible signals is finite (as in Section 13.3.1) or continuous (as in Section 13.3.2).

Proposition 13.4 (FH, Prop. 9.3)

If the owner can costlessly provide a verified report of his private signal, then he will do so if $y \in Y^*$. Furthermore, if he has observed $y \in Y^*$, he will sell the firm (i.e., bear no risk) and obtain net consumption $E[d|y] - q$, with certainty.

Inability to Verify that the Owner is Uninformed

Observe that our prior analyses (with or without report verification) can be interpreted as applying to settings in which there is a positive probability that the owner is uninformed. All that is required is the inclusion of the null signal y_o (for which the posterior belief equals the prior belief) as a member of the set of possible signals Y. However, the analysis changes if we follow Dye (1985) and assume that, while an owner can issue a verified report of any signal he has received, he cannot issue a verified report that he has not received any signal.

Dye considers this limitation on verified reports in a setting in which the owner is risk neutral, whereas, in this chapter, we assume the owner is risk averse. Under risk neutrality, the owner has no mechanism for disclosing his lack of information, but under risk aversion the owner can offer an outcome-contingent contract to convincingly disclose his lack of information. Consequently, the stable sequential equilibrium in our current setting is significantly different from the equilibrium in Dye's setting (which we present in Chapter 14).

To illustrate the effect of the ability to costlessly verify all but the null signal in a setting with a risk-averse owner we extend the FH-model. The set of possible signals is $Y = Y^v \cup \{y_o\}$, where $Y^v = \{y_1, ..., y_n\}$ is the set of costlessly verifiable signals and y_o is an unverifiable null signal. If informed, the owner receives signal y_i, $i = 1, ..., n$, with probability $\varphi(y_i)$, and his posterior belief is $\varphi(d|y_i) = (1-y_i)\underline{\varphi}(d) + y_i\bar{\varphi}(d)$. His belief given the null signal is $\varphi(d|y_o) = (1-y_o)\underline{\varphi}(d) + y_o\bar{\varphi}(d)$, where $y_o = \Sigma_{i=1}^{n} y_i\varphi(y_i)$. We assume $E[d|y_o] > q$, so that the investment is profitable if the owner is uninformed.

What does the owner do if he is uninformed? He cannot issue a verified report, but he can convincingly disclose his lack of information by issuing an outcome-contingent contract $\boldsymbol{c}_o$. To achieve full disclosure, this contract must be such that, for all verifiable signals $y_i \in Y^v$, the owner prefers to consume $\bar{c}_i^{**} = \max\{0, E[d|y_i] - q\}$ with certainty, rather issue the risky null information contract $\boldsymbol{c}_o$. Given the spanning condition, the optimal null signal contract $\boldsymbol{c}_o^{**}$ is the solution to the following problem, where y_k is such that $y_k \le y_o < y_{k+1}$.

$$U_i(y_o, c_o^{**}) = \underset{c_o}{\text{maximize}} \sum_{j=1}^{m} u(c_{oj})\, \varphi(d_j|y_o)$$

$$\text{subject to} \quad \sum_{j=1}^{m} [d_j - c_{oj}]\, \varphi(d_j|y_o) \geq q,$$

$$\sum_{j=1}^{m} u(c_{oj})\, \varphi(d_j|y_k) \leq u(\bar{c}_k^{**}),$$

$$c_{oj} \geq \underline{c}, \qquad \forall j = 1, ..., m.$$

Hence, there exist multipliers λ_o and μ_o such that

$$u'(c_{oj}) = \lambda_o \left[1 - \mu_o \frac{\varphi(d_j|y_k)}{\varphi(d_j|y_o)} \right]^{-1}, \tag{13.27}$$

subject to $c_{oj} = \underline{c}$ if $u'(\underline{c})$ is greater than the right-hand-side.

An informed owner obviously benefits from access to costless verification because he need not bear risk to disclose his signal. The informed owner's access to costless verification is also beneficial to the uninformed owner. A verified report cannot be issued to confirm the lack of information, but verification relaxes the incentive constraint underlying (13.27) relative to the incentive constraint underlying (13.5), since an informed owner with signal y_k bears no risk with verification while he bears risk without verification.

Costly Verification

Verified reports are generally provided by independent third parties, and they charge a fee for their services. Verrecchia (1983) considers the impact of a costly report in a setting in which the owner is risk neutral and, hence, he has no means of disclosing his private signal other than a costly report. Hence, Verrecchia obtains a partial disclosure equilibrium (which we present in Chapter 14) in which the owner does not disclose poor signals. In this chapter, we assume the owner is risk averse. Hence, he has the choice of disclosing his signal by either issuing a costly verified report or by issuing an outcome-contingent contract that imposes risk on him. Consequently, the stable sequential equilibrium in our setting differs from Verrecchia's equilibrium.

Let $\kappa > 0$ represent the direct cost of issuing a verified report of the owner's private signal. We introduce this costly report into the LP-model examined in Section 13.3.2 (with only firm-specific risk). Assume $q > \underline{y}$, so that $Y^* = [q, \bar{y}]$. Observe that if the owner observes $y \in Y^*$ and issues a verified report with the sale of his equity, he can set the offer price at $v = y$ and obtain a certain return of $y - q - \kappa$. Of course, since $z^\dagger(y)$, as characterized by (13.12b), equals zero for $y = q$ and is increasing in y, it is less costly for the owner to disclose his signal by retaining $z^\dagger(y)$, if $y \in [q, y_\kappa]$, where y_κ is such that

$$z^\dagger(y_\kappa) = \sqrt{\frac{2\kappa}{r\sigma^2}}. \tag{13.28}$$

Proposition 13.5

In the LP-model with the option of issuing a verified report at a cost κ, the stable sequential equilibrium involves no disclosure for $y \in [\underline{y},q)$, disclosure by retaining $z^\dagger(y)$ if $y \in [q, y_\kappa]$, and disclosure by issuing a verified report if $y \in (y_\kappa, \bar{y}]$.

Observe that empirically, it may appear that disclosure only occurs for $y \in (y_\kappa, \bar{y}]$. However, that fails to consider the indirect disclosure through contingent contracts for $y \in [q, y_\kappa]$.

13.4.2 Imperfect *Ex Ante* Reports

Verifying what an owner knows is a difficult task. However, auditors can often verify some of an owner's information. In that case, a verified report changes the investors' belief about the owner's private signal but does not fully reveal that signal. We initially consider the impact of mandatory imperfect reports, and then consider the impact of choices among alternative imperfect systems.

As before, $y \in Y$ represents the owner's private signal and $E[d|y]$ represents his posterior expected outcome from undertaking the investment q. Also, we again assume the owner can disclose his signal by offering an appropriate outcome-contingent contract. From the analysis in Section 13.3, it is obvious that a key factor affecting the outcome-contingent contract required to disclose a signal y is the set of worse signals for which the investment is profitable plus the worse signal (if any) for which the investment is weakly unprofitable. For example, based on the investors' prior beliefs in the LP-model, this set is $\underline{Y}(y) = [\max\{\underline{y},q\}, y)$. On the other hand, in the FH-model, if $E[d|y_k] < q < E[d|y_{k+1}]$, then $\underline{Y}(y_i) = \{y_k, ..., y_{i-1}\}$, for $i > k$. For simplicity, in this section we assume the investment is always profitable, i.e., $E[d|y] > q$, for all y, and $Y^* = Y$.

With imperfect verification, there is more than one signal that can result in a given report, and there may be more than one report that can result from a given signal. A report is denoted ψ and $\Psi(y)$ represents the set of reports that have a positive probability (density) of being produced if the owner has observed y, i.e., $\Psi(y) \equiv \{ \psi \mid \varphi(\psi|y) > 0 \}$, where $\varphi(\psi|y)$ is the likelihood function for ψ given y. We assume the report does not affect the owner's beliefs about the outcome d, but it does potentially change the investors' beliefs about both the outcome d and the owner's private signal y.

We focus on the impact of the report ψ on the investors' beliefs about y. These posterior beliefs, represented by $\varphi(y|\psi)$, are computed by Bayes' theorem. Prior to the report, the investors assign positive probability (density) to all signals in Y (by definition). After report ψ, they assign positive probability to the set

$$Y(\psi) \equiv \{\, y \in Y \mid \varphi(y|\psi) > 0 \,\},$$

which is the *support* of the investors' posterior signal beliefs. More importantly, the set of worse signals from which the owner must achieve separation given y is

$$\underline{Y}(y,\psi) = \{\, y' \in Y(\psi) \mid y' < y \,\}.$$

Non-discriminating Ex Ante Report Systems

A reporting system is defined to be *non-discriminating* if $\underline{Y}(y,\psi) = \underline{Y}(y)$ for all $y \in Y$ and $\psi \in \Psi$. That is, while a non-discriminating report may change the investors' signal beliefs, it does not change the set of worse signals from which a profitable signal must achieve separation.

There is full disclosure in the stable sequential equilibrium. A key feature of the full disclosure contract for each signal is that it depends only on the set of worse possible signals, but not the beliefs over that set. As a result, a non-discriminating reporting system has no value to the owner – he offers the same contracts with and without the report.

Proposition 13.6

The stable sequential equilibrium is unaffected by a non-discriminating reporting system.

To illustrate this point, consider the simple example illustrated in Figures 13.3 and 13.4. The owner may have observed either good or bad news. We established that the only stable equilibrium, irrespective of the probability of good or bad news, is a full disclosure equilibrium in which the owner bears no risk if he has observed bad news (i.e., contract a_b), but offers a risky contract (a_g) if he has observed good news. Observe that $\underline{Y}(y_b) = \emptyset$ and $\underline{Y}(y_g) = \{y_b\}$.

Consider a reporting system with $\Psi = \{\psi_\ell, \psi_h\}$, where $\varphi(\psi_h|y_g) = 1 - \varepsilon_g$ and $\varphi(\psi_\ell|y_b) = 1 - \varepsilon_b$. If ε_g and ε_b are close to zero, then there is very little noise in the reporting system, but if neither equals zero, then $\Psi(y)$ is independent of y and the system is non-discriminating. The system is also non-discriminating if $\varepsilon_g > 0$ and $\varepsilon_b = 0$, i.e., ψ_ℓ reveals y_b. The key point is that if $\varepsilon_g > 0$, then $\varphi(y_g|\psi_h)$ is less than one and $\underline{Y}(y_g,\psi_h) = \{y_b\}$ and the owner must offer contract a_g to convince the investors that he has not observed y_b. The fact that $Y(\psi_\ell) = \{y_b\}$ does not change the fact that $\underline{Y}(y_b,\psi_\ell) = \underline{Y}(y_b) = \emptyset$ – so the fact that ψ_ℓ reveals y_b is irrelevant.

Of course, if $\varepsilon_g = 0$ and $\varepsilon_b > 0$, then the reporting system is discriminating, since $\underline{Y}(y_g,\psi_h) = \{\emptyset\}$. In this case, the system has value to the owner if he has observed y_g since he need not bear any risk if ψ_h is reported. Of course, the system is not as valuable as a perfect system since $\underline{Y}(y_g,\psi_\ell) = \{y_b\}$ and the owner must offer a_g if ψ_ℓ is reported.

Discriminating Ex Ante Reporting Systems

The following result extends the simple example discussed above to the FH-model, in which there are a finite number of private signals, spanning, investment, and stable sequential equilibria. The proposition is stated for the setting in which $Y^* = Y$, but it is straightforward to remove that assumption.

Proposition 13.7

Assume $Y^* = Y$. In the FH-model, a verified *ex ante* reporting system is valuable to the owner who has observed signal $y_i \in Y^*$, $i > 1$, if, and only if, there is at least one report $\psi \in \Psi(y_i)$ for which there is at least one signal y_j, $j < i$, such that $y_j \notin Y(\psi)$.

That is, a reporting system need not totally eliminate risk retention to be valuable. However, there must be a positive probability that the risk required to disclose a given signal is reduced. Hence, a reporting system is valuable given signal y_i if there is at least one possible report that will eliminate at least one worse signal from which separation would otherwise be necessary. This result can also be applied to the LP-model, except that the discriminating report must eliminate a measurable set of worse signals to be valuable.

The Value of Discriminating Reporting Systems

We now consider the DFH-model (Datar *et al.*, 1991) which extends the LP-model to consider the value of an imperfect, but discriminating report by an independent auditor. The reporting system (e.g., auditor) is denoted $\eta \in H$ and the report from that system is ψ. The report ψ is scaled so that it equals the worst signal the owner could have received and obtained that report. We assume that if report ψ is received by an owner with signal y, then he uses equity retention to separate himself from $[\psi,y]$.[13]

In this setting it is useful to restate (13.12b) in a more generic form. Let δ be such that the set of signals from which the owner must separate, for any

---

[13] This implies that if signal y results in report ψ, then all signals in the set $[\psi,y]$ could also have obtained that report.

arbitrary signal y, is $[\underline{y}\text{-}\delta, y]$. That is, δ is a measure of maximum potential "under-valuation," which the owner "corrects" by retaining equity. It follows from (13.12b) that the retained equity, denoted $z^{\ddagger}(\delta)$, is such that

$$- r\sigma^2 [\ln(1\text{-}z^{\ddagger}(\delta)) + z^{\ddagger}(\delta)] = \delta. \tag{13.29}$$

If there is no report (or it is not discriminating), then $z^{\dagger}(y) = z^{\ddagger}(y - \underline{y})$.

The cost of risk to the owner of retaining z is $\frac{1}{2} r\sigma^2 z^2$. Therefore, the owner's equity retention cost, given signal y and report $\psi = y - \delta$ is

$$\kappa_r^{\ddagger}(\delta) \equiv \tfrac{1}{2} r\sigma^2 [z^{\ddagger}(\delta)]^2. \tag{13.30}$$

Obviously, this cost is strictly increasing in δ, since $z^{\ddagger}(\delta)$ is increasing in δ (see Proposition 13.3).

Let $\Phi(\psi | y,\eta)$ represent the likelihood distribution function for reporting system η and let $\Psi(y,\eta)$ be the support of that distribution. It then follows that the expected utility given signal y and reporting system η (ignoring audit costs) is

$$U_i(y,\eta) = - \exp[- r(y - q)]\, K(y,\eta), \tag{13.31a}$$

where
$$K(y,\eta) = \int_{\Psi(y,\eta)} \exp[r\kappa_r^{\ddagger}(y\text{-}\psi)]\, d\Phi(\psi | y,\eta). \tag{13.31b}$$

DFH focus on what they call consistent audit technologies, and which we call consistent reporting systems. The key characteristic of a consistent reporting system is that the distribution of potential post-report under-pricing levels is essentially independent of the signal. (For simplicity, we assume $Y = [\underline{y}, \bar{y}]$ with $\underline{y} \geq q$.)

Definition *Consistent Reporting System*

A discriminating reporting system η is *consistent* across signals if:

(a) there exists a constant $\bar{\delta}_\eta$ such that $\Psi(y,\eta) = [\max\{\underline{y}, y\text{-}\bar{\delta}_\eta\}, y]$, for all $y \in Y$; and,

(b) there exists a distribution function $G(\delta | \eta)$ with $G(0) = 0$ and $G(\bar{\delta}_\eta) = 1$, such that $\Phi(\psi | y,\eta) = 1 - G(y\text{-}\psi)$, for all $y \in Y$ and $\psi \in \Psi(y,\eta)$.

That is, the probability the report equals $y - \delta$, for all $\delta \in [0, \min\{\bar{\delta}_\eta, y - \underline{y}\}]$, is independent of the signal y. If $\bar{\delta}_\eta > y - \underline{y}$, then $\psi = \underline{y}$ has a strictly positive probability (i.e., a mass point) equal to $1 - G(y - \underline{y} | \eta)$. More intuitively, subject to the boundary conditions, the probability distribution with respect to the amount of under-pricing that must be overcome by equity retention is independent of the signal.

Assume the characteristics of the reporting system are mandated (e.g., by generally accepted auditing standards), so that the same system is used for each signal. In that case, the value of system η relative to the null reporting system η^o, given signal y, is

$$\pi(\eta|y) = \frac{1}{r}\{\ln[K(y,\eta)] - \kappa_r^{\ddagger}(y-\underline{y})\}. \tag{13.32}$$

Obviously, if $y > \underline{y}$ and η is discriminating with a positive probability of generating reports $\psi \in (\underline{y},y]$, then η has strictly positive value relative to η^o. The key, of course, is that with the null reporting system the owner must retain $z^{\ddagger}(y-\underline{y})$, whereas a report $\psi > \underline{y}$ reduces that equity retention to $z^{\ddagger}(y-\psi)$. Consequently, the value of a reporting system depends on the likelihood it will generate reports close to the owner's signal. In fact, the most valuable reporting system produces ψ equal to y with probability one – which is the perfect system considered in Section 13.4.1.

The value of a reporting system depends on the system's "quality", the owner's signal y, the riskiness of the investment σ^2, and the owner's risk aversion r. We consider each in turn.

A reporting system η is characterized by the likelihood distribution function $\Phi(\psi|y,\eta)$, and we employ the following definition of relative quality based on that function.

Definition *System Quality*

A reporting system η' is of *strictly higher quality* than η'' if $\Phi(\psi|y,\eta')$ strictly FS-dominates $\Phi(\psi|y,\eta'')$, for all $y \in (\underline{y},\bar{y}]$.

The first-order-stochastic dominance condition implies that η' is more likely to produce values of $\psi = y - \delta$ closer to y. Since smaller values of $\delta = y - \psi$ result in less equity retention, a higher quality system is more valuable.

Proposition 13.8 (DFH, Prop. 2)

If η' is of strictly higher quality than η'', then

$$\pi(\eta'|y) > \pi(\eta''|y), \quad \forall\, y \in (\underline{y},\bar{y}].$$

With signal y and no report, the cost of equity retention is $\kappa_r^{\ddagger}(y-\underline{y})$, which is increasing in y. With a consistent reporting system η, the distribution of equity retention is independent of y if $y - \underline{y} > \bar{\delta}_\eta$, in which case $K(y,\eta)$ is independent of y. If $y \in (\underline{y},\underline{y} + \bar{\delta}_\eta)$, then $K(y,\eta)$ is increasing in y since the range of values for

$\delta = y - \psi$ increases. However, since $y - \psi$ is never greater than $y - \underline{y}$, it follows that $\partial \ln[K(y,\eta)]/\partial y < \partial \kappa_r^\ddagger(y - \underline{y})/\partial \delta$.

Proposition 13.9 (DFH, Prop. 4)

(a) With consistent reporting system η,

$$\partial \pi(\eta | y)/\partial y > 0, \quad \forall\, y \in (\underline{y}, \bar{y}].$$

(b) If consistent reporting system η' is of strictly higher quality than η'', then

$$\partial[\pi(\eta' | y) - \pi(\eta'' | y)]/\partial y = 0, \quad \forall\, y \in [\underline{y} + \delta_{\eta''}, \bar{y}].$$

Proposition 13.8 establishes that the incremental value of using consistent system η' instead of η'' is strictly positive, whereas part (b) of Proposition 13.9 establishes that the incremental value is independent of y (for those signals for which both systems are fully discriminating).

Equation (13.30) specifies $\kappa_r^\ddagger(\delta)$, the cost of retaining equity to separate from $\psi = y - \delta$. Increasing the investment risk σ^2 has two effects on this cost. First, there is a direct increase since increasing the risk increases the cost of retaining a given level of equity. Second, given the higher cost, the owner can optimally hold less equity to disclose the same information, i.e., $z^\ddagger(\delta)$ is decreasing in σ^2 (see Proposition 13.2). The first effect dominates, so that more risk results in a higher cost:[14]

$$d\kappa_r^\ddagger(\delta)/d\sigma^2 = \tfrac{1}{2} r[z^\ddagger(\delta)]^2 + r\sigma^2 z^\ddagger(\delta)\, dz^\ddagger(\delta)/d\sigma^2 > 0, \quad \forall\, \delta > 0.$$

A discriminating system provides reports that reduce the amount of equity that must be held. Since the cost of retaining equity is increasing in σ^2, it naturally follows that the value of a discriminating system is increasing in σ^2. Furthermore, the incremental value of a more discriminating system is increasing in σ^2.

---

[14] Footnote 9 establishes that $dz/dL = (1-z)/z$ for $L = \delta/[r\sigma^2]$. Hence,

$$dz/d\sigma^2 = -(1-z)\delta/[rz\sigma^4] = (1-z)[\ln(1-z) + z]/[z\sigma^2] < 0,$$

$$d\kappa_r^\ddagger/d\sigma^2 = \tfrac{1}{2} rz^2 + r\sigma^2 z\, dz/d\sigma^2 = \tfrac{1}{2} rz^2 + r(1-z)[\ln(1-z) + z] > 0.$$

The first inequality follows from the fact that $\ln(1-z) + z < 0$ for $z \in (0,1)$. The second inequality follows from the fact that $d\kappa_r^\ddagger/d\sigma^2|_{z=0} = 0$, and

$$\partial[d\kappa_r^\ddagger/d\sigma^2]/\partial z = -r[\ln(1-z) + z] > 0.$$

Proposition 13.10 (DFH, Prop. 6 and 7)[15]

(a) For any discriminating reporting system η,

$$d\pi(\eta|y)/d\sigma^2 > 0, \quad \forall\, y \in (\underline{y}, \bar{y}].$$

(b) If consistent reporting system η' is of strictly higher quality than η'', then

$$\partial[\pi(\eta'|y) - \pi(\eta''|y)]/\partial\sigma^2 > 0, \quad \forall\, y \in (\underline{y}, \bar{y}].$$

The impact of an increase in the owner's risk aversion is more complex. Like σ^2, increasing r directly increases $\kappa_r^\ddagger(\delta)$ and decreases $z^\ddagger(\delta)$, with the first effect dominating the second. However, in (13.32), determining π also involves division by r. This reflects the fact that an increase in r has a negative impact on the value of a reporting system because there is risk with respect to the report that will be issued – it may be good news (close to y) or bad news (close to y-$\bar{\delta}_\eta$). The price the owner is willing to pay for that gamble decreases as his risk aversion increases. (Of course, despite the owner's risk aversion, the gamble always has positive value since all reports are at least as good as, and some are better than, no report.)

Reporting System Choice

In our earlier discussion of costly perfect reports, we established that the owner would not issue the report if his signal was close to its lower bound, since the cost of retaining equity to disclose his signal would be less than the cost of a perfect report. In our preceding discussion of the value of a discriminating reporting system we assumed the quality of the report is mandated for all signals. We now consider the impact of reporting system choice. To simplify the analysis we assume the choice is between a null (or non-discriminating) system η^o and a consistent discriminating system η. We again assume $Y^* = Y$, i.e., in the LP-model, $\underline{y} \geq q$.

Let κ_η represent the cost of system η and let $y_{\eta*}$ represent the signal for which the owner would be indifferent between no report and the mandating of reporting system η, i.e.,

$$\pi(\eta|y_{\eta*}) = \kappa_\eta.$$

[15] Footnote 14 establishes that $\partial[d\kappa_r^\ddagger/d\sigma^2]/\partial z > 0$. This plus $\partial z^\ddagger/\partial\delta > 0$ implies $d^2\kappa_r^\ddagger/d\sigma^2 d\delta > 0$. That is, the increase in the cost of equity retention due to more risk is greater the larger is δ. Hence, the benefit to reducing δ by obtaining a discriminating report is increasing in σ^2. Similarly, the incremental benefit of using a higher quality system is increasing in σ^2.

If a vote was taken whether to mandate the use of η instead of η^o, then the owner would vote yes if $y \in (y_{\eta*}, \bar{y}]$ and would vote no if $y \in [\underline{y}, y_{\eta*})$. However, if the choice of reporting system is made voluntarily, there are signals in the set $[\underline{y}, y_{\eta*}]$ for which the owner would choose η (e.g., would chose a higher quality auditor).

The key here is that the act of paying κ_η for η is itself informative to investors. Let $y_{\eta 0}$ represent the signal for which the owner would be indifferent between no report and a perfect report costing κ_η, i.e.,

$$\kappa_r^\ddagger(y_{\eta 0} - \underline{y}) = \kappa_\eta.$$

Since the owner would not choose η if he observes $y < y_{\eta 0}$, he need not retain any equity to disclose his signal if he observes $y = y_{\eta 0}$ and chooses η (i.e., pays κ_η). Now consider a signal $y > y_{\eta 0}$. If the owner chooses η^o, then he retains $z^\ddagger(y-\underline{y})$, but if he chooses η (and pays κ_η), then he need retain no more than $z^\ddagger(y-y_{\eta 0})$ if $\psi \le y_{\eta 0}$ and no more than $z^\ddagger(y-\psi)$ if $\psi \in (y_{\eta 0}, y]$. DFH establish that there exists a signal $y_{\eta 1} > y_{\eta 0}$ such that for $y \in (y_{\eta 0}, y_{\eta 1})$ the owner prefers η^o, while for $y_{\eta 1}$ he is indifferent between η^o and η. The analysis is then extended to signals $y > y_{\eta 1}$, leading to a finite sequence of isolated signals $y_{\eta 0}, y_{\eta 1}, ..., y_{\eta N} < y_{\eta*}$ such that for all $y \in [\underline{y}, y_{\eta N}]$ the owner weakly prefers η^o with strict preference for the identified finite sequence of signals. On the other hand, given those choices, the owner strictly prefers η for all $y \in (y_{\eta N}, \bar{y}]$.

Proposition 13.11 (DFH, Prop. 8)[16]

Given suitable regularity, the optimal full-disclosure equilibrium with voluntary choice between η^o and η (with cost κ_η), is characterized by a sequence of signals $y_{\eta 0}, y_{\eta 1}, ..., y_{\eta N}$, $N \ge 1$, such that:

(a) $y_{\eta 0} < y_{\eta 1} < ... < y_{\eta N} < y_{\eta*}$;

(b) the owner chooses η (but is indifferent between η^o and η) for all $y \in \{y_{\eta 0}, y_{\eta 1}, ..., y_{\eta N}\}$;

(c) the owner chooses η^o for all $y \in [\underline{y}, y_{\eta 0}) \cup ... \cup (y_{\eta N-1}, y_{\eta N})$;

(d) the owner chooses η for all $y \in (y_{\eta N}, \bar{y}]$.

---

[16] The analysis assumes that $G(\delta|\eta)$ is uniformly distributed on δ_η, and that κ_η is sufficiently small for $y_{\eta 0}$ and $y_{\eta*}$ to exist. In addition, there are some technical conditions, including $r\sigma \le 1$ (see DFH, p.28).

The most notable characteristic of this result is that the set of signals resulting in voluntary choice of η is larger than the set of signals that would result in a positive vote for requiring the use of η. The set of signals $y \in (y_{\eta N}, y_{\eta *}]$ benefit from voluntary choice, since the payment of κ_η partially separates them from $y \in [\underline{y}, y_{\eta N})$, reducing the equity that must be retained to complete the separation.

The complexity of the equilibrium makes it virtually impossible to analytically assess the impact of model parameters on the equilibrium choices. However, DFH conduct numerical analyses of the impact of investment risk on the choice of reporting systems, including choices between a low and high quality system. They provide the following summary statement of the examples they examined (DFH, p. 34):

(a) if the investment risk is sufficiently small, then the owner chooses the low quality system for all y;

(b) if the investment risk is sufficiently large, then the owner chooses the high quality system for all but a set of signals close to $\underline{y}$ (and that set shrinks as σ^2 increases).

These results are consistent with the earlier analysis of the value of alternative mandatory systems. More risk makes higher quality reporting systems more valuable due to the reduced equity retention. Hence, if the increased risk does not change the incremental cost of the higher quality system, increased risk can cause the owner to shift from preferring the low quality to the high quality system.

Titman and Trueman (TT) (1986) examine a model in which they exogenously assume there is no equity retention and there is a continuum of system (auditor) choices. The structure of their model is such that there is a full-disclosure equilibrium in which the quality of the chosen reporting system is increasing with the owner's signal y.[17] Furthermore, increasing the investment risk results in a decrease in the chosen quality for each signal (for essentially the same reason that more risk resulted in less equity retention in the DFH-model).[18]

[17] In the TT model, the reporting system provides new information about the value of the firm to both the owner and the investors. The owner's posterior mean is a weighted average of his prior mean and the report received. Hence, a report creates uninsured information risk. That risk is higher with a higher quality reporting system, since more weight is placed on a higher quality report. An owner is more willing to bear that risk if he has good news than if he has bad news. Hence, the quality of the system chosen is an increasing function of the owner's prior mean, e.g., better firms hire better auditors.

[18] An increase in σ^2, holding system quality constant, results in less weight being placed on the owner's prior mean and more weight on the report. This results in a lower quality system being chosen to signal the same prior mean.

Hence, the TT results are essentially counter to the DFH results with respect to the impact of investment risk on the choice of reporting system (e.g., auditor) quality.

Feltham, *et al.* (FHS) (1991) and Clarkson and Simunic (CS) (1994) conducted empirical studies directly motivated by the DFH analysis.[19] They assume that big and small auditors are proxies for high and low quality reporting systems,[20] and examine whether there is a positive association between investment risk and auditor size. FHS find very little evidence of either a positive or negative association in U.S. data. CS obtain a similar lack of positive association in U.S. data, but find a positive association in Canadian data. FHS conjectured that the lack of positive association in U.S. data is attributable to litigation in the U.S. that might cause the incremental cost of a big (higher quality) auditor to increase with investment risk. This led CS to examine both the U.S. and Canadian markets, since the latter is much less litigious. The results suggest that the benefit from a higher quality auditor increases with investment risk, but so does the audit fee. The latter effect may offset the former in the U.S., but not in the less litigious Canadian environment.

13.5 VERIFIED *EX POST* REPORTS

The analysis in Section 13.4.2 establishes that stable sequential equilibria are unaffected by non-discriminating *ex ante* reporting systems. Only full-disclosure equilibria are stable, and for each signal a full disclosure contract only depends on the set of worse signals, but not the beliefs over that set. However, a verified report after the owner has selected the contract offered to investors can be valuable even if it is non-discriminating.

Consider the FH-setting in which the contracts are supplemented by an *ex post* reporting system η that generates a verified *ex post* report $\psi \in \Psi(y,\eta) \equiv \{ \psi \mid \varphi(\psi|y,\eta) > 0 \}$. The reporting system η is part of the contract offered to investors. The owner can choose either to include η in his contract or exclude it, but he cannot influence the likelihood of the reports generated by that system, i.e., $\varphi(\psi|y,\eta)$. If η is included in the contract, then the owner's outcome-contingent contract is expressed as a function of both the terminal dividend d and the report ψ.

[19] We have ignored market risk in our discussion of the DFH model. However, there is clearly market risk in the empirical domain. Hence, FHS extend the DFH model to include market risk, in essentially the same way the LP-model included market risk (see Section 13.3.3).

[20] It would be very difficult to identify a continuum of auditor quality as would be required to directly examine the TT results.

Of course, if the *ex post* reporting system perfectly reveals the owner's signal in any full disclosure equilibrium, a manager with a profitable signal $y \in Y^*$ will include η in the contract and sell the firm (i.e., bear no risk). At the other extreme, if the reports provide no additional information about the owner's signal, then η will not be included in the contract. The key is the additional information generated by the reports.

Definition *Informative Ex Post Reporting Systems*

Ex post reporting system η is Y-informative if for all $y', y'' \in Y$, there exists some terminal dividends d and *ex post* report ψ such that

$$\varphi(\psi|d,q,y',\eta) \neq \varphi(\psi|d,q,y'',\eta).$$

If the *ex post* reporting system is costless, then including the system in the contract is weakly preferred to not including it, since the owner has the option to offer an outcome-contingent contract that does not depend on the *ex post* report. Hence, the reporting system is valuable if, and only if, the outcome-contingent contract depends non-trivially on ψ. The stable full disclosure contracts including η can be characterized as in the first-order conditions (13.7), i.e.,

$$u'(c_{ij}(\psi)) = \lambda_i \left[1 - \sum_{k=1}^{i-1} \mu_{ik} \frac{\varphi(d_j,\psi|y_k,\eta)}{\varphi(d_j,\psi|y_i,\eta)} \right]^{-1}.$$

If $y_i \in Y^*$ and $i > 1$, then for some $k < i$ it must be the case that $\mu_{ik} > 0$ (since an owner with a profitable signal y_i must separate himself from worse types). If η is Y-informative, there exists some terminal dividend d_j and report ψ such that

$$\frac{\varphi(d_j,\psi|y_k,\eta)}{\varphi(d_j,\psi|y_i,\eta)} \neq \frac{\varphi(d_j|y_k)}{\varphi(d_j|y_i)}.$$

Hence, the first-order conditions establish that the outcome-contingent contract offered by an owner with signal y_i depends non-trivially on the *ex post* report ψ.

Proposition 13.12 (FH, Prop. 9.8)

If a verified *ex post* reporting system is Y-informative in the FH-model setting, the reporting system is valuable to the owner who has observed signal y_i, if, and only if, $y_i \in Y^*$ and $i > 1$.

An Y-informative *ex post* reporting system has two benefits. First, it provides verified information that permits the owner to separate himself from worse signals more efficiently, i.e., he bears less risk. Chapter 18 provides a more detailed analysis of a similar role of *ex post* reporting systems in agency settings, as well as an analysis of the value of alternative reporting systems. A key result of that analysis is that the value of *ex post* reporting systems increases with the "variability" of the likelihood ratios that the systems provide. Second, the increased expected utility for owners with worse signals that would also use η relaxes the full-disclosure constraints associated with those signals.

13.6 EQUITY RETENTION AND REPORT CHOICE AS BIVARIATE SIGNALS

In the DFH model, equity retention is required even if the imperfect reports are costless because, for any signal and any report, there is a set of worse signals that could have generated the same report. A discriminating report provides partial disclosure, and equity retention is used to achieve full disclosure. Hughes (1986) extends the LP-model to consider a model in which equity retention and a report (e.g., a forecast) chosen by the owner are jointly used to provide full disclosure.

A distinctive feature of the Hughes model is that she assumes the owner has private information about both his posterior mean, denoted $y \in Y = [\underline{y}, \bar{y}]$, and his posterior variance, denoted $\sigma^2 \in \Sigma = [\underline{\sigma}^2, \bar{\sigma}^2]$.[21] The market price is independent of σ^2, since the investors are assumed to be risk neutral (i.e., well-diversified) with respect to firm-specific risk.[22] However, σ^2 affects the cost of using equity retention (see $\kappa_r^\ddagger(\delta)$ in (13.30)) to signal private information. Hence, the signal y inferred from z depends on σ^2.

Hughes assumes the owner can issue a report (e.g., a forecast) ψ at a cost

$$\kappa_\eta(\psi, y, \sigma^2) = k\psi^3/(y\sigma^2), \tag{13.33}$$

where $k > 0$ is a cost function parameter. In this setting, the owner directly chooses the report (instead of the reporting system), and the cost of the report is increasing in the report ψ that is issued, and decreasing in both his posterior mean y and variance σ^2. The first derivative with respect to the report is

---

[21] Grinblatt and Hwang (1989) provide another bivariate signaling model in which y and σ^2 are private information. In their model, equity retention and under-pricing are used to provide a bivariate signal.

[22] Hughes considers market risk, but it is largely irrelevant to the signaling issue, as demonstrated by our discussion of market risk in the LP-model (see Section 13.3.3).

$$\kappa_{\eta\psi}(\psi,y,\sigma^2) = 3k\psi^2/(y\sigma^2), \tag{13.34}$$

so that higher reports are incrementally less costly the better the agent's signal y or the more uncertain is the final outcome.

Hughes assumes the report is issued through a risk-neutral (e.g., large) investment banker who will incur litigation costs if the terminal dividend is significantly less than the forecast. The investment banker knows y and σ^2, but has no direct means of disclosing that information to investors. However, this information influences the fee the investment banker charges the owner. The specific shape of the function is chosen to reflect the key characteristics of the expected litigation cost if that cost is imposed, i.e., if $\psi > L(d,\sigma^2)$, where L is a confidence limit which is an increasing function of d and σ^2.

In this setting, the owner's certainty equivalent is

$$CE(y,\sigma^2,z,v,\psi) = zy + (1-z)v - q - \tfrac{1}{2}rz^2\sigma^2 - \kappa_\eta(\psi,y,\sigma^2). \tag{13.35}$$

Hence, the owner's first-order conditions, given $v = v(z,\psi)$ are

$$CE_z + CE_v v_z = y - v + (1-z)v_z - rz\sigma^2 = 0, \tag{13.36a}$$

$$CE_\psi + \mathrm{CE}_v v_\psi = -\kappa_{\eta\psi} + (1-z)v_\psi = 0. \tag{13.36b}$$

Using the full-disclosure equilibrium condition $v = y$ and (13.34), provides the following two differential equations in two unknowns:

$$v_z = r\sigma^2 z/(1-z), \tag{13.37a}$$

$$v_\psi = 3k\psi^2/[y\sigma^2(1-z)]. \tag{13.37b}$$

The solution to this system of equations provides the following full-disclosure valuation function:[23]

$$v(z,\psi) = [9rk\psi^3\{\ln(1-z) + z/(1-z)\}]^{1/3}. \tag{13.38}$$

Hughes derives the following comparative statics:

(a) a higher variance σ^2 results in a higher report ψ and lower equity retention z for each y;

[23] The solution of these differential equations is relatively complex. The interested reader is referred to the appendix in Hughes (1986).

(b) an increase in the penalty parameter k results in a lower report ψ and higher equity retention for each (y,σ^2);

(c) an increase in risk aversion r results in a higher report ψ and lower equity retention z for each (y,σ^2).

These comparative statics reflect cost and substitution effects. An increase in the variance or the owner's risk aversion increases the cost of retained equity. Hence, less equity is retained and this is offset by issuing a higher report. The converse occurs if the cost parameter is increased, since this makes issuing a given report more costly.

13.7 CONCLUDING REMARKS

This is the first of three chapters (Part D) which consider the disclosure of private information by the current owners of the firm. The distinctive feature of this chapter is that there is a single risk-averse owner[24] and he seeks to share the risk of ownership with well-diversified investors in the capital market. If the owner has no other mechanism for convincingly communicating his information to investors, then he can do so by offering a contract in which the amount of risk retained increases with the value of his firm. On the other hand, if it is possible to issue verified reports, then the reports may serve as substitutes for risk retention. The substitution is complete if the reports are costless and perfect. However, the substitution is incomplete (i.e., risk retention is still used for at least some signals) if the verification is incomplete (e.g., the lack of information cannot be verified), verification is costly, or the report imperfectly reveals the owner's information.

The distinction between firm-specific and market risk is important in this setting. Most models implicitly assume the owner's risk is firm-specific, so that risk retention is costly to the owner and the investors can costlessly absorb any of the risk transferred to them. On the other hand, if the outcome has both firm-specific and market-wide risk components, then only the former affects the owner's contract choice. This is because he can "shed" any market risk by appropriately adjusting his personal investment in the market portfolio, but he cannot avoid any retained firm-specific risk.

[24] We could readily extend this analysis to consider a setting in which the current owners are risk-averse *partners*. This would be relatively straightforward if all partners have HARA utilities with identical risk cautiousness. This would involve applying the results in Chapter 4 to the setting considered here.

APPENDIX 13A: Optimal Contracts in the LP-model

In the LP-model equity retention is used to disclose the initial owner's private information and, therefore, the outcome-contingent contract is restricted to be a linear function of the terminal dividend. However, in the LP-model setting the optimal outcome-contingent full disclosure contract is not linear. Even though there is a continuum of signals in the LP-model, the optimal outcome-contingent contract can be characterized in much the same way as in the FH-model which has a finite set of signals (and outcomes).

The set of signals is $Y = Y = [\underline{y}, \bar{y}]$, with $y \in Y$ set equal to the owner's posterior mean with respect to the terminal dividend, i.e., $d|y \sim N(y,\sigma^2)$. Assume, for simplicity, that the investment is profitable for all signals ($q < \underline{y}$) such that in any full disclosure equilibrium the investment will be undertaken for all signals, i.e., $Y^* = Y$. A full disclosure equilibrium is characterized by an outcome-contingent contract parameterized by the owner's signal, i.e., $\boldsymbol{c}: \mathbb{R}\times Y \to [\underline{c},\infty]$. For a given signal $y \in Y$ we write the outcome-contingent contract as $\boldsymbol{c}(y): \mathbb{R} \to [\underline{c},\infty]$. As in the LP-model with equity retention, there are many full disclosure contracts. The optimal full disclosure contract is the one that maximizes the owner's *ex ante* expected utility (before receiving his signal). Furthermore, the outcome-contingent contract for an owner with signal y, $\boldsymbol{c}(y)$, must be such that it is acceptable to investors, and such that the owner has no incentive to "mimic" the contracts offered by owners with signals $m \neq y$. That is, the optimal full disclosure contract $\boldsymbol{c}^*$ is a solution to the following decision problem

$$U_i(\boldsymbol{c}^*) = \max_{\boldsymbol{c}} \int_Y U_i(\boldsymbol{c}(y))\, d\Phi(y),$$

$$\text{subject to} \quad U_u(y,\boldsymbol{c}(y)) \geq 0, \qquad \forall\, y \in Y,$$

$$\boldsymbol{c}(y) \in \underset{m \in Y}{\operatorname{argmax}}\, U_i(y,\boldsymbol{c}(m)), \quad \forall\, y \in Y,$$

$$\boldsymbol{c}(d,y) \geq \underline{c}, \quad \forall\, (d,y) \in \mathbb{R}\times Y.$$

In general, the full-disclosure constraint is difficult to work with (since it is a continuum of constraints for each $y \in Y$). An approach commonly used is to assume that it can be substituted with its first-order condition, i.e.,

$$U_{im}(y,\boldsymbol{c}(y)) \equiv \int_{\mathbb{R}} u_i'(\boldsymbol{c}(d,y) - q)\boldsymbol{c}_m(d,y)\, d\Phi(d|y) = 0, \quad \forall\, y \in Y,$$

where $\boldsymbol{c}_m(d,y)$ denotes the partial derivative of the contract with respect to the choice of contract $\boldsymbol{c}(m)$. In Chapter 17 we discuss when it is appropriate to substitute an incentive constraint with its first-order condition in an agency setting. Essentially, this is justified if only the "local" incentive constraints are binding, as it is the case for the FH-model with spanning. Using the first-order condition for the full-disclosure constraint, the Lagrangian (ignoring the lower bound on the contract) is

$$\mathcal{L} = U_i(\boldsymbol{c}) + \int_Y \lambda(y) U_u(y,\boldsymbol{c}(y)) + \mu(y) U_{im}(y,\boldsymbol{c}(y))\, d\Phi(y).$$

Differentiating with respect $\boldsymbol{c}(d,y)$ yields the following first-order condition[25]

$$u'(\boldsymbol{c}^*(d,y) - q) = \lambda(y) \left[1 + \mu'(y) + \mu(y) \frac{\varphi_y(d|y)}{\varphi(d|y)} \right]^{-1}, \qquad (13\text{A}.1)$$

subject to $\boldsymbol{c}^*(d,y) = \underline{c}$ if $u'(\underline{c}\text{-}q)$ is greater than the right-hand-side. Observe that this characterization is similar to the FH-setting with a finite set of signals (see Proposition 13.1). We have replaced the likelihood ratio for a finite set of parameters with the likelihood ratio for a parameter from an interval on the real line (this change in form results in a change in sign). In addition, there is a $\mu'(y)$ term, which is similar to what we find in agency models with communication of private information (see Chapter 22).

The owner's signal is scaled such that it is equal to his posterior mean with respect to the terminal dividend, i.e., $d|y \sim \text{N}(y,\sigma^2)$. Hence, the likelihood ratio is (see Appendix 2B)

$$\frac{\varphi_y(d|y)}{\varphi(d|y)} = \frac{d - y}{\sigma^2},$$

i.e., the likelihood ratio is a linear function of the terminal dividend. However, with exponential utility the optimal full-disclosure contract is a concave function of the likelihood ratio, i.e., first-order condition (13A.1) can be rewritten as

$$\boldsymbol{c}^*(d,y) = \lambda(y) \frac{1}{r} \ln\left(\frac{r}{\lambda(y)}\right) + \frac{1}{r} \ln\left(1 + \mu'(y) + \mu(y) \frac{d - y}{\sigma^2}\right) + q.$$

[25] Due to the term $\boldsymbol{c}_m(d,y)$ in the first-order condition of the full-disclosure constraint, differentiation requires the use of Fréchet derivatives.

Consequently, the optimal full-disclosure contract is a concave function of the terminal dividend ($\mu(y) > 0$) for each signal y (where $\mu(y) > 0$) in the interval of dividends where $\boldsymbol{c}^*(d,y) > \underline{c}$.

REFERENCES

Akerlof, G. (1970) "The Market for Lemons: Qualitative Uncertainty and the Market Mechanism," *Quarterly Journal of Economics* 84, 488-500.

Banks, J. and J. Sobel. (1987) "Equilibrium Selection in Signaling Games," *Econometrica* 55, 647-661.

Cho, I., and D. Kreps. (1987) "Signaling Games and Stable Equilibria," *Quarterly Journal of Economics* 102, 179-221.

Cho, I. and J. Sobel. (1990) "Strategic Stability and Uniqueness in Signaling Games," *Journal of Economic Theory* 50, 381-413.

Christensen, P. O., G. A. Feltham, and M. G. H. Wu. (2002) ""Cost of Capital" in Residual Income for Performance Evaluation," *The Accounting Review* 77, 1-23

Clarkson, P., and D. Simunic. (1994) "The Association Between Audit Quality, Retained Ownership, and Firm Specific Risk in U.S. vs. Canadian Markets," *Journal of Accounting and Economics* 17, 207-228.

Datar, S., G. Feltham, and J. Hughes. (1991) "The Role of Audits and Audit Quality in Valuing New Issues," *Journal of Accounting and Economics* 14, 2-49.

Dye, R. A. (1985) "Disclosure of Nonproprietary Information," *Journal of Accounting Research* 23, 123-145.

Feltham, G., and J. Hughes. (1988) "Communication of Private Information in Capital Markets: Contingent Contracts and Verified Reports, *Economic Analysis of Information and Contracts*, G. A. Feltham, A. H. Amershi, and W. T. Ziemba (editors). Boston: Kluwer Publishers, 271-317.

Feltham, G., J. Hughes, and D. Simunic. (1991) "Empirical Assessment of the Impact of Auditor Quality on the Valuation of New Issues," *Journal of Accounting and Economics* 14, 375-399.

Fudenberg, D., and J. Tirole. (1991) *Game Theory*, Cambridge, Massachusetts: MIT Press.

Grinblatt, M., and C. Y. Hwang. (1989) "Signaling and the Pricing of New Issues," *Journal of Finance* 44, 393-420.

Grossman, S. J., and O. D. Hart. (1983) "An Analysis of the Principal-Agent Problem," *Econometrica* 51, 7-45.

Harsanyi, J. (1967-68) "Games with Incomplete Information Played by Bayesian Players," *Management Science* 14: 159-182, 320-334, 486-502.

Hughes, P. (1986) "Signaling by Direct Disclosure Under Asymmetric Information," *Journal of Accounting and Economics* 8, 119-142.

Kohlberg, E., and J.-F. Mertens. (1986) "On the Strategic Stability of Equilibria," *Econometrica* 54, 1003-1038.

Kreps, D., and R. Wilson. (1982) "Sequential Equilibrium," *Econometrica* 50, 863-894.

Leland, H., and D. Pyle. (1977) "Informational Asymmetries, Financial Structure, and Financial Intermediation," *Journal of Finance* 32, 371-387.

Mayers, D. (1972) "Nonmarketable Assets and Capital Market Equilibrium Under Uncertainty," *Studies in the Theory of Capital Markets*, edited by M. Jensen. New York: Praeger, 223-248.

Titman, S., and B. Trueman. (1986) "Information Quality and the Valuation of New Issues," *Journal of Accounting and Economics* 8, 159-172.

Verrecchia, R. E. (1983) "Discretionary Disclosure," *Journal of Accounting and Economics* 5, 179-194.

van Damme, E. (1987) *Stability and Perfection of Nash Equilibria*, Berlin: Springer-Verlag.

CHAPTER 14

DISCLOSURE OF PRIVATE INFORMATION BY DIVERSIFIED OWNERS

Chapter 13 examines disclosure of private information by a risk-averse owner of a firm who seeks to raise capital from, and share firm-specific risks with, well-diversified investors. We now consider a firm whose shares have been previously traded so that they are owned by well-diversified investors. We assume that the firm is operated by a manager who is exogenously motivated to act in the best interests of the firm's current owners. That is, as in Chapter 8, the manager is effectively an automaton, so that there are no incentive issues. In Volume II we consider agency theory models in which management incentives (including the incentives to reveal private information) are endogenous. The models in this chapter are generally called "disclosure models."[1]

We begin in Section 14.1 with a general discussion of key elements and issues in disclosure models. We provide a brief outline of the remainder of the chapter at the end of that section.

14.1 SOME BASIC DISCLOSURE MODEL ELEMENTS AND ISSUES

Most disclosure models can be viewed as having three dates. The initial date, $t = 0$, does not play a significant role in most analyses, but it represents the *ex ante* date at which the firm is owned by well-diversified investors, and the beliefs of all players (e.g., the initial equityholders, the manager, investors, competitors, and lawyers) are homogeneous. At $t = 1$, the manager may receive private information and may take actions that are observed by other players, such as investors and competitors. The other players then take actions, e.g., acquire shares issued by the firm or enter the firm's market, based on their

---

[1] Verrecchia (2001) provides an extensive review of the disclosure literature, and Dye (2001) provides a lengthy discussion of that review. Verrecchia's review of the voluntary management disclosure literature is largely contained in his Section 3, entitled "Discretionary-based disclosure," while Dye's discussion is in his Section 4.

beliefs given the manager's observed actions. At $t = 2$, the firm's terminal value is determined and distributed to the equityholders.

There are no risk sharing issues in the models considered in this chapter since we assume there is no market risk and investors (including the initial owners) are risk neutral (i.e., well-diversified) with respect to firm-specific risk. As a result, unlike the models considered in Chapter 13, ownership retention is not a viable signal of the manager's private information. We also exclude the possibility of other costly signaling devices, and as is typical in the disclosure literature, we assume the manager chooses between either truthfully disclosing his private information or making no disclosure. The incentive to report truthfully, if he does report, is exogenous.[2] This assumption is reasonable if the manager's information consists of verifiable "facts" and the manager believes there is a positive probability that a lie will be detected (with a sufficiently high penalty for lying about the "facts"). In Section 14.5 we briefly examine what are commonly called "cheap talk" models, which relax the truthfulness assumption.

In the initial disclosure papers in the accounting literature (e.g., Verrecchia, 1983, and Dye, 1985), the players consist of the manager, the initial equityholders, and the new investors at $t = 1$. The manager is assumed to make his disclosure choice (i.e., report truthfully or say nothing) so as to maximize the market value of the firm's equity at $t = 1$. This disclosure choice does not influence the terminal value of the firm's equity and does not affect the well-being of the initial owners who do not sell their shares at $t = 1$. However, it may influence the utility of the initial owners who choose to sell some or all of their shares at $t = 1$.

Typically, disclosure papers have not provided substantive reasons why risk neutral (e.g., well-diversified) owners would want a manager to maximize the market value of the firm's equity at $t = 1$. The analyses in Chapters 5, 6, 7, and 8 demonstrate that, in a general equilibrium setting, reporting more than dividends at $t = 1$ has no value if managers do not make production decisions, investors have homogeneous beliefs and time-additive preferences, and there is a sufficiently diverse set of marketable claims to permit investors to efficiently share risks. If investors' consumption plans are implemented by selling shares in the firm at $t = 1$, it will be as part of trading in well-diversified portfolios. These portfolios are accurately priced, whether or not managers withhold, partially disclose, or fully disclose their private firm-specific information. Observe that if there are any "deadweight" costs associated with disclosure, then the initial owners will be strictly better off with no disclosure.

---

[2] This assumption was also made in the perfect *ex ante* report models discussed in Section 13.4.1.

Some subsequent disclosure papers (e.g., Darrough and Stoughton (DS), 1990, and Feltham and Xie (FX), 1992) assumed that the initial owners plan to hold their shares until $t = 2$. However, to provide an incentive for the manager to be concerned about the market price at $t = 1$, it is assumed that the manager requires capital for investment in production at $t = 1$ and the only available source of this capital is the issuance of new equity. Obviously, the terminal value of the shares held by the initial owners is influenced by the number of new shares issued to obtain the capital required at $t = 1$. Hence, if the manager seeks to maximize the expected terminal value of the initial owners' equity (which we call the *intrinsic value*), he will be motivated to take actions that maximize the market value of the shares at $t = 1$.

The incentive to maximize current market value is endogenous in models in which new equity is issued, the initial owners retain their shares, and the manager is motivated to maximize the intrinsic value of the initial equity. Nonetheless, this does not imply that the initial owners are strictly better off relative to requiring the manager to issue the new shares with no disclosure. In fact, the *ex ante* expected value of the initial equity (i.e., at $t = 0$), is independent of the manager's disclosure choices, provided there are no deadweight costs of disclosure.

In most disclosure models, the manager's private information is single dimensional, e.g., the level of market demand, which varies from low to high. We represent that signal as $y \in Y = [\underline{y}, \bar{y}]$.[3] The prior probability distribution function over the signals is denoted $\Phi(y)$ and the *ex ante* expected signal is

$$y^o = \int_{\underline{y}}^{\bar{y}} y \, d\Phi(y). \tag{14.1}$$

After observing his signal, the manager chooses a publicly reported message $m \in M(y) = \{y, n\}$, where $m = y$ is truthful disclosure of his signal and $m = n$ is no disclosure. The set of possible reports that might be received by the recipient is

$$M = \bigcup_{y \in Y} M(y) = Y \cup \{n\}.$$

If $m = y$, then the recipient knows y. However, if $m = n$, then the recipient's posterior belief depends on his conjecture as to the manager's disclosure strategy $\boldsymbol{m}$: $Y \rightarrow M$. Let Φ^n: $Y \rightarrow [0,1]$ represent the recipient's posterior signal

[3] Many of the results also apply if Y is a finite set. However, most papers assume a continuum of signals (sometimes on the set $(-\infty, +\infty)$).

belief if the manager does not disclose his private signal. If the conjectured set of undisclosed signals is non-empty, i.e., $N \equiv \{ y \in Y \mid \boldsymbol{m}(y) = n \} \neq \emptyset$, then Bayes' theorem is applied, so that

$$d\Phi(y|n) = \begin{cases} d\Phi(y)/\Phi(N) & \text{if } y \in N, \\ 0 & \text{if } y \notin N. \end{cases} \tag{14.2}$$

Of course, if the conjectured set of undisclosed signals is empty, then the recipient does not expect to observe $m = n$, and his off-equilibrium belief in a sequential equilibrium is arbitrary.

The initial disclosure papers have only one type of recipient of the manager's report, e.g., new investors. However, subsequent papers (e.g., DS, Wagenhofer, 1990, and FX) have considered two types of report recipients (e.g., new investors and competitors). The equilibrium disclosure policies are distinctly different in the two settings. If there is only one type of recipient and there are no frictions, then the only equilibrium is full disclosure (see Grossman and Hart, 1980, Grossman, 1981, and Milgrom, 1981).[4] However, there is a partial disclosure equilibrium if message verification is costly (see Verrecchia, 1983) or if there is a positive probability the manager is not informed and he cannot verify to the recipient that he has no information (see Dye, 1985). In these settings, there is a single cutoff such that the manager discloses all signals above or all signals below the cutoff. For example, if new shares are sold to investors, the manager may report high demand but not low demand, whereas the reverse may hold if no new shares are sold but the terminal value depends on the response of competitors.

The results can be dramatically different if there are two recipients, e.g., new equity is issued and there is a potential entrant into the firm's product market. For example, there can be a partial disclosure equilibrium in which the manager does not disclose either high or low demand, but discloses his demand information for intermediate values. The key here is that there is a tension with respect to the type of information the manager would like to reveal to the two recipients.

In the disclosure literature the manager is generally assumed to make disclosure decisions at $t = 1$ that are in the best interests of the initial equityholders at that point in time. We refer to this as *ex post* disclosure choice. However, as our analysis demonstrates, the optimal *ex post* choice may not be optimal from an *ex ante* perspective. The *ex ante* perspective is represented by

[4] Fishman and Hagerty (1998) and Gertner (1998) provide an intuitive discussion of this result, and then provide short, insightful discussions of the nature of a variety of voluntary disclosure equilibria and possible effects of mandatory disclosure laws.

the market value of the firm at $t = 0$, given the disclosure policy that will be implemented by the manager at $t = 1$. In some models, the *ex ante* value is not affected by the disclosure policy, so that the *ex post* choice is as good as any other policy. However, in some models the *ex ante* value is maximized if the manager is committed to no disclosures, whereas in others it is maximized if he is committed to full disclosure. In those latter cases, papers focus on *ex post* disclosure choice because it yields partial disclosure and the authors are seeking to provide an economic rationale for the fact that managers appear to sometimes disclose and at other times withhold their information. Of course, the *ex post* choice assumption is justified if the initial equityholders cannot commit the manager to the *ex ante* optimal policy. Some papers make this assumption explicit, for others it is implicit.

Section 14.2 examines disclosure models with a single recipient (either new investors or a potential entrant in the firm's product market) in which all signals can be verified. Full disclosure results if verification is costless. However, if verification is costly, then the manager withholds bad news in the new equity model and withholds good news in the potential entrant model. Section 14.3 combines these two models, and obtains a disclosure equilibrium in which the manager withholds both good and bad news, and discloses intermediate news. Section 14.4.1 considers new equity and potential entrant models in which there is a positive probability the manager is uninformed and cannot credibly report that fact. As in the costly verification case, the probability of being uninformed results in the withholding of bad news in the new equity model and the withholding of good news in the potential entrant model. The new equity model is extended in Section 14.4.2 to include a lawyer who will undertake to sue the initial equityholders on behalf of the new investors if the outcome (i.e., terminal dividend) is such that he believes there is a sufficiently high probability the manager withheld information that would have reduced the market price at $t = 1$. This leads to a disclosure equilibrium in which the manager withholds poor news, but reports both bad and good news. Section 14.4.3 considers a setting in which the manager endogenously decides whether to become informed given costly information. In our basic new equity model, there is no production choice. Section 14.4.4 modifies the new equity model to consider a setting in which the firm is sold at $t = 1$ to investors who will make an endogenous investment decision based on the information disclosed by the manager. The disclosure equilibrium is qualitatively the same as in the basic new equity model. However, the *ex ante* value is maximized by full disclosure when there is endogenous production choice, whereas the disclosure policy had no effect on the *ex ante* value when production choice is exogenous. Finally, in Section 14.5 we consider a "cheap talk" setting in which the manager is not exogenously motivated to tell the truth if he discloses. If there is a single recipient, then there is no disclosure. However, we demonstrate the existence of a partial disclosure equilibrium in the new equity/potential entrant setting. In this equilibrium, the manager reports either that he has good news or bad news, but provides no details.

14.2 VERIFIABLE DISCLOSURE TO ONE RECIPIENT

In this section we consider settings in which there is only one type of disclosure recipient. The recipient's response is $\delta \in \Delta = [\underline{\delta}, \bar{\delta}]$. The intrinsic value at $t = 1$ of the initial equity given private signal y, disclosure m, and response δ is represented by $\pi_i(y,m,\delta)$.

For simplicity, we assume the recipient's response only depends on his expectation with respect to y, i.e., there exists a response function $\boldsymbol{\delta}^*: Y \rightarrow \Delta$, where $Y = [\underline{y}, \bar{y}]$ is the set of possible posterior expectations. Hence, the response function $\boldsymbol{\delta}: M \rightarrow \Delta$ is such that $\boldsymbol{\delta}(m) = \boldsymbol{\delta}^*(y)$ if $m = y$, and $\boldsymbol{\delta}(m) = \boldsymbol{\delta}^*(y^n)$ if $m = n$, where y^n is the recipient's posterior mean given no disclosure, i.e.,

$$y^n = \int_N y \, d\Phi(y|n). \tag{14.3}$$

A disclosure equilibrium $\mathscr{E} = (\boldsymbol{m}, \boldsymbol{\delta}, \Phi(\cdot|n))$ consists of the manager's disclosure policy $\boldsymbol{m}: Y \rightarrow \{y, n\}$, the recipient's response function $\boldsymbol{\delta}: M \rightarrow \Delta$, and the recipient's posterior belief given no disclosure $\Phi(\cdot|n)$. In equilibrium, the manager must not have an incentive to deviate from his disclosure policy given the anticipated response of the recipient. In addition, the recipient's response must be optimal given his posterior belief, which must be consistent with the manager's disclosure policy if Bayes' theorem can be applied.

Definition *Disclosure Equilibrium*

Given response function $\boldsymbol{\delta}$, $\mathscr{E} = (\boldsymbol{m}, \boldsymbol{\delta}, \Phi(\cdot|n))$ is a disclosure equilibrium if

(a) $\pi_i(y,y,\boldsymbol{\delta}(y)) \geq \pi_i(y,n,\boldsymbol{\delta}(n)), \quad \forall\, y \notin N,$

$\pi_i(y,y,\boldsymbol{\delta}(y)) \leq \pi_i(y,n,\boldsymbol{\delta}(n)), \quad \forall\, y \in N,$

(b) $\Phi(\cdot|n)$ satisfies (14.2) if $N = \{ y \in Y \mid \boldsymbol{m}(y) = n \} \neq \emptyset$.

Definition *Full- and Partial-disclosure Equilibrium.*

A disclosure equilibrium is defined to be a *full-disclosure equilibrium* if the no-disclosure set N is either empty or contains a single signal. A disclosure equilibrium is defined to be a *partial-disclosure equilibrium* if the no-disclosure set N is a measurable subset of Y and is not a singleton.

We initially demonstrate that full disclosure is the only equilibrium if the manager can costlessly verify all disclosures, the intrinsic value of the initial equity is a monotonic function of the recipient's response, and the recipient's response is a monotonic function of his posterior expectation given the manager's message. We then introduce costly verification, which results in partial disclosure characterized by a single cut-off.

14.2.1 Full Disclosure with Costless Verification

Assume the intrinsic value of the initial equity $\pi_i(y,m,\delta)$ is independent of m and a strictly monotonic function of δ. Further assume $\boldsymbol{\delta}^*$ is a strictly monotonic function of $y \in Y$. After characterizing the equilibrium in settings that satisfy these conditions, we provide specific examples of settings in which the monotonicity conditions are satisfied. The assumption that π_i is independent of m implies there is no cost of issuing a verified message.

The strict monotonicity assumptions create a setting in which the manager has an ordered preference with respect to the recipient's possible responses, and his signals are ordered so that the manager would like the recipient to believe he has observed a high signal not a low signal, or vice-versa. While the manager would like to withhold or disclose either high or low signals, the rational response of the recipient is such that "unraveling" occurs. That is, as is well-known in the literature, in this setting, the only equilibrium is a full-disclosure equilibrium.

Proposition 14.1

Assume $\pi_i(y,m,\delta)$ is independent of m and a strictly monotonic function of δ, and $\boldsymbol{\delta}^*(y)$ is a strictly monotonic function of y. The only equilibrium is a full-disclosure equilibrium. The non-disclosure belief $\Phi(\cdot|n)$ is concentrated at $y = \underline{y}$ if π_i is strictly increasing (decreasing) in δ and $\boldsymbol{\delta}^*$ is strictly increasing (decreasing) in y. On the other hand, $\Phi(\cdot|n)$ is concentrated at $y = \bar{y}$ if π_i is strictly decreasing (increasing) in δ and $\boldsymbol{\delta}^*$ is strictly increasing (decreasing) in y.

Proof: Assume, to the contrary, that N is a measurable subset of Y. If π_i is an increasing function of δ and $\boldsymbol{\delta}^*$ is an increasing function of y, then the manager is motivated to disclose all signals $y \in \mathrm{N} \cap (y^n,1]$, since $\boldsymbol{\delta}^*(y) > \boldsymbol{\delta}^*(y^n)$ for those types. Hence, N contains signals which the manager prefers to disclose. On the other hand, if π_i is a decreasing function of δ and $\boldsymbol{\delta}^*$ is an increasing function of y, then the manager is motivated to disclose all signals $y \in N \cap [0,y^n)$, since $\boldsymbol{\delta}^*(y) < \boldsymbol{\delta}^*(y^n)$ for those types. Similar proofs apply to the other two cases.

Q.E.D.

To illustrate the preceding discussion we consider a "new equity model" in which the recipient represents diversified investors in the capital market, and a "potential entrant model" in which the recipient is a competitor who may enter the firm's product market.

New Equity Model

In this model, the manager seeks to maximize the intrinsic value of the initial equity in a setting in which he issues new equity to investors in return for q units of capital. The signal y represents the firm's expected terminal value, and we assume $q < \underline{y}$, so that the investment is profitable for all signals. The manager issues a prospectus containing the message m and offers the fraction β of the firm's equity in return for the q units of capital, implying the firm has an *ex* investment market value of $v = q/\beta$.[5] The investors can accept or reject the offer. The manager anticipates the investors' beliefs given his message and we simplify the investors' response by letting δ represent the maximum price they will accept. Hence, the manager must issue a fraction $\beta = q/\delta$ of the firm's equity in order to obtain q units of capital. Therefore,

$$\pi_i(y,m,\delta) = y(1 - q/\delta). \qquad (14.4a)$$

The maximum price acceptable to the investors equals their posterior mean, i.e., $\delta^*(y) = y$. As a result, π_i is strictly increasing in δ and $\delta^*(y) = y$ is strictly increasing in y. The manager would like to disclose good news to investors, and withhold bad news. However, withholding information is not an equilibrium. The only equilibrium is a full-disclosure equilibrium with $\Phi(\cdot|n)$ concentrated at $y = \underline{y}$, i.e., the investors threaten to reject all offers of less than the fraction $q/\underline{y}$ if there is no disclosure.

Observe that the intrinsic value at $t = 1$ is

$$\pi_i(y,\boldsymbol{m}(y),\delta(\boldsymbol{m}(y))) = y - q. \qquad (14.4b)$$

Consequently, the *ex ante* full-disclosure equilibrium value of the initial equity is

$$v_0^* = y^o - q. \qquad (14.5a)$$

If the initial equityholders could require the manager to not disclose his private information (and this is known to the recipients), then new investors would require the fraction q/y^o of the firm's equity. The firm would be undervalued

---

[5] Note that β is the number of new shares issued divided by the total number of shares after the issue.

at $t = 1$ if $y > y^o$ and overvalued if $y < y^o$. However, the *ex ante* value would be unchanged, i.e.,

$$v_0^o = y^o(1 - q/y^o) = y^o - q. \tag{14.5b}$$

Hence, disclosure has no impact on the initial equityholders.

Potential Entrant Model

Now consider a setting in which the manager does not require any capital from investors, but is concerned about the entry of a competitor into his product market. The private signal y equals the firm's expected terminal value if the competitor does not enter, and α represents the fraction of the expected value that is lost if entry occurs, i.e., $(1-\alpha)y < y$ is the expected value of the firm if the competitor enters. Let αy be the gross value to the competitor of entering the firm's product market and let κ be the cost of entering that market. The competitor knows his cost κ when he makes his entry decision, but it is not known to the manager of the incumbent firm. Observe that entry occurs if the competitor's expected value of y is greater than his breakeven level $\gamma \equiv \kappa/\alpha$. Assume the incumbent manager's prior belief about the competitor's breakeven level is represented by the probability distribution function $G(\gamma)$, and (unless stated otherwise) it is strictly increasing for $\gamma \in [\underline{y}, \bar{y}]$ and independent of y.

The competitor's response δ is represented by the probability he will enter, i.e., $\boldsymbol{\delta}^*(y) = G(y)$ if y is the competitor's posterior expectation. Hence, $\boldsymbol{\delta}^*(y)$ is strictly increasing in y. The intrinsic value of the initial equity is

$$\pi_i(y,m,\delta) = [1 - \alpha\delta]y. \tag{14.6a}$$

Hence, π_i is strictly decreasing in δ. This implies the manager would like to disclose bad news to the competitor, and withhold good news. However, withholding information is not an equilibrium. The only equilibrium is a full-disclosure equilibrium with $\Phi(\cdot|n)$ concentrated at $y = \bar{y}$, i.e., the competitor threatens to enter with probability $G(\bar{y})$ if there is no disclosure.

Observe that given full disclosure, the intrinsic value of the initial equity is

$$\pi_i(y,\boldsymbol{m}(y),\boldsymbol{\delta}(\boldsymbol{m}(y))) = [1 - \alpha G(y)]y. \tag{14.6b}$$

Consequently, the *ex ante* full-disclosure equilibrium value of the incumbent firm is

$$v_0^* = y^o - \alpha \int_{\underline{y}}^{\bar{y}} G(y)\, y\, d\Phi(y). \tag{14.7a}$$

If the initial equityholders could require the manager not to disclose his private information (and could convey this to the competitor), then the *ex ante* value of the incumbent firm is

$$v_0^o = [1 - \alpha\, G(y^o)]y^o. \tag{14.7b}$$

Hence, in this setting, the *ex ante* value of the initial equity may differ between full and no disclosure.

Observe that if $G(y)y$ is a strictly convex function of y (e.g., $G(\gamma)$ is a uniform distribution on $[\underline{y}, \bar{y}]$), then Jensen's inequality implies

$$v_0^* < y^o - \alpha G(y^o)y^o = v_0^o.$$

Hence, in that setting, the initial equityholders are better off if they can require the manager not to disclose his private information, as opposed to making disclosure decisions at $t = 1$ in which he tries to maximize the intrinsic value of the initial equity.[6]

To illustrate the above comments, assume both y and γ are uniformly distributed on $[\underline{y}, \bar{y}]$. In that setting, $y^o = ½[\underline{y} + \bar{y}]$,

$$v_0^* = \left[1 - \frac{1}{3}\alpha\left(1 + \frac{\bar{y}}{\bar{y} + \underline{y}}\right)\right]y^o, \tag{14.8a}$$

$$v_0^o = [1 - ½\alpha]y^o. \tag{14.8b}$$

These two expressions imply $v_0^* < v_0^o$. The reason for this result is that the loss due to entry is larger for higher values of y than for lower values of y and, if there is full disclosure, the probability of entry is larger for higher values of y. No disclosure reduces the probability of entry for high values of y and increases the probability of entry for low values of y. Hence, no disclosure is strictly preferred. Of course, if γ is uniformly distributed on $[\underline{y}, \bar{y}]$ and the cost of entry is fixed, i.e., the value of the firm is $y - \alpha$ if entry occurs and y if it does not, then the *ex ante* value of the initial equity is the same with full and no disclosure.[7]

---

[6] If the probability of entry $G(y)$ is a sufficiently concave function such that the expected loss from entry $G(y)y$ is concave, the opposite result holds. In this case, the reduction in the probability of entry for high values of y is not sufficient to cover the loss from increased probability of entry for low values of y.

[7] With no disclosure, $v_0^o = y^o - \alpha G(y^o)$, whereas with full disclosure, $v_0^* = y^o - \alpha \mathrm{E}[G(y)]$, and $v_0^o = v_0^*$ if $G(\gamma)$ is uniformly distributed on $[\underline{y}, \bar{y}]$. Of course, with other distributions, either full or no disclosure can be preferred. For example, if G is concentrated at $\gamma^o < (>)\ y^o$, then full (no) disclosure is preferred.

The economics and accounting literature contain a number of papers that examine disclosure choice in product markets characterized as duopolies or oligopolies. In these models, the firms compete for a share of the market by simultaneously choosing either production quantities (Cournot competition) or selling prices (Bertrand competition). We consider the results from some of those papers in Chapter 15. Interestingly, the nature of the competition (Cournot versus Bertrand) and the nature of the private information (firm-specific versus industry-wide events) affect whether full disclosure dominates no disclosure, or the converse holds. The simple potential entrant model used in this chapter provides results similar to the product market competition models in which no disclosure dominates, and provides results that are opposite to product market competition models in which full disclosure dominates.

14.2.2 Partial Disclosure with Costly Verification

The fact that, empirically, managers do not fully disclose their information led accounting researchers to seek to identify factors that would induce partial disclosure. The initial work in the accounting literature was a paper by Verrecchia (1983),[8] in which the firm is assumed to bear an exogenous cost k if a disclosure is made. The most straightforward interpretation of this cost is that it represents the cost of verifying and transmitting the manager's message. Of course, such costs are not likely to be large, but one can also interpret this work as a preliminary step in introducing endogenous disclosure costs that stem from the actions of others, such as competitors.

New Equity Model

Verrecchia exogenously assumes the manager seeks to maximize the market value of the firm at $t = 1$. We modify his analysis by introducing the disclosure cost k into the setting in which the manager seeks to maximize the intrinsic value of the initial equity, and must obtain q units of capital by issuing new equity to investors. As before, δ represents the maximum price the investors assign to the firm's equity at $t = 1$. Hence,

$$\pi_i(y,m,\delta(m)) = \begin{cases} y - q - k & \text{if } m = y, \\ y(1 - q/y^n) & \text{if } m = n. \end{cases} \tag{14.9}$$

Observe that the introduction of the cost k implies that there are a set of signals which the manager will not disclose. Even if investors are pessimistic (i.e., they

---

[8] A disclosure cost paper by Jovanovic (1982) appeared in the economics literature slightly earlier.

set the price equal to $\underline{y}$ if there is no disclosure), the manager would prefer to accept that low price for the new shares instead of spending k to reveal $y \le \underline{y}(1 + k/q)$. Hence, the pessimistic posterior belief given no disclosure, $y^n = \underline{y}$, is inconsistent with signals $y \in [\underline{y}, \underline{y}(1 + k/q)]$ not being disclosed. In fact, since an equilibrium price will reflect the set of signals for which the manager chooses non-disclosure, there exists a cutoff $y^\dagger$ greater than $\underline{y}(1 + k/q)$ such that managers with signals $y \in [\underline{y}, y^\dagger]$ do not disclose.

The intrinsic value of the initial equity from disclosure and non-disclosure are depicted in Figure 14.1 for a setting in which y is uniformly distributed. The no-disclosure region is characterized by a cutoff $y^\dagger$ such that $y(1 - q/y^n) \ge y - q - k$ if, and only if, $y \in [\underline{y}, y^\dagger]$. Furthermore, the no-disclosure price y^n is consistent with the cutoff $y^\dagger$, i.e., in this example, $y^n = ½[\underline{y} + y^\dagger]$.

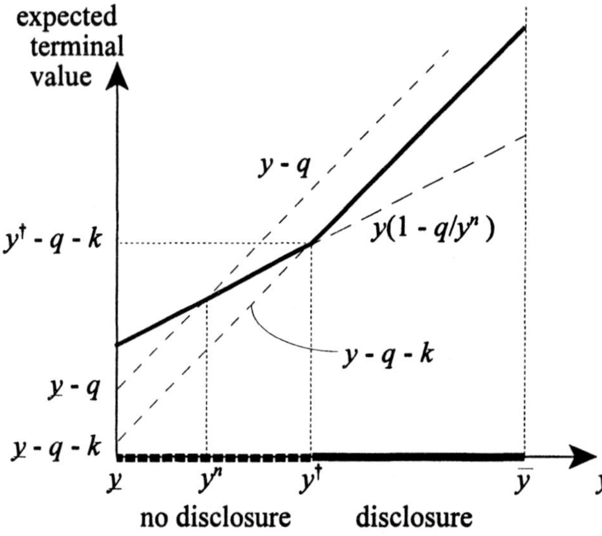

Figure 14.1: Partial disclosure in the new equity model with exogenous disclosure cost.

The firm's shares are overpriced if $y \in [\underline{y}, y^n)$ and underpriced if $y \in (y^n, y^\dagger]$. The manager withholds his information in the latter case, because the under-pricing is less than the disclosure cost k. And the investors are willing to accept the stock price y^n because, in expectation, the shares are fairly priced. If the disclosure cost is zero, then $y^\dagger = \underline{y}$, i.e., there is full disclosure. On the other hand, if k is sufficiently large, then $y^\dagger = \bar{y}$, i.e., there is no disclosure. The following proposition formalizes the above remarks.

Proposition 14.2

In the new equity model with disclosure cost $k \in (0, q(\bar{y}/y^o-1))$, the disclosure strategy $\boldsymbol{m}$ is an equilibrium if, and only if,

$$\boldsymbol{m}(y) = \begin{cases} y & \text{if } y \in (y^\dagger, \bar{y}], \\ n & \text{if } y \in [\underline{y}, y^\dagger], \end{cases} \qquad (14.10a)$$

$$y^\dagger = y^n(1 + k/q), \qquad (14.10b)$$

$$y^n = \frac{1}{\Phi(y^\dagger)} \int_{\underline{y}}^{y^\dagger} y \, d\Phi(y). \qquad (14.10c)$$

The *ex ante* value of the initial equity, given disclosure cost k, is

$$v_0^\dagger = y^o - q - (1 - \Phi(y^\dagger))k, \qquad (14.11)$$

where $1 - \Phi(y^\dagger)$ is the probability the manager will receive a signal which he is motivated to disclose. From (14.5b) and (14.11) it is obvious that $v_0^o > v_0^\dagger$, so that, if possible, it would be optimal for the owners to require the manager not to disclose any private information (provided this requirement can be made known to investors).[9] On average, the new shares are properly priced if there is no disclosure, and no disclosure avoids disclosure costs. That is, the manager's *ex post* incentive to incur deadweight disclosure costs so as to disclose good news and thereby reduce the "cost" of acquiring new equity capital, is not *ex ante* optimal.

If y is uniformly distributed on $[\underline{y}, \bar{y}]$, then $y^o = \frac{1}{2}(\underline{y} + \bar{y})$ and $y^n = \frac{1}{2}(\underline{y} + y^\dagger)$. Substituting the latter into (14.10b) implies

$$y^\dagger = \min \left\{ \underline{y} \frac{q + k}{q - k}, \bar{y} \right\}. \qquad (14.12)$$

There is partial disclosure if $k \in (0, q(\bar{y} - \underline{y})/(\bar{y} + \underline{y}))$. Furthermore, if there is partial disclosure, (14.12) implies that the no-disclosure set is increasing in the cost of disclosure k, but decreasing in the amount of capital q that is required. The latter effect follows from the fact that underpricing is more costly if more capital must be obtained.

---

[9] Verrecchia (1990) makes this point.

Verrecchia (1990) extends the analysis in Verrecchia (1983) to examine the impact of information quality on disclosure. The outcome x is assumed to be normally distributed and the signal equals x plus noise. We can reformulate this model so that $x = y + \varepsilon$, where y and ε are independently normally distributed random variables with variances σ_y^2 and σ_ε^2, respectively. An increase in information quality can then be represented as increasing σ_y^2 while $\sigma_x^2 = \sigma_y^2 + \sigma_\varepsilon^2$ is held constant. Verrecchia's Corollaries 1 and 3 can be interpreted as implying that both the cutoff $y^\dagger$ and the probability of no disclosure $\Phi(y^\dagger)$ decrease as σ_y^2 increases (and σ_ε^2 decreases). Furthermore, Verrecchia's Corollary 5 implies that, *ex ante*, the initial equityholders prefer that the manager receive no information, i.e., $\sigma_y^2 = 0$. Of course, the latter is equivalent to committing the manager to not disclose any information he receives.

Potential Entrant Model

Similar, but reverse, results occur if we introduce disclosure cost k into the potential entrant model. In this setting,

$$\pi_i(y,m,\delta(m)) = \begin{cases} [1 - \alpha G(y)]y - k & \text{if } m = y, \\ [1 - \alpha G(y^n)]y & \text{if } m = n. \end{cases} \tag{14.13}$$

From the manager's perspective, the worst case for no disclosure is that the competitor will believe the manager has observed $\bar{y}$. However, even in that setting, the manager would prefer the higher probability of entry rather than expend k to disclose his information if $\alpha[G(\bar{y}) - G(y)]y \leq k$. Since the competitor's probability of entry will be based on $y^n < \bar{y}$, it follows that there will be a non-disclosure set $[y^\dagger, \bar{y}]$, with a cutoff $y^\dagger < \bar{y}$.[10] This equilibrium is depicted in Figure 14.2 for a setting in which y and γ are both uniformly distributed on $[\underline{y}, \bar{y}]$.

[10] Note that if $m = n$ is preferred to $m = y$ for some signal y, i.e., $[1 - \alpha G(y^n)]y > [1 - \alpha G(y)]y - k$, then no disclosure is also preferred for all higher signals $y' > y$ (since $G(\cdot)$ is increasing). Hence, there is a single "upper-tail" no-disclosure set $[y^\dagger, \bar{y}]$ (implying that $y^n > y^o$).

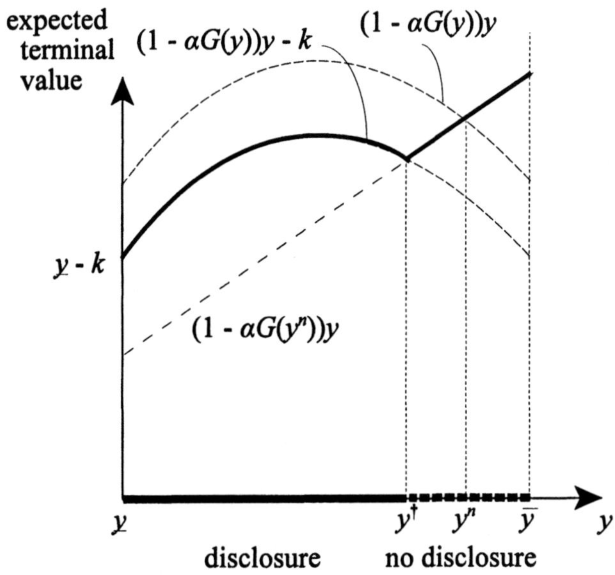

Figure 14.2: Partial disclosure in the potential entrant model with exogenous disclosure cost.

The following proposition formalizes the preceding comments.

Proposition 14.3

In the potential entrant model with disclosure cost $k \in (0, \alpha[G(y^o) - G(\underline{y})]\underline{y})$, disclosure strategy $\boldsymbol{m}$ is an equilibrium if, and only if,

$$\boldsymbol{m}(y) = \begin{cases} y & \text{if } y \in [\underline{y}, y^\dagger], \\ n & \text{if } y \in (y^\dagger, \bar{y}\,], \end{cases} \tag{14.14a}$$

$$\alpha[G(y^n) - G(y^\dagger)]y^\dagger = k, \tag{14.14b}$$

$$y^n = \frac{1}{1 - \Phi(y^\dagger)} \int_{y^\dagger}^{\bar{y}} y \, d\Phi(y). \tag{14.14c}$$

Again, there is full disclosure if the disclosure cost is zero (i.e., $k = 0 \Rightarrow y^\dagger = \bar{y}$), and there is no disclosure if the disclosure cost is too high (i.e., $k \geq$

$\alpha[G(y^o) - G(\underline{y})]\underline{y} \Rightarrow y^\dagger = \underline{y}$). The *ex ante* value of the initial equity given disclosure cost k is

$$v_0^\dagger = y^o - \alpha\left[\int_{\underline{y}}^{y^\dagger} G(y)y\, d\Phi(y) + G(y^n)y^n(1-\Phi(y^\dagger))\right] - k\Phi(y^\dagger). \qquad (14.15)$$

If $G(y)y$ is a strictly convex function of y (e.g., G is a uniform distribution) and $y^\dagger \in (\underline{y}, \bar{y})$, then Jensen's inequality implies

$$v_0^\dagger < y^o - \alpha G(y^o)y^o - k\Phi(y^\dagger) < v_0^o,$$

where v_0^o is the *ex ante* market value of the initial equity given the manager does not disclose any of his information (see (14.7b)). In this setting there are two benefits to no disclosure. First, as in the costless verification setting, the loss due to potential entry is less due to reduced probabilities of entry for higher values of y. Second, the deadweight costs of disclosure verification are avoided.

If y and γ are uniformly distributed on $[\underline{y}, \bar{y}]$, then (14.14c) implies $y^n = ½[y^\dagger + \bar{y}]$ and substituting this expression into (14.14b) and solving for $y^\dagger$ yields

$$y^\dagger = ½\left[\bar{y} + \sqrt{\bar{y}^2 - 8(\bar{y} - \underline{y})k/\alpha}\right], \qquad k \in (0, \alpha\underline{y}/2).$$

Hence, the cutoff $y^\dagger$ (i.e., the lower bound of the non-disclosure set) is decreasing with respect to the disclosure cost k and increasing with respect to the fraction of the firm's value α lost due to entry.

14.3 VERIFIABLE DISCLOSURE TO TWO RECIPIENTS

We now consider the disclosure equilibrium in a setting in which the value of the initial equity depends on the actions of two recipients for which the manager has conflicting disclosure incentives. In Section 14.3.1 we illustrate this setting by combining the new equity and potential entrant models examined above (but with no direct disclosure cost, i.e., $k = 0$). This is an adaptation of the model in Feltham and Xie (1992) (FX),[11] which extends the initial two-recipient model by Darrough and Stoughton (1990). In Section 14.3.2 we briefly describe some other two-recipient models.

---

[11] FX allow the cost of entry to have both a variable and a fixed component, whereas we restrict our analysis to the variable cost setting. Wagenhofer (1990) has a similar model but assumes the manager seeks to maximize the market value of the firm at $t = 1$.

14.3.1 New Equity/Potential Entrant Model

We refer to high values of y as good news and low values as bad news. The manager would like to disclose good news to investors and withhold bad news. However, disclosing good news to a potential entrant is costly, and disclosing bad news is beneficial. We assume all disclosures are public, so the disclosure choice is the same for both recipients. Hence, one recipient can be viewed as creating endogenous disclosure costs with respect to the other.

The manager again requires q units of equity capital from investors and loses a fraction α of the firm's value if competitor entry occurs. We let δ_p represent the maximum market price of equity that is acceptable to the investors and let δ_e represent the probability of entry by the competitor. The probability of entry is $G(y)$ if y is disclosed and $G(y^n)$ if y is not disclosed, where y^n is the expected value of y given no disclosure (see (14.3)).

The investors hold the same beliefs as the potential entrant, and rationally anticipate the potential entrant's response to the manager's disclosure decision. Consequently, the maximum *ex*-investment market value of the firm at $t = 1$ is

$$\delta_p(m) = \begin{cases} [1 - \alpha\delta_e(y)]y, & \text{if } m = y, \\ [1 - \alpha\delta_e(n)]y^n, & \text{if } m = n. \end{cases}$$

The manager must issue a fraction q/δ_p of the firm's equity in order to obtain q units of capital. Consequently, the intrinsic value of the initial equity at $t = 1$ is

$$\pi_i(y,m,\delta_e,\delta_p) = [1 - \alpha\delta_e][1 - q/\delta_p]y.$$

In this setting, the manager's message m does not directly affect the intrinsic value, but it does affect the responses of the two recipients. More specifically,

$$\pi_i^{\dagger}(y,m) \equiv \pi_i(y,m,\delta_e(m),\delta_p(m))$$

$$= \begin{cases} [1 - \alpha G(y)]y - q, & \text{if } m = y, \\ \left(1 - \alpha G(y^n) - \dfrac{q}{y^n}\right)y, & \text{if } m = n. \end{cases} \tag{14.16}$$

To illustrate the equilibria in this setting, we again assume the manager's signal y and the entrant's breakeven level γ are uniformly distributed on $[\underline{y}, \bar{y}]$. Observe that the intrinsic value of the initial equity given no disclosure, i.e., $\pi_i^{\dagger}(y,n)$, is an increasing linear function of y. On the other hand, the intrinsic value given disclosure, i.e., $\pi_i^\dagger(y,y) = [1 - \alpha G(y)]y - q$, is a concave function of y. In Figure 14.3 the two functions are such that, in equilibrium, they intersect twice. In the middle, disclosure dominates no disclosure, but no disclosure dominates in the two tails. In the bottom tail, denoted $N_1 = [\underline{y}, y_1^\dagger]$, the manager would like to disclose this bad news to the potential entrant (so as to reduce the probability of entry), but this would have a very negative effect on the market price at which new equity is issued to investors. On the other hand, in the upper tail, denoted $N_2 = [y_2^\dagger, \bar{y}]$, the manager would like to disclose this good news to investors (so as to obtain a higher price for the new equity that is issued), but this would have a negative effect on the intrinsic value due to a high probability of entry by the potential competitor.

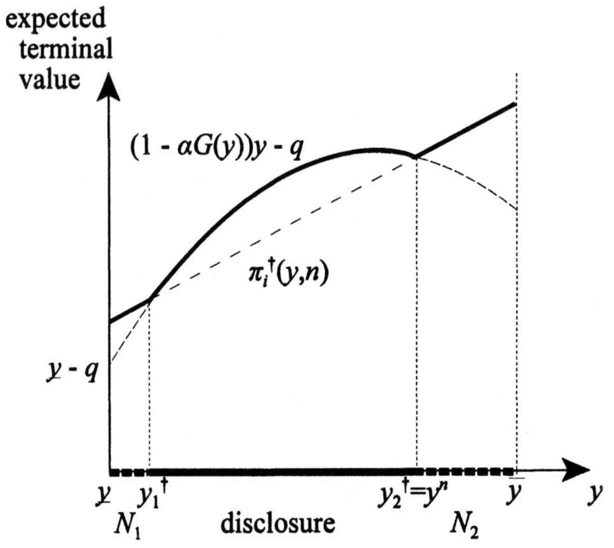

Figure 14.3: Partial disclosure in the new equity/ potential entrant model.

Proposition 14.3 (FX, Prop. 4.1)

In the new equity/potential entrant model, with y and γ uniformly distributed on $[\underline{y}, \bar{y}]$, any partial disclosure equilibrium is characterized by two no-disclosure sets $N_1 = [\underline{y}, y_1^\dagger]$ and $N_2 = [y_2^\dagger, \bar{y}]$, with either $y_1^\dagger$ or $y_2^\dagger$ equal to y^n. Furthermore, there is always a full-disclosure equilibrium whereas, generically, there is never a no-disclosure equilibrium.

In a partial disclosure equilibrium, there must be two disjoint sets of signals that are not disclosed. To prove this result, first observe that the linearity of

$\pi_i^\dagger(y,n)$ and the concavity of $\pi_i^\dagger(y,y)$ imply they cannot intersect more than twice. If they do not intersect, there is either a full-disclosure or a no-disclosure equilibrium. Assume they intersect once and no disclosure dominates for $y \in [y^\dagger, \bar{y}]$. This implies $y^n = \frac{1}{2}[y^\dagger + \bar{y}]$. To prove this cannot be an equilibrium, observe that $\pi_i^\dagger(y,n) = \pi_i^\dagger(y,y)$ if $y = y^n$, which can only occur if $y^\dagger = \bar{y}$, and this is not a partial disclosure equilibrium. A similar argument implies that there cannot be a partial disclosure equilibrium in which no disclosure dominates for $y \in [\underline{y}, y^\dagger]$. Since the no-disclosure intrinsic value must be equal to the intrinsic value with disclosure for $y = y^n$, the no-disclosure posterior mean must be either $y_1^\dagger$ or $y_2^\dagger$.

While a partial equilibrium may exist, as in the example depicted in Figure 14.3, there will always exist a full-disclosure equilibrium as well. For this to occur, the investors' and competitor's off-equilibrium belief given no disclosure, y^n, must be such that $\pi_i^\dagger(y,n) \le \pi_i^\dagger(y,y)$ for all $y \in [\underline{y}, \bar{y}]$. Let $\zeta(y) \equiv 1 - \alpha G(y) - q/y$ represent the fraction of the intrinsic value retained by the initial equityholders, so that $\pi_i^\dagger(y,y) - \pi_i^\dagger(y,n) = (\zeta(y) - \zeta(y^n))y$. Note that $\zeta(y)$ is a concave function of y and, thus, it is minimized at either $\underline{y}$ or $\bar{y}$. Hence, a full-disclosure equilibrium is sustained by a no-disclosure threat that either investors will assign the lowest possible price to the new equity, i.e., $y^n = \underline{y}$, or the competitor will enter with probability one, i.e., $y^n = \bar{y}$.

Since $\pi_i(y,n,G(y^o),y^o) = \pi_i^\dagger(y,y)$ if $y = y^o$, it follows that no disclosure can only be an equilibrium if $\pi_i(y,n,G(y^o),y^o)$ is tangent to $\pi_i^\dagger(y,y)$ at $y = y^o$. However, $\partial\pi_i(y,n,G(y^o),y^o)/\partial y = 1 - \alpha G(y^o) - q/y^o$ does not equal $\partial\pi_i^\dagger(y,y)/\partial y = 1 - \alpha G(y) - \alpha G'(y)y$ at $y = y^o$ unless $q = \alpha G'(y^o)(y^o)^2$, which is a knife-edge case. Hence, generically, there is never a no-disclosure equilibrium in this setting.

The *ex ante* value of the initial equity given the manager's *ex post* disclosure choice under a partial disclosure equilibrium is

$$v_0^\dagger = y^o - \int_{y_1^\dagger}^{y_2^\dagger} \alpha G(y)y\,d\Phi(y) - \alpha G(y^n)y^n[1 + \Phi(y_1^\dagger) - \Phi(y_2^\dagger)] - q. \qquad (14.17a)$$

On the other hand, under a full-disclosure equilibrium, the *ex ante* value is

$$v_0^* = y^o - \int_{\underline{y}}^{\bar{y}} \alpha G(y)y\,d\Phi(y) - q. \qquad (14.17b)$$

If the initial owners could preclude the manager from disclosing his information, then the *ex ante* value of the initial equity is

$$v_0^o = y^o - \alpha G(y^o)y^o - q. \qquad (14.17c)$$

Hence, the expected cost of obtaining new equity is again equal to q under all disclosure policies, so that the economic effect of the different disclosure policies depends on the impact on the cost of competitor entry. If $G(y)y$ is a strictly convex function of y and $\underline{y} < y_1^\dagger < y_2^\dagger < \bar{y}$, then applying Jensen's inequality to (14.17a) and (14.17b) establishes that

$$v_0^\dagger < y^o - \alpha G(y^o)y^o - q = v_0^o,$$

$$v_0^* < y^o - \alpha G(y^o)y^o - q = v_0^o.$$

Therefore, the initial equityholders strictly prefer no disclosure to both endogenous *ex post* disclosure choice (which leads to partial disclosure) and commitment to full disclosure.

14.3.2 Other Two-recipient Models

In the simple two-recipient model examined above, there are two disjoint no-disclosure sets, with disclosure of intermediate signals. The existence of disjoint no-disclosure sets or disjoint disclosure sets is a common feature in two-recipient models.

Potential Entrant Model with Common Knowledge of the Breakeven Level

FX consider a broader set of new equity/potential entrant models. In particular, they consider both fixed and variable costs of entry, and they consider settings in which the competitor's breakeven level γ is common knowledge. We do not provide a detailed analysis of these models, but it is instructive to briefly consider the potential entrant model in which the competitor's breakeven level is common knowledge, i.e., $G(\gamma) = 0 \ \forall \ \gamma < \gamma^o$ and $G(\gamma) = 1 \ \forall \ \gamma \geq \gamma^o$. In this setting, FX demonstrate that a partial disclosure equilibrium can exist in which there are three cutoffs, $y_1^\dagger < y_2^\dagger = \gamma^o < y_3^\dagger$, such that there are:[12]

(a) two disjoint no-disclosure sets, $N_1 = [\underline{y}, y_1^\dagger]$ and $N_2 = [y_2^\dagger, y_3^\dagger]$;

(b) two disjoint disclosure sets, $D_1 = (y_1^\dagger, y_2^\dagger)$ and $D_2 = (y_3^\dagger, \bar{y}]$;

(c) y^n equals either $y_2^\dagger$ or $y_3^\dagger$;

---

[12] A similar result is provided by Wagenhofer (1990) for a setting in which the manager is exogenously assumed to maximize the market value of the equity at $t = 1$ (there is no issue of new equity), the loss in value if the competitor enters the firm's product market is independent of y, and the entry threshold γ^o is common knowledge.

(d) the competitor plays a mixed strategy, entering with probability g^n if $m = n$.

This type of equilibrium is depicted in Figure 14.4. Observe that the manager does not disclose "bad" information (N_1) because the cost of increasing the probability of competitor entry from zero to g^n is offset by a lower cost of capital due to over-pricing by investors. He also does not disclose "better" information (N_2) because of the benefit of reducing the probability of competitor entry from one to g^n (the new equity is underpriced but the cost of capital would be even greater if he disclosed y due to the increased probability of entry). On the other hand, he discloses "poor" information (D_1) so as to avoid underpricing, even though the probability of competitor entry increases from zero to g^n. Finally, he discloses "good" information (D_2) in order to avoid underpricing, which provides more benefit than the cost of increasing the probability of competitor entry from g^n to one.

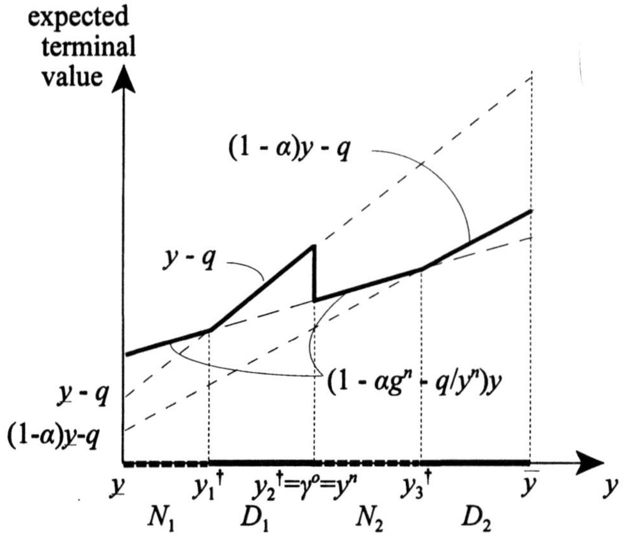

Figure 14.4: Partial disclosure in the new equity/ common knowledge-potential entrant model.

Investor Litigation

Trueman (1997) points out that no disclosure will result in a law suit if the realized outcome is such that the expected return from the law suit is sufficient to cover the costs of undertaking it. This threat will deter a manager from withholding bad news. In Trueman's model, this leads to a partial disclosure equilibrium characterized by two cutoffs, $y_1^\dagger < y_2^\dagger$, such that there is disclosure of bad and good news, i.e., if $y \in [\underline{y}, y_1^\dagger] \cup [y_2^\dagger, \bar{y}]$, and no disclosure of intermediate values, i.e., if $y \in (y_1^\dagger, y_2^\dagger)$. Hence, the results are effectively the opposite of the partial disclosure equilibrium in the new equity/potential entrant model depicted in Figure 14.3. We defer more detailed comments on Trueman's model until the next section because he assumes there is a positive probability the manager will not be informed.

Diverse Interpretation of Disclosed Information

Dutta and Trueman (DT) (2002) examine a model in which the manager has two types of information. One type can be credibly disclosed, whereas the other type cannot. Furthermore, the value implications of the former depend on the latter. For example, the first could be the firm's inventory level, whereas the second indicates whether that level is attributable to variations in past demand or variations in anticipated future demand. A high level of inventory is bad news if due to lower than expected past demand, whereas it is good news if due to an anticipated increase in future demand.

An analyst issues a forecast at $t = 0$ based on imperfect information about the manager' information and then issues a second forecast at $t = 1$, after observing the manager's disclosure (e.g., the inventory level, if reported). The manager wants to report high inventories and withhold a report of low inventories, if the manager believes the analyst will attribute the inventory level to the manager's demand forecast. On the other hand, the reverse holds if the manager believes the analyst will attributed the inventory level to an unanticipated variation in past demand. Hence, while there is a single recipient (the analyst), the recipient has two types (depending on his initial imperfect information about the source of variations in the inventory level) and the manager does not know the analyst's type. Hence, there is a tension similar to a two-recipient model and DT obtain disjoint disclosure sets.

14.4 POSITIVE PROBABILITY THE MANAGER IS UNINFORMED

Verrecchia (1983) obtained a partial disclosure equilibrium by introducing verification costs. This was followed by Dye (1985),[13] who obtained a partial disclosure equilibrium by assuming there is positive probability that the manager received no private signal and he cannot issue a credible report to

[13] Jung and Kwon (1988) extend the Dye analysis and correct a technical error in one of Dye's proofs. Dye (1998) further extends the model to include some investors who know whether the manager is informed or not.

reveal that fact. Obviously, if the manager could issue a verified statement that he has no information, then the model would be the same as in Section 14.2.1, with a positive probability that the manager has received "signal" y^o (the prior belief given no signal).

14.4.1 Single Recipient Models

In the basic model, $\Phi(y)$ represents the prior belief that the manager will receive signal $y \in [\underline{y}, \bar{y}]$ if he is informed and y^o represents his null signal if uninformed. Hence, the set of possible signals is $Y = [\underline{y}, \bar{y}] \cup \{y^o\}$. The probability the manager is uninformed is λ. The signal y again represents the expected terminal value of the firm (if there is no competitor) given signal y, and

$$y^o = \int_{\underline{y}}^{\bar{y}} y \, d\Phi(y).$$

The manager has no choice if he is uninformed (i.e., he receives the null signal) – he must send a message $\boldsymbol{m}(y^o) = n$. However, if he receives a signal $y \in [\underline{y}, \bar{y}]$ he chooses between issuing a truthful report (at zero cost) or not reporting, i.e., $\boldsymbol{m}(y) \in \{y, n\}$. The set of unreported signals is again denoted

$$N = \{\, y \in [\underline{y}, \bar{y}] \mid \boldsymbol{m}(y) = n \,\}.$$

The recipient's posterior mean given $m = n$ is

$$y^n = \frac{\lambda y^o + (1-\lambda)\int_N y \, d\Phi(y)}{\lambda + (1-\lambda)\,\Phi(N)}, \tag{14.18}$$

which is a weighted average of the posterior belief given that the manager is uninformed and the posterior belief given that he is informed but $y \in N$.

New Equity Model

Now consider the implications of a positive probability of being uninformed in the new equity model introduced in Section 14.2.1. Observe that if investors believe the manager will fully disclose his signals, then they will assign a price of y^o to the new equity if they observe $m = n$. However, if the manager anticipates that price, he will report $m = n$ for all $y \le y^o$. This would then lead to a price equal to y^n based on $N = [\underline{y}, y^o]$. However, this price is less than y^o and the manager would prefer to report $m = y$ for $y > y^n$. To achieve an equilibrium, we must find a no-disclosure set N such that $y \le y^n$ for all $y \in N$ and $y > y^n$ for all y

$\notin N$. It is obvious that, in this setting, the no-disclosure set is characterized by a cutoff $y^\dagger$ such that $N = [\underline{y}, y^\dagger]$. The following result and proof are found in Jung and Kwon (JK) (1988), but are very similar to Dye's Theorem 1.

Proposition 14.4 (JK, Prop. 1)

In the new equity model, with a positive probability the manager is uninformed, there exists a partial disclosure equilibrium characterized by a cutoff $y^\dagger = y^n \in (\underline{y}, y^o)$, with $N = [\underline{y}, y^\dagger]$.

Proof: The preceding discussion establishes that the partial disclosure equilibrium is characterized by a cutoff. The remaining issue is whether a $y^\dagger \in (\underline{y}, y^o)$ exists such that $y^\dagger = y^n$, where y^n is defined in (14.18). This condition can be restated as (using partial integration for the second equality)

$$\lambda(y^o - y^\dagger) = (1 - \lambda)\int_{\underline{y}}^{y^\dagger} (y^\dagger - y)\, d\Phi(y) = (1 - \lambda)\int_{\underline{y}}^{y^\dagger} \Phi(y)\, dy. \qquad (14.19)$$

The LHS of (14.19) is decreasing in $y^\dagger$ and the RHS is increasing in $y^\dagger$. At $y^\dagger = \underline{y}$ the LHS is positive and the RHS equals zero, whereas at $y^\dagger = y^o$, the LHS equals zero and the RHS is positive. Therefore, there must be a cutoff $y^\dagger \in (\underline{y}, y^o)$ at which LHS = RHS. **Q.E.D.**

Observe that (14.19) implies that the equilibrium cutoff $y^\dagger$ depends on the probability λ and the distribution function Φ, but is independent of the capital investment q. JK establish that the cutoff increases as the probability of not being informed increases. That is, increasing the probability of not being informed makes it optimal for the manager to withhold more information.[14]

---

[14] Penno (1997) extends the Dye/Jung/Kwon analysis to consider the probability of disclosure, i.e., $\lambda(1 - \Phi(y^\dagger))$, which he refers to as the "frequency of voluntary disclosure." In his Proposition 1, Penno establishes that this frequency is independent of the precision of the signal y with respect to the outcome x if that precision does not affect the probability λ of being informed. However, if increased precision makes it less likely that the manager will be informed, then the frequency of disclosure can be negatively related to the precision of the information (see Penno's Proposition 2).

Proposition 14.5 (JK, Prop. 2)[15]

In the new equity model, with a positive probability the manager is uninformed, the cutoff $y^\dagger$ is increasing in the probability λ.

While the capital investment q does not affect the cutoff $y^\dagger$, it does affect the intrinsic value of the initial equity at $t = 1$:

$$\pi_i^\dagger(y,m) = \begin{cases} y - q & \text{if } m = y, \\ y(1 - q/y^n) & \text{if } m = n. \end{cases} \tag{14.20}$$

Nonetheless, since there are no disclosure costs, the *ex ante* market price of the initial equity is the same as with full disclosure or no disclosure (see (14.5)):[16]

$$v_0^\dagger = y^o - q = v_0^* = v_0^o.$$

The equilibrium is depicted in Figure 14.5 for the case in which y is uniformly distributed on $[\underline{y}, \bar{y}]$. The cutoff $y^\dagger$ is always less than the prior mean y^o. The shares are overpriced if m equals n and $y \in [\underline{y}, y^\dagger]$, but is underpriced if the manager is uninformed with prior belief y^o. The manager would like to disclose he is uninformed, but we have assumed he cannot credibly do so.

Potential Entrant Model

The analysis is similar in the potential entrant model (as introduced in Section 14.2.1). If the competitor believes the manager will fully disclose his information, then he will enter with probability $G(y^o)$ if the manager does not disclose any information, i.e., $m = n$. However, if the manager anticipates this response, he will select $m = n$ for all $y \geq y^o$ so as to reduce the probability of entry. Following a line of reasoning similar to the discussion of the new equity model leads to the following disclosure equilibrium – the proof is similar to the proof of Proposition 14.4.

---

[15] **Proof:** Totally differentiating (14.19) yields

$$(y^o - y^\dagger)d\lambda - \lambda dy^\dagger = - \int_{\underline{y}}^{y^\dagger} \Phi(y)\, dy\, d\lambda + (1 - \lambda)\Phi(y^\dagger)\, dy^\dagger,$$

which implies $$dy^\dagger/d\lambda = [(y^o - y^\dagger) + \int_{\underline{y}}^{y^\dagger} \Phi(y)\, dy]/[\lambda + (1 - \lambda)\Phi(y^\dagger)] > 0.$$ **Q.E.D.**

[16] In this setting, a commitment to full disclosure involves direct disclosure of all $y \in [\underline{y}, \bar{y}]$ and indirect disclosure of y^o through $m = n$.

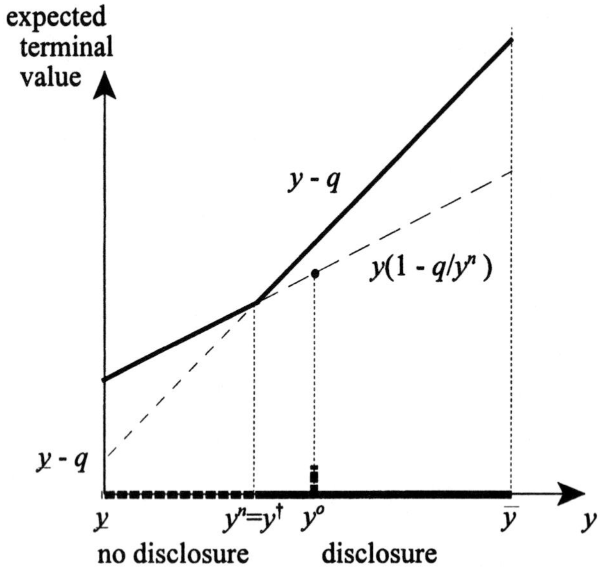

Figure 14.5: Partial disclosure in the new equity model with positive probability manager is uninformed.

Proposition 14.6

In the potential entrant model, with a positive probability the manager is uninformed and $G(y)$ strictly increasing for $y \in [\underline{y}, \bar{y}]$, there exists a partial disclosure equilibrium characterized by a cutoff $y^\dagger = y^n \in (y^o, \bar{y})$, with $N = [y^\dagger, \bar{y}]$.

The intrinsic value of the initial equity at $t = 1$ is

$$\pi_i^\dagger(y,m) = \begin{cases} [1 - \alpha G(y)]y & \text{if } m = y, \\ [1 - \alpha G(y^n)]y & \text{if } m = n. \end{cases} \tag{14.21}$$

The disclosure value is a concave function of y, whereas the no-disclosure value is a linear function of y. The *ex ante* market value of the initial equity is given in (14.7b) if the manager is required not to disclose his information. However, if the above disclosure equilibrium applies, the *ex ante* market value is

$$v_0^\dagger = y^o - \alpha\left[\lambda G(y^n)y^o + (1-\lambda)\left(\int_{\underline{y}}^{y^\dagger} G(y)\, y\, d\Phi(y) + G(y^n)\int_{y^\dagger}^{\bar{y}} y\, d\Phi(y)\right)\right]. \tag{14.22}$$

If $G(y)y$ is a strictly convex function of y, it again follows from Jensen's inequality that

$$v_0^\dagger < y^o - \alpha G(y^o)y^o = v_0^o.$$

That is, the initial equityholders strictly prefer to require the manager not to disclose his information.

Figure 14.6 depicts the partial disclosure equilibrium in a setting in which both G and Φ are uniform distributions on $[\underline{y}, \bar{y}]$. The cutoff $y^\dagger$ is always greater than the prior mean y^o. Disclosure is beneficial if $y < y^\dagger$ since it reduces the probability of entry, whereas no disclosure is beneficial if $y > y^\dagger$. The manager would prefer to reveal that he has no information (so that the prior mean y^o applies) because that would reduce the probability of entry. However, such disclosure is precluded in this model.

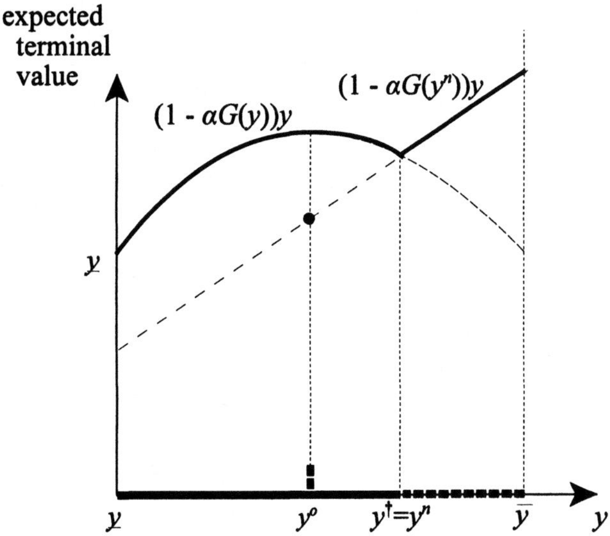

Figure 14.6: Partial disclosure in the potential entrant model with positive probability manager is uninformed.

14.4.2 Litigation

The new equity/potential entrant model discussed in Section 14.3.1 assumes the manager can always disclose his information. Of course, one could readily extend that model to include a positive probability that the manager is uninformed and has no mechanism for credibly disclosing that fact. In Section 14.3.2 we mentioned two-recipient models by Trueman (1997) and by Dutta and Trueman (2002) which assume there is a positive probability the manager is uninformed. We briefly examine a new equity model with some characteristics similar to Trueman's model.

The basic elements of the new equity model considered here are the same as in Section 14.4.1. The key innovation is the introduction of a potential cost of a law suit for "failure to disclose relevant information." More specifically, following Trueman, we assume the initial equityholders may be liable for damages if the manager (acting on their behalf) fails to disclose information that would have resulted in a market price less than the no-disclosure price paid by the new investors.[17]

There is a positive probability λ the manager is uninformed and must report $m = n$ (no disclosure). If informed, the manager's signal $y \in [\underline{y}, \bar{y}]$ represents the expected terminal value of the firm and he can report $m \in \{y, n\}$. The terminal value of the equity is $x \in X$,[18] and we assume $\Phi(x|y^1)$ is first-order-stochastically-dominated by $\Phi(x|y^2)$ if $y^1 < y^2$. There is no law suit if $m = y$ is reported, since it is known to be truthful. However, there may be a law suit if $m = n$. As before, $N = \{ y \in [\underline{y}, \bar{y}] \mid m(y) = n \}$ is the set of informative signals that are not disclosed and y^n represents the investors posterior expectation given no disclosure (see (14.18)). If the manager does not disclose and outcome x is realized, then the investors' lawyer holds the following posterior belief with respect to the manager's observed signal:

$$d\Phi(y|n,x) = \frac{(1-\lambda)\, d\Phi(x|y)\, d\Phi(y)}{\lambda d\Phi(x|y^o) + (1-\lambda)\int_N d\Phi(x|y)\, d\Phi(y)}, \quad \forall\, y \in N. \quad (14.23)$$

If the manager does not disclose, the investors provide capital investment q in return for a fraction q/δ^n of the firm's equity, where δ^n is the maximum price acceptable to investors given no disclosure. The investors' lawyer will incur a cost κ if he undertakes a law suit. If the law suit is undertaken and if the court uncovers the value of y observed by the manager, then the court will award damages proportional to the investors' overpayment for their shares, i.e., $\max\{0, q - yq/\delta^n\}$. Let θ represent the probability that the manager's signal y

[17] Trueman (1997) does not consider the issue of new equity. Instead, he assumes the manager is risk neutral and seeks to maximize the current market value of the firm's equity at $t = 1$ minus a multiple of the expected cost of the law suit. Using this objective function in our model would produce qualitatively similar results.

[18] Trueman assumes x can take on three values.

is uncovered times the damage rate used by the courts. Hence, if a law suit is undertaken, the expected net return to the lawyer (and the new investors) given n and x is

$$\pi_\ell(n,x) = \int_N \theta \max\{0, q(1 - y/\delta^n)\}\, d\Phi(y|n,x) - \kappa. \tag{14.24}$$

Given no disclosure at $t = 1$, the lawyer will undertake a law suit at $t = 2$ for all

$$x \in X_\ell = \{\, x \in X \mid \pi_\ell(n,x) > 0 \,\}.$$

Following Trueman, we assume, for simplicity, that the investors' anticipated share of the damages does not significantly affect the market price given no disclosure at $t = 1$.[19] Hence, the *ex* investment market price at $t = 1$ equals y if $m = y$ and y^n if $m = n$. The intrinsic value of the initial equity, given signal y and message m, is

$$\pi_i^\dagger(y,m) = \begin{cases} y - q, & \text{if } m = y, \\ y(1 - q/y^n), & \text{if } m = n \text{ and } y \geq y^n, \\ y(1 - q/y^n) & \\ \quad - \theta q(1 - y/y^n)\,\Phi(X_\ell|y), & \text{if } m = n \text{ and } y < y^n. \end{cases} \tag{14.25}$$

Clearly, the manager would never withhold his information if $y \geq y^n$, i.e., there is never any under-pricing for non-disclosed informative signals. In this setting, which is illustrated in Figure 14.7,[20] there can exist a disclosure equilibrium in which there are two cutoffs, $y_1^\dagger < y_2^\dagger = y^n < y^o$, such that there are two disjoint disclosure sets, $D_1 = [\underline{y}, y_1^\dagger]$ and $D_2 = [y_2^\dagger, \bar{y}]$, and an intermediate no-disclosure set $N = (y_1^\dagger, y_2^\dagger)$. In disclosure set D_1, the manager discloses bad news, despite its negative effect on the market price, so as to avoid a high

---

[19] We concur with Trueman's conjecture (see his footnote 11) that adjusting the no-disclosure market price at $t = 1$ for the investors' anticipated share of the damages would not affect the basic characteristics of the manager's equilibrium disclosure strategy.

[20] In Figure 14.7, $\Phi(y)$ is a uniform distribution on $[\underline{y}, \bar{y}]$, whereas

$$\varphi(x|y) = \frac{1}{\bar{x} - \underline{x}}\left(2\frac{\bar{y} - y}{\bar{y} - \underline{y}} + 4\frac{y - y^o}{\bar{y} - \underline{y}}\frac{x - \underline{x}}{\bar{x} - \underline{x}}\right), \quad \text{for } x \in [\underline{x}, \bar{x}],$$

with $\underline{x} = 2\underline{y} - \bar{y}$ and $\bar{x} = 2\bar{y} - \underline{y}$. This implies, for example, that $\varphi(x|y)$ is decreasing (increasing) in x for $y <$ (>) y^o and uniform for $y = y^o$. Furthermore, $E[x|y] = y$, $\forall\, y$.

probability of large damage claims for over-pricing. On the other hand, in disclosure set D_2, the manager discloses good news so as to obtain an appropriately high market price. The no-disclosure set N can be viewed as the withholding of poor news that would decrease the price if reported, but for which the expected damages are relatively small. This no-disclosure set takes advantage of the fact that the investors will not sue unless x is very low, since there is a strictly positive probability that the court will find that the manager was uninformed and, therefore, had nothing to disclose.

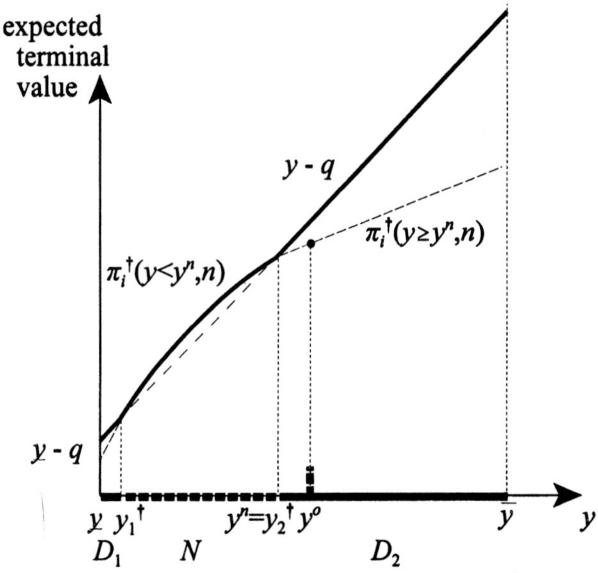

Figure 14.7: Partial disclosure in the new equity model with potential litigation for withholding bad news

Recall that in the new equity model with no litigation costs, the initial equityholders are indifferent between whether the manager fully discloses, partially discloses, or does not disclose his private information at $t = 1$. However, with litigation costs, they would strictly prefer that he fully disclose his information since this would avoid all litigation costs. That is, the initial equityholders strictly prefer a prior commitment to full disclosure instead of having the manager make an *ex post* disclosure decision, even though he is acting in their interests at that time. Of course, in a commitment to full disclosure, the manager still cannot directly disclose that he has no information, but in that setting $m = n$ indirectly discloses that he is uninformed.

Trueman demonstrates that, in his model, the probability of disclosure, i.e., $\Phi(D_1 \cup D_2)$, is increasing in the precision of the manager's information. The key here is that over-pricing is more readily inferred from the outcome if the manager's information is known to be more precise. Trueman also considers the impact of allowing the manager to make an unobservable choice between low and high precision information. If he receives high precision information, he chooses between disclosing that information, disclosing a noisy version of that information, or not disclosing his information. We do not explore the details of that model.

14.4.3 Endogenous Information Acquisition

The models discussed in the preceding sections all assume the manager's information is exogenously determined. Pae (1999) examines a model in which the manager endogenously decides whether to become informed and, if informed, whether to disclose his information. The manager's information is costly, and the cost is not known by investors (they have prior beliefs $F(k)$ over the set of possible costs $K = [\underline{k}, \bar{k}]$). The equilibrium is characterized by a cost cutoff $k^\dagger$ and a disclosure cutoff $y^\dagger$ such that the manager chooses to become informed if $k \in [\underline{k}, k^\dagger]$ and, if informed, discloses his signal if $y \in [y^\dagger, \bar{y}]$. Hence, the probability that the manager is uninformed is $\lambda = 1 - F(k^\dagger)$ and the probability he reports $m = n$ is $\lambda + (1\text{-}\lambda)\Phi(y^\dagger)$.

In this model, as in the other models in this chapter, the manager's information has no productive value. It merely influences the market price at $t = 1$ if reported to investors. In the context of our new equity model, the manager would be motivated, *ex post*, to acquire low cost information given that he can report good news and withhold bad news (as if he is uninformed) and thereby issue fewer shares to obtain the required capital. Of course, the market price given no disclosure reflects the investors' rational conjecture regarding $k^\dagger$ and $y^\dagger$, i.e., the price would equal y^n as specified in (14.18). As a result, the *ex ante* expected number of shares issued is the same whether the manager commits to not acquiring information (and hence commits to no disclosure) or makes an *ex post* information acquisition decision (i.e., after observing the information cost k). This implies, as Pae points out, that the initial equityholders will be better off, *ex ante*, if they can commit the manager not to acquire information *ex post*, since such acquisition has no *ex ante* benefit and it would result in deadweight information acquisition costs.

This is another example of a setting in which the *ex post* incentives induce a decision maker to "shoot himself in the foot." To provide insight why this occurs, assume the manager tells investors he will not acquire information. To see that this is not an equilibrium (if there is no means of enforcing this statement), consider the manager's *ex post* incentives if the investors "believe" the manager's initial statement unless he reports that he has changed his mind and truthfully reports what he has observed. In that case, the manager expects the price to equal y^o if he does not disclose. Hence, the expected intrinsic value of the initial equity if the manager acquires the information and reports all $y > y^o$ is

$$\Pi_i(k) = y^o - (q/y^o) \int_{\underline{y}}^{y^o} y \, d\Phi(y) - q\,[1 - \Phi(y^o)] - k.$$

The intrinsic value if information is not acquired is $y^o - q$. Hence, the manager will choose to become informed if

$$k < q \int_{\underline{y}}^{y^o} \left(1 - \frac{y}{y^o}\right) d\Phi(y).$$

The RHS is strictly positive, so that there can exist a cost k that is sufficiently small to induce information acquisition. Hence, if $\underline{k}$ is less than the RHS, no information acquisition (without commitment) is not an equilibrium.

For $k^\dagger$ and $y^\dagger$ to characterize an equilibrium, $y^\dagger$ must satisfy condition (14.19) for $\lambda = 1 - F(k^\dagger)$, and $k^\dagger$ must satisfy

$$k^\dagger = q \int_{\underline{y}}^{y^n} \left(1 - \frac{y}{y^n}\right) d\Phi(y),$$

for y^n as specified by (14.18).

Pae's model is slightly more complex in that he assumes the manager provides unobservable costly effort that increases the expected outcome. He demonstrates that information acquisition also induces the manager to select an inefficient effort level. We leave exploration of the impact of unobservable management actions to Volume II.

14.4.4 Endogenous Investment Choice

The new equity models discussed in the preceding sections all assume the investment level q is exogenous. Pae (2002) examines a model in which the initial equityholders sell all of their equity at $t = 1$, and the investors (i.e., the new owners) choose the optimal investment level based on their beliefs given the manager's disclosure.[21]

To briefly explore this type of model, let the production function be such that the market value of the firm at $t = 1$ given signal $y \in Y = [\underline{y}, \bar{y}]$ and investment $q \in [0,\infty)$ is truthfully reported is (assuming $y \geq \underline{y} > 0$)

$$V_1(y,q) = yf(q) - q,$$

where $f(q)$ is a strictly increasing concave function with $f(0) = 0$, $\lim_{q \to 0} f'(q) = \infty$, and $\lim_{q \to \infty} f'(q) = 0$. Given y, the investors' investment choice is $q^*(y)$ such that

$$y f'(q^*(y)) = 1,$$

and the market price is

$$V_1^*(y) = yf(q^*(y)) - q^*(y).$$

Let λ represent the prior probability that the manager is not informed[22] and let $\Phi(y)$ represent the prior signal belief, conditional on the manager being informed. As in the new equity model, the equilibrium disclosure strategy is characterized by a cutoff $y^\dagger$ such that $\boldsymbol{m}(y) = y$ if $y \in [y^\dagger, \bar{y}]$, $\boldsymbol{m}(y) = n$ if $y \in [\underline{y}, y^\dagger)$, and y^n is as specified by (14.18). Consequently, if there is no disclosure, the investor's investment choice is $q^\dagger(n)$ such that

$$y^n f'(q^\dagger(n)) = 1,$$

and the market price is

$$V_1^\dagger(n) = y^n f(q^\dagger(n)) - q^\dagger(n).$$

---

[21] Lanen and Verrecchia (1987) examine a disclosure model in which a risk-neutral owner makes operating decisions based on his private information and, subsequently, may have to sell his firm to investors. If he must sell, then he can choose to issue a costly verified report of his private signal or to not disclose. The key result is that the owner's operating decisions are not efficient for signals that will not be disclosed, i.e., the incentive to not disclose some signals leads to distortions in the operating decisions.

[22] Pae assumes that there are a large number of firms, with a fraction λ that are uninformed and a fraction $1 - \lambda$ that are informed. He then determines the social welfare of the entrepreneurs who are selling their firms. As Pae points out, this is mathematically equivalent to treating λ as the probability a given entrepreneur becomes informed and determining the *ex ante* value of the entrepreneur's equity.

Furthermore, as in Proposition 14.4, the equilibrium is such that $y^n = y^\dagger$ and $y^\dagger$ is characterized by (14.19).[23] Consequently, introducing endogenous production does not affect the qualitative characteristics of the partial disclosure equilibrium.

Recall that in the new equity model in Section 14.4.1, the initial equityholders are indifferent between full disclosure, partial disclosure, and no disclosure. That result changes in this model. The *ex ante* value of the firm in each case is:

full disclosure: $$v_0^* = \lambda V_1^*(y^o) + (1-\lambda)\int_{\underline{y}}^{\bar{y}} V_1^*(y)\, d\Phi(y);$$

partial disclosure: $$v_0^\dagger = [\lambda + (1-\lambda)\Phi(y^\dagger)]V_1^\dagger(n) + (1-\lambda)\int_{y^\dagger}^{\bar{y}} V_1^*(y)\, d\Phi(y);$$

no disclosure: $$v_0^o = V_1^*(y^o).$$

It is relatively straightforward to demonstrate that $v_0^* > v_0^\dagger > v_0^o$, i.e., more disclosure is strictly preferred to less disclosure. The key to this result is that information is used in the production choice and, in this model, the new investors are the decision makers while the old manager is the information source. If he does not provide them with information, then they must make an uninformed choice. They are "price protected," so the losers are the initial equityholders, i.e., the expected selling price of their shares is less if the manager discloses less (even though he seeks to maximize the *ex post* market price).

Pae examines the impact of increasing the informativeness of the manager's signal. Without going into the analytical details, Pae's results establish that moving from a less to a more informative system decreases the cutoff $y^\dagger$ and the no-disclosure posterior mean y^n, but increases the *ex ante* value $v_0^\dagger$. Of course, the more informative system also increases the full-disclosure value v_0^*, but has no impact on the no-disclosure value v_0^o.

Pae also extends his analysis to include endogenous information choice. There is an exogenous probability $1 - \lambda$ that the manager can acquire costly private information and, if he can, then he chooses its precision. The information cost is an increasing function of its precision. A key result is that, in a partial disclosure equilibrium, an informed manager acquires more precise information than is optimal if he is required to fully disclose his information.

---

[23] This holds even though the manager seeks to maximize the *ex post* selling price of the initial equity in this model.

14.5 UNVERIFIED DISCLOSURE TO TWO RECIPIENTS

In a single-recipient model, with appropriate monotonicity, the ability to costlessly issue credible reports of all signals leads to full disclosure (see Section 14.2.1). The costless credibility assumption is common in the disclosure literature, and may be justified by assuming there is a sufficiently high probability that a lie will be detected and the penalty for lying is sufficiently high to deter lying. However, this does not fit all settings.

As illustrated in Chapter 13, costly signals are a potential means for overcoming the lack of credibility of management forecasts or other unverified disclosures. In that chapter, we assumed the initial equityholder is risk averse and seeks to share his risk with diversified investors, so that risk retention is a credible signal. Risk retention is not a credible signal in this chapter since the initial equityholders are assumed to be risk neutral (i.e., well-diversified). The finance literature contains a number of signaling models in which dividend policy or capital structure are assumed to be credible signals.[24] However, we are primarily interested in the use of accounting reports (e.g., earnings forecasts) to disclose private management information.

There are a few papers that explore what are commonly called "cheap talk" equilibria. These papers have two recipients which create tension with respect to type of information the manager would like to disclose. The initial paper in the economics literature is by Crawford and Sobel (1982). Other papers in the economics literature include Farrell and Gibbons (1989) and Farrell (1993). In the accounting literature, Newman and Sansing (NS) (1993) and Gigler (1994) examine "cheap talk" in settings similar to our new equity/potential entrant model. The main difference between the NS model and our model, is that NS assume the initial equityholders issue debt (instead of equity) and use the manager's disclosure to "smooth" their consumption across two periods. The main difference between the Gigler model and our model is that, instead of considering a potential entrant, Gigler assumes the firm engages in Cournot

[24] Bhattacharya (1979) and Myers and Majluf (1984) are early examples of such models. For example, in Bhattacharya (1979), dividends are used as a credible signal due to a tax disadvantage of paying dividends. In Myers and Majluf (1984), issuance/non-issuance of new equity is used as the signal, and it is credible because positive NPV projects cannot be undertaken unless new equity is issued. In many of those models, the initial equityholders are better off if the manager is committed to (or given incentives to) follow a no-disclosure policy (as in many of the costly disclosure models of this chapter). Harris and Raviv (1991) provide a review of the capital structure theory based on asymmetric information, and Hart (2001) provides a critical perspective on this literature.

competition in a duopoly and the manager's private information pertains to the intercept of a downward sloping product market demand curve.[25]

We identify a "cheap talk" equilibrium in our new equity/potential entrant model. The manager receives an informative signal $y \in Y = [\underline{y}, \bar{y}]$, and for every signal y he can choose to send any message $m \in M = Y$. His reporting strategy (which may be mixed) is represented by the probability distribution function ψ_i: $M \times Y \to [0,1]$, which is expressed as $\psi_i(m|y)$. Let

$$M(\psi_i) \equiv \{ m \in M \mid d\psi_i(m|y) > 0 \text{ for some } y \in Y \}$$

represent the set of messages the manager might disclose if he employs disclosure strategy ψ_i.

The competitor's and investors' responses to the manager's message m depend on their posterior mean given the manager's message, which we denote as $\mu(m)$. If the competitor and investors have posterior mean μ after receiving the manager's message, then the competitor enters the firm's market with probability $G(\mu)$ and the maximum acceptable *ex* investment price to the investors is $[1 - \alpha G(\mu)]\mu$. Hence, the intrinsic value of the initial equity, given that the competitor and investors have posterior mean μ and the manager has observed y, is $\zeta(\mu)y$, where

$$\zeta(\mu) \equiv 1 - \alpha G(\mu) - q/\mu$$

is the fraction of the market's expected value that is retained by the initial equityholders. This leads to the following expression for the intrinsic value of the initial equity at $t = 1$, given signal y, disclosure strategy ψ_i, and competitor/investor posterior belief μ:

$$\pi_i(y,\psi_i,\mu) = \int_{\underline{y}}^{\bar{y}} \zeta(\mu(m))\, y\, d\psi_i(m|y). \tag{14.25}$$

Given the responses of the competitor and investors to their beliefs, $\mathscr{E} = (\psi_i,\mu)$ constitutes a *sequential equilibrium* if

(a) for every $y \in Y$, $d\psi_i(m|y) > 0$ only if $m \in \underset{m' \in M}{\operatorname{argmax}}\ \zeta(\mu(m'))$,

(b) μ satisfies Bayes' theorem for all $m \in M(\psi_i)$.

---

[25] Chapter 15 explores disclosure choice in duopolies.

It is straightforward to dispense with the two extreme cases of full disclosure and no disclosure.

Proposition 14.7 (NS, Prop. 1 and 2)
There is no full-disclosure equilibrium, and there always exists an equilibrium in which the same (uninformative) message m^o is reported for all y.

Full disclosure is impossible when there is no mechanism to enforce truthfulness. If the competitor and investors believe the manager is reporting truthfully, then he will be motivated to lie and report

$$m = \mu^* \in \underset{\mu \in Y}{\operatorname{argmax}}\ \zeta(\mu), \quad \forall\, y \in Y.$$

On the other hand, the no-disclosure (uninformative message) equilibrium can be sustained by the off-equilibrium threat by the competitor and investors to believe the "worst," i.e., to assign probability one to signal

$$y = \hat{\mu} \in \underset{\mu \in Y}{\operatorname{argmin}}\ \zeta(\mu), \quad \text{if } m \neq m^o.$$

In "cheap talk" models it is common to obtain partial disclosure equilibria that are called "partitioning equilibria." To illustrate this kind of equilibrium, assume $\Phi(y)$ and $G(y)$ are uniform distributions on $[\underline{y}, \bar{y}]$. Consider a disclosure strategy characterized by a cutoff $y^\dagger \in (\underline{y}, \bar{y})$, such that $m = \mu_1 = \frac{1}{2}(\underline{y} + y^\dagger)$ is reported with certainty for all $y \in [\underline{y}, y^\dagger]$ and $m = \mu_2 = \frac{1}{2}(y^\dagger + \bar{y})$ is reported with certainty for all $y \in (y^\dagger, \bar{y}]$. That is, the message equals the mean for the subset of signals that result in that message. If any other message is reported, then the competitor and investors threaten to believe the worst (i.e., to assign probability one to $y = \hat{\mu}$ if $m \neq \mu_1$ or μ_2).[26]

Observe that

$$\zeta(\mu) = 1 - \alpha \frac{\mu - \underline{y}}{\bar{y} - \underline{y}} - \frac{q}{\mu}$$

is a concave function which achieves its maximum at

---

[26] The disclosure strategy can also be represented as the disclosure of a set (instead of an expectation) or as the random choice among the signals within the set. The latter has the advantage of having no off-equilibrium messages.

$$\mu^* = \sqrt{\frac{q}{\alpha}[\bar{y} - \underline{y}]}.$$

Assume α and q are such that $\mu^* \in [\underline{y}, \bar{y}]$, as depicted in Figure 14.8. Now identify $y^\dagger$ such that

$$\zeta(\tfrac{1}{2}(\underline{y} + y^\dagger)) = \zeta(\tfrac{1}{2}(y^\dagger + \bar{y})).$$

As illustrated in Figure 14.8, the partitioning disclosure strategy characterized by that cutoff is a sequential equilibrium.

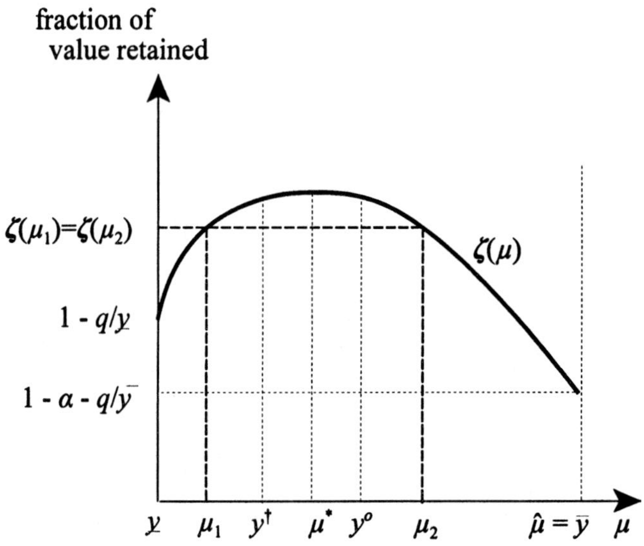

Figure 14.8: Partitioning equilibrium in the new equity/potential entrant model with no verification.

In this example, there is only one partial disclosure equilibrium, whereas in other settings (e.g., NS and Gigler), there are equilibria in which there is a sequence of partitions. The key here is that the model is such that manager's preferences over the possible competitor/investor posterior beliefs are independent of the manager's signal, whereas this is not the case in other models.

Recall that a no-disclosure equilibrium always exists. Hence, in this setting there are two possible equilibria. Furthermore, $\zeta(y^o) > \zeta(\mu_1) = \zeta(\mu_2)$, which implies that the manager prefers the no-disclosure equilibrium over the partitioning equilibrium.

14.6 CONCLUDING REMARKS

In this chapter we focus on *ex post* disclosure choice, i.e., the manager decides whether to disclose his private information after he has observed his signal. However, we also consider the disclosure policies that would maximize the *ex ante* market prices of the initial equity. The next chapter focuses on the equilibrium *ex ante* disclosure policies among competing firms, and then examines *ex post* disclosure choice. Throughout both chapters, we find some settings in which the *ex post* disclosure choices are the optimal *ex ante* policies, but frequently they differ. Hence, it is important to distinguish between the voluntary release of information as managers receive it, as opposed to the regular reporting of information under the terms of some policy to which management is committed to adhere.

In all of these models we assume investors are passive with respect to the acquisition of information. They merely receive the information disclosed by the manager, and do not expend personal resources to acquire private information. Obviously, the disclosure models in Chapters 13, 14, or 15 can be combined with the private investor information models in Chapters 11 or 12. In this type of model, the investors would all know what the manager disclosed, but may differ with respect to their private information. As discussed by Verrecchia (2001, Section 4.2), this type of approach can be used to explore the impact of disclosure policies on a firm's "information asymmetry component of the cost of capital."[27]

REFERENCES

Bhattacharya, S. (1979) "Imperfect Information, Dividend Policy, and "the Bird in the Hand" Fallacy," *The Bell Journal of Economics* 10, 233-254.

Crawford, V., and J. Sobel. (1982) "Strategic Information Transmission," *Econometrica* 50, 1431-1451.

---

[27] Zhang (2001), which is discussed in Section 12.2.3, provides a model in which the commitment to increased future disclosure increases the current selling price because of increased future prices due to reduced gains by privately informed traders at the future date.

Verrecchia (2001, Section 4.2) provides a model in which the manager and some investors are informed, whereas a competitor and other investors are uninformed. The model is idiosyncratic in its structure, but it does illustrate the potential for disclosure trade-off between gains from reduction in the cost of capital and increased proprietary costs.

Darrough, M. N., and N. M. Stoughton. (1990) "Financial Disclosure Policy in an Entry Game," *Journal of Accounting and Economics* 12, 219-243.

Dutta, S., and B. Trueman. (2002) "The Interpretation of Information and Corporate Disclosure Strategies," *Review of Accounting Studies* 7, 75-96.

Dye, R. A. (1985) "Disclosure of Nonproprietary Information," *Journal of Accounting Research* 23, 123-145.

Dye, R. A. (1998) "Investor Sophistication and Voluntary Disclosure," *Review of Accounting Studies* 3, 261-287.

Dye, R. A. (2001) "An Evaluation of 'Essays on Disclosure' and the Disclosure Literature in Accounting," *Journal of Accounting and Economics* 32, 181-235.

Farrell, J. (1993) "Meaning and Credibility in Cheap-Talk Games," *Games and Economic Behavior* 23, 514-531.

Farrell, J., and R. Gibbons. (1989) "Cheap-Talk with Two Audiences," *American Economic Review* 79, 1214-1223.

Feltham, G. A., and J. Xie. (1992) "Voluntary Financial Disclosure in an Entry Game with Continua of Types," *Contemporary Accounting Research* 9, 46-80.

Fishman, M. J., and K. M. Hagerty. (1998) "Mandatory Disclosure," *The New Palgrave Dictionary of Economics and the Law*, Volume 1, P. Newman (ed.), London: Macmillan Reference Limited, 605-608.

Gertner, R. H. (1998) "Disclosure and Unravelling," *The New Palgrave Dictionary of Economics and the Law*, Volume 2, P. Newman (ed), London: Macmillan Reference Limited, 605-608.

Gigler, F. (1994) "Self-Enforcing Voluntary Disclosures," *Journal of Accounting Research* 32, 224-240.

Grossman, S. (1981) "The Informational Role of Warranties and Private Disclosure about Product Quality," *Journal of Law and Economics* 24, 461-483.

Grossman, S., and O. D. Hart. (1980) "Disclosure Laws and Takeover Bids," *Journal of Finance* 35, 323-334.

Harris, M., and A. Raviv. (1991) "The Theory of Capital Structure," *Journal of Finance* 46, 297-355.

Hart, O. (2001) "Financial Contracting," Working Paper, Harvard University.

Jovanovic, B. (1982) "Truthful Disclosure of Information," *Bell Journal of Economics* 13, 36-44.

Jung, W.-O., and Y. K. Kwon. (1988) "Disclosure When the Market is Unsure of Information Endowment of Managers," *Journal of Accounting Research* 26, 146-153.

Lanen, W. N., and R. E. Verrecchia. (1987) "Operating Decisions and the Disclosure of Management Accounting Information," *Journal of Accounting Research* 25, 165-189.

Milgrom, P. (1981) "Good News and Bad News: Representation Theorems and Application," *Bell Journal of Economics* 12, 380-391.

Myers, S. C., and N. S. Majluf. (1984) "Corporate Financing and Investment Decisions when Firms have Information that Investors do not have," *Journal of Financial Economics* 13, 187-221.

Newman, P., and R. Sansing. (1993) "Disclosure Policies with Multiple Users," *Journal of Accounting Research* 31, 92-112.

Pae, S. (1999) "Acquisition and Discretionary of Disclosure of Private Information and Its Implications for Firms," *Journal of Accounting Research* 37, 465-474.

Pae, S. (2002) "Discretionary Disclosure, Efficiency, and Signal Informativeness," *Journal of Accounting and Economics*, forthcoming.

Penno, M. C. (1997) "Information Quality and Voluntary Disclosure," *The Accounting Review* 72, 275-284.

Trueman, B. (1997) "Managerial Disclosures and Shareholder Litigation," *Review of Accounting Studies* 2, 181-199.

Verrecchia, R. E. (1983) "Discretionary Disclosure," *Journal of Accounting and Economics* 5, 179-194.

Verrecchia, R. E. (1990) "Information Quality and Discretionary Disclosure," *Journal of Accounting and Economics* 12, 365-380.

Verrecchia, R. E. (2001) "Essays on Disclosure," *Journal of Accounting and Economics* 32, 97-180.

Wagenhofer, A. (1990) "Voluntary Disclosure with a Strategic Opponent," *Journal of Accounting and Economics* 12, 341-363.

Zhang, G. (2001) "Private Information Production, Public Disclosure, and the Cost of Capital: Theory and Implications," *Contemporary Accounting Research* 18, 363-384.

CHAPTER 15

DISCLOSURE OF PRIVATE INFORMATION IN PRODUCT MARKETS

Chapter 14 examines the disclosure of private information by a manager acting on behalf of well-diversified owners. The primary focus in that chapter is on models in which the firm issues new equity and, hence, the owners are concerned about the beliefs of the investors who will buy the new equity. The impact of a potential entrant into the firm's product market is examined in Sections 14.2.2 and 14.3.1. In the first instance, new equity is not issued but there is an exogenous cost of disclosing the manager's information. In the second instance, new equity is issued and disclosure is costless. Both settings yield partial disclosure. If the potential entrant is the only recipient of the manager's costly disclosure, then the manager discloses bad news and withholds good news. On the other hand, if new investors and the potential entrant are both recipients of the manager's costless disclosure, then there can exist an equilibrium in which the manager withholds both very bad and very good news, while disclosing the news between the two extremes.

The potential entrant model discussed in Chapter 14 is a relatively simple model of the potential effects of product market competition. In this chapter we consider more complex product market models that examine the impact of disclosure in settings in which competing firms simultaneously choose either production quantities or selling prices. The major development of these models has been in the industrial organization literature, but several accounting researchers have contributed to this literature. We limit our discussion to models and insights that have been of interest to accounting researchers.

Darrough (1993) provides an insightful review of disclosure policy and product market competition. More recently, the review of the disclosure literature by Verrecchia (2001), and its discussion by Dye (2001), include comments on disclosure in product markets.

In Section 15.1 we examine equilibrium disclosure policies in a two-stage game. In the first stage, at $t = 0$, the owners of the competing firms set their firms' *ex ante disclosure policies*. In the second stage, at $t = 1$, the firms' managers receive private information, disclose or withhold their information in accordance with the previously specified disclosure policies, and then simultaneously choose either their production quantities (if there is Cournot competition) or their selling prices (if there is Bertrand competition). The outcomes for the competing firms are realized at $t = 2$.

The owners of the firms seek to maximize the *ex ante* values of their firms. They are not concerned with the market prices at $t = 1$, e.g., they do not expect to sell their shares or issue new shares at that date. Since firms infrequently issue new equity, the product market disclosure models may capture a key aspect of the disclosure incentives that exist on an ongoing basis. Of course, one can combine the product market competition models considered in this chapter with the capital market disclosure models considered in Chapter 14 (see, for example, Section 15.2.3). As in Chapter 14, market risk is ignored, implying that the firms' owners are well-diversified and the risks are diversifiable.

We focus on duopoly models (i.e., there are two competitors), although many of the results can be extended to consider more than two imperfectly competing firms (i.e., an oligopoly). Section 15.1.1 considers Cournot competition, in which the managers of the two firms simultaneously choose their production quantities, and the market clearing prices are linear functions of the amounts produced. The variable production costs of the two firms and the intercept of their price functions are random variables. We initially assume the managers have private firm-specific cost information, and then consider private information about a parameter that affects the uncertain market clearing price of the common product sold by the two firms.

Section 15.1.2 considers Bertrand competition, in which the firms sell products that are imperfect substitutes and the managers simultaneously choose the selling prices for their products. We again initially assume the managers have private firm-specific cost information. Then we consider private information about a parameter that affects the uncertain demands for both products.

The analysis derives the well-known result that full disclosure is the equilibrium disclosure policy if there is Cournot competition with private firm-specific cost information or there is Bertrand competition with private industry-wide demand information. On the other hand, no disclosure is the equilibrium disclosure policy if there is Cournot competition with private information about the industry's market clearing price or there is Bertrand competition with private firm-specific cost information.[1] While we interpret the firm-specific information as pertaining to costs and the industry-wide information as pertaining to demand or prices, it should be noted that this is just for ease of expo-

---

[1] Darrough (1993) assumes managers report their private information with noise. She demonstrates that no noise is added if there is Cournot competition with firm-specific information or Bertrand competition with industry information, whereas maximum noise is added if there is Cournot competition with industry information or Bertrand competition with firm-specific information. Earlier analyses of disclosure choice under Cournot competition include Gal-Or (1985), Shapiro (1986), and Kirby (1988). Both Cournot and Bertrand competition are considered by Vives (1984) and Gal-Or (1986).

sition. The key distinction is between firm-specific versus industry-wide information, not between cost versus demand information.

The key to deriving the equilibrium in each setting is to consider general partial disclosure policies that have full disclosure and no disclosure as the extremes. For the general partial disclosure policies we initially derive the product market equilibrium by solving for the rational conjectures with respect to the choices made by the two managers. Each manager is assumed to maximize the firm's intrinsic value at $t = 1$, and identification of their equilibrium choices permits the calculation of the equilibrium *ex post* intrinsic values conditional on the signals received (i.e., the expected outcomes at $t = 2$ given what is known at $t = 1$). The *ex ante* values are then calculated by determining the expected *ex post* values. The final step is to establish that either full or no disclosure are the strictly dominating strategies for each firm at $t = 0$. That is, for example, with Cournot and private firm-specific cost information, full disclosure is strictly preferred to any other disclosure policy for both firms no matter which disclosure policy is chosen by the other firm.

The analysis in Section 15.1 assumes the firms' owners can make an enforceable *ex ante* commitment to the disclosure policy to be implemented by the firms' managers. Section 15.2 briefly explores the disclosure that will result if *ex ante* commitment is not feasible, and managers make the *ex post* disclosure choices that maximize the *ex post* intrinsic values of their firms.

15.1 *EX ANTE* DISCLOSURE POLICIES

As stated above, we begin by identifying the equilibrium *ex ante* disclosure policies under two types of duopoly competition: Cournot and Bertrand. Within each competitive environment we consider two types of private information: firm-specific cost information and industry-wide demand information.

In each of these settings there are two firms, and the information received by manager i at $t = 1$ is represented by signal $y_i \in Y_i$, $i = 1,2$. The signals are independently distributed, and the prior probability distribution function over manager i's signals is denoted $\Phi_i(y_i)$, $i = 1,2$. After observing his signal at $t = 1$, manager i chooses a publicly reported message $m_i \in M_i(y_i) = \{y_i, n_i\}$, where $m_i = y_i$ is truthful disclosure of his signal and $m_i = n_i$ is no disclosure. The set of possible reports that might be observed by manager j is

$$M_i = \bigcup_{y_i \in Y_i} M_i(y_i) = Y_i \cup \{n_i\}.$$

If $m_i = y_i$, then manager j knows y_i. However, if $m_i = n_i$, then manager j's posterior belief depends on his conjecture as to manager i's disclosure policy $\boldsymbol{m}_i$:

$Y_i \rightarrow M_i$.[2] The disclosure policies are chosen simultaneously by firms at $t = 0$, and then become common knowledge, i.e., manager j knows $\boldsymbol{m}_i(\cdot)$ at $t = 1$, $i,j = 1,2$, $i \neq j$. The disclosure policy for firm i induces a partition on the set of signals such that $Y_i = D_i \cup N_i$, where $N_i \equiv \{ y_i \in Y_i \mid \boldsymbol{m}_i(y_i) = n_i \}$ is the set of non-disclosed signals, and $D_i \equiv Y_i \backslash N_i$ is the set of disclosed signals. Full disclosure by firm i is represented by $N_i = \emptyset$, and no disclosure is represented by $N_i = Y_i$. The managers are committed to the disclosure policies chosen at $t = 0$, i.e., if $N_i = \emptyset$, $m_i = n_i$ is never observed, whereas if $N_i \neq \emptyset$, then manager j's posterior belief about manager i's information is

$$d\Phi(y_i|m_i) = \begin{cases} d\Phi_i(y_i)/\Phi_i(N_i) & \text{if } y_i \in N_i \text{ and } m_i = n_i, \\ 1 & \text{if } y_i \in D_i \text{ and } m_i = y_i, \\ 0 & \text{otherwise.} \end{cases} \qquad (15.1)$$

Hence, if $N_i \neq \emptyset$, manager j's posterior mean for manager i's information given no disclosure is

$$y_i^n = \int_{N_i} y_i \, d\Phi_i(y_i|n_i), \qquad (15.2)$$

and we let $n_i = y_i^n$ represent the no disclosure message.

After both managers have observed their own signals and the other's message at $t = 1$, they simultaneously choose their production quantities with Cournot competition or their product prices with Bertrand competition. We assume throughout this section that equilibrium production quantities and prices are strictly positive.

[2] Our disclosure policies differ from the disclosure policies considered in Darrough (1993). Her disclosure policies are represented as the manager's signal plus normally distributed noise, where full disclosure corresponds to zero noise and no disclosure is represented as the limit of the variance of the noise going to infinity. That representation does not allow her to consider partial disclosure policies where, for example, in the firm-specific cost information setting with Cournot competition, the manager reports low cost (to "scare the competitor away") and withholds high cost information (to prevent the competitors from taking advantage of that information by choosing a higher production quantity). These types of partial disclosure policies represent the *ex post* incentives of managers, and we want to include them in the set of possible disclosure policies in the *ex ante* setting as well.

15.1.1 Cournot Competition

We simplify our analysis of Cournot competition by assuming the two firms produce identical products. The firms simultaneously choose production quantities q_1 and q_2. The market clearing price ζ is represented by:[3]

$$\zeta = \theta - (q_1 + q_2), \tag{15.3}$$

where $\theta > 0$ is an industry-wide price function parameter.

Each firm's production cost is assumed to be a linear function of the amount produced by the firm.[4] We ignore the fixed costs since they are irrelevant to our analysis. The variable cost per unit for firm i is $c_i \geq 0$.

We initially assume the price parameter θ is known and consider firm-specific cost information. We then assume the firms have identical variable costs, i.e., $c_1 = c_2 = c$, and the managers have private information about the price parameter θ.[5]

Firm-specific Cost Information

In this analysis, we assume the variable costs c_1 and c_2 are independently distributed random variables with a common prior mean $\bar{c}$.[6] The information received by manager i pertains to the variable cost c_i, and the signal y_i is scaled so that it equals manager i's posterior mean with respect to c_i. Hence, $E[c_i|\mathbf{y}] = y_i$, where $\mathbf{y} = (y_1,y_2)$, and $Cov[y_1,y_2] = 0$. Since the costs have a common mean, it follows that $E[y_i] = \bar{c}$, and we assume $Var[y_i] = \sigma_i^2$, for $i = 1,2$, i.e., the signals may differ in their informativeness about their respective costs. If manager j observes the message $m_i = y_i$ then he knows that manager i's expected variable cost is y_i. On the other hand, if he observes the message $m_i = n_i$, his posterior mean for manager i's posterior expected cost is y_i^n.

When the manager of firm i chooses his production quantity at $t = 1$ he knows his own expected production cost y_i and the message m_j reported by firm

---

[3] The quantities are scaled, without loss of generality, such that the slope of the price function is one. We could generalize the model by considering firm-specific price functions of the form $\zeta_i = \theta - (q_i + \gamma q_j)$, as in Darrough (1993), where $\gamma \in (0,1]$ is a measure of the degree of product substitutability. However, assuming a single product allows us to explore most of the issues of interest.

[4] See Kirby (1988) for an analysis of the impact of convex costs on disclosure policy choice.

[5] It is not necessary for θ to be known in the cost information setting – the results are the same if θ is a common expectation with respect to that parameter. Similarly, it is not necessary for the firm-specific costs to be known in the price information setting – the results are the same if c is a common expectation with respect to the firms' variable costs.

[6] We assume the variable costs are sufficiently small that, in equilibrium, both managers will choose to produce, i.e., there are no corner solutions.

j. He does not know manager j's expected production cost if $m_j = n_j$, and he does not know firm j's production quantity even if $m_j = y_j$. However, manager i knows manager j's disclosure policy $\boldsymbol{m}_j(y_j)$ and has a conjecture of manager j's decision rule as a function of what he knows and has reported, which is represented by $\hat{\boldsymbol{q}}_j(m_i,m_j,y_j)$. This implies that manager i's conjecture of firm j's expected production quantity given messages m_i and m_j is $\bar{\boldsymbol{q}}_j(m_i,m_j) \equiv \mathrm{E}[\hat{q}_j|m_i,m_j]$. Hence, the intrinsic value of firm i at $t = 1$, given manager i's cost information, y_i, his production choice, q_i, and his conjecture of firm j's expected production choice, $\bar{\boldsymbol{q}}_j(m_i,m_j)$, is

$$\pi_{1i}(q_i|y_i,m_j) = \mathrm{E}[\zeta - c_i|y_i,m_j]q_i$$

$$= [\theta - (q_i + \bar{\boldsymbol{q}}_j(\boldsymbol{m}_i(y_i),m_j)) - y_i]q_i, \quad i = 1,2,\ i \neq j. \qquad (15.4)$$

Value function (15.4) is concave with respect to q_i, so that the optimal quantity for firm i, given the conjecture $\bar{\boldsymbol{q}}_j(m_i,m_j)$ and cost information y_i, is characterized by the first-order condition

$$\partial\pi_{1i}/\partial q_i = \theta - 2q_i - \bar{\boldsymbol{q}}_j(\boldsymbol{m}_i(y_i),m_j) - y_i = 0. \qquad (15.5)$$

Hence, given conjecture $\bar{\boldsymbol{q}}_j(m_i,m_j)$ and information y_i, manager i will choose

$$q_i = \frac{1}{2}[\theta - \bar{\boldsymbol{q}}_j(\boldsymbol{m}_i(y_i),m_j) - y_i], \quad i = 1,2,\ i \neq j. \qquad (15.6)$$

In a Nash equilibrium, the conjectures of the two managers are rational. It is obvious from (15.6) that q_i is reduced by ½y_i. Therefore, consider a linear conjecture of the form $\hat{\boldsymbol{q}}_j(m_i,m_j,y_j) = l_j + h_j m_i + k_j m_j - ½(y_j - m_j)$, which implies that $\bar{\boldsymbol{q}}_j(m_i,m_j) = l_j + h_j m_i + k_j m_j$, since $\mathrm{E}[y_j|m_j] = m_j$. Consequently, from (15.6), the conjectures $(\hat{\boldsymbol{q}}_1,\hat{\boldsymbol{q}}_2)$ constitute an equilibrium if

$$l_1 + h_1 m_2 + k_1 m_1 - ½(y_1 - m_1) = \frac{1}{2}[\theta - (l_2 + h_2 m_1 + k_2 m_2) - y_1],$$

$$l_2 + h_2 m_1 + k_2 m_2 - ½(y_2 - m_2) = \frac{1}{2}[\theta - (l_1 + h_1 m_2 + k_1 m_1) - y_2]. \qquad (15.7)$$

Collecting the coefficients for each variable in (15.7) implies that $l_i = ½(\theta - l_j)$, $h_i = -½k_j$, and $k_i + ½ = -½h_j$, $i,j = 1,2$, $i \neq j$, from which we obtain $l_i = ⅓\theta$, $h_i = ⅓$, and $k_i = -⅔$, $i = 1,2$.

Substituting these constants into (15.7) yields the equilibrium production quantities as specified in Table 15.1(a) as functions of the firm-specific cost information $\mathbf{y}$ given the disclosure policies $\boldsymbol{m}_1$ and $\boldsymbol{m}_2$. Substituting $\boldsymbol{q}_1(\mathbf{y})$ and $\boldsymbol{q}_2(\mathbf{y})$ into (15.3) yields the equilibrium price function, $\boldsymbol{\zeta}(\mathbf{y})$, as specified in Table

15.1(b). Furthermore, substituting $\boldsymbol{q}_i(\mathbf{y})$ and $\boldsymbol{\zeta}(\mathbf{y})$ into (15.4) and taking the expectation given y_i and m_j yields the equilibrium expected intrinsic value of firm i at $t = 1$, for given disclosure policies $\boldsymbol{m}_1$ and $\boldsymbol{m}_2$,

$$\mathrm{E}[\pi_{1i}|y_i,m_j] = \mathrm{E}[(\zeta - y_i)q_i|y_i,m_j]$$

$$= \frac{1}{9}\begin{cases} \left([\theta - 2y_i^n + m_j] - 2[y_i - y_i^n]\right)^2, & y_i \in D_i, \\ \left([\theta - 2y_i^n + m_j] - \frac{3}{2}[y_i - y_i^n]\right)^2, & y_i \in N_i, \end{cases} \tag{15.8}$$

for $i = 1,2$, $i \neq j$, where $y_i^n = \boldsymbol{m}_i(y_i) = \mathrm{E}[y_i|N_i]$ for $y_i \in N_i$. We assume an interior solution for each signal y_i if there is full disclosure, so that the equilibrium production quantity $\boldsymbol{q}^{fd}(\mathbf{y}) = ⅓(\theta - 2y_i + y_j) > 0$, for all $y_i \in Y_i$ and $y_j \in Y_j$. It follows by comparing the latter pair of terms in (15.8) that, *ex post*, a manager prefers to disclose "good news" (i.e., low costs, $y_i < y_i^n$) so as to induce the competitor to decrease his production. Conversely, disclosing "bad news" (i.e., high costs, $y_i > y_i^n$) has a negative effect (because it induces the competitor to increase production). However, the disclosure policy is chosen *ex ante* and, as we shall see, the *ex ante* optimal policy deviates from the manager's *ex post* incentives to disclose or withhold information.

Taking the expectation with respect to y_i in (15.8) yields firm i's *ex ante* value at $t = 0$, v_{0i}, given disclosure policies $\boldsymbol{m}_1$ and $\boldsymbol{m}_2$. These policies can be represented by the disclosure sets D_1 and D_2, and we express the *ex ante* value as a function of those two sets, $v_{0i}(D_i,D_j)$. The disclosure sets are chosen simultaneously at $t = 0$. To establish the equilibrium disclosure policy choices, consider firm i's optimal disclosure set D_i given disclosure set D_j.

We conjecture that the optimal disclosure set is $D_i = Y_i$, with $N_i = \emptyset$, i.e., full disclosure is optimal for manager i for all D_j. To prove this result, assume to the contrary that the optimal choice is less than full disclosure, i.e., $N_i \neq \emptyset$. From (15.8) we observe that disclosing (instead of not disclosing) all $y_i \in N_i$ does not affect the intrinsic value for any $y_i \in D_i$, but results in an increase in the intrinsic value of[7]

$$\mathrm{E}[\Delta\pi_{1i}|y_i,m_j] = \frac{1}{9}\{- (y_i - y_i^n)[\theta - 2y_i^n + m_j] + \frac{7}{4}(y_i - y_i^n)^2\}, \tag{15.9}$$

for all $y_i \in N_i$. Note that $\mathrm{E}[\Delta\pi_{1i}|y_i,m_j]$ is a decreasing convex function of y_i, so that the gains from disclosing low costs more than offset the losses from

[7] In determining this difference it is useful to note that the expression for $y_i \in D_i$ in (15.8) can be restated as $([\theta - 2y_i^n + m_j] - 2[y_i - y_i^n])^2$.

disclosing high costs (by Jensen's inequality). More specifically, taking the *ex ante* expectation of (15.9) yields

$$v_{0i}(Y_i,D_j) - v_{0i}(D_i,D_j) = \mathrm{E}[\Delta\pi_{1i}] = \tfrac{1}{9}\tfrac{7}{4}\mathrm{Var}[y_i|N_i]\,\mathrm{Prob}[N_i] > 0. \quad (15.10)$$

Table 15.1
Disclosure of Private Firm-specific Cost Information
Under Cournot Competition

(a) ***Equilibrium Production Quantities for given Disclosure Policies***

$$\boldsymbol{q}_i(\mathbf{y}) = \tfrac{1}{3}[\theta + \boldsymbol{m}_j(y_j) - 2\boldsymbol{m}_i(y_i)] - \tfrac{1}{2}[y_i - \boldsymbol{m}_i(y_i)], \quad i = 1,2,\ i \neq j.$$

(b) ***Equilibrium Price Function for given Disclosure Policies***

$$\zeta(\mathbf{y}) = \tfrac{1}{3}\,[\theta + \boldsymbol{m}_1(y_1) + \boldsymbol{m}_2(y_2)] + \tfrac{1}{2}[(y_1 - \boldsymbol{m}_1(y_1)) + (y_2 - \boldsymbol{m}_2(y_2))].$$

(c) ***Unique Sequential Equilibrium (Full Disclosure)***

(*i*) $\boldsymbol{q}_i^{fd}(\mathbf{y}) = \tfrac{1}{3}[\theta + y_j - 2y_i]$, $\quad i = 1,2,\ i \neq j.$

(*ii*) $\zeta^{fd}(\mathbf{y}) = \tfrac{1}{3}[\theta + y_1 + y_2]$.

(*iii*) $v_{0i}^{fd} = \tfrac{1}{9}[(\theta - \bar{c})^2 + 4\sigma_i^2 + \sigma_j^2]$, $\quad i = 1,2,\ i \neq j.$

The same result applies to firm *j*, so that a full disclosure policy is a *strictly dominating strategy* for both firms, which yields the following result.

Proposition 15.1
Full disclosure is the unique sequential equilibrium in the two-stage *ex ante* disclosure choice game under Cournot competition with firm-specific cost information.

Hence, even though the manager has *ex post* incentives to disclose "good news" and withhold "bad news," the *ex ante* value of a firm is maximized by requiring its manager to fully disclose his information.

The full disclosure equilibrium production quantities, price function, and *ex ante* equilibrium values of firms are as specified in Table 15.1(c).[8] The results in Table 15.1 reveal that the full-disclosure equilibrium prices are increasing in both expected costs. However, the equilibrium production choice by manager i is increasing in firm j's expected variable cost, but decreasing in his own firm's expected variable cost. Since we have scaled the signals so that they equal the posterior mean, we can view the variance of a signal as a measure of its informativeness.[9] Not surprisingly, the *ex ante* value of firm i is increasing in the variance of y_i, reflecting the fact that the manager can make better quantity choices if he has better information. Interestingly, these results also indicate that the *ex ante* value of firm i is increasing in the variance of y_j, $i \neq j$. That is, the manager of firm i benefits from knowing what the manager of firm j is choosing, and that benefit is larger if the manager j has better information. By disclosing their information, the two managers coordinate their actions to their mutual advantage.

Price Information

We now assume the managers do not receive any cost information (they have identical variable costs c), but receive private information about price function parameter θ (see (15.3)). To simplify the analysis, we assume the price parameter can be expressed as $\theta = \bar{\theta} + \varepsilon_1 + \varepsilon_2$, where ε_1 and ε_2 are random variations in the price parameter, with $E[\varepsilon_i] = 0$ and $Cov[\varepsilon_1, \varepsilon_2] = 0$. Furthermore, manager i's signal y_i is only informative about ε_i and is scaled such that $E[\varepsilon_i|\mathbf{y}] = y_i$, $i = 1,2$, which implies $E[y_i] = 0$. We again let $\sigma_i^2 \equiv Var[y_i]$ represent the informativeness of signal y_i. If manager j observes the message $m_i = y_i$, then his posterior mean for the price parameter is $E[\theta|m_i{=}y_i, y_j] = \bar{\theta} + y_i + y_j$. On the other hand, if he observes the message $m_i = n_i$, his posterior mean for the price parameter is $E[\theta|m_i{=}n_i, y_j] = \bar{\theta} + y_i^n + y_j$.

As in the firm-specific cost information setting, manager i knows manager j's disclosure policy and has a conjecture with respect to manager j's decision

---

[8] While many papers in this literature assume the variables are normally distributed, we have not made that assumption. The role of the variances in this analysis comes from the quadratic form of the value function. To see this, observe that the intrinsic value of firm i with full disclosure is 1/9 times $[\theta - 2y_i + y_j]^2 = [\theta - \bar{c} - 2(y_i - \bar{c}) + (y_j - \bar{c})]^2 = [\theta - \bar{c}]^2 - 2[\theta - \bar{c}][2(y_i - \bar{c}) - (y_j - \bar{c})] + [2(y_i - \bar{c}) - (y_j - \bar{c})]^2$. The first set of terms are not random, the expectation of the second set of terms equals zero, and, due to the independence of the two random variables, the expectation of the third set of terms equals $4\sigma_i^2 + \sigma_j^2$.

[9] The use of the variance as a measure of informativeness is clearly appropriate if the variables are normally distributed. As discussed in the preceding footnote, the use of the variance is appropriate in this setting (due to quadratic payoffs) even if the variables are not normally distributed. However, note that it is not the precision of the posterior beliefs about the random cost parameter which is important (since that risk is diversifiable). The key is the variance of the posterior mean for the cost parameter (and thereby the variability of production choices).

rule, $\hat{q}_j(m_i,m_j,y_j)$, from which he derives a conjecture of manager j's expected production quantity given messages m_i and m_j, $\bar{q}_j(m_i,m_j)$. Hence, the intrinsic value of firm i at $t = 1$, given manager i's price information, y_i, his production quantity, q_i, and his conjecture for firm j's expected production quantity, $\bar{q}_j(m_i,m_j)$, is

$$\pi_{1i}(q_i|y_i,m_j) = \mathrm{E}[\zeta - c|y_i,m_j]q_i$$

$$= [\bar{\theta} + y_i + m_j - (q_i + \bar{q}_j(\boldsymbol{m}_i(y_i),m_j)) - c]q_i, \quad i = 1,2,\ i \neq j. \tag{15.11}$$

Value function (15.11) is concave with respect to q_i, so that the optimal quantity for firm i, given the conjecture $\bar{q}_j(m_i,m_j)$ and price information y_i, is characterized by the first-order condition

$$\partial\pi_{1i}/\partial q_i = \bar{\theta} + y_i + m_j - 2q_i - \bar{q}_j(\boldsymbol{m}_i(y_i),m_j) - c = 0. \tag{15.12}$$

Hence, given conjecture $\bar{q}_j(m_i,m_j)$ and information y_i, manager i will choose

$$q_i = \tfrac{1}{2}[\bar{\theta} + y_i + m_j - \bar{q}_j(\boldsymbol{m}_i(y_i),m_j) - c], \quad i = 1,2,\ i \neq j. \tag{15.13}$$

In a Nash equilibrium, the conjectures of the two managers are rational, and we again consider linear conjectures of the form $\hat{q}_j(m_i,m_j,y_j) = l_j + h_j m_i + k_j m_j + \frac{1}{2}(y_j - m_j)$, so that $\bar{q}_j(m_i,m_j) = l_j + h_j m_i + k_j m_j$. Hence, the conjectures $(\hat{q}_1,\hat{q}_2)$ constitute an equilibrium if

$$l_1 + h_1 m_2 + k_1 m_1 + \tfrac{1}{2}(y_1 - m_1) = \tfrac{1}{2}[\bar{\theta} + y_1 + m_2 - (l_2 + h_2 m_1 + k_2 m_2) - c],$$

$$(15.14)$$

$$l_2 + h_2 m_1 + k_2 m_2 + \tfrac{1}{2}(y_2 - m_2) = \tfrac{1}{2}[\bar{\theta} + y_2 + m_1 - (l_1 + h_1 m_2 + k_1 m_1) - c].$$

Using a similar procedure as in the firm-specific cost information setting, it follows that consistency of the conjectures implies that $l_i = \frac{1}{3}[\bar{\theta} - c]$, $k_i = h_i = \frac{1}{3}$, $i = 1,2$.

Substituting these constants into (15.13) yields the equilibrium production quantities, as specified in Table 15.2(a), as functions of the industry-wide price information $\mathbf{y}$ given the disclosure policies $\boldsymbol{m}_1$ and $\boldsymbol{m}_2$. Substituting $\boldsymbol{q}_1(\mathbf{y})$ and $\boldsymbol{q}_2(\mathbf{y})$ into (15.3) yields the equilibrium expected price function, $\mathrm{E}[\zeta|\mathbf{y}]$, as specified in Table 15.2(b). Furthermore, substituting $\boldsymbol{q}_i(\mathbf{y})$ and $\mathrm{E}[\zeta|\mathbf{y}]$ into (15.11) and taking the expectation given y_i and m_j yields the equilibrium expected intrinsic value of firm i at $t = 1$, for given disclosure policies $\boldsymbol{m}_1$ and $\boldsymbol{m}_2$,

$$\mathrm{E}[\pi_{1i}|y_i,m_j] = \mathrm{E}[(\zeta - c)q_i|y_i,m_j]$$

$$= \frac{1}{9}\begin{cases} \left([\bar{\theta} + y_i^n + m_j - c] + [y_i - y_i^n]\right)^2, & y_i \in D_i, \\ \left([\bar{\theta} + y_i^n + m_j - c] + \frac{3}{2}[y_i - y_i^n]\right)^2, & y_i \in N_i, \end{cases} \tag{15.15}$$

for $i = 1,2,\ i \neq j$. It follows from (15.15) (and strictly positive equilibrium production quantities) that in the setting with industry-wide price information, *ex post*, a manager would like to disclose his information when he has "bad news" about the product market conditions, i.e., $y_i < y_i^n$, since that would lead the competitor to reduce his production. On the other hand, a manager would like to withhold "good news," i.e., $y_i > y_i^n$.

Table 15.2
Disclosure of Private Price Information
Under Cournot Competition

(a) ***Equilibrium Production Quantities for given Disclosure Policies***

$$\boldsymbol{q}_i(\mathbf{y}) = \frac{1}{3}[\bar{\theta} + \boldsymbol{m}_j(y_j) + \boldsymbol{m}_i(y_i) - c] + \frac{1}{2}(y_i - \boldsymbol{m}_i(y_i)), \quad i = 1,2,\ i \neq j.$$

(b) ***Equilibrium Expected Price Function for given Disclosure Policies***

$$\mathrm{E}[\zeta|\mathbf{y}] = \frac{1}{3}[\bar{\theta} + \boldsymbol{m}_1(y_1) + \boldsymbol{m}_2(y_2) + 2c] + \frac{1}{2}[(y_1 - \boldsymbol{m}_1(y_1)) + (y_2 - \boldsymbol{m}_2(y_2))].$$

(c) ***Unique Sequential Equilibrium*** (***No Disclosure***)

(*i*) $\boldsymbol{q}_i^{nd}(\mathbf{y}) = \frac{1}{3}[\bar{\theta} - c] + \frac{1}{2}y_i\,,$ $\qquad i = 1,2,\ i \neq j.$

(*ii*) $\mathrm{E}[\zeta^{nd}|\mathbf{y}] = \frac{1}{3}[\bar{\theta} + 2c] + \frac{1}{2}(y_1 + y_2).$

(*iii*) $v_{0i}^{nd} = \frac{1}{9}(\bar{\theta} - \bar{c})^2 + \frac{1}{4}\sigma_i^2,$ $\qquad i = 1,2,\ i \neq j.$

We conjecture that the optimal disclosure set is $D_i = \emptyset$, with $N_i = Y_i$, i.e., no disclosure is optimal for manager i for all D_j. To prove this result, assume to the contrary that the optimal choice involves at least some disclosure, i.e., $D_i \neq \emptyset$. From (15.15) we observe that disclosing $y_i \in D_i$ instead of not disclosing any $y_i \in Y_i$ has the following effect on the intrinsic value (note, $y_i^n = 0$ if $N_i = Y_i$),

$$\mathrm{E}[\Delta\pi_{1i}|y_i,m_j] = \frac{1}{9}\begin{cases} -y_i[\bar{\theta}+m_j-c] - \frac{5}{4}y_i^2, & y_i \in D_i, \\ -y_i^n[\bar{\theta}+m_j-c+\frac{5}{4}y_i^n+\frac{3}{2}(y_i-y_i^n)], & y_i \in N_i. \end{cases} \tag{15.16}$$

We now determine the change in the *ex ante* value by using (15.16) to compute the expected change in intrinsic value:

$$v_{0i}(D_i,D_j) - v_{0i}(\emptyset,D_j)$$

$$= \tfrac{1}{9}\{\mathrm{E}[-y_i[\bar{\theta} + \boldsymbol{m}_j(y_j) - c] - \tfrac{5}{4}y_i^2\,|D_i]\ \mathrm{Prob}(D_i)$$
$$+ \mathrm{E}[-y_i^n[\bar{\theta} + \boldsymbol{m}_j(y_j) - c + \tfrac{5}{4}y_i^n + \tfrac{3}{2}(y_i - y_i^n)]|N_i]\ \mathrm{Prob}(N_i)\}$$

$$= -\tfrac{1}{9}\{\tfrac{5}{4}\mathrm{E}[y_i^2|D_i]\ \mathrm{Prob}(D_i) + \tfrac{5}{4}[y_i^n]^2\ \mathrm{Prob}(N_i)\} < 0. \tag{15.17}$$

Hence, for firm i, the no disclosure policy, i.e., $D_i = \emptyset$ and $N_i = Y_i$, is a *strictly dominating strategy* for firm i. Of course the same holds for firm j, and we have the following result.

Proposition 15.2

No disclosure is the unique sequential equilibrium in the two-stage *ex ante* disclosure choice game under Cournot competition with price information.

This result is the opposite to the result in Proposition 15.1. If the information pertains to firm-specific costs, then the *ex ante* value of a firm is maximized by requiring its manager to fully disclose his information, whereas the *ex ante* value is maximized by requiring the manager not to disclose his information about the market price. The key to these results is that the change in expected intrinsic values with full disclosure versus no disclosure, i.e., $\mathrm{E}[\Delta\pi_{1i}|y_i,m_j]$, is a decreasing *convex* function of y_i with firm-specific cost information, while it is a decreasing *concave* function of y_i with industry-wide price information. Hence, in the latter setting, the gain from reporting "bad news" is lower than the loss from reporting "good news."

The no disclosure equilibrium production quantities, expected price function, and *ex ante* equilibrium values of firms are as specified in Table 15.2(c). Observe that Table 15.2(c*iii*) implies that firm i's *ex ante* value is increasing in the informativeness of manager i's signal, but is not affected by the informativeness of the other manager's signal.

15.1.2 Bertrand Competition

Under Bertrand competition, the firms sell different (but related) products and simultaneously choose the prices at which they will sell to customers. Those choices determine the demand quantities for the two products. To consider Bertrand competition we write the demand functions as

$$q_i = \alpha - \zeta_i + \gamma\zeta_j, \quad i,j = 1,2,\ i \neq j, \tag{15.18}$$

where $\gamma \in (0,1)$ is the degree of substitutability between the two products and $\alpha > 0$ is the demand function intercept.[10] Hence, the demand for firm i's product is decreasing in firm i's price and increasing in firm j's price.

Firm-specific Cost Information

We now consider the same firm-specific cost information as in Section 15.1.1. Recall that manager i observes y_i which is scaled so that it equals his expected variable cost, i.e., $\mathrm{E}[c_i|y_i] = y_i$, and $\mathrm{E}[y_i] = \bar{c}$, $i = 1,2$.

Let $\hat{\zeta}_j(m_i,m_j,y_j)$ represent manager i's conjecture with respect to manager j's pricing decision rule, and let $\bar{\zeta}_j(m_i,m_j) \equiv \mathrm{E}[\hat{\zeta}_j|m_i,m_j]$. Then the intrinsic value of firm i at $t = 1$, given manager i's choice of ζ_i, is

$$\pi_{1i}(\zeta_i|y_i,m_j) = (\zeta_i - y_i)(\alpha - \zeta_i + \gamma\bar{\zeta}_j(\boldsymbol{m}_i(y_i),m_j)), \quad i = 1,2,\ i \neq j. \tag{15.19}$$

The first-order condition for (15.19) characterizes manager i's optimal price:

$$\zeta_i = \frac{1}{2}[\alpha + \gamma\bar{\zeta}_j(\boldsymbol{m}_i(y_i),m_j) + y_i], \quad i = 1,2,\ i \neq j. \tag{15.20}$$

Applying the same approach as used to derive the results in Table 15.1(a) (i.e., assuming linear conjectures and finding the consistent constants) we obtain the equilibrium product prices for given disclosure policies as specified in Table 15.3(a). Substituting these prices into the demand function yields the equilibrium demand quantities as specified in Table 15.3(b). Furthermore, substituting these expressions into (15.19) yields the equilibrium expected intrinsic value of firm i at $t = 1$, i.e.,

$$\mathrm{E}[\pi_{1i}|y_i,m_j] = \mathrm{E}[(\zeta_i - y_i)q_i|y_i,m_j]$$

---

[10] As noted in footnote 3, we could have considered differentiated products in the Cournot competition setting. For example, Darrough (1993) obtains the same disclosure preferences using a price function of the form $\zeta_i = \theta - q_i - \gamma q_j$. The Bertrand demand function would be equivalent if $q_i = \alpha - \beta\zeta_i + \gamma\beta\zeta_j$, where $\alpha = \theta/(1+\gamma)$ and $\beta = 1/(1-\gamma^2)$. Our function is the same except we have rescaled by dividing by β and letting $\alpha = \theta(1-\gamma)$.

$$= \frac{1}{(4-\gamma^2)^2}\begin{cases}\left([(2+\gamma)\alpha - (2-\gamma^2)y_i^{\,n} + \gamma m_j] - (2-\gamma^2)[y_i - y_i^{\,n}]\right)^2, & y_i \in D_i,\\ \left([(2+\gamma)\alpha - (2-\gamma^2)y_i^{\,n} + \gamma m_j] - (2-\tfrac{1}{2}\gamma^2)[y_i - y_i^{\,n}]\right)^2, & y_i \in N_i,\end{cases} \tag{15.21}$$

for $i = 1,2$, $i \neq j$. Comparing the latter pair of terms in (15.21) yields that, with Bertrand competition, *ex post*, a manager would like to disclose when he has high costs, since that would inform the competitor that he is setting a high price and would induce the competitor to set a high price as well, implying that the demand for the firm's product would be higher. On the other hand, a manager would like to withhold low cost information. Note that these incentives are opposite to the *ex post* incentives with Cournot competition (with firm-specific cost information).

Table 15.3
Disclosure of Private Firm-specific Cost Information
Under Bertrand Competition

(a) ***Equilibrium Product Prices for given Disclosure Policies***

$$\zeta_i(\mathbf{y}) = \frac{1}{4-\gamma^2}[(2+\gamma)\alpha + \gamma \mathbf{m}_j(y_j) + 2\mathbf{m}_i(y_i)] + \tfrac{1}{2}[y_i - \mathbf{m}_i(y_i)], \quad i = 1,2,\ i \neq j.$$

(b) ***Equilibrium Demand Quantities for given Disclosure Policies***

$$\mathbf{q}_i(\mathbf{y}) = \frac{1}{4-\gamma^2}[(2+\gamma)\alpha - (2-\gamma^2)\mathbf{m}_i(y_i) + \gamma \mathbf{m}_j(y_j)]$$
$$- \tfrac{1}{2}[(y_i - \mathbf{m}_i(y_i)) - \gamma(y_j - \mathbf{m}_j(y_j))], \quad i = 1,2,\ i \neq j.$$

(c) ***Unique Sequential Equilibrium (No Disclosure)***

(*i*) $\zeta_i^{nd}(\mathbf{y}) = \dfrac{1}{2-\gamma}[\alpha + \bar{c}\,] + \tfrac{1}{2}(y_i - \bar{c}), \qquad i = 1,2,\ i \neq j.$

(*ii*) $\mathbf{q}_i^{nd}(\mathbf{y}) = \dfrac{1}{2-\gamma}[\alpha - (1-\gamma)\bar{c}\,] - \tfrac{1}{2}[(y_i - \bar{c}) - \gamma(y_j - \bar{c})], \; i = 1,2,\ i \neq j.$

(*iii*) $v_{0i}^{\,nd} = \dfrac{1}{(2-\gamma)^2}[\alpha - (1-\gamma)\bar{c}\,]^2 + \tfrac{1}{4}\sigma_i^2, \qquad i = 1,2,\ i \neq j.$

We conjecture that the optimal disclosure set is $D_i = \emptyset$, with $N_i = Y_i$, i.e., no disclosure is optimal for manager *i* for all D_j. To prove this result, we again assume to the contrary that the optimal disclosure policy involves some disclosure, i.e., $D_i \neq \emptyset$. From (15.21) we compute the impact of disclosing D_i instead of not disclosing any $y_i \in Y_i$:[11]

$$\mathrm{E}[\Delta\pi_{1i}|y_i,m_i]$$

$$= \frac{1}{(4-\gamma^2)^2}\begin{cases} \gamma^2(y_i-\bar{c})[(2+\gamma)\alpha-(2-\gamma^2)\bar{c}+\gamma m_j] \\ \qquad -\gamma^2(2-\frac{3}{4}\gamma^2)[y_i-\bar{c}]^2, & y_i\in D_i, \\ \gamma^2(y_i^n-\bar{c})[(2+\gamma)\alpha-(2-\gamma^2)\bar{c}+\gamma m_j] \\ \qquad -(2-\frac{1}{2}\gamma^2)(y_i-\bar{c})+\frac{1}{4}\gamma^4[y_i^n-\bar{c}]^2, & y_i\in N_i. \end{cases} \tag{15.22}$$

This implies that the difference in the *ex ante* value of firm *i* from using a no disclosure policy and a non-trivial partial disclosure policy D_i is

$$v_{0i}(D_i,D_j) - v_{0i}(\emptyset,D_j)$$

$$= -\frac{\gamma^2(2-\frac{3}{4}\gamma^2)}{(4-\gamma^2)^2}\{\mathrm{E}[(y_i-\bar{c})^2\,|D_i]\,\mathrm{Prob}(D_i) + (y_i^n-\bar{c})^2\,\mathrm{Prob}(N_i)\}$$

$$< 0. \tag{15.23}$$

Hence, no disclosure is indeed a strictly dominating strategy for firm *i* and, of course, also for firm *j*, so we get the following result.

Proposition 15.3

No disclosure is the unique sequential equilibrium in the two-stage *ex ante* disclosure choice game under Bertrand competition with firm-specific cost information.

---

[11] Observe that for $y_i \in D_i$ a comparison is made between the intrinsic value given disclosure versus no disclosure, where manager *j*'s expectation for y_i given no disclosure is zero. On the other hand, for $y_i \in N_i$ a comparison is made between the intrinsic value with no disclosure given a posterior expectation of y_i^n versus an expectation of zero. That is, the other manager's beliefs given no disclosure differ between the settings with partial versus "full" no disclosure.

This result is opposite to the result with Cournot competition, cf., Proposition 15.1. The key is that the change in expected intrinsic value with disclosure versus no disclosure is an increasing *concave* function of y_i with Bertrand competition, whereas it is decreasing and *convex* with Cournot competition.

The no disclosure equilibrium price functions, demand functions, and *ex ante* equilibrium values of firms are as specified in Table 15.3(c). Observe that Table 15.3(c*iii*) implies that firm *i*'s *ex ante* value is increasing in the informativeness of manager *i*'s signal (as represented by σ_i^2), but is not affected by the informativeness of the other manager's signal.

Price Information

We now consider the disclosure of price information under Bertrand competition. As in Section 15.1.1, the firms have identical variable costs c. The substitutability parameter γ is constant, whereas demand parameter α can be expressed as $\alpha = \bar{\alpha} + \varepsilon_1 + \varepsilon_2$, where ε_1 and ε_2 are random variations in the price parameter, with $E[\varepsilon_i] = 0$ and $Cov[\varepsilon_1,\varepsilon_2] = 0$. Manager *i*'s signal y_i is only informative about ε_i and is scaled such that $E[\varepsilon_i|\mathbf{y}] = y_i$, $i = 1,2$, which implies $E[y_i] = 0$. We again let $\sigma_i^2 \equiv Var[y_i]$ represent the informativeness of signal y_i.

If manager i has conjecture $\bar{\zeta}_j(m_i,m_j,y_j)$ with respect to manager j's pricing decision rule, the intrinsic value of firm i at $t = 1$, given his choice of ζ_i, is

$$\pi_{1i}(\zeta_i|y_i,m_j) = (\zeta_i - c)(\bar{\alpha} + y_i + m_j - \zeta_i + \gamma\bar{\zeta}_j(\mathbf{m}_i(y_i),m_j)), \quad i = 1,2,\ i \neq j. \quad (15.24)$$

The first-order condition for (15.24) characterizes manager *i*'s optimal price:

$$\zeta_i = \tfrac{1}{2}[\bar{\alpha} + (y_i + m_j) + \gamma\bar{\zeta}_j(\mathbf{m}_i(y_i),m_j) + c], \qquad i = 1,2,\ i \neq j. \quad (15.25)$$

Applying the same approach as used previously we obtain the equilibrium product prices for given disclosure policies as specified in Table 15.4(a). Substituting these prices into the demand function yields the equilibrium expected demand quantities as specified in Table 15.4(b). Furthermore, substituting these expressions into (15.24) yields the equilibrium expected intrinsic value of firm i at $t=1$,

$$E[\pi_{1i}|y_i,m_j] = E[(\zeta_i - c)q_i|y_i,m_j]$$

$$= \frac{1}{(2-\gamma)^2}\begin{cases} \left([\bar{\alpha} + m_j + y_i^n - (1-\gamma)c] + [y_i - y_i^n]\right)^2, & y_i \in D_i, \\ \left([\bar{\alpha} + m_j + y_i^n - (1-\gamma)c] + \tfrac{1}{2}(2-\gamma)[y_i - y_i^n]\right)^2, & y_i \in N_i \end{cases} \quad (15.26)$$

for $i = 1,2$, $i \neq j$. Comparing the latter pair of terms in (15.26) yields that the manager's *ex post* incentives are to disclose "good news," i.e., $y_i > y_i^n$, and to withhold "bad news," $y_i < y_i^n$. Of course, the incentive to disclose "good news" is to induce the competitor to set a high price which would lead to a higher demand for the firm i's product. The opposite occurs with "bad news."

Table 15.4
Disclosure of Private Demand Information Under Bertrand Competition

(a) ***Equilibrium Product Prices for given Disclosure Policies***

$$\zeta_i(\mathbf{y}) = \frac{1}{2-\gamma}[\bar{a} + c + \boldsymbol{m}_j(y_j) + \boldsymbol{m}_i(y_i)] + \tfrac{1}{2}[y_i - \boldsymbol{m}_i(y_i)], \quad i = 1,2,\ i \neq j.$$

(b) ***Equilibrium Expected Demand Quantities for given Disclosure Policies***

$$\mathrm{E}[q_i|\mathbf{y}] = \frac{1}{2-\gamma}[\bar{a} + \boldsymbol{m}_i(y_i) + \boldsymbol{m}_j(y_j) - (1-\gamma)c]$$

$$+ \tfrac{1}{2}[(y_i - \boldsymbol{m}_i(y_i)) + \gamma(y_j - \boldsymbol{m}_j(y_j))], \quad i = 1,2,\ i \neq j.$$

(c) ***Unique Sequential Equilibrium (Full Disclosure)***

(*i*) $$\zeta_i^{fd}(\mathbf{y}) = \frac{1}{2-\gamma}[\bar{a} + y_i + y_j + c], \qquad i = 1,2,\ i \neq j.$$

(*ii*) $$\mathrm{E}[q_i^{fd}|\mathbf{y}] = \frac{1}{2-\gamma}[\bar{a} + y_i + y_j - (1-\gamma)c], \qquad i = 1,2,\ i \neq j.$$

(*iii*) $$v_{0i}^{fd} = \frac{1}{(2-\gamma)^2}[\,(\bar{a} - (1-\gamma)c)^2 + \sigma_i^2 + \sigma_j^2], \qquad i = 1,2,\ i \neq j.$$

We conjecture that the optimal disclosure set is $D_i = Y_i$, with $N_i = \emptyset$, i.e., full disclosure is optimal for manager i for all D_j. To prove this result, we again assume to the contrary that the optimal disclosure policy involves some no disclosure, i.e., $N_i \neq \emptyset$. From (15.26) we compute the impact of disclosing $y_i \in N_i$ (this disclosure has no impact on the intrinsic value for $y_i \in D_i$)

$$\mathrm{E}[\Delta\pi_{1i}|y_i,m_i]$$

$$= \frac{1}{(2-\gamma)^2}\Big((\gamma[y_i - y_i^n][\bar{a} + m_j + y_i^n - (1-\gamma)c] + \tfrac{1}{4}\gamma(4-\gamma)[y_i - y_i^n]^2\Big), \quad (15.27)$$

for $i,j = 1,2,\ i \neq j$. Note that this is an increasing *convex* function of y_i so that the gain from disclosing "good news" exceeds the loss from disclosing "bad news." More specifically, the difference in the *ex ante* value of firm i from using a full disclosure policy instead of a non-trivial partial disclosure policy D_i is

$$v_{0i}(Y_i,D_j) - v_{0i}(D_i,D_j) = \frac{\gamma(4-\gamma)}{4(2-\gamma)^2}\mathrm{Var}(y_i|N_i)\,\mathrm{Prob}(N_i) > 0. \quad (15.28)$$

Hence, full disclosure is a strictly dominating strategy for firm i and, of course, also for firm j, i.e., we get the following result.

Proposition 15.4

Full disclosure is the unique sequential equilibrium in the two-stage *ex ante* disclosure choice game under Bertrand competition with price information.

Again, this result is opposite to the result with Cournot competition, cf., Proposition 15.2. The key here is that the gain from disclosing good news exceeds the loss from disclosing "bad news" due to the convexity of the change in expected intrinsic value with disclosure versus no disclosure.

The full disclosure equilibrium price functions, expected demand quantities, and *ex ante* equilibrium values of firms are as specified in Table 15.4(c). Observe that Table 15.4(c*iii*) implies that firm *i*'s *ex ante* value is increasing in the informativeness of manager *i*'s signal, as well as in the informativeness of the other manager's signal.

15.1.3 Discussion and Extension of Results

In the preceding analysis we have demonstrated that the equilibrium disclosure policy varies with the type of competition (Cournot versus Bertrand) and the type of information (firm-specific costs versus industry-wide demand or price parameter). We commented in the introduction that, as noted by Sankar (1995), the key aspect of the latter distinction is between information about firm-specific parameters versus industry-wide parameters, not the distinction between cost and demand or price parameters. To illustrate this point, we briefly consider private management information about an industry-wide cost parameter with Cournot competition.

Industry-wide Cost Information with Cournot Competition

Assume the firms have identical variable costs and that it can be expressed as $c = \bar{c} + \varepsilon_1 + \varepsilon_2$, where ε_1 and ε_2 are random variations in the cost parameter, with $\mathrm{E}[\varepsilon_i] = 0$ and $\mathrm{Cov}[\varepsilon_1, \varepsilon_2] = 0$. Manager i's signal is only informative about ε_i, and it is scaled such that $\mathrm{E}[\varepsilon_i | y_i] = y_i$. Applying the same approach as in the previous sections, the equilibrium production quantities and price function are given by

$$\boldsymbol{q}_i(\mathbf{y}) = \tfrac{1}{3}[\theta - \bar{c} - \boldsymbol{m}_j(y_j) - \boldsymbol{m}_i(y_i)] - \tfrac{1}{2}(y_i - \boldsymbol{m}_i(y_i)), \quad i = 1,2,\ i \neq j, \tag{15.29a}$$

$$\mathrm{E}[\zeta | \mathbf{y}] = \tfrac{1}{3}\, [\theta + 2\bar{c} + 2(\boldsymbol{m}_1(y_1) + \boldsymbol{m}_2(y_2))]$$

$$+ \tfrac{1}{2}[(y_1 - \boldsymbol{m}_1(y_1)) + (y_2 - \boldsymbol{m}_2(y_2))]. \tag{15.29b}$$

Substituting into the expression for the equilibrium intrinsic value of firm i at $t = 1$ and taking expectations given y_i and m_j yields

$$\mathrm{E}[\pi_{1i} | y_i, m_j] = \mathrm{E}[(\zeta - \bar{c} - y_i - m_j) q_i | y_i, m_j]$$

$$= \frac{1}{9}\begin{cases} \left([\theta - \bar{c} - y_i^n - m_j] - [y_i - y_i^n]\right)^2, & y_i \in D_i, \\ \left([\theta - \bar{c} - y_i^n - m_j] - \tfrac{3}{2}[y_i - y_i^n]\right)^2, & y_i \in N_i. \end{cases} \tag{15.30}$$

Note that in this setting, *ex post*, the manager would like to disclose high cost signals ($y_i > y_i^n$), and withhold low cost signals ($y_i < y_i^n$). Furthermore, evaluating the changes in intrinsic values with no disclosure and partial disclosure,

$$\mathrm{E}[\Delta\pi_{1i} | y_i, m_j] = \frac{1}{9}\begin{cases} y_i[\theta - \bar{c} - m_j] - \tfrac{5}{4} y_i^2, & y_i \in D_i, \\ y_i^n[\theta - \bar{c} - m_j - \tfrac{5}{4} y_i^n - \tfrac{3}{2}(y_i - y_i^n)], & y_i \in N_i, \end{cases} \tag{15.31}$$

and taking expectations yields

$$v_{0i}(D_i, D_j) - v_{0i}(\emptyset, D_j) = -\tfrac{1}{9}\{\tfrac{5}{4}\mathrm{E}[y_i^2 | D_i]\,\mathrm{Prob}(D_i) + \tfrac{5}{4}[y_i^n]^2\,\mathrm{Prob}(N_i)\} < 0.$$

These results are opposite to the results with firm-specific cost information with Cournot competition, and it follows that no disclosure is the strictly dominating strategy for both firms.[12]

Summary of Equilibrium Disclosure Policies

We do not formally consider Bertrand competition, but it should now be fairly obvious that in the Bertrand setting the strictly dominating strategy for both managers is to fully disclose their industry-wide cost information. To extend the analysis to firm-specific demand or price information we would have to view the firms as producing differentiated products with price or demand functions of the following forms:[13]

$$\text{Cournot:} \quad \zeta_i = \bar{\theta} + \varepsilon_i - (q_i + q_j),$$

$$\text{Bertrand:} \quad q_i = \bar{a} + \varepsilon_i - \zeta_i + \gamma\zeta_j,$$

for $i,j = 1,2$, $i \neq j$, where ε_1 and ε_2 are independently distributed random variables (with zero mean) about which the two managers are privately informed. Under Cournot competition, the strictly dominating strategy for both managers is full disclosure, whereas under Bertrand competition it is no disclosure.

Table 15.5 summarizes the above results.

Type of Information	Type of Competition	
	Cournot	Bertrand
Firm-specific	full disclosure	no disclosure
Industry-wide	no disclosure	full disclosure

Table 15.5: *Ex ante* disclosure policy equilibria.

---

[12] Dye (2001, footnote 58) observes that, under Cournot competition, no disclosure is preferred to disclosure if disclosure induces the outputs of the two firms to positively covary, whereas full disclosure is preferred if disclosure induces the outputs to negatively covary. With firm-specific information, there is negative correlation (see Table 15.1(a)), and with industry-wide information, there is positive correlation (see Table 15.2(a) and (15.29a)). Dye does not consider Bertrand competition. However, we observe that in both the firm-specific (see Table 15.3(a)) and the industry-wide (see Table 15.4(a)) settings, the prices of the two firms positively covary with disclosure.

[13] As noted earlier, we could also introduce a substitutability parameter into the Cournot competition setting. Here it is assumed to equal 1.

Low costs and high demand are "good news," while high costs and low demand are "bad news." It is useful to note how the type of information (firm-specific versus industry-wide) and the type of competition (Cournot versus Bertrand) affect the benefit from disclosure. That is, if the competitor thought firm i had made an *ex ante* commitment to not disclose any $y_i \in N_i$, would manager i prefer, *ex post*, to disclose good or bad news within that set?

One can establish this preference by comparing the expected intrinsic values at $t = 1$ for disclosure versus non-disclosure in, for example, (15.8). Here we observe that manager i would prefer to disclose $y_i < y_i^n$, i.e., low firm-specific costs (which is good news). On the other hand, from (15.30) we observe that manager i would prefer to disclose $y_i > y_i^n$, i.e., high industry-wide costs (which is bad news). The key, of course, is that reporting that you have low costs will inform the competitor your production will be high and thereby induce the competitor to reduce his production. On the other hand, reporting that you both have high costs will inform the competitor your production will be low, but this effect is more than offset by causing the competitor to reduce his production due to his high cost.

The desire to report good news about firm-specific information and bad news about industry-wide information under Cournot competition reverses with price information. For example, from (15.15) we observe that manager i prefers, *ex post*, to report $y_i < y_i^n$, i.e., low industry-wide prices (which is bad news). If we formally considered firm-specific price information, we would find that manager i prefers to report $y_i > y_i^n$, i.e., high firm-specific prices (which is good news).

Now consider Bertrand competition. From (15.21) we observe that manager i prefers, *ex post*, to report $y_i > y_i^n$, i.e., high firm-specific costs (which is bad news). Similarly, from (15.26) we observe that manager i again prefers to report $y_i > y_i^n$, but here that is high demand information (which is good news). If we formally considered industry-wide cost information and firm-specific demand information, we would find that manager i prefers to reveal high industry-wide costs (bad news) and high firm-specific demand (good news). The key force in the Bertrand setting is that manager i wants to induce manager j to increase his price. The competitor will do so if he believes manager i is setting a high price (due to either high costs or high demand).

Table 15.6 summarizes the above discussion. As we see here, the distinction between cost and demand information is irrelevant under Cournot competition – manager i can induce the competitor to reduce production by reporting that he has good news about his firm-specific parameters or by reporting that the industry parameters are unfavorable for both him and the competitor. On the other hand, as discussed above, under Bertrand competition, manager i can induce the competitor to increase his price by either reporting that costs are high or demand is high, and this occurs whether the information is firm-specific or industry-wide.

Type of Information		Type of Competition	
		Cournot	Bertrand
Firm-specific	- costs - demand	good news "	bad news good news
Industry-wide	- costs - demand	bad news "	bad news good news

Table 15.6: *Ex post* disclosure preferences.

Relating Table 15.5 and Table 15.6, we observe that under Cournot competition, gains from reporting good firm-specific news are greater than the losses of reporting bad firm-specific news, so that full disclosure is preferred *ex ante*. On the other hand, the losses from reporting good industry-wide information are greater than the gains from reporting bad industry-wide information, so that no disclosure is preferred *ex ante*. Under Bertrand competition, the gains from reporting good demand news are greater (less) than the losses from reporting bad demand news if the demand information is industry-wide (firm-specific). Conversely, the losses from reporting good cost news is greater (less) than the gains from reporting bad cost news if the cost information is firm-specific (industry-wide). Hence, under Bertrand competition, no (full) disclosure is preferred *ex ante* if the cost information is firm-specific (industry-wide).

Line-of-business versus Aggregate Reporting

In the analysis of disclosure policy equilibria, the firms are assumed to make an *ex ante* commitment to a disclosure policy that will be implemented irrespective of the manager's *ex post* incentives. Furthermore, any disclosures that are made are assumed to be credible. The initial exploration of disclosure under product market competition largely focused on the incentives to establish trade associations as a means of sharing information with competitors. Membership in a trade association can be viewed as a device to make an *ex ante* commitment to disclose information, and may make those disclosures more credible than information that is voluntarily released by firms through the press.

Accounting researchers have examined product market disclosure as part of their general interest in the impact of "proprietary costs" on *ex ante* commitments or lobbying with respect to disclosure policies, and on the *ex post* incentives to voluntary disclose information. While the basic models focus on one period of disclosure and production, an obvious extension is to consider two periods in which the reported results from the first period are informative about the parameters in the second period. In this setting, if the accounting policies are determined prior to the first period, then those accounting policies can be interpreted as *ex ante* disclosure policies.

Feltham, Gigler, and Hughes (1992) (FGH) use this approach in their exploration of the incentives to choose line-of-business (LOB) reporting instead of aggregate (AGG) reporting. In their model, a firm produces and sells in two product markets. In the first period, the firm is a monopolist in both markets, but a competitor enters into each market (at zero cost) at the end of the first period and, hence, the incumbent firm competes in a duopoly in the second period. Under LOB reporting, the incumbent separately reports (at the end of each period) the profits from the two product markets, whereas, under AGG reporting, the incumbent only reports the total profit from the two markets. Given that the first-period parameters for a given market are informative about the second-period parameters, LOB reporting is more informative about these parameters than is AGG reporting.

While FGH do not compare full disclosure to no disclosure, the results from LOB versus AGG reporting are comparable. FGH consider both Cournot and Bertrand competition, and both firm-specific and industry-wide parameters.[14] Their results are summarized in Table 5.7.

Type of Information	Type of Competition	
	Cournot	Bertrand
Firm-specific	line-of-business	aggregate
Industry-wide	aggregate	line-of-business

Table 15.7: *Ex ante* first-period reporting policy.

Information Manipulation

The introduction of an initial period has no significant effect if the incumbent's first-period choices of production or prices are observable by the competitor. The incumbent makes his optimal first-period choices (as a monopolist), and then the entrant makes inferences based on the observed choices and the reported results. However, the analysis becomes more complex if the first-period choices are not reported, so that the entrant must make his inferences based on the reported profits and rational conjectures about the incumbent's choices. In this case, the incumbent will be motivated to try to manipulate the competitor's inferences by selecting sub-optimal first-period choices. For example, if first-period industry demand is informative about second-period industry demand, then the incumbent is motivated to under-produce (under Cournot competition) in the first-period in order to reduce first-period profits

[14] FGH do not explicitly consider Bertrand competition with firm-specific information, but the results would be similar to the setting with Cournot competition and industry-wide information.

(relative to the optimal monopolistic level) and induce the competitor to underestimate second-period industry demand. Interestingly, due to rational expectations, the incumbent's attempts to manipulate the entrant's inferences will be fruitless. Nonetheless the incumbent will "shoot himself in the foot" by reducing output (unless he can provide the competitor with a verified report of his output choice).

To illustrate this latter phenomenon, we abstract from many aspects of the FGH setting and consider Cournot competition in a two period, single product setting, in which the incumbent ($i = 1$) is a monopolist in the first period, but faces a competitor ($i = 2$) in the second period.[15] We let θ represent the demand parameter (minus the variable cost) in both periods so that the first- and second-period outcomes are $x_{11} = [\theta - q_{11}]q_{11}$ and $x_{21} = [\theta - q_{21} + q_{22}]q_{21}$. The demand parameter θ is a random variable and at $t = 0$, when the incumbent makes his first-period choice, his expectation is $\bar{\theta}$. At $t = 1$, the incumbent learns θ and the competitor infers

$$\hat{\theta} = [x_{11} + \hat{q}_{11}^2]/\hat{q}_{11}, \tag{15.32}$$

where $\hat{q}_{11}$ is the competitor's conjecture with respect to the incumbent's choice.

At $t = 1$, the competitor acts as if both he and the incumbent believe the demand parameter is $\hat{\theta}$ and, hence, he chooses

$$q_{22}(\hat{\theta}) = \frac{1}{3}\hat{\theta}. \tag{15.33}$$

---

[15] Pae (2002) can be viewed as providing a somewhat more complex version of our simple example. In his setting, the incumbent operates as an monopolist in the first period, and then as a Cournot duopolist in the second period. The first-period profit is publicly reported, and is influenced by the incumbent's production choice as well as random variations in both the market demand and the firm's production cost (which is imperfectly correlated with the competitor's production cost). The incumbent knows his production choice and the two random variables (which are directly relevant to the second period competition). Pae considers the incumbent's *ex ante* disclosure choices with respect to three types of private information, and the distortion of first-period production each disclosure policy induces. In addition, he determines the social welfare (total firm profits plus consumer surplus) associated with each disclosure policy.

Other papers that examine the distortion of production decisions due to (unsuccessful) attempts to influence the inferences include Kanodia and Mukherji (1996), Kanodia and Lee (1998), and Sinha and Watts (2001). They consider settings in which managers make observable investment decisions based on unobservable private information and then sell the firm to new investors. The new investors make inferences about a manager's private information based on his observed investment choice and other information (e.g., accounting reports). These papers all demonstrate that a manager will distort his production choice (relative to first-best) in an attempt to manipulate investor beliefs. The distortions will be mitigated by the informativeness of other reports received by investors before the firm is sold.

However, the incumbent knows θ and believes the competitor will choose $q_{22}(\hat{\theta})$, so that it is optimal for him to choose

$$q_{21}(\theta,\hat{\theta}) = \frac{1}{2}[\theta - q_{22}(\hat{\theta})] = \frac{1}{2}[\theta - \frac{1}{3}\hat{\theta}]. \tag{15.34}$$

Now consider the *ex ante* value of the incumbent firm given the manager's first-period choice and the competitor's conjecture with respect to that choice:

$$v_{01}(q_{11},\hat{q}_{11}) = \mathrm{E}\left[(\theta - q_{11})q_{11} + \frac{1}{4}\left(\theta - \frac{1}{3}\,\frac{(\theta - q_{11})q_{11} + \hat{q}_{11}^2}{\hat{q}_{11}} \right)^2 \right]. \tag{15.35}$$

Differentiating (15.35) with respect q_{11} provides a first-order condition that characterizes the incumbent's first-period choice given the competitor's conjecture:

$$\mathrm{E}\left[\theta - 2q_{11} - \frac{1}{6}\left(\theta - \frac{1}{3}\,\frac{(\theta - q_{11})q_{11} + \hat{q}_{11}^2}{\hat{q}_{11}} \right) \frac{\theta - 2q_{11}}{\hat{q}_{11}} \right] = 0. \tag{15.36}$$

The competitor is rational, so that he is fully aware that the incumbent seeks to induce him to underestimate θ. Hence, in equilibrium, the solution to (15.36) must be such that $\hat{q}_{11} = q_{11}$. This implies that the equilibrium choice of q_{11} is characterized by

$$-\frac{1}{9}\,\frac{1}{q_{11}}\mathrm{E}[(\theta - 2q_{11})(\theta - 9q_{11})] = 0. \tag{15.37}$$

Observe that if the incumbent maximizes his first-period expected outcome (ignoring the second period), then he will choose $q_{11} = \frac{1}{2}\bar{\theta}$. This is the first-best production quantity. Substituting this choice into (15.37) establishes that the first-best choice is not an equilibrium unless there is no uncertainty about θ, so that $\mathrm{E}[\theta^2] = \bar{\theta}^2$. With uncertainty, $\mathrm{E}[\theta^2] - \bar{\theta}^2 = \mathrm{Var}[\theta]$ and $q_{11} < \frac{1}{2}\bar{\theta}$.

15.2 *EX POST* DISCLOSURE CHOICES

The analysis in the previous section establishes that even though managers may have *ex post* incentives to disclose some signals and withhold others, the strictly dominating *ex ante* disclosure policy is either to fully disclose or to withhold all signals depending on the type of competition and whether the information pertains to industry-wide or firm-specific components of costs or demands. However, if *ex ante* commitment to a disclosure policy is not feasible, then the *ex post* disclosure equilibrium will involve at least some disclosure, and quite possibly full disclosure.

15.2.1 The Basic *Ex Post* Disclosure Model

The analysis of *ex post* disclosure choices is unduly complicated if both competitors are privately informed. Hence, in the following analysis we assume only manager i receives private information – manager j is uninformed. We initially assume manager i's beliefs are based on a signal that can always be costlessly disclosed to manager j or withheld, i.e., manager i receives $y_i \in Y_i$ and then chooses a message $m_i \in M(y_i) = \{ y_i, n_i \}$.

Let $\pi_{1i}(y_i,m_i)$ represent the intrinsic value for firm i given that manager i has observed y_i and sent message m_i to manager j. As in Chapter 14, the disclosure set $D_i \subseteq Y_i$, with $N_i = Y_i \backslash D_i$, is an equilibrium if $\pi_{1i}(y_i,y_i) \geq \pi_{1i}(y_i,n_i)$ if, and only if, $y_i \in D_i$, and manager j's action given n_i is based on posterior expectation $y_i^n = \mathrm{E}[y_i|N_i]$ if $m_i = n_i$.

We consider *ex post* disclosure under Cournot competition, first with firm-specific information and then with industry-wide information. Recall that with firm-specific information, the *ex ante* equilibrium disclosure policy is full disclosure, whereas with industry-wide information it is no disclosure. The following analysis demonstrates that if the parameters are such that production is always strictly positive, then the *ex post* disclosure equilibrium is full disclosure in both settings. This result also holds for firm-specific information even if the output can be negative, but a partial disclosure equilibrium can exist if negative production is feasible in a setting in which the manager receives industry-wide cost information.

In the preceding analysis we exogenously assumed all production choices are strictly positive. If manager i receives firm-specific cost information (see Table 15.1) and manager j is uninformed, then production choices are always positive if $y_i^{max} \equiv \max\{y_i \in Y_i\} < \theta/2$.[16] Similarly, if manager i receives industry-wide cost information (see (15.29a)), then production choices are always positive if $\tfrac{1}{2}[3\, y_i^{max} - y_i^{min}] < \theta - \bar{c}$, where $y_i^{min} = \min\{y_i \in Y_i\}$.[17] These are not important assumptions in the analysis of *ex ante* disclosure policies, and

---

[16] Both y_i and m_i are no greater than the largest signal, and the production choice is $q_i = \frac{1}{3}[\theta - \frac{3}{2}y_i - \frac{1}{2}m_i] \geq \frac{1}{3}[\theta - 2\times\max\{y_i \in Y\}]$.

[17] In this setting, the signal is the incremental cost and the production choice is $q_i = \frac{1}{3}[\theta - \bar{c} - \frac{3}{2}y_i + \frac{1}{2}m_i] \geq \frac{1}{3}[\theta - \bar{c} - \frac{3}{2}\max\{y_i \in Y_i\} + \frac{1}{2}\min\{y_i \in Y_i\}]$.

they simplify the discussion.[18] However, in the analysis of *ex post* disclosure equilibria it is important whether we allow for the possibility of negative production (or corner solutions in which there is zero production for some signals and messages).

Darrough (1993), Sankar (1992, 1995), and Clinch and Verrecchia (1997) have examined settings in which the equilibrium production quantities and prices may be negative for some signals. Negative production can be interpreted as the purchase of the competitor's output. Of course, for the model to apply, we must assume the production technology is reversible, so that c represents the value to the firm from purchasing a unit of the competitor's output (e.g., the firm has other uses of the product and c is its opportunity cost).

Ex Post Disclosure with Firm-specific Information and Cournot Competition
Consider the setting with Cournot competition in which manager i receives firm-specific cost information and manager j is uninformed. The gain from disclosure versus no disclosure is given by (15.9). Assume there exists a no disclosure set N_i such that

$$G(y_i) \equiv \pi_{1i}(y_i,y_i) - \pi_{1i}(y_i,n_i) = -\tfrac{1}{9}(y_i - y_i^n)[\theta - \tfrac{1}{4}y_i^n - \tfrac{7}{4}y_i] \geq 0,$$

if, and only if, $y_i \in D_i$. The gain from disclosure, $G(y_i)$, is a convex, quadratic function with roots $y_i^\dagger = y_i^n$ and $y_i^\ddagger = [4\theta - y_i^n]/7$. The first root always exists, whereas the second may not (e.g., if the maximum signal and message are less than $\theta/2$). In any event, the convexity of the gain implies that for any y_i^n the disclosure set is $D_i = [y_i^{min},y_i^\dagger] \cup [y_i^\ddagger,y_i^{max}]$, where the last interval is null if $y_i^\ddagger \geq y_i^{max}$. The no disclosure set is $N_i = (y_i^\dagger, \min\{y_i^\ddagger, y_i^{max}\})$, so that y_i^n must be greater than $y_i^\dagger$, which is a contradiction! Hence, in this setting, the no disclosure set must be null, so that the *ex post* disclosure equilibrium is full disclosure – with or without the possibility of negative production.

Ex Post Disclosure with Industry-wide Information and Cournot Competition
Now consider the setting in which manager i receives industry-wide cost information, and manager j is again uninformed. The gain from disclosure versus no disclosure is computed using (15.30):

$$G(y_i) = \pi_{1i}(y_i,y_i) - \pi_{1i}(y_i,n_i) = \tfrac{1}{9}[y_i - y_i^n][\theta - \bar{c} + \tfrac{1}{4}y_i^n - \tfrac{5}{4}y_i]$$

[18] In that analysis, we used the assumption of positive production to discuss the manager's *ex post* incentives to disclose or withhold information, but not to determine the *ex ante* preferences for disclosure policies.

Assume there exists a no disclosure set N_i such that $G(y_i) \geq 0$, if, and only if, $y_i \in D_i$. In this setting, the gain from disclosure is a concave, quadratic function with roots $y_i^\dagger = y_i^n$ and $y_i^\ddagger = [4(\theta - \bar{c}) + y_i^n]/5$. Again, the first root always exists, whereas the second may not (i.e., $y_i^\ddagger$ may exceed y_i^{max}). For example, positive production for all y_i implies that $y_i^{max} < \theta - \bar{c}$ (see (15.29a)) and, thus, $y_i^n < y_i^\ddagger < \theta - \bar{c}$. However, it also follows from (15.29a) that positive production at $y_i^\ddagger$ implies that $y_i^\ddagger < [2(\theta - \bar{c}) + y_i^n]/3$, which is impossible when $y_i^n < \theta - \bar{c}$.[19]

Observe that if only the first root exists, then $D_i = [y_i^\dagger, y_i^{max}]$ and $N_i = [y_i^{min}, y_i^\dagger)$, and it is impossible for y_i^n to equal $y_i^\dagger$. Hence, if production is strictly positive for all y_i, then the only *ex post* equilibrium is *full disclosure*. On the other hand, if negative production is possible and the second root exits (or there is a corner solution with zero production and no disclosure for high costs), then $D_i = [y_i^\dagger, y_i^\ddagger]$ and $N_i = [y_i^{min}, y_i^\dagger) \cup (y_i^\ddagger, y_i^{max}]$, and there can be beliefs such that $y_i^n = y_i^\dagger$.[20]

The motivation for the low no disclosure region is obvious. Manager *i* does not want to reveal low industry-wide costs since that would induce manager *j* to increase production and drive down the industry selling price. The motivation for no disclosure of high industry-wide costs is more subtle. If manager *i*'s production is always positive, then he would want to disclose high costs so as to induce manager *j* to reduce his production. However, if the opportunity costs of selling in this market can be sufficiently high to induce manager *i* to be a buyer instead of a seller, then manager *i* will want to withhold high cost information from manager *j* so that he will not reduce production and manager *i* can acquire some of manager *j*'s output at a low price.

The following proposition summarizes the above results, and recognizes that they extend directly to firm-specific and industry-wide demand information.

Proposition 15.5

Assume there is Cournot competition, a single informed manager, and *ex post* disclosure choice. If the equilibrium production quantities are strictly positive for all signals and messages, then full disclosure is the equilibrium choice whether the information is firm-specific or industry-wide. If production can be negative (or zero with no disclosure), then full disclosure continues to be the equilibrium if the information is firm-specific. However, with negative (or zero) production and industry-wide information, there can exist an equilibrium characterized by a no disclosure set

$$N_i = [y_i^{min}, y_i^\dagger) \cup (y_i^\ddagger, y_i^{max}],$$

[19] $y_i^\ddagger = [4(\theta - \bar{c}) + y_i^n]/5$ is greater than $[2(\theta - \bar{c}) + y_i^n]/3$ if $y_i^n < \theta - \bar{c}$.

[20] In this discussion we assume that $y_i^n < \theta - \bar{c}$. However, if negative production is possible, it may be the case that $y_i^n > \theta - \bar{c}$ such that $y_i^\dagger > y_i^\ddagger$.

where y_i^n is equal to either $y_i^\dagger$ or $y_i^\ddagger$.

Although we only demonstrate these results for Cournot competition, similar results hold for Bertrand competition. No disclosure obtains as the *ex ante* optimal disclosure policy when the change in the expected intrinsic value with disclosure versus no disclosure is a concave function of the manager's information, and in those cases the preference for no disclosure occurs in the "tails." On the other hand, the full disclosure policy is *ex ante* optimal when the change in the expected intrinsic value with disclosure versus no disclosure is a convex function of the manager's information, and in those cases the preference for no disclosure occurs in the "middle." Furthermore, note that y_i^n is always at one of the end points of a no disclosure region (since a manager who has observed the signal y_i^n is indifferent between disclosing that signal or withholding it). Rational beliefs require that y_i^n is the expected signal for all non-disclosing firms. The latter two conditions imply that there must be at least two disjoint non-disclosure regions. Hence, partial disclosure policies can only be sustained as equilibria in the *ex post* setting when the *ex ante* optimal policy is no disclosure.

15.2.2 Positive Probability Manager *i* is Uninformed

In Section 14.4 we consider several disclosure models in which there is a probability $\lambda \in (0,1)$ that the manager will not be informed, and he will not be able to credibly reveal his lack of information. His only possible message, if he is uninformed, is $m_i = n_i$. The analysis in Section 14.4.1 establishes that, given appropriate monotonicity and a single recipient, a positive probability of being uninformed will result in a no disclosure set characterized by a single cutoff $y_i^\dagger$. If the manager prefers to reveal good news (e.g., to investors), then the no disclosure set consists of a "bad news tail," whereas if the manager prefers to reveal bad news (e.g., to a potential entrant into the firm's product market), the no disclosure set consists of a "good news tail."

Extending the analysis in Section 14.4.1 to the Cournot and Bertrand competition settings is straightforward if quantities and prices are strictly positive.[21] Hence, we merely comment on the results and do not formally derive them. From the analysis in Section 14.4.1 we know that the no disclosure set is either lower or upper tailed, i.e., N_i equals either $[y_i^{min}, y_i^\dagger)$ or $(y_i^\dagger, y_i^{max}]$. Furthermore, the no disclosure set never contains the prior mean (which is the mean given no information), i.e., $y_i^o \equiv \mathrm{E}[y_i] \notin N_i$. In addition, the cutoff is equal to the posterior mean given no disclosure, i.e.,

[21] Sankar (1992, 1995) and Darrough (1993) provide formal analysis of some of the settings mentioned here.

$$y_i^\dagger = \frac{\lambda y_i^o + (1-\lambda)\mathrm{E}[y_i|N_i]\mathrm{Prob}[N_i]}{\lambda + (1-\lambda)\mathrm{Prob}[N_i]}.$$

Low costs are good news, while low demand is bad news. Table 15.6 identifies whether the manager would prefer to reveal good news or bad news given each combination of competition type (Cournot or Bertrand), information applicability (firm-specific or industry-wide), and information type (cost versus demand). Applying the results from Section 14.4.1 to these settings yields the no disclosure sets specified in Table 15.8.

Type of Information		Type of Competition	
		Cournot	Bertrand
Firm-specific	- costs - demand	low costs high demand	high costs high demand
Industry-wide	- costs - demand	high costs low demand	high costs high demand

Table 15.8: *Ex post* no disclosure sets when there is a positive probability manager i is uninformed.

15.2.3 New Equity Model

As examined in Section 14.3.1, a compelling reason for equilibrium partial disclosure policies in the *ex post* setting is that there can be a tension between disclosure to product market competitors and disclosure to the capital market. If a firm must raise new equity to finance operations, *ex post*, it would like to disclose that it has low production costs or that product market conditions are favorable, and withhold information that production costs are high or product market conditions are unfavorable. These incentives are the same as the incentives for disclosure of firm-specific cost or demand information to Cournot competitors and firm-specific or industry-wide demand information to Bertrand competitors (see Table 15.6). However, there is a tension if the information is industry-wide with Cournot competition or pertains to costs with Bertrand competition. We illustrate the effect of a tension between capital and product market disclosure in the setting with industry-wide cost information and Cournot competition.

We assume that firm i has private information about the production cost, whereas firm j is uninformed. Firm i needs k_i units of new equity capital to operate production and, for simplicity, we assume that firm j is not issuing new equity capital. Manager i's message m_i is the only information available to the investors when they acquire the new equity. Let $\delta_i(m_i)$ represent the maximum equity price investors are willing to pay given message m_i such that manager i must issue a fraction $\beta_i(m_i) = k_i / \delta_i(m_i)$ of the firm's equity in order to obtain k_i units of capital. Therefore, the intrinsic value of firm i's initial equity at $t = 1$ given information y_i and disclosure policy $\boldsymbol{m}_i$ is[22]

$$\pi_{1i}(y_i, \boldsymbol{m}_i(y_i)) = \tfrac{1}{9}[\theta - \bar{c} - \mathrm{E}[y_j|\boldsymbol{m}_j(y_j)] - \tfrac{3}{2}(y_i - \mathrm{E}[y_i|\boldsymbol{m}_i(y_i)])]^2[1 - k_i / \delta_i(\boldsymbol{m}_i(y_i))].$$

Of course, the investors only know m_i, but make rational conjectures of the firm's disclosure and production strategies. Hence, the maximum equity price acceptable to investors is the expected *ex post* intrinsic value of the firm given the message, i.e.,

$$\delta_i(\boldsymbol{m}_i) = \tfrac{1}{9}[\theta - \bar{c} - \mathrm{E}[y_j|\boldsymbol{m}_j]]^2 + \tfrac{1}{4}\mathrm{Var}(y_i|\boldsymbol{m}_i),$$

where the latter term reflects the investors' uncertainty about the firm's signal given the reported message. Of course, if the manager discloses his signal, i.e., $m_i = y_i$, then $\mathrm{Var}(y_i|\boldsymbol{m}_i(y_i) = y_i) = 0$, whereas $\mathrm{Var}(y_i|\boldsymbol{m}_i(y_i) = n_i) > 0$ if there is a measurable set of signals that is not disclosed.

Observe that disclosing or not disclosing $y_i = y_i^n$ does not affect the *ex post* intrinsic value of firm i since the competitor's response depends on his posterior mean of firm i's cost parameter. Nonetheless, the maximum equity price acceptable to investors is higher with no disclosure than with disclosure. Hence, manager i will not disclose $y_i = y_i^n$, or signals "close to y_i^n." The key is that there is a cost of disclosure, since new investors "value uncertainty" given the convex quadratic form of the *ex post* intrinsic value function. In this sense, the model has similarities to the Verrecchia-type model with an exogenous cost of disclosure (see Section 14.2.2). In particular, the posterior mean given no disclosure, y_i^n, is not equal to one of the endpoints of a no-disclosure region. However, note that, in the current setting, the cost of disclosure is determined endogenously as the variance of cost signals given the no disclosure set N_i – which is endogenously determined.

The intrinsic values of the initial equity with and without disclosure is

---

[22] See (15.30) for derivation of the intrinsic value of the firm, i.e., both new and old equity.

$$\pi_{1i}(y_i,m_i) = \begin{cases} \frac{1}{9}[\theta - \bar{c} - y_i]^2 - k_i, & m_i = y_i, \\ \frac{1}{9}[\theta - \bar{c} - y_i^n - \frac{3}{2}(y_i - y_i^n)]^2\,[1 - k_i/\delta_i(n_i)], & m_i = n_i, \end{cases}$$

where

$$\delta_i(n_i) = \tfrac{1}{9}[\theta - \bar{c} - y_i^n]^2 + \tfrac{1}{4}\mathrm{Var}(y_i|N_i). \qquad (15.38)$$

The gain from disclosure is

$$G(y_i) = \pi_{1i}(y_i,y_i) - \pi_{1i}(y_i,n_i)$$

$$= \tfrac{1}{9}\{[y_i - y_i^n][\theta - \bar{c} - y_i^n][1 - 3k_i/\delta_i(n_i)] - \tfrac{1}{4}[y_i - y_i^n]^2[5 - 9k_i/\delta_i(n_i)]\}$$

$$- k_i\{1 - \tfrac{1}{9}[\theta - \bar{c} - y_i^n]^2/\delta_i(n_i)\}. \qquad (15.39)$$

Note from (15.38) that $\frac{1}{9}[\theta - \bar{c} - y_i^n]^2/\delta_i(y_i^n) < 1$ if $\mathrm{Var}(y_i|N_i) > 0$. Hence, if there is a measurable no disclosure set N_i (which is not a singleton), a manager who has observed the signal $y_i = y_i^n$ prefers to send the message $m_i = n_i$ instead of disclosing that he has observed $y_i = y_i^n$ (as discussed above). Continuity further implies that the no disclosure mean, y_i^n, is in the interior of the no disclosure set N_i. This differs from the result in the new-equity/potential-entrant models in Section 14.3 in which the equilibrium no disclosure mean is equal to one of the end points of the two disjoint no disclosure sets. However, it is similar to the result in Section 14.2.2 for settings with an exogenous cost of verified disclosure.

The fact that the no disclosure mean is in the interior of the no disclosure set N_i implies that there can be partial disclosure equilibria ranging from no disclosure to various one- and two-tailed no disclosure sets to full disclosure. However, if we restrict the parameters to be such that equilibrium production quantities are strictly positive, then a partial disclosure equilibrium in which there are disclosure in the tails and no disclosure in the "middle" cannot exist.

To demonstrate the latter, note that to have a partial disclosure equilibrium of this form, the gain from disclosure, $G(y_i)$, must be a convex function of y_i, i.e., the coefficient on the second-order term must be positive, which implies $5 - 9k_i/\delta_i(n_i)$ must be negative. This, plus strictly positive production (i.e., $\theta - \bar{c} > y_i^{max}$), implies that the coefficient on the first-order term is negative, i.e., $[\theta - \bar{c}$ -

$y_i^n][1 - 3k_i/\delta_i(n_i)] < 0$.[23] Consequently, the first term in $G(y_i)$ is a linear decreasing function of y_i, intersecting zero at $y_i = y_i^n$ and the second term is convex and positive, with a minimum of zero at $y_i = y_i^n$. The sum of the first two terms in (15.39) is negative for $y_i = y_i^{max}$, implying that it is not optimal to disclose y_i^{max} if it is not optimal to disclose $y_i = y_i^n$ (which follows from the fact that the first two terms are zero at $y_i = y_i^n$ and the third term is a negative constant).[24]

The preceding discussion implies that there can be an equilibrium in which the manager discloses good news (low costs) and does not disclose bad news (high costs) (see Figure 15.1). This result differs from Proposition 14.3, in which partial disclosure is always characterized by no disclosure in the lower and upper tails, with the no disclosure mean equal to one of the cutoffs. The

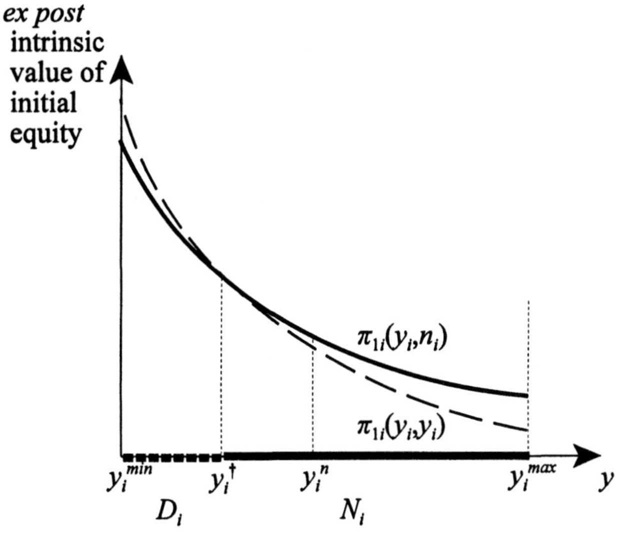

Figure 15.1: Lower-tail partial disclosure equilibrium in the new equity/Cournot competition model.

---

[23] $1 - 3k_i/\delta_i(n_i) = \frac{1}{3}(3 - 9k_i/\delta_i(n_i)) < \frac{1}{3}(5 - 9k_i/\delta_i(n_i)) < \frac{1}{4}(5 - 9k_i/\delta_i(n_i)) < 0$, where the last term is used in the next footnote.

[24] $\theta - \bar{c} > y_i^{max}$ implies that $[y_i^{max} - y_i^n][\theta - \bar{c} - y_i^n] > [y_i^{max} - y_i^n]^2$. Hence, given the result in the prior footnote,

$$[y_i^{max} - y_i^n][\theta - \bar{c} - y_i^n][1 - 3k_i/\delta_i(n_i)] - \frac{1}{4}[y_i^{max} - y_i^n]^2[5 - 9k_i/\delta_i(n_i)]$$

$$< [y_i^{max} - y_i^n]^2([1 - 3k_i/\delta_i(n_i)] - \frac{1}{4}[5 - 9k_i/\delta_i(n_i)]) < 0.$$

possibility of a single-tailed partial disclosure cutoff here is due to the fact that the no disclosure mean is in the interior of the no disclosure set.

15.3 CONCLUDING REMARKS

This chapter concludes our first volume, which has focused on the impact of information in capital markets. In Chapters 5 through 10 we assume all investors receive the same information and that the information received by investors is exogenously determined. With the exception of chapter 8, managers play no role in the analysis in those chapters. They have no private information to reveal and their production decisions are exogenously specified. Acquisition of private information by investors is considered in Chapters 11 and 12, and managers continue to play no role in the analysis.

In Chapter 8, managers make endogenous production decisions, but are assumed to be exogenously motivated to maximize the intrinsic value of their firms. For much of the analysis in Chapter 8, managers and investors are assumed to receive the same information, so that intrinsic value equals market value. However, Section 8.4.5 considers a setting in which investors are well-diversified and managers receive private firm-specific information. Interestingly, while disclosure of the managers' private information would affect the firms' market prices, it would not affect the managers' production decisions (if they maximize their firms' intrinsic values) and it would not affect the consumption plans of well-diversified investors. That is, while investors are better off if managers have better firm-specific productivity information, well-diversified investors are not made better off by the public reporting of that information.

In Chapters 13 through 15 we examine the disclosure of private management information in settings in which managers are exogenously assumed to act in the best interests of the firms' owners. In Chapter 13, the owner is the manager, so the alignment of their preferences is obvious. The owner is assumed to be undiversified and risk averse, and the disclosure of his private information is examined under the assumption that he seeks to share his risks with well-diversified investors. The investors know that the owner has private information, but they do not know what signal he has received, e.g., was it good news or bad news? The key issues in this setting center on the impact of the mechanisms the owner has available for convincing investors that what he reports is truthful.

In Chapters 14 and 15 we return to a setting in which the firm is owned by well-diversified investors and managers exogenously make decisions in accordance with the preferences of the owners. A key issue here is whether the investors can constrain the managers to implement a disclosure policy that is specified *ex ante*, or whether the managers will make disclosure decisions that are *ex post* optimal (from the investors' perspective). As is common in much of the accounting disclosure literature, the analysis in Chapter 14 assumes that the managers make their disclosure choices based on the owners' *ex post* preferences. However, in each case, we also consider the owners' *ex ante* preferences. As is also common in the accounting disclosure literature, the analysis generally assumes that managers either truthfully report their information, or do not disclose it – there is no lying. The mechanism for ensuring truthfulness is largely unspecified. Of particular interest in the accounting literature are the assumptions that provide equilibria in which the manager sometimes discloses his information, but not always.

Section 15.1 focuses on equilibrium *ex ante* disclosure policies in settings in which there is imperfect competition in a firm's product market. The type of information (firm-specific versus industry-wide) and the type of imperfect competition (Cournot versus Bertrand) are shown to influence whether the owners prefer their managers to fully disclose or not disclose their private information. Again, if a manager discloses his information, it is assumed that he is truthful, without specifying any mechanism for enforcing its truthfulness. Section 15.2 examines the *ex post* equilibrium disclosure policies. In some settings the *ex post* equilibrium disclosure choices are *ex ante* optimal, whereas in others they are not.

As emphasized in the preceding summary, the analyses in Chapters 8, 14, and 15 assume that managers exogenously act in the best interests of their firms' owners. There is no consideration of managers' personal preferences. Obviously, managers have personal preferences, and these preferences influence their actions, including their disclosure choices. Of course, the owners are aware of a managers' personal preferences and take them into consideration when they offer a manager a compensation contract. Compensation typically varies with one or more performance measures (e.g., accounting income or the firm's market value), and may be influenced by the information disclosed by the manager at the time of contracting.

Volume II examines the role of accounting measures in contracting between a principal (possibly acting on behalf of well-diversified owners) and an agent (e.g., a manager). The initial principal/agent models assume the agent has no private information other than his action (e.g., effort), which is personally costly. However, later in Volume II, we introduce private management information and the disclosure of that information as part of the compensation contract. These are typically referred to as *communication* models, but they are effectively *disclosure* models in which the manager's disclosure choices are based on his personal preferences and his compensation contract. A key feature of these models is that the well known *Revelation Principle* states that, under standard assumptions, there always exists an optimal contract which induces the agent to *truthfully disclose all of his private information.* That is, the optimal contract induces full disclosure. It should be noted, however, that one of the standard assumptions underpinning the Revelation Principle is that the principal is the only user of the information disclosed by the manager. Introducing other players, such as new investors or product market competitors, into a principal/agent model can result in contracts in which the manager is not induced to fully disclose his private information.[25]

REFERENCES

Christensen, P. O., and G. A. Feltham. (2000) "Market Based Performance Measures and Disclosure of Private Management Information," *Review of Accounting Studies* 6, 301-329.

Clinch, G., and R.E. Verrecchia. (1997) "Competitive Disadvantage and Discretionary Disclosure in Industries," *Australian Journal of Management* 22, 125-137.

Darrough, M. N. (1993) "Disclosure Policy and Competition: Cournot vs. Bertrand," *The Accounting Review* 68, 534-561.

Dye, R. A. (2001) "An Evaluation of "Essays on Disclosure" and the Disclosure Literature in Accounting," *Journal of Accounting and Economics* 32, 181-235.

Feltham, G. A., F. B. Gigler, J. S. Hughes. (1992) "The Effects of Line-of-Business Reporting on Competition in Oligopoly Settings," *Contemporary Accounting Research* 9, 1-23.

Gal-Or, E. (1985) "Information Sharing in Oligopoly," *Econometrica* 53, 329-343.

Gal-Or, E. (1986) "Information Transmission – Cournot and Bertrand Equilibria," *Review of Economic Studies* 53, 85-92.

Jung,. W.-O., and Y. K. Kwon. (1988) "Disclosure When the Market is Unsure of Information Endowment of Managers," *Journal of Accounting Research* 26, 146-153.

Kanodia, C., and D. Lee. (1998) "Investment and Disclosure: The Disciplining Role of Periodic Performance Reports," *Journal of Accounting Research* 36, 33-55.

Kanodia, C., and A. Mukherji. (1996) "Real Effects of Separating Investment and Operating Cash Flows," *Review of Accounting Studies* 1, 51-71.

Kirby, A. (1988) "Trade Associations as Information Exchange Mechanisms," *Rand Journal of Economics* 19, 138-146.

Sankar, M. (1992) *Corporate Voluntary Disclosures of Pre-Decision Information*, unpublished dissertation, University of British Columbia.

---

[25] For example, Christensen and Feltham (2000) consider a model in which the manager is induced to only partially disclose his private information so that new investors are induced to trade on non-contractible information, thereby making the market price a useful contractible source of information for incentive contracting. This model is discussed in Chapter 22 of Volume II.

Sankar, M. (1995) "Disclosure of Predecision Information in a Duopoly," *Contemporary Accounting Research* 11, 829-859.

Shapiro, C. (1986) "Exchange of Cost Information in Oligopoly," *Review of Economic Studies* 53, 433-446.

Sinha, N., and J. Watts. (2001) "Economic Consequences of the Declining Relevance of Financial Reports," *Journal of Accounting Research* 39, 663-381.

Verrecchia, R. E. (1983) "Discretionary Disclosure," *Journal of Accounting and Economics* 5, 179-194.

Verrecchia, R. E. (2001) "Essays on Disclosure," *Journal of Accounting and Economics* 32, 97-180.

Vives, X. (1984) "Duopoly Information Equilibrium: Cournot and Bertrand," *Journal of Economic Theory* 34, 71-94.

Vives, X. (1990) "Trade Association Disclosure Rules, Incentives to Share Information, and Welfare," *Rand Journal of Economics* 21, 409-430.

Author Index

Admati, A. R. 374, 382
Akerlof, A. 454
Amershi, A. H. 100, 132, 166, 467
Amir, E. 309
Ang, A. 326
Arrow, K. 48
Banks, J. 459, 463
Barth, M. E. 315
Beaver, W. H. 315
Begley, J. 274, 339, 344, 356
Berninghaus, S. 170, 172
Bhattacharya, S. 535
Billingsley, P. 34
Blackwell, D. 94, 97
Borch, K. 117, 157
Breeden, D. 161, 168
Brennan, M. 165
Buckman, G. 226, 231, 234, 236, 237
Bushman, R. M. 397, 409
Butterworth, J. E. 92
Caspi,Y. 170
Cho, I. 459-464, 469
Christensen, P. O. 168, 172, 215, 261, 270, 476, 578
Clarkson, P. 492
Clinch, G. 569
Collins, J. H. 306
Crawford, V. 535
Darrough, M. N. 503, 504, 516, 543, 544, 546, 547, 555, 569, 571
Datar, S. 485, 487-491
Debreu, G. 255, 260
Dechow, P. 344
DeGroot, M. H. 39, 41, 42, 77
DeMarzo, P. 413
Demski, J. S. 1, 85, 92, 132, 398, 401, 437
Duffie, D. 145, 188
Dutta, S. 522, 528
Dye, R. A. 481, 501, 502, 504, 522, 524, 543, 562
Easley, D. 373
Farrell, J. 535
Feltham, G. A. 1, 85, 168, 172, 261, 270, 274, 279, 280, 284, 293, 297, 316, 330, 339, 343, 344, 352, 356, 388, 398, 401, 409, 437, 463, 467, 469, 476, 481, 485, 487-493, 503, 504, 516, 518, 520, 565, 566, 578
Fishman, M. J. 504
Frankel, R. 348
Fudenberg, D. 453
Gal-Or, E. 544
Garman, M. B. 317, 319, 323
Gertner, R. H. 504
Gibbons, R. 535
Gigler, F. 535, 538, 565, 566
Girshick, M. A. 94
Gould, J. P. 101
Graversen, S. E. 168, 215
Grinblatt, M. 494
Grossman, S. J. 368, 372-374, 377, 383, 410, 419, 467, 504
Grundy, B. D. 405
Hadar, J. 61, 62, 65
Hagerty, K. M. 504

Hakansson, N. H. 138, 226, 231, 237
Hanlon, M. 307
Hanoch, G. 62, 65
Harris, M. 535
Harris, T. S. 307
Harsanyi, J. 453
Hart, O. D. 467, 504, 535
Hellwig, M. 375, 386, 398
Hirshleifer, J. 375
Holthausen, R. W. 315, 387
Huang, C. C. 92
Hughes, J. S. 463, 467, 469, 481, 485, 487-493, 565, 566
Hughes, P. 494, 495
Hwang, C. Y. 494
Indjejikian, R. J. 387, 397, 409
Jarrow, R. A. 373
Jovanovic, B. 511
Jung, W.-O. 522, 524, 525
Kanodia, C. 566
Kemsley, D. 307
Kim, O. 398, 405, 423, 424, 437
Kirby, A. 544, 547
Kirchenheiter, M. 309
Kohlberg, E. 459, 464
Kothari, S. P. 315
Kraus, A. 165
Kreps, D. 204, 413, 459, 461-464, 469
Kunkel, J. G. 138, 226, 231, 237, 264
Kwon, Y. K. 360, 432, 522, 524, 525
Kyle, A. S. 375, 419, 420, 423
Landsmen, W. R. 315
Lanen, W. N. 533
Lee, C. M. C. 315, 348, 566
Leland, H. 172, 471, 474, 497
Lev, B. 236
Levy, H. 62, 65
Litzenberger, R. H. 168
Liu, J. 326, 344
Lundholm, R. 292, 396
Magill, M. 159, 262
Majluf, N. S. 535
Malinvaud, E. 170
Marschak, J. 94, 97, 100, 135
Mayers, D. 478
McNichols, M. 398, 405, 437
Mertens, J.-F. 459, 464
Milgrom, P. 62, 413, 504
Miller, M. H. 277, 286
Miltersen, K. R. 168, 215
Miyasawa, K. 94, 97, 100
Modigliani, F. 277, 286
Morgenstern, O. 39, 113
Mukherji, A. 566
Myers, J. 307, 348
Myers, S. 535
Newman, P. 535, 537, 538
Ohlson, J. A. 138, 226, 231, 234, 236, 237, 278-280, 284, 291, 297, 316, 317, 319, 323, 327, 330, 333, 337, 339, 341, 343, 344, 349
O'Keefe, T. 292
Pae, J. 343, 352
Pae, S. 531-534, 566
Penman, S. H. 291
Penno, M. C. 524
Pfleiderer, P. 382
Pratt, J. 48
Pyle, D. 471, 474, 497
Quinzii, M. 159, 262
Radner, R. 135, 202, 261
Raiffa, H. 77
Raviv, A. 535
Ross, S. 169, 172
Rubinstein, M. 165, 323
Russell, W. R. 62, 65
Samuelson, P. A. 169
Sankar, M. 560, 569, 571
Sansing, R. 535, 537, 538
Savage, L. 39
Schlaifer, R. 77

Shapiro, C. 544
Shevlin, T. 307
Simunic, D. 492
Sinha, N. 566
Skiadas, C. 413
Sloan, R. 344
Sobel, J. 459, 460, 463, 535
Stiglitz, J. E. 368, 372, 374, 377, 383, 419
Stoeckenius, J. H. W. 132
Stokey, N. 413
Stoughton, N. M. 503, 504, 516
Swaminathan, B. 348
Sweeney, A. 344
Tirole, J. 453
Titman, S. 491, 492
Trueman, B. 398, 437, 491, 492, 521, 522, 528-531
Verrecchia, R. E. 132, 374, 375, 386, 387, 398, 405, 423, 424, 437, 449, 482, 501, 502, 504, 511, 513, 514, 522, 533, 539, 543, 569
Vertinsky, I. 92
Vives, X. 544
von Neumann, J. 39, 113
Wagenhofer, A. 504, 516, 520
Watts, J. 566
Watts, R. L. 315
Willard, K. 309
Wilson, R. 111, 117, 130, 132, 136
Wu, M. G. H. 388, 409, 476
Xie, J. 503, 504, 516, 518, 520
Yee, K. K. 317
Zhang, X.-J. 291, 333, 336, 339, 341, 356
Zhang, G. 317, 409, 423, 434, 539
Ziemba, W. T. 92

Subject Index

abnormal earnings 281
accounting accruals 339
  efficient accounting 341
  imperfectly reveal management information 343
  "other" information 339, 340
accounting model
  depreciation of investments 332
  "other" information 340
  R&D 357
  receivables and bad debts 354
accounting-value relation
  basic investment model 332
  basic proposition 281
  book value & operating income 333
  current accounting numbers and forecasts 348
  market risk 337
  mixed-equity 300
  no arbitrage 279
  operating income-value relation 289
  "other" information 341
  pure-equity 300
  R&D model 357
  receivables model 354
  risk-neutral probability model 283
  stationary model 326
  transitory model 350
  truncated forecasts 291
  valuation index model 283
  with privately informed investors 432, 434
accounts receivable 352
adapted stochastic process 187
aggregate consumption 161, 209, 229
  efficient sharing of 209
analysts' forecasts
  inferring "other" information 343
anticipated equity transactions 293
Bayesian equilibrium 453
Bayes' rule 194, 221, 460
Bertrand competition 545, 555
  firm-specific cost information 555
  price information 558
capital investment model 330
  accounting-value relation 332
  linear information dynamics 331
certainty equivalent 45, 239
cheap talk equilibrium 535
clean surplus relation 279
  book value of equity 279
  dirty 295, 298
  mixed 294, 297
  net income 279
  super-clean 294, 295, 297
comparative statics
  basic Grossman-Stiglitz model 384
  competitive acquisition of risk 377
  concurrent private information 394

concurrent public report 428, 430
endogenous informativeness of the public report 436
prior private information 404, 442
comparison of information systems 93
generally at least as valuable 93
competitive acquisition of risk 375
comparative statics 377
congruent preferences 126
action choice 127
definition 130
heterogeneous beliefs 136
information system choice 132
optimal partnership contract problem 128, 133
partnership utility function 131
consensus 387
conservative accounting 334
aggressive depreciation 334
economic - accounting income 336
market risk 336
positive NPV investments 334
price/earnings ratio 336
R&D model 356, 358
receivables model 356
risk-adjusted depreciation 338
consumption process 197
contingent claims 294
accounting relation 295
as debt 302
contract date 296
earnings-per-share 304
employee stock options 303
exercise date 296
mixed-equity 294
warrants 302, 304
Cournot competition 545, 547
ex post disclosure with firm-specific information 569
ex post disclosure with industry-wide information 569
firm-specific cost information 547
industry-wide cost information 561
price information 551
disclosure equilibrium 506
diverse interpretation of disclosed information 522
endogenous information acquisition 531
endogenous investment choice 532
full disclosure with costless verification 507
full- and partial-disclosure equilibrium 506
investor litigation 521, 527
new equity model 508, 511, 523
new equity/potential entrant model 517
one recipient 523
partial disclosure equilibrium 524
partial disclosure with costly verification 511
positive probability of uninformed manager 522
potential entrant model 509, 514, 525
disclosure game 452
diverse private signals models 372, 386
concurrent public report 396
consensus 387
informedness 387
private information prior to a public report 405
diversifiable risk 165, 173, 209, 475
diversified portfolio 172, 215

dividend-value relation 189, 194
auto-regressive example 323
general linear dynamics 321
general linear model 322
mixed-equity 300
pure-equity 299
stationary model assumptions 319
truncated forecasts 292
duopoly competition 545
economy-wide events 169, 215
economy-wide risk 181, 273
efficient accounting
sufficient conditions 342
efficient risk sharing 112, 154, 157, 201
contract curve 120
efficient risk sharing problem 116
linear risk sharing 122, 161, 206
Pareto efficiency 114
Pareto efficient partnership contract 117
Pareto preference 114
partners with homogeneous beliefs 112
risk-neutral partners 121
set of feasible sharing rules 114
set of possible of expected utility levels 114
sharing rule feasibility 113
entrant 509
equilibria in disclosure games 452
equilibrium refinement 459
Cho/Kreps-criterion 460-462
divinity and universal divinity 464
never weak best response 465
equity retention 471
and report choice 494
event-price 146, 159, 188
Arrow/Debreu security 149
date-event price 188
date-event security 189
deflator 151, 195, 219
event-security 148
ex ante disclosure policy 545
equilibria 562
ex post disclosure choice 567
new equity model 572
positive probability manager is uninformed 571
ex post disclosure preferences 564
exponential family of distributions 63, 69
exponential utility and normal distributions 106, 238, 472
expectation of a linear function 106
expectation of a quadratic function 107
mean-variance preferences 54
private investor information model 369
financing activities 286
book value 287
dividend policy irrelevance 286, 328
financial asset relation 288
financial income 288
marked-to-market 286, 288
firm value maximization 260
firm-specific events 169, 215
firm-specific risk 170, 215, 448, 454, 474
fully informed equilibrium 369
in a complete market 412
fully revealing rational expectations equilibrium 374
goodwill 334
Grossman-Stiglitz model 377
comparative statics 384, 394, 404
concurrent public report 388

endogenous information acquisition 381, 402
equilibrium price 381, 389, 391, 399
exogenously informed investors 378
investors shoot themselves in the foot 385
price-variability 394, 403
prior private information 397
rational beliefs 380, 390, 400
trading volume 392, 403
HARA utility functions 49, 52, 162, 207, 231
exponential 51, 52
identical risk cautiousness 122, 130
linear risk sharing 122
linear risk tolerance 50
linear sharing rule 124
logarithmic 51, 52
power 51, 52
heterogeneous beliefs 125, 227
side-betting 125
homogeneous beliefs 112, 226
stationary model 320
hurdle model
additively separable utility 59
information value 104
mean-variance approximation 56
multiplicatively separable utility 57
incumbent manager 509
inferring "other" information from forecasts
focusing on forecasts 347
general model 344
investment model 345
information economic model 84
beliefs 86
decision maker 84
decision strategy 88
expected utility 88
information 86
information system evaluator 84
null information system 90
optimal decision rule 89
optimal information system 90
perfect information system 90
information in teams 135
information manipulation 565
information representation
partition 81
information risk problem 180
risky endowment 375
informativeness 94, 177, 225
at least as Θ-informative 94
collapsing 95
garbling 100
more Θ-informative 98
redundant information 100
relation between informativeness and value 97
sufficient statistic 100
informed player 452
informedness 387
initial public offering 471
insurance informativeness 227
investment-disclosure game 466
investor 144
consumption set 152, 197
consumption transfer 152
endowed portfolio 152, 197
endowment 152, 197, 226
expected utility gradient 153, 155, 205
optimal portfolio choice problem 152, 198
issuance of new equity 294, 295
convertible debt 299
earnings-per-share 304
employee stock options 299, 303
mergers and acquisitions 298

non-monetary goods or services 298
warrants 298, 302, 304
Jensen's inequality 44, 45
Kyle model 420
comparative statics 428, 430, 436, 442
concurrent public report 424
differences from Grossman-Stiglitz model 419
endogenous information acquisition 423, 427
endogenous informativeness of the public report 434
equilibrium demand and price 422, 426
exogenously informed investors 421, 424
informativeness 422
liquidity traders 420
price-variability 430
prior private information 437
trading volume 429
law of large numbers 170, 216
Lebesgue-Stieltjes integral 35
line-item model
investment model 333
R&D 358
transitory model 351
line-of-business versus aggregate reporting 564
linear information dynamics
auto-regressive dividend model 323
basic investment model 331
basic residual income model 327
general dividend model 321
R&D model 357
receivables model 352
transitory model 350
valuation index 322
with privately informed investors 432
"other" information 339
linear value function
auto-regressive dividends 324
basic cash flow model 331
basic investment model 332
general 322
R&D model 357
receivables model 353, 354
transitory model 350
"other" information 340, 341
liquidity traders 375, 420
market equilibrium 154, 201
Arrow/Debreu-equilibrium in production economy 259
Arrow/Debreu equilibrium 202, 204, 228
individual optimality 154, 202
market clearing 154, 202
properties of equilibria in complete markets 159
properties of equilibria in dynamically complete markets 205
Radner sequential equilibrium 202
Radner sequential equilibrium in production economy 261
market portfolio 162, 207, 242, 475
Markov model 320
mean-variance preferences
exponential utility with normally distributed outcomes 54
hurdle model example 56
investment choice example 55
quadratic utility function 51
Taylor approximation 53
minimal aggregate consumption statistic 212
monotone likelihood ratio property (MLRP) 62, 467
multi-period economy 186

multi-variate normal distribution 77
conditional probability density function 77
conditional variance 78
joint density function 77
marginal distribution 77
Nash equilibrium 453, 548
no arbitrage 145, 188
accounting value 279
stationary model 319
noisy rational expectations equilibria 374
exogenously informed investors 378
off-equilibrium
actions 454, 460
beliefs 454, 458, 504, 519
operating activities 286, 328
book value 287
operating asset relation 289
operating cash flow-value relations 290
operating income 288
truncated forecasts 292
optimal portfolio choice 152, 238
plan 196
outcome-contingent contract 455
equity retention 471
full-disclosure constraints 470
full-disclosure equilibrium 469, 473
participation constraint 470
signaling with 466
with finite sets of outcomes and signals 467
with normally distributed outcomes 471
partition 81
f-relevant partition 84
f-sufficient partition 84
fineness and coarseness 82
noiseless information system 99
outcome-adequate 85
outcome-relevant 85
sigma-field 81
Y-measurable function 84
partnership
congruent preferences 126
efficient risk sharing 112
homogeneous beliefs 112
linear risk sharing 122
Pareto efficient partnership contract 117
partnership utility function 131
portfolio plan 187, 190, 197
posterior
covariance matrix 243
mean 243
posterior beliefs 72, 186
Bayes' theorem 73, 75
conditional probability 72
likelihood function 75
normal distribution 77
with random variables 74
preference assumptions 40
preference representation 38
concavity and convexity of preferences 43
expected utility 41
preference relation among gambles 39
preference relevant outcomes 39
Taylor approximation 47
time-additive 200
utility function 38
price taker 260
price-informativeness
basic Grossman-Stiglitz model 384
basic Kyle model 422
concurrent private information 394, 430
prior private information 404
price-taking informed investors 377

basic Grossman-Stiglitz model 377
price-variability
concurrent private information 394, 430
prior private information 403
private investor information 369
common signal model 371
competitive acquisition of risk 375
concurrent public report 388
diverse signal model 372, 386
fully informed equilibrium 369
in a complete market 410
liquidity traders 375
price-taking investors 377
residual income model 431
strategic investor model 420
unsophisticated equilibrium 369
probability
distribution 31, 32
probability space 31, 72
probabilizable events 32
product market 509, 543
production
alternatives 254
efficiency 256
feasibility 255
plan 255
production choice in dynamically quasi-complete market 268
with private management information 271
productivity events 269
proprietorship theory 293
pure-equity 294
public information 175, 223, 243
and prices 233
and trades 236
efficiency 177, 224
ex ante 180
ex post 176
in production economy 262
in securities market 228
incompleteness due to too much information 232
system change 230
public reports
concurrent private information 388, 424
endogenous informativeness 434
prior private information 397, 437
random variable 33
absolutely continuous distribution 36
discrete distribution 35
distribution function 33
family of p.d.f 38
generalized probability density function 35
joint distribution function 74
marginal distribution function 74
mixed distribution 37
posterior belief 74
probability (frequency) function 34
probability density function 34
research and development 356
residual income
capital charge 281
definition 281
Riesz Representation Theorem 150, 195
risk aversion 43, 241
asking price 46
bid price 46
concave utility functions 43
local risk aversion 47
risk cautiousness 50
risk premium 46
risk tolerance 49
risk cautiousness 161
risk sharing 112, 116, 143, 157, 454

risk tolerance 241
risk-adjusted cost of capital 284, 285
  auto-regressive dividend model 326
risk-neutral probability 149, 154, 167, 200, 283
  auto-regressive dividend model 325
  based on the bank account 219
  based on zero-coupon bonds 192, 205
riskless interest rate 147, 281
  discount factor 149, 281
  linear model 322
securities market 146
  complete 147, 190
  dynamically complete 189
  dynamically MAC-complete 214
  dynamically quasi-complete 218
  effectively complete 161
  effectively dynamically complete 206
  incomplete 158
  quasi-complete 168, 172
  Radner sequential equilibrium 230
security 145
  cum-dividend price 187
  dividend 145
  dividend matrix 147
  ex-dividend price 187
  portfolio of 145
  price of 145
separation of financing & operations 286, 328
sequence of partitions 186, 224
sequential equilibrium 453, 460, 550
  full disclosure equilibrium 457
  no-disclosure equilibrium 458
shooting oneself in the foot
  investor information acquisition 385
sigma-field 31
signaling game 452
spanning condition 467
spanning number 191
stable equilibrium 459
  non-credible threat 459
state
  partition 73
  state space 31
stochastic dominance 60
  first-order stochastic (FS) dominance 61
  FS-dominance theorem 62, 66
  second-order stochastic (SS) dominance 64
  SS-dominance theorem 65, 67
strategic investor model 420
strictly dominating strategy 550
sufficient statistic 78
  definition 80
  equivalent statistic 78
  factorization theorem 80
  "family" of likelihood functions 79
  garbling 100
  Markov model 321
  minimal sufficient statistic 80
  normal distribution 80
tax effects 306
  distribution of earnings & contributed capital 307
  dividends and interest 309
The First Welfare Theorem 156, 202
The Second Welfare Theorem 158
time-additive preferences 200, 210, 218, 226
trading volume
  concurrent public report 392, 429

prior private information 402
transfers
consistent 176, 224
efficient 176, 224
transitory earnings and investments 349
truncated forecasts 291
unbiased accounting 335
uncertainty representation 30
uninformed player 452
unsophisticated equilibrium 369, 373
common signal model 371
diverse signal model 372
in a complete market 410
unverified disclosure 535
sequential equilibrium 536
valuation index 150, 151, 160, 162, 200, 283, 321, 322
multi-period 196, 205
value of an information system 81, 90
buying price 91
conditions for positive value 92
hurdle model example 104
investment choice example 101
relation between informativeness and value 97
verifiable disclosure 506
new equity/potential entrant model 517
one recipient 506
two recipients 516
verified *ex ante* report 480
consistent reporting system 486
costless verification 480
costly verification 482
discriminating *ex ante* report 485
imperfect *ex ante* report 483
non-discriminating *ex ante* report 484
perfect *ex ante* report 480
positive probability of uninformed owner 481
reporting system choice 489
system quality 487
verified *ex post* report 492
informative *ex post* reporting system 493
windfall events 269